GUJARAT UNDER MODI

Dr Christophe Jaffrelot is Research Director at CERI-Sciences Po/CNRS, Professor of Indian politics and sociology at King's College (London), President of the French Political Science Association and Chair of the British Association for South Asian Studies. He works as a Non Resident Fellow at the Carnegie Endowment for International Peace and as a Permanent Consultant at the Centre for Policy Planning Staff of the French Ministry of Foreign Affairs. He is the author of several books, the most recent being *Modi's India: Hindu Nationalism and the Rise of Ethnic Democracy*.

CHRISTOPHE JAFFRELOT

GUJARAT UNDER MODI

THE BLUEPRINT FOR TODAY'S INDIA

context

cntxt

First published in the United Kingdom by C. Hurst & Co. (Publishers) Ltd in 2024

Published in India by Context, an imprint of Westland Books, a division of Nasadiya Technologies Private Limited, in 2024.

No. 269/2B, First Floor, 'Irai Arul', Vimalraj Street, Nethaji Nagar, Alapakkam Main Road, Maduravoyal, Chennai 600095

ISBN: 9789360456696

10 9 8 7 6 5 4 3 2

Typeset by Jojy Philip, New Delhi
Printed at Thomson Press India Private Limited

In memory of Jacques Pouchepadass (1942–2021),
who initiated me into the history of India,
forty years ago …

CONTENTS

ABBREVIATIONS

ABVP	Akhil Bharatiya Vidyarthi Parishad
ADG	assistant director general
AMC	Ahmedabad Municipal Corporation
ANHAD	Act Now for Harmony and Democracy
BAPS	Bochasanwasi Shri Akshar Purushottam Swaminarayan Sanstha
BJP	Bharatiya Janata Party
BPL	below the poverty line
BRIC	Brazil, Russia, India, China (group)
BRTS	Bus Rapid Transfer System
BSUP	Basic Services for the Urban Poor
CAG	Comptroller and Auditor General
CBI	Central Bureau of Investigation
CEPT	Centre for Environmental Planning and Technology
CII	Confederation of Indian Industry
CM	chief minister
CSDS	Centre for the Study of Developing Societies
CSE	Centre for Science and Environment
CWC	Congress Working Committee
DG	director general
DIG	deputy inspector general
EPZ	Export Processing Zone

FICCI	Federation of Indian Chambers of Commerce and Industry
FIR	first information report
GCZMA	Gujarat Coastal Zone Management Authority
GERC	Gujarat Electricity Regulatory Commission
GPP	Gujarat Parivartan Party
GSEB	Gujarat State Electricity Board
GSPC	Gujarat State Petroleum Corporation
GujCOC	Gujarat Control of Organised Crime
IAS	Indian Administrative Service
IFS	Indian Foreign Service
IMR	infant mortality rate
IPS	Indian Police Service
JCP	joint commissioner of police
JNNURM	Jawaharlal Nehru National Urban Renewal Mission
JNU	Jawaharlal Nehru University
KHAM	Kshatriyas, Harijans, Adivasis and Muslims
LCB	local crime branch
LeT	Lashkar-e-Taiba
MGNREGA	Mahatma Gandhi National Rural Employment Guarantee Act
MLA	member of the Legislative Assembly
MPCE	monthly per capita expenditure
MSME	micro, small and medium enterprises
MSU	Maharaja Sayajirao University
MU	mega unit
NCERT	National Council of Educational Research and Training
NCPRI	National Campaign for People's Right to Information
NCRB	National Crime Records Bureau
NDC	National Development Council
NIA	National Investigation Agency
NJAC	National Judicial Appointments Commission

NREGS	National Rural Employment Guarantee Scheme
NRG	non-resident Gujarati
NRI	non-resident Indian
NSS	National Sample Survey
NSSO	National Sample Survey Office
OBC	Other Backward Class
PIL	public interest litigation
POTA	Prevention of Terrorism Act
PUCL	People's Union of Civil Liberties
RBI	Reserve Bank of India
RSS	Rashtriya Swayamsevak Sangh
RTI	Right to Information
SC	Scheduled Caste
SEWA	Self Employed Women's Association
SEWS	Socio-Economically Weaker Sections
SEZ	Special Economic Zone
SIR	Special Investment Region
SIT	Special Investigation Team
SME	small and medium enterprise
SP	superintendent of police
SRFDC	Sabarmati River Front Development Corporation
SRP	State Reserve Police
ST	Scheduled Tribe
STP	Special Task Force
TLA	Textile Labour Association
UP	Uttar Pradesh
UPA	United Progressive Alliance
VC	vice chancellor
VHP	Vishva Hindu Parishad

PREFACE 2023

The trajectory of this book has been atypical. I submitted the manuscript in late 2013 in order to have it published before the 2014 Indian elections. For publishers, election campaigns are usually a good time for selling political books. However, their legal advisors considered that this manuscript was 'high risk'. The letter I received, summarising the legal assessments, claimed that some passages 'may be deemed as hurtful towards the people of Gujarat, containing an unyielding view of Narendra Modi's regime. While the manuscript had been carefully copy-edited, I was asked to cut so many passages that I decided not to move forward.

In 2020, Michael Dwyer and I decided not to let this book die because it was our duty to testify and present facts which were gradually fading away—because of censorship and self-censorship—regarding the rise to power of Narendra Modi in Gujarat and the specific political modus operandi he invented then.

In the meantime, I had worked on the Emergency for a book I co-authored with Pratinav Anil[1] and on Modi's governance as prime minister of India.[2] These two books have influenced my reading of Modi's Gujarat while revisiting this manuscript. I had also continued to visit Gujarat at least once a year till January 2020. But I have merely edited the original manuscript—not rewritten it—in order to show what was already known in 2013, one year before Indian voters decided to elect Narendra Modi as prime minister of India, and this is one important part of the archives that this book is intended to create.

While revising the manuscript in the late 2010s to early 2020s, I have been helped by Sharik Laliwala, Harald Tambs-Lyche, Sheba Tejani and Hemal Thakker—and I am grateful to them all!

PREFACE 2013

This book is based on twelve years of fieldwork in Gujarat, which I visited for the first time in February 2001. I have been to the state at least once a year since then and these trips have allowed me to collect sources and to interview many people from different walks of life, including NGO activists, politicians, bureaucrats, businessmen, journalists and ordinary citizens. Two phases of this research have been particularly intense—those coinciding with the 2007 and 2012 state election campaigns. In spite of my familiarity with Gujarat's landscape, this book draws more upon newspapers articles, reports and books than on interviews, not only because some of my interlocutors did not wish to be quoted, but also because open sources are particularly valuable when discussing Narendra Modi. First, they can be easily cross-checked by anyone; and, second, they show that the arguments advanced in this book could have been made by others.

This is a scholarly book on a topical subject. Social scientists are first and foremost public intellectuals, and to make substantial interventions, they must not content themselves with the occasional newspaper article but should instead write books. It is not just their duty—it is their professional obligation. Those who have been trained to apply their mind to subjects of some significance to society as a whole must make use of their training and not only for the benefit of their peers who read specialised academic journals.

I am especially grateful to the following people for their contribution in helping this book see the light of day: J.S. Bandukwala, Shabnam Hashmi, Ashish Khetan, Rita Kothari, Martin Macwan, Father Cedric Prakash, Mallika Sarabhai, Teesta Setalvad, Gagan Sethi, Ghanshyam Shah and Mukul Sinha. Miriam Périer and Michael Dwyer, my publisher for thirty years who has greatly improved the original manuscript, have also made the completion of this book possible in a short span of time. But naturally, the mistakes and the shortcomings remain mine alone.

INTRODUCTION

This book deals with a unique political object: the transformation of Gujarat into what I called, in 2001, 'a laboratory for Hindu nationalism'[1] and what Howard Spodek in 2010 called 'the Hindutva laboratory'[2] after the rise to power of Narendra Modi, who governed the state for a record number of years—between 2001 and 2014. While Spodek and I published our work in which these quotations appeared before Modi became prime minister, we are today in a position to identify elements of continuity between the political model he invented in Gujarat and the way he transposed them to the national level. To understand this model is particularly important because of its remarkable efficacy. Never before had a man who had never won an electoral mandate become chief minister of an Indian state and won three successive state elections; never before had a chief minister become prime minister and been re-elected (at least) once without occupying any elective national post before; and never before had the Bharatiya Janata Party (BJP), governed a state of the Indian Union for so long—since 1998 till now.

This list of 'firsts', reflecting a major shift in Gujarat as well as Indian politics, is puzzling and this book seeks to elucidate what may seem like an enigma. The hypothesis we are going to test in the following pages assumes that the ground for the rise to power of the BJP in Gujarat was prepared by the characteristics of the state itself but that the party's rule in this state was largely due to Modi's very specific modus operandi, which was to be transposed—in an unprecedented step—to the national scene after 2014.

GUJARAT: AN *ASMITA* SHAPED BY GEOGRAPHY, HISTORY, RELIGION AND CASTE

Gujarat was officially created in 1960 as one of the new linguistic states of the Indian Union. It was formed from a myriad of former princely states and carved out, like Maharashtra, from the old Bombay Presidency of the British Raj. But there was a Gujarat before Gujarat, and a clear understanding of how its identity was shaped constitutes a useful background to its twenty-first-century politics.

While each region of India is specific, Gujarat is a unique state in many respects, including its extreme valorisation of an economic ethos, its peculiar caste hierarchies and its relationship with Islam. These characteristics, which can only be understood in a historical perspective, are largely due to geography. Indeed, the location of the Gujarat peninsula at the crossroads of trade routes linking the plains of North India and the Indian Ocean and therefore tilted towards the Middle East and Africa, largely explains the intensity of the commercial links that emerged there as early as Antiquity. These only intensified when European trading companies established themselves in India, and later benefited from relatively early industrialisation in the colonial era. Many Gujarati merchants became entrepreneurs and transformed Ahmedabad into the 'Manchester of India'. These economic achievements went hand in hand with a broader cultural admiration for mercantile values, which continues to this day, with business being eulogised uninhibitedly in Gujarat. Referring to Gujaratis, the director of the Entrepreneurship Development Institute of Ahmedabad declared in 2013: 'Entrepreneurship is in their blood. No doubt in that. Gujarati children are exposed to money-making businesses early on. Even in social gatherings people talk about business rather than bureaucracy, politics, or literature. By the time a person comes out of college he would have a role model in one or other successful businessman.'[3]

Historically, Hindu merchant castes, the Vanyas, played a major role in the economic development of Gujarat. Among them, the dominant community has comprised the followers of Vaishnavism, known as Vaishnav Vanya.[4] From the fifteenth century onwards, this group played a key role in society, in stark contrast to what happened elsewhere in India where the caste system is generally dominated by Brahmins and Kshatriyas. Hence the development of what Harald Tambs-Lyche called a 'Vanya model of culture', which emphasises not only a business ethos but also asceticism and vegetarianism[5] and places the trading castes on a par with Brahmins, and even above them sometimes.[6]

However, elite groups of Gujarat are represented by 'two poles, the martial and the mercantile'.[7] The latter, led by the Vaishnav Vanyas, tended to prevail not only because of their wealth and influence but also because of their location since they were entrenched in the central plains around Ahmedabad, whereas the warrior castes (mostly Rajputs) dominated the periphery formed by Kathiawad (now known as Saurashtra), where they ruled a constellation of 232 princely states till 1947.[8]

But the caste system of Gujarat also worked differently because the very notion of caste as we know it in neighbouring North India has always been more elastic in this region. Clear-cut *jatis* (sub-castes) were not established as elsewhere in India because some hypergamous relations—marrying someone of a different caste or status—cut across social boundaries.[9] In central Gujarat, members of the dominant caste, the Patidars (Patels), who were the most numerous and owned most of the land, have traditionally had matrimonial links with lower-caste peasants, like the Kanbis; and in Saurashtra, Rajputs have done the same with similar lower peasant castes, the Kolis.[10] These matrimonial relations have somewhat blurred social frontiers among these two caste complexes, which became antagonistic after they aligned themselves in two rival poles, the martial and the mercantile. The latter crystallised in central Gujarat, comprising the Vaishnav Vanyas, Patidars, Kanbis and Brahmins, while the former, consisting of Rajputs and Kolis, took shape in Saurashtra.[11] Harald Tambs-Lyche suggests that this polarisation benefited the central Gujarat bloc because it was richer and more educated and won the anti-colonial struggle.[12] Indeed, the Congress party was led by Vanyas (including Mahatma Gandhi), Patidars (including Sardar Patel) and Brahmins (including Indulal Yagnik, K.M. Munshi and Morarji Desai), whereas the Rajputs and Kolis of Saurashtra remained identified with various princely states.

The pre-eminence of the bloc based in central Gujarat has played a major role in shaping social identity. Its ethos not only emphasised economic values, but promoted also a rather exclusive form of Hindu Vaishnavism which found expression in the Pushtimarg *sampradaya* (sect) and, in the nineteenth century, in new sectarian developments, such as the Swaminarayan movement, founded by Sahajanand Swami.[13] In 1907, a breakaway fraction of this *sampradaya* established the Bochasanwasi Shri Akshar Purushottam Swaminarayan Sanstha (BAPS), which developed a more centralised network of temples and body of ascetics.[14] In the twentieth century, this movement, which was massively supported by the Patidars (or Patels as they now started to call themselves), propagated a 'kind of Gujarati religiosity in which uniformity and homogeneity are the ideal'.[15] The hegemonic aspirations of Vaishnavism have pushed the Shakti cults (goddess cults), followed by the warrior castes (Kshatriyas), on the defensive, to such an extent that their goddesses have sometimes become vegetarian. Moreover, vegetarianism is a cardinal principle of Vaishnavism in Gujarat, where this dietary option is also fostered and supported by the influence of Jainism.

This variant of Hinduism tended to become dominant in Gujarat also because of the response of the region to Islam, geography once again playing a major role. It explains why Gujarat witnessed one of India's first encounters with Muslims. Social scientists read this encounter in different ways: some emphasise the role of Sufi saints who attracted scores of Hindus who eventually converted to Islam,[16] while others dwell on its violent aspects. Achyut Yagnik and Suchitra Sheth, for instance, point out that the 'first raid took place only four years after the death of the Prophet in AD 635'.[17] Then came, in the early years of the eleventh century, the 'sack of the Somnath temple',[18] one of the most important places of worship for the Hindus of Gujarat, by Mahmud of Ghazni. In 1411, a Sultanate in Gujarat was established by Ahmed Shah, who also founded the capital city, Ahmedabad. Samira Sheikh convincingly argues that this political entity prepared the ground for the making of a form of 'proto-nationalism' in Gujarat.[19] According to Yagnik and Sheth, the

> forceful imposition of jiziya [a poll tax levied on non-Muslims] was another watershed in the social history of Gujarat. Even though Muslims had been a constituent element of society since the eleventh century and large numbers of mosques were already a part of the landscape, for the first time, the state distinguished between its citizens along the lines of religion. In one stroke, Gujarati society was divided into two blocs not only in the cities but also in rural areas.[20]

This reading of history tends to minimise significant forms of religious interaction (evident from the popularity of Sufi saints among Hindu devotees and of certain gurus among Muslims) and cultural synthesis (as in the invention of a Gujarati version of Urdu, for instance).[21] But this narrative lent itself to political instrumentalisation and to the construction, in the nineteenth century, of a regionalist ideology that now needs to be deciphered.

This ideology relied primarily on the close association of Gujarati identity (or *asmita*, a word also translated as 'pride', which became commonplace in the twentieth century) with Hinduism. The architects of this *asmita*, mostly literary figures who codified the Gujarati language in the nineteenth century, were all Hindus.[22] The key figures were Narmadashankar Lalshankar Dave (popularly known as Narmad), Kavishwar Dalpatram Dahyabhai (better known as Dalpatram), his son Nanalal Dalpatram Kavi, Mahipatram Rupram and Karsandas Mulji. Narmad—along with Dalpatram—heralded the modern age of Gujarati literature.[23] He wrote the first essay published in Gujarati in 1851, compiled the first lexicon of the Gujarati language, and coined the famous watchword '*Jai jai garvi Gujarat*' (Hail, hail, proud Gujarat) with which he prefaced his dictionary.[24]

These pioneers endowed the Gujarati *asmita* with an ethno-religious content. In his seminal poem '*Koni koni chhe Gujarat?*' (Whose is Gujarat?), Narmad writes that it 'belongs to all those who speak Gujarati; to those who observe Aryadharma [Aryan religions] of all varieties; and also to those who are foreigners but nurtured by this land; and to those who follow other religions [*paradharma*] but are well-wishers of Mother Gujarat and therefore our brothers.'[25] While this definition of a Gujarati is inclusive, it has a certain ethno-religious flavour, particularly given the fact that Narmad, as much as Dalpatram, 'attributed the decline of Gujarati culture and knowledge to Muslim rule'.[26] After some hesitation, Narmad adopted a conservative view of society, eulogised 'birth-based caste hierarchy and advocated that "all castes should follow the duties ascribed to them in the Varnashrama Dharma"'.[27] A contemporary of Narmad, Nandshankar Mehta, published the first Gujarati novel along these lines in 1866. *Karan Ghelo: The Last Rajput King of Gujarat* tells the story of the Chaulukya–Vaghela dynasty, which was defeated by the army of Alauddin Khilji in the thirteenth century, and 'equates the "post-Rajput" period or the "Muslim" period with the degradation and decline of Gujarat'.[28] This periodisation was not only present in novels, but gradually permeated the consciousness of the Hindu public sphere.

The cultural and social characteristics of Gujarat thereby endow the majority Hindu community with the key features of ethnic nationalism: ethnic ties, common values, a shared historical narrative and a pervasive fear (as well as stigmatisation) of the Other. In fact, the promotion of vegetarianism reflected an attempt by the Brahmin–Vanya–Patidar bloc of central Gujarat to impose their lifestyle over the Rajput–Koli of Saurashtra and the lower castes, as well as religious minorities. Subsequently, the enforcement of Prohibition—Gujarat remains one of the only 'dry' states in India today—reflected the same ethos.

But in contrast to other Indian states which have acquired a strong subnationalist identity—like Maharashtra, for instance—Gujarat has not been the crucible of a regional party. Despite the strength of its subnationalist identity, there is no space in the state for a regional party. This contradiction vanishes if one admits that Gujarati identity is rooted in Hinduism and directed against Muslims.[29] Hindu Gujaratis regard themselves as Hindus par excellence—opposed to Muslims—and have never seen the need for a regionalist polity after the formation of the state of Gujarat in 1960. Certainly, Indulal Yagnik created the Mahagujarat Janata Parishad in 1956 for Gujarat to be carved out from the Bombay province, but the party vanished after this state was formed.[30]

The creation of Pakistan reinforced the already latent equation between Hindus and Gujaratis. Even before 1947, Hindus considered Gujarat to be a frontline state. During the Raj, this geopolitical configuration crystallised with the formation of Sindh, which was lopped off from the Bombay Presidency in 1936. After Independence, the location of Gujarat became even more strategic, and exposed, since it bordered Pakistan. According to Parvis Ghassem-Fachandi: 'The national border with Pakistan is a barrier that generates psycho-geographical effects. Whatever its actual porosity or asserted impenetrability, it is psychologically more momentous than any desert could ever be.'[31] That the desert offered no protection is evident from Gujarat's position at the forefront of the 1965 war that started in the Rann of Kutch. Not only that, but the plane carrying its then chief minister, Balwantrai Mehta, who was inspecting the border with his wife, was shot down by the Pakistani Air Force, killing them both.[32]

Inhabiting a frontier state and endowed with a regional identity which promoted Hindu values against the Muslim 'Other', the majority community of Gujarat has tended to invest its subnationalism in national parties—including the Indian National Congress—rather than in regional forces. Its Gujarati leaders, in effect, evolved a peculiar variant of the Congress in this region. The first chapter of this book deals, in particular, with the very specific trajectory of the Gujarat segment of the Congress until the 1990s, since this detour will help us to understand the rise to power of the BJP, the Hindu nationalist party that has dominated politics in the state since the mid-1990s.

HINDU NATIONALISM, AN IDEOLOGY AND A MOVEMENT[33]

Hindu nationalism took shape in the 1920s and even goes back to the nineteenth century—like the Gujarati *asmita* whose development ran parallel to it in many ways. The first expression of Hindu revivalism emerged in the nineteenth century, as an ideological reaction to European domination and later to Muslim proselytisation. It developed under the aegis of the Arya Samaj (the Aryan Society), which was founded in 1875 by Swami Dayananda, a Gujarati Brahmin. Arya Samajis argued that Indian antiquity, which they called the 'Vedic Golden Age', was imbued with cultural greatness,[34] like the glorious Gujarati *asmita*.

In the early twentieth century, the Arya Samaj of Punjab—the movement's stronghold—was the crucible of a political party, the Hindu Sabha (the Hindu Association), which drew support from like-minded activists in the Hindi belt to create the Hindu Mahasabha (the Great Hindu Association) in 1915. This organisation took shape *within* the Congress party as its right wing, but remained dormant until the 1920s.[35] It was rekindled then at a time when the ideology of Hindu nationalism crystallised in reaction to a Muslim threat felt subjectively if not experienced concretely.[36] Indeed, Muslim mobilisation in the framework of the Khilafat movement—in defence of the Constantinople-based Caliph—resulted in a wave of anti-Hindu attacks that exacerbated a feeling of vulnerability in some Hindu quarters.[37] Hindu nationalism was codified in this context by V.D. Savarkar, who wrote *Hindutva:Who Is a Hindu?* in 1923.[38]

Savarkar drew his definition of Hindu identity from Western theories of the nation. The first criterion of the Hindu nation, for him, was the sacred territory of the Aryavarta described in the Vedas—and by Dayananda, whose book *Satyarth Prakash* (The Light of Truth) Savarkar read extensively.[39] Then comes race: for Savarkar, Hindus are the descendants of the 'Vedic fathers' who occupied this land in Indian antiquity; they form a people more than a community of believers following the same creed. In addition to land and race, Savarkar mentions language as a pillar of Hindu identity. In doing so, he refers to Sanskrit but also to Hindi: hence the equation he finally established between Hindutva and the trio 'Hindu, Hindi, Hindustan'—typical of an ethnic nationalism in which religion, ultimately, plays a secondary role. This ideology was at odds with the brand of multiculturalism promoted by Gandhi and Nehru within the Congress party.

For Savarkar, who became the leader of the Hindu Mahasabha in the same year, the majority community was supposed to embody the nation, not only because it was the largest but also because it comprised the sons of the soil. For his followers (until today), Hindus are the autochthonous people of India, whereas the religious minorities are outsiders whose members must adhere to the Hindu culture, presented as *the* national culture. In the private sphere, they may worship their gods and follow their rituals, but in the public domain they must pay allegiance to Hindu symbols. This applies especially to Muslims and Christians, the proponents of the allegedly un-Indian religions in India.[40]

While Savarkar shaped the ideology of Hindu nationalism, he did not explain how Hindus could concretely react to the Muslim threat, or reform and organise themselves. This task was taken up by one of his followers, K.B. Hedgewar, who founded the Rashtriya Swayamsevak Sangh (RSS) in his home town, Nagpur (in today's Maharashtra).[41] This movement—which quickly became the largest Hindu nationalist organisation—was intended not only to propagate Hindutva ideology but also to infuse new physical and martial strength into the majority community.

To achieve this twofold objective, Hedgewar decided to work at the grassroots level in order to reform Hindu society from below. He created local branches (shakhas) of the movement in towns and villages according to a standardised pattern: young Hindu men gathered in the open air for games with martial connotations and ideological training sessions every morning and evening. The men in charge of the shakhas, the pracharaks (preachers), dedicated their life to the organisation; as RSS cadres they could be sent anywhere in India to develop the organisation's network. By 1947, there were about 600,000 of these swayamsevaks (volunteers).[42] The RSS had become the most powerful Hindu nationalist movement, but it had little impact on public life in India, simply because it remained out of politics. M.S. Golwalkar, who succeeded Hedgewar as sarsanghchalak (head) of the organisation in 1940, had made apoliticism a mandatory rule.[43]

However, soon after Independence, the RSS's leaders realised that they could no longer remain apart from politics. In January 1948, Mahatma Gandhi was killed by (an alleged former *swayamsevak*)[44] Nathuram Godse, and Prime Minister Jawaharlal Nehru immediately banned the organisation, whose leaders then realised that they could expect no help from any political party. A section of the movement's leaders who favoured the RSS's involvement in politics argued that this situation justified the launch of a party of its own. Though reluctant, Golwalkar allowed the opening of talks with Shyama Prasad Mookerjee, then Hindu Mahasabha president, negotiations that resulted in the establishment of the Bharatiya Jana Sangh in 1951, on the eve of the first general elections.[45] This party is the ancestor of the BJP, which was formed in 1980.

The Jana Sangh was to be only one of the front organisations set up by the RSS, its aim no longer being merely to penetrate society directly through *shakhas*, but also to establish organisations working among specific social categories. Hence, in 1948 RSS cadres based in Delhi founded the Akhil Bharatiya Vidyarthi Parishad (ABVP), a student union whose primary aim was to combat communist influence on university campuses. In 1964, in association with Hindu clerics, the RSS set up the Vishva Hindu Parishad (VHP), a movement responsible for bringing together the heads of various Hindu sects to lend coherence to this very unorganised religion and endow it with a centralised structure.[46] Taken together, these initiatives—among many others—were presented by the mother organisation as forming the Sangh Parivar, 'the family of the Sangh', that is of the RSS.[47]

The Sangh Parivar remained a secondary actor in Indian public life till the 1980s when it launched the Ayodhya movement. A town in Uttar Pradesh, Ayodhya is described in the Hindu tradition as the birthplace and capital of the god-king Lord Ram, an avatar of Vishnu. A Ram temple supposedly once occupied the site until it was allegedly destroyed in the sixteenth century on the orders of Babur, the first Mughal emperor, in order to build a mosque, the Babri Masjid. In 1984—35 years after idols of Ram and Sita had been installed in the mosque by Hindu activists[48]—the VHP called for the site to be returned to Hindus. In 1989, the BJP rallied to this ethno-religious mobilisation strategy, which contributed to its success at the polls, taking it from 2 to 88 seats.[49] In 1990, while the party was a major component of the coalition in power that had just ousted the Congress party, its president, L.K. Advani, led a 10,000 km 'chariot journey' (Rath Yatra), its goal being the construction of the Ayodhya temple. Advani was turned back before crossing into Uttar Pradesh and police opened fire on activists who had attacked the mosque, leading to a dozen or so deaths. This episode reinforced the 'champion-of-Hinduism' image that the BJP was trying to inculcate among the majority community. In the 1991 general elections the party won 20.08 per cent of the vote and 120 seats in the Lok Sabha, the lower house of the Indian parliament. Hindu nationalist militants tried to put an end to this deadlock by demolishing the mosque on 6 December 1992.

By the mid-1990s, the BJP had reverted to a moderate line, which allowed it to build a coalition of more than 15 parties in the late 1990s. This National Democratic Alliance enabled the BJP president, A.B. Vajpayee, to form a government after the 1998 and 1999 polls.[50] While the BJP lost the general election of 2004, the party remained well entrenched in several states, including Gujarat, where Narendra Modi had become chief minister in 2001.

NARENDRA MODI OF GUJARAT?

The political career of Modi in Gujarat is exceptional in the sense that he was the first RSS *pracharak* seconded to the BJP to become a chief minister and, then, the first chief minister to be re-elected twice. This book's primary objective is to account for his rise to power and his making of a new polity, which was to be transposed to the national scene in 2014. While Modi's achievements owe much to the man himself, they have to be analysed in the broader historical perspective of Gujarat's politics and society.

The very fact that, as mentioned above, the Congress adopted in Gujarat a Hindu traditionalist overtone prepared the ground for the rise of Hindu nationalism. But Congress politics helped the BJP even more when, turning their back on their rather conservative roots, some Congress leaders tried to woo low-caste voters—thereby alienating their traditional supporters, including the Patels, who then joined the BJP in the 1980s, at a time when Hindu–Muslim riots were fomenting communal polarisation. The BJP took power in the 1990s in this context, as chapter 1 will show, but the chief minister at the time, Keshubhai Patel—who had lost almost every local election and by-election in 2000–01—was replaced by Narendra Modi in 2001.

Modi had been the chief organiser of the party for many years in the 1980s and 1990s but had been exiled from Gujarat in 1995 after party leaders accused him of organisational shortcomings[51]. In 2001, he needed to rebuild a base for himself as he was not even a member of the Legislative Assembly (MLA). While he had been chief minister since October 2021, he was elected an MLA[52] in February 2002, three days before the beginning of the Gujarat riots that coincided with his assertive rise to power.

Gujarat has long been a riot-prone area owing to prolonged communal tensions between Hindus and Muslims, but the Hindu–Muslim violence of 2002 was of a different intensity (at least in terms of its geographical spread and duration), hence its characterisation as a 'pogrom', a word that also applies to the Congress-led anti-Sikh violence that followed Indira Gandhi's assassination in 1984.[53] In Gujarat, in 2002, the exceptional nature of the communal clashes can only be explained by the role of the state apparatus, including the police; this resulted in an equally unprecedented religious polarisation that helped the BJP win the state elections in December 2002, as we shall see in chapter 2.

While these abnormal circumstances may explain the initial massive electoral success of BJP in Gujarat, we need to turn to other, additional factors to understand his political resilience. The BJP's standard explanation for this achievement is spelt out in terms of governance, a word that refers here to development as well as the rule of law. Regarding the latter, the Gujarat government of that time was in fact largely responsible for de-institutionalising the rule of law. First, as we will see in chapter 3, in the wake of the 2002 pogrom, it 'saffronised' the police by rewarding policemen who had let the pogrom happen and punishing those who had resisted the Hindu nationalist forces in the street, and tried to influence the judicial process. Second, chapter 4 shows that the rule of law was also badly affected by the carte blanche given to Hindu nationalist vigilante groups by the corruption of the police and by the lack of investment in both the police and the judiciary. As a result, the level of criminality remained very high in Gujarat, among politicians as well—and even among ministers, who indulged in illegal surveillance of their political opponents and others.

If the de-institutionalisation and politicisation of the rule of law formed the first pillar of Modi's style of governance in Gujarat, the second one pertained to his economic and social policies. In contrast to his predecessors, Narendra Modi did not capitalise mainly on the Gujaratis' sense of entrepreneurship, which had resulted in the making of a dense network of small and medium-sized enterprises, but as chapter 5 demonstrates, on big investors, who were attracted to Gujarat by all kinds of concessions (and by the creation of Special Economic Zones) and who became, in some cases, crony capitalists. While this strategy generated a high growth rate and endowed Gujarat with robust infrastructure, the highly capital-intensive industrialisation it promoted brought with it relatively few good jobs, Gujarat being known for its casual labour practices. Chapter 6 scrutinises the social characteristics of the so-called Gujarat model that Modi invented, which relied on jobless growth, low levels of developmental state expenditures (including education), and growing inequalities, both between urban and rural Gujaratis but also among both urban and rural Gujaratis.

The third dimension of Modi's politics in Gujarat concerns the way in which he succeeded in concentrating power. In contrast to most BJP leaders, who have cultivated a collegial style of governance and reported to the RSS, Modi relied primarily on the state bureaucracy, emancipated himself from the Sangh Parivar, and fought some of its components, including the VHP. Chapter 7 shows that he established his own channels of communication with the people, the populist way, against the Delhi-based cosmopolitan Establishment. But chapter 8 qualifies this populism, as Modi's style is, in fact, *national*-populist: indeed, 'Moditva', a term coined by the Gujarati media, combined populism and Hindu nationalism, as the people he defended comprised the sons of the soil, the Hindus, against the others—namely Muslims, first and foremost. Among Hindus, the BJP attracted primarily upper-caste voters, as usual, as well as low-caste voters, especially those who had joined the emerging 'neo-middle class' as a result of the urbanisation process, a plebeianisation trajectory that we'll study in chapter 9. But the whole of Gujarat did not support the ruling party—it never won more than 50 per cent of the votes in state elections. Chapter 10 analyses the opposition, the dissenting voices and the victims of the BJP government in Gujarat, a state polarised along social as well as religious lines, at the expense of secularism.

The characteristics of Modi's win in Gujarat make it clear that the state was truly the testing ground where he learnt the techniques that were to be applied to the whole of India after 2014. In the following pages, I'll make this point at the end of each chapter in order to show that Modi repeated as prime minister most of the strategies he had pioneered as chief minister, including communal polarisation, the de-institutionalisation of the state, the promotion of crony capitalism and, of course, a national-populist style. This modus operandi has resulted in a similar kind of personalisation of power, saffronisation of the state and society, and inequalities along socio-economic and ethnic lines. The very fact that techniques that have been tested regionally could be replicated on such a large, semi-continental scale makes their analysis even more necessary.

PART ONE

FROM HINDU TRADITIONALISM TO HINDUTVA VIA CASTE AND COMMUNAL VIOLENCE

Under Narendra Modi, Gujarat became the stronghold of Hindu nationalism: never before had the BJP won so many elections in a row in a state of the Indian Union. This exceptional development resulted from a unique combination of factors. On the one hand, the Congress party, dominant till the 1980s, prepared the ground for the Sangh Parivar in two, contradictory ways. Some of its leaders—including Sardar Patel, K.M. Munshi, Gulzarilal Nanda and Morarji Desai—were imbued with Hindu traditionalism, a conservative ideology promoting the regional *asmita*. Instead of fighting Hindu nationalism in the name of secularism, they accommodated this political culture and even strengthened it. But there were also progressive Congressmen, like Indulal Yagnik, who defended a social justice-oriented agenda. This group asserted itself when Mrs Gandhi took power, especially after the 1969 split within the Congress which resulted in the making of an explicitly Hindu traditionalist Congress (O) and a socialist, secular Congress (R). While the latter and its successor— the

Congress (I)—gained power in the 1980s, its progressive policies polarised society in such a way that, by alienating a dominant caste—the Patels—it helped the BJP to assume power in the 1990s, partly because many Congress leaders were not prepared to embark fully on a social justice agenda.

Besides social polarisation, religious polarisation played a major role in Gujarat. The state, indeed, was devastated by recurring communal riots in 1969, 1985 and 1992, which were engineered or triggered by the Sangh Parivar. Such violence reflected a deep-rooted Hindu–Muslim conflict, accentuated even further every ten years or so. This process reached its culmination in 2002, in the wake of what has to be described as an anti-Muslim agenda. Narendra Modi was the newly appointed chief minister at the time of this event, which marked the crystallisation of an unprecedented form of communal polarisation.

The two chapters of the first part of the book, therefore, present the two faces of the same coin: social polarisation and communal polarisation, two processes which took shape primarily in Gujarat and which have become mainstays of BJP's politics.

1

GUJARAT BEFORE MODI

HOW THE CONGRESS PREPARED THE GROUND FOR HINDUTVA POLITICS

> The danger is that the emerging Gujarat with its provincial, middle class, upper caste Hindu restrictive outlook seems to have forgotten even the old. Without a recovery of its one-time welcoming, accommodating and adaptive culture, the Gujarat of the 21st century is unlikely to be a nice place to know.
>
> 'The Problem', *Seminar*, October 1998, p. 13

Until the 1990s, Gujarat was not a stronghold of Hindutva politics; quite the contrary. The Jana Sangh won only 1.4 per cent of valid votes in the 1962 Lok Sabha elections and 2.2 per cent in 1971. However, some of the party's ideas, including its opposition to state ownership of the economy,[1] were promoted by the Swatantra Party as early as 1962. This party, formed in 1959 by senior Congressmen, including C. Rajagopalachari and N.G. Ranga, who opposed Nehru's economic policy by offering a more liberal approach, made significant inroads in Gujarat in the 1960s. In 1962 it became the largest opposition party in the state Assembly with 25 per cent of the votes and remained so in 1967 with almost 40 per cent of the votes.

Not only that, the Congress itself shared some important dimensions of the Sangh Parivar's programme. This was largely due to the ambivalent legacy of Mahatma Gandhi in a state whose political culture he had largely shaped. On the one hand, Gandhi promoted social reform and labour organisation; on the other, his discourse was conducive to Hindu traditionalist attitudes. The tension between these two trends fostered factionalism and resulted in splits and defections in the late 1960s and 1970s with the creation of the Congress (O) and the Congress (R), which in Gujarat competed neck and neck in elections in the 1970s. Indira Gandhi's Congress (I)—the heir of the Congress (R)—then unwittingly prepared the ground for Hindutva politics by exploiting the policy of reservations for the lower castes and the tribals in the 1980s. In response, the upper castes joined hands and supported Hindu nationalism in order to counter reservation politics. But the Sangh Parivar rose to power in the 1990s on its own 'merits' too. In the 1980 and 1990s it reaped the harvest of fifty years of political activism at the grassroots and benefited from communal polarisation resulting from a series of Hindu–Muslim riots that its activists had triggered.

GANDHI'S NOT SO AMBIVALENT LEGACY

Gandhi is mostly remembered in Gujarat for the popular movements that he orchestrated after settling down in his Ahmedabad ashram in 1915. In 1917 he took up the cause of textile mill workers in Ahmedabad. He even became 'a union leader'[2] by launching the Majoor Mahajan Sangh, better known by its English name, the Textile Labour Association (TLA), in February 1920. This federation of craft unions organised the unskilled labourers in Ahmedabad's cotton mills, while working for harmony between industrialists and their employees. If caste discriminations continued within the TLA itself, its leaders—all professionals from the upper castes—made a point of interacting with and helping Dalits.[3]

The Mahatma fought against the ostracism which affected the Dalits too. He insisted that everyone who stayed there had to clean the toilets in his Sabarmati ashram. Under his guidance, the Congress voted in the early 1920s for a motion declaring the work of Bhangis (sweepers) as respectable,[4] and at its Nagpur session, which was held in December 1920, a resolution was passed condemning 'the sin of untouchability'.[5] However, that very month he published in *Young India* an article defending certain aspects of the caste system:

> I believe that caste has saved Hinduism from disintegration [...] The caste system is not based on inequality, there is no question of inferiority, and so far as there is any such question arising, as in Madras, Maharashtra or elsewhere, the tendency should undoubtedly be checked [...]
>
> Interdrinking, interdining, intermarrying, I hold, are not essential for the promotion of the spirit of democracy. I do not contemplate under a most democratic constitution a universality of manners and customs about eating, drinking and marrying. We shall ever have to seek unity in diversity, and I decline to consider it a sin for a man not to drink or eat with anybody and everybody ...[6]

Clearly, Gandhi's campaigning on behalf of the exploited did not mean that he was egalitarian—at least not in an individualist manner. In the 1920s his ambiguity was probably the root cause of the Janus-faced aspect of the Congress in Gujarat, the conservative wing being epitomised by Sardar Patel, K.M. Munshi, Gulzarilal Nanda and Morarji Desai and the progressive one by Indulal Yagnik.[7]

Indulal Yagnik, the Lonely Progressive Face of the Congress in Colonial Gujarat

Yagnik was drawn to Gandhi immediately after the latter returned from Africa in 1914.[8] He then contributed to *Young*

India, the newspaper launched by Annie Besant. When Gandhi took over the newspaper, Yagnik settled in Ahmedabad and worked for him. However, he was more interested in serving the poor in the countryside. In 1917 he was involved in famine relief with the Bhils. He then discovered, as he writes in his autobiography, that 'depressed communities, like Rabaris and Bhois, potters and Chamars, Untouchables and Bhangis, were shouting for help from the terror of the constant oppressions of compulsory labour.'[9] He was also enthused by Gandhi's plea in favour of vernacular languages[10] and wanted to start a school for Dalits, for which he submitted a provisional budget of Rs 5,000 to the Congress Provincial Committee. Its president, Vallabhbhai Patel, turned down his request, arguing that 'while the Congress was committed to a campaign against untouchability, it had to direct its resources to the struggle against the British'. Yagnik turned to Gandhi, who supported him, thus angering Patel. As a consequence, 'Feeling that there was little point staying in the Congress in the face of such hostility, Yagnik submitted his resignation, which Gandhi promptly accepted',[11] by saying: 'There is no doubt that there is no other person as industrious as Bhai Indulal. There is also no doubt that one would not easily come across a sincere person like him. But because of their different natures he and Vallabhbhai cannot work together. Therefore, it is my suggestion to accept Bhai Indulal's resignation with great regret ...'[12]

Yagnik concentrated on his work in the villages and co-founded the Kisan Sabha (Peasant Association) in 1936. He later reflected upon this parting of the ways, for which Patel was largely responsible—and described him in the following terms:

> Collecting money raining on the Congress table—thanks to Mr Gandhi and his propaganda in his great political movement—and influenced by the conservative and petty-minded counsels of his new-found allies [the businessmen rallying around the Congress], sitting at the headquarters, stationary and immobile

> like a great god, he increasingly tended to develop into a bureaucratic and centripetal force charged with the onerous responsibility of guarding the people's treasure in the name of the great Mahatma. While, though I had made Ahmedabad the headquarters of all my public and political activities, I instinctively represented the centrifugal tendency and could not help identifying myself with the needs, the views, and the feelings of the mass of the workers and people in the districts and the village.[13]

This quotation is particularly interesting in the light of the opposition between the central social bloc (discussed in the introduction) and the periphery.[14] The former was indeed mostly drawn from Vanya Vaishnavs and Patidars based in Ahmedabad, and the Congress under Patel identified with these groups.

Sardar Patel, Social Conservatism and Hindu Traditionalism

Sardar Patel was elected municipal councillor for an Ahmedabad ward (and was then mayor of the city) and joined Gandhi in 1917. He became president of the Gujarat Congress in the early 1920s, a position he held for about two decades.[15] His relations with Indulal Yagnik revealed his political priorities. His proximity to the businessmen who funded the Congress in Gujarat after Gandhi became its party leader reinforced his social conservatism. This dimension of his personality, which was to find expression in his opposition to 'the socialist faction' which emerged in the Congress in the mid-1930s,[16] and in his defence of private property rights in the Constituent Assembly, was well in tune with the mercantile aspect of the 'central Gujarat bloc'. Not only was he less sensitive to the Dalit question than Yagnik was, but he was also more favourably inclined towards the Hindu Mahasabha, including its main leader in Gujarat, Vamanrao Mukadam.[17]

This was partly a reflection of Patel's ambivalent attitude towards the Muslim minority. In 1919–21 he supported the Khilafat movement,[18] considering that the abolition of the Caliph 'has, as a matter of fact, been a heart-breaking episode for the Indian Muslims, and how can Hindus stand by unaffected when they see their fellow countrymen thus in distress?'[19] This sense of solidarity was fostered by his belief that Muslims 'originally belonged to India and were converted from Hindus'.[20] Yet Patel also complained to Gandhi that 'the manners and customs of Muslims are different. They take meat while we are vegetarians. How are we to live with them in the same place?' Gandhi replied, 'No, sir, Hindus as a body are nowhere vegetarians except in Gujarat.'[21]

Patel's attitude towards Muslims also changed after the Muslim League's separatism developed in the 1940s. According to Ghanshyam Shah, 'though he was in the know about the active participation of some Congress leaders like Vamanrao [Mukadam] in instigating communal riots, Patel did not even reprimand these leaders'.[22] This inclination intensified after Partition took place. When he became deputy prime minister and home minister in the Nehru government, Patel explained in a letter he wrote to Rajendra Prasad on 5 September 1947 that, as home minister, he had 'already given licenses to two or three Hindu dealers for the sale of arms', suggesting that he was helping anti-Muslim militias.[23]

Soon after Independence, in November 1947, Patel came to Junagadh, a princely state of Saurashtra, whose Muslim ruler wanted to accede to Pakistan, so that he could direct the occupation of the state by the Indian army.[24] He seized this opportunity to visit the ruins of the temple of Somnath. According to his close associate V.P. Menon, he 'was visibly moved to find the temple which had once been the glory of India looking so dilapidated. It was proposed then and there to reconstruct it so as to return it to its original splendour.'[25] He declared, 'The restoration of the idols would be a point of honour and sentiment with the Hindu public.'[26] While Gandhi and Nehru disapproved of a decision that, in their view, transgressed the religious neutrality of the Indian state,[27] Patel was backed by the Hindu nationalists.

He himself manifested some sympathy for the RSS. In December 1947, during a speech in Jaipur, he expressed his will 'to turn the enthusiasm and discipline of Rashtriya Swayam Sevak Sangh into right channels'.[28] On 6 January 1948, he made an even more important speech at Lucknow, inviting the Hindu Mahasabha to amalgamate with the Congress on the ground that its members could not pretend to be 'the only custodians of Hinduism'. He held out the same invitation to members of the RSS and justified this move while criticising Nehru obliquely: 'In the Congress, those who are in power feel that by the virtue of authority they will be able to crush the RSS. You cannot crush an organisation by using the danda [stick]. The danda is meant for thieves and dacoits. They are patriots who love their country. Only their trend of thought is diverted. They are to be won over by congressmen, by love.'[29]

Gandhi was assassinated by Nathuram Godse three weeks later and the organisation was banned. Home minister Patel was in charge of the repression, which he justified in eloquent terms to Shyama Prasad Mookerjee, his colleague from the Hindu Mahasabha in the Nehru government:

> The activities of the RSS constituted a clear threat to the existence of the Government and the State. Our reports show that those activities, despite the ban, have not died down. Indeed, as time has marched on, the RSS circles are becoming defiant and are indulging in their subversive activities in an increasing measure. The number of persons arrested is not large; it is just above 500 throughout India. This would show that generally only those are in detention whose release is prejudicial to security.[30]

Still, Patel was prepared to engage with the RSS. In December 1948, while the RSS was still banned he made a speech, in Jaipur, in which he 'advised members of the RSS to join the

Indian National Congress if they had the good of the country uppermost in their hearts'.[31] As home minister, Patel negotiated with the RSS leaders who demanded the lifting of the ban. He was convinced that the RSS could be legalised after it adopted a constitution complying with the Indian Constitution. He then considered that 'the only way for them [the leaders of the RSS] is to reform the Congress from within, if they think the Congress is going on the wrong path'.[32] On 10 October 1949, while Nehru was abroad, Patel had a resolution passed by the Congress Working Committee (CWC) authorising RSS members to be part of the party. The prime minister rescinded the decision soon afterwards.[33]

While Patel appreciated some of the qualities of the RSS, he was not in favour of letting the organisation penetrate the state apparatus. In January 1948—a few weeks before the assassination of Gandhi—he declared that he approved the action 'of the Bombay Government banning the employment of Rashtriya Swayam Sevak men in Government service [...] because it was not proper for Government servants to identify themselves with a communal organization'.[34] Similarly, as the chairman of the Minorities Committee of the Constituent Assembly, Patel never considered Muslims second-class citizens. Instead, he asked them to show their allegiance to the Indian Republic and to be fully loyal to it. He justified his rejection of the old separate electorate in terms of this sense of patriotism and national unity.[35]

Sardar Patel epitomised the category of Congressmen that Bruce Graham calls 'Hindu traditionalists'.[36] For Graham, these politicians were not as radical—and, in particular, not as xenophobic—as Hindu nationalists, but were close to them when it came to defending their culture. In certain cases, such sympathies led them to join the Vishva Hindu Parishad (VHP) or to support the Sangh Parivar (including the RSS) while remaining in the Congress. Even when they did not do so, these respectable personalities who derived some of their prestige from their association with Gandhi actively aided the RSS and its offshoots. Manu Bhagavan, therefore, has convincingly argued that these people 'used their status and their position to make a range of extremist, belligerent right positions acceptable to the mainstream'.[37]

After 1947, Sardar Patel wanted to take the Congress in this direction contra Nehru. He had Purushottam Das Tandon, another Hindu traditionalist, elected Congress president in place of Nehru, who then resigned from the CWC. But Patel died in 1950 and Nehru forced Tandon to resign the following year. Before the 1951–52 elections, Nehru was fully in control and described the Hindu nationalists as the main enemy of the Congress during the first Indian election campaign.[38] But in Gujarat, lieutenants of Patel, including K.M. Munshi, were to continue his work in the same vein within the party.

K.M. Munshi and Gujarati *Asmita*: From Gandhi to the VHP—via Somnath

K.M. Munshi played a major role in the shaping of the political culture of Gujarat before as well as after Independence. He was a prolific novelist, whose work had a strong impact on society,[39] his most popular novel, *Gujarat No Nath* (The Lord of Gujarat), being published in 1917. The story is set in twelfth-century Patan, the capital of King Munjlal Mehta (a Jain), whose aim was to build a territorial state for all Gujarati speakers. In the novel Munshi argues that Hindu (and Jain) kings had succumbed to Muslim invaders because of their disunity. However, he eulogises Vedic India and claims that Gujaratis had much in their history to be proud of. According to Ajay Skaria, however, he presents the province as the land of an 'exclusionary upper caste martial and male Hinduism'.[40] Munshi was to revisit these themes in *Gujaratni Asmita* (1939), *The Early Aryans in Gujarat* (1941), *The Glory That Was Gurjara Desa* (1943) and *Somanatha: The Shrine Eternal* (1951).

Many years later, Meghnad Desai, who was born in the city of Baroda in 1940, confided:

> A more general consciousness of being a Gujarati came from reading K.M. Munshi's novels. It is hard now to describe what a thrill it was to read *Gujarat No Nath*. Almost everyone I knew in my family circles had read it more than once. I probably first read it when I was seven and then every now and then yet again. Munshi's history of Gujarat is of course a total concoction but I was not to know that then. The sheer power of his style, his ability to build up Patan as some great capital city, the grandeur of his character [...] made me proud to be a Gujarati.[41]

Munshi joined the Congress in 1928 and took part in the Salt March[42] in 1930, though he never fully adhered to Gandhi's ideas, including that of non-violence. This was obvious as early as 1929 when, appearing as a witness in the Bombay Hindu–Muslim riots inquiry, he declared: 'I believe that the time has come for the hindus that if they want to be safe from these fanatic mahomedans they all should join the Arya Samagists [*sic*] movement and retord [*sic*] the mahomedans in the same way as they are retording [*sic*] the hindus.'[43] Clearly hostile to the Muslim League, he launched a campaign on behalf of Akhand Hindustan (United India) from 1938 to 1941 in response to Jinnah's demand for Pakistan. The RSS, which campaigned against Partition, naturally backed this movement. Its leaders 'invited Munshi to preside over the "Gurupornima"[44] celebrations and to parade of the RSS [*sic*] in Poona on August 4th 1941'.[45] He told RSS volunteers: 'your first and foremost duty is therefore to teach fearlessness to the Hindus ... in the name of tolerance we have let the social system grow nerveless'.[46] The same year Munshi was asked to resign by Mahatma Gandhi because of his involvement in the Akhara movement,[47] named after gymnasiums (*akharas*) where young Indians received physical training. Munshi then received the backing of the Hindu Mahasabha, which invited him to speak at its Working Committee meeting in 1942.[48]

In 1946, Gandhi asked him to re-join the Congress—for mysterious reasons.[49] He was soon after elected to the Constituent Assembly where he was to be one of the most active members of the Drafting Committee, arguing forcefully in favour of Hindi as a national language and against conversion, until 1949.[50]

As a Congress leader, Munshi was asked by Patel to direct the massive operation that was to result in the integration of Hyderabad state in 1948.[51] However, he is mostly remembered in Gujarat for his contribution to rebuilding the Somnath temple—a task with which he had been entrusted by Sardar Patel on account of his long-standing interest in the site. He had visited the temple in 1922 'and gradually became obsessed with the idea of rebuilding it'.[52] In 1937, he wrote a book called *Jaya Somanath*, which focused on the sack of the temple by Mahmud of Ghazni. Recreating this episode, Munshi wrote: 'Fifty thousand Indian warriors laid down their lives in defence of their beloved shrine. Mahmud captured the fort, entered the temple sanctified by centuries of devotion, broke the Linga [symbol of Lord Shiva] to pieces, looted the temple and burnt it to the ground.'[53] The ruins of the old temple were pulled down in October 1950 and in May 1951 Rajendra Prasad, the president of the Republic of India, performed a re-installation ceremony, in the face of opposition from Nehru[54] and Yagnik.

Munshi not only wanted to restore the religious grandeur of Hinduism, he also wanted to defend its social traditions. For both reasons he focused on building up the Bharatiya Vidya Bhavan, which he had established in 1938.[55] Through this institution and its publishing house—which became very popular in the 1950s—the history that Munshi wished to propound to young Indians drew only upon Hindu, Buddhist and Jain sources, something that was already evident from his preface to C. Rajagopalachari's translation of the Ramayana,[56] in which he wrote that the Ramayana and the Mahabharata were the 'collective unconscious of India'.[57] Besides religion, social norms mattered a great deal to Munshi, who declared during a lecture in 1950: 'We, who are blinded by an admiration of the social apparatus of the West, fail to realise that chaturvarnya [the caste system based on the four varnas] was a marvellous social synthesis on a countrywide scale when the rest of the world [was] weltering in a tribal state.'[58] He added that India's 'modern Renaissance' could be traced to the end of the seventeenth century when Shivaji rose against 'alien rule'.[59] In Munshi's rewriting of Indian history, Muslims are often described as 'barbaric'[60]—in spite of the numerous examples of cultural synthesis that had existed in Gujarat itself.[61]

Munshi was a misfit in Nehru's Congress given its emphasis on secularism. After spending two years in Delhi as Union minister for agriculture and food (1952–53) and five years in Uttar Pradesh as governor (1957–59), he left the party and joined the Swatantra Party. He was not the only Congressman from Gujarat to do so. In addition to another follower of Patel, V.P. Menon, the son of Sardar Patel himself, Dahyabhai, did the same.[62] The Swatantra Party was not only a conservative party, as the title of Howard Erdman's book, its 'biography', suggests; it was also liberal in the economic sense of the word, as its name made clear. It did very well in Gujarat, which became one of its strongholds, so much so that one of its founders, Piloo Mody, successfully contested the elections in Godhra in 1967 and 1971. Another co-founder of the party, M.R. Masani, was elected MP for Rajkot in 1967.

As well as favouring a more liberal approach to the economy, Munshi also wanted to promote Hindu culture. In parallel with his commitment to the Swatantra Party, he drew closer to the Sangh Parivar. In 1963 he published in the mouthpiece of the RSS, *Organiser*, an article whose title was self-explicit: 'Wanted: an active Hindu religion'.[63] The next year he helped in founding the VHP in Bombay, the city where, many years before, he had met the architect of the VHP, an RSS *pracharak* named Shivram Shankar Apte.[64] Munshi remained a VHP member till his death in 1971.

Gulzarilal Nanda: From Gandhian Trade Unionism to the VHP via the Bharat Sadhu Samaj

Gulzarilal Nanda had a similar trajectory. In 1921 he left Punjab for Ahmedabad in order to work with Gandhi—after having taken part in the Non-Cooperation movement—and became one of the driving forces of the Textile Labour Association. He became its secretary in 1922 and worked in this capacity till 1946. He was elected to the Lok Sabha from Sabarkantha in 1952,[65] and again for two more consecutive terms in 1957 and 1962. He was Nehru's labour minister in 1946–50 and then minister for planning (1951–57), labour (1957–63) and home (1963–66) before acting twice as interim prime minister in 1964 and 1966.

By that time, Nanda had drawn closer to the Sangh Parivar. A Hindu traditionalist, he had the odd idea, when minister for planning and labour in the mid-1950s, of enrolling *sadhus* (Hindu ascetics) in the economic development of India, and set up the Bharat Sadhu Samaj (BSS) 'to act as a unifying force for re-organising all religious sects and orders for utilising in the maximum the spiritual and moral potentialities for all-round development of the country'.[66] Nanda's role in the BSS (he was chairman of its Central Advisory Committee) reflected his Hindu traditionalist inclinations, which were also apparent in his promotion of Ayurvedic medicine.[67] But it also showed his willingness to see Hindu religious figures play a role in the public sphere. In 1964 he even approached Swami Karpatri, the founder of the reactionary Ram Rajya Parishad, to invite him to join him in the battle against corruption. *Organiser* hailed the initiative.[68] Simultaneously, Nanda launched a Sadachar Samiti in order to gather together representatives of religious associations and upstanding worthy citizens, and again *Organiser* heartily welcomed the idea.[69]

A few months later, Nanda defended the RSS in the Rajya Sabha, insisting that it was not a political but rather a cultural organisation. What lay behind this intervention was the possibility that RSS members might be allowed to join the government administrative services. The left was then objecting that the RSS was a political movement and that, therefore, as in the case of Communist Party members, the status of *swayamsevak* (an RSS member) was incompatible with that of a civil servant.[70] The following year he invited the RSS chief, M.S. Golwalkar, to a meeting at which he informed him of the growing tensions with Pakistan just before the 1965 war and asked for his help in maintaining law and order.[71] In the end, the way he handled the clampdown on the VHP's demonstrations against cow slaughter outside the Indian parliament in late 1966 left so much to be desired that Indira Gandhi, who had retained Nanda reluctantly as home minister, dismissed him.[72] Later, Nanda drew closer to the Sangh Parivar and eventually joined the VHP in 1982.[73]

Morarji Desai's Affinities with the Jana Sanghis

During the 1970s, the career of another Gujarati politician illustrated the links between traditionalist Congressmen and the Sangh Parivar: Morarji Desai. Hailing from South Gujarat, Desai had been MP for Surat for 23 years (for five consecutive terms from 1957 to 1980), having joined Gandhi and the Congress after resigning from the civil service in 1930.[74] A conservative Gandhian, he was one of the staunchest opponents of Nehru and, later, Indira Gandhi in the 1950s and 1960s. He was especially critical of their economic policies but did not share their brand of secularism either. Morarji Desai was one of the driving forces behind the 1969 split in the Congress that resulted in the setting up of the Congress (O), whose main stronghold was Gujarat. In the 1971 elections, of Gujarat's 16 MPs (including Desai) 11 went to the party, and with 11 seats the Congress (O) was doing as well as the Congress (R), a case unique in India.

Morarji Desai grew closer to the Jana Sangh during the Navnirman (Reconstruction) movement of 1973–74 when all the opposition parties demanded the resignation of the Congress (R) chief minister, Chimanbhai Patel, and fresh elections because of the corruption of his government. The Congress (O) and then the Jana Sangh MLAs resigned in protest. Both parties worked together, along with socialists and others, within a new party, Janata Morcha. With their support, Morarji Desai began a high-profile fast demanding that the Assembly be dissolved and new elections held. Both demands were eventually met. After the Emergency, during which the same groups united against their common enemy, Indira Gandhi, Morarji Desai's Congress (O) and the Jana Sangh merged within the Janata Party along with Charan Singh's Bharatiya Lok Dal (a party that championed the interests primarily of peasant landholders) and some socialists. Desai became prime minister with the support of the ex-Jana Sanghis and others, he and they sharing the same views on many issues.

First, they were not in favour of the policy of positive discrimination for the lower castes that the socialists of the Janata Party were eager to implement in the two North Indian states they governed, Bihar and Uttar Pradesh. Second, Desai had long backed the controversial Freedom of Religion Bill that a former Jana Sanghi MP introduced in December 1978 in order to regulate conversions. He eventually withdrew his support for the bill after entreaties from Christian leaders.[75] Third, Desai revealed the intensity of his Hindu traditionalist outlook in the 'textbook controversy'. In May 1977, he received an anonymous memorandum demanding the withdrawal from public circulation of four history books, of which three were intended for use in teaching. The books in question were *Medieval India*, by Romila Thapar, *Modern India*, by Bipan Chandra, *Freedom Struggle*, by Bipan Chandra, A. Tripathi and Barun De, and *Communalism and the Writing of Indian History*, by Romila Thapar, Harbans Mukhia and Bipan Chandra. The memorandum criticised these works above all for not condemning forcefully enough certain Muslim invaders in the medieval period and because they emphasised that freedom struggle leaders such as B.G. Tilak and Aurobindo were partly responsible for antagonism between Hindus and Muslims. The RSS campaigned separately for the withdrawal of these textbooks.[76] In May 1977, Desai's secretariat indicated to the Ministry of Education that the prime minister was willing to have the books withdrawn. As Susanne Hoeber Rudolph and Lloyd Rudolph put it, 'Desai's Hindu cultural revivalism, noblesse oblige high-caste attitudes and economic conservatism, provided the political and ideological conditions for an evolving rapport between him and the like-minded members of the Jana Sangh faction.'[77]

Soon afterwards, the Janata Party was harmed by the dual membership controversy. This occurred when socialists in the party protested that ex-Jana Sanghis should not pay allegiance to both the RSS and Janata. Charan Singh backed them, but Desai supported the Hindu nationalists almost until the party split, sealing the fate of his government in 1979.

The legacy of Mahatma Gandhi varied from state to state. In Bihar, as the prestige of Jaya Prakash Narayan clearly showed, the socialist variant prevailed. In Gujarat, the conservative version became hegemonic at the expense of the progressive one that Indulal Yagnik represented for only a few years. Sardar Patel, K.M. Munshi, G. Nanda and Morarji Desai are four exemplars of 'Hindu traditionalism'. At the very least, their cultural inclinations were in tune with social conservatism, as is evident from Sardar Patel's lack of interest in Dalit education and Morarji Desai's distinct coolness towards positive discrimination. These ideological affinities with some features of the Sangh Parivar—a political constellation which the four Congressmen either supported or even joined—helped the Hindu nationalists to develop their network in Gujarat from the 1950s to the 1970s and to polarise the state along communal lines at the expense of secularism.

This is evident from the 1969 Hindu–Muslim riots. This wave of violence, which resulted in the death of more than a thousand people—mostly Muslims—after it had been triggered by Hindu nationalists, reached unprecedented levels because of the mismanagement and communal bias of the Congress government. In his account of the riot, Ghanshyam Shah points out:

> A highly placed Congress leader of Gujarat, in a public meeting, exhorted the youth in these terms: 'There are anti-national elements in this country whose loyalty is towards Pakistan. Police, having some limitations, cannot trace these elements. Therefore, it is your duty to find them out. You should enter their houses, catch hold of them, then do whatever you want to do.' A few Congressmen even took part in the riots—directly or indirectly. Some deliberately misguided the administration.[78]

The guilty men were mostly conservative Congressmen who were to form the Congress (O), which remained in office after the 1969 split. But Indira Gandhi's Congress also contributed to the Sangh Parivar's rise after her party took power in the 1970s and began promoting quotas in favour of the lower castes in the 1980s. After polarising Gujarat along religious lines, the state Congress helped to polarise it along social lines.

THE ANTI-RESERVATION MOVEMENT, SPRINGBOARD OF HINDU NATIONALISM

If Hindu traditionalists remained dominant within the Congress in Gujarat till the 1969 split, things naturally changed afterwards. The Congress (R) of Indira Gandhi, faithful to its socialist (or rather populist) agenda, brought back into the fold those who had been eased out or alienated, and also attracted progressives. Indulal Yagnik was one of those who rallied around the Congress

(R); he was re-elected on this ticket in 1971, to the same Ahmedabad seat he had held since 1957.[79] He died the following year, but the man who succeeded him in that very constituency, Ehsan Jafri, represented the same school of thought.

Jafri was a freedom fighter, trade unionist and literary figure. While still at R.C. High School in Ahmedabad, he published a magazine in Urdu and then joined the freedom movement in the 1940s. Influenced by communism, he became a labour union leader and was jailed for a year in 1949 because of his 'calls for revolution'.[80] Upon his release, he became the general secretary of the Progressive Editors' Union and completed his law degree, after which he practised as a lawyer in Ahmedabad. In the 1969 communal riots that ravaged the city, his house was burned down and his family moved to stay in a relief camp. He rebuilt his house in almost the same place in Ahmedabad, in the industrial belt, and even established a Bohra housing association, Gulberg Society, of 14 dwellings. These events prompted him to get involved in the promotion of secularism and, attracted by Indira Gandhi's political manifesto, he joined the Congress and even became president of the Ahmedabad branch in 1972. He was elected MP for Ahmedabad in 1977 with 50.6 per cent of the valid votes cast at a time when the Congress (R) was so unpopular that it returned an unprecedentedly low number of MPs in Gujarat (10 out of 26). No Muslim candidate had ever been elected MP for Ahmedabad before or, indeed, since. He never contested elections again but remained involved in public affairs, even though literature (including Urdu poetry) played an increasingly important part in his life.

In Gujarat, the Congress (R), renamed Congress (I) in 1978, endorsed the caste-related repertoire of quota politics instead of class-based socialism. This was with good reason if one recalls the decline of the proletariat: in the late 1970s the closing of one mill after another, a process that had begun in the early 1960s, resulted in what Jan Breman calls 'the unmaking of an industrial working class'.[81] And even if the borders of caste groups were fuzzier in Gujarat than in other states of India, caste mattered all the more as post-Independence India's land reforms had fostered some of the caste-related social dynamics that already emerged in the colonial era.[82]

Vanyas (merchant castes) remained predominant, not because of their numbers (they represented only 3 per cent of society) but rather on account of their prestige and influence, clearly related to the importance of business in Gujarat. Brahmins, 4.1 per cent, as elsewhere in India were over-represented among professionals, politicians and in the bureaucracy. Rajputs, 4.9 per cent, were still considered as Savarnas (upper castes), but most of them were not rich and about a fifth were landless.[83] Increasingly, they had to compete against the Patidars, 12.3 per cent of the population, a dominant caste of farmers that benefited from the abolition of the zamindari system of landownership (especially in Saurashtra) in the 1950s and quickly seized the opportunity of growing and marketing commercial cash crops such as tobacco, cotton, sugar cane and groundnuts, with some of them moving to the cities as their businesses prospered. Ghanshyam Shah emphasises the fact that 'the Patidars follow[ed] many of the cultural practices of the Vanyas and consequently elevated their position from the middle to high caste'[84]—through a process reminiscent of M.N. Srinivas's notion of 'Sanskritisation'. Among the practices responsible for this upward move, strict vegetarianism played a major role.

Further down the hierarchy, backward castes (mostly peasants, pastoralists and artisans) accounted for about 40 per cent of society, but among them the Kolis formed a huge group of about a quarter of the state's population. The other low castes were the Thakors, the Patanvadias and the Bareeyas (who were often bracketed together with Kolis). At the bottom of the pyramid, Scheduled Castes (or Dalits) represented only 7.2 per cent of the population (half of the national average), whereas

Scheduled Tribes (Tribals or Adivasis), at 17.7 per cent, were twice as numerous proportionally as elsewhere in India.

Table 1.1: Caste distribution in Gujarat

Castes and communities	*Per cent*
Higher castes	13.1
– Brahmin	4.1
– Vanya	3.0
– Rajput	4.9
– Other	1.1
Middle castes	12.3
– Patidar & Kanbi	12.2
– Other	0.1
Lower castes	40.3
– Koli	24.2
– Artisan castes	6.1
– Other	10.0
Scheduled Castes	7.2
Scheduled Tribes	17.7
Muslims	8.5
Other minorities	1.0
Total	100

Source: Ghanshyam Shah, *Caste Association and Political Process in Gujarat*, Bombay, Popular Prakashan, 1975, p. 9 (adapted from the 1931 census).

The rise of the Patidars at the expense of the Rajputs, and their social acceleration after the abolition of the zamindari system in the 1950s, fostered a unique caste realignment and even the creation of a 'caste federation'.[85] From the turn of the twentieth century, Rajput leaders in Gujarat had established caste associations to promote education.[86] In the late 1930s,

Natvarsingh Solanki extended these associations to other castes that he described as 'Kshatriyas'.[87] He tried to refashion the social identity of those groups in order to allow others to join hands with the Rajputs and, in this way, to acquire more weight to cope more effectively with the Patidars.

His most natural target was the members of Gujarat's largest caste, the Kolis, who had been classified by the British as a 'criminal caste', but he claimed that they were Kshatriyas and resorted to genealogists to provide evidence of their aristocratic lineage. Some Koli clans had already established matrimonial alliances with Rajputs, as they practised hypergamy.[88] These relations had given birth, in Saurashtra, to a rural caste complex cultivating a rivalry with the richer, urban 'bloc' of central Gujarat, comprising mostly Vanyas, Patidars and Brahmins. Before the beginning of the Raj, some Kolis had established small principalities and, after the British took over, they had retained some control over land as landowners or rather big tenants. Many of them met the necessary conditions for being enfranchised when the British established provincial legislative councils. The right to vote therefore enabled the Kolis to use their main asset, their numbers: in 1931, according to the census, they represented about 20 per cent of the population, almost double that of the Patidars. Solanki opened his caste association to the Kolis precisely in order to transform it into a mass organisation.

In 1947, the Kutch, Kathiawar, Gujarat Kshatriya Sabha (Association of the Kshatriyas of Kutch, Kathiawar and Gujarat, the three geographical units which were to form Gujarat in 1960) was created. The word 'Kshatriya' was a useful umbrella label to bracket the Rajputs and the Kolis together against their common rivals, the Patidars. The Rajput leaders of the Kshatriya Sabha emphasised that a Kshatriya was to be defined not by descent but by martial attributes. Political calculations therefore had social implications and several taboos were abolished. Rajputs and Kolis of the Kshatriya Sabha could eat together,[89] while the

Koli elite—mostly made up of landed families—married their daughters to lower Rajputs. Kshatriyas therefore tended to form a new caste, although the use of terms like 'Koli Kshatriyas' and 'Rajput Kshatriyas' revealed that the merger was far from complete.[90]

In the early 1960s, the Kshatriya Sabha offered its electoral support to the Congress in exchange for party candidate tickets for several of its members. The Congress was not entirely responsive, especially given the opposition of Patidars, who were very influential in the party.[91] The Kshatriya Sabha then split, some of its members supporting the Congress and some supporting the Swatantra Party during the 1962 elections. The Congress suffered a setback, whereas the Swatantra Party became the leading opposition party in the state, with 26 seats—as against 113 (out of 154) to the Congress. The Swatantra Party continued to perform well in 1967, with 66 seats, as against 93 (out of 166) to the Congress. This development persuaded the Congress to change its strategy, and hence it sponsored a parallel Kshatriya organisation and gave tickets to their candidates before the 1967 elections.[92]

Yet, the Congress remained upper caste-oriented, as revealed by the large proportion of its MLAs who came from the upper castes (for the profile of MLAs by caste and religion from 1962 to 2012, see Appendix A): in 1967 Congress upper-caste MLAs accounted for 47.6 per cent of all members (including 15 per cent Brahmins and 15 per cent Vanyas) and Patidars for 18.3 per cent, totalling almost 66 per cent.[93] The elitist character of the Congress was even more evident from the social profile of the Congress state administration: in the government that was formed by Hitendra Desai after the 1967 election, more than 71 per cent of the ministers and ministers of state were from the upper castes (for the social profile of the government of Gujarat between 1962 and 2012, see Appendix B).

After the 1969 split, most upper-caste party leaders joined the Congress (O). The Congress (R) had to be (re-)built almost from scratch to form an alternative social coalition. It turned to the Kshatriyas and promised that it would appoint a commission to look into the socio-economic problems of the Backward Classes of Gujarat (the administrative category under which the Kshatriyas fell) if voted into power.[94] This deal and Mrs Gandhi's popularity enabled the Congress, in the 1972 state election, to win 140 seats out of 168 while the Congress (O) obtained only 16. The face of the ruling Congress was changing. While the percentage of upper castes and Patidars remained almost the same among its MLAs (19.3 per cent), those of the low castes including the Kshatriyas rose from 11.9 per cent to 19.3 per cent.[95] These trends were further accentuated in the 1975 elections—which the Congress lost—when Patidars deserted the party to rally round the opposition: they represented only 6.7 per cent of the party's MLAs whereas lower castes accounted for 21.3 per cent of the total.[96]

In 1972, the Congress government appointed the state's first Socially and Educationally Backward Classes Commission, under the chairmanship of A.R. Baxi.[97] In 1976, after Mrs Gandhi's Congress staged a comeback in Gujarat in the context of the Emergency, Madhavsinh Solanki, a low-caste Rajput from the Kshatriya group who had been a protégé of Indulal Yagnik since 1946,[98] became chief minister.[99] In his government, upper castes represented less than 45 per cent of the ministers and ministers of state (see Appendix B). Solanki promised to implement the recommendations of the Baxi Commission regarding reservations for the Other Backward Classes (OBCs), the standard name for these groups according to the Indian Constitution—a category whose main component comprised the Kshatriyas in Gujarat. The commission recommended that 10 per cent of the positions in technical colleges (medicine, engineering, agriculture, etc.) be reserved for OBCs and that the same quota should be applied in class III and IV of the administration (only 5 per cent were to be reserved for OBCs in class I and II).[100]

The Congress lost the 1977 elections in the state, four months after Solanki had formed his first government. But during the electoral campaign he established a formidable social coalition incorporating Kshatriyas, Harijans (Scheduled Castes), Adivasis (Scheduled Tribes) and Muslims (hence the acronym KHAM). This KHAM coalition could not deal with the unpopularity of the post-Emergency Congress, but Solanki and his colleagues insisted on pursuing the same strategy, one that was clearly an expression of the peripheral, martial bloc. Besides Solanki, who hailed from Bharuch, the other Congress (R) leaders of Gujarat included Sanat Mehta, who came from Saurashtra, and Jinabhai Darji, an OBC who was from the tribal belt of South Gujarat. Darji, who had concentrated his energies on defending the poor, the Adivasis in particular, by creating forest and milk cooperative societies as well as cooperative societies for diamond cutters and fishermen,[101] was the mentor of Solanki, who described him as 'a man of the poor just like Indulal Yagnik'.[102] Darji had become president of the Congress (R) in 1972, and is usually considered 'the father of the KHAM concept'.[103] These men drew their pro-reservation inspiration from the socialist leader who had promoted this policy more than anyone else hitherto, namely Rammanohar Lohia.[104]

Their strategy largely explained the Congress's success during the 1980 elections. For the first time, OBC MLAs formed a larger group than Patels in the Legislative Assembly of Gujarat with 20.4 per cent (the Patels formed 18.8 per cent), and this was largely due to the victory of the Congress, of whose numbers in the Assembly OBC MLAs represented 19.6 per cent (as against 11.9 per cent of Patels).[105] The government of Solanki was overwhelmingly lower caste in composition (see Appendix B): 27.3 per cent of its members were OBCs and 12.1 per cent SCs—as against 12.1 per cent of Patels (not more than Dalits).[106]

After Solanki's victory, OBCs were soon admitted to quotas that had been established in the 1970s at postgraduate medical faculties.[107] In response, students from B.S. Medical College in Ahmedabad launched a protest in December 1980 and submitted to the government a memo seeking to dilute the reservation policy. Solanki immediately made concessions, but these were rejected by the students, who demanded the abolition of all employment and education reservations. The slogan 'Abolish all reservations everywhere' was especially popular among Patidars, in particular in the districts of Ahmedabad, Kheda and Mehsana. There, in only four months, the protests resulted in the deaths of 31 people. Dalits—who were more vulnerable than STs and OBCs because of their small numbers—were targeted by the Patidars.[108]

The upper castes and the Patidars, who were now part of the same group, the Savarnas, opposed the reservations because they symbolised the questioning of a social order—in what I have called elsewhere a 'silent revolution'.[109] As I.P. Desai pointed out, the problem for the Savarnas could have been expressed through one crude question: 'How can these "Dheds" [Dalits, shoemakers and leather workers] demand equality with us? But the upper castes also want to be called progressive. Hence the argument of "merit" above "caste".'[110] Indeed, they demanded that reservations be abolished because their beneficiaries did not deserve the jobs they got.

In the early and mid-1980s, Solanki, who was now known as 'the messiah of Gujarat's poor' (not only because of reservations but also thanks to measures such as a midday free-meal scheme),[111] continued with his 'quota politics'.[112] He appointed a second Backward Classes Commission, whose report was submitted in 1983. It recommended that caste be abandoned as a criterion for the definition of quotas and that the existing quota should be increased from 10 per cent to 28 per cent. Solanki kept this report secret until January 1985—two months before the state elections—and then supported an increase of quotas up to 28 per cent, without abandoning the caste criterion. These 28 per cent, added to the 14 per cent reservations for STs and the 7 per cent to SCs, meant that 49 per cent of positions in higher education and in state government employment were now 'reserved'.[113]

These decisions partly explained the success of the Congress (I) in the March 1985 state elections where it won a record number of seats: 149. Among the party MLAs, OBCs represented 25.5 per cent (the same proportion as among the party candidates); and in the ministry, more than 29 per cent of the ministers were OBCs, as against 12.5 per cent of Patels (see Appendix B).[114]

Anti-reservation demonstrations had erupted in February 1985, but they spread widely after the election and the formation of the government, in which only one Patidar had a senior post.[115] Once again, students were in the forefront of the protests, but the key organisation, the Vali Mandal, was made up of students' parents and other political activists. Its leader was a professor of sociology, Shankarbhai Patel, who was a member of the Janata Party.[116] Students took their protest to the streets and attacked symbols of the state, including buses, post offices and schools.[117] For the first time in this context, middle-class men and women took to the streets, showing no qualms about targeting their low-caste neighbours.[118] They also demonstrated and '20,000 residents of high caste pockets like Naranpura and Vijaynagar [two Ahmedabad neighbourhoods] spilled out onto the streets daring the police to "fill the jails".'[119] As the police responded with tough counter-measures the like of which the middle classes had not experienced before, the BJP tried to project itself as their protector.[120]

To begin with, Solanki tried to capitalise upon the polarisation of society that the violence reflected. He was 'the mastermind behind a Kshatriya Sammelan', a huge congregation of Kshatriyas that was organised near Baroda, 'where Kshatriyas dramatically pulled out their swords saying that it was the Kshatriyas' birth right to rule and any move to remove Solanki would be opposed even by the use of force'.[121] But eventually, Solanki had to resign on 5 July since, by that time, 180 people had been killed, 6,000 made homeless and 1,600 shops destroyed.[122] The caste bloc of central Gujarat had once again defeated the caste bloc of the periphery—and even the KHAM coalition. Note that the former was then still dominated by Congress leaders belonging to the caste of Patels, including Chimanbhai Patel. Solanki accused the Patidars at large of being responsible for his ousting, an accusation corroborated by the fact that Shankarbhai Patel, who headed the student movement, worked under the aegis of Chimanbhai Patel, the strongest Patidar leader in the state in the 1980s. Solanki explains that these faction leaders

> approached [Rajiv Gandhi] and requested him to change the Chief Minister. Rajiv argued that I had won with an overwhelming mandate, why should I change him? They said that many communal riots had taken place between Hindus and Muslims, so its effect would be in Pakistan who would take it to the United Nations. That is the argument they made. Rajiv did not directly tell me, but he told V.P. Singh who told me indirectly about it [...] I tendered my resignation as Chief Minister of Gujarat on a small piece of paper, which Rajiv Gandhi accepted.[123]

Solanki's successor, Amarsinh Chaudhary, declared that there would be no increase in the percentage of seats reserved for OBCs until a 'national consensus' emerged.[124] Chaudhary also appointed a notable Patel personality to his government, Vallabhbhai Patel.[125] Pravin Sheth and Ramesh Menon conclude: '1985 will probably go down in history as the year which heralded the re-emergence of the political clout of Patels in Gujarat. The anti-reservation stir heralded their deeply casteist attitudes coupled with intolerance. Their aggressiveness, determination and, of course, economic power were more than evident. Patel-dominated areas in the state were the major arenas of violence.'[126]

However, violence took a different turn after 18 March 1985. Two days before, Solanki had made major concessions to the students, but instead of letting the agitation ebb, demonstrators relaunched it in the Old City of Ahmedabad, this time on a different, anti-Muslim platform. Their objective was to repair the damage caused to Hindu unity in the course of the anti-reservationist campaign by transforming Muslims into scapegoats for the upper castes as well as Dalits and OBCs—and to preserve not only Hindu unity but the social order. Ornit Shani, in her book on the 1985 riots, argues that 'in spite of an inter-Hindu caste reservation conflict and prevailing class tensions among them, an all-Hindu consolidation against Muslims emerged'. And Shani concludes: 'The aftermath of the Ahmedabad riots of 1985 marked the beginning of the political shift in Gujarat from Congress rule to the rise of the BJP, which further strengthened the upper castes' position.'[127]

In fact, the Parivar were already trying hard to reach out to Dalits in different ways. For example, on the birth anniversary of Dr Ambedkar, on 14 April 1983, the RSS had launched a Samajik Samrasta Manch to attract Dalits in the name of Hindu unity. The Sangh Parivar, and more precisely the VHP, received the support of prominent religious sects in this endeavour, including the Swaminarayan movement.

The planning of the 1985 Gujarat riots leaves no room for doubt: the only houses which were torched were those of Muslims, while the others were marked 'Hindu' in white paint.[128] Muslims in the Old City were attacked by Hindus shouting 'Muslims should go', 'This is a Hindu Raj, come out and bow down'.[129] A similar scenario unfolded in the industrial areas and in slums further east. The climax of this anti-Muslim agitation occurred on 20 June 1985 when Hindu priests led the annual procession celebrating Lord Jagannath, flouting a curfew.

They made a point of including Dalits in this Rath Yatra, in which Dalits had never previously participated.[130] The procession, which eventually swelled to 100,000 people, was a show of force, with demonstrators shouting anti-Muslim slogans while passing by a mosque in the Old City.[131] Some Muslims threw stones in retaliation.[132] In the industrial suburb, the riots set Muslims against Dalits, who were fighting the 'Other' alongside their former adversaries, the police and the Patels.[133] Not only did violence reunite Hindus against Muslims, but Hindu nationalist organisations made a point of helping Dalit families which had been affected by the riots, such as with legal aid.[134]

In the communal violence of 1985, 220 people were killed, including 'only' 100 Muslims, if one goes by the official report. But 12,000 of them were made homeless since 2,500 houses had been destroyed and 900 Muslims arrested.[135] These riots made the Muslims of Ahmedabad realise that they were socially isolated, with even Dalits turning against them, not only because they felt more 'Hindu' now, but also because they could loot Muslim properties during the riots.

After 1985, the Sangh Parivar used religious processions and Hindu–Muslim riots in a more systematic manner to promote majoritarian unity. The 1986 Rath Yatra is a case in point. As the procession was disrupted along its return route, the VHP protested against the 'attack' and violence spread throughout the city. Dalits and OBCs were among the main aggressors in the industrial belt, and low-caste organisations like the Kutch Rajput Sabha and the Saurashtra Garasiya Sangh supported the bandh orchestrated by the VHP.[136]

The VHP was not the only Hindu organisation to promote Hindu solidarity. More traditional Hindu sects were also engaged in similar activities, including the Swaminarayan movement. BAPS was involved in the 1985 events and its leader, Pramukh Swami Maharaj, played an important role, as a self-proclaimed mediator, in sealing the fate of the reservation policy for instance.[137]

The year 1985 is an important turning point in the post-Independence political history of Gujarat. After that, the Congress lost ground while the BJP's rise was almost linear because the Sangh Parivar capitalised on the rallying of the upper castes and the Patidars around the Hindutva agenda *against* the reservation policy of the Congress and social change at large. The Congress alienated the upper castes (in particular the Patels) with its quota politics in the 1980s, but the strategy would probably have worked had the party persisted with its implementation. But it did not, as is evident from the way in which Solanki's successor changed track.[138] In the Hindi belt, in spite of violent anti-reservation agitations—in the late 1970s and early 1990s, in Bihar, for instance—the promoters of quota politics persisted with their policy. These leaders were not from the Congress but from caste-based parties with socialist leanings, like the peasant farming Yadav-dominated Janata Party and Janata Dal. In contrast, the Congress in Gujarat, as elsewhere, could not resign itself to being associated with OBCs, for two main reasons: first, it had always regarded itself as a catch-all party (or a rainbow-like coalition); and, second, it was still dominated by the upper castes: even in Solanki's governments, in the 1980s, the upper castes predominated over OBCs (30.30 per cent as against 27.3 per cent in 1980; 41.7 per cent as against 29.2 per cent in 1985).[139] Rather than embarking on a strategy of confrontation, therefore, the Congress ended up losing the support of the upper castes as well as the Patels (only 9.7 per cent of its MLAs came from this caste group in 1989)[140] and could not retain, in the medium term, the support of the low castes, who felt betrayed.

THE RISE TO POWER OF THE SANGH PARIVAR

In Gujarat, the Sangh Parivar benefited till the 1970s from the strength of Hindu traditionalist leaders (in the Congress as well as in the Swatantra Party) and, from the 1980s, from the Congress's inability to sustain progressive policies. But its rise to power in the 1990s also reflected decades of grassroots activism.

THE RISE OF THE HINDUTVA MOVEMENT IN GUJARAT: FROM THE MAKING OF RSS TO THE ABDUL LATIF MOMENT

The RSS developed in Gujarat according to its standard procedures, with *pracharaks* being sent from Nagpur to organise *shakhas* (local branches). The *pracharaks* were the products of officers' training camps that the RSS founder, K.B. Hedgewar, had set up in 1927 to build a network of full-time workers, which became the backbone of the organisation.

Hedgewar sent the first *pracharak* to Gujarat in 1938,[141] where the 'epicentre of the RSS'[142] was then Baroda, a princely state whose dynasty, the Gaekwad, hailed from Maharashtra and could be traced back to Shivaji's Maratha Confederation.[143] For Hedgewar's emissaries, who were mostly Maharashtrian Brahmins, Baroda had the advantage of being a strongly, though not overwhelmingly, Marathi-speaking city. Five years after the first *pracharak* was sent to Baroda, in 1943 another one was dispatched to Ahmedabad, where the first officers' training camps in Gujarat were set up in 1945. Madhukarrao Bhagwat, the father of the current RSS chief, went to Ahmedabad around the same time to become *prant pracharak* (supervising the work of a number of *pracharaks* working in several districts).[144] It was under M. Bhagwat that L.K. Advani completed the second year of his OTC training. Subsequently, Narendra Modi was to credit him with being 'a major influence in his political education'.[145]

The RSS expanded in Gujarat partly because of the help of Hindu activists. Besides the Congress traditionalists mentioned above, notables of the Hindu Mahasabha also supported the Sangh. The Hindu Mahasabha had been part of the Congress till 1937, at which point it represented its right wing, whereas the Congress Socialist Party represented its left wing. In Gujarat, the main leader of the Hindu Mahasabha was Vamanrao Mukadam, whom Yagnik and Sheth describe as 'a prominent leader of the Congress'.[146] A Maharashtrian Brahmin from Godhra, he was explicitly anti-Muslim. In 1928 he led a procession in Surat in honour of Lord Ganesh, 'which provoked a violent conflict between Hindus and Muslims'.[147] Beatriz Martinez-Saavedra points out that the 'unproblematic actuation of the Hindu Mahasabha was allowed from some sectors of Congress in Gujarat. For instance, even the most fervent of Gandhi's followers such as Vallabhbhai Patel, leader of the Gujarat Provincial Congress Committee for many years (1921–1946), never disqualified the Mahasabha regardless of its aggressive stance and its being openly opposed to the Gandhian notion of ahimsa [non-violence]'.[148]

After 1947, offshoots of the Sangh Parivar took shape one after another in Gujarat—along with specific channels of communication like the RSS weekly, *Sadhana*, which was founded in 1956.[149] In his history of the Sangh in Gujarat, Ghanshyam Shah emphasises the creation of the Bharat Vikas Parishad, which was established in the wake of the 1962 Sino-Indian war as a '"service-cum-samskar[150] oriented" socio-cultural voluntary organisation to penetrate the Savarna-dominated civil society. Its stated objective was to attract "the elite, intellectuals and the well-to-do citizens" in social welfare work for promoting "a sense of patriotism, national unity and integrity".'[151] Soon after, in 1964, 'the VHP launched the journal *Vishwa Hindu Samachar* to propagate its ideology among the upper and middle castes'.[152]

But other offshoots of the RSS were soon set up to reach out to non-elite groups, including the Bharatiya Kisan Union and the Bharatiya Mazdoor Sangh, the peasant and labour unions of the Sangh Parivar. The RSS itself capitalised on this communal polarisation: after the 1969 riots, the number of RSS *shakhas* 'increased from less than thirty to forty-five in 1973'.[153] It also organised, as elsewhere in India,

> health relief and income generation welfare programmes on a regular basis in more than 200 locations in the state of Gujarat. It has adopted few villages for 'total development'. Though the RSS claims that it does not encourage rituals, various activities carried out by it are not free from them. The VHP and other

> similar outfits also undertake several welfare programmes, and involve upper-caste professionals like doctors and teachers in philanthropic work for the poor. They also often coordinate their functions with other sects like Swaminarayan, Swadhyay, Gayatri Pariwar, Pushtimargis, and also, occasionally, caste organizations.[154]

The Gujarati unit of the Jana Sangh was created in November 1951, independently from the rest of Bombay province.[155] The party made no inroads in the first general election of 1951–52 and in 1957 it nominated only five candidates to the Assembly elections, all of whom lost.[156] In the 1960s, even though the Jana Sangh formed some kind of agreement with the Swatantra Party,[157] its growth was blocked by this party, which attracted voters belonging to the Jana Sangh's core constituency—traders and professionals from the 'middle world', a category comprising non-salaried middle-class people, according to Bruce Graham.[158] In 1967, the Jana Sangh won only one seat and 1.9 per cent of the valid votes in the state Assembly election. In the early 1970s, like its Congress (O) allies, it could not cope with the Congress wave created by Indira Gandhi: it won only three seats in the 1972 state Assembly elections, but increased in terms of valid votes from less than 2 per cent to 9.3 per cent of the total votes cast because it fielded 100 candidates as against 16 five years before.[159]

In the 1970s, the Jana Sangh started to assert itself thanks to the overtures of mainstream opposition parties—mostly breakaway factions of former Congressmen—which were prepared to dilute their (often shallow) commitment to secularism to win the support of a disciplined group like the Sangh Parivar. What was true at the national level as early as the 1960s, when the opposition's watchword became 'non-Congressism', was confirmed in the 1970s in Gujarat, where the Congress (O) had its stronghold and shared deep affinities with Hindu nationalism. In 1970–71, the Jana Sangh supported the government that the Congress (O) had formed after the 1969 split, but this rapprochement really gained momentum during the Navnirman movement, which emerged in 1973 in reaction to the corruption and authoritarianism of the Congress.[160] Students were at the forefront of the agitation, and among the student unions the offshoot of the RSS, the ABVP, was particularly active. The Jana Sangh benefited from this agitation and united with all opponents of Indira Gandhi, including Morarji Desai. After Desai forced the Congress government to resign and organise elections in 1974, the Jana Sangh's representation jumped from 3 to 18 seats (with 8.8 per cent of valid votes) and contributed to the rise to power of the Janata Front subsequently formed by the Congress (O), the Bharatiya Lok Dal of Charan Singh, the Socialist Party and the Jana Sangh. This coalition closed ranks after Indira Gandhi imposed the State of Emergency in June 1975, during which Jana Sanghis and other party members found common cause, either because they were in jail together or had gone underground, resisting Nehru's daughter.[161] This grouping won the 1977 elections comprehensively in Gujarat too.

The disintegration of the Janata Party, which resulted in the creation of the Bharatiya Janata Party by former Jana Sanghis, opened a new era of Congress domination marked by Solanki's KHAM coalition in the 1980 and 1985 elections. The BJP won 9 seats (out of 182) and 14 per cent of the valid votes in 1980, and 11 seats and 15 per cent of the valid votes in 1985.[162]

Things started to change in the second half of the decade after the collapse of the KHAM coalition and the communal polarisation of society.

POLARISING GUJARAT: HINDU NATIONALISM, RIOTS AND MUSLIM MAFIAS

The Sangh Parivar had gradually acquired a certain expertise in fostering polarisation by exploiting (or creating) communal tensions, having tried their hand at these techniques as early as the

1960s. The 1969 riot, which was the deadliest wave of Hindu–Muslim violence since Partition, is a case in point.[163] Officially, 660 people were killed (including 430 Muslims)—unofficially 1,000 to 2,000[164]—while 1,074 were injured (including 592 Muslims), over 48,000 people were made homeless, and property worth 42 million rupees was destroyed in Ahmedabad alone, including 32 million rupees worth belonging to Muslims (the riot also spread to neighbouring districts).[165]

The 1969 riots have been attributed by several analysts to socio-economic factors.[166] Indeed, from the mid-1960s onwards, the textile industry began a slow decline that has continued ever since. Entrepreneurs turned away from Ahmedabad's big cotton mills to Surat's smaller units, which fitted in better with new means of production and, more importantly, specialised in synthetic textiles that were in greater demand. Consequently, the Textile Labour Association lost its secular influence over the labour force, and Ahmedabad's under-qualified workers—among whom Hindus were over-represented compared with Muslim skilled craftsmen turned factory employees—were hit by a first wave of unemployment.

But the riot had political roots too. It started in the eastern part of Ahmedabad where the RSS had established its local strongholds and which M.S. Golwalkar, the RSS chief, chose as the location for a massive three-day rally, from 27 to 29 December 1968, in Maninagar. This meeting prepared the ground for the riot, which almost happened in March 1969 when a policeman knocked a copy of the Koran from a handcart stacked with books. The actual riot was triggered six months later when another police officer, who happened to be a Muslim, accidentally dropped a copy of the Ramayana while dispersing a Ramlila audience. RSS leaders then formed a Hindu Dharma Raksha Samiti (Committee for the Protection of the Hindu Religion), which organised demonstrations during which vitriolic slogans were chanted.[167] The Jana Sangh leader Balraj Madhok came to Ahmedabad to deliver a rabble-rousing speech on 14 and 15 September. One typical incident then sparked the full-blown riot. This occurred after Muslims entered the Jagannath temple to protest against the disruption of one of their processions by cows belonging to the temple. Immediately, Hindu nationalists orchestrated not only protests but also attacks. Their first targets were the Muslims of the walled city where 118 people were killed and 1,979 shops destroyed. But the worst-hit area was the industrial belt where the Muslim-dominated *chawls* (one-room housing units built for factory workers) were singled out by the assailants: 712 people were killed and 3,891 properties destroyed.[168] A distinctive feature of this riot was the attacks on Muslim *chawls* by their Dalit neighbours who formerly lived peacefully alongside them but who, all of a sudden, killed and raped Muslims.[169]

In the 1960s, there were officially 2,938 registered cases of communal violence in Gujarat.[170] The 1970s were much more peaceful, but again, in the 1980s, starting with the 1985 riots, the number of casualties increased tremendously: in 1986, it was still above 130, as a sequel of the 1985 event; in 1990, the toll was even worse, this time because of the mobilisation of the Sangh Parivar in the context of the Ram Janmabhoomi movement.[171] The VHP, as mentioned above, had launched the movement in 1984 seeking to mobilise the masses in order to reclaim the site of the Babri Masjid in Ayodhya. This culminated in 1990 in a grand nationwide procession led by the BJP president, L.K. Advani. His Rath Yatra was intended to take him to Ayodhya after a 10,000-kilometre-long 'procession' that left from Somnath. Indeed, for the Sangh Parivar, what had been achieved in Somnath had to be repeated in Ayodhya.[172] In this tense and febrile atmosphere, Ganesh Chaturthi processions precipitated outbreaks of rioting in Surat, Anand and Baroda.

The 1992–93 riots marked the end of this cycle of violence. They were sparked by the demolition of the Babri Masjid on 6 December 1992 by Hindu nationalist activists. In Ahmedabad,

134 people were killed. While in places like Bombay riots were fostered by Muslim attacks on public institutions in protest against the demolition of the Babri Masjid, in Ahmedabad the assailants were Hindu nationalists. Groups of 200 to 1,000 men, armed with tridents, swords, spears and petrol bombs shouted slogans like '*Musalman ko kato maro*' (Cut and kill Muslims) and attacked Muslim houses and businesses in the walled city and in industrial areas. Similar incidents took place in Surat, where clashes led to around 200 deaths and 19,000 people were made homeless.[173] According to the Varshney–Wilkinson database, between 1950 and 1995, of all Indian states, Gujarat recorded the highest number of deaths per million urban inhabitants: almost 120, compared with 80 in Bihar.[174]

Communal violence was not the only reason for the growing polarisation of Gujarat along religious lines: the role of the 'Muslim mafias', those related to bootlegging in particular, need to be factored in too. Gujarat being a 'dry' state since its formation, illegal consumption of alcohol gave birth to a very lucrative underground trade, with the blessing of policemen who collected their baksheesh (*hafta*), as Ornit Shani has shown.[175] The stereotype of the 'Muslim goonda' is an old one. As early as 1970, in his account of the 1969 riot, Ghanshyam Shah pointed out that

> there was a widespread belief in Gujarat that most of the street-corner bullies and goondas (thugs/hooligans) belong to the Muslim community. It was said that although these goondas harassed the common citizen, the government took no action against them because they had the protection of some Congress leaders as they secured votes for them. Moreover, some of the goondas were bootleggers and gamblers who had links with the police. Thus the ordinary Hindu felt he was helpless against anti-social elements that, according to him, came from the Muslim community.[176]

The stereotype of the Muslim bootlegger can be examined through the career of one of the liquor mafia dons, Abdul Latif, who hailed from the Old City of Ahmedabad and was part of the Bombay-based gang of Dawood Ibrahim. Latif helped members of his community in 1985: he 'started charitable work during the communal riots and distributed essential goods to poor people';[177] as a result, 'particularly for Muslims in the old city area, he became a local Robin Hood'.[178] So much so that in 1987, in spite of being barred, he was elected on an independent ticket by five wards. The political assertiveness of Latif—at the expense of the Congress, a party many Muslims no longer trusted—was used by the BJP to help polarise politics in Gujarat. This strategy was applied first in the 1987 municipal elections. Analysing the role of Latif, Howard Spodek points out: 'The BJP demonized both the man and the community by campaigning on a platform contrasting "Ram Raj" against "Latif Raj". Among some Hindus, indignation over Latif's candidacy was a factor in the BJP victory in the 1987 municipal elections in Ahmedabad.'[179] Many party members who had been actively involved in the 1985 riots were elected to the municipal corporation.

This modus operandi was repeated in 1993 during a key by-election in Ahmedabad, in the Ellisbridge constituency. The BJP candidate was Haren Pandya, the rising star of the party, whose campaign was managed by Narendra Modi, then organising secretary of BJP in Gujarat. Chimanbhai Patel wanted to defeat Pandya, who had accused him of corruption on the basis of some hard evidence. But Patel was close to Latif, and Modi exploited this weak point: in its door-to-door campaigning, the BJP's activists asked everyone 'not to forget Latif' as they went to vote.[180] This slogan referred to the illegal activities, including extortion, of a man who had become a hero to many Muslims. Pandya won the seat—previously held by the Congress—by 48,000 votes.[181]

This provided the blueprint for the 1995 state elections. In 1995, the BJP won not only the local elections but also the state elections, for the first time, and its strategy was very similar. During the election campaign, the party exploited the relations that some Congress leader had developed with Abdul Latif, who, for instance, 'aided the Muslim Congress MLA, Muhammad Hussin Barej'[182] and was, much more importantly, close to Chimanbhai Patel's faction.[183] Prashant Dayal, one of the best-informed journalists in Gujarat, points out: 'BJP did not have any real issue for the 1995 election, but they had Latif. They construed the Congress as the party of Latif and hence Muslims. This strategy of polarization was devised by Narendra Modi who had first set up the issue of Ram Janmabhoomi in Gujarat and now the issue of Latif.'[184] The *Times of India* emphasised: 'No election speech of a BJP leader was complete without the mention of Latif and his connections with Dawood Ibrahim and the Congress',[185] all the more so as Latif had absconded to Pakistan and could therefore be presented not only as a criminal who terrorised Hindus, but also as a fifth columnist.

A retired director general of Gujarat Police concluded: 'It would not be wrong to say Abdul Latif laid the foundations of the BJP's climb to power on its own strength in Gujarat.'[186] Another retired senior policeman, R.B. Sreekumar, concurs: from the late 1980s onwards, 'the bulk of citizens in Gujarat nurtured an impression of a Muslim underworld being sheltered, promoted and used as a mafia by many Congress party leaders, who were getting substantial share of black money generated by criminals'.[187] When in 1996 the BJP chief minister Keshubhai Patel arrested Latif, he was 'hailed as a "Hindu Hriday Samrat" [Emperor of Hindu hearts] and felicitated by the BJP in many districts for this achievement'.[188] Latif was killed in 1997, but the BJP could continue to polarise Gujarati society along communal lines by promoting a politics of fear so long as Latif's gang remained active, as is evident from this press report:

> In 1997, kidnappers purportedly sought to take advantage of [Gautam] Adani's riches by kidnapping him. The billionaire was allegedly held for a ransom of US$1.5 million. As per the charge sheet filed by police, on January 1, 1998, Adani and Shantilal Patel were abducted at gunpoint after they left Karnavati Club here in a car and headed for Mohammadpura Road. It was alleged that a scooter forced the car to stop, and then a group of men came in a van and abducted both of them. They were taken to an unknown place in a car before being released, the charge sheet said [...] In 2018, Ahmedabad court acquitted two main accused—former gangsters Fazlu Rehman and Bhogilal Darji alias Mama. [189]

Fazlu Rehman is generally described in the media as 'one of the most-feared extortionists and underworld don'.[190]

Violent communal polarisation was intended to unite the Hindus against the Muslims, as an article in the VHP's *Vishwa Hindu Samachar*, edited by K.K. Shastri, the former president of the Gujarati Sahitya Sabha, made clear: 'All Hindus should unite against "*vidharmis*" [people of other religions].'[191] But, in parallel, the Sangh Parivar co-opted lower-caste Hindus. First, in 1983, the RSS established the Samajik Samrasta Manch (SSM, Social Assimilation Platform) to woo Dalit supporters in the name of social harmony.[192] In Gujarat, this organisation and the VHP exploited the craze of some low-caste groups for Sanskritisation by organising inter-caste dinners. It also took Dalits to Ayodhya in 1992 to take part in the demolition of the Babri Masjid.[193] Second, the BJP appointed some Dalits to its party apparatus. One new cadre told Ghanshyam Shah in 1987: 'the BJP subscribes to Brahminical ideology but the Congress in practice is no way different. Moreover, I worked in the Congress for ten years but I did not get a position, whereas the BJP has given me a party position.'[194] Third, OBCs and Dalits were recruited by the Bajrang Dal,[195] the youth wing of the VHP which had been created in 1984 to become an instrument for plebeianising the Sangh Parivar because of its loose discipline and absence of emphasis on the RSS *samskara* (good influences).[196]

The polarisation of Gujarat along communal lines was one of the reasons why the BJP finally won the state elections in the 1990s.

THE KESHUBHAI PATEL INTERLUDES: CASTE POLITICS AND THE MAKING OF A HINDUTVA TEST SITE[197]

The communalisation of the public sphere was not the only explanation for the electoral success of the BJP. The way it cleverly factored in caste in its political strategy, in the post-KHAM context, is another. While the Jana Sangh was an even more Banya (or Vanya)–Brahmin party in Gujarat than elsewhere, the BJP wisely accommodated the emergence of the Kshatriyas as a political force in the 1980s, in a counter-intuitive move given the anti-OBC bias of its Savarna upper-caste base. The party already had Kshatriya cadres in its ranks because the RSS had attracted youths from that caste, for whom the *shakhas* (local branches) offered a vector for Sanskritisation. One of them, Shankarsinh Vaghela, a Rajput leader who had joined the RSS in his youth, became general secretary and then president of the BJP throughout the 1980s, at a time when most presidents of BJP state units were still from the upper castes. Moreover, Vaghela had developed an alternative Kshatriya Sabha to compete with the pro-Congress Gujarat Kshatriya Sabha and the KHAM coalition. His successor at the helm of the BJP in Gujarat, Kashiram Rana, was also an OBC. In the 1980s, the BJP fielded between 15.5 per cent and 17.5 per cent OBC candidates in the Vidhan Sabha elections, and in 1990s, 20 per cent to 24 per cent.[198] In 1990, out of 67 BJP MLAs, 24 per cent were OBCs, as against 25.5 per cent Patels and 31.3 per cent upper castes.[199]

Nor did the BJP ignore the Patels. In the 1995 elections, the party nominated many Patel candidates (28 per cent of its candidates, as against 20.3 per cent of upper castes) and put forward one of them, Keshubhai Patel, as its chief minister-in-waiting. Keshubhai was also a veteran RSS member who had developed a base among his segment of the Patidars, the Leuva Patels of Saurashtra, the province from which he hailed. While in the 1995 state elections as many OBCs (38 per cent) supported the BJP as the Congress, 67 per cent Patidars voted BJP (as against 20 per cent for the Congress).[200] Patels now represented 29 per cent of the 121 MLAs of the BJP, while the OBCs had declined from 24 per cent to 20.5 per cent and the upper-caste MLAs had dropped from 31.3 per cent to 26.4 per cent.[201] They were also well represented in the government of Keshubhai Patel that was formed in March 1995: at 25 per cent, the percentage of Patel ministers and ministers of state was still below the share of upper castes (32 per cent), but above the proportion of OBCs (23 per cent) (see Appendix B). Sharik Laliwala, in his detailed study of the sociology of the governments of Gujarat, goes beyond such aggregates and analyses the kind of portfolios that Patels got: in the 1995 government, Patels received the chief ministership and 'three-fourth of cabinet spots'.[202]

Vaghela never reconciled himself to the appointment of Keshubhai Patel as chief minister: the man who had 'built the BJP in Gujarat, brick by brick over long years, was sidelined'.[203] He revolted, and in September 1995 he airlifted 47 MLAs (his supporters in the state Assembly) to Khajuraho in Madhya Pradesh, which allowed him to claim that Patel had lost his majority.[204] Atal Bihari Vajpayee intervened, Vaghela backtracked and Patel stepped down. He was replaced by a compromise candidate, Suresh Mehta.

In 1996, Vaghela was asked to contest the Lok Sabha seat for the Godhra constituency, but his enemies within the Sangh Parivar—including RSS cadres who had been upset by his alleged lack of discipline—ensured that he lost. Kashiram Rana was removed from the party presidency and replaced by a follower of

Keshubhai Patel. In August 1996, Vaghela launched a forum that was supposed to focus only on cultural issues, the Mahagujarat Asmita Manch (Forum for the Pride of Greater Gujarat). He was expelled from the BJP soon afterwards and formed a separate party, the Rashtriya Janata Dal (National People's Party), which his supporters in the Gujarat Assembly joined immediately. Keshubhai Patel lost his majority and Vaghela became chief minister with the support of the Congress.[205]

But the Congress resented the manner in which Vaghela began asserting his authority over state politics and building a base for himself. He had to step down, and in 1997 he took the risk of dissolving the Assembly in order to hold state elections two years ahead of schedule, in 1998. They marked the triumph of the BJP—which won 117 seats with 44.8 per cent of the valid votes—and of Keshubhai Patel, who was appointed chief minister once again.

In 2001, I called Gujarat 'a laboratory for Hindu nationalism',[206] not only because it was, at the time, the only place where the BJP ruled with the benefit of an absolute majority, but also because it had been the focus of a massive attempt to develop the Sangh Parivar. First, the VHP benefited greatly from the rise to power of the BJP, which, from this position, could protect the organisation. As early as 25 December it organised anti-Christian rallies in different districts of South Gujarat,[207] including Dangs (where, out of 144,091 inhabitants, 135,376 were Tribals in 1991).[208] Soon afterwards, ten or so churches and prayer halls were burned or damaged.[209] Then, sixteen churches were burned and eight were damaged in the days that followed. The National Commission for Minorities submitted to President K.R. Narayanan a report on these attacks which blamed the state BJP government for its "inept handling of the situation".[210] Indeed, the state machinery did nothing to check Hindu nationalist propaganda.[211] As a result, the December 1998 scenario unfolded once again in December 1999.

In parallel, the Sangh Parivar continued to publicly abuse Muslims. In June 1998, a communal riot took place at Bardoli. Ghanshyam Shah points out: 'Before, during and after the riots, a number of RSS, VHP and Bajrang Dal leaders made provocative speeches against the Muslims.'[212] One such leaflet claimed that 'Every year about five lakhs [500,000] of Hindu girls are allured, trapped, raped and married by Muslim rogues and children are given birth by them. They are enslaved and sold to Arab countries'; or that 'Muslims are destroying Hindu Community by slaughterhouses, slaughtering cows and making Hindu girls elope. Crime, drugs, terrorism are Muslim's empire.'[213]

Gujarat was badly affected by communal violence in the late 1990s. In July 1999 a Hindu–Muslim riot took place in Ahmedabad in which eight people were killed, mainly Muslims.[214] In September that year violence erupted in Surat when the Ganesh Chaturthi procession was prevented by the police from parading outside a mosque. The processionists protested so vehemently that the police opened fire, killing seven people and injuring twenty others.[215] In March 2000 a Muslim was killed in Ahmedabad during a riot that broke out owing to the way 'some self-styled volunteers of the VHP' tried to 'check' on minorities slaughtering cows during the festival of Eid al-Adha.[216]

Gujarat under Patel also implemented a policy that the RSS had long cherished, namely the rewriting of history textbooks. The Gujarat State Board of School Textbooks published a Standard IX social studies textbook in which Muslims, Christians and Parsis were presented as 'foreigners' and in which it was said that 'in most of the States the Hindus are a minority and the Muslims, Christians and Sikhs are in a majority'.[217]

By the late 1990s, Gujarat had become the stronghold of Hindu nationalism, the only state where the BJP was in a majority and where other components of the Sangh Parivar were flourishing, and dared to implement a starkly communal and violent agenda directed against the minorities. The situation was deteriorating so quickly that the monthly publication *Seminar* devoted its October 1998 issue to the state. A senior Gujarati, Lord Meghnad Desai, wrote about his home state in the first article: 'In the 1950s and early 1960s, it was a tolerant, polite, civilised and cultured place [...] Gujarat has over the last 30 years become a nasty, violent, intolerant, communalist place [...] the majority of Gujarat, especially the affluent Hindu middle classes, have so changed that it is difficult to be proud of them.'[218]

2

HINDUTVA VERSUS 'ISLAMIST THREATS'

NARENDRA MODI, 'EMPEROR OF HINDU HEARTS'

> Actually, even now I have not completely returned to the material world.
>
> Narendra Modi to Nilanjan Mukhopadhyay[1]

In 2000–01, Keshubhai Patel's government had to cope with two events that threatened its survival. In 2000, the BJP lost heavily in the municipal elections, even in its strongholds (such as Ahmedabad, which it had held since 1987, and Rajkot, since 1983), and retained a reduced majority in the four other municipal corporations. The setback was even more dramatic in rural areas since the party, which held 24 of 25 district councils (panchayats), hung on to only 2 of them.[2] The number of BJP seats dropped from 599 to 192 in the District Panchayat boards while those of the Congress jumped from 111 to 513.

On 26 January 2001, a massive earthquake with its epicentre near Bhuj (in Kutch) affected various parts of the state, including Ahmedabad.[3] Unsurprisingly, given the magnitude of the natural disaster, the government could neither deliver relief in the way it should have nor meet its citizens' expectations. However,

Gujaratis resented more the fact that many of the buildings that were destroyed—in the process killing thousands of people—had often been built with no regard for basic safety procedures, lending currency to the suspicion that 'contractors and the government were in collusion and that money had changed hands for building permits'.[4] There was also controversy regarding the 2001 report of the Comptroller and Auditor General (CAG) 'over expenses relating to the Chief Minister's foreign trip to garner NRI [Non-Resident Indians] funds'.[5]

In this context, in September 2001 the BJP lost by-elections in two of its strongholds: the Sabarmati Vidhan Sabha seat, which was part of Advani's Lok Sabha constituency, and the Sabarkantha Lok Sabha seat. On 2 October, Keshubhai Patel met the BJP high command in Delhi, which, while describing him as 'Lok Hriday Samrat' (Emperor of people's hearts),[6] also demanded his resignation. He reluctantly agreed, and, having failed to promote one of his lieutenants to succeed him, eventually accepted the choice of the national leadership, Narendra Modi, who was sworn in as chief minister on 7 October 2001. The circumstances of Modi's elevation to the apex position in Gujarat are not unimportant for understanding his strategy in the following months, including during and after the communal violence which engulfed the state in 2002. But this strategy can also only be understood in the light of the new incumbent's past record and career.

A PRACHARAK MORPHED INTO A POLITICIAN?

Modi has always claimed that he was 'an apolitical CM'.[7] This claim extends back to his first faltering steps in the public arena, which, undeniably, have endowed him with a unique pedigree. But this claim needs to be scrutinised because it does not mean that the new chief minister had no ideology; on the contrary, it reflected his sense of doctrinal purity.

Narendra Damodardas Modi was born on 17 September 1950 in the small town of Vadnagar (Mehsana district). He hails from the low caste of Modh Ghanchis (oil pressers), which was added to Gujarat's Socially and Economically Backward Classes list in 1994 and to the central Other Backward Classes (OBC) list in 1999. His father sold edible oil, but also had a tea stall where Narendra used to work as a child. He joined the local RSS *shakha* when he was seven or eight years old 'because this was the only extra-curricular activity open for him outside his peer group'.[8] According to the biography of Modi by M.V. Kamath and K. Randeri, he very early on showed 'an inclination towards becoming a *sanyasi* [world renouncer]'.[9] Such a calling is not uncommon in the RSS. M.S. Golwalkar himself renounced the world before becoming number two in the organisation. Like him, Narendra Modi went to the Belur Math, headquarters of the Ramakrishna Mission in Calcutta (today's Kolkata), and then to the Himalayas. In an interview he gave to Nilanjan Mukhopadhyay he explained: 'I went to the Vivekananda Ashram in Almora, I loitered a lot in the Himalayas. I had some influences of spiritualism at that time along with the sentiment of patriotism—it was all mixed. It is not possible to delineate the two ideas.'[10] This collapsing of religion and a certain political culture is typical of Hindu nationalists who, since Savarkar, look at India as their *punya bhoomi* (sacred land) and *matri bhoomi* (mother land).[11]

Another biographer of Modi, Kingshuk Nag, does not mention this episode at all but highlights the fact that Modi left Vadnagar in 1967, when he was 17 years old, to escape a child marriage that had been arranged years before.[12] In this version, Modi went to his uncle's place in Ahmedabad (about 110 km away) directly from his home town.

Modi became a full-time RSS worker by the late 1960s or early 1970s. He then started living at Hedgewar Bhawan (RSS headquarters) in the residential area of Maninagar (Ahmedabad) and became the assistant to the *prant pracharak* in charge of Gujarat and Maharashtra, Lakshmanrao Inamdar, a former lawyer who regarded him as his *manas putra* (a son born out of the mind)[13] and whom he regarded as his mentor.[14] It seems that Modi became a *pracharak* as early as 1972. The following year he was involved in the Navnirman agitation, after being dispatched by the RSS to the ABVP, then at the forefront of this movement. Around that time, it seems that Modi registered as an MA student at Gujarat University after passing his BA as an external student of Delhi University.[15] In 1974 or 1975, he became close to one of his professors, Pravin Sheth, who writes: 'As an external student of post-graduate programme in Political Science at Gujarat University, Modi used to come to me, collect reading material from me, grasp the matter. He applied them in examinations and achieved first class first. After acquiring good understanding of Political Sociology and Indian Politics, with his unique sense, he had applied the theory of Political Science in practice with appropriate adaptations.'[16]

Modi was then absorbed by the Emergency, working underground after its declaration. He was put in charge of disseminating information, including counter-propaganda against Indira Gandhi's (and Sanjay Gandhi's) dictatorial regime. He also took care of the families of those RSS leaders who were in prison and maintained 'links between Indians abroad and at home'.[17]

Immediately after the Emergency, he was 'assigned the role of key researcher for a resource book on the Emergency'.[18] This episode is important because it enabled Modi not only to interact with many politicians, but also to tour India.[19] But he soon returned to his home state to pursue a career within the local RSS. As early as 1978 he had been appointed *vibhag pracharak* (the head of RSS units in six districts), and then *sambhag pracharak* (which involved the supervision of two vibhags, or divisions, those of Surat and Baroda). In 1981, he became *prant pracharak*, a role that consisted in coordinating various organisations of the Sangh, including the Vishva Hindu Parishad (VHP), the Bharatiya Kisan Sangh and the ABVP throughout Gujarat.[20] By the mid-1980s, he had been recognised as a skilled organiser and, when in 1986 L.K. Advani became BJP president, he considered taking Modi on for party work. Deputed to the BJP in 1987, he became the *sangathan mantri* (organising secretary) of the Gujarat unit of the party. The organising secretaries had formed the backbone of the Jana Sangh since the 1950s, after Deendayal Upadhyaya created the post in the 1950s and occupied it for years at the national level. As the state party organiser-in-chief, Modi was the architect of a whole series of programmes in the form of 'Yatras' (literally pilgrimages or processions, but in practice mass demonstrations). For instance, the Nyay Yatra aimed to 'demand justice for Hindu riot victims',[21] and the Lok Shakti Yatra mobilised street protests against the liquor mafia in the Old City of Ahmedabad—a demonstration that exemplified the strategy of polarisation.

Then Modi managed the Gujarat leg of Advani's 1990 Rath Yatra, which started from Somnath. Subsequently, his skills as an organiser were used for Yatra politics at the national level. In late 1991, he was in charge of the Ekta Yatra, which Murli Manohar Joshi, the BJP president who had just taken over from Advani, led from Kanyakumari to Srinagar in order to reaffirm the national unity of India. His colleagues in the BJP office in Delhi noticed that on this occasion 'he did not function the way a full-time RSS *pracharak* should. He was seen as projecting himself and seeking the limelight.'[22] Indeed, during the Ekta Yatra, 'not only was Modi accompanying Joshiji on his vehicle, but would, at every stop, address the crowds along with the BJP president. As an organiser of the yatra, he should have consciously kept a low profile.'[23] Besides his taste for interacting with the Indian public which the Ekta Yatra revealed, it also afforded him a new opportunity to broaden his national, pan-Indian political experience.[24]

Even before becoming the main party organiser of the BJP in Gujarat, Modi concentrated on one particular objective in the 1980s: the conquest of local power structures. He had concluded that 'the route to Gandhinagar went through local power structures that had to be won'.[25] As mentioned above, the BJP took the municipality of Rajkot in 1983 and that of Ahmedabad four years later, when Modi was in charge of all BJP election campaigns, including local ones.[26] These successes were achieved largely thanks to the growing political polarisation resulting from communal violence. Ahmedabad is a case in point. The BJP rose to power there after the 1985 conflagration, before which Modi had told his professor, Pravin Sheth:

> Muslims are spreading fear among the mixed localities of walled city areas in Ahmedabad. Their intention is to force evict 70% of Hindu population out of the *pols* [lanes of the Old City forming sub-local communities] in the walled city by spreading fear, and put the rest in minority so that they also sell their houses to Muslims and migrate to safer places in despair. Thus, they plan to convert the entire area of the walled city into a Muslim dominated town. But our RSS volunteers have reached there. We will educate Hindus about Muslim intent, try to raise their morale and prevent them from being evicted. We will inspire them to preserve our ancient heritage of the walled city structures and *pols*.[27]

The Sangh Parivar was indeed effective in Ahmedabad, as large numbers of Muslims fled during the 1985 riots and sought refuge in the ghetto of Juhapura.[28] The polarisation strategy worked elsewhere too, and this is one of the reasons why in 1995 the BJP won six municipal corporations, including that of Surat where the BJP took all the seats. The party also won a majority in 18 of 19 District Panchayat boards. Achyut Yagnik and Suchitra Sheth point out that in the rise to power of the BJP in the state, 'the crucial factor was the Sangh Parivar's penetration into the local power structures of Gujarat, which began in the 1980s and continued in the 1990s'.[29]

In 1995, Modi appeared as a major architect of the rise to power of the BJP in Gujarat after the party for the first time won a majority of seats in the state Assembly. BJP's strategy continued to rely on communal polarisation, a process that was nurtured, in the wake of the 1985 riot, by targeting the 'Muslim mafia' of Abdul Latif.

Modi was also successful in eliminating political rivals and winning powerful patrons in Delhi, as the 1996 episode of Advani's election in Gandhinagar shows. The BJP president was then looking for a safe berth, given that in 1991 he had won his New Delhi seat by a small margin: 'it was Modi who suggested to Advani that he should contest for Lok Sabha from Gandhinagar … that was until then represented by Modi's peer-turned-foe Shankarsinh Vaghela (he won in 1989). It was a masterstroke as BJP got charged up in the state and Vaghela was relegated to the fringes. The relationship grew with Advani frequently visiting Gujarat after becoming MP from the state.'[30] Modi had killed two birds with one stone, displaying a political acumen that is not usually the main hallmark of RSS *pracharaks*, who make a point of eschewing politics—by definition, a dirty game.

Gradually, Modi became a semi-public figure, to such an extent that he was called 'super chief minister' after Keshubhai Patel formed the government and became its official head.[31] He took part in cabinet meetings and remained in the room when senior bureaucrats came to report to the chief minister, for instance.[32]

However, Modi failed to keep the party united, despite this being a major responsibility of a *sangathan mantri*. After the 1995 electoral triumph, Keshubhai Patel and Shankarsinh Vaghela were locked in fierce rivalry for the post of chief minister. In spite of his close long-term relationship with the latter (Vaghela was, like him, one of the few low-caste RSS veterans, and when he was the party president, Modi was his secretary), Modi threw his weight behind Patel, ensuring that Vaghela would get none of the spoils that were distributed to party workers.[33] This move further alienated Vaghela, who created a difficult situation for Keshubhai Patel after defecting with 'his' 47 MLAs. After this episode, Patel, who came increasingly under the influence of Sanjay Joshi, another *pracharak* assigned to the BJP who was also a rival of Modi, persuaded the party's national leaders that Modi had to be banished from Gujarat.[34]

Narendra Modi went to Delhi when he was appointed national secretary in November 1995, in charge of Himachal Pradesh. Advani, who had become BJP president again in 1993, had been keen to promote him to that post, but his increasingly influential right-hand man, Pramod Mahajan, did not see eye to eye with Modi, and Modi had to spend most of his time in Chandigarh. However, when Kushabhau Thakre, another *pracharak* turned BJP cadre,[35] became party president in 1998, Modi was promoted to the post of general secretary and became, from Delhi, de facto head of the party's organisation with official responsibilities for the states of Punjab, Haryana, Jammu and Kashmir, Chandigarh and Himachal Pradesh, as well as the Bharatiya Janata Yuva Morcha, the youth wing of the party.[36] He was retained in this capacity by Bangaru Laxman when the latter took over from Thakre in 2000.

His biographers M.V. Kamath and K. Randeri emphasise that by becoming *All-India Bharatiya sangathan mahamantri*, Modi was following in the steps of three prestigious figures: Deendayal Upadhyaya, S.S. Bhandari and Kushabhau Thakre.[37] However, none of them became public figures in the way he did: as organisers, they remained the power behind the throne, even though Upadhyaya and Thakre contested elections once, by default. Modi, on the contrary, had evinced some interest in the life of a politician. He liked public meetings and interacting with both the masses and the media. Other differences pertained to

Modi's tendency to side in faction fights at the expense of party unity and his abrupt behaviour with colleagues, two things that precipitated long-lasting antagonisms. Modi made two enemies in the 1990s: Shankarsinh Vaghela and Sanjay Joshi. Pravin Sheth attributed these developments to 'his egoistic nature and abrasive behaviour with his fellow workers. Sometimes it appears that he has a Hubris complex. In this state, he tends to believe that his level of understanding is more than anyone else.'[38]

Furthermore, Modi played the politician's game when it served his interests. Not only did he sideline Vaghela by suggesting to Advani that he stand for his constituency, but he also tried to dislodge Keshubhai Patel as chief minister of Gujarat. In his memoirs, Vinod Mehta, then editor-in-chief of *Outlook*, recalls: 'When he was working at the party office in Delhi, Narendra Modi came to see me in the office. He brought along some documents that indicated the chief minister of Gujarat, Keshubhai Patel, was up to no good. The next thing I heard was that he had become the chief minister in place of Keshubhai.'[39] However, Modi continued to present himself as an organisation man par excellence and, when Vajpayee asked him to take over from Keshubhai Patel, he replied: 'That is not my work. I have been away from Gujarat for six long years. I am not familiar with the issues. What will I do there? *It is not a field of my liking* [my emphasis]. I don't know anyone.'[40] Although he liked mass meetings, Modi did not like politics and did not consider himself a politician. This factor was to play a role when he took his first steps as chief minister.

Modi knew that it would be a challenging task to arrest the BJP's declining trend before the state elections that were due to be held in February 2003.[41] Just before his swearing-in as chief minister he told his colleagues: 'We have only 500 days and 12,000 hours before the next election for the state assembly.'[42] That the BJP was under such pressure probably explains why communal polarisation appeared particularly relevant to its pursuit of power in 2002.

THE RIOTS OF 2002 AND ITS POLITICS[43]

On 27 February 2002, three days after Modi won a by-election that allowed him to join the state Assembly and be confirmed as chief minister of Gujarat, violence broke out in Godhra, a district headquarters town in eastern Gujarat.[44] As a result, 59 Hindus were killed, including 25 women and 14 children, who were burned alive aboard the Sabarmati Express. The train was returning from Faizabad in Uttar Pradesh carrying many *kar sevaks* (literally servers-in-action)—VHP activists who had travelled to Ayodhya to try, once again, to build the Ram temple on the ruins of the Babri Masjid. The undertaking had once again been postponed through central government intervention, mediation and judicial decisions, a process which had been going on since the demolition of the Babri Masjid in 1992 and which was increasingly frustrating the *kar sevaks* and their backers.

Of the train's 2,000 passengers, about 1,700 were *kar sevaks* from Gujarat who were returning home. They chanted Hindu nationalist songs and slogans throughout the journey, all the while harassing Muslim passengers. One family was even made to get off the train for refusing to utter the *kar sevaks'* war cry: 'Jai Shri Ram!' (Hail to Lord Ram!) More abuse occurred at the halt in Godhra, a Gujarati town known for its large Muslim population and history of communal riots. A Muslim shopkeeper was ordered to shout 'Jai Shri Ram!' He refused and was assaulted until the *kar sevaks* turned on a Muslim woman and her two daughters. According to several accounts, one of them was forced to board the train before it moved off.[45]

The train had hardly left the station when one of the passengers pulled the emergency chain. The train came to a halt in the middle of a Muslim neighbourhood inhabited by Ghanchis, a community from whom many of Godhra's street vendors are drawn. Hundreds of Muslims surrounded the *kar sevaks*' coaches and attacked them with stones and burning torches, an assault that resulted in many deaths.[46]

Anatomy of Mass Violence

On 27 February, Chief Minister Narendra Modi reached Godhra at about two in the afternoon, along with members of his government, including Ashok Bhatt. He spoke on TV that evening. The testimony of Parvis Ghassem-Fachandi, who was then conducting fieldwork in Ahmedabad, is particularly telling:

> In the evening [of 27 February], Chief Minister Modi proclaimed on TV, not without a certain pathos in his voice, that the Godhra incident was a 'pre-planned attack', explicitly contradicting the [local] Collector's statement released just a few hours earlier, also on TV, which had described the incident not as planned but as an 'accident'. Senior members of the central government in New Delhi echoed Modi's words, speculating that the 'foreign hand' of the infamous Pakistani intelligence services (ISI) [Inter-Services Intelligence, the Pakistani military intelligence service] was involved.[47]

That evening, on the government's orders, most of the bodies of those who had died in Godhra were taken to Ahmedabad for a post-mortem and public ceremony.[48] The arrival of the corpses was broadcast on television, generating considerable emotion, all the more so since they were shown merely covered with a sheet. The next morning, 'Modi alleged that no ordinary group could have committed such a "cowardly act". The Godhra incident was, he argued, "not a communal incident" caused by long-standing hostility between two communities, but a "one-sided collective violent act of terrorism from one community".'[49] This authoritative gloss immediately circulated on radio and television and in the newspapers.'[50] The reference to terrorism justified the way the Gujarat government resorted to POTO (the Prevention of Terrorism Ordinance, which later became an Act in 2002), ignoring the protests of the National Human Rights Commission.[51]

On 28 February, the VHP organised a bandh, or shutdown of the city, which established the conditions for a Hindu offensive, particularly in Ahmedabad. Hindu nationalist activists started to engage in violence, targeting minorities. The local policemen remained passive when rioters took control of the streets,[52] some of them sending away cars driven by locals from the neighbourhoods the Hindu nationalist activists had targeted for their misdeeds.[53]

The assault on the Gulberg Society, a housing complex in Ahmedabad, offers the most telling illustration of the attitude of the activists and the police. The report of the Concerned Citizens Tribunal points out that what happened there was 'probably the first carnage to have been unleashed after the Godhra tragedy'.[54] Indeed, it set a pattern. It was surely the first target because it was there that Ehsan Jafri lived. He had just canvassed against Modi in the campaign that had taken place a few days before in Rajkot, for a by-election that the chief minister had won.[55] In the locality his compound was considered a safe haven. After all, he was a former MP and during the 1985 riots high-profile officials had protected him. As a result, when the bandh was declared, people from the neighbourhood came to take refuge behind the high walls of Gulberg Society. There were about 200 men, women and children there at 7.30 a.m. when a large crowd gathered in front of the compound. At ten thirty, according to some of the survivors who testified before the Concerned Citizens Tribunal, the commissioner of police (CP) of Ahmedabad, P.C. Pandey, visited Jafri 'and gave him a personal assurance that they would send reinforcements and that he would be fully protected'.[56] But 'within five minutes of the CP's departure, at 10.35 a.m., the

Zahir Bakery and an auto-rickshaw just outside Gulberg society were burnt' and the attack on Gulberg Society began.

I have analysed elsewhere the extreme form that communal violence took in the 2002 riots.[57] Though I do not want to downplay it here, this chapter will focus on the "governance" dimension. In that respect, the attack on Gulberg Society is a case in point. According to eyewitnesses, including a Parsi woman who stayed with him till the end, Ehsan Jafri had

> made repeated frantic calls pleading for police assistance against a huge mob in a murderous mood. He kept calling the control room for several hours [...] Pleading anonymity, police officials who met the Tribunal confirmed that Shri Jafri had also made frantic calls to the director general of police, the police commissioner, the chief secretary and the additional chief secretary (home) among others. Three mobile vans of the city police were on hand around Shri Jafri's house but did not intervene [...] It was only nine hours later that the Rapid Action Force (RAF) of the central government intervened, by which time it was far too late.[58]

Former chief minister Amarsinh Chaudhary himself told the team of the National Human Rights Commission which held an inquiry in Gujarat in March 2002 under the stewardship of the former chief justice of the Supreme Court, J.S. Verma, that he 'spoke to the CM Narendra Modi in the afternoon and found him well informed about the presence of a violent crowd outside Shri Jafri's house'.[59]

In Gulberg Society, 69 people were killed, including Ehsan Jafri, three of his brothers and two nephews. The inaction of the police explains how the Hindu nationalist activists managed to unleash communal violence and maintain their flow of hateful propaganda on 28 February and during the days that followed, in Ahmedabad and elsewhere.

Propaganda unchecked

The VHP used a radical discourse to mobilise anti-Muslim sentiment. A pamphlet distributed during the riots opened with this characteristic assertion: 'Today the minority community is trying to crush the majority community.'[60] Another declaration, made by the Bajrang Dal (the VHP's youth wing), began the same way: 'Fifty years after independence it appears that Hindus are second [class] citizens of this country. Religious conversions, infiltration terrorism and bomb blasts have surrounded Hindustan.'[61] The Bajrang Dal further justified their feeling of insecurity by identifying a culprit: 'Jehad is being carried out in order to establish an Islamic state in Hindustan.'[62]

While some reporters from English newspapers and television channels were prevented by the police from getting to key locations like Gulberg Society,[63] others amplified the VHP's propaganda. In contrast to the English media, which took a secular line, Gujarati newspapers published sensationalist, inflammatory stories, among them the two main daily newspapers, *Sandesh* and *Gujarat Samachar*.

The Press Council later initiated an inquiry[64] which concluded that Gujarat's press had endorsed the conspiracy theory that the government had propagated as early as 27 February.[65] On 1 March, the Vadodara edition of *Sandesh* ran with headlines claiming that 'A mob of 7–8 thousand was waiting for the Sabarmati Express to arrive at Godhra', giving its readers good reason to believe that there was indeed a conspiracy.[66] On 6 March, a report was headlined: 'Torching of the train at Godhra was pre-planned. Kalotta [one of the accused] was tipped by a railway officer how to cut open the vacuum pipes'.[67] The Muslim threat was described as an outcome of the support given by Islamist groups and Pakistan to Gujarati Muslims. On 1 March the headline of a news item published by *Sandesh*[68] claimed that a 'mini-Pakistan' existed in Baroda, when describing one of the Muslim pockets of the city that were developing there, as in many other Gujarati urban areas, because of the ghettoisation of the minority.

The chief managing director and editor of *Sandesh*, Falgun Patel, estimated that during the violence the circulation of his newspaper increased in terms of receipts by Rs 150,000.[69] The electronic media also played a part in promoting communal sentiment. For example, on 27 February, JTV kept showing, non-stop, images of the burnt bodies from the Sabarmarti Express in Godhra. Second, they interviewed—sometimes live—Hindu nationalist cadres who spoke their mind. Ajay Dave from the VHP declared, 'We will retaliate with violence and create history.'[70]

Neither the propaganda of the VHP–Bajrang Dal nor the disinformation peddled by the media prompted any administrative reaction.

The unleashing of violence

The passivity of the police not only allowed Hindu nationalist propaganda to circulate, but also enabled the Hindu nationalist militias to strike almost everywhere with impunity. While previous riots had usually been confined to a few places, the 2002 riot was pervasive throughout Gujarat, across dozens of districts.

In urban areas prone to violence, local Sangh Parivar activists played a key role, as Ward Berenschot has shown.[71] Indeed, Hindu nationalist leaders had become increasingly influential at the local level as intermediaries (or *dalal*s) between ordinary citizens and state resources (such as jobs and subsidies). Berenschot explains the significance of this new form of 'access to state resources' in terms of the decline of the Congress and its trade unions, which used to offer similar services.[72] Yet the BJP did not develop this local network by default; it was also the outcome of a long-term agenda intended to capture power at the municipal level.

Whatever the reason for the creation of this network of BJP local municipal councillors and other *dalals*, the clientelistic links on which it relied were activated to unleash communal violence. As Berenschot points out, 'the capacity of local leaders to access state resources generates the necessary authority and influence to mobilize large groups of people for rioting'.[73] By contrast, as Berenschot shows, a neighbourhood like Ramrahim Nagar, where no *dalals* could be mobilised, remained unaffected by violence.

In some places, the assaults were military-like in their planning. The troops were perfectly disciplined and incredibly numerous: groups of attackers sometimes numbered thousands of men.[74] These squads generally arrived in Muslim neighbourhoods by the truckload. They wore a basic uniform—khaki shorts and a saffron headband—and carried daggers, swords and trishuls (tridents).[75] But they used gas cylinders too, and observers were struck everywhere by 'the widespread use of cooking gas cylinders in blowing up places of worship, factories, houses and other business establishments throughout the state'.[76] The shortage of gas cylinders in the market before any violence had begun was interpreted by the investigators as a sign of premeditation. But there were other signs. The lists that the ringleaders had in hand attested even more clearly to the pre-planned nature of the assault: these indicated Muslim homes, businesses and shops, some of which bore Hindi names, thereby proving that research had been undertaken beforehand to ascertain the owners' identity. The lists, on computer printouts, had been drawn up on the basis of voter registration rolls.[77]

The main targets were not the Muslims of the Old City, but rather those living in isolated smaller groups, in industrial suburbs, like Naroda Patiya and, to a lesser extent, in the residential areas of West Ahmedabad, including Paldi.[78] In all these places women were often attacked first,[79] rape being systematic in the affected localities.[80] The rioters' desire to eradicate Islam—and not only to displace the Muslims—also explains the many attacks against places of worship. Altogether, 527 mosques, madrasas, cemeteries and other *dargahs* (mausoleums of Sufi saints) were damaged or destroyed.[81] The tomb of Wali Gujarati, known as the founder of Urdu poetry, who died in 1707, was also destroyed in Ahmedabad. Many places of worship that were demolished were 'replaced' by a statue of Hanuman and a saffron-coloured flag.

Beyond the City

Traditionally Hindu–Muslim riots have been an urban phenomenon.[82] Yet the violence in 2002 spread to villages, even, in many cases, those where very few Muslims resided.[83] The districts of Mehsana and Gandhinagar, for instance, which had only 6.6 per cent and 2.9 per cent Muslim residents respectively according to the 2001 census, were heavily affected, even in the rural areas.

This phenomenon can largely be explained by the fact that in rural Gujarat the small Muslim minority often comprised shopkeepers and moneylenders. This social class among Muslims is primarily from the Bohra, Khoja and Memon communities. In many villages, these groups owned several businesses and were the main moneylenders (*sahukar*), to whom peasants would become indebted, sometimes to pay their daughters' dowry, sometimes to buy seed. They became one of the attackers' prime targets, often pinpointed by Hindu nationalist activists drafted in from the cities. They exploited the peasants' resentment towards this small economic elite and raised their hopes of benefiting financially by looting shops. This led the sociologist Dipankar Gupta to interpret the spread of rioting to rural Gujarat as being mainly due to economic reasons.[84] The findings of Bela Bhatia in Sabarkantha partly corroborate this analysis. She observed a shift in violence from urban to rural between 28 February—when the small towns of Khedbrahma and Bhiloda were hit—and the evening of 1 March, when it spread to the villages.[85] Again it was Hindu nationalist activists from the city or nearby towns who were responsible. These *tolas* (groups) arrived in villages on tractors or in jeeps. The assailants—most of them were Patels—split into three groups, *todwavalla* (those who were destroying), *lootwavalla* (those who were looting) and *baadwavalla* (those who were burning). In all, 2,161 houses, 1,461 shops, 71 workshops and factories, and 38 hotels were looted and entirely or partly destroyed in Sabarkantha district. In addition, 45 places of worship met the same fate, which suggests that beyond the purely economic aspect, the violence reflected other forms of resentment. One of the slogans heard most frequently was '*Muslai ne gaam ma thi kado*' (Get rid of the Muslims from the village), chanted by both local villagers and outside activists.

Altogether, hundreds of villages were affected, particularly in the districts of Panchmahal, Mehsana, Sabarkantaha, Bharuch, Bhavnagar and Vadodara. In the last-mentioned, the army had to be called in on 5 March and thousands of Muslims from 22 different villages were evacuated to refugee camps.[86]

Still, the most surprising development occurred elsewhere in the 'tribal belt' bordering Madhya Pradesh. Never before had there been such massive participation of indigenous tribal peoples (Adivasis) in anti-Muslim riots alongside Hindu nationalist activists. Bela Bhatia's research in Sabarkantha—a district where tribals made up 17 per cent of the population—led her to conclude that the Adivasis 'were used by upper caste and [upper] class Hindus in their program against the Muslims'. In testimonies she gathered in the field from Muslim survivors, they even made excuses for the violence the Adivasis perpetrated, saying that it was not surprising to see them loot Bohra, Khoja and Memon shops, given the area's structural drought and the febrile atmosphere generated by the rioting.

But Adivasis were not only instrumentalised; they sometimes showed their own agency in the riots. For even if, from the outset, the violence came from outside, some Adivasis devised their own versions of it. This was particularly noticeable in the first tribal village in Gujarat to be affected: Tejgadh, in Panchmahal district. There again, outsiders torched the first shops, but 'once the first attack was over, other villagers joined in on their own with no further need for instigation and the looting continued'.[87] This involvement of Adivasis in the rioting reflected the influence of the Sangh Parivar and especially the VHP and the Vanavasi Seva Sangh (Vanavasi Service Association), a question we will return to in the final chapter of this book.[88]

If rural Gujarat was torn by communal violence for the first time and on such a scale, the post-Godhra riots remained mostly an urban phenomenon, and towns that had not previously experienced riots were also affected. Late on 28 February, Gandhinagar, the capital of Gujarat, some 30 km from Ahmedabad, was the scene of Hindu–Muslim violence for the first time in its history. Twenty-six towns in all were subject to curfew. Ahmedabad and Godhra saw the most serious clashes, with 350 and 100 victims respectively in early March, according to official figures. Next were two riot-prone cities, Mehsana (50 dead) and Sabarkantha (40 dead).[89]

Reviewing the chronology of events gives an idea of the forces of destruction that were unleashed in Gujarat during those few days. On 28 February, in Ahmedabad, in the Naroda Gaon and Naroda Patiya areas, an armed horde of several thousand people attacked Muslim houses and shops, killing 200 people. Six other neighbourhoods in the city were subject to similar attacks on a lesser scale. Three other districts, namely Vadodara, Gandhinagar and Sabarkantha, suffered comparable violence. From 1 March, mainly rural districts were added to the list of hotspots: Panchmahal, Mehsana, Kheda, Junagadh, Banaskantha, Patan, Anand and Narmada. On 2 March, Bharuch and Rajkot, which had yet to be affected by communal violence, were hit in turn. On the 4th, riots broke out in Surat, a city that had seen considerable Hindu–Muslim violence in the 1990s and that was much less affected this time. Violence, by then, had affected 151 towns and 993 villages.[90]

The clashes could not have spread so quickly and taken on such proportions had not well-organised actors orchestrated them. Nor were they a spontaneous reaction since they took place more than 24 hours after the Godhra carnage and in the framework of the VHP's bandh—spontaneous anti-Muslim reactions had been confined to Godhra itself on the 27th and were rather limited.[91]

Though it is widely believed that the official statistics concerning casualties of the Gujarat riots are underestimates, they provide some valuable indications: the official death toll is 1,169, but NGOs have mentioned the figure of 2,000 victims[92] on the basis of information gathered from families about missing persons—those whose bodies were never found.[93]

'WE HAVE NO ORDER TO SAVE YOU':[94] THE PERPETRATORS AND THEIR PROTECTORS

In contrast to what happened in previous episodes of communal violence, the faces of the perpetrators of the Gujarat riots are known. They appear in footage taken in a sting operation by a reporter for *Tehelka* magazine, Ashish Khetan, who in 2007 approached Sangh Parivar leaders posing as a sympathetic PhD student. He recorded interviews with dozens of people involved in the massacres using a camera hidden in his laptop.[95] In 2008 the National Human Rights Commission directed the Central Bureau of Investigation (CBI) to authenticate *Tehelka*'s tapes, a work it completed on 10 May 2009.[96]

The Bajrang Dal leader Babu Bajrangi,[97] accused of being deeply involved in the clashes that officially claimed 89 lives on 28 February 2002 in Naroda Patiya, is thus seen declaring to Khetan:

> In Naroda and Naroda Patiya, we didn't spare a single Muslim shop, we set everything on fire, we set them on fire and killed them [...] We believe in setting them on fire because these bastards say they don't want to be cremated, they're afraid of it [...] It has been written in my FIR [First Information Report] ... there was this pregnant woman, I slit her open ... Showed them what's what ... what kind of revenge we can take if our people are killed ... I am no feeble rice-eater. Didn't spare anyone ... they shouldn't even be allowed to breed ... I say that even today ... Whoever they are, women, children, whoever. Nothing to be done with them but cut them down. Thrash them, slash them, burn the bastards [...] I came back after I killed them, called up the [state] home minister [Gordhan Zadaphia][98] and went to sleep ... I felt like Rana Pratap, that I had done something like Maharana Pratap [a Rajput king who fought the Mughals in the sixteenth century].[99]

In Naroda Patiya and Naroda Gam, the local BJP MLA, Maya Kodnani, was directly involved, as is evident from what Khetan was told by Suresh Richard, one of the Dalits (from the Chhatri caste) who attacked local Muslims:[100] 'Mayaben was moving around all day in an open jeep ... [...] [She was saying] Jai Shri Ram, Jai Shri Ram ... wearing a saffron headband ... She kept raising slogans ... She said, carry on with your work, I'm here [to protect you].'[101]

Haresh Bhatt, who in 2002 was vice president of the Bajrang Dal, told Khetan how the assailants were armed: 'I have my own gun factory ... I used to make firecrackers ... We made all the bombs there ... Diesel bombs, pipe bombs, we made them there ... and we used to distribute them from here as well ... We ordered two truckloads of swords from Punjab ... right here, in a village called Dhariya, we readied everything there ... and then we distributed the samaan [arms].'[102]

The testimonies the attackers gave about the role of the police were consistent.[103] As Babu Bajrangi told Khetan, they 'shut their eyes and their mouths'.[104] Ramesh Dave, the VHP district secretary of Kalupur (Ahmedabad), declared that 'they even gave us cartridges',[105] and Anil Patel, another state VHP leader, claimed that not only cartridges but also weapons were provided by the police: 'They would come and take *samaan* [weapons] and deliver it safely to the places it was supposed to go ... The police gave us so much support ... Some even said, do something ... loot them, break them, finish them.'[106] Several top civil servants, on condition of anonymity, admitted to National Human Rights Commission investigators that senior politicians were directly or indirectly involved in the 2002 violence:

> While in previous riots politic elements did play a major part and the police and administration failed to control violence, they were not accused of direct involvement in the carnage. The failure of police and administration in the current riots is attributed not to their professional incompetence but to their attitude of apathy and callousness in general and the accusation of connivance and complicity was made in some cases.
>
> A number of persons holding responsible positions in public life alleged involvement of some Ministers and MLAs in these riots.[107]

The Concerned Citizens Tribunal explains this in the following terms:

> On the evening of February 27, after visiting Godhra, Shri Modi announced that there would be a state bandh the next day. This was after the VHP and BD had already given the bandh call. Thereafter, the chief minister called a meeting of senior police officers. At this meeting, specific instructions were given by him in the presence of cabinet colleagues, on how the police should deal with the situation on the bandh day. The next day, i.e., on the day of the bandh, there was absolutely no police bandobast. The state and city (Ahmedabad) police control rooms were taken over by two ministers, i.e., Shri Ashok Bhatt

> and Shri Jadeja. Repeated pleas for help from people were blatantly turned down.[108]
>
> Senior ministers from Shri Modi's cabinet organised a meeting late in the evening on February 27, in Lunavada village of Sabarkantha district. Shri Ashok Bhatt, the state health minister, and minister Prabhat Singh Chauhan from Lunavada attended. At this meeting, a diabolical plan was drawn and disseminated to the top 50 leaders of the BJP/RSS/BD/VHP, on the method and manner in which the 72-hour-long carnage that followed was to be carried out.
>
> According to confidential evidence recorded by the Tribunal, these instructions were blatantly disseminated by the government, and in most cases, barring a few notable exceptions, methodically carried out by the police and IAS administration.[109]

These conclusions are based on the testimony of a 'highly placed source' given under condition of anonymity.[110] Later on, in January 2010, Sanjiv Bhatt, a senior policeman, explained to the Special Investigation Team appointed by the Supreme Court that as deputy commissioner (intelligence) of the Gujarat Intelligence Bureau from December 1999 to September 2002 and as nodal officer to dispatch useful information to the various intelligence agencies and armed forces, on 27 February 2002, following the Godhra incident, he had taken part in the meeting Narendra Modi convened at his residence. This meeting was, according to Bhatt, the point of departure for 'the official orchestration of the 2002 riots in Gujarat':

> The Chief Minister Shri Narendra Modi said that the bandh call had already been given and that the party had decided to support the same, incidents like the burnings of kar sevaks at Godhra could not be tolerated. He further impressed upon the gathering that for too long the Gujarat Police had been following the principle of balancing the actions against the Hindus and Muslims while dealing with the communal riots in Gujarat. This time the situation warranted that the Muslims be taught a lesson to ensure that such incidents do not recur

> ever again. The Chief Minister Shri Narendra Modi expressed the view that the emotions were running very high among the Hindus and it was imperative that they be allowed to vent out their anger.[111]

Not only were the police paralysed, but the army too. While troops had been airlifted from Jodhpur to Ahmedabad, there was no vehicle to take them from the airport to the city. Lt General Zameer Uddin Shah, the officer in charge of this operation, called Operation Aman, points out in his autobiography: 'By 7 a.m. on 1 March 2002, we had about 3,000 troops landed, but no transport, so they remained at the airfield. These were crucial hours lost.'[112] According to a Human Rights Watch report, the army's ability to intervene rapidly was also hindered by the state government's failure to provide 'information regarding areas where violence was occurring'.[113]

The state's partiality was also evident from the orders the police received from the government. The testimony of R.B. Sreekumar, the additional director general of police (intelligence), is most valuable here.[114] This officer kept a diary between April and September 2022 which he entitled 'Register for recording verbal instructions from higher officers viz. DGP and above'. This document records his interactions with Narendra Modi and his entourage. For instance, an excerpt from the entry dated 22 April 2002 reads: 'I also suggested that the police should arrest soon Hindu leaders involved in the heinous crimes committed during the recent communal riots. The Chief Secretary said such action is not possible immediately as it is against the state Govt policy.' This 'policy' was confirmed by Modi himself on 7 May, as Sreekumar's diary entry states:

> [The CM] asked me to concentrate on Muslim militants. After assuring him to do the needful, I requested him to initiate action to win confidence of minority community as delineated in my note.[115] He was annoyed about my insistence on this point and argued that Muslims are on the offensive, keeping alive

> their belligerent posture. Quoting statistics of high casualty of Muslims due to police firing, riots etc., I appealed to him to see reason and accept that Hindus are on the offensive. The CM instructed that I should not concentrate on Sangh Parivar as they are not doing anything illegal.

This policy was endorsed by K.P.S. Gill, the 'supercop' who had tamed the Sikh guerrilla campaign in Punjab in the 1990s, and who had just been appointed Modi's security advisor in early May at the suggestion of the home minister, L.K. Advani, who was anxious to strengthen the chief minister of Gujarat. On 8 May:

> DGP informed [R.B. Sreekumar] that in his last meeting with Shri Gill, the latter [had] told him the following (1) We should not try to reform politicians—that means BJP and Sangh Parivar will continue to pursue their policy of suppressing, terrorizing and attacking Muslims to make them accept the status of being second class/rate citizens of India and we should not take (viz. police) any action. (2) There is no need for taking action against vernacular press, who are publishing communally inciting news items in favor of the Sangh Parivar.

These entries confirm that the government was using the police to achieve its political—and even ideological, communal—objectives: the military alone could restore law and order. Finally, Operation Aman brought Gujarat back to normality, but it 'took two months of firm and even-handed measures by the Army for passions to be brought under control and peace and sanity restored'.[116] The troops left in two phases in April–May.

NARENDRA MODI, BETWEEN RESIGNATION AND ELECTION

Narendra Modi submitted his resignation at the BJP National Executive meeting that was held in Goa on 12 April 2002. This move was a response to criticisms that emanated from within the BJP itself. Among his main detractors was Shanta Kumar, the food minister in Vajpayee's government.[117] But Vajpayee himself was in favour of Modi's resignation. When he came to Ahmedabad, the week before the BJP National Executive, he endorsed the idea that what had happened in Godhra was a 'pre-planned' attack, but also said: 'Gujarat is a puzzle for me because civilised society does not target and kill women and children.'[118] Just before the Goa meeting, Vajpayee told Advani that 'Modi should have at least offered to resign',[119] and Advani conveyed this message to him. This was the reason why he finally made the move.

However, according to Advani, 'The moment Modi said that, the meeting hall reverberated with a thunderous response from the hundred-odd members of the party's top decision-makers and special invitees: '*Isteefa mat do, isteefa mat do*' (Don't resign, don't resign).'[120] The party president himself, Jana Krishnamurthi, resisted Modi's offer to resign. He 'strongly condemn[ed] the hue and cry of those who demanded the head of the chief minister of Gujarat',[121] and added:

> If the message can go to everyone in the society that whosoever provokes another, and whoever takes initiative in provoking or attacking another, whatever religion he may belong to as goondaism does not have religion, the state as well as society will come down on him heavily to punish him, then the whole society and everyone in society will remain assured that there is justice rendered to all with no appeasement of anyone.[122]

Moreover, Krishnamurthi attributed the violence to Pakistan's military intelligence, the ISI, an idea that K.P.S. Gill was to propagate.[123] As a result, Shanta Kumar faced a disciplinary committee and Vajpayee defended Modi. According to *India Today*, 'there was absolutely no way he could go against the ferocity of the pro-Modi sentiment'.[124] As Vinod Jose would comment later on: 'For perhaps the first time, a prime minister fell in line behind a chief minister—and from that point onwards, Vajpayee lived in fear of Modi.'[125] Twenty years later, in his autobiography, Shanta Kumar, who had to resign from Vajpayee's government in 2003, wrote: 'His [Vajpayee's] opinion on Gujarat riots was completely different than that of the party. Once he did try to discuss "*raj dharam*" (duty of the ruler) within the party but stayed quiet afterwards. I still remember what he had told Shri Arun Jaitleyji before the meeting of the Working Committee in Goa, but he did not say anything during the meeting.'[126]

Moreover, Rajiv Shah, a senior Ahmedabad-based journalist, convincingly argues that Modi was never inclined to bow to Vajpayee's attempt to remove him from Gujarat's chief ministership.[127] One of his aides told Shah: 'He is dead scared that once he ceases to be chief minister, he might lose control over the administrative apparatus which otherwise may support him in an effort to hide facts that point the finger of suspicion at him.'[128] That Modi considered he was fighting for political survival—and more—was subsequently to over-determine many of his decisions.

With the BJP behind him, Modi successfully asked the National Executive for permission 'to dissolve the state assembly and seek a fresh mandate from the people of Gujarat'.[129] In the past, when communal violence polarised society along religious lines, it had generally led the majority community, with a heightened sense of its Hindu identity, to vote in greater numbers for the BJP. This is one of the reasons explaining the correlation between the election calendar and the cycle of riots, as Steven Wilkinson points out: 'both riots and deaths do tend to cluster in the months before elections, and then drop off sharply in the months after an election is held'.[130] This scenario, according to Wilkinson, was more likely to occur in the context of competition between two parties, as in Gujarat: 'In this case, we would expect the party that has the strongest antiminority identity to foment antiminority violence in order to attract swing voters away from its main competitor.'[131] Gujarat itself was accustomed to pre-election riots. Between 1987 and 1991, 40 per cent of the 106 Hindu–Muslim riots that afflicted the state occurred at election time.[132]

While elections were not scheduled till February 2003, Modi saw advantages in anticipating them in order to benefit from the post-riots religious polarisation,[133] especially since the BJP had suffered repeated electoral setbacks.[134] As early as March 2002, Modi had an opinion poll conducted that showed that if elections were organised then, the BJP would win two-thirds of the seats in the Gujarat Assembly.[135] Vajpayee, when he met him on 28 March, refused to 'prepone' state elections.[136] But after the Goa meeting, the balance of power changed. Modi recommended that the governor, S.S. Bhandari, another RSS cadre, dissolve the Gujarat Assembly on 19 July. At the same time, he resigned as chief minister, while remaining at the helm to handle routine proceedings. And he immediately set about calling for early elections even though violence had far from subsided everywhere.[137] The open letter he addressed to the citizens of Gujarat to explain his decision is worth citing at length:

> In the pretext of [the] Godhra incident and its aftermath, efforts were made to pressurise Gujarat. Power-hungry forces stooped to the lowest possible level and made a united effort to devour the prestige of Gujarat [...] Those elements which failed in opposing [the] Narmada [dam] project [see below], now try to portray Gujaratis as rapists to the rest of the world. Those who nurture such elements, insulted five crore [50 million] Gujaratis by describing Gujarat as Godse's Gujarat. [...] The best spirit of democracy is to go to the people. So we again seek your blessings in the form of people's mandate. After the elections, we want to march forward with fresh air and new trust ... The people of Gujarat are awaiting an opportunity to teach a lesson to those who play with the pride of Gujarat. [...] And so, I submit my resignation of my Cabinet at the feet of the five crore [50 million] people of Gujarat.[138]

This speech inaugurated Modi's populist style of politics, which came to rely primarily on a constant cycle of legitimation of his rule by gaining an elective mandate. However, the chief election commissioner, James Michael Lyngdoh, who visited 12 of the state's districts between 31 July and 4 August, was reluctant to organise any polls, especially since many voters, a vast majority of them Muslims, were still living far from their homes in refugee camps. There were 125,000 or so Muslims sheltering in refugee camps at the height of the violence. Officially, they still numbered 87,000 in April 2002, 66,000 of them in Ahmedabad alone.[139] Most of the assistance they received came from Muslim NGOs.[140] The Gujarat government strove to demonstrate that calm had been restored and hurriedly closed the refugee camps or reduced the number of their occupants as reported in official statistics, and argued that in accordance with Article 174 of the Constitution, the time between dissolving the Assembly and holding new elections could not exceed six months. National BJP leaders, starting with Deputy Prime Minister L.K. Advani, joined in the call for early elections. Given the objections of the Election Commission, which preferred that President's Rule[141] be declared because the election could not be organised under normal conditions and because, in this case, Article 174 did not apply, the BJP brought the case before the Supreme Court. The court upheld the Election Commission's order on deferring Gujarat polls but said that 'ordinarily law and order should not be a ground for deferring holding of elections so that the Assembly meets again within six months of its dissolution'.[142] When Lyngdoh resisted political pressure in favour of elections, he became the main target of Narendra Modi. In the *Asian Age*, Deepal Trivedi pointed out:

> Mr. Lyndoh's name reveals [that] he is Christian. This, according to Mr. Modi, means that Mr. Lyngdoh is a Congress agent since its president, Mrs Sonia Gandhi is, 'after all', a Christian. At a nondescript village in Baroda [Vadodara] district, Mr. Modi, addressing a massive tribal rally reportedly joked about how

> Mr. Lyngdoh and Mrs Gandhi could be 'meeting each other in church'. [...] Since last week, a campaign by a faceless Gujarat Gaurav Samiti [Committee for Gujarat's Pride] has been initiated in Gujarat where all vernacular papers have been splashing massive advertisements stressing that if elections could be held in Jammu and Kashmir despite having over three-lakh (300,000) pandits living as refugees in and outside the state, and in the Northeast where 30,000 Reangs (Hindus) live as refugees, why can't there be elections in Gujarat which only has '5,000 Muslim refugees'.[143]

Lyngdoh eventually succumbed to the pressure and in early November the Election Commission set a date for the elections to begin on 12 December.

On 8 September, Modi toured the state in a manner that was highly reminiscent of L.K. Advani's Rath Yatra of 1990. Like that political 'pilgrimage' which had departed from the Somnath temple, Modi's Gaurav Yatra (Pride Procession) left from the Bhathiji Maharaj temple in Phagval (Kheda district). This tour instantly met with great popular success. On 9 September in Himmatnagar, a huge crowd gathered along the roadside and at the place where Modi was to hold his rally, though he did not arrive till two in the morning. One of Modi's campaign slogans cast him as the Hindu Hriday Samrat, a title that had hitherto been accorded to the Shiv Sena leader, Bal Thackeray.[144]

Throughout this tour, Modi's speeches were peppered with communal references. On 9 September, at Bahucharaji (Mehsana district), he said: 'The Muslim philosophy is: "hum paanch, hamare pachchees" [We are five (an allusion to Muslim polygamy), we will have twenty-five children (an open criticism of the high Muslim birth rate that many Hindus fear)].'[145] The fact that this speech was put on record resulted in the transfer of three Intelligence Bureau officers 'on punishment postings',[146] but the VHP distributed thousands of copies of this declaration. Praveen Togadia, the VHP international general secretary, held 220 rallies during the election campaign, making 'jehadi terrorism' his main target. The VHP not only handed out CDs describing the massacre in Godhra, but also had T-shirts printed stating: 'We will not allow our area to be converted into Godhra.'

The BJP campaign resorted to a politics of fear of Islamism and terrorism, which calls to mind its 1995 campaign when it focused on Abdul Latif's crimes and his relations with the Congress. As early as May, during a public function in Unjha (Mehsana district), Modi expressed his 'government's zero tolerance against "traders of death that are supported by Pakistan", power-hungry politicians and pseudo-secularists in Gujarat'. He accused Pakistan of resorting to 'semi-terrorism' and the Congress of 'tarnishing [the] state's image'.[147] He castigated Pakistan's 'semi-terrorism' while speaking at the Indian Air Force headquarters in Jamnagar and 'warned of dire consequences and unimaginable destruction to Pakistan if it attempt[ed] an air attack on the state'.[148] On another occasion, he pointed out that 'besides the proxy war in Jammu and Kashmir, Pakistan has perpetrated semi-terrorism in Gujarat and the beginning was made by Godhra carnage'.[149]

In June, Modi declared that Gujarat's madrasas had to be reformed after arms, including the explosive compound RDX and AK-47s, had been recovered from one of them.[150] In July, Muslim youths were arrested in Ahmedabad, linked to this alleged discovery, but in September R.B. Sreekumar, the additional director general of police in charge of intelligence, sent a report to the Ahmedabad commissioner of police 'informing that the recovery of indigenous firearms and arrest of Muslims in July 2002, on the eve of the Rathyatra, was stage-managed by city Crime Branch DIG Vanzara'. According to his sources, 'the recovered firearms were manufactured in a factory owned by local politicians (supporters of religious organisations) in Sabarkantha district and they were planted on the arrested Muslims'.[151]

During the election campaign, one of the BJP's television commercials began with the sound of a train pulling into a station, followed by the clamour of riots and women's screams before the ringing of temple bells was blocked out by the sound of automatic rifle fire. A few frames later Modi's reassuring countenance appeared, hinting to voters that only he could protect Gujarat from such violence.

Terrorism became an even more relevant theme after the Akshardham attack. On 24 September, in Gandhinagar, two armed men entered the Akshardham Swaminarayan temple, a huge complex that can accommodate up to 5,000 worshippers. With Chinese AK-56s they shot at everything that moved and launched grenades, killing 28 people, and remained holed up in the temple till a National Security Guard commando flushed them out the next morning. Three members of the police were killed in the siege. The Modi government immediately declared that the terrorists were connected to Pakistan and, indeed, the three accused were eventually sentenced to death after an investigation proved they were linked to the militant groups Lashkar-e-Taiba and Jaish-e-Mohammed.[152] But the accused appealed the verdict and the Supreme Court quashed the judgment of the special 'POTA' (Prevention of Terrorism Act) court and the Gujarat High Court, two courts that had deliberated on the basis of evidence provided by the Gujarat police investigation.[153] Six of the accused who had been convicted of this attack were acquitted eleven years after being jailed, after the Supreme Court justices who examined the case file found it contained no evidence.[154] The judgment came many years after the event, but at the time the attack had fostered polarisation by exacerbating fear of Islamism and Pakistan among the Hindus of Gujarat.

This context explains the attacks against Pervez Musharraf, president of Pakistan, in Modi's election campaign. For example, at a rally in Ahmedabad on 1 October—which he dubbed 'Anti-Terrorism Day'—he declared that 'India will continue to refer to him as Mian Musharraf [Musharraf the Muslim]. If the pseudo-secularists don't like it, they can go and lick Musharraf's boots. I dare him to send more terrorists to Gujarat, we are prepared this time. *Arey mian, taari goli khuti jashe* (Mian, your bullets will run out).'[155]

Modi covered 4,200 km during the Gaurav Yatra and held 400 rallies in 146 of the state's 182 constituencies. In the end, the BJP garnered a majority with a record tally of 126 out of 182 seats (compared with 117 in 1998) and almost 50 per cent of the votes cast. The Congress won only 51 seats (2 fewer than in 1998 despite a slight increase in votes, 38 per cent compared with 34 per cent).[156] Only the post-Godhra and post-riot context made this landslide possible. As Sanjay Kumar pointed out, Narendra Modi's party 'did gain from the polarisation of the voters after the riots', as is evident from the fact that 'the vote share of the BJP had increased much more in riot affected constituencies'.[157] Indeed the BJP won 42 out of 50 seats in the three districts most heavily affected by this violence, Panchmahal, Dahod and Vadodara (where it won all the 13 MLA seats). Kumar's interpretation was reconfirmed by the findings of Aseem Prakash, who showed that in the 13 districts affected by the communal violence, which represented 66 per cent of total electors, the BJP did well: it won 71 per cent of its votes there—and 91 seats out 116—registering an increase of 21 seats. The situation prevailing in the seven districts which had seen the most acute violence, Ahmedabad, Panchmahal, Vadodara, Mehsana, Dahod, Anand and Sabarkantha, is even more telling: there, the BJP won 60 out of 68 seats. In contrast, the Congress made progress in 'riot free districts' (+9 per cent in terms of valid votes and an increase of 17 seats compared with 1998), at the expense of the BJP (–3 per cent and 18 seats fewer).[158] In their even more specific study, Raheel Dhattiwala and Michael Biggs have shown that 'violence was worst in districts or constituencies where the BJP faced the greatest electoral competition' and that in the places where violence was the most acute, it increased the 'BJP vote by more than 12 percentage points'.[159]

Polarisation had such an impact partly because it allowed the BJP to transcend caste cleavages and attract the Hindu masses. A Dalit interviewee from Ahmedabad told Ward Berenschot: 'After the riots there were elections. At that time, Vankars and Chamars (Dalit castes) had become Hindus [though in fact their religion was Hinduism already], so they voted for a Hindu. So the Hindu won. The riots were over. Then they stopped being Hindus and again became Vankars and Chamars.'[160] An exit poll mentioned that while 76 per cent of upper castes and 82 per cent of Patels voted BJP, OBC castes also supported the party—between 54 per cent and 61 per cent according to their *jati*.[161] Another survey showed that 59 per cent of respondents did not wish to have someone from another community as a neighbour, indicating just how deep the divide had become.[162]

The impact of Modi's discourse went beyond Gujarat. In August 2002, a national survey of 17,776 Indian citizens in 98 parliamentary constituencies showed that for a relative but nearly absolute majority of respondents, the Gujarat riots were due not to the state government or Hindu nationalists or even to local rabble-rousers, but to 'Muslim fundamentalists' and 'Muslims aggressors from Godhra' (29 per cent and 20 per cent of the respondents respectively).[163] Such data showed that Modi's narrative had worked: a very large proportion of Hindus (in Gujarat particularly) considered that he had protected them from the threat posed by Muslims, a sentiment which echoed a complex of vulnerability discernible already at the time of the origins of the Hindu nationalist movement in the 1920s.[164]

According to scholars who did fieldwork during or after the 2002 riots, this 'event' had liberated many Hindus from their fear of Muslims, which the activities of criminals like Latif had created in the first place. Howard Spodek, mentioning the impact of these

'Muslim mafias', observes: 'Repeatedly, in formal interviews and in general conversations, I heard the remark that until 2002 "we Hindus lived in fear of the Muslims, now they will live in fear of us. We have taught them a lesson."'[165] One of Ghassem-Fachandi's interviewees, a Gujarati teacher, told him something similar about the Muslims: 'They finally learned what it is to get hurt, what it feels to get tensed. To have fear, they have finally learned vulnerability.'[166] These words dovetail with my analysis of the crystallisation of Hindu nationalism as an identity-building process, based on the stigmatisation and emulation of 'threatening' Others, that was intended to solve a deep sense of vulnerability.[167] For Hindu nationalist ideologues, their community was divided into castes and sects and the Hindus were therefore weak, while the Muslim minority, because of its sense of unity, was dominant. Another psychological variable needs to be factored in, too: while Hindus were traditionally seen by the British as effete, Muslims have often been considered as part of the martial 'races'—and their practice of animal sacrifice stood in stark contrast with the Hindu ideal of vegetarianism, so pervasive in Gujarat.[168] The unleashing of violence was sometimes perceived as an imitation of Muslim techniques, was greeted with relief, evident proof that Hindus could 'teach Muslims a lesson'.[169]

Few Hindus of Gujarat showed compassion after the 2002 violence, and K.P.S. Gill himself said that he had been 'disturbed by the absence of the "Kalinga effect" in Gujarat, an allusion to the remorse felt by Emperor Ashok after he had killed thousands on the battlefields of Kalinga'.[170] Many middle-class Hindus, in particular, approved of what had happened and continued to support those to whom the violence had been attributed.

A NATURAL REACTION

Six months before Narendra Modi became prime minister of India, Ashis Nandy very convincingly argued that 'the Gujarat riots mark the beginning of a new phase in Indian politics'.[171] Not only did they catapult Modi to the forefront of Gujarat politics, but they also demonstrated that polarisation could help him politically on a large scale. Hindu nationalists knew this, and that is why, according to the British officials who investigated the incident, the 2002 violence was pre-planned.[172] A *pracharak* with little experience of electoral politics, he showed that religious polarisation could resuscitate the BJP, which was a declining political force when he became chief minister in 2001. He had promoted this strategy in previous local elections in Ahmedabad where Muslims—partly because of the role of Abdul Latif—could be represented as a threat. But to use religious polarisation to generate electoral dividends in a state where Muslims represented less than a tenth of the population was no easy task. The Godhra episode created the right context. As Modi pointed out on 2 March 2002, in the middle of it all: 'Every action has an equal and opposite reaction.' In Gujarati, he described the latter as '*svabhavik pratikriya*', a 'natural reaction or remedy'.[173] This Newtonian construct calls to mind another metaphor, the one Rajiv Gandhi used after the killing of his mother and the anti-Sikh riots that followed: 'When a big tree falls, the earth shakes!'[174] In both cases, metaphors were equated to justifications, and the subsequent polarisation of communities resulted in substantial electoral gains.

Modi's position was more precarious. After all, he had been in office for less than a year when he decided to organise state elections. But his unswerving commitment to his cause was to become a political asset. The new, dominant narrative in Gujarat presented 2002 as a landmark, a turning away from violence and insecurity to peace and safety: 'Hindu nationalists characterize the time after 2002 as a time of peace while they refer to the time before 2002 as a time of violence, outlining a narrative of messianic time. The Hindu nationalist messianic time is clearly embedded in the messiah figure of Narendra Modi and the Hindu religion.'[175]

Modi routinised this repertoire in one election campaign after another in Gujarat (as we'll see below) and, finally, transposed it to the national scene. The 2014 election campaign offers several illustrations of this modus operandi. While he did not go to Ayodhya, he held one meeting in the neighbouring town of Faizabad in May 2014, with a huge portrait of Lord Ram hung as a backdrop. He also made a point of visiting Hindu temples and holy places on the campaign trail.[176] He appeared repeatedly with many religious figures, including Baba Ramdev, a saffron-clad guru who taught yoga every morning to millions of people on television channels.[177] More importantly, Modi decided to contest elections in the constituency of Varanasi, the spiritual capital of Hinduism, to answer the 'call' of the sacred river Ganges.[178] In the speech he gave in December 2013 in Varanasi, he 'exhorted the voters of UP to help usher in *Ram Rajya* [the Kingdom of Ram]'. After him, Kalyan Singh, former BJP chief minister of Uttar Pradesh, bellowed, 'I do not say that every Muslim is a terrorist. But I ask why every terrorist is a Muslim.'[179]

Such utterances fitted well with Modi's strategy of polarisation, without exposing him. Indeed, in 2014, he usually let others pronounce them and, instead, cultivated a certain moderation, as his reputation as the 'Emperor of the Hindu hearts' was already well known. But he occasionally indulged in this register too. While campaigning in Jammu and Kashmir, he tweeted, '3 AKs are very popular in Pakistan: AK 47, AK Antony & AK-49.' The first term of this three-part alliteration (one of Modi's favourite stylistic devices) referred to Islamic terrorism from Pakistan; A.K. Antony was the Congress defence minister under Manmohan Singh; and, lastly, Modi made fun of Arvind Kejriwal by dubbing him 'AK 49' in reference to his brief, 49-day stint as chief minister of New Delhi in 2013–14. In a rally in Hiranagar, Modi said that these three AKs were helping Pakistan.

In the case of Antony, this was a way of presenting him as a traitor to the nation out of weakness. In the case of Kejriwal, the accusation stemmed from the fact that his website showed half of Kashmir as belonging to Pakistan—a geopolitical reality that India continues to deny, as it claims the entire state.[180]

In 2014, Modi's polarisation strategy relied also on the exploitation of local conflicts such as the Muzaffarnagar riots and their aftermath. In August 2013, this outbreak of violence had caused the death of 55 people, most of them Muslims, and the displacement of 51,000 others—a record in Uttar Pradesh.[181] BJP MLAs who had been formally implicated by the police, in particular owing to anti-Muslim provocations they had posted on social media, were 'felicitated by the BJP at an Agra rally addressed by Narendra Modi, where they were hailed as "heroes" who had "ensured the safety of Hindus" at the time of riots'.[182] When it came time to distribute tickets to candidates, the party nominated three of these MLAs who were under investigation for their role in the Muzaffarnagar riots.[183]

After becoming prime minister of India, Narendra Modi cultivated his image of protector of the Hindus in many different ways. This strategy culminated in the role he played in Ayodhya when the foundation stone of the Ram temple was laid in August 2020. He was 'not only the chief guest but also the master of ceremonies and the official *yajmaan* [patron of a religious ritual]'.[184] Modi appeared here as the high priest of the majority community. He also spoke as gurus do during the monthly radio programme '*Maan ki baat*' (Words from the heart), which he initiated in 2014.[185]

PART TWO

DE-INSTITUTIONALISING THE RULE OF LAW

In the wake of the 2002 riots, the Modi government pursued a strategy of politicisation of the police and the judiciary which was the direct result of this episode of mass violence: to avoid any meaningful inquiry was vital for the BJP in Gujarat and for Hindu nationalists at large. The most professional policemen who had done their duty in 2002 were sidelined whereas the others were promoted. Some of them were also implicated in a new politics of fear targeting so-called jihadi terrorists, who were victims of extra-judicial killings. The judicial process itself was affected by the nomination of prosecutors belonging to the Hindu nationalist movement itself and the infiltration of the judiciary more generally speaking. The Supreme Court of India tried to resist these trends, as is evident from the creation of a Special Investigation Team, but this could not make much difference.

In parallel with the politicisation of the police and the judiciary, the Modi government failed to fight against deep-rooted corrupt practices and the criminalisation of politics. Not only were the police and the judiciary not strengthened for fighting these evils, but whistleblowers were targeted and the state indulged in new forms of surveillance. More importantly, the de-institutionalisation of the rule of law found expression in the promotion of Hindu vigilante groups, which exerted a form of cultural policing in the streets as well as on university campuses.

These groups benefited from the protection of the government and became well entrenched at the grassroots level. Their penetration of society resulted in the making of a 'deeper state' propagating the Hindu nationalist ideology at the expense of the rule of law.

3

THE CAPTURE OF INSTITUTIONS

> The Gujarat Police have, with great courage and risk to their own lives, arrested 400 terrorists and got many of them convicted. Not only the Gujarat government but also five-and-a-half crore [55 million] Gujaratis congratulate them.
>
> Narendra Modi, 15 August 2010[1]

In order to polarise Gujarat beyond the events of 2002 and to protect himself from legal challenges, Narendra Modi needed to exert stronger control over the rule of law. Such a move was important, in particular, for perpetuating the politics of fear which had emerged in 2002. Hence the need to de-institutionalise state power.

Gujarat had traditionally been plagued by a poor law and order record. In this 'dry' state, as mentioned above, bootleggers have prospered. Ghanshyam Shah pointed out as early as 1970 that 'it is an open secret in Gujarat that the police and anti-social elements have close ties. More often than not, illicit liquor, gambling and smuggling—which are rampant in the towns and villages of Gujarat—run under police protection. For this, policemen get a regular amount every month, which is often many times their salaries.'[2] In 2007 a *Times of India* reporter pointed out:

'According to senior police officials in the state and the prohibition department, liquor smuggling business is worth nearly 2 billion rupees[3] in Gujarat and there are at least 1,500 habitual offenders (against prohibition laws) in Ahmedabad city alone.'[4] This 'business' flourished with the blessing of the police, who generally earned generous commissions (*hafta*) in exchange for their silence. During the 1980s, the police allegedly received a cut of 40 per cent of the profits from such deals.[5] Nor did the politicians lag behind: they earned their own share in exchange for the protection they extended to so-called anti-social elements.[6] When Julius Ribeiro, the director of the Central Reserve Police Force, was asked to take command of Gujarat Police in 1985, he realised that 'the police force here ha[d] been ruined due to heavy politicisation [...] Police officers were pressurised to do what politicians wanted',[7] to such an extent that officers resisted his orders to arrest bootleggers as they 'were friends of different ministers'.[8]

Ribeiro could not radically transform this state of affairs when he worked in Gujarat. In fact, when the army had to intervene to restore peace in 2002, Lt General Zameer Uddin Shah observed that 'the higher police hierarchy was totally politicised'[9] and the state remained prominent on the national crime graph of India. When Narendra Modi took power, reducing crime was one of his electoral promises. Yet the BJP government further de-institutionalised the police in the wake of the 2002 riots, by fostering the communalisation of 'law and order'. Similarly, particular attention was paid to the legal cases pending in courts that followed in the aftermath of the 2002 violence. This had a debilitating structural impact on the state machinery.

POLICE AND RULERS AS PARTNERS IN CRIME

The Gujarat police force had undeniably been transformed already by previous governments, including Keshubhai Patel's. But the Modi government damaged this institution in an unprecedented manner. Not only were the policemen who had made the riots possible rewarded—and others punished—but police officers were used by the government to further polarise society along religious lines, owing to a series of 'fake encounters'—a category of crimes we'll analyse below.

Rewarding Guilty (Police)Men, Punishing Law-abiding Officers

Immediately after the 2002 riots, the Modi government signalled how it was to proceed: in spite of the failure of the state to maintain the rule of law, the chief minister argued that the police had done their job,[10] and none of the senior policemen in charge of law and order were transferred or suspended; on the contrary, some of the guilty men were promoted. The case of Ahmedabad Police Commissioner[11] P.C. Pandey is emblematic, all the more so as he was the top policeman of the city with close to five million people under his jurisdiction, who had failed (or did not try) to control the violence. On 2 March, when interviewed, he partly justified the attitude of the police: 'Police were not insulated from the general social milieu ... [When] there's a change in the perception of society, the police are part of it and there's bound to be some contagion effect'—a very revealing argument that he later made before the National Human Rights Commission.[12] Far from being punished, Pandey was promoted by BJP leaders, including L.K. Advani, who was home minister. He was first dispatched to New Delhi in May 2002 as additional director general of the Central Bureau of Investigation (CBI) and then came back to Gujarat as director general of police, being appointed by the Gujarat government. On retirement, he was appointed chairman of the Gujarat State Police Housing Corporation. He then joined the Adani Group,[13] as part of the emerging nexus between the Gujarat government, the bureaucracy and industrial houses.

One of his subordinates, M.K. Tandon, was also promoted to various posts and ended his career as additional director general of police. In 2002, he was joint commissioner in the area of Ahmedabad where the Gulberg Society was located, along with Naroda Gam and Naroda Patiya (the neighbourhoods where about 200 Muslims perished). He was then 'promoted and posted as IGP [inspector general of police] in charge of the prestigious Surat range and later as ADGP [additional director general of police] (Law and Order)'.[14] Similarly, K.K. Mysorwala, head of police headquarters in the area where Naroda Gam is located, might have been held partly responsible for the deaths of the 110 people who perished there on 28 February 2002.[15] But he was reassigned to Gandhinagar before becoming deputy superintendent of police of Rajkot. Deepak Swaroop, who in 2002 was IGP in charge of the districts of Vadodara (Rural), Godhra, Dahod and Narmada 'where mob violence took virulent form due to lukewarm posture of police to rioters', was also subsequently promoted as ADGP (Law and Order).[16] K. Nityanandam, who was home secretary at the time, was 'promoted to the post of Commissioner of Police, Rajkot city, in the rank of ADGP'.[17] The full list of IPS cadres who in 2002 neither tried to keep the situation under control nor protected Muslim citizens, yet were promoted or benefited from post-retirement jobs has been established by R.B. Sreekumar, a former senior police officer, one of those who, on the contrary, were punished because of their completely different attitude to what occurred during the riots.[18]

This list is long too. Rahul Sharma, superintendent of police (SP) in Bhavnagar district, was transferred three days after having protected a mosque from a mob on the verge of destroying it; he became deputy commissioner of police, in charge of the Ahmedabad city Police Control Room.[19] Vivek Shrivastava, SP of Kutch district, met with the same fate for having arrested a BJP leader who had attacked a Muslim family. He was 'transferred in the thick of riots'[20] and made deputy commissioner (prohibition and excise) for the Ahmedabad region. Himanshu Bhatt, SP in Banaskantha district, was also transferred after having taken action against one of his sub-inspectors who participated in the violence. He was transferred to the State Intelligence Bureau at Gandhinagar 'during riots in March 2002'.[21] He resigned and left India shortly afterwards. Satish Chandra Verma, deputy inspector general in charge of the Indian border for Bhuj district, who had ordered the arrest of BJP MLA Shankar Chaudhary for having killed two Muslims, was reassigned to the State Reserve Police Training Centre in Junagadh. There were many others.[22] Steven Wilkinson thus concludes that the Modi government 'acted in a biased and partisan way throughout, even going so far as to transfer 27 officials for taking too aggressive a stance towards Hindu rioters'.[23]

That none of the police officers in charge of localities badly affected by violence were brought to book parallels the stand Modi adopted immediately after the 2002 riots: the state machinery had done its best to maintain peace. A first step had thus been taken in the transformation of the police into a communalised force paying allegiance to an ideology, a party and even an individual leader. The next one found expression in a series of 'fake encounters'.

Fake Encounters and the Politics of Fear: Polarising by Other Means

In India, the term 'fake encounters' denotes extra-judicial killings in which the police execute people who, they claim, were threatening them or were trying to flee arrest.[24] In Gujarat, between 2002 and 2006 a series of such encounters resulted in the killing of several young Muslims who were portrayed as Islamists. In 2012, ten years after the first such encounter occurred, the Supreme Court heard a public interest litigation (PIL) petition filed by the journalist B.G. Verghese and screenwriter Javed Akhtar in 2007 and recognised the need to probe 21 such 'encounters',[25] including the three most infamous: the Sadiq Jamal, Ishrat Jahan and Sohrabuddin cases.

Before returning to these three cases, it is important to note that the monitoring of the probe was a bone of contention between the Gujarat government and the Supreme Court. The latter had first appointed former judge M.B. Shah to take the helm of the Special Task Force (STF) which had been formed on an ad hoc basis, and the former had endorsed him, but after only one month he resigned. The Modi government then appointed the former chief justice of the Bombay High Court, K.R. Vyas. But the Supreme Court did not confirm him because it wanted 'someone whose integrity is completely beyond any question'.[26] Instead, the court appointed Justice Bedi.[27] The Modi government objected that fake encounter cases in all the states—and not only in Gujarat—should be brought within the ambit of the Supreme Court. The court responded: 'You bring human rights violations from other states. You will find we will respond with same alacrity.'[28] As head of the STF, Justice Bedi finally filed five sealed reports before the Supreme Court. In July 2013 the court decided to share this material with the parties in view of the ongoing judicial process. In 2014, the STF submitted to Justice Bedi a report in which the policemen accused in ten encounters were given a 'clean chit' or certificate of exoneration.[29] In 2019, out of the remaining seven cases, four were settled with compensation being given to the survivors,[30] and three were considered 'fake encounters'.[31] All of them concerned Muslim men: Sameer Khan, Kasam Jafar and Haji Haji Ismail. The Bedi Committee report gives detailed information about the first case:

> As per the police version the deceased had come in contact with Muslim Jehadi organizations and on the basis of a passport illegally obtained from Bhopal had got one month's visa to visit Pakistan, had gone, stayed there and had [*sic*] in that country

for three years during which period he had obtained training in weapons from the Jaish-e-Mohammad at places such as Karachi, Lahore, Rawalpindi etc. and had thereafter re-entered India through Nepal with the assistance of the ISI [Pakistan military intelligence] and established hide outs in Mumbai, Rajkot and Bhopal etc. It is further [*sic*] the police version that after the attack on the Akshardham Mandir, the deceased had been directed by Rizvan of the Jaish-e-Mohammad who was a resident of Pakistan to go to Ahmedabad and kill the then Chief Minister Mr. Narendrabhai Modi.[32]

Referring to the medical and other reports, the Bedi Committee said that the police officers who killed Sameer Khan 'were close and towering over the deceased and he was probably sitting on the ground'.[33] Justice Bedi concluded: 'the killing of the deceased was indeed the result of a fake encounter. I am, therefore, of the opinion that Inspector K.M. Vaghela and Inspector T.A. Barot at the first instance be prosecuted for murder'.[34] This scenario was typical of the three fake encounters that I have singled out because of their specific importance, and because they were not monitored by the Bedi Committee.

The Sadiq Jamal incident took place on 13 January 2003, near the Galaxy cinema at Naroda (Ahmedabad). A reliable source in understanding this case is the confession of Ketan Tirodkar, a Mumbai-based journalist who was arrested by the CBI in July 2012. He declared before the MCOCA[35] court in Mumbai in two paragraphs of his affidavit:

In the first week of January 2003, Accused No. 1 [Daya Nayak, a policeman from Mumbai][36] told me that he wanted to oblige a big politician in Gujarat by giving an ISI [Pakistan military intelligence] agent or some similar militant for an encounter killing ... I had met one Sadiq Mehtar aged about 18 years in Dubai, who was a house-help of Said Tariq Parveen.[37] This Sadiq had lost some of his dear ones and his house in the Gujarat ethnic riots ... Accused No. 1 saw him and thought him to

> be the only easy target available after some drafting to build his profile as a militant. So Accused No. 1 and myself made a profile of Sadiq about his being in Dubai in the company of 'D' [Dawood Ibrahim] gang members Salim Chiplun and others and had come to India on the contract of LeT for eliminating Gujarat Chief Minister Narendra Modi.
>
> Then on 11.1.2003, as planned by Accused No. 1 I asked Sadiq to come to the Traffic Police Post on the Andheri Flyover where Accused No. 1 had kept the Gujarat Police in wait. Said came there and we both boarded the vehicle and came towards National Park dressed like journalists, carrying shoulder bags. I introduced them to Sadiq and alighted from the vehicle and they went towards Gujarat. Two days thereafter I read in newspapers that Sadiq was killed in police encounter in Gujarat.[38]

Many years later, the CBI investigated this case and in December 2012 eight policemen were arrested, accused of fake encounters.[39] In November 2013, four additional police officers from Maharashtra were implicated by the CBI investigating team in its report to the agency's head office.[40]

The Ishrat Jahan case refers to an encounter that took place on 15 June 2004 on the Ahmedabad–Gandhinagar Road. Four people were killed by a team of the Crime Detection Branch of the Ahmedabad City Police. They were presented as jihadists targeting Narendra Modi in the first information report (FIR) that the police filed in June 2004:

> I, JG Parmar, Police Inspector, Crime Branch, Ahmedabad City, declare in person that I am working in the Crime Branch since 11/06/2002, and lodge my complaint as follows.
>
> Pakistan based terrorist outfits like Lashkar-e-Taiba and Jaish-e-Mohammad are very active in India in association with ISI of Pakistan for quite some time with intention to spread terrorism in India. Especially after the Godhra train tragedy and the communal riots that followed, they have made Gandhinagar and Ahmedabad City their main targets.

> About 15 days back, Shri KR Kaushik, Commissioner of Police (CP), Ahmedabad City, received information from intelligence sources that two Pakistani *fidayeens* had left from Kashmir for Ahmedabad by different routes. They are (1) Jishan Johar @ Jaanbaj @ Abdulgani R/o [resident of] Narnanak Kalerbadi, Dist. Gujranwala, Punjab, Pakistan and (2) Amjadali Akbarali Rana @ Salim @ Rajkumar R/o Haveli Diwan, Bhalwal, District Sargodha, Punjab, Pakistan. It was also learnt that one Javed r/o Pune, Maharashtra was arranging their local network. Their aim is to attempt a suicidal attack on Shri Narendra Modi, Chief Minister of Gujarat.[41]

According to the police, the car of the terrorists was intercepted in Ahmedabad and the four occupants were killed when they opened fire on the policemen who were trying to apprehend them.

The incident is known as the 'Ishrat Jahan case' because one of the four victims was Ishrat Jahan, a 19-year-old college girl who was studying for her BSc in Mumbai, at the Guru Nanak Khalsa College. She had travelled to Ahmedabad with Pranesh Pillai, alias Javed Ghulam Sheikh, who had come from Kerala to Mumbai in search of work. He had already been booked for assault by the Mumbai police and charged with involvement in a fake currency racket. The nationality of the two others has not been ascertained. After the encounter, Gujarat Police claimed that they were Pakistanis. But in 2009 the metropolitan magistrate, S.P. Tamang, submitted to the Metropolitan Court of Ahmedabad a report indicating that the Pakistan IDs that had been found on the corpses were forged,[42] and that the four people had in fact been killed by bullets fired from close range while they were sitting. Tamang also argued that they had been held in custody for days before the fake encounters and that weapons—including an AK-56—had been planted on them to make people believe they were terrorists.[43] Tamang mentioned the names of several senior policemen as being implicated in the fake encounter: D.G. Vanzara, the chief of the Detection of Crime Branch, Narendra K. Amin, then Vanzara's deputy, K.R. Kaushik, the Ahmedabad police commissioner, P.P. Pandey, who was the chief of the Crime Branch, and Tarun Barot, an inspector whose name has already been mentioned in relation to the Sadiq Jamal case.[44]

In August 2010 the High Court, one year after the Tamang report, asked the Special Investigation Team (SIT) which had been appointed by the Supreme Court to probe the 2002 violence, to take up the case. Its head expressed his inability to do so and the High Court formed a new SIT. The Gujarat government challenged the High Court order to create such an SIT and requested it to leave the investigation to Gujarat Police, but the Supreme Court rejected its petition. In October 2010, two senior policemen decided to cooperate with the CBI just after the arrest of the home minister of the state, Amit Shah. N.K. Amin, who had close relations with the VHP leader Praveen Togadia,[45] turned 'approver' or witness on behalf of the state, while G.C. Raiger, former additional director general of police, also became a witness. In January 2011, after a year of investigation, the SIT member Satish Varma—who was to pay for his stand[46]—filed an affidavit stating that the encounter was fake and accusing the two other members of the SIT 'of not allowing the probe to be done in an unbiased manner'.[47]

On 8 April 2011, the Gujarat High Court told the state government that it would hand over the case to the CBI or to the National Investigation Agency (created three years before) if the SIT was not in a position to investigate the case the way it wanted. On 21 November 2011, the SIT reported to the High Court that the encounter was not genuine. Ishrat Jahan and Javed had been intercepted by Gujarat Police a few days before the encounter from a toll booth near Anand and held at a farm nearby. In December 2011, the SIT filed an FIR in which all this information was presented.[48]

The court ordered that a charge of murder should be filed against twenty policemen, including those Tamang had already mentioned two years earlier. In January 2012, the High Court asked the CBI to take over the case and justified its decision with these words: 'Keeping in view the paramount consideration of instilling confidence in the investigation and for maintaining credibility of investigation with the aim to book the real offenders, it appears to us that it would not be a case to be assigned to the state agency.'[49]

The CBI immediately filed a charge sheet against twenty policemen, including some of those who had already been formally accused in the Sadiq Jamal case. The CBI charge sheet stated that the police officers entered into 'criminal conspiracy and in pursuance thereof, they abducted the deceased, kept them in illegal confinement and thereafter killed all of them in [a] fake encounter'.[50]

Two years later, in February 2013, the CBI also arrested Gujarat IPS officer G.L. Singhal, who was then assistant commissioner of police in the Crime Branch. At the same time it expressed its wish to arrest Rajendra Kumar, then joint director of the Central Intelligence Bureau in Gujarat, who, according to the CBI, 'colluded with the then Gujarat DGP K.R. Kaushik and then joint commissioner P.P. Pandey to generate the IB [Intelligence Bureau] input that led to the encounter and was also involved in planning it'.[51] However, the IB chief, Asif Ibrahim, opposed such a move.[52]

The fake encounters reviewed so far illustrate the politics of fear that politicians have implemented in other countries, in particular after 9/11.[53] A human rights activist speaking under the condition of anonymity makes this point very clear:

> The BJP Government in Gujarat knew that it could not risk another riot similar to 2002, as its credibility to govern efficiently and maintain communal harmony would be completely eroded. At the same time, it was important to sustain the sharp

> polarization between Hindus and Muslims for electoral gains. The Government used the encounters as a proxy for the riots to reproduce polarization between Hindus and Muslims. The police encounters that took place in Gujarat were spectacles. The public consumed the media accounts of these encounters and started fearing Muslims and Islamic terror.[54]

This analysis echoes the interpretation of the encounters under review by both the police and the BJP. Regarding the former, the FIR filed in the Sadiq Jamal case revealingly established a relation between the 2002 violence and the 'logical' attempts by Pakistanis and Islamists at terrorising India:

> The ISI and jihadi organizations from Pakistan, in association with underworld gangsters and notorious gangs, took advantage of the situation arising from the riots to target Gujarat. This fact is clearly established by various acts of terrorism such as the attack on Akshardham, the conspiracy to kill Narendra Modi, and Praveen Togadia in Ahmedabad by local L-e-T terrorists, namely Shahid Bakshi and Samir Khan Pathan, and the firing on VHP general secretary Dr. Jaideep Patel ... Meanwhile, Jamal had seen on television channels the news regarding communal violence in Gujarat that had erupted after the Godhra carnage. On seeing such incidents, he had made up his mind to kill Narendra Modi.[55]

According to the investigating officer, Tarun Barot, Shahid Bakshi and two other cadres had sent '33 riot-affected youths from Gujarat to Pakistan via Moradabad for terrorist training to avenge the Gujarat riots'.[56] Seven years later, after the police failed to provide evidence, the three accused were acquitted.[57]

The media amplified the politics of fear with sensationalist headlines and illustrations. Its favourite targets were the Muslim mafia dons, including Dawood Ibrahim. On 3 December 2008, the front page of the Ahmedabad edition of *DNA* published an article entitled 'Fidayeen may be closing in on Modi: Intelligence'. Such speculation was based on unverifiable claims.

Another ran with the headline 'One of the intelligence intercepts said that Pakistan-based LeT [Lashkar-e-Taiba] was determined to kill 5,000 in Gujarat to avenge the 2002 riots'. Such pieces of 'information' enabled the newspaper to ask alarmist questions in the wake of the trauma of the 2011 Mumbai terror attack:

> After Mumbai, where will the fidayeen strike next? If important intelligence intercepts and top police officials are to be believed, the next big terror focus is Gujarat, with chief minister Narendra Modi being the target of a suicide attack [...] Another senior Maharashtra police officer went one step further and said that a group of LeT operatives was already in Gujarat trying to penetrate Modi's inner cordon.[58]

On 3 June 2009, the Ahmedabad edition of *DNA* claimed, in the title of an article, that 'Dawood planned to kill Narendra Modi for '02 riots'—with 'Target Modi' as a catchy intertitle—and, in a separate box, that 'Dawood had sent 3 men to kill Modi'.[59] But these pieces of 'news' were based on the confession of the culprits that had been obtained by the police. On 6 December 2010, the Ahmedabad edition of the *Indian Express* had the catchy title 'After 26/11 [the Mumbai attack], LeT target was Modi', despite the fact that WikiLeaks, on which this claim was founded, mentioned 'a possible operation against Gujarat Chief Minister Narendra Modi'.[60] In 2013, *Outlook* used a quote to title an op-ed—'Indian mujahideen: "Modi is one to 10 in the list of targets"', even though his name was not even mentioned in the article.[61] After fake encounters came to an end in 2007 owing to Satish Verma and Rajnish Rai, the two police officers who conducted a thorough investigation as directed by the judiciary, the trauma of the Mumbai attack and speculation fostered by revelations coming from the police and the intelligence services helped the BJP to sustain an atmosphere of fear with the help of the media's sensationalism. The politics of fear continued to operate.

BJP politicians went one step further when they referred to the Ishrat Jahan case: they presented Modi not only as a target, but also as the man who resisted these attacks. By establishing also a direct relation between the events of 2002 and the fake encounters, but in a different perspective, one of them declared:

> Pre-2002 era, before Modi became the Chief Minister, Gujarat witnessed recurrent riots between Hindus and Muslims. However, Hindus asserted themselves in 2002 and finally gave a strong signal to the Muslims that they would not tolerate their crimes against Hindus silently. Ishrat Jahan and several other terrorists came to Gujarat to kill Narendra Modi because they could not tolerate Hindus becoming strong and assertive under Modi's rule. When these Human Rights groups, NGOs, and Congress raise questions regarding the legitimacy of Ishrat's killing, they are actually supporting the terrorists' conspiracy of killing Modi and weakening Hindus.[62]

Fake encounters were a sound means of keeping Gujaratis on edge and projecting Modi as their protector against not only Islamists (or Muslims at large) but also the secular Hindus who opposed Modi politically. A big role in propagating this climate of fear was played by the police, not only by perpetrating fake encounters, but in talking to the media. Several weeks before the death of Sadiq Jamal, in December 2002 the deputy commissioner of police in the Crime Branch of Ahmedabad city, D. G. Vanzara, had already presented a case against three young Muslims arrested in Delhi in August 'on charges of plotting to kill Chief Minister Narendra Modi and VHP leader Praveen Togadia by recruiting boys from riot relief camps and training them for jihad [...] [Allegedly] these three had visited Ahmedabad to recruit some 33 boys from relief camps. The plan, according to the police, was to send the boys to Pakistan for training.'[63] After seven years in jail, the three were acquitted by the Ahmedabad Sessions Court because there was insufficient evidence against them to prosecute. But soon afterwards Mohammed Viquar

Ahmed, hailing from Gujarat, was arrested in Hyderabad because, according to the police, 'he was part of a jihadi plot to kill top cops and politicians of Gujarat including Chief Minister Narendra Modi'.[64] These disinformation operations in which policemen engaged repeatedly—Vanzara gave several press conferences himself—helped cultivate a climate of fear. This strategy continued for years. In 2016, Rajendra Kumar—the IB officer against whom the CBI had submitted a supplementary charge sheet alleging that he was 'a key conspirator' in the Ishrat Jahan case—declared on TV:

> A person called Meraj, who is an Indian was the main conspirator in the plan to assassinate Narendra Modi. He came from UAE to India, but he has never been investigated properly.
>
> Kumar alleged that Meraj planned the terror conspiracy along with Javed, two Pakistanis, and Ishrat Jahan. Kumar said that Meraj fled India to go to the Middle East a few days after Ishrat Jahan and Javed visited him in his village in the Indian State of Uttar Pradesh. He said that Meraj was an L-e-T cadre, and there was enough evidence to show that Ishrat Jahan and others often visited Meraj's village in Uttar Pradesh. Kumar argued that if the BJP had not defended the interests of Hindus after the Godhra incident, Muslims would have continued to kill Hindus through various acts of violence.[65]

In his report, Tamang attributed the attitude of the policemen to 'their personal interest which included to secure their promotion, to maintain his [*sic*] posting, so as to falsely show excellent performance, to get special appreciation from the Hon'ble Chief Minister and to gain popularity'.[66] But the police officers would not have behaved the way they did, talked to the media and remained unpunished had they not benefited from political protection. In fact, some policemen and politicians were partners in crime, as the former, to cite one of the three statements of R.B. Sreekumar before the Special Task Force, were 'enjoying extra hierarchical accessibility and closeness to

Minister of State Shri Amitbhai Shah and Chief Minister Shri Narendra Modi, in Gujarat State Govt.'[67] Similarly, the inspector of police, Tirth Raj, who investigated the Sameer Khan case, concluded that 'the deceased had [not only] been killed in a fake encounter, but on instructions from the then Minister of State for Home and Law and Justice [Amit Shah] and the DGP [director general of police], Chakraborty'.[68] According to Justice Bedi, his 'report and all inculpatory material had been destroyed' when he re-investigated the case himself.[69]

The involvement of key members of the Gujarat government in fake encounters became even more obvious in the Sohrabuddin case. Sohrabuddin Sheikh—like Javed, Ishrat Jahan's companion—was part of the underworld—probably linked to Dawood Ibrahim's gang—when he was killed in an alleged fake encounter on 26 November 2005. He was known in particular for extorting protection money from marble factories in Gujarat and Rajasthan. He was travelling with his wife, Kauser Bi, on 23 November 2005, between Hyderabad (Andhra Pradesh) and Sangli (Maharashtra) when their bus was stopped by the Gujarat Police Anti-Terrorist Squad. His wife was taken to a farmhouse outside Ahmedabad and he was killed a few days later on a highway at Vishala Circle near Ahmedabad.[70]

Sohrabuddin was immediately described as a terrorist by D.G. Vanzara, who, by then, had been promoted as Gujarat's Anti-Terrorist Squad chief. He held a press conference to explain that Sohrabuddin was an LeT jihadist who wanted to assassinate Narendra Modi.[71] But the younger brother of Sohrabuddin, Rubabuddin, petitioned the Supreme Court in December 2005, in spite of intimidation,[72] claiming that his brother had been killed in a fake encounter, while an investigative journalist, Prashant Dayal, gathered important revelations from policemen who had participated in the fake encounter, which were published in *Divya Bhaskar* (a Gujarati newspaper) in 2006.[73] It seems that influential figures in Rajasthan who were paying protection money to Sohrabuddin wanted to get rid of him. Interestingly, they contacted Gujarat Police after the 2003 and 2004 fake encounters mentioned above. Some police officers apparently thought that they could kill two birds with one stone: remove from circulation a notorious extortionist and claim that they were also protecting the state from a terrorist. In addition, Sohrabuddin Sheikh 'was reportedly involved in the death of Haren Pandya', to which we'll return below.[74]

In March 2007, the Supreme Court ordered the Criminal Investigation Department (CID) to probe the case. Inspector General Geetha Johri, Gujarat's first female officer,[75] was tasked with reporting to the court. She gathered enough evidence to enable deputy inspector general (DIG) of police, Rajnish Rai, who was formally in charge, to arrest three accused on 24 April 2007: D.G. Vanzara, who had recently become DIG Border Ranges,[76] Rajkumar Pandian, superintendent of police with the Intelligence Bureau, and M.N. Dinesh, a police officer from Rajasthan (he was then superintendent of police of Udaipur district). In May 2007, Geetha Johri submitted a report in which she mentioned 'the collusion of [the] state government in the form of Shri Amit Shah, MoS [minister of state] for Home' and said that this case 'makes a complete mockery of the rule of law and is perhaps an example of the involvement of [the] state government in a major crime'.[77] Johri was then told to suspend the inquiry.[78] The Supreme Court reinstated her but eventually, in January 2010, directed the CBI to take over the investigation. The reasons for this decision were similar to the previous ones: 'We feel that police authorities of the state of Gujarat failed to carry out a fair and impartial investigation as we initially wanted them to do. It cannot be questioned that the offence the high police officials have committed was of grave nature which needs to be strictly dealt with.'[79]

In July 2010, the CBI filed a 30,000-page-long charge sheet that resulted in the arrest of several additional policemen as well as Amit Shah. The latter was accused of being implicated not only in the fake encounter targeting Sohrabuddin, but also in an extortion racket.[80] In this alleged illegal activity Sohrabuddin and senior police officer Abhay Chudasama were also involved[81]—a clear illustration of the nexus between criminals, police officers and politicians in Gujarat.[82]

Among other things, the court was frustrated by the fact that the Gujarat police had failed to analyse the call records properly.[83] When the CBI was finally in a position to scrutinise the hundreds of phone calls Amit Shah had exchanged with the policemen accused in the fake encounters, the CBI was also able to implicate them in one more encounter, involving Tulsiram Prajapati. Prajapati, who was part of the same network of extortionists, had witnessed the killing of Sohrabuddin and some of his accomplices. The police as well as politicians feared that he might blackmail them. Accused of involvement in another murder, Prajapati was jailed in Udaipur, but was then transferred to Gujarat after the Ahmedabad police issued a summons to the Rajasthan police in order to present him in some other case in an Ahmedabad court. On his return, he was murdered on 26 December 2006 in a fake encounter in Banaskantha.[84]

The CBI had Amit Shah arrested on 25 July 2010. He was one of Narendra Modi's most influential lieutenants, as is evident from the fact that he was in charge of ten portfolios in the Gujarat government,[85] including—besides the Ministry of State for Home—the ministries and departments of transport, prison, law and justice, legislative and parliamentary affairs, police housing, border security, civil defence, home guard, as well as prohibition and excise.[86] The son of a rich businessman, Shah—who was the chairman of Ahmedabad District Cooperative Bank and who became MLA for Sarkhej (Ahmedabad) in 1996 after a by-election—was a VHP activist turned BJP politician. Known for the handling of L.K. Advani's electoral campaigns in Gandhinagar, he 'advised Modi on almost all matters related to party management and political strategy'.[87] Unsurprisingly, the chief minister—who, like all his predecessors, had decided to keep the home portfolio for himself and replaced Haren Pandya with Gordhan Zadaphia when he became chief minister in 2001—handed Shah the most sensitive job of Ministry of State for Home after he was first elected as an MLA in 2002 in Ahmedabad.[88] In this capacity, he piloted the Gujarat Control of Organised Crime (Amendment) Bill through the Gujarat Assembly after the repeal of the POTA (Prevention of Terrorism Act) by the Congress-led UPA government.

Shah was granted bail in October 2010 but was ordered not to reside in Gujarat by the judges, who feared he might interfere with the ongoing judicial process. Ultimately, the Supreme Court transferred the Sohrabuddin case from Gujarat to Mumbai in September 2012 after the CBI stated that 'witnesses were intimidated and a free and fair trial was not possible in Gujarat'.[89] Consequently, the accused who were not on bail were also transferred to Mumbai.

During a bail hearing, which resulted in the rejection of the bail plea of one of the accused, the retired deputy superintendent of police M.L. Parmar, Justice Abhay Thipsay of the Bombay High Court made an important statement about this fake encounter: 'It was a very ambitious plan to eliminate Sohrabuddin who was being too troublesome for some wealthy and influential people who then approached political leaders. The plan satisfied the wealthy as also the political leaders. And at the same time, it enhanced the prestige, popularity and importance of the concerned political leader.'[90] This assessment led Congress leaders to offer their interpretations of the fake encounters in terms of the politics of fear. The then leader of the opposition, Shaktisinh Gohil, declared that the 'encounters were used by Modi and company to—(a) show Gujarat's commitment in controlling Muslim terrorism; (b) project a clear threat to Modi by pan-Indian Muslim militants'. Gohil stressed that his argument was substantiated by the fact that the encounters stopped after Vanzara was arrested.[91] Another Congress leader, Arjun Modhwadia, went one step further when he pointed out that the publicity built up around the fake encounters and their sheer volume were part of a strategy to exploit a politics of fear, thereby enabling the Hindu nationalists to perpetuate the communal polarisation inherited from the 2002 riots.[92] Indeed, Josy Joseph points out that 'the encounter culture of Gujarat had an explicit political aim: creating a narrative of a terror threat, especially targeted at Modi, and whipping up Islamophobia'.[93]

The other conclusion one can draw from these fake encounters relates to the nature of the rule of law in Gujarat. They represent one entry point into the 'collusion' (to use Geetha Johri's word) between politicians, criminals and policemen. The resignation letter of D.G. Vanzara is of great interest in this respect. In September 2013, Vanzara (who had just been rearrested because of his role in the Ishrat Jahan case)[94] resigned from Gujarat Police. In his resignation letter he said that he had suffered silently till then 'only because of my supreme faith in and highest respect for Narendrabhai Modi, the chief minister of Gujarat, whom I used to adore like a God. But I am sorry to state that my God could not rise to the occasion under the evil influence of Amit Shah.'[95] Vanzara's letter is revealing of the implications of the reigning collusion. He said that he assumed that 'mutual protection and reciprocal assistance was the unwritten law between police and government in such cases'. Indeed, Vanzara had benefited from the government's benevolent attitude: in only five years, from 2002 to 2007, he was promoted from deputy commissioner of police in the Crime Branch of Ahmedabad city to deputy inspector general of police in the Anti-Terrorism Squad, Ahmedabad, and then deputy inspector general of police, Border Range, Kutch–Bhuj.

However, his expectations were disappointed after his arrest and that of his men—since, as he said, most of the 31 policemen under arrest had 'served under me as my juniors in the past'.

> With the passage of time, I realized that this government was not only not interested in protecting us but it also has been clandestinely making all efforts to keep me and my officers in the jail so as to save its own skin from CBI on one hand and gain political benefits on the other. It is everybody's knowledge that this government has been reaping very rich political dividends, since last 12 years, by keeping the glow of encounter cases alive in the sky of Gujarat.

The last sentence suggests that the government of Gujarat was instrumental in perpetrating fake encounters to exploit the politics of fear—a fear of jihadists who were allegedly after Narendra Modi. This interpretation is reinforced by another sentence: 'The only fault, if that is to be construed as a fault, which they [the policemen in jail] committed was that they performed their duties diligently and served their country well under the direct instructions from this government.' Vanzara returned to this theme in greater detail a couple of pages later:

> Gujarat CID/Union CBI had arrested me and my officers in different encounter cases holding us to be responsible for carrying out alleged fake encounters, if that is true, then the CBI Investigating officers of all the four encounter cases of Sohrabuddin, Tulsiram, Sadiq Jamal and Ishrat Jahan have to arrest the policy formulators also as we, being field officers, have simply implemented the conscious policy of this government which was inspiring, guiding and monitoring our actions from the very close quarters. By this reasoning, I am of the firm opinion that the place of this government, instead of being in Gandhinagar, should either be in Taloja Central Prison at Navi Mumbai or in Sabarmati Central Prison at Ahmedabad.

If fake encounters were, indeed, 'the conscious policy' of the Gujarat government, the guilty men were in fact the politicians and the policemen were merely the executioners. Between 2002 and 2006, fake encounters helped the Modi government to maintain an atmosphere of fear in Gujarat—a fear attributable to the Islamist threat. For Josy Joseph, Vanzara's letter 'is proof of how the unaccounted part of the security establishment is deployed by politicians to construct political narrative, terrorise ordinary citizens, muzzle critics and bury the rule of law'.[96]

To sum up: from 2002 onwards, the Modi government established a very specific relationship with the police. They were partners in crime in two different ways. First, the government rewarded those officers who had shown some communal bias during the riots and punished the others. Second, the series of fake encounters mentioned above created (or reflected) new forms of illicit relations, which were probably unprecedented in India. While Gujarat was a test site for the communalisation of the police, a similar attempt was being made with the judiciary.

FOCUS ON THE JUDICIARY

The 2002 riots appear to have had almost the same debilitating effect on the judiciary that it had on the police. As has been established earlier, it was the government's objective to erase the responsibility of the guilty men and even to protect the criminals. It meant that forms of impunity had to become the norm and, therefore, the courts, too, became a target. This was bound to have long-term effects—was supplemented by the general undermining of the rule of law in respect of the staffing of the High Court and the appointment of the Lokayukta, or anti-corruption ombudsman.

What Justice for the Victims of the 2002 Violence?[97]

Among victims of the 2002 violence, the search for justice immediately became paramount, obsessive even. They were helped by NGOs in dealing with the judicial process, including Citizens for Peace and Justice, ANHAD (Act Now for Harmony and Democracy) and Janvikas, whose leaders and supporters,

Teesta Setalvad, Harsh Mander, Shabnam Hashmi, Gagan Sethi, Father Cedric Prakash, Mukul Sinha and others, occupied the front line for years.[98] They faced huge challenges. Not only did the attitude of the police prevent many victims from arguing their case because their FIRs (first information reports prepared by the police) had not been registered, the evidence lost and potential witnesses intimidated, but even those who could attain the judicial phase of the process with the support of NGOs had to contend with the state's hostility.

The first shortcoming of Gujarat's justice system came to light in the investigative procedure that always follows communal violence in India. For the past several decades, each of these episodes has resulted in the appointment of a commission of inquiry, usually presided over by a retired judge. Some cases are extremely well documented (such as the inquiry conducted after the 1969 riots in Ahmedabad); others dragged on (such as that in the wake of the clashes in Bhagalpur in 1989). None of them has really led to prosecution, but for the victims the existence of an official document that establishes the facts is already a victory. Therein lies the major difference between the riots in Gujarat and the violence that broke out in Mumbai in 1993, for instance. In the latter case, even if the Srikrishna Commission (named after its chairman) took five years to issue a report and even if nothing came of this, as Rowena Robinson writes, 'it provided a public, legitimate space for the articulation of suffering'.[99]

In Gujarat, nothing of the sort was achieved. On 6 March 2002, the government appointed a commission whose principal mandate was to investigate the circumstances surrounding the Godhra incident, hence its name: the Godhra Inquiry Commission. However, victims' families and the media protested that its chairman and sole member, Justice K.G. Shah, was close to the government. Another retired judge, G.T. Nanavati, was appointed alongside him and took over the commission chairmanship. In an interview—recorded by hidden camera—

that Ashish Khetan conducted with Arvind Pandya, advocate general of Gujarat, the latter, who was close to the chief minister, confided that Shah was 'our man' and that Nanavati was in it 'for the money'.[100] Nanavati proved complacent indeed, declaring during a press conference shortly after his appointment that he had noticed no shortcomings by the police in their handling of the riots.[101]

The Shah–Nanavati Commission waited till the spring of 2007 to ask the Gujarat government to analyse CDs containing recorded phone conversations between Hindu nationalist leaders and bureaucrats as well as policemen in areas devastated by the 2002 riots.[102] The CDs had been handed over to the commission (which had not bothered to request them) by the superintendent of police Rahul Sharma, an officer who was anxious to shed light on the matter. He was deputy commissioner of police in Ahmedabad in April 2002 when he was charged with collecting data for the investigation into the massacres that took place in Naroda Patiya and Gulberg Society. He asked AT&T and Celforce to provide him with all the communications that had taken place in these areas on 28 February. They contained evidence of the presence in Ahmedabad district of police officers who had claimed to be elsewhere and of Hindu nationalist cadres whom the survivors indicated as being among their attackers. Rahul Sharma compiled CDs of these recordings, constituting a wealth of incriminating evidence, and handed them over to his superiors in the Crime Branch—who misplaced them. He also gave a copy to the Shah–Nanavati Commission, which, in the end, made little use of them.[103]

Justice Shah died in March 2008. He was replaced by another retired judge, Justice Akshay Mehta, and the Gujarat government extended the commission for a year in December 2008—continuing to do so every year subsequently till 2019.[104] In 2004, in an interview with Shekhar Gupta, Narendra Modi declared: 'I am waiting for the inquiry commission so that we can get a third party's objective view and then work on the shortcomings.'[105]

The Congress-led coalition that came to power in New Delhi in 2004 strove to counter the former Shah–Nanavati and the subsequent Nanavati–Mehta Commission. The minister of railways, Lalu Prasad Yadav, took advantage of his portfolio to appoint a commission of inquiry into the actions of the railway police. Its chairman, U.C. Banerjee, a retired judge, concluded in 2005 that the fire in the coach that killed 59 in Godhra in 2002 was accidental and not premeditated.[106] Immediately afterwards, the Gujarat High Court issued a stay order against the implementation of the U.C. Banerjee Committee report in March 2006, after having received in September 2005 a complaint disputing the legitimacy of this committee, given that the Gujarat government had already appointed the Shah–Nanavati Commission.[107]

The Supreme Court rejected the stay order in a decision handed down on 3 July 2006. In October, the Gujarat High Court declared the Banerjee Committee 'illegal'.[108] Manmohan Singh's government counter-attacked by asking the Gujarat High Court for permission to make the Banerjee Committee report public, by submitting it to parliament. The Gujarat High Court delayed its decision and in March 2009 postponed the hearings on this issue *sine die*.[109]

The Nanavati Commission finally submitted an interim report in September 2008, which concluded, contrary to the Banerjee Committee, that outside criminal elements had been involved in the Godhra blaze and thus described it as resulting from a conspiracy.[110] The final report, more than 2,000 pages long, was submitted in November 2014, but it was not fully tabled in the Gujarat state Assembly till 2019.[111] It exonerated the Modi government.[112]

Judiciary Under Orders?

Within the Indian court system, criminal justice has four components: investigation, prosecution, adjudication and appeal.

Investigation is handled by the police, prosecution by public prosecutors, adjudication by the lower judiciary (for example, the Sessions Court), and appeal to the High Court (with a possible second appeal to the Supreme Court). It is important to evaluate the relative independence of these four links in the chain, to assess the kind of justice that has been delivered in post-2002 Gujarat.

The second link in the criminal justice chain is the prosecution services. Sections 24 and 25 of the Code of Criminal Procedure of 1973 deal with the appointment of public prosecutors. In the case of prosecutors in the sessions courts, appointment powers lie unambiguously with the state government. Though some Supreme Court judgments have suggested that prosecutors are beholden only to the Criminal Code and not to the state, in practice prosecutors are viewed as arms of the state.

Indeed, members of the Sangh Parivar have exerted greater influence on Gujarat's legal bodies since the BJP came to power in the state. As early as 1996—following the formation of the Keshubhai Patel government—Piyush Gandhi, a former ABVP and VHP leader, was made prosecutor for Panchmahal. Such examples abound in districts that would be hardest hit by violence in 2002. In Mehsana, Dilip Trivedi, VHP secretary general in Gujarat, was appointed district public prosecutor, a position he held from April 2000 to December 2007. This is one of the most obvious reasons why, whereas about 3,000 people were arrested in 2002 in the district, only between 100 and 150 remained accused in 2007—all of whom were out on bail. As for complaints, out of the 182 lodged, only 76 were heard and only 2 of these resulted in charges (because in these two cases the judges were Muslims, according to Trivedi).[113] In his responses to journalists, Trivedi did nothing to hide his political leanings. He retorted: 'Do people expect the BJP to appoint the supporters of the Congress as public prosecutors? Whichever party comes to power, it appoints its men in key positions.'[114]

After applications were filed in the High Court, another VHP lawyer, Rajendra Darji, replaced Trivedi in the Dipda Darwaja massacre case, yet he remained district prosecutor until 2007.[115]

In Sabarkantha, another district that was hard hit by the 2002 riots, the public prosecutor appointed in 2003, Bharat Bhatt, was also president of the district branch of the VHP. He explained that the six other prosecutors were also BJP sympathisers, for a very simple reason: 'since the ruling party makes the appointments, all of them are with us'.[116] The accused—whom he was supposed to punish—being his friends, he advised them 'not to smile when they [would] see [him] in court'. To get as many cases dismissed as possible, he did all he could to convince Muslims to withdraw their complaints:

> Whenever I feel that there is a need to scold … I tell them you live in the village … settle the issue and keep each other's honour intact, you have all your property there … live peacefully, whatever had to happen has happened … the tongue and the teeth are both inside the mouth. Even if the teeth cut the tongue, we don't break the teeth … Similarly, if you want to live in this village where your fathers and your grandfathers have lived … and anyway, you won't leave this village and go to Pakistan … forgive him, he has committed a mistake … He will say sorry … you also say sorry … keep each other's honour […] Some agree after taking money but some also agree on their own … […] In almost 25% of the cases they agreed.[117]

In Panchmahal—where 121 riot FIRs had been filed—the public prosecutor, Piyush Gandhi, who was, as we have seen, the VHP district president, revealed in an interview with the *Indian Express*:

> The state government appoints people as public prosecutors who it feels are honest and experienced. No political or organisational affiliations work in this. I am associated with the RSS since 1964. In 1982, I joined the Ram Mandir movement and since 1985 I am president of VHP Panchmahal district unit.

> The VHP is not a political organisation so I don't consider mine as a political appointment.[118]

In the Ode case—in Anand district—regarding the disappearance of 27 people, the public prosecutor was also an RSS sympathiser, who was more candid about his role: 'What is new in public prosecutors being political appointees? It has always been like this.'[119] In Vadodara, one of the prosecutors, Sanjay Bhatt, was not only a 'VHP advocate', but also the nephew of the VHP city unit president, Ajay Joshi, who defended the 21 accused in the Best Bakery case (see below).[120]

The most controversial cases were in Ahmedabad. There, Chetan Shah, a VHP lawyer, had procured bail for hundreds of Hindu arsonists and rioters, and till 2003 he was defending all 35 accused in the Gulberg Society case. A press report tells the rest of the story:

> Now, Shah has been appointed the chief public prosecutor at Ahmedabad sessions court where more than 950 riot-related cases will come up for hearing. Shah, who has secured freedom of many of the accused, is now expected to lead the prosecution against the same people. Speaking to Times News Networks, Shah said he would not appear in cases involving the persons whom he had helped secure bail earlier. However, in his capacity as the chief public prosecutor, Shah would still decide which prosecutor handles the cases against persons who were earlier his clients. Incidentally, Shah is defending state law minister Ashok Bhatt in another case, where the latter is accused of leading a mob which killed a police constable in the mid-80s.[121]

H.M. Dhruv, who had acted as attorney for Chetan Shah, was appointed 'special prosecutor' for the Gulberg Society and Naroda Patiya cases after having been the defence attorney in the first case.[122] As for Arvind Pandya, the special prosecutor or advocate general acting as the government's counsel for the defence before the Shah–Nanavati Commission, he turned out to be a convinced ideologue, as was evident when he justified the 2002 violence in the following terms: '[In Godhra, Muslims] thought they could get away with it because the Gujarati is mild by nature [note that Muslims are not considered as Gujaratis]. In the past, they had beaten the Gujarati, they have even beaten the whole world, and nobody has shown any courage … […] But this time, they were thrashed … It is Hindu rule now … All of Gujarat is ruled by Hindus, and that too from the VHP and the BJP.'[123] The prosecutor, who uttered words so unbefitting of a lawyer, also confessed that during the hearings, 'Every judge was calling me in his chamber and showing full sympathy for me … giving full cooperation to me, but keeping some distance … the judges were also guiding me as and when required … how to put up a case and on which date … because, basically, they are Hindus.'[124]

This overview suggests that there was not even one Muslim public prosecutor in the districts that had been most badly hit in 2002,[125] and that many of the prosecutors were members of (or were linked to) the Sangh Parivar. Taking stock of this situation, the Special Investigation Team chairman, R.K. Raghavan, in his report to the Supreme Court in 2010 wrote: 'It has been found that a few of the appointees [of the judiciary of Gujarat] were in fact politically connected, either to the ruling party or organisations sympathetic to it.'[126]

Supreme Court versus Gujarat Government and the High Court

Thanks to the tenacity of some plaintiffs backed by equally determined NGOs, a few trials finally began in 2003, such as that concerning the murder of 14 Muslims in Ghodasar in Anand district. Hindus had attacked Muslim houses on 3 March 2002, killing 14 people, 12 of them women who were trying to flee through the fields. Of the 63 accused on the stand, 48 were acquitted and 12 received a life sentence handed down by the

Nadiad sessions court in Kheda district, in November 2003.[127] But most complaints came to nought.

Transfer of trials and (re-)opening of cases

The difficulties encountered by Muslim victims resulted not only from the attitude of the prosecutors, but also from intimidation tactics employed against the witnesses. The most telling illustration of this state of affairs is what is known as the Best Bakery case, from the name of a bakery in Vadodara where 14 people were burned alive on 1 March 2002. The police began their investigation on the basis of a complaint lodged by a young woman, Zahira Sheikh, who was 18 years old at the time, and who was one of the 73 eyewitnesses called to the stand. The trial began at the Vadodara courthouse in February 2003 and went on for several weeks. The government pleader, Raghuvir Pandya, who had recently been appointed in 2002 to the district and sessions court in Baroda, was a VHP sympathiser.[128]

In June 2003, the 21 accused were acquitted because 37 of the 73 key witnesses, including Zahira, her mother and her brothers, retracted their statements before the judges. Shortly afterwards they said they had 'lied in court because they had been threatened with death unless they did so'.[129] It was then that the legal rights group Citizens for Justice and Peace helped Zahira record her statement before the National Human Rights Commission and thereafter co-petitioned with her in the Supreme Court to request a reopening of the investigation and a retrial of the case outside Gujarat. The Supreme Court persuaded the government of Gujarat to request a retrial before the state's High Court, but the appeal was dismissed in December 2003. In January 2004 Zahira filed an appeal with the Supreme Court, which decided in her favour on 12 April 2004, thereby invalidating the High Court decision, and ordered a retrial outside Gujarat. Such a transfer seemed the best way to lift all manner of pressures.[130]

The Supreme Court took this opportunity to remind the High Court of its duty 'in a case where the role of the prosecuting agency itself is put in question and is said to be hand in glove with the accused, parading a mock fight and making a mockery of the criminal justice system itself'.[131] The judges of India's highest court even took their colleagues in Gujarat to task:

> When the investigating agency helps the accused, the witnesses are threatened to depose falsely and the prosecutor acts in a manner as if he was defending the accused, and the Court was acting merely as an onlooker and there is no fair trial at all, justice becomes the victim … The modern day 'Neros' were looking elsewhere when Best Bakery and innocent children and women were burning, and were probably deliberating how the perpetrators of the crime could be saved or protected.[132]

A retrial was held in Mumbai starting in October 2004. But on 3 November, Zahira held a press conference stating that the first judgment was correct. In November and December, Zahira, her mother and her brothers once again retracted, telling the judges that, owing to the dense smoke, they had no idea how their relatives died. On 22 December, the online edition of *Tehelka* broadcast a video purportedly showing Zahira and her family receiving a large sum of money from the hands of one of Vadodara's BJP MLAs—who denied it. The trial nevertheless continued and at last, in February 2006, on the basis of incriminating evidence gathered by the CBI (which was finally charged with the investigation), 9 of the 17 accused were given life sentences while 8 others were acquitted for lack of evidence. The Supreme Court sentenced Zahira to one year in prison for having lied under oath.[133]

The Supreme Court also deemed it necessary to transfer the trial of the Bilkis Yakub Rasool case. This woman was five months pregnant when she was gang-raped in her village of Limkheda (Dahod district) by neighbours she knew, on 3 March 2002.[134] She had already witnessed the rape of three of her family members and the murder of 15 family members including her three-year-old daughter. She lodged a complaint the following day for rape and the murder of 14 members of her family. While recording her complaint, the police only mentioned seven of the deaths, claiming that the bodies of the other people could not be found, and refused to record her complaint of rape. The case was closed in January 2003 for lack of evidence. Bilkis, with the support of several NGOs, including Janvikas, and the National Human Rights Commission, petitioned the Supreme Court, which ordered the government of Gujarat to reopen the case in September 2003. The police then began a campaign of harassment against the victim, even waking her in the middle of the night to return to the scene of the rape and murders to re-enact the events. Then, in December 2003, the Supreme Court directed the CBI to reopen the case.[135] It finally arrested 12 people for rape and murder and 6 police officers for obstruction of justice. Facing threats, Bilkis sought the transfer of the case in July, something to which the Supreme Court agreed, and a public prosecutor was appointed by the central government in August 2004. Eventually, the case was tried in Mumbai and 13 of the 20 accused were convicted, with 11 of them being given life sentences.[136]

From the Godhra Riots Inquiry Committee to the Special Investigation Team

Drawing their own conclusions from the failure of the judicial process in Gujarat, the Supreme Court finally appointed a Godhra Riots Inquiry Committee, which re-examined 2,107 cases that had been closed within months after the violence. In view of the committee's report, it concluded in February 2006 that 1,594 cases should be reopened and required further investigation. Another 13 complaints were lodged and 41 police officers involved in the riots were charged. Over 600 accused were thus arrested while waiting to stand trial.[137] This action, however, did not take the judicial process very far owing to the obstructionist practices on the part of the Gujarat government.

In March 2008, the Supreme Court decided to circumvent the obstacle by appointing a Special Investigation Team (SIT). The terms of reference of the SIT, outlined by the court in May 2009, restored the victims' hopes.[138] This new body was called upon to concentrate on only a half-dozen cases, which amounted to an admission that full justice was impossible but concurred with the 'realism' recommended by some NGOs from the start.[139] The cases in question were Naroda Patiya, Naroda Gam, Gulberg Society, Sardarpura, Dipda Darwaja, Sabarkantha, Ode and Godhra.

The biggest weakness of the new approach lay in the role it granted to local actors. Not only was the Gujarat High Court responsible for appointing judicial officers, including the public prosecutors, who were to make up the SIT, but half of the six members in charge of 'leading the investigation', in already extremely difficult conditions,[140] were to be recruited from among Gujarat police officers. It was no surprise that the local authorities' choice fell on officers who not only depended upon but had actually sometimes been protected by the Gujarat government. Indeed, the appointment of Ashish Bhatia, former additional commissioner of police in Surat, Shivanand Jha, former additional commissioner of police of Ahmedabad, who had become home secretary, and Geetha Johri was criticised by the victims and their sympathisers. In an open letter to the SIT chairman, R.K. Raghavan, Shiv Visvanathan, an Ahmedabad-based academic, asked, with regard to one of the people appointed, 'How is a man seen as accomplice to murder to guarantee justice?'[141]

Many of the public prosecutors appointed by the Modi government remained in place. Such was the case, for instance, of Suresh Shah, who had been special public prosecutor in the Mehsana massacre case since 2004. But others were appointed by the SIT after allegedly taking advice from NGOs such as Citizens for Justice and Peace.[142] However, at least two of those who were nominated in an impartial fashion after the SIT was established ultimately resigned, as they were unable to complete their task. R.K. Shah, who had been named special public prosecutor for the Gulberg Society case, and his assistant public prosecutor, Naina Bhatt, sent their letters of resignation to the Supreme Court on 25 February 2010. In an interview, Bhatt explained:

> Generally, I found the judge (B.U. Joshi) unsympathetic to the victims and eyewitnesses. Also, the SIT investigating officer, James Suthar (a deputy superintendent of police), was not cooperating much either [...] All the papers pertaining to the case were not given to me by various investigating agencies handling the matter. At the eleventh hour they would give the papers to me and I would not have enough time to study the papers, to talk to witnesses on that aspect of the case.[143]

The SIT was particularly dysfunctional from three viewpoints. First, it refused to make use of incriminating evidence such as recordings of telephone conversations between police officers, senior civil servants and Sangh Parivar leaders, or footage recorded by Ashish Khetan with a hidden camera for *Tehelka*.[144] Secondly, it left the vast majority of accused out on bail. This was so for 51 of the 65 accused in the Gulberg Society case, for 54 of the 63 accused in the Naroda Patiya case, for 80 of the 89 accused in the Naroda Gam case, for 26 of the 37 accused in the Ode case, for 65 of the 73 accused in the Sardarpura case, and for all 84 accused in the Dipda Darwaja case. This bias—contrasting with the record number of Muslims in custody for the Sabarmati Express case in Godhra by virtue of POTA (the Prevention of Terrorism Act)[145]—enabled the accused to threaten witnesses.[146]

Thirdly, the SIT made no systematic effort to protect the witnesses, most of whom were Muslim victims or surviving relatives who generally lived in utter poverty, a situation already conducive to an attitude of resignation or of accepting bribes. In November 2011, a key witness in the Naroda Patiya case was knifed to death in Juhapura (Ahmedabad). Nadeem Saiyed was a Right to Information (RTI) activist who had made many enemies after exposing their wrongdoings. Three months before, he had confided to Mallika Sarabhai: 'Ben, my life is under constant threat. I am afraid they will get to me before I can testify.'[147] A few days later, Saiyed was killed, while two other witnesses in the Ode case said they were receiving death threats and had written to the SIT for protection.[148]

After 2007, the Modi government benefited from the support, within the judicial machinery, of Tushar Mehta. As a junior lawyer, Mehta had assisted Krishnakant Vakharia, an advocate specialising in cooperative law. Amit Shah had got in touch with Mehta (who worked for Vakharia till 2004) for this very reason in the 1990s and he then became 'the point-man for Amit Shah'.[149] He was involved in all the legal procedures that mattered in Gujarat after the 2002 riots.[150] After Modi won the 2007 election, Mehta was designated a senior advocate by the Gujarat High Court and appointed as the additional advocate general of Gujarat in 2008, thanks to Amit Shah.[151] When Amit Shah was arrested in 2010, Tushar virtually gave up his practice and became Shah's 'eyes and ears'.[152]

> Mehta, as the additional advocate general, received confidential reports of the investigation into the riot cases from the SIT's official email account. He forwarded these reports to Swaminathan Gurumurthy, an influential ideologue of the Rashtriya Swayamsevak Sangh with close links to the BJP leadership. Gurumurthy read the reports, prepared a note in response and sent it to Ram and Mahesh Jethmalani, the lawyers for many of those accused of playing a role in the 2002 riots. No one besides the state's counsel and the amicus in the case was supposed to have seen the reports, least of all the lawyers of the people that the SIT was constituted to investigate.[153]

The Supreme Court called the SIT to order and attempted to put the investigation back on track in 2009–10.

The SIT and Narendra Modi

Unable to ignore Rahul Sharma's CDs, which established that BJP and VHP officials were present near Gulberg Society, Naroda Patiya and Naroda Gam when the violence occurred (and moreover were in cellphone contact with police officers), the authorities finally made some arrests in 2009. Among the policemen, only a minor figure, K.G. Erda, who was in charge of the Gulberg Society area in 2002, was arrested.[154] But at the same time, the Gujarat government submitted an affidavit to the High Court indicating that, 'in spite of being an MLA, Kodnani was a leader of the mob instigating them to commit the crimes and in fact even fired her pistol'.[155] Maya Kodnani, the local MLA, was arrested as well as Jaideep Patel, a VHP leader who had allegedly also led attackers in the Naroda area. While the SIT ignored some key actors, it interrogated others, including Narendra Modi[156] after the widow of Ehsan Jafri filed a petition implicating him.

In June 2006, Zakia Jafri and Citizens for Justice and Peace filed a 119-page complaint with the director general of police of Gujarat, P.C. Pandey, making a case for criminal conspiracy to commit mass murder, destruction of evidence, intimidation and subversion of the criminal justice system. It read, on pages 100–01:

> The present accused no. 1 is The Chief Minister, Mr. Narendra Modi, then and Presently Chief Minister, Gujarat State, The Constitutionally elected head of the state and responsible for the Fundamental Rights, Right to Life and Property of all Citizens regardless of caste, community and gender. Alleged to be architect of a Criminal Conspiracy to subvert Constitutional Governance and the rule of law; unleash unlawful and illegal practices during the mass carnage and thereafter protecting the accused who played direct as well as indirect role and abetted the commission of the crime.[157]

Since the Gujarat police took no action, on 28 February 2007, exactly five years after the events, Mrs Jafri and Citizens for Justice and Peace filed a petition in the Gujarat High Court. In November that year, the court dismissed the petition. On 8 June 2008, the same petitioners filed a criminal complaint with the Supreme Court. It levelled charges against 63 persons, including the chief minister, Narendra Modi, 11 cabinet ministers and 3 BJP MLAs, 6 members or cadres of other Sangh Parivar organisations, and 38 high-ranking IPS (Indian Police Service) and IAS (Indian Administrative Service) officers. What was at stake was a catalogue of misdemeanours on the part of the state in Gujarat that explained the high human toll and massive destruction of property in the riots. In March 2009, the court directed the SIT to investigate further.[158]

On 28 March 2010, Narendra Modi testified before the SIT. The SIT member who questioned him, A.K. Malhotra (the inquiry officer), was not a member of the Gujarat police force. Nevertheless, he did not have the means to interrogate the state's chief minister, who claimed to know nothing at all about the reports the Intelligence Bureau sent him about what was brewing in February 2002.[159]

Ultimately the 600-page report that the SIT filed with the Supreme Court in December 2010 merely deplored the 'sweeping' and 'offensive' comments Modi made against Muslims, deeming that they 'showed a measure of thoughtlessness and irresponsibility on the part of a person holding a high public office'.[160] It concluded—what was still an interim report—by saying: 'As many as 32 allegations were probed into during this preliminary inquiry. These related to several acts of omission and commission by the state government and its functionaries, including the Chief Minister. A few of these alone were in fact substantiated [...] The substantiated allegations did not throw up material that would justify action under the law.'[161]

The lawyers defending the victims of the 2002 riots were already disillusioned by the functioning of the SIT when it submitted its report. They had asked the Supreme Court to transfer the case to the Central Bureau of Investigation, but in vain.[162]

Contrasting Verdicts

The first trial that was completed after the appointment of the SIT was that concerning the burning of the Sabarmati Express in Godhra. While 63 of the surviving 94 accused were released on 22 February 2011 after nine years in prison (5 other prisoners died in jail) where they had been detained under POTA charges,[163] 31 accused were found guilty and 11 of them—a record—were sentenced to death while 20 others got life imprisonment. This harsh verdict was due to the conclusion that the judge, P.R. Patel, had drawn from the first Shah–Nanavati Commission report, that it was a planned attack. However, Justice Patel contradicted himself by acquitting the two men the police considered to have masterminded the operation, Maulvi Umarji and Mohammed Hussain Kalota, the president of the municipality at the time of events. How could they have been acquitted if they were behind the conspiracy? Second, the conspiracy theory contradicted a previous decision by the High Court. In 2005, the central POTA review committee had concluded that POTA could not apply to the accused in the Godhra case since it was not a case of terrorism or conspiracy.[164]

The frustration of those who had been condemned stemmed from two additional factors. First, the police officer placed in charge of the investigation by the SIT, Noel Parmar, had not only described Muslims as 'all complete fundamentalists',[165] but was one of the state police officers who had been well treated by Modi's government. He had been granted four extensions of service beyond retirement in 2004. The SIT's response was to nominate his right-hand man, Ramesh Patel, in his place. Second, in August 2010 the trial court had rejected an application by some of the accused to summon Ashish Khetan as a defence witness. Their counsels argued that the court would learn much from his interview—during his sting operation—with the two men from the Kalubhai garage who, allegedly, sold the petrol that was used to set the train ablaze .[166] In his article on the subject,[167] Ashish Khetan argues that (a) two of the nine BJP men who testified that they had seen Muslims setting the train ablaze admitted during the sting operation that they were actually at home that day; and (b) the two petrol pump attendants mentioned above initially declared to the police that they had not sold any petrol, but one of them, Ranjit Singh, had been caught 'admitting on camera that he and Pratap [the other witness] had been bribed Rs 50,000 by [one] police office [...] to do that'—that is, to change their testimony.

Another disturbing element in this case concerns Husain Mulla. On 14 July 2002, he was arrested 'and upon threat of death, forced him to sign a number of confessional statements, among them that he had pulled the chain of the Sabarmati Express and that he saw two Muslim men set fire to the bogey (S6)'. Subjected to torture, Mulla managed to escape.[168] Last but not least, the lawyer and scholar Nitya Ramakrishnan points out that the judge considered the confession of one man, Jabir, a 'proof of the conspiracy' whereas, according to the law, 'use of a post arrest confession to prove conspiracy is forbidden'.[169]

The second trial completed after the SIT had been appointed concerned the Sardarpura case. On 10 November 2011, the special court sentenced 31 people to life imprisonment and acquitted 42 others. The judgment rejected the accusation by defence lawyers that witnesses had been tutored by the rights activist Teesta Setalvad.[170] In fact, it said of her: 'In the present case, the injured witnesses were in such a state of mind that without the active support of someone they might not have come before the court to give evidence.'[171] This verdict has been described as unprecedented,[172] and was welcomed by NGOs supporting the victims even though it did not consider, contrary to their firm belief, whether the Sardarpura violence resulted from a Hindu nationalist conspiracy.[173]

The Ode case—named after a locality where 23 people, including 9 women and as many children, were killed—also resulted in a trial. In April 2012, 18 of the accused were found guilty of murder and criminal conspiracy and sentenced to life imprisonment.[174] One month later, 9 other men who had been found guilty of burning to death three people in the village of Ode received the same sentence.[175]

The fourth trial to take place was the Naroda Patiya case. On 31 August 2012, a special trial court acquitted 29 people and convicted 32 others of murder, criminal conspiracy and rape; 22 were sentenced to a minimum of 14 years of imprisonment, 7 to a minimum of 21 years, Maya Kodnani to 28 years (including 18 years under the charge of murder), and Babu Bajrangi to life imprisonment. The court seized this occasion to criticise the police inspector in charge of Naroda Patiya in 2002, K.K. Mysorewala, whose attitude resulted in mass murder, 'which has brought shame for the entire nation and shame to the secular feature of the Constitution of India'. It also lambasted the poor quality of the investigation, something, the court said, one would not expect from senior policemen—but, it added, 'they must have been over-shadowed by some element'.[176] The judge, Jyotsna Yagnik, went one step further when Maya Kodnani—who had been appointed to the Gujarat government after the 2007 state elections—complained that she had been a victim of politics. The judge said that, on the contrary, Kodnani had been 'tremendously favoured by the then investigating agencies [before the Supreme Court-appointed SIT took over]. All care, at the cost of the duty of the investigating officer and even the interest of the victims, was taken to see to it that Kodnani's involvement does not come on the books. This, in fact, comes in the way to believe that Kodnani was ever a victim of any politics.'[177]

However, the most significant case remained that relating to the Gulberg Society massacre, which had resulted from a petition filed by Zakia Jafri against Narendra Modi and others. The main issue there pertained to the notion of conspiracy (already used in some of the trials mentioned above), which had become prominent after the leaking to the press of the SIT report and, therefore, of senior policeman Sanjiv Bhatt's deposition before the team (see chapter 2). In April 2011, Bhatt used the term in his affidavit in which he said that the SIT should concentrate on ascertaining the existence of a 'larger conspiracy or official orchestration behind the Gujarat Riots of 2002'.[178] The meeting he claimed he took part in was held at Narendra Modi's residence on 27 February 2002.[179]

In May 2011, the Nanavati–Mehta Commission finally summoned Bhatt for a hearing. Narendra Modi immediately counter-attacked, saying that he had indeed held a 'law and order meeting' at his residence on the evening of 27 February 2002, but that Sanjiv Bhatt did not attend. Bhatt's chauffeur, on the other hand, declared that he clearly remembered having driven his boss to the chief minister's residence that evening, and a former BBC journalist who had interviewed Bhatt on the same day filed an affidavit before the Supreme Court that corroborated his schedule.[180]

Bhatt, who had already been transferred first to the post of principal of the Sabarmati jail and then to that of principal of the State Reserve Police Training School at Junagadh, was suspended in August 2011. In November, the government of Gujarat went further: it withdrew a revision petition in an alleged case of custodial death against Bhatt,[181] a procedure similar to that followed against Satish Verma—who, incidentally, had taken over from Bhatt as principal of the training school at Junagadh.

In a parallel move, after receiving the SIT report in May 2010, the Supreme Court submitted it in October 2010 to the *amicus curiae*, Prashant Bhushan. He was about to complete his report when the state of Gujarat accused him of bias. He resigned immediately. His successor, Raju Ramachandran, submitted a ten-page report, which led the Supreme Court to direct the SIT to investigate further. Then, in May, the court allowed the *amicus curiae* to bypass the SIT and to meet witnesses, including police officers. In July, Ramachandran submitted his report and in September, in its judgment regarding the petition by Zakia Jafri and the Citizens for Justice and Peace, the court, while it decided to cease monitoring the case, directed the trial court to decide whether the 63 persons mentioned in the petition—including Modi—had to be probed. This judgment was celebrated by the BJP as an exoneration whereas, for some other people, it meant that the 'trial court is now to "begin"'.[182]

In his report the *amicus curiae*, Ramachandran, who accepted the testimony of Sanjiv Bhatt as valid, considered that Narendra Modi could be formally charged:

> In my opinion, the offences which can be made out against Shri Modi, at this prima facie stage, are offences inter alia under Sections 153A(1)(a) & (b) of IPC [which concern promoting enmity among different groups on grounds of religion], 153B(1)(c) [against assertions prejudicial to national integration], 166 [directed against public servants disobeying the law with the intent to cause injury to any person] and 505(2) [regarding statements creating or promoting enmity, hatred or ill-will] of the IPC [Indian Penal Code].[183]

Ramachandran also indicted several policemen. However, the SIT rejected his interpretation of the case. It 'virtually exonerated the then Police Commissioner, P.C. Pandey, his deputies M.K. Tandon and P.B. Gondia and some other police officers of the charge of dereliction of duty, and said the investigation proved that they had tried to curb the riots to the best of their ability given the limited resources available at their command to deal with the rapidly deteriorating situation'.[184] A closure report was therefore submitted to the Supreme Court. However, that court did not close the case,[185] and in September 2013 Zakia Jafri made a final submission challenging the SIT's decision in favour of Modi.[186]

The *post facto* judicial activities suggest important conclusions about the rule of law in Gujarat. Certainly, some judges have made history by condemning a record number of guilty men (and women) to an unprecedented number of severe sentences (including the death penalty). Never before had communal violence resulted in such verdicts. But the magnitude of this state-sponsored violence was also unprecedented since Partition, and, moreover, justice had not been achieved for most of the victims. Not only have many politicians and policemen responsible for the carnage (if not actively involved in it) been spared, but the number of cases investigated has been very small compared with the FIRs that have (or should have) been registered. This anomaly reflects the communalisation of the state machinery, in spite of the resilience of some institutions like the National Human Rights Commission.

Last but not least, the preceding narrative suggests that a sort of judicial federalism has evolved, a phenomenon that had perhaps never yet manifested itself in this form in India. While the Gujarat police and judicial system appeared to display all kinds of bias and limitations, the Centre, whether it was the government in Delhi or the Supreme Court, could not overcome the resistance put up at the state level. The appointment of SITs and the transfer of trials to Maharashtra showed how unreliable Gujarat's institutions had become in the eyes of the Supreme Court—but they were no solution.

THE PROCESS OF DE-INSTITUTIONALISATION

From 2002 onwards, Modi's discourse emphasised that he had restored law and order and guaranteed peace and security in Gujarat, whereas the state had previously—or so he claimed—used violence and curfews because of Muslim criminal elements. He therefore projected himself as the protector of the Hindu majority beyond the 2002 episode, which was presented as a turning point. The orchestration of fake encounters with jihadis who allegedly intended to kill him helped Modi to consolidate this image of saviour of the majority community—and of a man who risked his life in order to promote collective safety. On 15 August 2010, Modi's Independence Day speech eulogised the police of Gujarat:

> While the country is besieged by terrorism, Maoist and Naxalite violence, the Gujarat Police have, with great courage and risk to their own lives, arrested 400 terrorists and got many of them convicted. Not only the Gujarat government but also five-and-a-half crore [55 million] Gujaratis congratulate them.
>
> I want to laud the Gujarati Police. While nobody in the country was able to stop bomb blasts happening all over, the Gujarat Police detected the nexus of gangsters, which then caused fewer bomb blasts.
>
> I would say there is an entire battalion of protectors of terrorists. They have many faces. Sometimes these people talk sweet and enter into the field to defend terrorists. Tricks to safeguard terrorists and dislodge this government are being played. Like terrorists, their protectors are also spread throughout ... we need to recognize them.[187]

This speech is typical of the politics of fear and Modi's security-oriented discourse, which we will encounter again when analysing his election campaigns. The discourse went hand in hand with a growing de-institutionalisation of the police forces, which were not only used in fake encounters, but also invited to adopt and engage in communal attitudes—as the promotion of the guilty officers of the 2002 riots showed.

A similar de-institutionalisation of the judiciary occurred in parallel, due to the infiltration of the judicial machinery and a sophisticated strategy of appointing reliable men to key posts. This policy, which was intended to cope with the fallout of the events of 2002—as in the case of the police—had equally debilitating long-term effects.

More importantly for us, this policy prepared the ground for what Modi and Amit Shah, his home minister from 2019, were about to do at the Centre. To exert systematic control over the police and the judiciary was, indeed, a priority as early as 2014. And some of the techniques—as well as key players—used to that effect were drawn directly from the test site that Gujarat had become for twelve years under Modi and Shah.

First, they tried to appoint to key positions police officers who had been part of their entourage in Gujarat. In 2015, Y.C. Modi became additional CBI director.[188] He had spent eight years on secondment to the CBI between 2002 and 2010 and had been part of the SIT that probed Modi's role in the Gujarat riots and investigated the murder of Haren Pandya. Regarding the latter investigation, in September 2011 the Gujarat High Court declared that it had been 'botched up and blinkered'.[189] In 2016, another IPS Gujarat cadre, Rakesh Asthana, was appointed additional director of the CBI. He had also been part of the SIT. A few months after becoming additional CBI director, Asthana became acting or interim CBI director. R.K. Dutta, who, on the basis of seniority, should have replaced Anil Sinha—the outgoing director, who was retiring—had been transferred to the Ministry of Home Affairs as special secretary (a post specially upgraded for him) two days before Sinha retired.[190] This transfer, which made Asthana's appointment possible, was ordered without following the rule that the government must secure the Central Vigilance

Commission's approval before altering the tenure of any CBI officer. The CBI, as an institution, resisted and Asthana could not take up the post—he was therefore appointed director general of Civil Aviation Security.[191] Instead, Alok Verma, then Delhi police chief, became CBI director. But Asthana's rise to power did not end there. A few months later, in 2017, he was appointed 'special director' of the CBI in spite of opposition from the CBI director himself,[192] who accused Asthana of corruption[193]—and the latter did the same to the former. The government sent both on indefinite leave in late October 2018.[194] On 7 January 2019 the Supreme Court reinstated Verma as CBI director, but a committee headed by Prime Minister Modi removed Verma from the post on 10 January 2020 'on charges of corruption and dereliction of duty'.[195] Alok Verma took early retirement and in 2021 Modi could appoint Praveen Sinha, a Gujarat cadre of the 1988 batch—till then the CBI additional director—as acting director. At the same time, Asthana was appointed police commissioner of Delhi—an officer reporting directly to the home minister because Delhi is not a full-fledged state.

Secondly, Modi and Shah focused their attention on the judicial process. For that, they again brought to Delhi people who had helped them in Gujarat. Tushar Mehta, who had also defended Amit Shah in the Sohrabuddin Sheikh case, is a case in point: he followed Modi and Shah to Delhi where he was appointed additional solicitor general in 2014 and solicitor general of India in 2018. Another 'rising star', S.V. Raju, who had been practising at the Gujarat High Court and had been Amit Shah's lawyer in different cases, was appointed too as additional solicitor general at the Supreme Court of India in 2020.[196]

But the Supreme Court judges were the real target. The very first bill that was introduced in parliament by the Indian government in 2014 dealt with the reform of their appointment. The idea was to abandon the collegium system (by which Supreme Court justices were selected by the five most senior judges, including the chief justice of India) and to create a National Judicial Appointments Commission (NJAC) in which lawyers would be in a minority. When this bill was passed as an amendment to the Constitution in parliament, the Supreme Court quashed it. Then, the government refused to appoint several judges that the collegium had selected and used several other techniques to curb the independence of the judiciary,[197] a practice already initiated by the government immediately after Modi took over.

In June 2014, the central government was asked to appoint four judges to the Supreme Court selected by the collegium. The Modi government appointed all of them except Gopal Subramanium, because of Intelligence Bureau and CBI reports questioning his integrity.[198] Subramanium wrote a nine-page-long letter to the chief justice in which he pointed out that the court had appointed him *amicus curiae* in the Sohrabuddin case but added that he bore 'no personal vengeance or any kind of grudge' against the then prime accused, Amit Shah.[199] The same could not be said of Shah vis-à-vis Subramanium. In his letter, in which he withdrew his candidacy for the Supreme Court, Subramanium wrote, rather prophetically, 'The events of past few weeks have raised serious doubts in my mind as to the ability of the Executive Government to appreciate and respect the independence, integrity and glory of the judicial institution. I do not expect this attitude to change with time.'[200]

Maya Kodnani was acquitted in 2018, while the Supreme Court granted bail to Babu Bajrangi in 2019. In 2022 the 11 men who had been given life sentences in the Bilkis Bano case were released after 14 years in jail. A panel appointed by the BJP government of Gujarat had approved the application for remission of these men, but approval had also been granted by Amit Shah, the home minister of the central government.[201] One year later, a special SIT court in Ahmedabad acquitted all 67 accused, including former BJP MLA Maya Kodnani, ex-

Bajrang Dal leader Babu Bajrangi, and Vishwa Hindu Parishad leader Jaydeep Patel, in the 2002 Naroda Gam massacre case.[202] In many cases investigated by the CBI, the agency abstained from filing any appeal against the judicial decisions.

4

CREATING A DEEPER STATE

FROM CRIMINALISATION OF POLITICS TO VIGILANTISM AND SURVEILLANCE

> I and my state of Gujarat are indebted to you for the courage and conviction you showed in saying good words for me and my state.
>
> Narendra Modi's open letter to Anna Hazare, 2011

The saffronisation of the police and the judiciary that we have studied in chapter 3 is only one dimension of the decline of the rule of law observed in Gujarat. These two institutions were also weakened by the state government. This process was twofold, as it resulted from the protection of corrupt policemen by the government as well as from its refusal to strengthen the custodians of the rule of law, including the judiciary. Unsurprisingly, crime and corruption remained very high in the state, this trend affecting in particular the whistleblowers who tried to use the Right to Information Act to fight both evils.

While this trend perpetuated existing tendencies, during Modi's terms two other phenomena gained momentum: the making of a police state relying on new forms of surveillance, and the creation of a deep state—or deeper state—based on the growing influence of Hindu vigilante groups. Surveillance was not an unprecedented practice, as is evident from the role of the Intelligence Bureau in Gujarat, as in other states, but the government targeted new victims. Similarly, while vigilante groups were already active in Gujarat from the 1980s and 1990s, they could now exert a more systematic form of cultural policing with the blessing of the government, so much so that in some towns and cities they controlled society at the grassroots level.

HOW NOT TO STRENGTHEN LAW AND ORDER

Corruption and Criminalisation of Gujarat Police

In his autobiography, Julio Ribeiro, the chief of Gujarat Police in the mid-1980s, criticised the force not only for its politicisation, but also for its corrupt practices,[1] which were largely due to their illicit relationships with bootleggers. The BJP exploited this nexus and claimed that it would restore the rule of law as well as clean up the police. However, the Modi government hardly delivered on that front. In March 2007, Gujarat government records tabled in the state Assembly showed 'the police department as the most corrupt', compared with the revenue department, for instance: 'In the last three years, nearly 25 per cent of cases of corruption registered in Gujarat relate[d] to the police department.'[2]

Surprisingly, policemen connected to the Muslim bootlegging mafia continued to benefit from government protection. In May 2008, O.P. Mathur was appointed Ahmedabad police commissioner in spite of his poor reputation. In the 1990s, Mathur had been charged with running the 'Latif Squad' which the Gujarat government had formed to bring down the eponymous gang. However, documents that the CBI compiled in the case of the murder of Rauf Valiullah, a Congress worker who was gunned down on 9 October 1992 in Ahmedabad, showed that Mathur and the Latif gang were part of the same nexus. Valiullah had denounced Latif's liquor trafficking, to the consternation of Mathur, who, like many other policemen, got a cut (or *hafta*) in exchange for exercising benign neglect.[3] In a remarkable piece of investigative journalism, Prashant Dayal wrote:

> As addl [additional] CP [commissioner of police], Mathur was in charge of the entire eastern belt of the city [of Ahmedabad], including Dariapur, which was Latif's stronghold. The [CBI] documents, especially the statement of Abdul Khurdush, the right-hand man of Latif, who is still in Sabarmati jail, show how the entire police force was on the payroll of the Latif gang. While Khurdush has spoken about Latif's close links with Mathur, and that it was Mathur who had allegedly told Latif about Valiullah being a thorn in his side, Khurdush also gave CBI a detailed list of the regular payments (ranging from 25,000 rupees to 30,000 rupees per month) made by Latif to various police officers serving in Ahmedabad at that time to allow the gang to conduct its liquor business freely.[4]

Prashant Dayal explains that the promotion of Mathur in 2008 was partly related to the case of Sohrabuddin, a former Latif gang member who had continued with his extortion racket after Latif was killed. When, in 2007, the Supreme Court handed over the Sohrabuddin case to the police deputy inspector general Rajnish Rai, the Modi government 'panicked' and appointed O.P. Mathur CID chief. Rai 'handed over the case papers to Mathur which included a CD containing telephone records of police officers, businessmen and politicians which indicated towards a possible nexus behind the elimination of Sohrabuddin'.[5] The CD subsequently disappeared when Mathur was promoted as commissioner of police of Ahmedabad in 2008.

Besides Dayal's articles, the *Times of India* reacted by organising a poll asking readers whether they wanted Mathur to stay or to go: 98 per cent of the respondents replied that he had to resign, and some of them even asked for his suspension.[6] In response, Mathur filed charges of sedition and conspiracy against the editor of the newspaper (a move that resulted in a judicial imbroglio to which we'll return).

Mathur's rejection by the readers of the *Times of India* reflects the unpopularity of the police in Gujarat.[7] In 2007, the Anti-Corruption Bureau of the Gujarat government had revealed that the police was the most corrupt sector in government: nearly a quarter of the 433 corruption cases registered were related to this department (the Panchayat and Revenue departments were second and third).[8] Some policemen were indeed engaging in unprofessional practices—part of a long tradition. An Ahmedabad-based journalist reported in the *DNA*:

> There are many cops who allegedly support the criminal activities and also get the lion's share of the loot by literally being partners in the illegal business. A bootlegger told *DNA* that the days when he could smuggle liquor into the city easily are gone. 'Now we not only have to give the *haftas* [commissions] but also a healthy share to "strict" cops to do our business [...] These cops first target a bootlegger or operator of a gambling den and tell him or her to offer them a partnership. If the bootlegger does not agree, then a new competitor is created with the support of such cops.'[9]

In 2010, to improve their image, the police of Ahmedabad decided to expose the officers who were guilty of all kinds of crime, suggesting that after nine years at the helm of the state government, Narendra Modi was not in a position to clean up the police force. This operation resulted in an impressive list of 350 cases of policemen 'caught helping criminals in one way or other'.[10]

Disinvesting from the Rule of Law

In spite of Modi's commitment to restoring the rule of law in Gujarat, he invested neither in the police nor in the judiciary, and did not even appoint a Lokayukta (ombudsman) for several years.

The transformation of Gujarat Police into a somewhat privatised and ideological force was made easier by its comparatively small size—a state of things which also partly explains the decline of law and order. Indeed, the state police, under Modi, were as understaffed as they were underpaid.[11] In 2010, the Comptroller and Auditor General (CAG) published a report showing that Gujarat Police had '58,158 personnel against the sanctioned strength of 76,780 personnel including state reserve police'.[12] Things had not improved by 2011, as is evident from Table 4.1, which shows that Gujarat lagged behind many other states in terms of police vacancies.

In 2012, less than 56 per cent of sanctioned posts in the police force were actually occupied in Gujarat. Its vacancy rate—a little more than 44 per cent—was 30 percentage points higher than the national average, and higher than that in every other state except Uttar Pradesh. The situation was so strained that during the 2012 Assembly elections, the state police 'faced acute shortage of IPS officers, field officers and constables'. As a result, the Election Commission had to send 'a force of 65,000 men from the paramilitary forces and other armed police from different states to help the Gujarat police'.[13]

The state judiciary was also understaffed, to such an extent that the Gujarat government created night court sittings, which were intended to speed up the disposal of pending cases. This new judicial system saw the light of day thanks to the 'Evening Courts Rules—2006', which had been drawn up by the state law department, under the aegis of Ashok Bhatt, the law minister. According to this new disposition, courts would continue working for two hours after 6.15 p.m. and the judges functioning at that time would get an additional 25 per cent remuneration.[14] For *India Today*, the 'biggest advantage of evening courts is that the litigants don't have to take leave from work or, in case of a non-permanent employee or a small businessman, lose a day's earning'.[15] This experiment, which was launched in the presence of the chief justice of India, Y.K. Sabharwal, was extended to half a dozen districts in less than six months. There, 44 such night courts disposed of 39,000 cases from November 2006 to March 2007.[16]

However, the judiciary could not cope with the burden of cases because it continued to remain understaffed throughout Modi's chief ministership. In 2012, the situation regarding vacancies in the judiciary had not improved, as is evident from Table 4.2.[17] Vacancies represented a third of the sanctioned strength of the High Court in Gujarat, whereas they stood at 30 per cent on average all over India. Only 6 states, out of 21, had more vacancies in their High Court than Gujarat. This was one of the major reasons for the backlog that the night courts were unable to reduce significantly. The Gujarat High Court had 139,467 pending cases in 2005, and 115,394 two years later.[18]

Judges were not the only ones missing from the courts: the judiciary was also understaffed as far as clerks were concerned. Ahmedabad consumer courts are a case in point: of the 295 clerical positions sanctioned, 83 were still vacant in 2013. Besides, out of the 186 employees, 170 were on contract, most of them 'retired people who [were] working for 60 per cent of their last withdrawn salary'.[19]

In the mid-2000s Bibek Debroy and Laveesh Bhandari awarded a poor grade to Gujarat as far as 'legal structure and property rights' were concerned. In 2005, Gujarat came 14 out of 20 states in that regard. In 2007 it was still number 9, behind Chhattisgarh.[20] No review of that kind took place subsequently.

Who's Afraid of the Lokayukta?

Not only was the judiciary weak, but Gujarat did not benefit from the services of a Lokayukta (ombudsman), although, by the end of Modi's last term as chief minister, the BJP was arguing that Lokayuktas at the state level and a Lokpal at the national level were badly needed for fighting corruption and the criminalisation of politics. In fact, the institution of the Lokayukta had been set up in many states to address grievances about the integrity and efficiency of the government or the bureaucracy. Politicians were naturally apprehensive of the role of Lokayuktas, who could not be dismissed or transferred by the government, and could only be removed by an impeachment motion passed by the state assembly. In spite of his vocal support for the creation of a Lokpal in Delhi, the BJP government in Gujarat for years abstained from appointing one in his own state.

In 2010–11, the social activist Anna Hazare became the instigator and symbol of a quest for moral rigour and transparency in public office. Modi immediately backed his arguments and supported Hazare's demand for the creation of a Lokpal, an ombudsman who would be empowered to investigate irregularities committed by bureaucrats and politicians, including the prime minister. In an open letter to Hazare, the chief minister of Gujarat wrote:

> Respected Annaji, my respect for you is decades old. Before I entered politics, I was full time RSS pracharak. At those times, national leaders of the RSS who came to attend our meetings invariably discussed your rural development activities so that it could be emulated. It has tremendous impact on me. In the past, I also had the good fortune of meeting you.
>
> I and my state of Gujarat are indebted to you for the courage and conviction you showed in saying good words for me and my state. In this show of courage, you exhibited commitment to truth and a soldier-like conviction. And because of this, your opinion has been universally accepted.
>
> I request you to also bless me that your praise shall not make me complacent and commit mistakes.
>
> Your blessings have given me the strength to do what is right and it is good. At the same time, my responsibility has also gone

> high. Because of your statement, crores [millions] of youth would be having great expectations and therefore even a small mistake on my part will disappoint them. Therefore, I have to remain vigilant and seek your blessings for the same.[21]

Such a discourse should have found expression in the promotion of the Lokayukta in Gujarat, which, like the Lokpal demanded by Anna Hazare at the national level, was designed to fight corruption among politicians and civil servants through state-level investigations. The Gujarat Lokayukta Act had introduced this new institution in 1986. According to the Act, the Lokayukta was to be appointed by the governor after consultation with the chief justice of the Gujarat High Court.[22]

The third Lokayukta of Gujarat, S.M. Soni, resigned in 2003. Three years later, in 2006, the chief justice of the Gujarat High Court approved the candidature of Justice K.R. Vyas, whose name had been suggested by the government of Gujarat. However, the Congress-appointed governor of Gujarat, Naval Kishore Sharma, did not respond for many months, and Justice Vyas was meanwhile appointed chairman of the Maharashtra Human Rights Commission. The post of Lokayukta continued to remain vacant.

In November 2009, the new governor, Mrs Kamla Beniwal, asked the chief justice to put together a selection panel to appoint the next Lokayukta. The Gujarat government then went to court, claiming that the governor could not take the initiative in this matter but could only follow the recommendations of the Council of Ministers. The court agreed and Narendra Modi then asked the chief justice to suggest four names in February 2010, out of which the Council of Ministers supported that of Justice J.R. Vora.[23] The attorney general objected that only one name should have been recommended, something the government of Gujarat rejected but the Supreme Court upheld. Then, Mrs Beniwal asked the chief justice who was the best candidate between Justice R.P. Dholakia, the president of the Gujarat

Consumer Disputes Redressal Commission, and Justice J.R. Vora. The chief justice, S.J. Mukhopadhyay, opted for the former, but the governor, instead of appointing him, asked Mukhopadhyay to recommend one name only.[24] Mukhopadhyay then recommended the name of the retired Justice S.D. Dave on 31 December 2010. The governor submitted his name to the government of Gujarat, which rejected it and suggested Justice Vora instead. The chief justice replied that the man was not available anymore, since he had been appointed director of the Gujarat State Judicial Academy. Then Justice Dave said that he was not interested in the position. Following this, Mukhopadhyay suggested the retired Justice R.A. Mehta and the governor asked the chief minister to appoint him. However, Modi objected that Justice Mehta, who had displayed an antagonistic attitude towards the government, was too old (he was 75). The chief justice responded in August 2011 that he had investigated the case personally and considered that Justice Mehta had 'a high reputation, great integrity and his neutrality is well acclaimed, besides the fact that he has not shown any aspiration to any government post whether central or state'.[25] The state government filed a writ petition in the High Court, challenging Justice Mehta's appointment. In October 2011, a two-member bench delivered a judgment with differing views. The matter went to a third judge, Justice V.M. Sahai, who declared that the 'pranks of the Chief Minister demonstrate destruction of our democracy and the questionable conduct of stonewalling the appointment of Justice Mehta as Lokayukta threatened the rule of law'.[26] For Sahai, 'open resistance of the council of ministers headed by the chief minister in not accepting the primacy of the opinion of the chief justice of the Gujarat high court in the matter of appointment of Lokayukta has created a crisis situation'.[27] The Gujarat government then applied to the Supreme Court.

Given the absence of a Lokayukta, the Gujarat government appointed an ad hoc commission to probe 15 allegations of corruption that the Congress had raised, regarding deals that had been offered to companies investing in Gujarat, including Tata, the Adani Group and Essar. What was at stake in many of these cases was the price of the land that had been sold to the companies. But the one-man commission headed by former Justice M.B. Shah, which was appointed in June 2012, concluded in October of the same year that no irregularity had occurred.[28]

Six months later, in early 2013, the Supreme Court upheld the appointment of Justice Mehta as Lokayukta and dismissed the review petition filed by the Gujarat government. In response, in April 2013, the Gujarat Assembly passed a new Gujarat Lokayukta Aayog Bill,[29] whose aim was to dilute the role of the governor and the chief justice in the appointment procedure of the Lokayukta. According to this law, the Lokayukta would be selected by a panel headed by the chief minister and comprising a minister chosen by the chief minister, the Speaker of the state Assembly (also from the ruling party or at least the majority), the leader of the opposition, a High Court judge appointed by the chief justice of the High Court, and the state vigilance commissioner.[30]

Three months later, Justice Mehta announced that he had turned down the office of Gujarat Lokayukta after new criticisms emanating from the BJP: 'How can I take up the responsibility and become the Lokayukta when my objectivity and credibility are not accepted by the government and by the public functionaries whose conduct the Lokayukta may have to investigate?'[31]

In September 2013 Governor Beniwal returned the Lokayukta Aayog Bill for review to the government of Gujarat. At that time, the state had established another record: no other Indian state having passed a Lokayukta Act had failed to appoint someone to the post within ten years. Finally, in November 2013, because Narendra Modi (as BJP candidate for the prime ministership) could no longer afford to be at the helm of one of the few states without a Lokayukta, the government of Gujarat recommended to Governor Beniwal the appointment of a retired justice of the Gujarat High Court, D.P. Buch, as Lokayukta of the state. His name had apparently been proposed by the chief justice, Bhaskar Bhattacharya, allegedly on the suggestion of Shankarsinh Vaghela, the Congress leader of the opposition.[32] Kamla Beniwal completed the appointment process in December 2013, and it was confirmed on 11 December 2013 that Justice Buch would take the oath as the new Lokayukta of Gujarat.[33]

This delayed appointment was all the more problematic as most of the major allegations of corruption against the Gujarat government pertained to acts that were already more than five years old—whereas the law allowed the Lokayukta to probe cases arising from only the previous five years.[34]

CORRUPTION AND CIVIL INSECURITY

The failure of the Modi government to pay more attention than its predecessors to the police, the judiciary and the Lokayukta dovetailed with the persistence of corruption and the criminalisation of politics in Gujarat, a trend against which whistleblowers tried to fight, at great cost to themselves.

The Diversification of Criminal Activities

By the end of Modi's first five-year term, in 2007, the citizens of Gujarat were rather dissatisfied with the state government's performance in the domain of law and order. An Indian Express–CNN-IBN–CSDS survey showed that for 36 per cent of respondents, corruption had increased in the state, whereas only 14 per cent considered that it was under control or had decreased.[35] One year later, similar results emerged when Transparency International surveyed the prevalence of corruption in Indian states by interviewing more than 22,700 Below Poverty Line households. The organisation categorised Jammu and Kashmir,

Bihar, Madhya Pradesh and Uttar Pradesh in the 'alarmingly corrupt' category, Karnataka, Rajasthan and Tamil Nadu as 'very highly corrupt', Chhattisgarh, Delhi, Gujarat, Jharkhand, Kerala and Orissa as 'highly corrupt', and Andhra Pradesh, Haryana, Himachal Pradesh, Maharashtra and Punjab as 'moderately corrupt'. In Gujarat, while 25 per cent of urban interviewees and 29 per cent of their rural counterparts said that their knowledge of corruption was more the product of hearsay than actual fact, 75 per cent and 69 per cent of respondents respectively from both parts of the state answered that it was a reality of which they had first-hand experience.[36] About 70 per cent of interviewees considered that it had increased or remained the same over the previous twelve months (the rest thought it had decreased).[37] The assessments of the grievance redressal mechanisms were highly polarised. On the one hand, interviewees considered they had improved in the education, electricity, public distribution system and water supply sectors. On the other hand, they found that the situation had deteriorated in the police, housing, land records and registration sectors.[38] Interestingly, 65 per cent of them attributed corruption to government officers and only 18 per cent to politicians,[39] which suggests that the Anti-Corruption Bureau, which had taken action against several civil servants,[40] remained largely ineffective.

Criminality did not significantly decline in the first decade of Modi rule either.[41] In fact, crime was as pervasive in Gujarat as in many other states of a similar size (see Table 4.5).[42] A comparison of Gujarat and 27 other states of India, and more especially of the ratio of crime to population, shows that it was not performing better than most other Indian states as far as fighting crime was concerned. With 0.0019 cognisable crimes per head every year on average between 2006 and 2010, Gujarat occupied 12th place, on a par with Chhattisgarh and Himachal Pradesh (see Tables 4.3, 4.4 and 4.5).

The Gujarati media highlighted some of the most dramatic manifestations of the resilience of crime in the state. The issues of rape and 'missing persons'—including children[43]—are worth mentioning here.[44] In 2005, 236 people disappeared in Ahmedabad alone; in 2006, there were 249; and in 2007, 642, most probably victims of kidnapping for extortion or human trafficking.[45] In this context, many Gujarati entrepreneurs have armed themselves in self-protection.[46]

The largest city of Gujarat, Ahmedabad, was especially affected by the rise of criminality.[47] In 2003, according to the National Crime Records Bureau (NCRB) report, the city had the lowest crime rate of the 35 Indian cities with more than a million inhabitants. By contrast, in 2012 the NCRB stated that the city ranked fourth with 21,347 registered criminal cases. Between 2003 and 2012, there was a 32 per cent increase in registered cases. The crime rate (complaints registered per 100,000 people) in Ahmedabad for 2012 was 336.1; higher than the national crime rate of 294.9.[48] Crimes against women were especially high. Among 53 cities, Ahmedabad ranked fourth in this category.[49]

This rising insecurity was also the result, paradoxically, of the violent ways and means of the Gujarat police. In its 2009 third annual report, the state Human Rights Commission declared that violations of human rights by the police had increased from 163 cases in 2006 to 602 in 2009, including 10 cases of 'torture and violence', 3 of 'abduction and kidnapping', 4 of death in police custody, 1 of rape, 1 of attempted murder, 8 of illegal arrests, 16 of unlawful detention, 58 of prolonged trial, and 266 of 'failure in taking lawful action'.[50]

Two years before, at a time when 'fake encounters' had recently become a public controversy, an editorial of the Ahmedabad edition of the *Times of India* explained that they were simply a 'confirmation of what has already been suspected: close links between the police on the one hand and politicians and criminals on the other'.[51] The journalist attributed this symbiosis to the fact that Gujarat had not reformed the police in the same way that other states had in order to insulate them from political influence, as was evident from 'the pernicious practice of transferring police officers on the whims of state governments'. But politicians had no incentive to reform the police if they benefited from joint corrupt practices—and they did: in spite of Modi's claim, the politicians of Gujarat were not cleaner than under his predecessors.

Cleaner Political Personnel?

The criminalisation of politics is an important factor to take into account when analysing the dysfunctional nature of policing in Gujarat, as elsewhere. All Indian parties and states have been affected by criminality, whose magnitude has increased in parallel with economic growth. Gujarat's political class is no exception. In the state Assembly elected in 2002, 34 of the 182 MLAs (28 from the BJP, out of 127; and 6 from the Congress, out of 46) had criminal records.[52] Things did not improve subsequently. According to the Association for Democratic Reforms (ADR), in 2007, 27 per cent of the newly elected MLAs were facing criminal cases: 25 of them belonged to the BJP and 19 to the Congress,[53] while 18 MLAs were even accused of 'heinous crimes' such as murder or rape. The ADR published reports showing that between 2007 and 2012 the average assets of Congress and BJP candidates who contested on both occasions and who filed the required affidavits (99 people in total) had jumped, respectively, from about 60 million rupees, 74 million rupees and 46 million rupees to 73 million rupees.[54] In another report focusing on criminal charges, the ADR revealed that out of 135 sitting BJP MLAs, 32 (28 per cent) had declared criminal cases in their affidavits, including 14 (12 per cent) for serious cases such as murder or attempted murder. On the Congress side, the figures were similar: of 61

MLAs, 20 (33 per cent) declared criminal cases, including 7 (12 per cent) with serious cases.[55]

Milan Vaishnav[56] arrived at similar conclusions on the basis of investigating MLAs' affidavits.[57] Of the 117 BJP MLAs elected in 2007, 25 (21.3 per cent), according to his research, were facing criminal charges.[58] For the Congress, the figures were, respectively, 23 out of 59 MLAs (39 per cent), including 11 for serious and 13 for heinous crimes.[59]

Besides Amit Shah and Maya Kodnani, to whom we will return later, other members of Modi's government were among the BJP MLAs facing criminal charges during his three terms. Babu Bokhiria, the Porbandar MLA and water resources minister, was sentenced to three years in jail in 2013 for illegal mining.[60] Parshottam Solanki, the Bhavnagar MLA who had been appointed fishery minister in 2007, was also accused of corruption for awarding contracts in 2009 for fishing in 58 reservoirs without following the legal procedures.[61] The fishing licences were granted at the expense of the state exchequer, which allegedly lost 4 billion rupees. In September 2012, the Gujarat High Court decided to allow the prosecution of Solanki, which Governor Beniwal had initiated, to follow its course.[62] In addition to ministers, the Gujarat BJP retained in its ranks an ex-MP, Babubhai Katara—a close associate of the VHP—who was arrested at Indira Gandhi International Airport in 2007 on charges of human trafficking while he was 'trying to send a teenaged boy and his mother out of the country to Canada using the passport of his wife and son'.[63] In 2013 Katara was appointed to the BJP National Council.[64] The BJP also welcomed several Congressmen with criminal records, including Vitthal Radadia, who had 32 criminal charges against him in 2007.[65]

To sum up, while Debroy and Bhandari ranked Gujarat first for its efforts against corruption in 2001–05 and second (behind Bihar) for the following five years,[66] these efforts did not bear fruit so far as the criminalisation of politicians was concerned.

And we will see in the next chapter that it made no significant difference to corruption in the corporate sector either. Nor has the number of crimes diminished significantly, compared at least with those in some other states of India. These results reflect the state of the police and the judiciary, as well as the political class. In this context, the defence of the rule of law came to depend even more than before on whistleblowers, including Right to Information activists, who were more exposed.

The Fate of RTI (Right to Information) Activists in Gujarat[67]

RTI activists are at significant risk of violence all over India. Between the mid-2000s and the mid-2010s, 69 of them were killed according to the National Campaign for People's Right to Information (NCPRI). In addition, the NCPRI presented in its database the cases of 133 RTI activists who were hurt and 170 others who were harassed or threatened.[68] According to this database, in 2017 the states with the largest number of casualties were not those of the Hindi belt known for law-and-order problems, but rich states, namely Maharashtra, Gujarat and Karnataka, with (respectively) 13, 13 and 7 murders, 31, 14 and 11 cases of assault, and 36, 14 and 12 cases of harassment. Gujarat had the highest ratio of RTI activists murdered per capita.

The stories of RTI activists who were murdered in Gujarat after 2010 provide a telling commentary on the state of law and order in the state. We will not recount all these cases but focus on those involving the state, the corporate sector and politicians.

Vishram Laxman Dodiya, who was killed on 11 February 2010, was a bookseller on the sidewalk in Surat, working in front of the local office of Torrent, a private energy company providing electricity to the city. Although he was not well educated (7th or 8th Standard pass), he was intellectually alert and read a lot. An RTI activist, he used to file applications for information for himself and others. He filed one about the price of electricity in Surat, one of the two cities of Gujarat—along with Ahmedabad—where electricity was then supplied by a private company. He did so because the Gujarat Energy Regulation Commission had allowed the private company in question, Torrent, to increase the price of electricity, even though electricity was already more expensive in Surat and Ahmedabad than in other cities of Gujarat. The RTI that Dodiya filed was intended to help him understand the reasons for the alleged loss that was affecting the company and that justified the rates hike. He filed another RTI after one of his neighbours obtained an electricity connection with false documents. Dodiya then went to the power distribution company 'to find out how'—in vain. He was shown the door, but then filed another RTI. A *Tehelka* investigative journalist adds: 'The company officials tried to persuade Dodiya to withdraw the RTI. He refused. His son, Girish, remembers that on 11 February 2010 the local police officer called saying that company officials wanted to meet him. Dodiya ate dinner and left. A few hours later, his mutilated body was found on a street near his home.'[69] The investigation into his murder was suspended after a year when his widow withdrew the case.[70]

The murder of Amit Jethwa, a famous RTI activist, took place against the backdrop of the illegal use of land by a private company. The case had a political dimension. Jethwa was an environmental activist who for years had raised the issue of illegal mining inside the Gir Lion Reserve in Junagadh.[71] He protested, in particular, against the extraction of limestone inside the sanctuary by two big companies associated with the BJP and the Congress, Ambuja and Gujarat Heavy Chemical respectively. In mid-2010, he filed a PIL in the Gujarat High Court accusing local BJP MP Dinu Solanki and several relatives of involvement in illegal mining in the Gir forest. On 20 July 2010, he was shot at by two men on a motorbike near the High Court. Gujarat Police exonerated

Solanki and arrested only his nephew. But on appeal the Gujarat High Court had the case transferred to the CBI, which arrested Dinu Solanki in November 2013.[72] Soon after, Solanki was out on bail and sought actively to influence witnesses.[73]

The police were even more deeply implicated in other cases, as is evident from that of Shailesh Patel. On 15 June 2015 Patel, a journalist reporting for a small newspaper in Surendranagar, filed an RTI with the district superintendent of police against a notorious bootlegger, Rafik Yunus, alias Haji: he wanted to know the details of the cases registered since 2011 against this man and the action taken by the police in response. According to Patel's sister, a police constable herself, a few hours later, on the same day, he was summoned by the local Crime Branch (LCB, next to the police station) and asked to withdraw the RTI. He refused and headed off. Later that evening, he was asked again to come to the Crime Branch. There, the two sons of the bootlegger—who had probably been informed about his RTI by the police themselves—started to beat him badly. When he shouted, they stuffed a rag in his mouth and he died of suffocation. A local shopkeeper commented on this affair in the following terms: 'Several complaints have been filed so far, and even women took out rallies against bootlegging. But when police have strong nexus with bootleggers, how can they take action against them? We feel here LCB and police both are in partnership with illegal liquor distilleries owners.'[74]

Some women have also become RTI activists and had to deal with assaults and harassment. Manisha Goswami fought first against the pollution affecting Vapi, a city in Valsad district where factories making chemical products had rendered the groundwater unfit for drinking and killed the rivers. In 2014 Manisha filed an RTI with the local collector's office in order to hasten the formation of the Valsad District Level Coastal Committee, which was supposed to protect the coastal environment.[75] But it seems that she was assaulted on account of another RTI that she filed with the local municipality about illegal constructions, mentioning three shopping complexes in the town. She was attacked while taking her 12-year-old daughter to school on her scooter. Although injured, she continued to fight.

Not only did the state fail to protect RTI activists but, in some cases, it was responsible for their ongoing harassment and even their death. This was largely due to the nexus linking politicians, mafias and even businessmen. Instead of implementing the law, the police maximised their 'monopoly of legitimate violence' (to paraphrase Max Weber) by dealing directly with local mafias or bargaining with political rulers as well as businessmen.

Thus, the failure of the Gujarat government to invest in the rule of law and to protect whistleblowers led inevitably to a relatively high level of corruption and crime, not only in society at large, but among the political class in particular. In other words, Modi's Gujarat was not very different from what the state used to be under his predecessors, or from other states of the same size.

THE MAKING OF A DEEPER STATE

The notion of a 'deep state'—which has been mostly used, in South Asia, about Pakistan—refers to a political system where power is ultimately exerted in a secret manner by security forces in conjunction with (or without) politicians. Lately, Josy Joseph has applied this category to contemporary India in that sense. Unsurprisingly, he devotes one full chapter to the 'Gujarat model'.[76] But in the Gujarat of this time, state authority did not only rely on a 'deep state'; it also ruled over people through the network of the Sangh Parivar and, more specifically, through vigilante groups which had penetrated and permeated society in such a way as to fashion a 'deeper state'.

A 'Big Brother-like State'

Any deep state is a surveillance state—and Gujarat tended to become such a one in the early 2000s. The Gujarat government revealed its intention to resort to phone tapping soon after coming into power in 2001 and then allegedly resorted to the technique despite it being illegal to do so. In December 2001, three months after he was appointed chief minister, the Gujarat cabinet approved the draft of the Gujarat Control of Organised Crime (GujCOC) Ordinance and sent it for approval to the Government of India. The latter approved it—after some minor amendments in 2002—but asked the state government to have it passed as a law in March 2003. It did so and in April sent the bill to the Ministry of Home Affairs for Presidential assent. Then, interestingly, the BJP-led government of A.B. Vajpayee returned the bill to the Gujarat Assembly and asked the Modi government to remove two sections: the one which allowed phone tapping (in the original GujCOC bill, district collectors and police were permitted to intercept and record phone calls) and held that intercepted telephone conversations could be considered legitimate evidence; and the section according to which a confession made before a police officer could also be considered as evidence. The original bill was sent again to Pratibha Patil in 2008[77] and to Pranab Mukherjee in 2015, but they returned it too. In 2019, President Kovind finally gave his assent.[78]

Even though this practice had not been legalised, the Gujarat Government asked Intelligence Bureau officers to tap phones of political opponents soon after taking over power in Gujarat. On 16 April 2002, he instructed R.B. Sreekumar, the additional director general of police in charge of intelligence, 'to start tapping the telephone of Shri Shankarsinh Vaghela [who had just become the head of the Gujarat state Congress]'. This demand was reiterated on 26 July 2002, when, incidentally, the chief minister also asked Sreekumar 'to prepare Assembly Constituency Profile of [the] 182 ACs [Assembly constituencies]'.[79]

When Modi was chief minister, his government was accused of having tapped the phones of other senior politicians, including Shaktisinh Gohil and Haren Pandya.[80] Most of the time, this illegal surveillance was archived on the instruction of Modi's principal secretary, P.K. Mishra. The total budget for spying operations was no less than 200 million rupees in 2008, according to former chief minister Suresh Mehta, who protested against what he regarded as a Big Brother-like state.[81] In 2013, Gujarat Police 'obtained nearly 90,000 telephone-call data records (CDRs) of people and entities in three months', something India's intelligence agencies found intriguing.[82]

As is often the case in such political systems, politicians were not the only target. In 2013, the minister of state for home, Amit Shah, was 'accused of misusing his powers and police machinery for illegal surveillance of a young woman in August 2009 "at the behest of his saheb".'[83] These accusations resulted from the publication of a statement, before the CBI, of Gujarat IPS officer G.L. Singhal, who was an accused in the Ishrat Jahan fake encounter case; he had handed over to the investigating agency 267 recorded telephonic conversations that revealed 'how three key wings of the Gujarat Police—the State Intelligence Bureau, also known as CID Intelligence, the Crime Branch and the Anti-Terrorist Squad—misused their powers to stalk an unmarried young woman from Bangalore, who had her parents staying in Gujarat'.[84] Singhal declared:

> In the latter half of 2009, when I was posted as SP (Operations) in the Anti-Terrorist Squad (ATS) at Ahmedabad, Shri Amit Shah had directed me several times to watch the movements of Shri Pradeep Sharma,[85] who was then posted as Municipal Commissioner, Bhavnagar. He had also asked me to put a watch on a young woman named Madhuri [not her real name]. I had deputed some men of the Crime Branch (as ATS was short of subordinate staff) to follow her, as directed by Shri Amit Shah.[86]

Narendra Modi had allegedly met this woman in 2005 during the inauguration of a public recreation park that she designed. They communicated subsequently by email and text messages and, according to the media, 'All along, Madhuri [name changed], who looked upon Pradeep Sharma as a guide and mentor whom her family trusted, kept him in the loop, even showing him bits of the text messages she had exchanged with Modi.'[87]

The transcripts of the recorded conversations between Singhal and Shah[88] show that Madhuri was followed by policemen everywhere she went (while shopping, at the hospital where she visited her mother, on a plane) and that her phone, as well as the phones of relatives and of Sharma, were tapped. These transcripts also show that Amit Shah was kept informed and monitored this spying operation. When she met a boy at an Ahmedabad ice-cream parlour, he told Singhal: 'I want him in jail for as many days as Vanzara has been jailed for [...] No matter how big the person, put him in jail.'[89]

Pradeep Sharma, who had been praised by Modi as 'one of the state's brightest collectors' because of the way he contributed to the rebuilding of Bhuj after the 2001 earthquake, fell from favour at exactly the same time: 'in January 2010, Shah's police arrested Pradeep Sharma on charges of criminal conspiracy and breach of trust. There was no notice, no summons.'[90] Not only had an IAS officer been kept under surveillance on the mere oral order of the minister of state for home, but he was sent to jail and accused of corruption in land deals which had allegedly taken place between 2003 and 2007. He was granted bail by the High Court in 2018.[91] This 'snoopgate' phenomenon, to use the phrase coined by the media, raised a question that Prashant Bhushan addressed immediately: 'whether there is any rule of law in the state or whether the administration is run on the whims and fancies of one individual'.[92]

Those who resort to surveillance tend to cultivate secrecy to hide their illicit modus operandi. Singhal's statement before the

CBI is very telling in this respect. He revealed, for instance, that 'expensive encrypted cell phones were purchased and distributed to select government officials like G.C. Murmu (Secretary to Chief Minister), P.P. Pandey (suspended ADG [additional director general] of Gujarat Police and now prime accused in the Ishrat Jahan encounter case), A.K. Sharma (JCP [joint commissioner of police], Ahmedabad city) and Singhal himself, who could then discuss over these secured phone lines the tactics of subverting the investigations into encounter killings'.[93]

This list identifies only a small number of the core group of Gujarat's deep state: some of its members occupy senior positions today in New Delhi, some twenty years later. But the Gujarat of this time was more than a deep state, because the government and the security apparatus operated in synergy with vigilante groups.

The Bajrang Dal, the State and Cultural Policing

Gilles Favarel-Garrigues and Laurent Gayer define vigilantism as

> a voluntary and apparently autonomous practice, minimally routinized, involving the use of force to right wrongs or enforce norms (both legal and moral precepts), in the name of a community of reference that is the primary audience of the self-styled law enforcers. Vigilante activity has a temporality of its own: it is not eruptive, as in some cases of lynching, or stable over the long term, unlike the regular police. Having various sociological profiles, but usually linked to conservative or reactionary circles, vigilantes have no qualms about breaking the law to maintain the order in the name of which they patrol, hunt and punish their prey.[94]

Vigilantes act as 'outlaw law enforcers' (to borrow another formula from Favarel-Garrigues and Gayer),[95] whether in self-defence groups or ideological militias, setting up people's courts or handing their victims over to the police. Although this repertoire covers a variety of modi operandi, two types stand out: for one, vigilantes attack individuals or groups whose customs are perceived as deviant or who arouse fear among the local majority;[96] second, these same groups (and others) go after members of their own community on the ground that they are betraying the community and its traditions (be they religious, cultural, social or other). In both cases, the method used involves a degree of physical or psychological violence.

While the Gujarat police engaged in forms of communalisation, communal organisations have likewise specialised in cultural policing and worked in tandem with the police. This convergence, which resulted in a certain privatisation and ideologisation of the rule of law, was partly due to the activities of the Bajrang Dal, a component of the Sangh Parivar which was allowed by the Modi government to discipline society, on behalf of Hindu orthodoxy and orthopraxy. In Gujarat, as elsewhere,[97] the Bajrang Dal's primary targets were, firstly, artists who, it was believed, were disrespectful of Hindu culture. Its growing influence predated the rise to power of Modi. In 1996, Bajrang Dalis attacked the Herwitz gallery of the famous painter Maqbool Fida Husain in Ahmedabad.[98] They destroyed canvases and wall hangings worth 15 million rupees representing the Buddha, Hanuman and Ganesh. But the real object of their fury was something else: a canvas dating from 1976 that depicted the goddess Saraswati far too scantily clad for their tastes.[99] The Bajrang Dal became even more active under the Modi government, as is evident from the role of some of its cadres (including Babu Bajrangi) in the 2002 violence.

Later, the Bajrang Dal persuaded some witnesses to the violence not to file complaints. A few of the latter defied the intimidation as long as the authorities guaranteed them police protection,[100] but most of them abandoned the idea. Recourse to intimidation was not limited to the victims of 2002. In 2006, Babu Bajrangi, the most famous Bajrang Dal leader of Gujarat—who had originally created his own organisation, Navchetan[101]—informed theatre owners throughout Gujarat that he opposed the screening of a film entitled *Parzania* that portrayed the riots of 2002 through the true story of a Parsi family from Gulberg Society whose child had been missing ever since. All the cinemas caved in to the pressure, and the film was not screened in the very state that served as its backdrop. N.K. Acharya, a retired civil servant from Mehsana district, lodged a complaint with the courts and became a victim of intimidation after being kidnapped and held hostage for two weeks in March 2007.[102]

Babu Bajrangi extended his 'parallel government'[103]—to borrow N.K. Acharya's phrase—to moral issues. In the mid-2000s, Bajrangi had started showing up on the campus of Gujarat University in Ahmedabad to deal with young Muslims who were looking at female Hindu students too intently for his taste. He then launched a campaign to 'rescue' Hindu girls who had married a Muslim or a man of a different caste.[104] One of his pamphlets explained that love marriages harmed Hindu traditions, and that rescuing a Hindu girl was equal to saving 100 cows.[105] In the space of a few months, Hindu girls were thus 'rescued', persuaded to abort when they were pregnant, and remarried to a man of their caste. Some parents whose daughters had 'married beneath their station' without their approval and run away, usually to Mumbai, used Babu Bajrangi's services to find them and return them home. Some husbands responded by filing criminal cases with the tribunals of Gujarat and Maharashtra—to no avail since the police refrained from carrying out an inquiry into Bajrangi's activities.[106] Finally the Supreme Court initiated an inquiry that prompted the Bajrang Dal to expel him from its ranks in February 2007.[107]

Besides the Supreme Court, private associations and NGOs came to the aid of the Bajrang Dal's victims. In April 2007, members of the NGO ANHAD helped Mausami Shah to lodge a complaint. She had been kidnapped by Bajrangi's shock troops, brought home and forced to resume living with her husband, a Hindu, whom she had left for a Muslim. A police inspector and Bajrangi received her at the Ellisbridge police station to advise her to return to her marital home.[108]

Even after Bajrangi was expelled from the Bajrang Dal, the organisation continued to exert some degree of cultural policing, as is evident from the way Hindu artists became the targets of its wrath for their 'immoral' treatment of Hindu deities. On 29 January 2004, a gang of militants attacked the Garden Art Gallery in Surat and destroyed eight canvases by M.F. Husain, K.H. Ara, N.S. Bendre and Chittrovanu Mazumdar. The instigators of this act of destruction gave no justification for their deed: such gratuitous violence was aimed at art considered deviant by its very nature.[109] These activities continued after Bajrangi was expelled from Bajrang Dal.

In May 2007, Hindu nationalists burst into the Fine Arts Department at Maharaja Sayajirao University (MSU) in Vadodara (which has one of the most renowned art departments in India) where the best student artworks of the year were being exhibited. A master's student, Chandra Mohan, had made a painting that one Niraj Jain, who had held various positions in the Bajrang Dal, the VHP, the BJP and the ABVP, found offensive because of the way it showed Hindu gods and goddesses. He called the police, who arrested Mohan immediately,[110] accusing him of painting obscene pictures of religious subjects.[111] The dean of the faculty was asked to shut down the exhibition, which he refused to do. The university president, Manoj Soni, whom Narendra Modi had just appointed as vice chancellor of the university, suspended him and the show was cancelled.[112]

Such developments were made possible not only by the political protection the Bajrang Dal received from the government, but also because the boundary between the police and the Bajrang Dal had become extremely blurred, to the point of enabling Bajrang Dalis to join the police and vice versa. For instance, the paramilitary Home Guards, a force consisting of civilians used by the authorities to maintain order at the local level, enrolled in their ranks RSS and Bajrang Dal members. A high-ranking police officer admitted that the district commanders of the Home Guards began to change as soon as the BJP came to power in Gujarat.[113] When the army intervened in Gujarat to restore peace in 2002, Lt General Zameer Uddin Shah observed that 'most of the 25 Home Guard Commandants were primary members of right wing organisations'.[114]

The role of the Bajrang Dal in cultural policing contributed to the making of a parallel state, one that was protected and abetted by some police officers. In his portrait of a Bajrang Dali from Ahmedabad—Kunal—Moyukh Chatterjee has shown how both vigilantes and policemen worked together. From a fairly high-caste group—Kunal was a Rajput—but practically illiterate, this young man lived in a Dalit neighborhood whose inhabitants he despised. Having no stable job, he and the group of Bajrang Dalis he led lived from hand to mouth. To compensate for his lack of status, he posted pictures of himself on Facebook in warrior-like poses, clutching a trishul (Shiva's trident). Kunal described himself as a 'fanatic' (*kattar*), because he was a 'tough guy'. He proved this during the 2002 riots when he helped burn down a mosque (with police complicity) and continued to flex his muscles by forcibly preventing Muslims from dating young Hindu women. This is how Moyukh Chatterjee analysed his actions: 'In Ahmedabad—where everyone has finer clothes, smarter phones, and better paying jobs—Kunal and his boys are proud of saving Hinduism from effete Hindus and treacherous Muslims.'[115] For those with no social capital, muscular devotion to the cause of the majority religion was their only claim to fame.

This modus operandi was a contributory factor in the formation of a deeper state, a state in which the police and vigilante groups worked in unison to enforce not the law but the societal norms in which Hindu nationalists believed. These norms were rooted in the upper-caste ethos and, therefore, found expression not only in the promotion of Hindu culture as reinterpreted by the

Hindutva ideologues, but also in the defence of Brahminical values. This state was deeper than the bureaucratic apparatus to which the police belonged not only because these norms were more demanding in terms of social hierarchy (between Hindus and Muslims as well as between castes), but also because those who were in charge of enforcing them formed a denser network: besides the police forces, vigilantes criss-crossed society at the grassroots level.

A DE FACTO HINDU RASHTRA

The specific kind of saffronisation we see of the Gujarat institutions in the wake of the 2002 riots and the making of a new, 'deeper' state at the expense of the rule of law are like two sides of the same coin.

In the Gujarat of this time, the rule of law was, first of all, the victim of the government's lack of will to reform and strengthen the police and the judiciary, which resulted in a persistently high level of criminality and corruption. But this situation was also a consequence of the fact that the ruling party was so tainted that it had a vested interest in weakening the police and the judiciary. While RTI activists were among the last whistleblowers, they were also among the first casualties of corruption and the criminalisation of politics. These developments were not particularly new, nor exceptional compared with other Indian states. What was new was the kind of state that the BJP started to create in Gujarat—a state that was 'deeper' than its predecessor because it relied not only on forms of surveillance but also on Hindu vigilante groups which imposed a de facto Hindu Rashtra (state or nation) on the ground.

This unique combination foreshadowed two major features of post-2014 India. On the one hand, mechanisms of surveillance gained momentum in Delhi, especially after Amit Shah became home minister in 2019. That the central government was using surveillance techniques rather massively surfaced during the 'Pegasus affair', named after a spyware developed by NSO, an Israeli company whose customers can only be governments agencies.[116] Among the many Indian personalities whose phones were tapped were politicians like Rahul Gandhi, civil servants like Ashok Lavasa (former member of the Election Commission) and Alok Verma (former head of the CBI), and journalists like Siddharth Varadarajan, co-founder of *The Wire*.[117]

A similar technique was used against a group of intellectuals, lawyers, trade unionists, human rights activists and a Christian priest, Father Stan Swamy (who died in jail), who were accused of conspiracy aimed at overthrowing the government and assassinating the prime minister on the basis of letters recovered from the computers of two of those arrested. Amnesty Tech, the Amnesty International's digital security team, discovered subsequently that one of these computers contained malware allowing remote access, and alleged that the letters could have been planted.[118]

The Government of India also initiated a more systematic surveillance system by resorting increasingly to facial recognition. After the 2020 Delhi riots, the home minister declared that 'police ha[d] identified 1,100 people through the facial recognition technology. Nearly 300 people came from Uttar Pradesh. It was a planned conspiracy.'[119] How could the police know? It seems that 'the footage procured from CCTV, media persons and the public was matched with photographs stored in the database of Election Commission and e-Vahan, a pan-India database of vehicle registration maintained by Ministry of Road Transport and Highways.'[120] Gautam Bhatia points out that 'such 'dragnet' screening is a blatant violation of privacy rights, as it essentially treats every individual like a potential suspect, subject to an endless continuing investigation'.[121] This technique has been more and more systematically used by the government, while the Indian parliament has yet to enact a personal data protection law.[122]

On the other hand, after 2014 the government came to rely on the vigilante groups of the Sangh Parivar for disciplining society. As in Gujarat, these groups—including the Bajrang Dal—worked in tandem with the police. Their first targets were Muslims, who were at the receiving end of recurring campaigns against 'love jihad' (when young Muslim men were supposed to seduce Hindu girls in order to marry them and convert them to Islam), or for promoting reconversion to Hinduism or 'homecoming' (*ghar vapsi*), or to defend bovines (including sacred cows) that Muslim farmers were suspected of taking to slaughterhouses. Vigilante groups like the Bajrang Dal or the Gau Raksha Dal (Cow Protection Movement) watched everybody at the grassroots level: they not only kept an eye on Muslims, but also made sure that Hindu girls did not date Muslim men or that Hindus did not sell their dwellings to Muslims (who were suspected of indulging in 'land jihad' in order to infiltrate mixed neighbourhoods). Vigilantes not only sought to defend Hinduism, but to enforce the Brahminical ethos, as is evident from their promotion of vegetarianism. This cultural policing developed in conjunction with the state: not only were laws passed to 'ban beef' and make inter-religious marriages very difficult, but on the ground policemen and vigilantes often patrolled together, the latter being deeply entrenched in the social fabric which the Sangh Parivar has permeated over the course of a hundred years.

The deeper state that resulted from this alchemy created a de facto Hindu Rashtra,[123] whose prototype was invented in Gujarat. In addition to the mechanisms of communal polarisation that we have analysed in the first part of the book, Gujarat was thus a blueprint for the rest of the nation in respect of the subversion of the rule of law.

However, in our study of the transformation of the rule of law in the Gujarat of that time, there was one missing category of player: businessmen. Given their role in Gujarati society, they have inevitably contributed to the level of corruption in the state. In 2010, the chief justice of the Gujarat High Court, S.J. Mukhopadhyay, felt 'concerned about the future of Gujarat judiciary, where money [had] become the main source and where you [could] buy anybody with the power of money'.[124] Money, indeed, played an increasingly important part in society and the state.[125] Anna Hazare himself, when he visited the state in 2011, lamented that there was 'nothing but scams in Gujarat'.[126]

In Gujarat, the dominant role of businessmen has traditionally existed alongside 'grand corruption',[127] involving large economic transactions. For *Business India*, Gujarat has been renowned for the corruption associated with an economically developed society: 'If Gujarat is flooded with investment it is partly due to a corrupt but well-organized regime. Industrialists know that in Gujarat everything has a price. Land, water and power concessions, not to mention environmental clearances are hassle free if one has the right political connections. Similarly, files move fast and lengthy duplicate procedures are simply non-existent if one knows which palms to grease.'[128]

According to Jennifer Bussell, nothing changed when the BJP came to power. In 2005, Gujarat was second only to Delhi in terms of the existence of 'grand corruption', whereas it did better than all other states (except Himachal Pradesh and Kerala) in terms of 'petty corruption'.[129] For Bussell this state of affairs can be explained by the eagerness of Gujarati politicians not only to attract big investors, but also to outsource public services, in the name of reform, to private firms. This 'company model', as Bussell explains,

> provides three important potential benefits to politicians and bureaucrats [...] First there may be only one or two companies signing contracts, limiting the number of occasions in which state officials might be caught receiving a bribe. Second, the scale of the partner and the contracts [...] implies that state

> actors may be able to acquire a much larger single payment from the transaction [...] Finally, because this model deals with high-profile contracts, it is also more likely to involve state leadership directly, thereby limiting the number of hands through which bribes will have to pass before reaching the highest political levels and maximizing the rents for top officials.[130]

Here again, Modi inherited a time-tested legacy and refined it so extensively that, in the end, the difference with the past was not one of degree, but of kind. Modi, indeed, reshaped the political economy of Gujarat to a large extent, creating a new model of crony capitalism as well as greater inequalities.

PART THREE

DEVELOPMENT OR GROWTH?

Gujarat has traditionally been trade-oriented and, more recently, a place where industry has flourished under the aegis of entrepreneurial communities whose remarkable influence has already been referred to. After Independence, it was one of the states where the businessmen's sense of entrepreneurship resisted most effectively the Nehruvian system. Aseema Sinha has shown how this business community circumvented some of the adverse consequences of the state-owned economy in the 1950s and 1960s.[1] Under the Licence Raj, Gujarat promptly allocated the quota permits decided by the Planning Commission to the private sector and then played a pioneering role in the 1970s when it created an 'investment promotion cell' which fostered a hybrid form of state capitalism. This achievement resulted as much from the resilience of its capitalists as from the mindset of the bureaucrats who were immersed in a business-oriented milieu.

The state was so business-friendly that Sinha has described its economic model as one of 'bureaucratic-liberalism'. Congress chief ministers trained under Indira Gandhi like Madhavsinh Solanki had no inhibition in following this 'ism' even before the much-vaunted liberalisation of 1991. In the mid-1980s he claimed that he would turn his state into a 'mini-Japan'. At that time, Gujarat had become the second most industrialised state in India, as 'its government, in cooperation with the private sector, launched many projects in power development, electronics, fertilizers and many other industries'.[2] Then, in the 1990s, Gujarat liberalised its economy more quickly than most other states in India.[3] This was partly an unintended consequence of a deep fiscal crisis (the fiscal deficit represented 7.37 per cent of the state's net domestic product in 1990–91). To cope with this crisis, Gujarat turned to the Asian Development Bank, which in 1994 'approved a US$250 million loan for public sector restructuring and fiscal reform in Gujarat, with a two-year implementation window'.[4] The government of Gujarat used this money to assist the downsizing of loss-making PSUs (public sector undertakings).[5] Similarly, in the mid-1990s, Gujarat evolved a ports policy by which the government would give 'complete control of two ports to the private sector'.[6] The chief minister who presided over this policy was a Congressman, Chimanbhai Patel. The total traffic was 2 million tons at the time. Keshubhai Patel continued with the same policy and, by 2000, it had reached 71 million tons.

Narendra Modi promoted infrastructure too, including ports and roads, but he shifted from the traditional Gujarati policy of supporting entrepreneurship by protecting mega projects handled by big companies. The state, therefore, became the crucible of a new form of crony capitalism which generated growth but not development. Inequalities increased, not only between the urban and rural parts of the state, but also between social classes, as good jobs remained few.

5

A NEW BRAND OF CRONY CAPITALISM

> The industry friendly, hassle free, single door clearance policy of the [Gujarat] government has ensured that the investment flow continues in the state.
>
> Sanjay Gupta, CEO of the Adani Group, 2003

In 2001, when Narendra Modi became chief minister, Gujarat accounted for about 15 per cent of India's exports. Still, the economy was not doing well in the early 2000s, even before the 2001 earthquake, which damaged it further. The annual growth rate had dropped from 12 per cent in 1991–95 to 3 per cent in 1996–2000.[1] Gujarat's financial situation was also on the slide, the revenue deficit jumping from 28.63 billion rupees in 1998–99 to more than 80 billion rupees in 2000–01.[2] As a result, in December 2001 Modi announced a ten-point plan to relaunch the economy.[3]

A few months later, not only did the events of 2002 affect the economy of Gujarat because of the loss of life and property, but it also paralysed industry and commerce for weeks.[4] Prime Minister Vajpayee, during his visit to Gujarat in early April 2002, conceded in the course of a press conference that 'Gujarat has suffered "serious" economic losses due to the recent riots in the state'.[5] He regretted that 'a large number of investors, including foreign investors, were willing to invest heavily in the state but for the trouble'.[6]

The Gujarat Chamber of Commerce and Industry, in a rather alarmist communiqué, estimated that the state's economy might lose 300 billion rupees in 2002.[7] Businessmen also feared that investors were less eager to put their money in the state. The Confederation of Indian Industry (CII) was especially vocal. Rahul Bajaj, a senior member of the CII, described 2002 as a 'lost year for Gujarat' and challenged Modi with several 'tough questions' during a CII meeting in February 2003 in Delhi, where the industrialist Jamshyd Godrej also raised the issue.[8]

Given the influence of business interests on the public sphere in Gujarat, Modi knew that he needed to restore their confidence. 'Development' (*vikas*) was the mantra of the BJP in the local election campaign of February 2003,[9] and in the name of development Modi launched business-friendly policies. These measures catered more to the needs of the industrialists and the urban middle class than to the poor; and while he projected himself as the 'Vikas Purush' (Development Man), what he called 'the Gujarat model' found expression in growth without development and in a new form of crony capitalism.

POWER, PORTS AND ROADS: GUJARAT'S SUCCESS STORIES

Infrastructure was the priority of the Modi government. In 2010, this approach found expression in a series of documents called 'BIG 2020',[10] which envisaged an investment of 11.81 trillion rupees across 19 infrastructure sectors, but the promotion had started before, at least in three areas, power, ports and roads, which the government tried to develop with the support of the private sector, a process that often involved reforms of the public sector. Indeed, Modi claimed that he was not a politician but an organisation man who sought to promote efficiency. Hence his desire to reform the public sector—which was supposed to be badly managed—even if he had to take on the trade unions. Power was a case in point.

The reform of the power sector was the first test for Modi's economic policies. In 2000–01, the Gujarat State Electricity Board (GSEB) recorded a deficit of 22.46 billion rupees. Transmission and distribution (T&D) losses were particularly high, because of power thefts and bad management. The Modi government decided to meter the supply of power and make theft of electricity a criminal offence—'and the law was enforced',[11] thanks to the creation, among other things, of special police stations. However, the GSEB was also affected by the power purchase agreements (PPAs) that had been signed with private companies, as these companies inflated the price at which they sold power to the state. The Modi government appointed a new chairperson for the GSEB, Manjula Subramaniam, who was asked to renegotiate the PPAs—which she did—and, more broadly, to reform the board. She did this too after a new law was passed in 2003, the Gujarat Electricity Industry (Reform and Reorganisation) Act, which separated the lines that supplied power to the rural areas into two, one to supply power for agricultural needs and the other for households. This was because the tariff for power used for agricultural purposes was much lower, and many people used this subsidised supply for their household needs. In addition, power tariffs increased and were revised every year. As a result, the GSEB posted its first profit of 2.03 billion rupees in 2005–06.

In parallel with the reform of the public sector, the Modi government sought to attract private investors. Atul Sood points out that 'in 2002, the new industrial units which generate electricity for captive requirements have been exempted from payment of excise duty for the first five years and in 2005, the transmission service agreements have been streamlined by introducing intrastate availability-based tariff. All this has given big boost to the power sector in Gujarat, wherein a large part of its industrial load is being met by captive power plants.'[12] And this was due to private investment: 'Private players, once reluctant to invest in Gujarat's power generation, [were] now rushing in.'[13] Indeed, private companies started to invest massively in the power sector. While the installed capacity increased by 12.87 per cent from 2006–07 to 2010–11, the contribution of the private sector to this capacity grew by 33.24 per cent over the same period, reaching 7,178 MW.[14] As a result, its share in installed capacity jumped from 36.15 per cent in 2001–02 to 54.75 per cent in 2010–11.[15] In 2011–12 the role of the private sector remained almost the same, representing 41,290 MUs (million units) out of a total of 78,651—about 52.5 per cent of the total.[16] P. Vashist and G. Arya explain this development by the deregulation process which made it possible for Torrent Power, for instance, to transmit and distribute electricity in the areas of Ahmedabad and Surat. But they also argue that 'high industrial tariffs have led many large manufacturing plants to choose captive generation and leave the grid system'[17]—something small and medium enterprises (SMEs) could not do so easily.

The completion of the Narmada dam also contributed to the growing production of electricity by the state of Gujarat. As Gujarat's installed capacity in the power sector almost doubled between 2005–06 and 2011–12,[18] the state—which had imported power in 2001—was able to sell on 14.5 billion rupees worth of power to 13 other states in India in 2008–10.[19]

Peasant unions resisted reforms that resulted in more expensive electricity.[20] Their pressure had forced Modi's predecessors (and his peers in most neighbouring states) to postpone reform of the power sector. In Gujarat in 2003–04, their protest was orchestrated by the Bharatiya Kisan Association (the Association of Indian Peasants), an offshoot of the RSS, but, as we will see in chapter 7, Modi made no concession. By the mid-2000s, Gujarat was among the states which were providing the 'lowest subsidy to domestic and agriculture sector'.[21] Partly because of these reforms, the transmission and distribution losses peaked in 2004–05 and then declined substantially, from 30.43 per cent to 22.74 per cent in 2010–11.[22] Modi's biographers celebrate the 'courage' he showed when he 'cracked down on more than 1.22 lakh [122,000] farmers for power thefts' and conclude that the way he 'dared to establish law even if it hurt farmers showed his spirit of fairness'.[23] The business community appreciated this move as well, as it was an expression of what Nandan Nilekani called Modi's 'non-populist policy'.[24] In 2011, *Business Today* pointed out that 'Modi runs Gujarat like a benignly tyrannical CEO.'[25]

The corporate sector—and many other people—also appreciated the development of roads under the Modi administration. Gujarat invested a lot of money in transport infrastructure in the first decade of the twenty-first century, partly as a result of a World Bank loan.[26] From 2000–01 to 2011–12, the state allocated 96.69 billion rupees for the construction of roads and bridges.[27] In the 1992–97 plan, the budget allotted to roads was about 1 billion rupees per year, whereas with the last plan Modi implemented as chief minister, it jumped to 20 billion rupees a year—with even more, 42.60 billion rupees, being spent in 2012–13.[28] The World Bank, in a very positive report assessing road construction in Gujarat, was impressed by the figures it produced itself for a similar period: 'The annual road sector allocation has grown from US$30 million in 1995–96 to an impressive US$610 million in 2010–11.'[29] The percentage allocation for roads in the overall annual plan in Gujarat grew from 4.9 per cent in 1995–96 to 8 per cent in 2007–08 and 9.3 per cent in 2008–09[30]—figures that we will later compare with the funds allocated to education and public health.

As a result, the length of the national highways doubled in ten years, from 1,570 km in 1999 to 3,229 km in 2009.[31] Almost half the extent consisted of four or six lanes. State highways were also comparatively well developed. The percentage of state highways—26 per cent of all roads—was substantially higher than in Maharashtra (18 per cent), Andhra Pradesh (13 per cent) and Karnataka (8 per cent). Moreover, in 2005 the government launched the Pragatipath Yojana programme, to 'connect tribal belts, coastal, industrial and rural areas with mainstream areas and the extremities of the state'. The total length of construction under the project was 3,710 km at a total cost of 24.88 billion rupees.[32] In addition to the quantity and length of roads, the World Bank emphasised their quality, as 90 per cent of them were paved in Gujarat, as against 81 per cent in Punjab, 76 per cent in Tamil Nadu and 68 per cent in Karnataka.[33] These achievements were hailed by the World Bank, which had partly financed them. In its report on the roads of Gujarat, it declared: 'Gujarat has been lucky to have a reform-minded government exhibiting strong political will and clear vision of its ambitious goals for the development and prosperity of the State. During the launch of the Infrastructure Vision, the State's Chief Minister assured industrialists to provide the infrastructure needed to serve industries operating in the state.'[34]

In contrast to other states of a similar level of development that also built many roads in the same period, Gujarat attracted private investment in road-building amounting to more than 70 billion rupees for various projects.[35] Similarly, according to P. Vashisht and G. Arya, 'Gujarat [was] the only state which has witnessed a significant growth in its rail infrastructure through PPP [public–private partnership].'[36] This development was largely meant to connect industrial areas to ports, which were also created or enlarged by private companies. The incentives offered by the state government were many: concessions on stamp duties and registration fees, full freedom to fix tariffs or rates for services provided at the port, zero state equity participation, no state involvement in the management of private developers, and government responsibility for land acquisition.[37]

As mentioned above, this liberalisation of the state ports policy had been initiated in 1995, but the Modi government accelerated it. As a result, from 1995 to 2010–11, the state's maritime sector received 394.17 billion rupees of investment proposals, which found concrete expression—among other things—in the building of four new ports.[38]

The Modi government attracted private investors in the infrastructure sector within the framework of a new law, the Gujarat Infrastructure Development (Amendment) Act of 2006. Atul Sood emphasises that the Act was the first institutional arrangement of its kind in India for private sector participation:

> A concession period of maximum 35 years is allowed under this act. It provides three modes for private sector participation in infrastructure projects: competitive bidding, comparative bidding and direct negotiation. There is also a provision for financial support for the development of infrastructure projects, with a subsidy up to 40 per cent (Government of Gujarat, 20 per cent & Government of India, 20 per cent) of the total project cost for the developers via the Viability Gap Funding (VGF) Scheme.[39]

Narendra Modi became one of the favourite chief ministers of the corporate sector because of the way he developed Gujarat's infrastructure—but for other reasons too. While he claimed to be in favour of economic liberalisation, he was more business-friendly than market-friendly, as is evident from the industrial policy he initiated.

A NEW INDUSTRIAL POLICY: FROM SMALL IS BEAUTIFUL TO BIG IS BEAUTIFUL[40]

Gujarat has traditionally been a land of entrepreneurs where the state has assisted small and medium enterprises (SMEs) and where some positive discrimination was implemented for smaller-scale entrepreneurs as well as measures favouring workers.[41] Archana

Dholakia and Ravindra Dholakia point out that the 1990, 1995 and 2000 industrial policies of the government of Gujarat 'focused largely on interest subsidies and incentives for small and tiny manufacturing sectors. Industries that were employment-intensive, export-oriented, using modern technology, ready to locate in backward regions, and set up by social groups like Scheduled Castes and Tribes and other backward castes were given incentives'.[42]

The 2003 industrial policy introduced by Narendra Modi broke with this tradition, including the special attention that had been paid to backward areas till then.[43] First, 'Inspections carried out under the labor department substantially reduced in numbers'—something big entrepreneurs, who resented what they had considered a form of harassment, greatly appreciated. Second, 'a large number of industries were exempted from obtaining No-Objection Certificate (NOC) from Pollution Control Board'. And third, 'Relatively easy and quick possession of land through the "urgency" clause, simplification of administrative processes to release agricultural land for industrial use, liberal land pricing strategy for unused government land and efficient land acquisition policy were all fallout of the 2003 policy'.[44]

In 2009 a new industrial policy was announced by the state government. The Gujarat Special Investment Region Act was passed in order 'to come up with a legal framework to enable development of mega investment regions and industrial areas in the State'.[45] Its ultimate aim was to create 'global hubs of economic activity supported by world class infrastructure, premium civic amenities, centers of excellence and proactive policy framework'. The Act was the mainstay of the 2009 Industrial Policy, which was explicitly designed for 'making Gujarat the most attractive investment destination not only in India but also in the world'.[46] It targeted not only 'prestigious units' (above 3 billion rupees), but even more so 'mega projects', which denoted more than 10 billion rupees of project investment and direct employment of only 2,000 people—hence a ratio of Rs 500,000 per job, a clear sign of capital intensity.[47] To attract big companies, access to land was considered a key element in 2009.[48] The Gujarat Industrial Development Corporation (GIDC) therefore started to acquire land to sell to industrialists, in some cases on a 99-year lease, or in Special Economic Zones. While in 1990–2001 it had acquired 4,620 ha, this figure rose to 21,308 ha between 2001 and 2010–11.[49]

The new industrial policy would not only impact the peasantry because of its provisions regarding land, it also affected the workforce. While, till the 1990s, it was mandatory for businesses benefiting from state subsidies or incentives in the context of some new investment to employ 100 permanent workers, 'the condition of employing 100 permanent workers turned into 100 regular workers and then *just* 100 workers'[50] in the 2000s.

To attract big investors, the Gujarat government also made significant concessions in terms of tax deductions and other fiscal subsidies. The amount of such subsidies per year (in terms of sales tax incentives and sales tax deferment),

> which was on an average 12.54 billion rupees between 1990–91 and 1999–2000, jumped by almost five times to 59.66 billion rupees per year during the period from 2000–01 to 2006–07. Also, there was a big jump in the total sales tax subsidy per unit in the second period. It rose from 33.7 million rupees in 2000–01 to 830 million rupees per unit in 2004–05 and to 2006–07 [...] This means that the state government let go of 40 per cent of its revenue from its main source of income.[51]

The new industrial policy of Gujarat, in so far as it aimed at making the state a model of economic modernity, reflected a decidedly pro-business approach to development.

Market-friendly or Business-friendly?

In the last page of his book whose title, *Gujarat: Governance for Growth and Development*, echoed Narendra Modi's programme,

Bibek Debroy summarised the state's economic policy as follows: 'What is the Gujarat model then? It is one of freeing up space for private initiative and enterprise and the creation of an enabling environment by the state.'[52] This liberal interpretation of the 'Gujarat model' needs to be qualified. In fact, Modi's policies continued to remain faithful to the close relations that had always existed between Gujarat's robust business community and its politicians as well as the bureaucracy.[53] The state continued to maintain a business-friendly[54] approach, more than a market-friendly one. But this trend increased further under Modi, as the CEO of the Adani Group admitted in the epigraph at the beginning of this chapter.[55]

The policy of the post-1995 BJP governments regarding access to land illustrates this state of affairs well, as Nikita Sud has demonstrated. The reform of the Bombay Tenancy and Agricultural Land Rules is a case in point here. This piece of regulation, on the statute books since the British Raj, prohibited the purchase of agricultural land by anybody not residing within eight kilometres of a plot.[56] This meant that urban dwellers could not easily buy land, which therefore remained in the hands of agriculturists. In 1987, the Congress government amended this provision, restricting it to drought-affected areas. When the BJP took over in 1995, the party removed this restriction and amended another section of the rules: 'Now no permission would be required from the revenue officials for the conversion of farmland up to 10 hectares to 'N[on] Agricultural status for setting up a "bona fide industrial unit".'[57] In 1999, the BJP government tried to liberalise the selling of *gauchar* (village common-property pastoral land) as well. Large protests by the Maldhari pastoralist community forced the government to abandon this measure, but Narendra Modi issued a government resolution sealing the fate of this kind of land as well as all wasteland. This resolution 'indicates the intention to allot plots from among 4.6 million hectares of state-controlled wasteland to the corporate sector for establishing industries and to large farmers for technology-intensive and corporate farming'.[58] Such deregulation reflected a clear choice in favour of industry (and industrialists) at the expense of agriculture.

However, the pro-business attitude of Narendra Modi found expression in several other ways. Besides the biennial investors' summit 'Vibrant Gujarat', which epitomised this attitude, it resulted in all sorts of concessions to industrial houses, especially in the context of the creation of new Special Economic Zones.

'Vibrant Gujarat': The 'Sow a Rupee and Harvest a Dollar' Formula[59]

In order to attract Indian investors, including those residing abroad, and to burnish his economic credentials, Modi conceived a special event in conjunction with chambers of commerce and industry. The Federation of Indian Chambers of Commerce and Industry (FICCI), which had remained neutral after the 2002 riots (whereas the CII had been critical), was asked to organise this event, known officially as the Global Investors Summit or, more casually, as the 'Vibrant Gujarat' meeting. The programme was scheduled for 28–30 September 2003, to coincide with Navratri (the popular Hindu festival) and to benefit from the return visits that non-resident Gujaratis (NRGs) usually make around that time of the year.

In contrast to the policy of previous governments, the programme did not rely on competitive bids, but on calls for projects. Hundreds of companies were drawn to this get-together and promises of investment were made totalling 660 billion rupees.[60] Despite this being a good start, it was still something of a disappointment because NRGs did not show up in large numbers. Hence the decision to move the biennial event to January, during the Christmas break, which made more sense for Gujarati businessmen based in the United States and in Europe. In January 2005, 1.06 trillion rupees of investment commitments were made in the form of memorandums of understanding (MoUs), of which 60 per cent allegedly materialised.[61] Two years later, the promises of investment reached 4.65 trillion rupees;[62] in 2009, 12.4 trillion rupees;[63] and in 2011, 20.83 trillion rupees.[64] Most of them came to naught, but Gujarat was indeed vibrant during Vibrant Gujarat and in terms of the state's political marketing (see Table 5.1).

The realisation of promised investments declined steadily over the course of time, but by the mid-2000s investment in Gujarat had risen significantly and Modi had become one of the favourite chief ministers among Indian capitalists. They made a point of attending the Vibrant Gujarat meetings and of showering praise on him. Among them, the Gujaratis were usually the first to appear on the platform, the most prominent ones including Mukesh and Anil Ambani, Shashi Ruia (of Essar Group) and Gautam Adani, who was the closest of all to the chief minister. Other investors also took part in later editions of the Vibrant Gujarat summits, including Anand Mahindra and Ratan Tata. Vibrant Gujarat had become a place where, one after the other, the big capitalists of India eulogised the 'Vikas Purush' (Development Man).

SEZs and the Rest

Indian industrialists had already taken note of the state's infrastructure and policies before Modi took over power, but they appreciated one of his policies in particular: the multiplication of Special Economic Zones (SEZs). Gujarat, which had been the first state to develop an Export Processing Zone (EPZ) in Kandla in 1965, was also the state that had the first private EPZ, in Surat.[65] Unsurprisingly, it was one of the first states to pass an SEZ Act, in 2004.[66] Bibek Debroy points out that 'the attractiveness of SEZs in Gujarat had quite a bit to do with the SEZ Act's provisions on the labour market. For example, there is easier exit, more flexible provisions on hiring and terminating labour and the concept of fixed term employment.'[67] Besides relaxing labour laws, SEZs are also areas in which industrialists are invited to set up production units (generally export-oriented) in exchange for various tax concessions and subsidies. Bibek Debroy and Laveesh Bhandari point out that 'tax breaks are given [and] regulations are also fewer and less intrusive in SEZs. SEZs offer a free-market atmosphere to traders, implying a higher level of economic freedom.'[68] Taking stock of the development of these SEZs, in 2005 the Rajiv Gandhi Foundation 'adjudged Modi's Gujarat as the Number 1 state in economic freedom index'.[69] By June 2010, the Government of India had given 'approval to 60 SEZs in Gujarat covering an area of 31,967 hectares'.[70] By that time, the government had 'allotted more than 20,000 acres of land to the roughly 27 SEZs that had already been notified'.[71]

Within SEZs or out of them, Indian investors appreciated the speed of administrative procedures and decision-making as well as the concessions made to them in Gujarat. The manner in which Tata Motors could build the Nano factory is a case in point. In August 2008 Ratan Tata abandoned the idea of making this low-cost car in Singur (West Bengal) when agriculturists' protest against the expropriation of villages was backed by Mamata Banerjee, a powerful state politician. It seems that Modi then sent a one-word SMS to Ratan Tata: 'Suswagatam' (Welcome). Ratan Tata said later in an interview that his company had been contacted by seven state governments, but that Modi had delivered land more quickly: 'The speed and the fact that Gujarat could transfer possession of the land without any hassles to Tata Motors was perhaps the singular reason that made us decide on Gujarat.'[72] Ratan Tata added that 'Narendra Modi is an extremely easy person to deal with—very informal, compatible and pleasant, and capable as well. It is very difficult not to feel comfortable with him. The fact remains that he has taken a personal interest in the project to ensure that everything moves smoothly.'

Traditionally, in the 2000s, politicians used to keep industrialists waiting at arm's length—a legacy of the Licence Raj era. And here was a chief minister who took a 'personal interest' in business and businessmen and expedited matters on their behalf. The Nano deal was wrapped up in fifteen days, Tata Motors opting for the site at Sanand that Modi had pre-selected (among others) for the new factory. To woo Tata, the chief minister not only moved very fast but also offered many concessions: 'for 1,100 acres of land allegedly sold at 900 rupees per sq. m, while its market rate was around 10,000 rupees per sq. m, the Tatas were given facility of payment through instalments'.[73] It also received exemption from stamp duty of '20 crore rupees levied on the sale of land [and] deferred payment of Value Added Tax (VAT) on the sale, of twenty years'.[74] According to a report based on a leaked version of the agreement, 'Besides this, loans amounting to 95.70 billion rupees against an investment of 29 billion rupees—330 per cent of the total invested—will be made available to it which will be payable at 0.1 per cent interest after 20 years'.[75]

While this deal became publicly known, others were made with similar conditions, according to investigative journalists. The conglomerate Larsen and Toubro was, for instance, 'allotted 8,00,000 sq. m of prime land in the industrial zone of Hazira, Surat, without auction, at the rate of Re 1 per sq. m [...] thereby costing the state exchequer a few hundred crore rupees'.[76] In the same vein, the Essar Group was 'allotted 2.08 lakh [208,000] sq. m of disputed land for a steel plant on the CRZ [Coastal Regulation Zone] and forest land that can't be allotted as per Supreme Court guidelines [...] The occupier is unauthorised but no action has been taken by the state machinery.'[77] Similarly, a comprehensive study showed in 2012 that in one case Reliance Industries had paid for land it acquired between Rs 21 and Rs 390 per hectare—that is, less than the market price.[78]?

The Comptroller and Auditor General (CAG) noticed these 'irregularities'.[79] In a highly detailed report, it accused the Gujarat government of causing a loss to the exchequer of about 5.8 billion rupees by bestowing 'undue' favours on large companies, including Reliance Industries, Essar, the Adani Group, Larsen and Toubro, and Ford.[80] Land allotment was the main issue,[81] but not the only one: 'During the last five years, the audit reports have highlighted cases of non/short levy, non/short realization, underassessment/loss of revenue, incorrect exemption, concealment of turnover, application of incorrect rate of income tax, incorrect computation, etc worth 52.88 billion rupees.'[82] This indictment came after the CAG posed more than 5,000 queries and made 15,100 audit observations.[83] But the CAG's reports hardly made any difference. The state government continued to present 'the Gujarat model' as a success story, with the help of some of its main beneficiaries—Gujarat-based companies which have generally recorded good results under Modi's chief ministership. Between 2002 and 2012, the market capitalisation of Essar increased by 4,507 per cent and that of Reliance Industries by 1,357 per cent—but that of the Adani Group rose by 8,615 per cent,[84] a meteoric trajectory that is scrutinised below.

Gautam Adani, or the Rise of a Regional Oligarch

If the name of Gautam Adani was frequently mentioned in the CAG reports, it was because he exemplified the type of capitalism that took shape in Gujarat in the 2000s. By the end of Modi's chief ministership, the combined market value of Adani Enterprises, Adani Power and Adani Ports and Special Economic Zones (APSEZ) was close to the value of Reliance Industries, whereas the Adani Group had been 500 times smaller, only 13 years before, in 2001.[85] The media explained this prosperity by pointing to Gautam Adani's close relations with Narendra Modi, which became apparent when Modi used Adani's chartered plane on his campaign trail across India in the run-up to the 2014 elections.[86] Gautam Adani had already shown the nature of his proximity to Modi when he was chief minister of Gujarat (at that time they visited China, Japan, Singapore and Russia together). At the same time, the turnover of the group rose more than twentyfold, from 37.41 billion rupees in 2001–02 to 756.59 billion rupees in 2013–14.[87]

Gautam Adani was born in 1962 in a Jain family, in Ratanpol (in the Old City of Ahmedabad), his parents having migrated from North Gujarat. At the age of 18, he dropped out of Gujarat University and moved to Bombay, served a stint as a diamond sorter at Mahindra Bros, and then became a diamond trader.[88] He moved to Ahmedabad in 1981 to help his brother Mahasukh, who was starting a plastic-film manufacturing business. This company was heavily dependent on supplies of PVC, whose sole producer in India at the time was IPCL. They used to supply the Adani brothers two tons per month, but their rapidly growing business soon needed over 20 tons per month. Adani thus began importing plastic granules through Kandla port, which was India's largest port till 2013, when it was superseded by Adani's adjacent Mundra port. The Adani Group then diversified. In 1988, Gautam Adani set up a commodities trading venture called Adani Exports. In the next four years, his import orders grew from 100 metric tons (MT) to 40,000 MT.[89]

In 1991–92, Adani and the agribusiness group Cargill were given 3,000 acres of coastal land in Kutch by the Chimanbhai Patel government for salt production. The project fell through after protests, and Cargill pulled out. Adani held on to his land and began thinking of converting Mundra into a big port. In the context of the nascent liberalisation policy, the Gujarat Maritime Board decided to allot ports to private companies in a joint venture with the state. An initial list of ten ports was created, including Mundra, which was 14 metres deep (deeper than Kandla at 12 metres) and could berth larger ships of 200,000 MT and above.[90] In 1993, the business was incorporated as a limited company with two backers, Adani himself and Rajesh S. Adani, his younger brother. In 1997, Adani Exports entered into a joint venture with the Gujarat government to build a mega port at Mundra. Around that time the Adani Group established a base in Dubai, where two of the five Adani brothers were primarily in charge of the supply chain of Adani Exports. In 1999, Adani ventured into coal trading for the first time, with a shipment landing at Mundra. In 2000 Adani allowed P&O Australia, one of the world's largest port operators, to set up a container terminal in Mundra.

There is no evidence that Gautam Adani and Narendra Modi knew each other before the latter became chief minister, but they became very close soon afterwards. In the aftermath of the events of 2002, which disrupted the state economy for weeks, after businessmen (including senior members of the CII) criticised Modi,[91] CII members from Gujarat formed the Resurgent Group of Gujarat to counter what they regarded as 'a concerted attempt by a section to defame Gujarat'.[92] Among them were Dr Karsan Patel and Ambubhai Patel (Nirma Group), Indravadan Modi (Cadila Pharmaceuticals), Pankaj Patel (Cadila Healthcare), Chintan Parikh (Ashima), Anil Bakeri (Bakeri Group) and, last but not least, Gautam Adani, who was a newcomer to the world of medium to big companies,[93] yet took a leading role.

When the first Vibrant Gujarat meeting took place in September–October 2003, Adani went further than his colleagues, and pledged 150 billion rupees of investment.[94] This was a major turning point in the Adani–Modi relationship. The Adani Port and SEZ (APSEZ) at Mundra (Kutch district) was created the same year to provide cargo handling and other port services. It soon became India's first multi-product port-based SEZ, after Adani was granted 3,585 ha of land, including 2,008 ha of forest and 990 ha of *gauchar* (village grazing) land. Two converging investigations have alleged that the Adani Group bought this land, in one particular area, at a rate ranging from 1 to 32 rupees a square metre when the market rate was over 1,500 rupees per square metre,[95] and, in another area, at the cost of 10 rupees per square metre, when the market price there was between 700 and 800 rupees per square metre.[96]

In Mundra, Adani acquired up to 7,350 ha of land. *Forbes* argues, on the basis of the signed agreements, that for most of this area 'he got the 30-year, renewable leases for as little as one U.S. cent a square meter (the rate made out at 45 cents a square meter). He in turn has sublet this land to other companies, including state-owned Indian Oil Co., for as much as $11 a square meter. Between 2005 and 2007 at least 1,200 hectares of grazing land was taken away from villagers.'[97]

During the 2009 Vibrant Gujarat summit, the Modi government

> signed MoUs allowing the Adani group a 150-billion-rupee expansion of its SEZ over the next 15 years. The government topped off its largesse of land to the Adani group with five-years tax breaks of over 32 billion rupees, almost four times what it had marked for redeveloping Kutch after the 2001 earthquake. Government data shows an investment of 1.32 trillion rupees in the Adani SEZ, port, and power plant, but only 38,875 jobs created. That comes to an astonishing figure of 33.8 million rupees for creating one job.[98]

This is a clear indication of capital intensity, an issue we'll return to later.

In 2013 a CAG report pointed out that in the Adani Group's SEZ in Mundra, '14 lease deeds for an area of 4,84,326 sq. m in MPSEZ were registered during the period from December 2008 to November 2011. However, the Collector had given permission to only one unit [...] Accordingly, the transfers of land admeasuring 4,65,728 sq. m by way of lease in the remaining 13 cases were irregular.'[99] The CAG also criticised the Gujarat government for purchasing electricity from the Adani Group at an abnormally high price. It pointed out that this 'non adherence to the terms of Power Purchase Agreement led to short recovery of penalty of 1.60 billion rupees and passing of undue benefit to a private firm'.[100]

In 2012, the Modi–Adani connection was targeted by Arvind Kejriwal, the leader of the Aam Aadmi Party, who, the year before, had taken part in anti-corruption campaigns along with Anna Hazare. He accused the Gujarat government of buying power from the Adani Group at 5.45 rupees per unit when the Gujarat Mineral Development Corporation had made a better offer.[101] Gas was another source of income for the Adani Group, as it had also acquired a monopoly in the supply of CNG in Ahmedabad.

In its last report dealing with the Modi government in Gujarat, the CAG reiterated the critique it had made in 2012 of the Adani Group and criticised the Essar Group too:

> the purchase of power from the private sector increased to 37.22 per cent (2012–13) from 15.22 per cent (2008–09). Of this increase, the share of Private IPPs in power purchased from private sector [the Adani and the Essar groups] increased to 82.75 per cent (i.e. 22,562.17 MUs) in 2012–13 from 66.59 per cent (i.e. 5,653.24 MUs)[102] indicating an increase of 300 per cent in purchase of power from them during 2008–09 to 2012–13.[103]

The Adani group was also targeted by environmentalists. The Gujarat Coastal Zone Management Authority (GCZMA) in May 2006 formed a subcommittee which reported that the Adani Group had built many bunds (embankments) in the intertidal area and blocked many creeks feeding water to the mangrove patches. Nothing came of this report. Four years later, in December 2010, the Ministry of Environment and Forests sent an inspection team to investigate complaints from local inhabitants. The report presented after the visit found many instances of non-compliance. It made the same observations regarding large-scale destruction of mangroves and the obstruction of creek systems and natural flow of seawater because of reclamation. All this made no difference. On 14 September 2012 the minister of state for environment and forests, Jayanthi Natarajan, formed a committee under the chairmanship of Sunita Narain, director general of the think tank Centre for Science and Environment (CSE), to inspect Mundra port. It reached the same conclusions as its predecessors.[104]

All the inspectors and experts also observed that the Mundra thermal plants of Adani and Tata released fly ash, despite the terms of the 2007 clearance. In 2011 a Gujarat Pollution Control Board inspection revealed that about 27,127 MT of fly ash was found to be dispersed in low-lying areas of the MPSEZ. The Sunita Narain committee made a similar observation. When Megha Bahree visited the place, she noticed that 'fly ash and saline water from Adani Power and a nearby Tata Power Co. Ltd plant are spoiling the crops and making the soil less fertile'.[105]. The Sunita Narain committee recommended a 2 billion rupee environment restoration fund (ERF), but no penalty was imposed on either company by the government.[106] In 2016, the Gujarat High Court appointed another committee to inquire into the degradation caused by the Mundra port. It came to the same conclusion as its predecessor but, says environmentalist Mahesh Pandya, 'if you ask the Gujarat Pollution Control Board or the state environment and forests department how many notices they have served to the company, you will find none'.[107]

A PRO-RICH AND BUSINESS-FRIENDLY POLICY RESULTING IN DEBTS, INVESTMENTS AND GROWTH

Partly because of Modi's business-friendly policy, the financial situation of Gujarat did not improve, and the government developed a strategy of (sustainable) indebtedness. Nevertheless, the state attracted enough investments to record a robust growth rate.

A Pro-business as well as Pro-rich Taxation Policy—and Indebtedness

The fiscal liabilities of Gujarat increased from 453.01 billion rupees in 2001–02 to 964.52 billion rupees in 2007–08 and 1.39 trillion rupees in 2011–12.[108] The internal debt of Gujarat represented 76 per cent of these liabilities, making Gujarat the third most indebted state of India, behind Uttar Pradesh (1.58 trillion rupees) and West Bengal (1.92 trillion rupees).[109] In 2013, the Gujarat government was paying an interest charge of 345 million rupees every day, while the state's per capita debt reached 23,000 rupees in the same year.[110] By 2009–10, debt represented 288.7 per cent of the total revenue receipts of Gujarat's budget, the second highest in the country after West Bengal (the national average being 203.5 per cent).[111] In 2013–14, the government planned to raise fresh loans of 260.09 billion rupees. Of this amount, 198.77 billion rupees—that is, 76 per cent—was to be used to pay the principal and the interest of existing debts.[112]

This state of affairs was partly due to the concessions made by the Modi government to industrialists. But it resulted also from its supply-side taxation policy, which found expression, as we've seen, in the development of SEZs, which all proved very costly for the exchequer. Focusing on stamp-duty exemptions and duty forgone on customs and imports, Manshi Asher points out that between 2006 and 2014 the Treasury lost 'tens of billions of rupees. Reliance Group's Jamnagar SEZ benefited from more than Rs 50 billion worth of exemptions; the Adani Group's Mundra SEZ Rs 18 billion; the Kandla SEZ Rs 8 billion; and the Dahej SEZ Rs 1.3 billion.'[113] In 2007, Modi removed the octroi, a local tax, in a decision immediately hailed by his core constituency of traders and entrepreneurs.[114] The government made up for the loss of this revenue and others by increasing indirect taxes, the most socially insensitive ones, since everybody pays the same percentage irrespective of their income. In 2013, VAT and sales taxes represented more than 70 per cent of total tax receipts.[115] By contrast, land revenue represented less than 3 per cent of total tax receipts.[116] Debroy points out that in the Gujarat budget 'one would have expected land revenue, stamps and registration and taxes on vehicles to account for a much larger share of state taxes than they [do] presently'.[117] Clearly, industrialists and the urban middle class had been spared.

But another reason for the poor fiscal situation of the Gujarat of this time was that some of those who were supposed to pay taxes did not—whether captains of industry or ordinary citizens. Companies, for instance, owed 120 billion rupees in taxes to the state in 2011.[118] In 2012, Essar alone owed 80 billion rupees of sales tax.[119] The total amount due from the individual taxpayers of Ahmedabad, Surat, Baroda and Rajkot represented 75.55 billion rupees in 2010—more than the annual tax receipts of Bihar.[120]

The fiscal situation of Gujarat was not alarming so long as the growth rate remained high. The important ratio here was of debt to GDP. In 2013 it had only reached 20.87 per cent and therefore the state complied with the Fiscal Responsibility and Budget Management Act, which stipulates a maximum debt level of 30 per cent.[121]

Some FDIs, a Lot of Domestic Investments—and Growth

The main achievement of the Gujarat economic policy was to attract investment. Foreign investors did not rush to the state—while Gujarat was in the 'top five', it did not attract investors massively, compared with other states. In twelve years, from 2000 to 2012 (including eleven years under Narendra Modi), Gujarat attracted $8.5 billion in foreign direct investments (FDI), which represented 4.5 per cent of the national total—much less than Maharashtra at $61.4 billion and Delhi at $37.8

billion, a little less than Karnataka at $10.5 billion and Tamil Nadu at $9.8 billion, and slightly more than Andhra Pradesh at $7.6 billion. And by the end of Modi's second term, the attractiveness of Gujarat to foreign investors declined from 10.3 per cent of the total of FDIs in India in 2008–09 to 2.7 per cent in 2011–12.[122] But Gujarat could rely on Indian investors.

In 2003 Gujarat represented 16.43 per cent of the total domestic investments of India and was second only to the much larger state of Maharashtra (21.11 per cent).[123] This flow continued in the framework of the Vibrant Gujarat meetings and beyond. These investments mostly came from Indian companies already familiar with Gujarat. Reliance Industries, for instance, developed a petroleum refinery with a final capacity of 62 million metric tons per annum. Essar also established its 11 million tons per annum capacity plant close by and set up a big steel mill in Hazira in South Gujarat.[124] These investments accounted for most of the main achievements of the Gujarat economy and its growth, although the impact of the Modi government needs to be qualified because growth did not accelerate significantly under him (see Tables 5.2 and 5.3).[125]

While in the 1990s Gujarat was already ahead economically of most of the other states of India, it remained among the front runners in the following decades. In the years 2005-06–2011-12, when the impact of Modi's policies fully registered, the state remained among the top six (of the twenty largest states), except in 2006–07 and in 2008–09, when it fell out of the top ten (see Table 5.4).

This performance needs to be disaggregated sector-wise. Unsurprisingly, the most dynamic sector was industry, in which most investments were concentrated. With an average yearly growth rate of 10.64 per cent in 2005-06–2011-12, Gujarat's industry recorded the fourth best performance in India—the national average being 7.5 per cent.[126] As a result, in 2013 it accounted for 20 per cent of India's industrial output, including 24 per cent of its textile production, 35 per cent of its pharmaceutical products, 51 per cent of its petrochemical production, and 22 per cent of its exports.[127] But the services sector did equally well—with a 10.86 per cent average growth rate—and as a result, this sector also ranked fourth in India, the national average being 9.95 per cent.[128]

The performance of agriculture was also remarkable as its average growth rate in 2005-06–2011-12 ranked fourth too in India. While the productivity of industry and services could largely be explained by investments in the private sector, the trajectory of agriculture partly reflected the impact of the Narmada dam. As the *Socio-economic Review* of Gujarat state for 2012–13 admitted, the Modi government was fortunate in benefiting from a key decision of the Supreme Court exactly one year before he took over as chief minister. Indeed, on 18 October 2000, the court delivered a judgment backing the completion of the Sardar Sarovar Dam on the Narmada River up to a height of 95 metres, a project that the Narmada Bachao Andolan and other NGOs had contested bitterly till then. This dam had first been envisioned by Sardar Vallabhbhai Patel (hence its name) in 1946–47 in order to use the water of the river Narmada, primarily to irrigate Gujarat. The building of the dam was contested before the courts by several NGOs defending local peasants whose villages and lands were to be submerged, but eventually the project was cleared in 2000. Narendra Modi, who was to successfully agitate in favour of a higher dam,[129] gave credit to his predecessors, including Keshubhai Patel, for this achievement.[130]

Costing 392 billion rupees, this is the world's second largest concrete gravity dam with the third largest spillway capacity. It was supposed to irrigate up to 1.8 million ha in Gujarat, to bring drinking water to 9,633 villages (or 53 per cent of the 18,144 villages of Gujarat) and 131 towns (with 29 million people in total), and generate 1,450 MW of hydropower. The first two objectives involved the construction of a main canal of 458 km.[131] While only 332 km of the Sujalam Suphalam Spreading Canal had been completed by 2012, the Modi government considered that the state had by then achieved '82.39 per cent of ultimate irrigation potential of surface water'.[132] According to figures of the Directorate of Economics and Statistics, Narmada water was supplied to 4,002 villages and 92 towns.[133]

The completion of the Narmada project was largely responsible for the remarkable growth rate in agriculture. According to a survey by the Associated Chambers of Commerce and Industry of India (ASSOCHAM), from 2000–01 to 2009–10 this sector attained an average annual growth rate of 10.97 per cent.[134] However, this statistic has been contested by the Planning Commission,[135] whose data situate the annual growth rate of agriculture in Gujarat at 8.46 per cent as an average over the years 2005-06–2011-12—while the national average was only 3.82 per cent.[136] These statistics were similar to those of the International Food Policy Research Institute.[137]

The performance of these three sectors of the state's economy explains its remarkable per capita growth rate between 2004–05 and 2011–12 (see Table 5.4). From 2007–08, Gujarat had the third highest per capita net domestic product of Indian states. and the yearly growth rate of GDP was among the top six, five times out of seven between 2005–06 and 2011–12. However, it must be remembered that these per capita figures are averages that conceal wide disparities.

THE COST OF GUJARAT'S POLITICAL ECONOMY

While Gujarat had always performed better than most of the Indian states economically, Narendra Modi, during his chief ministership, not only capitalised on these past achievements, but transformed the local political economy too.

First, his economic policy did not rely only on massive public investments in infrastructure, but was also designed to attract big investors, including multinationals, whereas Gujarat was traditionally known for its SMEs and their entrepreneurship. This strategy, which translated into the making of dozens of SEZs, gave birth to what Modi's former professor, Pravin Sheth, called a 'corpo-state'.[138] Indeed, in the Gujarat of this time, a handful of crony capitalists became influential oligarchs, thereby creating a new relationship between politicians and businessmen, in a state where this form of integration was already commonplace but had never reached such a level. So much so that Sheth and Pradeep Mallick point out that these big players avoided the democratic oversight of the Indian state by carving out their own domains ('corpo-doms'). 'If weakly regulated, Gujarat with 60 SEZs will become an informal set of SEZ's corpo-doms (new rajwadas). Autonomous status of SEZs in terms of limited unionism, defunct local elected bodies and enormous clout of corporates to control local dissent by raw power at their disposal will hinder free and fair democratic process in their jurisdiction.'[139]

Here again, Gujarat appears to have been the testing ground for the rest of the nation for different reasons. First, some of the same men who had flourished during his chief ministership continued to prosper during his prime ministership. Gautam Adani is a case in point. While in 2012 he ranked fourth on the list of the ten richest Gujaratis[140]—a list topped by Mukesh Ambani[141]—by 2022 he had become the richest man not only in India, but also in Asia, and second only to Jeff Bezos in the world.[142] As early as 2014, his proximity to Narendra Modi was confirmed by the fact that he accompanied him as his private guest on most of his foreign travels.[143] Subsequently, he was one of the most obvious beneficiaries of the government's policies, including the privatisation of airports and seaports.[144]

Second, Modi's supply-side policy in Gujarat prefigured his economic strategy as prime minister. This approach was not unrelated to his business-friendly attitude, but it also reflected another facet of his ideology, namely, the belief that the private sector should be prioritised. As early as 2015, in his first national budget, Modi lowered corporate tax:[145] for existing companies it was reduced from 30 per cent to 22 per cent, and for manufacturing firms incorporated after 1 October 2019 that started operations before 31 March 2023, it was reduced from 25 per cent to 15 per cent—the biggest reduction in 28 years. He also abolished the wealth tax that had been introduced in 1957. By contrast, taxes on alcohol and petroleum products increased dramatically, so much so that indirect taxes (the most unfair ones) rose quickly under the Modi government to reach 50 per cent of total taxes—as against 39 per cent under the first UPA government and 44 per cent under the second UPA government.[146] This trajectory emulated that of Gujarat under Modi, where indirect taxes had already increased a lot.

Prime Minister Modi's supply-side policy also resulted after 2014 in the same dilution of environmental laws and regulations as in Gujarat. In 2020 the Ministry of Environment and Forests drafted an environmental impact assessment (EIA) notification that allowed public or private entities to apply for environment clearance *ex post facto* for projects which, till then, had had to be submitted to the public before they started. Several large-scale industries (including chemical manufacturing, petroleum products, modernisation of irrigation, buildings, construction and area development, and large-scale renewable energy projects like dams) were also exempted from public hearings. And from 2022 mining firms extracting iron, manganese, bauxite and limestone were no longer required to conduct public hearings while expanding production capacity by as much as 20 per cent.[147]

The economic policy of Modi in Gujarat had direct and indirect social consequences. By investing heavily in infrastructure and hardly at all in education, as well as by promoting highly capitalistic companies at the expense of labour-intensive enterprises, the Modi government failed to reduce inequalities. More generally speaking, the political economy of the Gujarat of this time fostered social polarisation.

6

SOCIAL POLARISATION

JOBLESS GROWTH AND THE WIDENING OF THE URBAN–RURAL GAP

> In the ten years of our journey of development, Gujarat has emerged successful in many areas through numerous initiatives. But without the blessings of six crore Gujaratis it would not have been possible to achieve this feat. This is the outcome of the determination of six crore Gujaratis for development.
>
> Narendra Modi, 2011[1]

The impressive growth rate of Gujarat under Modi—founded upon its previous economic achievements, the capitalist structures (and culture) of the state, and its capacity to attract investors led some analysts to regard its successes as 'miraculous'.[2] Modi used grandiloquent words like this to refer to the economic achievements of his state repeatedly. On his website, for instance, he explained in 2011 how Gujarat had emerged as 'a Model for Development' over the previous ten years.[3]

Yet his experiment with the economy of Gujarat became the heart of a debate between social scientists. Jagdish Bhagwati and Arvind Panagariya consider that what they call the '"Gujarat model" is the metaphor for a primarily growth and private-entrepreneurship driven development',[4] which was bound to benefit society at large. Amartya Sen and Jean Drèze, in their book *An Uncertain Glory*, contend that Gujarat exemplified growth without development, a syndrome that prevailed throughout India in the first decade of the twenty-first century but was particularly pronounced in Gujarat.[5]

Indeed, the Gujarat 'model' has not reduced social inequalities; quite the contrary. And this was bound to happen, according to Bibek Debroy, since for him 'any period of rapid economic growth results in increased income inequalities'.[6] In fact, the political economy of Gujarat resulted in a very inegalitarian and socially polarised 'model'.[7] First, industry—the engine of growth—did not create many (good) jobs. Second, growth did not bring significant benefits either to the rural part of the state or to the weaker sections. While the growth rate of Modi's Gujarat was remarkable, the state recorded poor results in terms of social indicators, largely because the government was not interested in fighting inequalities by investing in pro-poor policies, such as public health and education.

WHAT JOBS? THE SOCIAL COST OF CAPITAL-INTENSIVE INVESTMENTS

By focusing on infrastructure and 'mega projects' and promoting big companies, Modi's 'Gujarat model' boosted the growth rate but created few good jobs, not only because the rules pertaining to job creation—for attracting investors—were relaxed, as mentioned above, but also because the infrastructure and the big projects supported by the Gujarat government were all very capital-intensive. Atul Sood shows that in the 2010s Gujarat 'investment in infrastructure projects account[ed] for more than 37.59 per cent of the total ongoing investment and create[d] only about 21.5 per cent of total employment'.[8] The petrochemical industry and the chemical industry were other cases in point. They were so dynamic that they represented 34 per cent and 15 per cent respectively of the industrial output in 2009,[9] but they were not labour-intensive sectors.[10] Manufacturing was more labour-intensive, but automation was also gaining momentum in the large factories. For instance, the Nano plant never had more than 2,200 employees—for an investment worth 29 billion rupees, or a ratio of more than 13 billion rupees per job created directly (indirect job creation needs to be taken into account but is more difficult to measure). Sangeeta Ghosh points out that even if we remove the petrochemical industry 'from the analysis, Gujarat's manufacturing process is highly capital absorbing, in fact the highest among all states'.[11]

Indeed, between 2009–10 and 2012–13, Gujarat was the state where investment in industry was the highest in India (above Maharashtra and Tamil Nadu),[12] but this performance did not translate into job creation as much as in the states where enterprises tended to be smaller and (therefore) more labour-intensive. A comparison between Gujarat and Tamil Nadu is illuminating in this respect: in 2013, the Gujarat industrial sector represented 17.7 per cent of India's fixed capital and only 9.8 per cent of factory jobs, whereas the industry of Tamil Nadu represented 9.8 per cent of fixed capital but 16 per cent of factory jobs.[13] In Gujarat, fixed capital increased fourfold in five years, but the annual growth rate of employment declined from 2.4 per cent to 0.1 per cent between 1999-2000–2004-05 and 2004-05–2009-10. Joblessness was especially pervasive in the rural areas; by contrast, the growth rate of urban employment increased slightly, from 4 per cent to 4.9 per cent, but because of construction work, not because of manufacturing, where the job market registered a negative growth rate of 2.23 per cent per annum between 2004–05 and 2009–10.[14]

This was partly due to the crisis afflicting the SMEs (small and medium enterprises), which are four times more labour-intensive than big enterprises on average. A study by the Institute of Small Enterprises and Development, which the Gujarat Industrial Development Corporation sponsored, showed that in 2013 the non-performing assets of the SMEs of Gujarat had grown by 43.9 per cent. Besides the economic slowdown (which affected exports too), this was attributed mainly to the rise in the price of gas and electricity (sometimes decided to please big companies, as the Comptroller and Auditor General argued) and the poor financial support that the SMEs received because of the indifference shown to them by local banks.[15] The share of the credit of MSMEs (micro, small and medium enterprises) as a percentage of gross bank credit declined continuously from 12.98 per cent in 1997–98 to 6.34 per cent in 2006–07. It started to rise again and reached 10 per cent in 2009–10, but for many companies it was too little—and too late.[16]

These financial tensions were partly due to the crisis affecting the district cooperative banks, which were in bad shape after financial irregularities almost sealed the fate of eight of them in the early 2000s.[17] The failure of the Madhavpura Mercantile Cooperative Bank—to which we'll return—had the largest repercussions on the sector. Four of the eight banks mentioned above had to be liquidated. This financial situation precipitated the crisis that afflicted many MSMEs. According to the Ministry of MSMEs and Startups, the number of ailing entities jumped from 4,321 in 2010–11 to 20,615 in 2012–13 and 49,382 in 2014–15—a trend second only to that of Uttar Pradesh.[18] Between 2004 and 2014, 60,000 MSMEs shut down in Gujarat.[19] Clearly, the MSMEs were in no position to hire as many people as before.

Not only did the growth rate of jobs not increase in proportion to the growth rate of the state GDP under Modi—something the government of Gujarat admitted in 2009[20] and even more explicitly in 2016[21]—but the quality of jobs did not improve either, as is evident from the informalisation process at work in the job market.[22] Formal employment remained almost stagnant (+0.3 per cent) between 1999–2000 and 2009–10. By contrast, informal employment increased by 4.47 per cent between 2000 and 2006.[23] According to the National Sample Survey Office, in 2009–10 the informal sector represented 84.1 per cent of the working force in Gujarat and only 74.9 per cent in Maharashtra. The proportion of male workers in the urban informal sector increased in Gujarat from 74.1 per cent in 2004–05 to 80.6 per cent in 2009–10, whereas it decreased in Maharashtra (from 72.3 per cent to 61.3 per cent), in Tamil Nadu (from 76.7 per cent to 74.7 per cent) and in India at large (from 73.9 per cent to 68.5 per cent).[24] In the Nano plant, for instance, out of 2,200 employees, 430 were 'permanent workers' in 2016. They earned 12,500 rupees, whereas informal workers earned about 3,300 rupees a month.[25] While in 2007–08 the regular employment growth rate in the formal sector had remained the same since 1993–94 (2.7 per cent), the share of contractual work in the informal sector increased to 34 per cent from 19 per cent in 1993–94.[26]

While those working for the state government had secure jobs, their wages remained quite low. In 2009, 19,000 labourers on daily wages—mostly working in the Roads and Buildings Department—who earned between 2,550 rupees and 3,200 rupees a month, benefited from a revised pay scale after 11 years without any increase in real terms.[27] But the situation of informal sector workers was much worse. In 2011, according to the National Sample Survey Office, the average wages per day received by casual labourers aged 15–59 was 144.52 rupees among urban workers (other than those in public works) and 130 rupees among rural workers (other than those benefiting from the Mahatma Gandhi National Rural Employment Guarantee). Only Chhattisgarh and Uttar Pradesh were worse off (see Table 6.1). This, and the informalisation of work, explain in part the low rate of unemployment (the lowest in India), also shown in Table 6.1.

This 'casualization of the workforce'[28] resulted in some tensions. In 2011, the *Economic Survey of India* listed Gujarat as the worst state for labour unrest in 2010–11, as it had witnessed the highest number of strikes and other forms of labour unrest on account of various financial and disciplinary issues: 'Wage and allowance, bonus, personnel, indiscipline and violence, and financial stringency were the major reasons for these strikes and lockouts.'[29] In 2014, Gujarat was the Indian state where the number of strikes was the highest, at 26 (as against 19 in Tamil Nadu).[30] One of the longest strikes took place in the Nano factory. In February 2016, 422 of the 420 workers went on strike. They protested against the suspension of other workers for indiscipline, but besides the reinstatement of the 28 suspended workers, they had other demands, including union formation and wage increases.[31] A compromise was reached after one month, by which time most of the suspended workers were reinstated, unions were recognised and negotiations on wages began.

The informalisation of work was one of the reasons why Gujarat's social indicators continued to show such disparities.

SOCIAL INDICATORS: THE 'MODEL' IN QUESTION

The social indicators of Gujarat contrast starkly with its economic achievements. Indeed, the Gandhinagar-based Directorate of Economics and Statistics conceded in its 2013 report that 'the improvement in the human development scenario in the state is [...] not commensurate with the economic progress that the state has witnessed since 2000–01'.[32]

In fact, social indicators varied considerably in the 2000s. The state significantly improved literacy under Narendra Modi, who emphasised girls' education. Every year he visited girls' schools in order to publicise female educational initiatives. He even initiated a Vidya Laxmi bond programme whereby, in areas where female literacy rates were less than 35 per cent, a bond of

1,000 rupees was provided at the time of admission in Standard 1, repayable after completion of Standard 7. Bibek Debroy highlights another key policy decision: the appointment of 'para-teachers', known as *vidhyasahayakas*, which contributed to a good pupil–teacher ratio in primary schools (30, when the national average was 42).[33] For the first time in the history of Gujarat, the literacy rate increased by more than ten percentage points in the ten years from 2001 to 2011, with the gender education gap and urban–rural education gap diminishing significantly (see Table 6.2). However, other states did better, and therefore Gujarat's position sank 'from sixteenth in 2001 to eighteenth in 2011 in terms of growth in literacy'[34]—and an in-depth report from the NGO Pratham showed that rural Gujarat lagged behind states like Haryana.[35]

This state of affairs was partly due to the legacy that the Modi government inherited from its predecessors, but also to its own policies. The ratio of state expenditure on education to the Gujarat state domestic product (GSDP) dropped from more than 2 per cent in 1999–2000 to less than 2 per cent in 2007–08.[36] In 2010–11, Gujarat spent 15.9 per cent of its budget on education, while Bihar, Chhattisgarh, Haryana, Kerala, Maharashtra, Orissa, Rajasthan, Uttar Pradesh and West Bengal spent between 16 per cent and 20.8 per cent, the national average being 16.6 per cent.[37] Over the years 2001-02–2012-13, Gujarat spent 13.22 per cent of its budget on education, whereas the national average was slightly above 15 per cent (see Table 6.3).[38] In fact, between 2000–01 and 2012–13, only 4 states out of the 21 listed in Table 6.3. spent less than Gujarat on education. If, nevertheless, the literacy rate increased significantly—though not as much as in other states—this achievement may have been due less to the fact that the educational system had become more effective, irrespective of the financial means at its disposal, than to the growing number of families sending their children to private schools—which represented more than 18 per cent of all primary schools in Gujarat in 2011–12[39]—mostly in urban areas.[40]

Gujarat's social indicators other than education were even less positive under Modi. While the per capita income growth rate was remarkably high, the poverty reduction rate was not as satisfactory as in other states. With 23 per cent of its citizens living below the poverty line in 2010, Gujarat did better than the Indian average (29.8 per cent), but it had reduced this proportion by less than ten percentage points in five years, whereas six other states had done better (see Table 6.4). According to the Planning Commission of India, 31.8 per cent of Gujaratis lived below the poverty line in 2011, more than in Kerala, Punjab, Himachal Pradesh and Haryana.[41] The relatively low poverty reduction rate of Gujarat had something to do with the average wages of casual workers in urban and rural areas.[42] According to a report of the National Sample Survey (NSS) of 2011, Gujarat had some of the lowest average daily wages for casual labourers in urban areas. These wages were not only much below the national average, but on a par with those in Uttar Pradesh. The NSS report, *Employment and Unemployment in India*, showed that in 2007–08 average wages or salaries of regular workers or salaried employees were 199 rupees per day, while they were 267 rupees in Bihar.[43]

Poverty went hand in hand with malnourishment in the Gujarat of this period. One of the social indicators in which Gujarat lagged the most dramatically behind other states was the 'hunger index'. This is based on three indicators: the prevalence of calorie undernourishment, the proportion of underweight children below the age of five, and the under-five mortality rate. In 2007, with 23.3 per cent, 44.7 per cent and 6.1 per cent respectively per 1,000 of its population, Gujarat came number 13 in a list of 17 states, below Orissa.[44] In 2011, the Indian Institute of Public Administration published a report showing that at least one of these three indicators had not improved. The situation was so bad that in 2012 the Gujarat government asked for 4.5 billion rupees of aid from the Government of India to fight malnourishment.[45] This demand was justified by the drought conditions—for which the government of Gujarat had already asked 187.23 billion rupees.[46]

With only 43 per cent of its children achieving a normal weight, Gujarat came last among 17 Indian states—and remained behind the national average by ten percentage points (see Table 6.5).[47] In 2013 the Comptroller and Auditor General (CAG) indicated that a third of the children of Gujarat remained 'underweight'. The CAG conceded that the state government had made efforts to improve the situation, but some of them were misplaced: 'The government focused more on nutritional status of children in the age group of 3–5 years, whereas the highest malnourishment was noticed in children between 0–3 years.'[48] Similarly, according to the 66th round of the National Sample Survey that took place in 2009–10, out of 35 states and Union territories, Gujarat came 34th in terms of consumption of cereals.[49]

Nor was the state doing very well in terms of the infant mortality rate (IMR). The situation did improve on that front. The state ranked 25th in 2001 and it was 22nd (on a par with Jammu and Kashmir) in 2011. However, while the IMR of Gujarat was below the national average by six percentage points in 2001, the difference had reduced only to three percentage points in 2011—many states had done better, as is evident from Table 6.6. Out of the 15 largest states of India, Gujarat ranked seventh as far as IMR was concerned in 1990–94, and it remained at the same level in 2005–10. Writing in the early 2010s, Sandeep Sharma pointed out that 'IMR in Gujarat is 63 compared to 57 at the national level and U5MR [under-five mortality rate] is 77 compared to 74 at the national level'.[50]

This situation was not unrelated to the way public health was neglected by the government. With 2.8 per cent of its budget devoted to health-related expenditures, Gujarat ranked last out of 17 large states in 2000–01; according to the Reserve Bank of India, it ranked seventh in 2010–11 when 4.2 per cent of the budget went to health.[51] The comparison between the average figures over three five-year-long periods is even more telling: health expenditure as a share of total expenditure declined in Gujarat from 4.39 per cent in 1995-96–1999-2000 to 2.02 per cent in 2000-01–2004-05 and 0.77 per cent in 2005-06–2009-10.[52] As a result, the 'ratio of doctors in public sector health care to population [was] 1:19,000, as against 1:9,000 in Tamil Nadu'.[53] In 2013, the deputy chairman of the Planning Commission, Montek Ahluwalia, tried to draw the attention of Narendra Modi to this issue, but he replied that his state spent 42 per cent of its budget on the social sector,[54] without providing a breakdown of this aggregate figure.

Infant mortality and malnourishment are not unrelated to gender ratios since they both partly reflect the treatment of girls. In 2011 the child sex ratio in the 0–6 age group was three percentage points above that of 2001 (886 girls per 1,000 boys, as against 883 three years before), but it was still below those of Uttar Pradesh, Himachal Pradesh, Madhya Pradesh and Orissa. And the overall sex ratio continued to decline, from 921 per 1,000 ten years before to 918 in 2011. At that time, Gujarat ranked 25th among 35 Indian states and Union territories.[55]

As a result of all these factors, in terms of the human development index (HDI) Gujarat slipped from 10th place in 1999–2000 to 11th in 2011.[56]

To sum up: the statistical picture of Modi's Gujarat was rather puzzling. While the rise of per capita revenue was remarkable, many social indicators were out of step with the state's economic success. This discrepancy can best be understood if one disaggregates the average per capita revenue: in 2013, 12,000 Gujaratis declared a taxable income of more than 10 million rupees—and there would be many more super-rich to be counted if undeclared revenues were taken into account[57]—

whereas almost a third of the population lived below the poverty line. In conclusion, the rise of inequalities resulted from the pro-rich policies analysed in the previous chapter and the lack of social expenditures that we have just examined. The state was particularly indifferent to the poor of rural Gujarat.

THE GROWING URBAN–RURAL DIVIDE

The gap between peasants and urban dwellers became more pronounced all over India after the economic liberalisation announced in 1991. This is evident from the National Sample Survey data, including the average monthly per capita expenditure (MPCE), one of the most reliable indicators for measuring standards of living. The rural–urban differential, in terms of MPCE, grew dramatically between 1993–94 and 2007–08: the MPCE was already 62.9 per cent higher in towns and cities than in the villages of India in 1993–94, and the gap reached 90.7 per cent fourteen years later, before a decline to 83.9 per cent in 2011–12 (see Table 6.7). In contrast to this trajectory, the Gujarat differential climbed from 49.8 per cent in 1993–94 to 68 per cent in 2007–08 and remained the same in 2011–12. Gujarat was not the state where this differential was the most marked; far from it. Haryana (because of satellite cities like Gurgaon), Karnataka (because of Bangalore) and even Rajasthan, Uttar Pradesh and West Bengal saw the gap between urban and rural standards of living increase more dramatically. But Gujarat was also unable to reverse this trend, in contrast to Andhra Pradesh, Kerala, Tamil Nadu and Bihar.

Not only had the rural population of Gujarat lost ground vis-à-vis the urban population of the state—even if the gap was no longer widening—but it also started to lag behind the rural populations of other states. In 1993–94 and 2007–08, rural Gujaratis were ranked fourth in terms of MPCE. In 2011–12, they occupied the ninth place, behind the rural populations of Haryana, Karnataka,

West Bengal, Andhra Pradesh, Tamil Nadu, Maharashtra, Punjab and Kerala. Urban dwellers did not do better, though they had not been highly ranked beforehand (seventh and eighth places respectively in earlier surveys).

The socio-economic story of Modi's Gujarat is partly summarised in Table 6.8, which shows that in 1993–94, just before the BJP took power, 24.21 per cent of the population lived below the poverty line (BPL), and the percentage was more significant in urban Gujarat (27.89 per cent) than in the rural areas (22.18 per cent).[58] Of 17 states only 2 did better as far as the proportion of the rural BPL population was concerned (Andhra Pradesh and Punjab), and only in 5 other states (Andhra Pradesh, Karnataka, Madhya Pradesh, Rajasthan and Tamil Nadu) was the percentage of the rural BPL population less than that of the urban. By 1999–2000, the situation had changed dramatically. The share of the rural BPL population of Gujarat had declined from 22.18 per cent to 13.17 per cent, but that of the urban BPL population had diminished even more significantly, from 27.89 per cent to 7.52 per cent. As a result, the gap between the urban and the rural poor widened significantly: of 17 Indian states, 9 had more effectively contained urban–rural inequalities.

In 2004–05, the methodology used by the Planning Commission to measure the poverty line changed. India now began to use what is known as the 'Tendulkar methodology' (named after Suresh D. Tendulkar). However, this change did not affect the trend mentioned above. The proportion of rural poor did not decrease significantly in Gujarat: out of 17 states, only 6 were worse off in this regard and 10 others were doing better, including Rajasthan, Tamil Nadu, Karnataka and Andhra Pradesh. As a result, the gap between the percentage of the rural poor and that of the urban poor was one of the largest in India: out of 17 states, 12 were doing better.

In 2009–10, the situation had improved marginally. The proportion of the BPL rural poor in Gujarat remained high: with

26.7 per cent, the state was number 10 (out of 17 states), even though it remained below the national average (33.8 per cent). The proportion of urban poor, on the other hand, continued to diminish. In fact, in terms of urban poverty reduction, Gujarat was doing well: it occupied the fifth place out of 17 states. As a result, the gap between the proportion of urban poor and rural poor remained very pronounced (Gujarat ranked number 11, which meant that ten states on our list had contained urban–rural inequalities more effectively).

The situation hardly changed in 2011–12. The proportion of BPL rural dwellers in Gujarat remained high but had diminished: with 21.54 per cent, Gujarat occupied ninth place out of 17. Though the proportion of the urban poor had decreased, this trend was slower than in the past: Gujarat now ranked eighth. As a result, the gap between the proportion of urban poor and rural poor was larger than in most Indian states (Gujarat ranked number 13, which meant that 12 states had contained the urban–rural divide more effectively).

The urban–rural differential found expression in several indicators, including health-related ones. The IMR is a case in point. Till 2000–04, the rural–urban gap in this domain was lower than the national average, but in 2005–10 it exceeded it.[59] The Sample Registration System (SRS) survey, in a September 2014 report, showed that things did not improve during Modi's last term as chief minister: Gujarat's rural IMR was 4.3 per cent, as against the urban IMR of 2.2 per cent, suggesting a gap of 2.1 points, higher than that of 20 major Indian states, with the exception of Assam.[60]

This state of affairs reflected the gap between the agricultural growth rate and that of other sectors.[61] In 2014 the National Sample Survey Office (NSSO) published the results of the 70th round of its *Key Indicators of Situation of Agricultural Households in India*, which showed that in Gujarat the average monthly net receipts from cultivation per agricultural household stood at

Rs 2,933 rupees, which was less than the national average of Rs 3,081 rupees; the state ranked twelfth in a list of 21 major Indian states.[62] This situation largely explains the high level of rural indebtedness. In 2015, the NSSO's report *Key Indicators of Debt and Investment in India* revealed that in Gujarat 65 per cent of rural households had taken loans with interest rates above 25 per cent (for half of these households, the rate was even more than 30 per cent). Only one state in India—Jammu and Kashmir—had a higher share of its rural population affected by this kind of indebtedness.[63]

The gap between urban and rural Gujarat can also be explained by the policy of the state government. In 2007, Urban Resource Centres were created to provide one-stop-shop services in several poor townships of Ahmedabad. This 13.2 million rupee initiative was part of the Garib Samruddhi Yojna scheme, a 130 billion rupee state government programme for 500,000 poor urban families. In 2011, the government went further. The urban development minister, Nitin Patel, announced additional assistance: 910 million rupees were given to the urban poor for building homes in the municipal areas.[64] Similar financial support was not provided to the rural poor.

While some urban bias was rather routine in Modi's Gujarat, the urban poor were not its main beneficiaries: the government catered systematically to the needs of towns and cities because of the electoral support it received from the middle class (see chapter 9)—and this inclination made the urban–rural gap more pronounced. For instance, Jennifer Bussell has shown that the reforms aimed at modernising the administration focused on cities in Gujarat:

> For example, the Civic Centre initiative, Gujarat's first state-led one-stop services program, was launched in the largest city, Ahmedabad, and then extended only to other urban centres. These centres offer services almost entirely targeted to middle and upper class [...] Only one service, hawker's licenses, has

> a clear appeal to lower-class groups [...] A similar initiative in Gujarat, which was initiated by the District Collector's office in Ahmedabad, was selected by the state government to be implemented across all district offices. Because this initiative was intended to reach rural districts, it had the potential to provide services to a broader group of citizens and in particular to poorer constituents [...] However, there has been little pressure to implement this directive, resulting in a failure by collectors in other districts to actually initiate the project [...] this reflects the lack of attention to, and political support for, service development in areas that would most likely benefit poor, rural citizens rather than the urban middle and upper classes.[65]

The urban bias highlighted by Jennifer Bussell is also discernible in the preference given to industry. Water is a case in point. While the opening of the Narmada dam reduced water stress affecting peasants, the canals carrying water had yet to reach all the fields, especially in Saurashtra, at the end of Modi's second five-year term as Gujarat chief minister. This was due to bad planning, but also to the fact that priority in water distribution went to industry and to cities. Second, prime agricultural land was given over to industry. Big companies received some of this land, as mentioned above, and their industrial (or port-oriented) activities sometimes harmed the interests of peasants. In Mahua, a Special Economic Zone (SEZ) of 268 ha was granted to Nirma 'to set up a cement plant besides a mining lease on more than 3,000 hectares in areas across the coastline in Bhavnagar district'.[66] The local BJP MLA, Dr Kanubhai Kalsariya, objected that the water tank upon which the villagers depended would be seriously damaged. He was sidelined and therefore resigned from the party to fight the government's policy.[67] Half-a-dozen equally large projects were responsible for the loss of thousands of hectares of agricultural land.[68]

Access to land also became more difficult for peasants because of the liberalisation measures mentioned above. Taking stock of the implications of this policy, Nikita Sud points out:

> The state has given up on the poor as active agents of development. It has ceased to consider them as owners of productive assets. The failure of land-to-the-poor schemes is in practical terms blamed on them, rather than on the politics of redistribution, and the role of dominant castes and classes and the state in this failure. Indeed, as a senior government official suggested in an interview, Adivasis and lower castes have not been able to realise the potential of land—even when they have had access to it. They cannot adopt appropriate technologies or access adequate inputs.[69]

Peasant leaders in Gujarat went so far as to claim that 'Agriculture is being systematically "killed" so that when industry comes, farmers are not only willing, but desperate to sell their lands'.[70] While these arguments sound alarmist, the primary sector indeed declined from 19.5 per cent of the gross state domestic product in 2004–05 to only 14.6 per cent in 2010–11, whereas the share of industry went up from 36.5 per cent to 39.4 per cent and the tertiary sector from 44 per cent to 46 per cent.[71] While development economists would interpret this as a sign of structural transformation, with the share of output shifting to more productive sectors, this evolution was not so positive because the shift was limited to output, as employment did not move to more productive sectors.

Not only was the rural part of Gujarat not supported by the state as much as the urban areas, but agriculture in the state became more polarised in socio-economic terms. These growing social inequalities were primarily due to the widening of the gap between peasants growing cash crops—which were promoted by the state—and those cultivating food grains. S. Sen and C. Mallik emphasise that

> the market reforms undertaken by the state to enable farmers to directly sell their produce to wholesalers, exporters and large trading companies, i.e., without operating through commission agents, have acted as an inducement to farmers to cultivate high

> value crops on one hand and facilitated contract farming on the other. As a result, Gujarat's non-food agricultural economy has been growing fast, much faster than that observed at the all-India level.[72]

Cotton is a case in point. It benefited from 'highly remunerative MSP [minimum support prices]' and from 'improvement in the irrigation conditions promoted by the state'.[73] Its yield grew by 217 per cent between 2001–02 and 2008–09.[74] However, cotton could only be cultivated by richer farmers, partly because of the cost of irrigation, and partly because of the 'high cost of BT cotton cultivation'.[75] In contrast, Sen and Mallik in the early 2010s observed that 'there are clear evidences of further marginalization of the already vulnerable economic and social groups in terms of access to cultivated land over the last five years in the state [of Gujarat]'.[76] The relative boom of cash crops like cotton, sugar cane and groundnuts largely explains the growth rate of agriculture in the state, but it aggravated inequalities among the peasantry.

GIVING UP ON THE POOR

From the point of view of social indicators, the very notion of a 'Gujarat model' is a 'myth'.[77] But though there is no model, there is in fact a pattern, as the poor social indicators of Modi's Gujarat reflect the policies he championed.

First, the priority given to mega projects and the supply-side policy (or business friendliness), which, as the previous chapter showed, were two mainstays of Modi's economic strategy, attracted big firms which were highly capitalistic, and therefore not labour-intensive. They also invested in Gujarat because of the low level of wages and the flexibility that prevailed in the job market—as was evident from the large number of contracted labourers.

Second, the Modi government did not spend much on the poor as a rule. In fact, Gujarat was one of the states where funds allotted to the social sector were not only limited, but also not fully disbursed.[78] In a 2010 report, the Reserve Bank of India showed that in 2005–10 Gujarat spent 5.1 per cent of its annual budget as an average in the social sector—less than all other states, except Haryana and Punjab (the national average being 5.8 per cent). Education and public health were cases in point, as we have seen. But the government of Gujarat did not even utilise large amounts of the money that had been budgeted: in 2010, 42 per cent of plan money remained unutilised.[79]

That the Modi government was unwilling to spend more on social expenditures chimes with the objective of a minimal state, which has always been an ideal of Hindu nationalist ideologues.[80] Unsurprisingly, the state came first out of 20 states in a study by Bibek Debroy and Laveesh Bhandari of 'economic freedom' in terms of 'size of the government': no other state had so little public expenditure, had downsized its public sector undertakings (PSUs) to such an extent, or collected so few taxes.[81] Since it does not spend much, a minimal state has indeed one major benefit: low fiscal pressure on the corporate sector and on taxpayers. From a social point of view, limited social expenditure reflects a tolerance of profound inequality. When it had to spend, the Modi government did not necessarily consider social spending as a priority, compared with infrastructure—which, from its point of view, should bring development for all, once entrepreneurs (freer to invest than elsewhere because of the minimal state) could best display their true capabilities. This supply-side approach has clear affinities with the trickle-down theory that liberals promoted in post-1991 India. Unsurprisingly, the World Bank director himself endorsed this policy during a three-day visit to India in 2014.[82]

The strategy of the Modi government in Gujarat in terms of social expenditures was in tune with its fiscal policy, whose redistributive potential was barely used to reduce inequality. Indeed, the government's policy did not contain inequalities in

Gujarati society, where the weaker sections were concentrated among villagers. Nor was it intended to do so since in a liberal dispensation, a disproportionate amount of the benefits of growth are bound to be captured by the minority with capital who can benefit from the relaxation of state regulations. This capital can be intellectual or financial or consist of land.

The Modi government itself acknowledged that it had failed to help the poor during the 2009 annual Chintan Shibir (literally, introspection camp or brainstorming session) gathering of ministers, MLAs and 250 senior bureaucrats. The report that was discussed then emphasised that 'non-availability of houses for the poor in urban as well as rural areas [was] acute and [was] an immediate source of concern'.[83] The situation was reportedly worse in the villages, where 1.137 million BPL families were 'homeless'. According to the report, the poor represented about a third of society; the middle class was roughly of the same size (as we'll see in chapter 9).

How far was Gujarat the testing ground for Prime Minister Modi's government policies after 2014 from the point of view of its socio-economic programmes? The continuity between the regional experiment and the national policy of Modi's administration during his first term as prime minister is again striking. First, the idea of a minimal government reflected in Modi's 2014 campaign slogan 'minimum government, maximum governance' resulted, as in Gujarat, in a centralisation of economic power and a corresponding de-institutionalisation of economic policy.[84] If, in Gujarat, Modi could personally bring the Nano factory to his state, as prime minister he could impose the 2016 demonetisation of Rs 500 and Rs 2000 banknotes unilaterally, without consulting the Reserve Bank of India. This decision resulted in a prolonged cash shortage that badly affected the informal sector.

Secondly, the job problem, which was one feature of the 'Gujarat model', has become one of the most acute issues in Modi's

India, where the 'worst ever rate of joblessness in the country'[85] was recorded by the National Sample Survey during 2017–18. While the puzzle of jobless growth had already been present before 2014, it was aggravated by the support big companies received, at the expense of the SMEs—the largest providers of jobs in industry, handicrafts and services. For instance, big companies received loans from public banks and accumulated debts they could not reimburse,[86] making the situation of many banks so precarious that the Reserve Bank of India prohibited them from granting loans, thereby penalising small and medium-sized enterprises whose access to credit had already started to shrink because of the decline in bank resources. A number of these SMEs—some of them very small—went bust. The crisis this sector experienced partly explains the crunch in the labour market.

Thirdly, Modi, as prime minister, did not consider inequalities as a priority any more than he did as chief minister and, therefore, did not use the mechanisms at his disposal for correcting them. Besides his fiscal policies, which we have already mentioned in the previous chapter, his attitude to the rural poor was revealing in this regard. A case in point is the vast programme initiated by Manmohan Singh in 2005 under the Mahatma Gandhi National Rural Employment Guarantee Act (MGNREGA).[87] This scheme brought millions of people out of poverty, not only by giving them an income, but also by revising the minimum wage in rural areas.[88] Partly for this reason, per capita rural income grew from 2.7 per cent per year between 1999 and 2004 to 9.7 per cent between 2006 and 2011.[89] Yet Modi and the BJP considered the programme a disaster because it assisted the poor instead of fostering entrepreneurship. In the first BJP government's parliamentary budget session in February 2015, Modi concluded that MGNREGA was nothing but a 'monument' to the 'failures' of previous governments.[90] Enormous amounts continued to be allocated to the programme, but during the fiscal year either the funds were not distributed or else drastic cuts were made. The Supreme Court was obliged to intervene in May 2016 to compel the government to disburse the funds earmarked for MGNREGA. Year after year, most of the MGNREGA funds vanished midway through the fiscal year.[91] Other rural development programmes have also had their budgets cut drastically, starting with those designed to develop irrigation, despite rural areas being in dire need of them.[92] The assessment made by Himanshu Kaushik, an expert in this matter, captures the essence of the problem: 'Real investment in agriculture declined by one percentage point per annum during the first four years of the Modi government.'[93]

The BJP did not even come to the aid of farmers, those who—unlike farm workers—own parcels of land and sell their surplus. In his campaigning, Modi had promised farmers that the state would buy their products on agriculture markets at 1.5 times the production costs. But the means of calculating such costs was never specified, and, in fact, minimum support prices proved to be not high enough.[94] Worse still, when market prices rose, the government tried to reduce them by importing more of the commodity in question or by preventing farmers from exporting so as to maintain an abundant supply.[95] As a result, the wholesale price index declined and even became negative in 2018.[96] Why? The 'people' the BJP represented were primarily urban and the party displayed an 'urban consumer bias'.[97]

The tensions between the Modi government and farmers culminated in the 2020–21 farmers' movement which, echoing the mobilisation of the Bharatiya Kisan Sangh against the Gujarat government during Modi's first five-year term as chief minister, protested against three laws which were seen by the demonstrators as promoting agro-food companies, like those of Mukesh Ambani and Gautam Adani, at the expense of the peasantry.

In addition to communal polarisation, social polarisation based on two reinforcing fault lines—the divide between rural and urban and, within these two worlds, that between rich and poor—appears as another key feature of Modi's politics that crystallised into a Gujarati test site (a feature that was also closely linked to his pro-business attitude). How has Modi circumvented—or mitigated—the risk of alienating large sections of society by adopting such policies? Primarily by inventing in Gujarat a populist repertoire that has remained the trademark of his politics till today.

PART FOUR

THE MAKING OF MODITVA

The RSS was conceived of as an organisation in which individuals had to sacrifice their identity: the Sangh was above the man. This is why *swayamsevaks* all have to wear the same uniform, from foot soldiers to the supreme leader, the *sarsanghchalak*. Nor was the *sarsanghchalak* supposed to dominate in any sacralised or absolute manner, because the guru of the organisation was its saffron flag rather than an individual. The RSS's founder, K.B. Hedgewar, never wanted to be considered as a guru, and even his successor, M.S. Golwalkar, in spite of his nickname, Guruji, did not break with this tradition. They were probably both aware that their organisation might not continue to grow, or even survive, after their deaths if it were too closely associated with them as individuals. The secondary role of its leader vis-à-vis the organisation explains the collegiality of the RSS decision-making process; and institutions like the Akhil Bharatiya Pratinidhi Sabha and the Akhil Bharatiya Kendra Mandal remain key to the functioning of the organisation. Nor are *sarsanghchalaks* high-profile public figures.

Narendra Modi, though he was trained in this tradition as a *pracharak*, has abjured such a collegial style of functioning. That he was seconded to the BJP and appointed chief minister made this transition partly necessary because political leaders must project themselves as public figures to win popular support. However, no Hindu nationalist leader had gone so far in this direction before. At the state level, despite faction fights, a more collective modus operandi—under the aegis of local RSS leaders—had remained the rule. At the national level, not only did Deendayal Upadhyaya (the most important face of the Jana Sangh in the 1960s) remain a rather unassuming thinker rather than a crowd-puller, but his successors, A.B. Vajpayee and L.K. Advani, worked a double act for almost four decades. Even the Rath Yatra (in 1990), during which Advani was presented as a Hindu national hero, a man with a mission on his way to Ayodhya, did not result in the marginalisation of Vajpayee, who became the BJP's candidate for prime minister six years later.

The rise to power of Narendra Modi in Gujarat reflects a different trajectory and strategy. Never before had the BJP seen such a concentration and personalisation of power at the state level. This was evident not only in the way Modi controlled the bureaucracy, his first instrument, and established—gradually—his authority over the party, but also in his style of campaigning and mobilisation. This national-populist style, combining Hindu nationalism and a direct relationship with the people, gave birth to a new concept: Moditva.

7

PERSONAL POWER VERSUS HINDUTVA'S COLLEGIALITY

> The Newsmaker, we believe, must be someone who occupies mindspace, shapes public opinion, generates column inches and clocks time on the airwaves.
>
> Aroon Purie, explaining why Modi was designated 'Newsmaker of the Year' in 2003[1]

Narendra Modi managed to concentrate power in his hands very quickly in the first half of the 2000s. The first group to fall in line was the bureaucracy. Indian civil servants consider that they cannot resist their political masters easily because they can be transferred, penalised and even dismissed. The conquest of the Gujarat state BJP was more difficult, not only because state party leaders resisted, but also because they were supported by personalities within the RSS. Modi surmounted all these opponents and ultimately exerted a largely personal authority because he developed a parallel power structure and built networks allowing him to relate directly to the people.

This pattern calls to mind Indira Gandhi's achievements in the 1970s. After the 1969 split that deprived her of most of the Congress machinery, Indira tried to reform her newly founded party, the Congress (I), but failed to transform it into an effective cadre-based organisation. Hence her decision to rely more on the bureaucracy—a move which culminated during the Emergency[2]—and to go to the people. Narendra Modi, in Gujarat, followed the same route after he realised that the state BJP and the Sangh Parivar at large were unreliable.

(EX-)CIVIL SERVANTS AS INSTRUMENTS OF PERSONAL POWER

After becoming chief minister, Modi declared that he wanted to restore a work ethic and sense of discipline in the bureaucracy. In June 2002 he organised a meeting of the district collectors and district development officers and exhorted them 'to create a "distinct work culture" in government offices and warned that officials would be held responsible if people from *talukas* [sub-units of a district] and districts [were] forced to bring their problems to the Sachivalaya [headquarters of the state bureaucracy] for their solution'.[3] In 2003, it became clear that the bureaucracy was to be Modi's main instrument when he announced that he would personally review every year the performance of each of the 29 government departments. This review, spread over a month, looked into 'past performance, targets and their achievability'.[4] In order to ensure the bureaucracy became more directly involved in the government's policy, Modi introduced an annual three-day Chintan Shibir bringing together his ministers, BJP MLAs, 'and every bureaucrat and senior police official'.[5]

His modus operandi alienated several senior bureaucrats. One of them told Rajiv Shah: 'Modi decides on every issue and wants his officials to carry out his wishes. CMO [Chief Minister Office] officials have been reduced to making PowerPoint presentations to Modi on how his schemes can be put into practice.'[6] According to Shah's calculation, 'the number of IAS bureaucrats who have resigned in the last five years [between

2001 and 2006] is more than the total of the previous 40 years since Gujarat became a state'.[7] Indeed, between 2001 and 2008, a record number of 11 IAS officers resigned. One of them spoke on condition of anonymity: 'It is not possible for a sensible and hard-working IAS officer to work in the hostile environment created by Modi's autocratic style of functioning.'[8] The leader of the opposition in the Gujarat state Assembly, Arjun Modhwadia, explained this change differently. He declared in 2006, about Modi: 'He is the first chief minister in 45 years who insists that bureaucrats make all file notings in deference to his wishes. If any file noting is not of his liking, Modi returns the file instructing the official to jot down his viewpoint.'[9] In addition to those who resigned, 24 IAS officers were transferred to Delhi by 2008.[10] Some bureaucrats also resented the way Modi publicly exposed those administrators who were guilty of various irregularities—there were 13 in 2010, for example.[11]

Modi clearly imported the RSS culture he had acquired as a *pracharak* into the state machinery. When Nilanjan Mukhopadhyay asked him how he learnt 'the ropes of administration and governance after he became chief minister', he responded: 'I had learnt from the Sangh the basic skill of running an organization.'[12] In the RSS, the line of command is notoriously hierarchical, even military. Indeed, several army officers expressed their admiration for Modi. For instance, Major General I.S. Singha of the Golden Katar division declared in 2011, at the inauguration of the 'Know Your Army' exhibition in Ahmedabad: 'Chief Minister Modi has all the qualities of a successful army commander. His programmes are aimed at development of both the state and the nation [...] Like in the army he keeps deadline for completion of work, and ensures that target is achieved by the set time.'[13]

Modi's style of governance did not rely only on the state apparatus. He seemed not to fully trust independent minded civil servants; and he did not believe in state power only, as was evident from the growing role of the private sector in the development of Gujarat. This lack of reliance on the state apparatus was reflected in the decline in the number of state functionaries. In 2008, six key departments—including Finance and Urban Development—had no director,[14] and in the Department of Finance, 2,635 positions out of 9,727 were vacant in 2011.[15]

Instead of investing in the bureaucracy at large, he gradually selected a handful of civil servants who became part of his personal entourage. G.C. Murmu is a case in point. A 1985 Gujarat-cadre IAS officer, he was made joint secretary of the Home Department, in the ministry of Amit Shah, in 2004. He then worked with Modi and Shah during the post-violence investigation. According to R.B. Sreekumar, Murmu in 2004 was 'authorised and entrusted with the task of tutoring and briefing government officials deposing before the Nanavati Commission by the highest authorities of the government and Home Department'.[16]

Another senior bureaucrat who became a close associate of Narendra Modi in Gujarat was P.K. Mishra. A 1972-batch IAS officer belonging to the Gujarat cadre, Mishra was Modi's personal secretary in 2001–04. In his comments on the Special Investigation Team's preliminary report into the Gujarat riots, the head of the SIT, R.K. Raghavan, noted that Mishra was one of the bureaucrats who 'had been accommodated in post-retirement jobs, and [were] therefore obliged not to speak against the Chief Minister or State government'.[17] Indeed, after retirement in 2008, Mishra was appointed head of the Gujarat Electricity Regulatory Commission (GERC), an important institution responsible for fixing the price of power. But journalists considered that he would also 'work as the most formidable advisor to Modi—especially on how to "manage" state-based IAS babus [officials] and where to transfer them'.[18]

Not only did key bureaucrats become part of Modi's inner circle, but they also solidified the nexus between his government and the corporate sector. This triangular relationship is exemplified by the role of former bureaucrats in the Adani Group. Indeed, beyond the political connections of the Adani Group, the link between the Gujarat state and Adani became almost organic after several ex-IAS officials in Gujarat went on to join Adani companies. In 2002, Sanjay Gupta, a 1985-batch IAS officer who had played a pivotal role in the Gujarat State Petroleum Corporation (GSPC), resigned from the administration to become the CEO of Adani Infrastructure Project.[19] P.N. Roy Chowdhury, a former head of the Gujarat Maritime Board and principal secretary to the Gujarat Department of Agriculture and Cooperation, became joint president of strategic planning at Adani Ports and Special Economic Zone Limited.[20] In 2006, Adani Ports recruited Vipul Mittra, an IAS officer who had recently resigned from the service; he had been vice chairman of the Kandla Port Trust.[21]

In addition to IAS officers (and police officers), lawyers were part of this nexus too: we have already mentioned the case of Tushar Mehta. In July 2013, the additional advocate general of Gujarat, Kamal Trivedi, represented Rajesh Adani in a duty evasion case launched by the Enforcement Directorate. When asked if this amounted to a conflict of interest, his answer was: 'I do not cease to be a lawyer just because I am the advocate general.' According to the lawyer Anand Yagnik in 2013, over twenty lawyers who had fought cases against the Adanis were now retained by the group.[22]

In the words of Ghanshyam Shah, Narendra Modi 'leaned on the government machinery' (and more especially on a select number of bureaucrats) to 'reduce his dependence on and "interference" from the party [the BJP] and Parivar *karyakartas* [workers]', whom, in many cases, he did not trust—to such an extent that he 'evolved an informal surveillance system to keep track on [their] political movements'.[23] Indeed, Modi was in control of the state apparatus of Gujarat before prevailing over his own party. In fact, the BJP was still to be fully conquered by the mid-2000s, partly because of the opposition of senior leaders, and partly because of the resistance of other constituent elements of the Sangh Parivar.

THE MAN ABOVE THE ORGANISATION: A NEW CONCEPT FOR THE SANGH PARIVAR

The Conquest of the State BJP

When Modi returned to Gujarat in 2001, he no longer commanded the party apparatus of the state BJP. Some of those with whom he had built the party in the 1980s and 1990s were now in control but were not prepared to collaborate with him anymore. Among them was Sanjay Joshi. An engineer from Nagpur and a full-time *pracharak*, Joshi had worked under Modi when he was organisation secretary of the state BJP. When Modi was banished from Gujarat, Joshi took over from him. According to Bharat Desai, at that time Modi 'thought he would be able to operate through his protégé, but Joshi only kept the party's interest supreme'.[24] In the process, Joshi also became closer to the chief minister, Keshubhai Patel. When Modi was sent back to Gujarat by the New Delhi headquarters, Joshi became national secretary. This kind of swap made things easier for the new chief minister although Modi still continued to spar with Joshi.[25]

But other state BJP leaders resisted Modi's rise to power. Among them, Haren Pandya was probably the most determined. Home minister in the government of his mentor Keshubhai Patel, Pandya was asked by Modi to vacate his seat in the safe constituency of Ellisbridge (Ahmedabad), to enable him to be elected MLA in a by-election—something he needed in order to remain chief minister. Pandya, who had been shifted to the post of revenue minister by Modi, refused. But Vajubhai Vala agreed to oblige and Modi became one of the MLAs for Rajkot in his place.

Vala was subsequently rewarded by being appointed minister of finance in the Modi government and state party president in 2005, while Pandya was excluded from pre-poll meetings,[26] and failed to get a ticket to stand for Ellisbridge in 2002.[27] Pandya's fate was probably sealed because of his testimony before the Concerned Citizens Tribunal. Vinod K. Jose narrates what followed in a rare piece of investigative journalism:

> In May 2002, three months after the start of the riots, Pandya secretly gave a deposition to an independent fact-finding panel led by Justice V.R. Krishna Iyer. Modi could not have known what Pandya said, but written records show that Modi's principal secretary, P.K. Mishra, instructed the director-general of state intelligence to track Pandya's movements, and in particular those related to the fact-finding panel. The intelligence director took down the instructions in a register—the entry for 7 June 2002 reads as follows: 'Dr P.K. Mishra added that Shri Harenbhai Pandya, minister for revenue, is suspected to be the minister involved in the matter. Thereafter, he gave one mobile number 9824030629 and asked for getting call details.'
>
> Five days later, on 12 June 2002, there is another entry in the register: 'Informed Dr P.K. Mishra that the minister who is suspected to have met the private inquiry commission ([named after] Justice V.R. Krishna Iyer) is known to be Mr Haren Pandya. I also informed that the matter cannot be given in writing as this issue is quite sensitive and not connected with the charter of duties given to State Intelligence Bureau vide Bombay Police Manual. It is learnt that the telephone number 9824030629 is the mobile phone of Shri Harenbhai Pandya.'
>
> News reports soon revealed that an unnamed minister in Modi's cabinet had deposed before the Iyer commission and described for the first time the meeting at Modi's residence after the train conflagration, at which Modi allegedly told his top police and intelligence officers that there would be justice for Godhra the next day, and ordered the police not to stand in the way of the 'Hindu backlash'.

The leak provided sufficient evidence for Modi to press a case of indiscipline against Pandya within the BJP, and two months later Pandya was forced to resign from the cabinet. But Modi had not finished. The state elections were due in December 2002, and Modi saw an opportunity to deny Pandya the Ellisbridge seat that he had refused to vacate a year earlier. 'Modi never forgets, and never forgives,' the BJP insider close to the chief minister told me. 'It doesn't help a politician to have such long-term vengeance.'

And so Modi denied Pandya the constituency he had represented for 15 years. The leadership of both the RSS and the BJP objected and asked Modi to relent, but he refused. At the end of November, RSS leader Madan Das Devi went to meet Modi at his home, bearing a message from the RSS supremo K.S. Sudarshan, his deputy Mohan Bhagwat, L.K. Advani and A.B. Vajpayee: Stop arguing, don't create division before the elections, and give Pandya his seat. Devi stayed late into the night, but Modi held his ground, the state party functionary said: 'He knew he would start getting phone calls from [RSS headquarters in] Nagpur and Delhi, since he did not listen to Devi. So that night, by 3 a.m., he got himself admitted into the Gandhinagar Civil Hospital for exhaustion and fatigue.'

Pandya, according to the party functionary, charged to the hospital to confront Modi. 'Haren told him, "Don't sleep like a coward. Have the guts to say no to me."' Modi refused to budge, and the RSS and BJP leaders finally gave in. After two days Modi was discharged from the hospital and handed Pandya's seat to a newcomer. And in December, he came back to power, riding the post-Godhra wave of communal polarisation.

Pandya, for his part, started to meet with every senior leader in the BJP and RSS—in Delhi and in Nagpur—telling them that Modi would destroy the party and the Sangh for his own personal gain. Senior BJP figures, who still regarded Pandya as a valuable asset to the party, decided to transfer him to headquarters in Delhi as a member of the national executive or a party spokesman. 'Modi even tried to scuttle that,' [Gordhan] Zadaphia [a man who had worked in the VHP before joining

BJP] told me. 'Pandya going to Delhi was going to be harmful for Modi in the long run.'

Three months later, on 26 March 2003, the day after Pandya received a fax from the party president instructing him to move to Delhi, he was murdered in Ahmedabad. The Gujarat police and the Central Bureau of Investigation (CBI) announced that Pandya had been assassinated in a joint operation between Pakistan's Inter-Services Intelligence, Lashkar-e-Taiba, and the Dubai-based underworld don Dawood Ibrahim. Twelve men were arrested and charged with Pandya's murder, but eight years later, in September 2011, the Gujarat High Court acquitted every single one and rubbished the entire case. 'The investigation has all throughout been botched up and blinkered,' the judge said. 'The investigating officers concerned ought to be held accountable for their ineptitude resulting in injustice, huge harassment of many persons concerned and enormous waste of public resources and public time of the courts.'[28]

Indeed, the judges considered that the investigation had not been conducted properly.[29] Soon afterwards, police sources were cited by the newspaper *DNA*, attributing the murder to Sohrabuddin and Prajapati, two victims of fake encounters.[30] Sanjiv Bhatt declared in a 2011 affidavit to the High Court of Gujarat that, while he was in charge of Sabarmati Central Prison, he had come across 'very important documentary evidence regarding the role of certain highly placed State functionaries/politicians and senior police officers of the State of Gujarat in the killing of Shri Haren Pandya'.[31] Bhatt added that Amit Shah, then home minister of state, ordered him to destroy the report, and that Modi and Shah 'were highly disturbed and agitated'[32] when he decided not to do so. D.G. Vanzara subsequently 'hinted at a political conspiracy behind Pandya's killing'.[33]

Pandya's successor at the home ministry, Gordhan Zadaphia, was in office during the 2002 riots and he too was eased out of Modi's government after the 2002 elections. Their differences apparently arose from questions of political style, as Zadaphia told Vinod Jose:

'Modi understands only one alphabet, and that is capital I,' Zadaphia told me. 'I was threatened with death by Modi himself.'

'It was in February 2005,' Zadaphia continued. 'I noticed an intelligence man from the state police following me, and when I confronted him, he told me he was instructed by the home minister's office to shadow me.' A few days later, Zadaphia said, there was a meeting of BJP legislators with the chief minister. 'I asked Modi in the meeting, Narendrabhai, what kind of spy activities are you doing against your own party legislators?' I asked, why is an intelligence man following me? Then Vajubhai Vala, a senior minister, took the microphone and said 'Okay Gordhanbhai, cool down. We will look into it, but this is not a question to be asked now.' Modi didn't speak at all, but I got a note from his secretary that said 'Please meet the CM'.

'I met him at his chamber after the meeting. Amit Shah was sitting there. Modi asked me, 'Why are you asking these kinds of questions in public?' I said, 'What shall I do? It is not a private matter.' Then he looked sternly into my eyes and said, 'Khatam ho jaoge Gordhanbhai ...'—You're going to get finished Gordhanbhai.

'I asked him, What kind of finishing? Physically or politically?

'He said, 'You complained against me to L.K. Advani and Om Mathur [a senior BJP leader] in Delhi.'

'I said, of course. There's no option for me other than to complain to the people in Delhi. But if you're saying you will finish me off, let me tell you, I'll die when my time comes. Don't try to threaten me again.'

Zadaphia moves around with a police escort and a dozen armed security men; as a former deputy home minister—and a controversial one at that—he was offered protection by the government after the riots. Pandya, however, did not have security guards. 'Haren was bold,' Zadaphia said. 'He thought nothing would happen to him. That was a mistake.'[34]

Eventually, Zadaphia left the BJP and formed his own party, the Mahagujarat Janata Party, in 2007, before the state elections.

Splits and faction fights were not new in the BJP. They developed at the state level and sometimes took an acute form. What was remarkable about the BJP in Gujarat in the 2000s was not only the unprecedented intensity of personal animosities but the ability of Narendra Modi to ignore the party organisation (including the high command) and the RSS.

This process gained momentum when Modi clashed with Keshubhai Patel for control of the state party machinery. In 2001, Patel silently resented the way he had been replaced by Modi.[35] He was to respond later, along with other veterans, including Kashiram Rana, the former party president, and Suresh Mehta, the former chief minister, when they realised that they were being completely marginalised by the new rulers of Gujarat.[36] This process was engineered by Modi partly in reaction to the emergence of a rebel camp after the 2004 Lok Sabha election when the BJP fared poorly (it won only 14 seats). At a birthday function for one of the dissidents, Dr A.K. Patel (a former Union minister), 'more than 50 MLAs had remained present when some MLAs had even gone to the extent of calling Modi "Hitler"'.[37]

One of the techniques by which Modi undermined his opponents was to promote rival candidates against them in their own strongholds in the 2005 local elections. For instance, in Surat, 'most of the sitting councillors, having allegiance to Kashiram Rana [a former mayor of Surat and its sitting MP, for the sixth time], were denied ticket'.[38] And the BJP swept the poll—in Surat too, where the municipal corporation was recaptured by the party—which meant that the new batch of councillors across Gujarat owed their allegiance to Modi. The chief minister also appointed local rivals of his opponents at the helm of party bodies. For instance, by 'appointing Tarachand Chheda as district president in Kutch, which is Suresh Mehta's bastion, Modi cut Mehta to size'.[39]

The final battle for the control of the Gujarat state BJP took place in the mid-2000s when BJP veterans and MLAs mobilised around Keshubhai Patel.[40] The decisive moment came in 2006 when the president of the Gujarat BJP had to be replaced.[41] Patel was himself a candidate for the post. Narendra Modi supported an alternative contender, Purshottam Rupala, whom Keshubhai Patel had not included in his government in 1998–2001, but whom Modi had made cabinet minister in 2001.[42] The party elections were intensely contested. Rupala won, but Patel objected that the election had not been free and fair. He went to Delhi in order to make representations about the irregularities committed during the polls. As a result, the BJP high command had to ask the party vice president, Bal Apte, an RSS old-timer, to investigate and submit a report. The nomination of the state party president was postponed until this report was submitted.[43] Twelve days later, Rupala was appointed president of the Gujarat BJP without any further explanation. Soon afterwards Pravin Sheth, Modi's former political science teacher, wrote that 'Modi's biggest foes are the RSS men on loan to the party (Sanjay Joshi from Gujarat) and Bal Apte'.[44]

Keshubhai Patel, who resented the way Modi was ignoring his own achievements as chief minister,[45] denounced the style of his successor more and more violently: 'It is like dictatorship in the state,' he said.[46] Other BJP men made similar criticisms. Govindacharya, the former right-hand man of L.K. Advani, declared during a meeting of the Mahagujarat Janata Party that 'Gujarat Chief Minister Narendra Modi functions like a dictator'. He believed that this style affected the bureaucracy: 'Government officers are low on morale and are averse to take initiatives because they fear reprimand.'[47] These were the bitter words of a now marginalised politician.

From 2007 onwards, Modi was fully in control of the Gujarat BJP party apparatus, particularly after the state elections, which gave him the opportunity not to nominate again many outgoing MLAs—47 out of 117[48]—and could induct newcomers who owed their position to his political patronage. In 2010, at the end of Rupala's term, another protégé of Modi, R.C. Faldu, took over from him. He was the only candidate and was re-elected at the helm of the state BJP in 2013. The year before, in the aftermath of the 2012 state elections, Keshubhai Patel left the BJP and formed a new party, with which Zadaphia's party merged immediately.

Sidelining the Non-BJP Parivar

In the course of his first term as chief minister, Modi not only conquered the BJP in Gujarat but also stamped his authority over other components of the Sangh Parivar. This unprecedented move was facilitated by the parallel communications and power structure that he established.

Modi against the VHP

In the 1990s and early 2000s, the VHP was a very powerful organisation in Gujarat, as is evident from its role in the 2002 violence. Its leader, Praveen Togadia, had been a highly prominent participant in the Ayodhya movement. He and Modi were contemporaries and worked together in the movement, for instance in the 1990 Rath Yatra, which was largely successful because of the VHP's inputs. After Modi took power, instead of joining hands, the two leaders became locked in fierce rivalry. As Nilanjan Mukhopadhyay rightly points out: 'The reasons for the distancing between the two that happened slowly over the years was due to the fact that in the Hindutva pantheon there was not enough space for both of them to co-exist, because both had political ambitions and were youthful. Beyond a point, Modi could not allow Togadia to grow and the VHP leader would not have played second fiddle to Modi.'[49]

To prevent Togadia from gaining further power, Modi did two things. First, he continued to project himself as a 'Hindu Hriday Samrat'. Second, he undermined the VHP by targeting the objectives and leaders of the organisation. To show the world that the organisation was powerless, Modi's administration destroyed Hindu temples in the name of an anti-encroachment drive whereas the VHP was supposed to defend them. Furthermore, when Babu Bajrangi and Maya Kodnani, as well as eight others, were condemned to many years of imprisonment, the state government appealed for the death sentence. In response, the VHP came out to defend 'its' people, after which the state government eventually abandoned its attempt to seek the death sentence for Kodnani,[50] although the VHP was just as interested in the fate of Babu Bajrangi, the Bajrang Dal activist. The general secretary of the organisation wrote a letter to Modi alleging that 'Bajrangi and other convicts were framed in the case and seeking death penalty for them would be injustice to them and the Hindus in general'.[51] Right to the end of Modi's chief ministership, this lobbying was carried out in vain since the state government never budged.

While the national leader of the VHP, Ashok Singhal—who had accused Modi of being another Mahmud of Ghazni because of the way he destroyed temples in 2008—was mollified by the Gujarat chief minister's justification for his actions,[52] Togadia could not accept this. He repeatedly attacked Modi at VHP meetings on this issue and others, such as the shrinkage of pasture for cows that resulted from selling off agricultural land to industrialists.[53]

Like some of the BJP old-timers mentioned above, Togadia turned to the RSS as an arbiter. In 2008, the VHP told the Sangh Parivar that the Gujarat government had razed to the ground 200 temples. When Modi went to the RSS headquarters in Delhi, this problem was raised and he declared that 'no more temples [would] be razed by the state government'.[54]

The VHP was even more successful with the repeal of the Gujarat Public Trusts Act. This law, passed in 2011, was intended to increase the control of the government over inheritance rules, financial transactions and the working of trusts. Religious trusts supported by the VHP, the Swaminarayans and the *Shankaracharya* of Dwarka (a personality notoriously hostile to the Sangh Parivar) opposed this Act, which was bound to limit the freedom they enjoyed in managing their activities and their temples. Eventually, after 'hearing trustees, religious leaders and saints',[55] Modi bowed to their pressure, but this drawn-out year-long 'tug of war'[56] further harmed relations between the VHP and the Gujarat government.

Alienating the Bharatiya Kisan Sangh

Another offshoot of the RSS, the Bharatiya Kisan Sangh (BKS), lost several battles against Narendra Modi, in spite of the RSS's intervention. Tensions emerged soon after Modi took power when he implemented on 10 October 2000 an award of the Gujarat Electricity Regulatory Commission (GERC) intended to hike electricity prices. The BKS, the largest peasants' union in Gujarat, founded in 1979 (ironically by one of Modi's former mentors, the RSS senior figure D.B. Thengadi), immediately opposed this move, filing no less than seven petitions against the proposal because of the increase in the electricity price it involved.[57] All previous governments had postponed the implementation of the award, but Modi was more decisive because of the serious fiscal crisis and his larger plans for reform. He introduced close to 250 per cent hike in the power tariff. In July 2003, the BKS asked farmers 'to boycott the payment of all new bills'[58]; the organisation would later mobilise huge crowds. In September 2003, more than 50,000 farmers took part in a rally in Gandhinagar where the BKS leader, Prafull Senjalia, 'criticised Modi for following in the footsteps of Pandit Nehru by giving more importance to industry rather than agriculture'.[59] Three months later, the BKS was 'forced to vacate its state-level office, located in the MLAs' quarters for the past eight years'. The national secretary of the BKS, Jivanbhai Patel, reacted strongly to this decision, which forced the organisation to work from a tent:

> Modi has triggered a hornet's nest. He will pay for his act. If he has come to power with our support, now he should know we can even push him out of power. He should not undermine our strength [...] We think our tough stand on the farmers' [electricity] rate has irked Modi. Lately, it had become impossible to talk to him, quite unlike former chief minister Keshubhai Patel, who always used to give us an audience, despite our differences with him.[60]

The agitation took a dramatic turn when a BKS senior leader, Laljibhai Patel, started a fast. On 23 January 2004, the RSS intervened. A team of five mediators, including Ramdas Agarwal (a Rajya Sabha member from Rajasthan), Madan Das Devi (the RSS joint general secretary in charge of relations between the Sangh and the BJP), Bal Apte and Arun Jaitley (a senior BJP member, then a member of the Vajpayee government), came to Ahmedabad,[61] but faced an uphill struggle. Modi refused to modify his stance on the power tariff,[62] but offered compensation: the state government would take water from the Narmada canal via 15 pipes to fill dams, which would save 2,000 MW of power for use in extracting underground irrigation water.[63] Laljibhai Patel ended his hunger strike and the mediators returned to Delhi. But the deal made sense in the long run only. The BKS leaders were so bitter that they chose not to help the BJP in the 2004 Lok Sabha elections, in which it secured poor results. Soon after these elections, the general secretary of the organisation declared:

> Modi's ego has been the main reasons for BJP's poor showing [...] Modi's repugnant utterances, anonymous advertisements, show off during festivals, flaunting of public money to gather crowds, anti-rural mindset and false promises [...] Modi has even lost the right to resign on moral grounds. He should be just

> dumped. This is the collective demand of BKS. And this should be done understanding people's feelings, and particularly that of Gujarat farmers.[64]

The BKS finally agreed to negotiate and admitted that surface water had to replace ground water for irrigation.[65] But the organisation remained a determined opponent of Modi and continued to criticise his policy regarding electricity during his second term. In 2007, when the government claimed that the situation was rapidly improving on the power front, the BKS regretted that 'the state government has passed on the burden of shortage of electricity supply of nearly 600 MW from the western grid onto the farmers'.[66] The BKS also accused the state electricity board of cutting off power to farmers' water pumps after complaints of meter tampering and thefts.[67] While the situation improved markedly in the early 2010s, the BKS continued to argue with the state government about electricity. In 2011, targeting a governance issue—when Narendra Modi had adopted 'good governance' as his motto—it claimed that '3.75 lakh [375,000] applications of farmers seeking electricity connections have been awaiting clearance',[68] and that the way in which power was distributed to farmers was incoherent.[69]

Second, the BKS attacked the Modi government on the question of farmers' suicides. In 2007, the general secretary of the organisation lamented: 'The police stations do not register farmers' suicide deaths. These suicides are brushed aside as resulting from domestic problems. But the problems arise because of the farmers' plight in rural Gujarat.'[70] These accusations were made at a time when the Modi government boasted that 'the outgoing fiscal year's agricultural production has been a stupendous 320 billion rupees'. Commenting on these achievements, the president of the BKS, Prafull Senjalia, said: 'These are all fudged figures.'[71]

Third, the BKS defended farmers who were illegally drawing water from canals because of persistent water shortages in 17 of the state's 26 districts. It criticised the 'Narmada battalion' that the government had created for seizing farmers' pumping sets and penalising the violators in 2013.[72]

Last but not least, the BKS initiated several campaigns against the establishment of Special Economic Zones (SEZs) and Special Investment Regions (SIRs), which resulted in the granting of land to industrialists at the expense of farmers. The organisation protested against the Mandal Becharaji SIR, which, in its view, would divert 50,880 ha of fertile land for the use of industrial concerns such as Maruti.[73]

To sum up, the extent to which Modi alienated key components of the Sangh Parivar as chief minister of Gujarat was unprecedented. While faction fights had become commonplace in the BJP, their intensity in Gujarat was unique, as was the animosity between the chief minister and the VHP as well as the BKS. On different sides—be it among BJP dissidents or offshoots of the Parivar—Narendra Modi's style of functioning was one of the root causes of resentment. Indeed, his capacity to make individual decisions and to stick to them in spite of criticisms from within his own political fold stood in stark contrast with the tradition of collegiality that the Sangh had always cultivated.

THE RSS'S DILEMMA

The RSS was forced to mediate with Modi several times, but it usually failed to fashion compromises, something almost unprecedented in the annals of the Sangh Parivar. As Nilanjan Mukhopadhyay points out,

> the bone of contention was a hierarchical matter—who was senior—Modi or the RSS' top brass in the state? RSS leaders felt that since Modi had been a relatively junior functionary when he was deputed to the BJP, he should be reporting to them as in the RSS, seniority is determined by the last position held. Modi in contrast felt that after the RSS deputed a Pracharak to

> one of the affiliated organisations where they have to adhere to rules and a style of power-politics, it is wrong to expect daily briefings.[74]

As a result, state RSS leaders increasingly distanced themselves from the chief minister of Gujarat. According to Mukhopadhyay, the rebels who mobilised behind Keshubhai Patel in the first half of the 2000s had 'more than token backing from the state RSS leaders including Prant Pracharak Manmohan Vaidya'.[75] A 'senior leader of the RSS' also told Mukhopadhyay that he was 'disturbed' by the possibility that 'the chain of events in Gujarat' might eventually give a 'bad name' to the Sangh Parivar.[76] This person was concerned that the state of Gujarat was not fulfilling its 'basic duty—to act in a non-partisan and non-sectarian manner as it has to provide law and order, safety and security to the helpless people to whichever community they might belong to. This is particularly true after the counter provocation like the Godhra incident stopped. Muslims now are too weak to do anything so why continue with this?'[77]

Obviously, some RSS senior leaders disapproved of the direction in which Narendra Modi was taking the Sangh Parivar. That he decided on initiatives without necessarily referring to the Sangh was a problem for them; in addition, he was regarded as being accomplished at self-promotion, as Manmohan Vaidya admitted to Nilanjan Mukhopadhyay: 'Narendrabhai has managed the project of Vibrant Gujarat very efficiently and also introduced several innovative ways for investment which did not exist earlier—like tourism. But the main reason why it has got talked about so much is that he has been very successful in marketing his development model.'[78]

Modi was both a blessing and a problem for the RSS because of his capacity to reach out to people and win supporters, among the Sangh Parivar as well, while short-circuiting the organisation in the process. This issue was especially acute at the state level, where the post of Gujarat BJP president was a major bone of contention. In early 2004, when the term of the last party president, Rajendrasinh Rana, had expired by one year, Modi resisted the Sangh Parivar's 'rather strong pressure in favour of a person who could hold in check the Narendra Modi government and also ensure coordination with the Sangh'.[79] According to Rajiv Shah, a close observer of Gujarat's politics, by 2005–06 RSS circles resented 'Modi's attempt to emerge as the sole torch-bearer of the Hindutva legacy'.[80] The rift was partly due to the way, according to press reports, associates of Modi fabricated a 'sex CD' showing his rival Sanjay Joshi 'in a compromising position'. As mentioned above, the CD led Joshi, all-India BJP secretary, to resign from his post, but it was then found to be fake. Joshi was allowed back into the party, but because of tensions between Modi and the RSS, Joshi did not attend RSS meetings in 2006.[81]

Finally, Modi prevailed and captured the BJP, but the tensions remained. While Sangh Parivar leaders mediated successfully to keep Keshubhai Patel in the BJP,[82] some Gujarat RSS cadres abstained from backing the chief minister during the 2007 elections.[83] Their disenchantment stemmed partly from the fact that he did not even submit the list of candidates nominated by the BJP to the RSS state headquarters, as state party leaders would routinely do in such circumstances. He also reduced coordination with the state's *prant pracharak* to a bare minimum. As a result, one of the RSS's strongmen in the Gujarat RSS, the *prant prachar pramukh* (head of ideological work at the state level), Mukund Deobhankar, declared in the press that this time his organisation would abstain from electoral work.[84] One of his colleagues, a co-founder of the RSS in Rajkot and its *sampark pramukh* (communications head) for the western region,[85] Pravin Maniar, explained in an interview that the RSS would indeed adopt a different attitude from that of 2002: 'This time around, we have not asked our workers to get involved in any poll related work [...] We have always extended our support for the cause of Hindutva. But we are wedded to an ideology and not any individual [...] None of the Sangh Parivar organisations have benefited from this government.'[86]

The RSS was clearly reproaching Modi for personalising power and it resented that he had not rewarded other components of the Sangh Parivar, the VHP and the BKS, despite their having helped him so much in the past. The VHP was particularly hostile to Modi because its leaders believed that he had won largely because of the organisation's support in 2002 but had never repaid his debts. Praveen Togadia apparently let his brother canvass in favour of the Congress. Leaders of organisations close to the RSS also distanced themselves from the government of Gujarat. Devendra Das, the secretary general of the Akhil Bharatiya Sant Parishad (All India Association of Ascetics) and the Ram Janmabhoomi Nyas Raksha Samiti (Committee of the Trust for the Defence of Lord Ram's Birthplace), accused Modi of the killing of 100,000 cows.[87] Das proclaimed a staunchly anti-Modi slogan in his stronghold of Baroda: 'Narendra Modi is not the protector of Hindus, but their destroyer.'[88] The vice president of the Sant Parishad, Swami Avichaldasji Maharaj, who was also the leader of the Gyan Sampradaya, a popular sect in Gujarat, justified his rejection of Modi in three words: 'We feel cheated.'[89]

The tensions between Modi and other leaders of the Sangh Parivar partly explain the decline of some of the mainstays of the family, including the mother organisation. According to press reports, in ten years the number of RSS *shakhas* (branches) had diminished from 1,500 to 1,000 and attendance was 'down by an estimated 50%'[90]—a decline which may have been due to social factors, including the growing irrelevance to middle-class youths of gathering in khaki shorts before dawn. In the early 2000s, the student association ABVP had 94,000 members; it apparently retained only half of them in 2012.[91] The Bharatiya Kisan Sangh, which had 2,225,000 members in 2003, allegedly numbered only 600,000 nine years later.[92] This trend was sometimes due to direct conflicts (including the way Modi had defeated the BKS). But it also reflected Modi's desire to rid himself of the BJP's fellow travellers—Praveen Togadia being just one who was totally marginalised.

In spite of all this, the RSS's top leaders supported Modi and even sometimes gave way to him. Manmohan Vaidya, the Gujarat *prant pracharak*, 'was ultimately removed from Gujarat at Modi's behest and was shifted to Chennai'.[93] Similarly, the RSS accepted Modi's demand to sideline Sanjay Joshi once again in 2012. In 2011, Nitin Gadkari, the BJP president, had appointed Joshi to the BJP National Executive and as party coordinator for the Uttar Pradesh state elections. But in May 2012 Modi allegedly threatened to boycott a meeting of the BJP National Executive if Joshi was not removed from the body. Joshi had to resign, and Modi immediately announced he would participate in the meeting.[94]

Modi, after 2002, was so independent minded that he stopped reporting to the RSS and had no hesitation in alienating the VHP and the BKS. Even though, eventually, the Sangh Parivar refrained from sabotaging the prospects of the BJP in Gujarat,[95] for the complex reasons listed above, the support of the state leaders of the RSS, VHP and BKS was far from optimal, if not minimal, in 2007. The relative estrangement of Modi from the Sangh Parivar therefore intensified his natural inclination towards short-circuiting the leaders of this 'family' and personalising his grip on power. The control of Modi over the BJP was such that he personally selected the party candidates, not only at the state level, but also at the local level, implementing what came to be known as the 'no repeat' rule according to which many outgoing MLAs and members of municipal corporations were not nominated again. In 2007, notes Ghanshyam Shah:

> 43 per cent of sitting MLAs were given tickets. All of them were Modi loyalists. For the Parliament, out of sixteen sitting

> BJP MPs, only three were repeated. In choosing candidates, Modi took into account a combination of factors: loyalty, caste identity and financial power. Individual character and record of work in the party were not the major considerations. Of the twenty-six candidates for the Parliament elections, two were not even members of the BJP on the day of selection.[96]

These actions provide a clear indication of the manner in which Modi dominated the party.

THE BUILDING OF AN AD HOC NETWORK: MODI'S PYRAMID AND POLITICAL MARKETERS

Narendra Modi belongs to the Hindutva movement, but the media felt the need to coin a new word, 'Moditva', to describe the variant of this movement that the chief minister of Gujarat represented. This unprecedented personalisation of Hindu nationalism found an expression in the organisation as well as in the leadership and messaging style that Modi evolved.

Local Notables and Cooperatives

Modi gradually gained control of the state BJP apparatus and started to micro-manage party affairs—something he was in the right position to undertake, given that he had run the party organisation in Gujarat for many years in the 1980s and 1990s. As mentioned above, he systematically tried to appoint local rivals of his adversaries at the municipal level. He also took a personal interest in the nomination of candidates contesting local and state elections, and even panchayat and municipal elections, something very few chief ministers take pains to do, at least to the extent he did.[97] It was also something that RSS leaders appreciated.[98] In 2010, when local elections took place in Gujarat, Modi addressed as many as 21 public meetings.[99] The BJP swept the polls—in former Congress strongholds as well[100]—and, naturally, the newly elected representatives considered that they, at least partly, owed their good fortune to Modi, who had campaigned for them.[101] Modi's interest in local politics went back to the 1980s, when he was building the BJP in Gujarat. However, it also had to do with an even older Gujarati tradition: the influential role of cooperatives.

During the Raj, establishing cooperatives was part of the attempt by Indians to emancipate themselves from British domination. In Gujarat, this sense of self-help found expression in Amul (the dairy products cooperative founded in 1946), which became a symbol of the economic modernisation of the peasantry. The self-made men who ran cooperatives gradually became notables and for many of them it was a launch pad for a political career, within the Congress or beyond the party. Indeed, cooperative leaders played a key role in the clientelistic political economy of Gujarat because 'the sector that touched maximum number of people across rural and urban areas'[102] enabled these leaders to receive the people's support in exchange for their protection (including that of their jobs). As Nikita Sud points out, 'Control over co-operatives is an important signifier and reproducer of local power and an announcement of bigger ambitions.'[103] Atul Dev was even told in Gujarat, by an Ahmedabad-based academic: 'No political party has been able to achieve anything in Gujarat without first getting a grip over the cooperative units.'[104]

Many senior Jana Sangh and BJP leaders in Gujarat had begun their careers as leaders of local cooperatives. Keshubhai Patel, 'a farmer-turned-small-flour-mill-owner',[105] became director of the Rajkot Citizens Co-operative Bank before taking over as president of the Gujarat Jana Sangh in 1969.[106] He then became an MLA for the first time in 1972. But Keshubhai Patel belonged to a faction hostile to Modi, who thus had an added reason to gain a foothold in the cooperative milieu. Among his first partners, it was Amit Shah who realised very early on the political importance of the cooperatives and tried to take control of them. He was especially interested in the cooperative banks, which financed a large number of SMEs. He got in touch with the lawyer Krishnakant Vakharia for this reason after the BJP won the 1995 election:

> Though the Congress was out of power, it maintained its hold over some cooperative units. The most important of these was the Ahmedabad District Cooperative Bank. When elections were announced for the bank's governing body, the Congress and the BJP began an all-out battle for control. Amit Shah, already close to Modi and fighting on his side in the BJP's internal wars [against Keshubhai Patel], led the BJP camp in the dispute […] To draft a petition, Vakharia directed Shah to [Tushar] Mehta […] Mehta argued the case in court for several years, and became close to Shah in the process.[107]

The Ahmedabad District Cooperative (ADC) Bank was the biggest cooperative society in the state. In the mid-1990s its head was Ghanshyam Amin, the elder brother of Narhari Amin, a close confidant of former chief minister Chimanbhai Patel. Eventually, Shah won control of the bank at the age of 36—and 'it is only after that Amit Shah could conquer all the cooperatives'.[108] After he joined the Modi government in 2002, Shah bequeathed charge of the ADC Bank to Ajay Patel, but he 'gradually worked at the other district cooperative banks which were generally headed by Congress leaders and, over the years, established BJP's supremacy in most of them'.[109] Then, 'Shah's realisation of the political importance of cooperatives soon took him to the dairy sector in the state'.[110] It was in this sector that the stars of Gujarat's 'White Revolution' were to be found. Amul was internationally known, but there were also the Banas and Dudhsagar dairies. When in 2006, the octogenarian 'milkman of India', Verghese Kurien, resigned as president of the Gujarat Cooperative Milk Marketing Federation, a BJP candidate, Parthi Bhatol, took over from him.[111] In 'three years', Shah managed to 'wrest control of the co-operative societies from the Congress'.[112]

Thus, thanks to Amit Shah, his right-hand man, Narendra Modi completed the establishment of a power structure based on local bodies that relied not only on the Panchayati Raj (village self-government) and the municipal corporations, but also on powerful cooperatives. Modi and Shah went on to build their network at the grassroots level by combining bottom-up and top-down processes: they relied on existing notables and created new ones by nominating them for all kinds of elections, for which they canvassed personally. This modus operandi recalls the techniques that Indira Gandhi implemented at the national level in the 1960s and 1970s when she short-circuited the notables of the Congress (O) to build her own 'pyramid'.[113] But Modi and Shah worked more systematically in Gujarat, making it easier for them to exercise remote control of the state from Delhi after 2014.

Spin Doctors and High-tech Political Communication

In parallel with this bottom-up kind of pyramid making, the government of Gujarat resorted to a top-down strategy of communication relying on some of the most up-to-date options available. Modi's first innovation consisted in hiring a Washington-based PR and lobbying firm, APCO Worldwide.[114] In August 2007, while Modi was having difficulties with the RSS, this company, 'the second largest independent PR firm in America, took on the responsibility of taking care of PR for both the government of Gujarat as well as the biennial industrial summit, "Vibrant Gujarat" [...] The Gujarat government has been paying nearly 1.5 million rupees a month since 2009 in order to bring about the image makeover.'[115] When the contract was signed, APCO had already worked for the Nigerian dictator Sani Abacha, the life-president of Kazakhstan, Nazarbayev, and the Russian oligarch Mikhail Khodorkovsky.[116] It seems that this contract was renegotiated in 2010. According to findings made possible by an RTI enquiry, for

22.5 million rupees per year, at the dollar rate of 2010, 'APCO will also gauge the tonality of coverage and identify journalists who can further be Media Ambassadors for Gujarat'.[117]

Similarly, before the 2012 elections, engineers and other professionals played a major role in Modi's team besides BJP followers.[118] Sunil Khilnani points out that 'the real masterminds of Modi's political campaigns are not shadowy figures wearing RSS uniform under their plainclothes. They are smart, cheery IIT-ians [alumni from Indian Institutes of Technology]: men like Rajesh Jain.'[119] Rajesh Jain was indeed a pillar of Modi's team. A postgraduate from Columbia University, and a staunch supporter of Modi, he revolutionised the internet in India by creating his IndiaWorld web portal and then started Netcore.[120] His company ran not only the website of Narendra Modi but also 'Gujaratriots.com', a website explaining the 2002 riots in a way that glossed over almost all the findings of the Indian judiciary.[121]

Still younger people formed a dense circle of confidants around Modi, to the bewilderment of the Indian media. In 2012, for instance, Prashant Kishor, a US-educated Bihari in his thirties, became one of his key advisors. A journalist was surprised to see that 'even close Modi aides [were] directed first to him'.[122] Kishor played a pioneering role in the emerging world of political consultants in India and was to be a major asset in 2013–14 when Modi became the BJP candidate for prime minister.[123]

Besides these young US-educated aides, Dhiren Avashia, a former journalist and director of the Educational Media Research Centre at Gujarat University, was for many years 'Narendra Modi's key media advisor and the brain behind his many publicity projects'.[124] These and other young, modern aides helped Modi greatly online and were especially active in countering his critics on the internet. While their arguments were often shallow and their tone dismissive, the style of most of their messaging was extremely aggressive. B. Raman, a former bureaucrat and security analyst, whose blog was a reference point for some of those who followed Indian affairs, made his objections known in 2012:

> The style of the online blitzkrieg adopted by his [Modi's] die-hard followers in India and abroad reminiscent of the methods of the Nazi storm troopers, continues to add to the disquiet [...] I have repeatedly urged that he should openly dissociate himself from them and condemn their methods. He has not done so thereby giving rise to an unfortunate suspicion that he may be politically benefiting from them.[125]

Narendra Modi was probably the first BJP chief minister who, after only one term, depended so little on the Sangh Parivar and instead relied heavily on an alternative team comprising local leaders owing him allegiance as well as communication experts—including those whom Raman called his 'storm troopers'—dedicated to promoting him as an individual.

ON A LARGER CANVAS

Narendra Modi initiated a new governance style in Gujarat, characterised by a clear centralisation of power, at the expense of traditional Hindu nationalist collegiality and institutional mechanisms.

Firstly, Modi's pyramid relied on bureaucrats from among whom, along with some police officers, he recruited his close guard; a number of them were also part of the nexus between businessmen and politicians that we've studied in chapter 5. The chain of command he used relied largely on the government administration. Secondly, his style of leadership was not as collegial as the standard practices of the BJP. In fact, Modi not only dislodged Keshubhai Patel, but also sidelined him and other senior leaders, who were then systematically marginalised. Thirdly, Modi also managed to emancipate himself from the Sangh Parivar, including the VHP and the BKS, two organisations against which he fought. Moreover, he emancipated himself from the state RSS leaders and imposed his terms on the organisation on several occasions, even when senior Sangh leaders tried to mediate between him and other components of the Parivar. Fourthly, in order to make up for the (partial) loss of the Sangh Parivar's support (on which he did not want to depend anyway), Modi created his own network of supporters consisting of local bodies (ranging from cooperatives to municipal corporations) and spin doctors as well as tech-savvy communicators who reported directly to him.

Although this outcome went against the traditional hierarchy and collegiality of the Sangh Parivar, the RSS's top leaders preferred not to antagonise him. Modi's ability to prevail over RSS leaders and to get away with it—a very important development which we need to ponder—can be explained in several ways.

According to one of his more determined opponents, Shankarsinh Vaghela, Modi was able to dictate terms to the Sangh Parivar because of his financial muscle. Vaghela alleges: 'Under the influence of money, it [the RSS] has become a pitiable organisation of spineless people. The BJP's Delhi leadership dances to Modi's tunes because he has asked all industrial houses to send funds to Gujarat.'[126] Certainly, Modi was so close to Indian business elites that he occupied the kind of position in the BJP that Pramod Mahajan left vacant when he died in 2006. Still, money cannot be the only explanation.

Nilanjan Mukhopadhyay offers another point of view: the RSS leaders, after Modi won the 2012 Gujarat elections, were 'willing to court Modi because—in their assessment—he appeared to be the most dependable person to galvanize the cadre and make electoral dents outside the traditional support base'.[127] The Sangh Parivar cadres had indeed become increasingly supportive of Modi by the beginning of his third five-year term. This was especially true of the young *swayamsevaks* who no longer identified with the only alternative available in the BJP, namely the ageing leadership that L.K. Advani embodied. The octogenarians, in their view, had become irrelevant, whereas Modi epitomised an effective brand of modern leadership. As far as the electoral reach of Modi was concerned, the RSS realised that in Gujarat—as we will see in the next chapter—he had succeeded in attracting not only upper-caste and Patel voters but Other Backward Classes (OBCs) as well.

This analysis needs to be complemented by a third explanation: the RSS leaders resigned themselves to the rise of Narendra Modi not only because of his popularity among *swayamsevaks*, but also because they recognised him as a true, staunch Hindu nationalist. In fact, even if the style of Modi was not to the liking of RSS leaders, it probably helped them to overcome some of the organisation's past inhibitions. He dared to say—and do—things RSS old-timers would have hesitated to articulate, partly because they had experienced state repression under Nehru and Indira Gandhi. Modi, for instance, asserted a new style when he openly declared that he was a 'Hindu nationalist'—something no one had expressed till then.[128] Traditionally, the Sangh Parivar claimed that it was a truly secular organisation because Hinduism was a tolerant religion and that the real 'pseudo-secular' organisation was the Congress because of the way it pampered its Muslim 'vote bank'.[129] In 2012, emulating Modi's unapologetic Hindu nationalist discourse, the RSS changed course. The Sangh's mouthpiece in Hindi, *Panchajanya*, reacted strongly to the idea promoted by the chief minister of Bihar that the prime minister of India should be secular. An anonymous columnist objected:

> Our Constitution makers did not give any such 'distinguished identity' to the prime minister's post, perhaps because they believed that India has always stood for eternal values, religion and culture, and the basis of our society and national life is the feeling of all-inclusiveness and mutual existence [...] Leaders who are eager to establish a secular rule by laying atrocities

> on Hindus should be asked why India should not have a government and a prime minister who is concerned about the majority Hindus.[130]

This explicit Hindu majoritarianism was fully in tune with Modi's message. In addition, the RSS, which had traditionally shunned violence,[131] started to advocate it less indirectly—and even adopted an aggressive tone—during and after the Gujarat riots. While this was not so apparent among the RSS's top leaders, there were signs of such a development among local cadres. After the events of 2002,[132] Modi began transforming Hindu nationalism by entrenching a new radicalism that struck a chord among *swayamsevaks* and RSS cadres.

Lastly, and even more importantly, RSS leaders wanted the BJP to win the 2014 elections more desperately than ever before because of the way the CBI and the National Investigation Agency (NIA) had been directed by the Manmohan Singh government—and home minister P. Chidambaram in particular—to investigate terrorist attacks in which RSS cadres—including Indresh Kumar, a member of the national executive of the RSS—were implicated. In addition to the two famous Malegaon cases of 2006 and 2008,[133] RSS men were accused of having engineered the blasts on the Samjhauta Express (2007), and at Hyderabad's Mecca Masjid (2007), Ajmer Dargah (2007) and Modasa (2008), which were responsible for the death of 121 people.[134] The RSS chief Mohan Bhagwat himself worried that 'the Hindu terror investigation, which became intense since 2010, might lead up to him'.[135] D.K. Jha points out:

> The Central Bureau of Investigation's interrogation of Indresh Kumar, a member of the RSS national executive, in December 2010, brought the investigation to Nagpur's doorstep. It was in connection with the Mecca Masjid bombing and had come during the CBI's interrogation of Aseemanand, a long-time RSS member who had been arrested in November 2010 on charges

> of masterminding a series of saffron terror cases [and who confessed in 2011 that he had been implicated in most of the cases mentioned above].[136]

As a result, a senior RSS cadre remembers: 'At the time, winnability was the only thing everyone [among the organisation's leaders] was concerned of', and Modi appeared to be in a better position than anyone else to beat the Congress and its coalition.

For all these reasons, Narendra Modi, in spite of developing a very personal style as chief minister of Gujarat, received the backing of the RSS leaders, who supported his candidacy for the post of prime minister in 2013–14.

Once he became prime minister, Modi replicated some of the strategies (reviewed in this chapter) that he had experimented with in the testing ground of his home state. He relied on bureaucrats to govern India in a more systematic manner than his predecessors had. First, some of those who had been part of his close guard in Gujarat followed him to Delhi. G.C. Murmu is a case in point. In 2015, he was appointed joint secretary in the Department of Expenditure; in 2017, he was made special secretary in the Department of Revenue; in 2019, he became secretary of the Department of Expenditure and, then, lieutenant governor of Jammu and Kashmir, a clear sign of the trust he enjoyed at the highest level. Less than one year later, he was appointed chief auditor general of India, an equally sensitive post.[137] In parallel, P.K. Mishra was named Modi's additional principal secretary and has retained the post since then. There were many other examples. In addition, several ex-IAS and IFS officers joined Modi's government, including Hardeep Singh Puri, S. Jaishankar, Raj Kumar Singh, Satyapal Singh, A. Vaishnaw and Ram Chandra Prasad.

Secondly, when he moved to Delhi, Modi sidelined the old guard in the same way he had marginalised Keshubhai Patel, Suresh Mehta, Kashiram Rana and Gordhan Zadaphia in Gujarat.

Capitalising on his 2012 state election victory, he was appointed to the BJP Parliamentary Board in March 2013 and then became president of the Central Election Campaign Committee in June, over objections from L.K. Advani. Instead of accommodating his former mentor in any meaningful position, Modi marginalised him, like most other members of the old guard, including Jaswant Singh, minister for external affairs under Vajpayee, who was denied a ticket in 2014, and M.M. Joshi, who was persuaded to change constituencies to let Modi contest the seat he held in Varanasi. The list of candidates that Modi and Shah prepared for the 2014 elections was theirs and reflected a new balance of power. Veteran politicians were either totally ignored (like Yashwant Sinha and Arun Shourie) or invited to join a purely consultative body called the Margdarshak Mandal.[138]

Thirdly, Modi, as prime minister, prevailed over the RSS national leaders in the same way he had prevailed over the RSS state leaders in Gujarat. This was very clear even before the 2014 elections. While the election campaign was starting, Mohan Bhagwat invited him to Nagpur to 'discuss with him how the RSS could contribute to his election campaign'.[139] Modi refused to go to the organisation's headquarters and Bhagwat had to travel to Ahmedabad, where he was told by Modi that he did not need any help. Immediately after the election, Modi had Amit Shah appointed party chief in spite of the reservations of the RSS. Finally, the RSS itself was subjugated by Modi. Not only did the members of the organisations pay allegiance to Modi, with the RSS chief appearing merely to amplify his discourse, but the prime minister decided the nomination of some of the key officers of the organisation. In 2021, for instance, Dattatreya Hosabale, 'Modi's man in the RSS',[140] was elevated to the post of general secretary.

Lastly, until he fully captured the BJP apparatus—and even after he did so—Modi relied on a parallel pyramid made up of consultants and 'vote mobilisers'. In the case of consultants, or political marketing professionals, the continuity between Gujarat and India is complete since the same organisation, Prashant Kishor's Citizens for Accountable Governance, was in charge of his 2012 state election campaign and his 2014 Lok Sabha election campaign.[141] This organisation worked in tandem with two networks, 'Modi 4 PM' and 'Mission 272' (whose name referred to the number of seats needed to give the BJP a majority in the Lok Sabha),[142] which paid direct allegiance to the BJP candidate. Pradeep Chhibber and Susan Osterman show that 'vote mobilizers'[143] canvassing for Modi were particularly active on social media and the internet, and had been recruited beyond the pool of BJP activists. A CSDS opinion poll found that only 19 per cent of them were party members,[144] and that 32 per cent of them would have voted for another party had Modi not been the BJP candidate for prime minister.[145]

Besides this modus operandi, Modi replicated as prime minister something else he had experienced as chief minister: the attempt to conquer power at the lower level. While as chief minister he had canvassed to win local elections, as prime minister he invested an exceptional amount of energy in state election campaigns.

Thus, after 2014 Narendra Modi transposed to the national level a governance style that echoed Indira Gandhi's, but whose personalised version he had invented in Gujarat. In contrast to Indira Gandhi, he imposed this culture of command and compliance over the state and society at large in the name of a clear-cut ideology. In terms of content, this process can best be described as a form of national populism.

8

RELATING TO THE PEOPLE THE NATIONAL-POPULIST WAY

> Local issues are not important during the campaign in the forthcoming polls. There is just one issue with us—Modi.
>
> Purshottam Rupala, Gujarat BJP president, on the 2007 elections[1]

In the previous chapter, we analysed how Narendra Modi built a parallel network that helped him to relate directly to the people. This technique is typical of populism, a political approach that relies more than others on an unmediated communication between the leader and the masses, at the expense of intermediate bodies, including political parties. Modi resorted to all kinds of channels to reach out to the people and create a state of quasi-permanent popular mobilisation.

But the content of his message also fits the definition of populism. For Cas Mudde, this 'ism' 'considers society to be ultimately separated into two homogeneous and antagonistic camps, 'the pure people' versus 'the corrupt elite', and argues that politics should be an expression of the *volonté générale* (general will) of the people'.[2] Moreover, Modi projected himself as the spokesman of the people against the Delhi-based

Establishment and the Nehru–Gandhi family in particular. However, his populism relied wholly on the ideology of Hindu nationalism, such that the people he was defending consisted only of the majority community. This combination has been theorised by Gino Germani, who calls it 'national-populism'.[3] In Gujarat, this variant found expression in the notion of 'Moditva', a formula coined by the media to capture this very specific alchemy combining Hindutva, Gujarati identity and the figure of its interpreter.

SATURATING THE PUBLIC SPACE PERSONALLY

Narendra Modi resorted to political techniques that no BJP leaders had tried before. Until then, indeed, the culture of collegiality implied consultations with other Sangh Parivar leaders, and the sense of belonging to the RSS family went hand in hand with reliance on the help of *pracharaks*, especially when canvassing. Modi broke with these old practices in order to reach out to Gujaratis directly. In a way, as we have mentioned, this mini-revolution emulated that of Indira Gandhi in the late 1960s and early 1970s when she freed herself from the shackles of the Congress bosses who controlled regional or local vote banks. However, she had to split with the Congress in 1969 to achieve this populist revolution in 1971, whereas Modi did not form a breakaway faction—and eventually the Sangh Parivar rallied around him.

From Yatra Politics to High-tech PR

Modi rearranged the politics of the BJP and of Hindu nationalism *ad hominem*. During the 2007 election campaign Purshottam Rupala, the BJP state president in Gujarat, admitted that his party had a one point-programme: Modi. This naturally meant that Modi became the chief campaigner, as was evident from his brand of 'Yatra politics'.

A key player in Advani's Rath Yatra in Gujarat in 1990 and Joshi's Ekta Yatra at an all-India level in 1991, Modi continued to rely on Yatra politics. In 2002, the Gaurav Yatra was a major component of his electoral campaign. In 2012, again, he took his campaign caravan on a cavalcade throughout the state before the Congress even started to hold meetings. By 9 October, his Swami Vivekananda Yuva Vikas Yatra was over: he had held 135 rallies. But touring the state was physically demanding, time-consuming and insufficient to fully saturate Gujarat's public space. As early as 2007, therefore, Modi turned to more sophisticated modes of communication.

He allegedly owned three laptops—one in his office, one at home and one for travelling—and was supposed to spend several hours reading the 200 to 250 emails he received every day from citizens of Gujarat. He was said to respond to a tenth of them directly and let the bureaucracy take care of the others.[4] Modi's 2007 campaign not only used the internet but also the mobile phone, of which Gujaratis were early users compared with the rest of India (14 million out of 52 million Gujaratis had a cell phone in 2007). Phone networks enabled Modi to send thousands of SMSs and MMSs to potential voters as well as party cadres.

In 2012 he continued in this vein,[5] but took another step by initiating a TV channel in his name, NaMo. More importantly, he held a series of virtual meetings: Modi's hologram appeared on stage in 3D simultaneously in different locations (26 localities on 2 December, for instance) to deliver his speeches to massive audiences, which were sometimes mesmerised (some of his supporters even wondered, Is this real?). While Modi continued with more conventional forms of outreach too—he addressed 125 rallies in the first half of December 2102, or ten meetings a day[6]—his use of 3D techniques is revealing of his awareness of the exceptional power that images have in politics (and in Indian civilisation).[7] He held 132 holographic shows during the 2012 election campaign in order to communicate directly with a huge number of citizens, at a cost of 1.5 billion rupees, according to some estimates.[8]

Narcissism, Image-building and Populism

The iconographic material on which BJP propaganda and the state government's communications were based portrayed Modi's image constantly.[9] This also reflected his narcissistic inclination.[10] Indeed, Modi has a very high opinion of himself. When Nilanjan Mukhopadhyay asked why he was so good at conceiving original ideas, he responded: 'I think it is probably a God-gifted ability.'[11] This was perfectly in tune with his reference to himself as not fully present in the mundane, everyday world (as we mentioned in chapter 2).

While he dedicated much energy to image-building,[12] he acknowledged that there was only one Indian leader who could really be associated with a 'brand', and that was Mahatma Gandhi.[13] To 'brand' was so much part of his communication strategy that he resorted to the services of the actor Amitabh Bachchan to promote 'Gujarat's brand'. Indeed, in 2010, Bachchan was appointed 'brand ambassador' for Gujarat to promote tourism through video clips.[14]

In Gujarat, Modi tried to create his own brand by means of his body language. All his biographers mention his interest in fashion, even from a very young age.[15] Mukhopadhyay devotes one full chapter to what is known in Gujarat as 'the Modi kurta'. This long shirt has only one distinctive feature: its short sleeves. Modi told Mukhopadhyay that when he was an itinerant RSS worker, he had little time to wash his clothes, which is why he decided to cut his sleeves in half. After becoming a public figure, he had his style of kurta designed by an Ahmedabad-based tailor, Jade Blue. By 2004, the 'Modi kurta' was so popular that this company asked Modi for permission to sell it under that name. Modi concluded: 'it was part of my simplicity and has become a fashion for the outside world today'.[16]

Such brand awareness reflects a form of narcissism,[17] but it also reveals a specific sense of communication: Gujarati citizens could think about their chief minister not only when they saw his picture on a wall (or on their child's school bag),[18] but also when they saw someone wearing 'his' kurta. More importantly, they could wear it themselves and look like him, in accordance with the populist's motto 'I am you, you are me'.[19]

This is what happened, almost literally, in 2007 when the BJP distributed masks of Modi. His supporters canvassed while wearing masks of him as if hundreds and even thousands of Modis were campaigning together. Sympathisers started to do the same and repeated the trick in the 2012 election campaign, as if to say: 'we are all Narendra Modi'.[20] This technique of mass communication indicates that a more sophisticated style of populism was taking shape when Modi invited his supporters to identify with him by wearing the same shirt and masking their face with his—thereby suggesting that he was ubiquitous.

Populism has recently tended to be defined as a form of demagogy, but the populist leader is not only the politician who promises the moon to voters and distributes subsidies at the expense of the state exchequer. He is primarily the one who tries to relate directly to the people, by circumventing all intermediaries—including his party—and even tries to embody the people and look like their mirror image.[21] This mimetic dimension of populism is central to Pierre Ostiguy's theory.[22] For Ostiguy, the first step in achieving populist alchemy is when the leader appears to the masses as one of them, creating a sense of togetherness which usually is developed in opposition to elite groups.[23]

Celebrating Gujarat and Modi: A State of Quasi-permanent Mobilisation

Besides the use of sophisticated techniques of communication, Modi saturated the public sphere by introducing a state of quasi-permanent or recurrent mobilisation in Gujarat. As an astute commentator observed in 2007: 'Modi is not just a man or [a] Chief minister, but an "event" in Indian politics after Indira Gandhi to present that sole authoritative model of leadership. With wider vision of brand building and systematic strategies of image positioning than Indira. So, in a way Gujarat has seen non-stop round the clock election campaign by him in the past five years.'[24]

Indeed, the organisation of events mobilising Gujarati society was not confined to election campaigns. Instead, Modi tried to keep society in a state of constant mobilisation, the same way that the fear engineered by fake encounters kept people in a permanent state of tension. On every occasion, the masses were invited to immerse themselves in some grand show organised to celebrate the glory of Gujarat and its chief minister for one reason or another—its economic achievements, its cultural traditions—or simply to take part in some recreational entertainment or festival. Each of these staged events offered Modi an opportunity to promote a form of personality cult, as was evident from the omnipresence of his photographs at every minor crossroads or garage forecourt or in newspaper advertisements.

To give a full list of these events would be tedious, but to do so for a three-year period only (with a couple of exceptions), from 2003 to 2006, is informative.[25] In 2003, Modi celebrated Gujarat Foundation Day as 'Gaurav Day' (Day of Pride): 'Thereafter, till 2012, every year this celebration was organized in different cities.'[26] (In the same spirit, in 2010, the 50th anniversary of the creation of the state of Gujarat was celebrated in a grand manner during Swarnim [Golden] Gujarat functions.) In 2003–04, more than 20 'Vibrant Gujarat' shows were organised throughout Gujarat; in October 2004, Vibrant Navratri took place in Ahmedabad. Then came the Vibrant Gujarat Global Investors Summit in January 2005. When *India Today* declared Modi 'the best Chief Minister' of India on the basis of a 2006 survey, he launched a huge billboard campaign. Soon after, five functions were held to publicise the Jyotigram power scheme intended to give continuous power to the rural parts of Gujarat round the clock. The most remarkable event was still to come at Sidhpur, where the mythical Saraswati River was revived with Narmada water. A government officer in charge of the programme said the administration spent 50 million rupees mobilising people from far-flung areas. Over 5,000 *sadhus* attended. 'Five crore is a one-time expenditure the government has incurred. But what remains hidden is the electricity bill the state would have to cough up for keeping river Saraswati flowing. The water flowing in Saraswati is pumped from 80 km away at a daily cost of 300,000 rupees,' the official said.[27]

This permanent state of mobilisation was indeed costly, but it was an investment from which Modi derived political dividends. The Sadbhavana (Goodwill or Harmony) Mission is a case in point, which deserves a detailed analysis. On 17 September 2011, on his 62nd birthday, Modi embarked on a new kind of programme aimed at promoting harmony in the face of all forms of social division based on caste and religion, including vote bank politics.[28] It consisted in Modi visiting all the districts in Gujarat and fasting for one day in each of them to promote this new mindset of social harmony. Given the packed diary of the chief minister, this programme could not be achieved in one fell swoop, so it had three legs, the last of which ended a few months before the 2012 state elections. The conclusion that Modi drew from this campaigning is worth quoting at length:[29]

> Dear friends,
> A journey called Sadbhavana Mission that began from Ahmedabad concluded at the auspicious Ambaji Shaktipith [the shrine of Shri Amba] after the observance of 36 fasts.
>
> Personally, the experience of interacting and observing one-day fasts in all districts across Gujarat was extraordinary.
>
> We can calculate people's support at the time of election through ballot boxes, but they are not sufficient to assess the

intensity of people's emotions. During the Sadbhavana fasts, I was overwhelmed to personally witness the deep bond that all Gujaratis share with each other. The pride and satisfaction of an election victory dwarfs in comparison to the fulfilment of seeing people treat each other with utmost respect and deep regard.

I am used to being told repeatedly by elders and peers about the philosophy of Janta Janardhan (People are God) but have seldom seen it being put to practice anywhere. Sadbhavana Mission provided me the fortune of witnessing this.

I fall drastically short of words to explain the powerful experience of seeing the poor and the rich, the old and the young, the educated and the uneducated classes come together without any inhibitions during the Sadbhavana Mission.

After completion of the 36 Sadbhavana fasts, the country and the world have to take note of the fact that Gujarat's atmosphere of unity, peace and brotherhood is the main reason behind our rapid progress.

On one hand, we have our nation being dominated by the poison of caste, religion-based vote-bank politics that has deeply disappointed and broken the trust of every Indian. The 'Divide and Rule' philosophy adopted by the Centre has caused irreparable damage to the image of our great nation.

On the other hand, Gujarat has adopted the path of peace, unity and brotherhood. Gujarat has shunned vote-bank politics and adopted the politics of development. 'Collective Efforts, Inclusive Growth' has replaced the age-old divisive practice of 'Divide and Rule'.

Gujarat's present decade has presented a model of development based on Sadbhavana and progress and our successful experiment in the form of the Sadbhavana Mission has given a new ray of hope to our countrymen who are immersed in deep disappointment.

It is often difficult for one to understand the good motives behind such noble initiatives as there is a tendency of some to see these public events from just a political perspective.

There were a host of incidents that touched my heart during the Sadbhavana Mission. I am at a loss of words to express my heartfelt gratitude for the phenomenal love and support extended by the people. However, I feel you would certainly like to know certain details which will acquaint you with the scope and depth of Sadbhavana Mission.

- It was no small feat for a state that representatives from all states and well-wishers from many political parties were present at the Sadbhavana fast held at Ahmedabad from 17th–19th September 2011.
- At least one member from 70 per cent to 75 per cent of the families in Gujarat participated during the 36 Sadbhavana fasts.
- The presence of over 5 million people from 18,000 villages reflects the scale and public participation in the Sadbhavana Mission.
- Shaking hands and personally meeting over 1.5 million people is perhaps a sort of record in the history of public life. But personally, to me it is a never-before kind of experience which deeply touched my heart.
- It had been my personal decision to observe fasts. But thousands of my fellow citizens voluntarily observed fast with me. Over 450,000 people including 150,000 women observed fasts and gave moral support to the Sadbhavana Mission.
- It is our culture to go for pilgrimage on foot. But during Sadbhavana Mission, hundreds of padyatras [pilgrims] arrived to the venue of fast from various holy places. Over 100,000 people, especially the youth, joined the mission as padyatris.
- Sadbhavana Marches (Prabhat-Pheris [early morning communal singing]) were organized in thousands of villages despite cold weather and saw a participation of over 1.6 million people, thus spreading the message of Sadbhavana across the state.
- Sadbhavana Mission energized the society to fight against malnutrition. As a result, about 40,000 Tithi Bhojans [community midday meals] were organized in villages through which around 4.2 million poor children were provided with nutritious meals.

- With an intention to serve the poor, more than 600,000 kgs of foodgrains were distributed to poor families in rural areas.
- Substantial sum of more than 40 million rupees were donated to Kanya Kelavani Nidhi, which will promote girl child education in the state.
- Thousands of citizens pledged to contribute for the welfare of society. Youth and newlyweds denounced social evils like dowry and child infanticide and pledged to adopt Anganwadis [rural child care centres].
- Thousands of drawing, elocution and essay writing competitions on the theme of Sadbhavana were held, which motivated around 1 million children to participate and imbibe the spirit of peace, unity and brotherhood.

Friends,
I don't wish to assess the success of Sadbhavana Mission in mere numbers.

Sadbhavana Mission has reflected the inner strength of our social fabric and touched the hearts of people in every nook and corner of Gujarat.

It is this energy of six crore [60 million] Gujaratis which has been the vital force behind Sadbhavana Mission.

It gives me immense satisfaction to see that my effort to show the nation and world the strength of Sadbhavana Mission has been successful.

Today, the blessings and well-wishes of lakhs [hundreds of thousands] of my fellow citizens received in support of my pledge have infused me with fresh vigour to serve my people.

Yours,

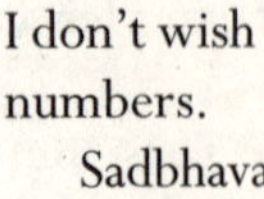

The newspapers of Gujarat trumpeted this achievement in similar terms. As in Modi's account, it was all about the numbers. A couple of them, published as banner headlines, are worth citing: 'New record: above 15 lakh citizens personally met the chief minister'; 'A heartfelt thanks to all six crore Gujaratis who were part of 36 Sadbhavana fasts'. The latter suggests that even those who did not participate in the movement were part of it. In that sense it was an all-encompassing, total mobilisation during which Modi was in direct contact with society as a whole and through which society came to form an undifferentiated whole—as Modi says plainly, all kinds of social divisions in terms of caste or caste were erased during the Sadbhavana Mission. Indeed, 'unanimism'—the idea that the people are one and that they and their leader share the same consciousness and collective emotions—is an important aspect of populism. It could allow Modi to claim 'I am the people' and the masses to identify with him. But Modi's populism relied on other principles, as was evident from the content of his speeches and his body language.

The Messenger Is the Message

The cognitive dimension of the personality cult that Modi introduced as chief minister of Gujarat did not rely on discourse only, but on symbols too. Whatever the language he used, he promoted a sense of strength, an anti-Establishment ethos and Hindu majoritarianism, so much so that his populism was akin to *national* populism.

Non-verbal Populism, Body Language and Sarcasm

To some extent, Modi's messages relied on non-verbal communication: Modi the messenger was the message, because of his body language and the very channels he used.

When on stage—and 'the bulk of Modi's political draw comes from his performances on the stage'[30]—Modi's body language, including his voice, had a distinctively masculine, muscular overtone. As Nalin Mehta points out, 'his rallies came to be marked by umpteen references to his "chappanese chaattee" or his 56-inch chest and how it would protect Gujarat'.[31] Mehta added, 'Modi had turned into somewhat of a sex symbol in Gujarat', 'part folk-hero, part superstar'.[32]

Modi's channels of communication were technologically advanced, and conveyed his capacity for epitomising modernity. Besides the use of 3D holograms mentioned above, he was innovative in his reliance on social networks, not only the internet, but also Twitter. But his use of technology was not the only way through which he communicated non-verbally. Vivek Desai, one of the men who photographed Modi, explained that he was very particular about each and every detail of his image: outfits, colours, attitudes and gestures that could carry some specific meaning—for instance, he never showed the palm of his right hand because this was the Congress electoral symbol.[33] Similarly, 'Modi actually does not ever wear green and is very careful about the blacks also'.[34] His favourite colour was, of course, saffron, and he wore typically Gujarati clothes, including the Gujarati turban. This was a way of telling his fellow countrymen, 'I'm one of you'—as was also evident from his definition of CM (chief minister) as meaning the 'common man'. This non-verbal message was in tune with the discursive one on the 'Gujarati *asmita* [identity]' and his defence of Gujarat against the Centre, as we'll see below.

If non-verbal communication matters a lot in politics, oratorical skills are key to the mass appeal of populists. These skills pertain as much to their style as to the themes they articulate. Modi's style conveyed a subtle form of authority in the garb of dismissive sarcasm. This was evidenced by the harsh rhetoric he reserved for his adversaries, whom he treated as enemies, as populists routinely do. In 2012, during the state election campaign he said: 'We have banned *gutka* in Gujarat. We want to banish cancer from this land. We want to banish Congress too.'[35] This formula was made of words, but it not only belonged to the discursive genre, it was a metaphor evoking pathological images.

Such formulas, halfway between discourse and visuality, were part of the sarcastic repertoire that Modi had no inhibitions in deploying. In 2005 he told the reporter Shekhar Gupta, who objected that he was not raising the level of political debate, that he 'believe[d] in sarcasm'.[36] For populists, sarcasm kills two birds with one stone: first, it differentiates them from the usual rhetoric of politicians—who belong to the Establishment—because it has a provocative and vulgar overtone. Secondly, it is supposed to reflect their popular—plebeian—identity. Populists, in relating to the masses, must show that they share their culture, their manners and their language, in contrast to the elites' 'propriety',[37] as Pierre Ostiguy has shown. Modi's sarcasm embodied a twofold technique of address: he was supposedly speaking like ordinary people and transgressing the codes of good behaviour of the Establishment in the name of an authenticity that the elites had betrayed. Sonia and Rahul Gandhi were the prime targets of Modi's sarcasm when he was Gujarat's chief minister. He called Sonia 'Pastaben' (Sister Pasta, in reference to her Italian origins) and 'Shetangana' (literally, the white woman). As for Rahul, Modi nicknamed him 'Jersey Cow'.[38]

Such sarcasm reflected a masculine—if not macho—and dismissive attitude towards his opponents and a remarkable capacity to stick to one's position under pressure. As we have seen, no RSS or senior BJP leader could twist Modi's arm in Gujarat and no journalist could get him to express any regret about what had happened in his home state in 2002. In Gujarat this attitude was often attributed to his *marut*, a form of virility which was associated with his failure ever to apologise for the riots of 2002, unlike Advani, who said that the demolition of the Babri Masjid on 6 December 1992 had been the saddest day in his life.

The Making of a Hero

Pierre Ostiguy convincingly argues that the successful populist is the leader who is perceived by the people not only as someone 'like me' against the Establishment, but also as an 'ego ideal',[39] a hero who protects them. The political style reflected in Modi's body language and other forms of non-verbal communication aimed at building the image of a hero. Max Weber's canonical definition of charismatic authority needs to be quoted here at length: it is a 'certain quality of an individual personality, by virtue of which he is set apart from ordinary men and treated as endowed with supernatural, superhuman, or at least specifically exceptional powers or qualities. These are not accessible to the ordinary person but regarded as of divine origin, or as exemplary.'[40] Modi had already achieved something exceptional in 2002 in Gujarat; he had then been projected by his supporters as the Hindu Hriday Samrat. To tend and cultivate this heroic image remained his priority from then on.

On his website, Modi appeared endowed with supernatural powers during his chief ministership. His online biography, for instance, included sentences such as: 'His outstanding memory of addressing lakhs of people, even common men, by their first name has made him the darling of the masses.'[41] But it was even more evident from his capacity to project himself as the protector of Gujaratis almost in a literal, physical sense. This is what one needs to understand about his claim that he is Hanuman, in response to the opposition leader Arjun Mohrwadia's speech in which Modi was compared to a monkey.[42] 'A Congress leader recently called me a monkey. Probably he hasn't read the Ramayana or he would have known about the power of monkeys. I am Hanuman and six crore Gujaratis are my Ram whom I serve.'[43] Such a statement resonates in a particular way among the Hindus of Gujarat.

This (partly supernatural) strength to protect his fellow citizens, and his embodiment, in the eyes of his supporters, as an ideal of strength vis-à-vis the Muslim threat, partly explain the fascination and adoration that he has generated. This was particularly evident from media coverage of the 2007 election campaign. Let's take the example of the Ahmedabad edition of the

Times of India's front pages on four successive days. A 23 November article recalled, on the basis of testimonies by old teachers of his, how good he was as an actor in school plays in his village.[44] On 24 November the newspaper narrated how as a child he liked to swim in the lake near his house amid crocodiles, and would even have brought home a baby crocodile, had his mother not asked him not to do so.[45] The following day, a front-page article was devoted to one of the sentences on Modi's website: 'I can digest any kind of poison.' The journalist who authored this piece then compared Modi and a sultan of Ahmedabad who had similar powers.[46] On 26 November we learned that Modi, when he was ten, helped his father to sell tea on the platform of a small railway station.[47] These accounts of his private life presented Modi as a man endowed with supernatural powers and, at the same time, as a perfectly ordinary and meritorious child.

That one of the most influential newspapers in India—at least in its Ahmedabad edition—should devote such front-page articles to Modi during an election campaign seemed suspicious. Referring to the television coverage of Modi's transition to the national scene in 2013, Harish Khare suggested that to explain 'the Indian media's current obsession with Narendra Modi', the 'only reasonably cogent answer to give was the convergence between the corporate ownership of the electronic media and Mr Modi's corporate bank-rollers'.[48] But the obsession with Modi in which some sections of the Indian media indulged reflected only some convergence between the BJP and the corporate sector; and it did not begin in 2013 either, as is evident from the way, ten years before, *India Today* explained to its readers a survey that prompted the magazine to designate Modi 'Newsmaker of the Year':

> Once in a while in a nation's life, one man emerges from the shadows and shatters the idyll. Suddenly he is an emperor amidst the wreckage, his eyes surveying a grand tomorrow and his feet trampling on the dead residue of yesterday. He becomes

> the sole arbiter of that space between fear and freedom, anxiety and adoration. The man becomes a force, an idea, that storms the minds and hearts of a people, and forever shifts the centre of political gravity. The national script is rewritten: he against the Other. He divided and dominates. Such men are the frontbenchers of history. There are many synonymous for them. Dictator. Liberator. Redeemer. Revolutionary [...] Narendra Damodardas Modi shook India. And how. Look at him, look at him up close. For so long, he was just another politician. Then one day, he was just another chief minister. Today, he is just Modi.[49]

While the title of the article was 'Narendra Modi, master divider', the text does not reflect any particular communal perspective. Modi was eulogised because of the stamina he had shown. This is typical of a 'heroisation' process whereby a character impresses others through an image of strength. Modi offered here a great illustration of Ostiguy's theory that a successful populist 'leader is both *like me* [...] *and* an ego *ideal*'[50]—or is perceived at least as embodying this alchemy. That is why body language often plays a key role in manufacturing the image of the populist, who must appear as a strong man to convince the populace that he is the right conduit for expressing revenge: the revenge of 'those at the bottom' against the elites and those they protect.

However, in order to understand the appeal of Modi in Gujarat, one needs to look beyond his capacity to saturate the public space with his image, tours and meetings, and scrutinise the content of his message.

A GUJARATI VARIANT OF NATIONAL POPULISM

Narendra Modi's message first emphasised his achievements in terms of development and governance. During the 2007 election campaign, he projected himself as a 'Vikas Purush', and he continued to do so thereafter. Welcoming the economist Jim

O'Neill, who had predicted, as a Goldman Sachs expert, that the BRIC countries would overtake the G6 countries by 2050, he summarised his whole trajectory (and strategy) in 2013:

> Many of you may recollect that we started our journey with strengthening governance. It was a bad time in 2001 as we were hit by a devastating earthquake. Among our initial steps were setting up mechanisms for inter-departmental sharing and coordination. E-governance, system re-engineering and rigorous monitoring were other areas of focus. Transparency, openness and people's participation were also insisted upon right from the beginning. The overall idea was to move from Government to Governance.[51]

Hence his slogan 'Pro-people, Pro-active Good Governance', or P2G2. The promotion of his economic achievements was replete with statistics—sometimes very specifically so. For instance, to highlight the work of cattle camps he had set up to treat sick cows, he went as far as noting that Gujarat had 'eradicated 112 diseases out of 169 diseases that afflict animals'.[52]

However, these governance- and development-oriented themes systematically receded into the background during Modi's election campaigns, when polling days were approaching and more emotionally laden issues prevailed, including the defence of Gujarat and the promotion of Hindutva.[53]

Protecting Gujarat against the Congress-dominated Centre

Modi sought to be identified with Gujarat as if there was a genuine osmosis between him and Gujaratis. This strategy was facilitated by the strength of Gujarati subnationalism[54] and its reinvigoration during the Narmada movement, which literally prepared the ground for rejuvenating the Gujarati *asmita*. As mentioned above, the Narmada dam project was finally approved by the Supreme Court in 2001, just before Modi took power, but for years all the parties of the state of Gujarat had supported it. When the

Sardar Sarovar project was initiated in 1959—Nehru laid the foundation stone in 1961—it met with strong opposition from villagers whose lands and homes were bound to be submerged in the neighbouring state of Madhya Pradesh. Suffering as they did from acute water shortages, Gujaratis mobilised in favour of this dam in what is known as the Narmada movement. As Mona Mehta convincingly argues, its promoters came from all political parties and 'perceived Gujarat as the object of external persecution and identified an oppositional "Other" that was believed to impede the state's interest'.[55]

This opposition crystallised in the early 1990s when the Narmada Bachao Andolan announced that its activists would walk from Madhya Pradesh in order to stop the building of the dam, which had begun ten years before. Then the supporters of the dam in Gujarat planned a counter-rally, the driving force of which was none other than the chief minister, Chimanbhai Patel, and the Gujarat Chamber of Commerce and Industry.[56] At that time, the *Gujarat Samachar*, in an editorial, called the Narmada project the 'lifeline of Gujarat'. In December 1990, 200,000 people 'led by the Chief Minister marched to the Gujarat side of the border'.[57] No dissenting voice could be heard. In fact, as the social scientist Himmat Patel said, 'The Narmada fever in the state is so widespread that nobody is ready to hear anything except news of its early implementation.'[58] For Mona Mehta, who points out that 'dissenters were deemed "enemies" of the state', this moment of unity against 'others' fostered Gujarati nativism (or subnationalism) to such an extent that 'the Narmada consensus profoundly shaped subsequent debates in the state'.[59]

Indeed, Modi capitalised on this past experience in order to project himself as the protector of Gujarat, like Chimanbhai Patel. He exploited Gujarati subnationalism not only by identifying himself with the 'Gujarati *asmita*', but also by claiming that he was defending the state against the Centre—and against Congress rule in particular.

Victimised by the Congress-led government and the Nehru–Gandhi dynasty

As early as his first five-year term as chief minister, Modi tried to embody and represent Gujarat against the Centre, and more especially against the Nehru–Gandhi family, as if the state's adversaries were not the state Congress but located in Delhi. He went as far as saying: 'I have been facing negativism of the centre at every front. It often appears as if they are dealing with an enemy nation when it comes to Gujarat.'[60] During the 2012 election campaign, he claimed that he had been victimised by the Centre: 'Of all the Chief Ministers that the country has seen in the last 60 years, I have suffered the maximum injustice at the hands of the centre.'[61] This sense of victimisation was justified, among other things, by economic considerations. For instance, Modi accused the Centre of resisting his demands to raise the height of the Narmada dam. In 2013 he declared at a farmers' mass convention in Rajkot district: 'I have met the Prime Minister 15 times, asking for the permission to allow installation of gates on Narmada Dam. However, every time he says, "Oh really! Has it still not been done?" [...] When installed, the gates would increase the water storage capacity of the dam by 70 per cent.'[62]

He tried hard to appear as the protector of Gujaratis, sometimes by inventing discriminatory measures. During the 2012 election campaign, he said: 'We want justice—we want gas at Delhi and Mumbai rates. We want them to restore 32 per cent kerosene quota for Gujarat.'[63] The Congress had to remind Modi that 'the Centre has released more funds for Gujarat than that released by the NDA government [in 1999–2004]'.[64] And the Union government responded by publishing adverts in Gujarati newspapers explaining that if gas was so expensive in the state, it was because of the high VAT rate. In contrast, the Modi government avoided mentioning the help it received from the Centre. In 2012, for instance, the Gujarat government had to turn to the Centre for help because of a severe drought.[65]

Populists routinely argue that they are victimised by Establishment people (including the intelligentsia) so as to appear closer to the people—who are supposed to be victims of the elite too.[66] But, at the same time, in order to be their ego ideal, they claim to be strong men. Modi embodied this Janus-like figure in Gujarat.

The Strong Modi versus the Weak Manmohan Singh

During his 2007 and 2012 election campaigns, Modi concentrated his attacks on the Congress-led government in New Delhi—as if the Congressmen of Gujarat were not worth targeting (and as if New Delhi was his final destination)—because he could more effectively articulate his state versus Centre programme by projecting himself as the strong chief minister against the weak prime minister.

He criticised the inaction of Manmohan Singh—whom he called 'Maun [Silent] Mohan Singh',[67] accusing him of saying and doing nothing about issues like inflation and poverty. He even more stridently denounced the weak stand of New Delhi vis-à-vis Pakistan. Alleging, in 2012, that the head of a Pakistani delegation, Rehman Malik, had compared the 2008 Mumbai attack to the demolition of the Babri Masjid in New Delhi, he slammed the UPA government for 'lacking the guts' to take on the interior minister of Pakistan:

> The government in Delhi is so weak that a senior minister from a Pakistan delegation equated 26/11 Mumbai terror attack with the 1992 Babri Masjid demolition.[68] The demolition is our country's internal matter—a matter that arose due to differences between the people of the country—while 26/11 was an act of aggression. By defending the act and comparing it to the Ayodhya incident, Pakistan has signed it. Yet, the Delhi government did not have the guts to ask this delegation to apologise, or send them back.[69]

Modi seized this opportunity to refer to other security issues, including the negotiations on Sir Creek, a disputed area on the border of Sindh and Gujarat: 'Neither the prime minister nor Congress has responded to my questions on Sir Creek issue. They are cheating the country and Gujarat by keeping everyone in the dark about details of the talk [...] Elections will come and go. But I am more concerned about the security of the country. Sir Creek is to western India what Siachen is to north India.'[70] The fact that Pakistan had a border in common with Gujarat naturally helped Modi to exploit popular fear of this neighbour.

Economically Lagging Behind versus Decisively Moving Forward

Modi also attacked the Centre for its lack of economic dynamism, compared with Gujarat. In the early 2010s, while India's growth rate was declining, he emphasised this point even more strongly. But in many of his speeches he cited statistics that were inconsistent with the official ones. For instance, after his 2012 victory, he delivered an address in this vein at the BJP headquarters in New Delhi:

> Brothers and sisters, today I came here to attend NDC [National Development Council] meeting and in the meeting I put my point before the Prime Minister and said that it is the country's misfortune that [in] the post where you are, [in] the place from where you are speaking, an atmosphere of despair is being created in the country. Whatever you are saying is taking the country to the bottom of deep despair. I put my point very strongly and said that you neither have any thought nor vision, there are no diligent people or any action plan to take the nation forward ...! And if this continues, we do not know how much would the country suffer. You will be shocked that before one year [last year?] the Planning Commission and Indian Govt. had decided a 9% growth rate. We [in Gujarat] are much ahead of them but they could not even achieve 9% and got stuck at 7.9%. Friends, the matter of sadness is different, this time they have even stopped thinking about 9% and decided to achieve

> 8.2% growth rate [...] They have to struggle so much for this mere 0.3%, this is the condition of Delhi Government ... while Gujarat is growing at 11% plus rate. In the field of agriculture, they are not able to cross 2.5%–3% whereas Gujarat is not coming below 10%.[71]

This speech, typical of the growth mystique he propagated, was based on figures that official statistical agencies would not corroborate. In a humorous vein, Abheek Barman declared: 'Modi does not need [the infrastructure company] APCO to lie.'[72]

A similar problem occurred during the Sadbhavana Mission when Narendra Modi, during his tour which took him from one district to another for his fasts, made a substantial series of promises. As it ended, the media reported that 'the series of announcements made by the chief minister during the fast [420 billion rupees] [were] even bigger than the state's annual plan [371.2 billion rupees for 2011–12]' and partly consisted of money from central government and other local bodies.[73]

Modi's speeches illustrate the demagogic dimension of populist discourse, in which most politicians indulge routinely, but which populists take to another level because of their capacity to lie and propagate fake news.

'Mr Clean' versus Congress Corruption

In 2012, Modi tried to exploit the anti-corruption movement launched by Anna Hazare against the federal government in order to project himself as 'Mr Clean'. In his speech concluding his Vivekananda Yatra, he declared: 'Friends, in the last eight years, have you heard any good news coming out of Delhi? All that you get to hear about is corruption, scams and favouritism.'[74]

Modi also presented himself as the protector of Gujarat against the Centre's predatory instincts, as 'the chowkidar' [gatekeeper] of the Gujarat Treasury, guarding it from the greed of the Congress.[75] And he added: 'Earlier, this money used to get swallowed. *Maaru koi Vhalu-dahalu nathi* (I don't have near and dear ones). The six crore Gujaratis are my family and their happiness is mine.' His dedication to his chief ministership, with all the sacrifices it implied, was one of his favourite themes. In another electoral speech he said: 'I am a labourer who has not taken a break for an hour in the past 11 years in order to work for the development of Gujarat.'[76] Here, Modi was suggesting a contrast with the Nehru–Gandhi dynasty whose members were not only born with a silver spoon in their mouths but who were allegedly corrupt because of their desire to redistribute money within the wider family.

Aam Aadmi Son of the Soil against a Cosmopolitan and Anti-Gujarat Privileged Family

Modi also attacked the Nehru–Gandhi family on three other grounds. First, Sonia Gandhi was a foreigner while Modi himself was 'from this country only'. He once wondered: 'What kind of people are these Congressmen? They can regard an Italian woman as their own but they find a son of the soil like me an outsider.'[77] In 2012, during the Gujarat election campaign, he related this quality of his to patriotic virtues when he declared: 'I am the son of this soil. I was born and grew up there. I don't require your certificate of nationalism.'[78] For Modi, the Congress's cosmopolitanism stemmed not only from Sonia's origins, but also from the way the party indulged in Muslim 'appeasement'. This critique was encapsulated in two other sarcastic formulas coined by Modi, when he called Manmohan Singh's government 'the Delhi Sultanate' and Rahul Gandhi '*shehzada*' (the crown prince of the Muslim dynasties, especially during the Mughal Empire).

Second, Modi argued that the Gandhi–Nehru family had never favoured doing justice to Gujarat because of its tendency to centralise power in its own hands. In 2012, again, he conveniently ignored the politics of Morarji Desai and appropriated the legacy of Indulal Yagnik, saying: 'It was not for nothing that Indulal Yagnik had to launch Mahagujarat Andolan [to establish Gujarat as a separate state]; and people of Gujarat launched Navnirman Andolan [the 1974 protests against the economic crisis] against the family's corrupt dynastic rule in the past.'[79] Modi went one step further when he accused the Nehru–Gandhi family of cultivating an old anti-Gujarati prejudice. In 2012 he declared: 'Historically, the Nehru Parivar doesn't like any Gujarati leader. They treated Sardar Vallabhbhai Patel badly. They treated Morarji Desai badly. Now it's my turn to be targeted by them.'[80] Such a discourse reconfirms that Modi oscillated between flexing his muscles and claiming he was a victim.

Moreover, Modi always tried to present himself as an *aam aadmi*, a common man, in contrast to the Nehru–Gandhi family, whom he conveniently associated with a political elite or aristocracy. During the 2013–14 Lok Sabha electoral campaign, after becoming the BJP's unofficial prime ministerial candidate, Modi elaborated on this theme by emphasising his lowly background as an OBC and former *chaiwala* (tea boy).[81]

The discourse of victimisation that Modi articulated vis-à-vis the Centre and the Nehru–Gandhi family also fits neatly in Ostiguy's theory of populism. As populist leaders claim to be like the common people, they must appear as victims of the elites too. The repertoire of victimisation is even more powerful when the political Establishment is perceived as betraying the people because of its cosmopolitan origins.

Modi combined this repertoire of victimisation and a nationalist register by exploiting the way the United States cancelled his visa in 2005. This decision had been made in response to the Gujarat riots of 2002. Modi immediately replied that the denial of a visa was 'an insult to the Constitution of India and its people and [a] threat to [the]sovereignty and democratic traditions of the country'. For him, this decision by the US was aimed at 'browbeating India into submission to its whimsical way of interpreting democracy'. He also denounced the US's 'double standards' as it maintained good relations with Pakistan in spite of 'genocide and wanton killing of Hindus'.[82] Last but not least, Modi urged the Delhi government to challenge the American decision—and the Manmohan government indeed reacted, in the name of nationalism. Foreign secretary Shyam Saran lodged a 'strong protest' against the American decision and the Government of India expressed 'deep concern and regret'.[83] In this way Modi successfully projected himself as a national victim of a foreign government. Vir Sanghvi made this point clear: 'He may be a mass murderer, but he's our mass murderer.'[84]

Modi also projected himself as a victim during election campaigns while judicial investigation was continuing into the events of 2002. In 2009, on the first day of polling in Gujarat, a BJP advertisement showed a woman tying a *rakhi* on Modi and below appeared this sentence: 'Our Narendra Bhai in jail? Do you accept this? Uproot the Congress today by voting for BJP. Defeat all those who are against Gujarat.'[85] This advertisement tried not only to present Modi as a victim of the Congress, but also to associate him with Gujarat.

Gujarati *Asmita*: Hinduising a Regional Culture

Gujarati *asmita* is an old literary formula that K.M. Munshi used repeatedly before and after Independence in his politico-cultural writings. It was used to refer to Gujarati 'identity', but has been more accurately translated as 'pride'. The content of this Gujarati *asmita* remained highly elusive in Modi's speeches. It was usually associated with another formula, 'Garavi Gujarat' (Glorious Gujarat), which recalled the early, golden days of Gujarati history—hence the naming of universities after Gujarati literary figures like Narmad and Hemchandra.[86]

During Modi's chief ministership, Gujarati *asmita* was primarily associated with the 'pre-Muslim' period of Gujarati history. As early as 2003, Modi decided to celebrate Independence Day at Patan, the ancient capital of the Rajput Chalukya dynasty. This was an occasion to celebrate not only the glorious past of the state, but also its Hindu traditions. Press reports announced in July that on 15 August, 'Bells will ring in each of the temples of Patan at 6.15 am. This will be followed by an "Asmita" (Pride) rally with the participation of Gayatri Parivar, Swadhyay Parivar, Brahmakumaris, Swaminarayan sect, etc. [all Hindu religious movements].'[87]

The promotion of Gujarati *asmita* drew also upon the legacy of one of the state's major political figures, Sardar Patel, the man Modi referred to the most when he was chief minister—so much so that the 'BJP glorified Modi as "*chhote sardar*" (junior sardar)'.[88] Modi chose to appropriate Patel in opposition to Nehru, his bête noire. For him, Patel had been a victim of India's first prime minister, whom he depicted as the embodiment of the Congress—its main rival—whereas the party had been created by Patel himself in Gujarat. In October 2010, Modi announced that a statue of Patel (also known as the 'Iron Man of India') would be built near the Narmada dam using metal collected by the peasants of India—they were then invited to send in tools they were no longer using. This Statue of Unity would be 182 metres high, a world record.[89] Modi laid the foundation stone on 31 October 2013, on the 138th anniversary of Sardar Patel's birth.

Modi also celebrated another Gujarati hero, the revolutionary Shyamji Krishna Varma, whose ashes he brought back from England (where Varma had founded India House in 1905). Upon arrival, 'Modi paraded Varma's ashes through Mumbai before taking it to Mandvi through several districts of Gujarat in a trademark chariot-style coach and the sojourn was given the heavily Sanskritised name of Veeranjali Yatra (a *yatra* to pay an ode to a revolutionary)'.[90] If Patel was promoted as the Gujarati alternative to Nehru, Varma was set against Gandhi and his doctrine of non-violence.

As chief minister, Modi promoted Gujarati culture by giving a new, official dimension to regional festivals such as Uttarayan and Navratri. The former was presented as 'predominantly a Hindu festival marking the awakening of the gods from their deep slumber',[91] while, in fact, it had been introduced by the Persians and had grown in Gujarat because of the patronage of Muslim kings, who enjoyed what it is really all about: a kite-flying competition. In 2012 Modi inaugurated the International Kite Festival, which the Ahmedabad Municipal Corporation had first established in 1989.

In terms of political communication, Modi strove to be associated with Gujarati subnationalism in many other ways during election campaigns. In 2002, he coined the slogan 'Aapanu [Our] Gujarat, Aagavu [Distinct] Gujarat'.[92] In 2007, he called the first TV channel that he launched during the election campaign 'Vande Gujarat' (Praise Gujarat!—an adaptation of a patriotic anthem with Hindu overtones, 'Vande Mataram!' (I bow to thee, Mother [India]!) whose origins lay in a poem by Bankim Chandra Chatterjee (1838–94)). His main slogan at that election was 'Jitega Gujarat!' (Gujarat will win), as if his victory could only be that of Gujarat. In 2009, during the Lok Sabha election campaign, his slogan was 'Swarnim [Golden] Gujarat' and one of the advertisements, containing Modi's photograph, declared: 'Body is dedicated. Mind is dedicated. For your sake this life is dedicated. O God, give me that strength so that my life is dedicated to Gujarat.'[93] As we have seen, his desire to be one with Gujarat also found expression in the dress code that he adopted occasionally. Moreover, Modi tended to be typically Gujarati in another, subtler and, at the same time, more powerful way, by emphasising his strict vegetarianism. In 2003, he commemorated the 135th anniversary of Mahatma Gandhi, saying: 'Gujarat's main strength lies in its vegetarianism.

Most Gujaratis are strict vegetarians. The concept of "Chappan Bhog" or 56 different dishes is native only to the Indian context and more especially to the Gujarat culture. The beauty of the Gujarat palate lies in its variegatedness [*sic*]. Vegetarianism is the first step for a healthy society.'[94] This quasi-equation between vegetarianism and Gujarati identity excluded Muslims from the bounds of 'Gujaratihood'. Modi was in a position to equate Gujarati *asmita* and Hindutva precisely by claiming that his state epitomised the culture of the majority community. Indeed, to conclude this analysis of Modi's national-populist repertoire in Gujarat, it is necessary to demonstrate that his politics remained rooted in Hindu nationalism.

The Routinisation of Hindutva

After the events of 2002, the BJP eschewed the promotion of any aggressive versions of Hindutva. Ten years later, Modi even initiated the Sadbhavana (Goodwill) Mission, which was intended to gather all Gujaratis together, beyond divisions of caste and religious community. Nevertheless, the government remained closely associated with Hinduism, and the electoral campaign of the ruling party in 2007 and 2012 was not free of communal connotations.

Soon after he took office as chief minister, Modi's identification with the religion of the majority found expression in the invitation he extended to Hindu clerics and holy figures to public functions. For instance, in 2002 *sadhus* took part in the grand celebration of the mixing of water in Ahmedabad when new canals took the Narmada dam water to the Sabarmati in the city. During the function, known as the Narmada-Sabarmati *sangam*, he performed a puja from a boat near Ellisbridge, along with Pramukh Swami Maharaj, then president of the Hindu organisation BAPS, which was 'telecast live on four giant screens along with pyro techniques'.[95]

Similarly, in 2010 Modi inaugurated the new, post-earthquake Swaminarayan temple in Bhuj (Kutch), emphasising in his speech that 'Cultural nationalism is once again [taking] our country on the right path that was shown by saints and sages centuries ago'.[96] Three years later, he was the chief guest at the 60th anniversary celebration of BAPS's youth activities.[97] This grand function, which gathered together 60,000 people at the Sardar Patel Stadium in Ahmedabad on 6 January 2013, was opened by Modi and Pujya Mahant Swami, who was to become the chief of BAPS in March 2013. The latter garlanded the former on stage and they both lit the lamp.[98]

Modi was not the only leader of the Sangh Parivar to be closely associated with the Swaminarayans and other religious organisations. For instance, in November 2012 he took part in a three-day Sant Sammelan at the Swaminarayan *gurukul* (school of pupils and their guru) at Chharodi, near Ahmedabad, along with the RSS chief Mohan Bhagwat and Ashok Singhal from the VHP.[99] Achyut Yagnik and Suchitra Sheth write:

> In fact, just as the lines between the state and the Sangh Parivar were blurred, the demarcation between the Sangh Parivar and the Hindu sects are equally fuzzy. This development was reflected in a newspaper announcement on the day of assembly elections in December 2002 when *Fulchah*, a widely circulated Gujarati daily from Saurashtra, carried a prominent advertisement by the VHP which exhorted all Hindus to vote for the 'protectors of Hindu culture'. In the list of the signatories to the advertisement, the local swamis of the Swaminarayan sect topped the list, followed by the local head of the Asram sect.[100]

While Modi claimed that he was the embodiment of Gujarat, he defined the state identity (*asmita*) as much in cultural as in religious terms. In contrast to the strategy of the other chief ministers, who articulated a subnationalist ideology by using language as the main vector of unification in their region, Modi—as a true RSS man—emphasised the role of religion. Thus, the 'Other' par excellence was the Muslim[101]—a doxa Modi inherited from the founders of Gujarati identity, including Hemchandra.[102]

Similarly, Modi's equation of Gujarati-ness and vegetarianism prepared the ground for several attacks on the meat industry, one of the economic mainstays of the Muslim community. In 2012 he criticised the central government, which 'was putting a cap on export of cotton but had been encouraging a "pink revolution" by promoting export of mutton by huge subsidies'. Nilanjan Mukhopadhyay perceptively writes:

> Pink is euphemism for blood and mutton is used to imply all non-vegetarian food items. Without using the word Hindutva, Modi argued that duty is imposed on export of cotton but not on mutton, an indication of the Centre's orientation towards those engaged in the trade of flesh (*maans*). He used words carefully, ensuring that he would not get accused of inflaming passions but prompted listeners to wonder on the religious identity of those engaged in beef export [...] Throughout 2012, 'pink revolution' was a recurring theme in various speeches of Modi and was aimed at generating revulsion towards those who were engaged in the trade of meat export.[103]

In contrast, Modi promoted vegetarianism. The quasi-equation between Gujarati-ness and vegetarianism generally excluded the Muslim minority from 'Gujaratihood.'

Hindutva-related Themes in the 2007 and 2012 Election Campaigns

Unsurprisingly, Modi tried to mobilise support with his tried-and-tested Hindutva repertoire during state elections campaigns, by exploiting fear of the 'Other'—be it Pakistan or Islamists, or even Indian Muslims—usually in response to the opposition's secularism.

In 2007, while state Congress leaders chose not to confront him on the communalism issue, lest they alienate Hindu voters, the national leaders of the Congress who campaigned in Gujarat articulated a different discourse. In November 2007, Sonia

Gandhi launched the official campaign of the party in Anand at a women's meeting, using an offensive tone:

> We all know the misdeeds committed during his [Modi's] rule in 2002. The truth makes us hang our heads in shame. Which civilised society would want such a ruler? [...] After all we all are mothers, wives and daughters of those who have been killed and jailed.[104] We have to raise our voice against barbarians. *Maujuda kushasan badalne ka mauka hain* (We have the opportunity to change the present government).[105]

In her second tour of Gujarat a few days before the polls, Mrs Gandhi again repeated the same argument. On 7 December, she said during her Amreli meeting: 'The Gujarat election is not about one election, but about the protection of democracy, rule of law and humanity itself.'[106] And she added that Gujarat was known as the place where the belly of a pregnant women had been split open. She had earlier argued, in Navsari and Rajkot, that 'those who run the government are liars, corrupt and peddlers of religion and death'.[107] Local Congressmen suggested that this comment was not aimed at Modi. Yet Digvijay Singh, the general secretary of the Congress, insisted that a 'Hindu terrorist' had misbehaved in 2002 in Gujarat.[108]

Till then, Modi's campaign had mostly focused on economic issues. But his Hindu nationalist image remained one of his assets and he had already started referring frequently in election meetings to the Ram Setu controversy (after the Indian government declared there was no historical proof that Lord Ram had built this natural formation).[109] He hit back immediately after Congress national leaders attacked him on the grounds of communalism. He first intensified his propaganda on security issues. As in 2002, he projected Muslim terrorists as an immediate threat and himself as the protector of their Hindu targets. One of his video clips broadcast online started off 'with a bomb blast, followed by sirens, dead bodies strewn about and Modi threatening unseen terrorists with "*int no jawab patthar thi*"—a stone for every brick'.[110] The BJP released another political advert in which Modi declared: 'I will not spare the merchant of death in Gujarat'—the jihadis.[111] He had one advert published in the English press headlined 'In 4 years, acts of terror claimed 5,619 lives in India. But in Gujarat, only 1'.[112] Citizens were then invited to restore a safe India 'by trouncing soft-on-terror Congress'. Among other things, the advert criticised the repeal of the Prevention of Terrorism Act (POTA), a drastic anti-terrorism law passed in 2002, during the Vajpayee government. In a meeting in Godhra, Modi harangued the crowd in typical fashion:

> the Congress says you are terrorists. Are you terrorists? This is an insult to Gandhi's and Sardar Patel's Gujarat. Teach the Congress a lesson for calling the people of Gujarat terrorists [...] Sonia Behn, it is your government that is protector of merchants of death. In Gujarat, we have eliminated the merchants of death [a reference to Sohrabuddin and other Muslims accused of terrorism] [...] Sonia Behn, if you cannot hang Afzal, hand him over to Gujarat. We will hang him.[113]

Afzal Guru had been found guilty of taking part in the plot that led to the attack on the Indian parliament by an Islamist terror group in December 2001. The Indian courts sentenced him to death in 2006. But many observers criticised the way the investigation had been conducted.[114] Afzal remained in jail on death row for many years till his execution in 2013. This explains why Modi volunteered to do the job the Centre was not doing, allegedly because it did not want to antagonise the Muslim community.

A few days before the first round of elections, Modi further radicalised his campaign by mentioning Sohrabuddin explicitly. During a meeting in South Gujarat on 4 December, he declared: 'I am thumping my chest and declaring that Sohrabuddin's encounter took place on the dharti [soil] of Gujarat.[115] If I have done something wrong, hang me. But these people [Congressmen], next they will offer a chadar [cloth worn by Muslim women] at Sohrabuddin's grave.'[116] This was a way to claim full responsibility for the crime in order to receive all the credit for this 'achievement'. Such a strategy contradicted the previous line taken by Modi, whose government had till then considered Sohrabuddin's death as an error on the part of the police, had put the guilty men behind bars and turned to the Supreme Court on 23 March 2007.[117]

As far as a trial by an international court was concerned, Modi declared in his Godhra meeting: 'Why not a court in Pakistan? The Centre talks of imposing Article 356 [President's Rule][118] in Gujarat but the Gujaratis will give me an AK-56 to fight it.'[119] This was an interesting variation on the victimisation theme: while there was absolutely no rumour of imposing President's Rule on Gujarat and suspending the state government, Modi claimed that he would resist such an assault on the state not by resorting to legal procedures, but by seizing arms. Shortly after, while campaigning in Rajkot, he described Manmohan Singh's government as 'the Delhi Sultanate'[120]—for the first time, to my knowledge.

The shift in Modi's campaign was duly noticed in the media, though it was never interpreted as a response to the campaign of national Congress leaders.[121] Modi also denounced the way the Congress allegedly promoted Christianity, because of Sonia Gandhi. In one of his meetings, he produced two two-rupee coins from his pocket, one from the pre-2004 period and one made under the UPA government, on which a cross was visible. He said: 'The Cross has appeared on the coin after Sonia-backed Government took over. Doesn't it amount to using the government machinery to spread Christian beliefs?'[122]

This new context resulted in the mobilisation of Sangh Parivar activists who had till then played a marginal part in the BJP's campaign. Now Modi appeared once again—as in 2002—as the rallying point of anti-Congress and anti-'Muslim appeasement' forces. Early in December, a thousand RSS cadres joined the BJP campaign.[123]

During the 2012 elections campaign, Modi eschewed this rabid communal repertoire as much as he could. In fact, he tried to make himself more acceptable to the minorities, as is evident from the 2011–12 Sadbhavana programme. He highlighted his record on law and order and communal harmony and linked both, albeit in a paradoxical way, in his Ahmedabad speech delivered at the end of his Vivekananda Yatra. Arguing that in the past 'Ahmedabad's identity was curfew', he claimed that he had been the one who re-established peace: 'It has been 11 years ... has the curfew gone or not? Have the riots disappeared or not? [...] Today we have embraced the road of peace and brotherhood.'[124]

Still, in practice, Modi's election campaign was replete with communal references—though not to the extent of earlier campaigns—and his speeches were suffused with Hindutva rhetoric. Speaking before the Jain International Trade Organisation (JITO), he accused the central government of heavily subsidising the opening of slaughterhouses—which was immediately interpreted in the media as an attack against cows.[125] One of his supporters, the BJP MP Navjot Singh Sidhu, went one step further by accusing Keshubhai Patel of eating *gaumans* (beef).[126] Patel retorted that the BJP was itself the 'biggest killer of cows and the largest seller of *gauchar*'.[127] Modi also received support from another media-savvy mass communicator, Baba Ramdev, who was closely linked to the Sangh Parivar.[128]

In a more communal vein, Modi referred to Ahmed Patel, Sonia Gandhi's right-hand man from Gujarat, as 'Ahmedmian' and tried to persuade voters that the Congress had decided to promote him as the party's candidate for the post of chief minister: 'Ahmedmian Patel says he does not want to be Chief Minister. But the Congress has already set the stage to make him the chief minister.'[129] The

Congress had apparently no intention of promoting a Muslim leader in the state. In fact, it nominated an unprecedentedly small number of Muslim candidates in 2012 (see chapter 6).

MODI'S POPULIST TACTICS

By the end of his first five-year term, Modi had invented a political repertoire that he could propagate by relying on the state BJP, which he had progressively conquered, on the Sangh Parivar cadres who had rallied around him (in spite of their leaders' inclinations sometimes) and, even more, on a network of supporters paying allegiance to him personally, as well as on channels of communication specially designed by and for him, in particular the social media.[130] By saturating the public sphere and projecting his image in a systematic manner, he intended to keep Gujarat in a state of quasi-permanent mobilisation. Visuality played a key role in the politics of Narendra Modi, as is evident from the role of his mask or his kurta as well as from his body language, which signified a masculine, omnipresent Gujarati whose gestures and dress code were intended to 'speak' to every fellow countryman. All these measures fitted with populist politics.

In terms of substance, Modi claimed that he represented the masses, politically and socially, as he was 'like them', but at the same time he appeared as an exceptional chief, as the people's hero, who protected them from the Delhi-based Establishment and politicians at large. Like many populists, Modi also claimed that he was not a politician[131]—and therefore was 'clean'. Indeed, for his supporters, as Swapan Dasgupta would declare, he was someone who 'has shown the possibilities of an alternative approach to politics'.[132] According to Dasgupta, Modi adopted efficiency as the only criterion of his actions, as in the world of business—hence the idea that Modi was Gujarat's CEO.

However, Modi defended Gujaratis not only politically and socio-economically, but also culturally, in the name of their *asmita*. In that sense, his populism exemplified the notion of national populism. While national-populist leaders claim that they represent all the people, their people are in fact the sons of the soil only. In the case of Modi, this autochthonous view relied on an ideological equation between the Gujarati *asmita* and Hinduism. As a result, Hindutva could be used as a form of subnationalism and in the name of Moditva. The chief minister attacked the Congress as the ruling party in Delhi that discriminated, he said, against Gujarat politically and economically, but also as a cosmopolitan organisation, headed by a foreigner, and as a protector of Muslims—the group that was excluded from Modi's definition of Gujarati-ness. Hence his definition of the Delhi government as the 'Delhi Sultanate'.

This 'anti' dimension was key to Modi's strategy in Gujarat. He often spoke *against* something or someone. He was not only against the Union government, but also against the Nehru–Gandhi family, which was ruling there because it was anti-Gujarat (since Jawaharlal Nehru had prevailed over Sardar Patel), because it was corrupt whereas he was clean, because it was cosmopolitan whereas he was *desi*, because it was well-off for at least three generations while he had been brought up as a *chaiwala*. But Modi was also against the meat-eaters and, more importantly, the Muslims (and their Pakistani supporters), who imperilled Gujarat. While the 2007 and 2012 election campaigns were not as communally laden as that of 2002, the BJP again used polarisation to its advantage.

However, Modi's rhetoric was far from being only negative. His campaign in the state elections was based on his priority of 'governance for growth and development', to paraphrase the title of Bibek Debroy's book. At times, while canvassing, he inflated some of the many statistics which peppered his speeches, as demagogues often do, but the spirit in which he spoke was clear:

he wished to modernise Gujarat by developing its infrastructure, its cities and its economy at large. This was well in tune with the aspirations of the urban middle class, who formed the core group of his supporters, as the next chapter will show.

But Modi claimed that he represented all the Gujaratis—hence his reference to his 55 million or, subsequently, 60 million 'brothers and sisters', as if the whole state was one with him. While this was clearly an exaggeration, like most successful national-populist leaders, Modi was able to perform many different roles—of protector, victim, aggressor, sage and so on—simultaneously and with ease. This is an ability that he successfully retained after becoming prime minister, when, incidentally, he continued to change his clothes according to the traditional dress code of the region he was visiting. Hence his different names: Hindu Hriday Samrat, Vikas Purush, Vishva Guru and so on. This made his persona something of a screen on to which people could project whatever fantasies they wished. In Gujarat, he learnt that he could be all things to all men, and he continued to apply this stratagem after 2014.

The continuity between Modi's politics in his Gujarat years and his Indian years is fascinating for other reasons, not only because he capitalised in 2014 on what he called the 'Gujarat model'.[133] More importantly, he asserted himself as the chief campaigner after capturing power within the BJP and still relied on the favourite techniques and themes of his Gujarat years. This kind of 'nationalisation' of a state leader who had never been a minister in the Union government, who had never been at the helm of his party and who had never been elected to parliament before, was totally unprecedented.

The style was the same, as was evident from the way Modi related to people. He travelled 186,411 miles to hold 475 regular rallies,[134] and 3D holographic projections delivered 12 speeches across 1,350 venues during the months of April and May 2014.[135] In addition, Modi made a direct connection with voters at thousands of tea stalls where he held *chai pe charcha* (informal chats over tea) with Indian citizens who wished to interact with him via the internet.[136] At 4,000 tea stalls scattered across 24 states, he connected with them using technologies such as video-conferencing and mobile broadband.

The substance also remained the same, Hindutva replacing the Gujarati *asmita*—which was in any case already rooted in Hindu nationalism and the rejection of Islam. During the 2014 election campaign, for instance, the BJP invited Muslims to attend his rallies but, in some places, reserved space for them in the audience—and distributed skullcaps to men and burqas to women at the entrance before they were directed to a corner.[137] While polarisation played a role in the 2014 elections, it did so even more in 2019 after the Pulwama attack on security forces by a suicide bomber: the fight against jihadis and Pakistan became even more important than during Modi's campaigns in Gujarat.[138] Despite the mixed results of retaliatory Indian air strikes against Pakistan—which were hardly reported in the media—Modi managed to portray himself as India's protector in a campaign dominated by nationalist and even warmongering rhetoric.[139]

As in Gujarat, Modi presented himself during his campaigns for prime minister as a victim of the Establishment, against whom he was eager to defend people 'like him'. Responding to Congress accusations regarding his role in the events of 2002, he declared from the stage in April 2014, resorting to the vocabulary of victimisation and heroisation:

> I am convinced that if there is even a grain of truth in the allegations, I feel for India's bright future and traditions, Modi should be hanged in the street square [...] There is a small coterie who think they have worked hard and created a storm. But Modi does not lose, does not die [...] Now, I am in the people's court and I am waiting to hear from them, and their verdict.[140]

These remarks tick another box on the populism checklist, the rejection of institutions in favour of the people's voice, which is the only legitimate one, as if voting for a leader amounted to exonerating him.[141] And he continued to project himself as a common man against the dominant elite represented by the Nehru–Gandhi family. He now called Rahul 'Mr Golden Spoon'.[142] He also attacked Rahul's sister Priyanka, explaining at a rally that the only reason she was in politics was out of filial piety. Priyanka retorted that the level of such a remark was 'low', a word Modi immediately—and tactically—interpreted as a reference to his caste. In a television interview with Arnab Goswami, he went on the defensive: 'Don't I have the right to at least state the truth? Is it because I come from a humble background, from a humble family? Has this country become like that? Has my democracy submitted itself to one family? And when a poor man says something, there is uproar.'[143] Gujarat was thus also the incubator of a major asset of Modi's on the Indian national scene, his command of the national-populist repertoire.

Between elections too, Prime Minister Modi has applied policies he had experimented with in Gujarat. Saturating the public space with his image is one of them, as one could see on television every day, especially before the G20 meeting in Delhi in September 2023. This technique fitted with the orchestration of a personality cult that reflected a persistent narcissism; and it found expression in a revealing anecdote in 2015: Modi wore a suit decorated with his own name to meet President Barack Obama.

More importantly, his attacks on the opposition were equally radical at the national level, as could be seen from his desire to eradicate the Congress from the political scene altogether and create a 'Congress Mukt Bharat' (a Congress-free India), as if the party was not a rival but an enemy (a theme we'll return to in the last chapter).

Similarly, the promotion of Hinduism, which almost became an official religion when Modi played the role of high priest while laying the first stone of the Ayodhya temple in 2020, echoed his role as patron of the Swaminarayan movement and the majority creed in Gujarat. Moreover, the same saffron-clad yogis (including Baba Ramdev) supported him before and after 2014.

Last but not least, Muslims were once again at the receiving end of the BJP government after 2014 too, something we will return to in the last part of this book.

PART FIVE

GAINING AND EXERTING DOMINATION: SUPPORTERS, OPPONENTS AND VICTIMS

In Gujarat, Modi's BJP broke its record in all other states by winning three elections in a row between 2002 and 2012 (see Table 9.1). Historically, the core base of the party, as in other states, comprised the upper-caste urban middle class, which remained over-represented among the supporters of Narendra Modi when he became chief minister. Still, this group was not numerous enough to win elections on its own. Under Modi, it was part of a larger coalition that also included what the state BJP designated as the new 'neo-middle class' in its 2012 election manifesto. This unprecedented coalition reflected an erosion of the political role of caste identities, which have always been more malleable in Gujarat than in other states, as is evident from the making of the 'Kshatriya' caste federation after Independence.

Nevertheless, castes, tribes and religious communities continued to play a role in Gujarat politics. Unsurprisingly, Modi's BJP was unable to make substantial and sustainable inroads among three categories of voters: Dalits, Adivasis and Muslims.

This shortcoming reflected a polarisation of the electorate that stemmed from the polarisation of society after years of uneven development and growing inequalities. It was also a result, to a lesser extent, of the attempts of opposition parties to resist the rise of Modi.

Our survey of the supporters and the opponents of Modi in Gujarat during his chief ministership will not concentrate on electoral politics only. The polarisation mentioned above affected Gujarat and Gujaratis more widely, as is evident from social processes like ghettoisation and by the fact that the corporate sector and many non-resident Gujaratis were pro-Modi whereas sections of the intelligentsia were not (and suffered accordingly)

9

THE BACKING OF THE ELITE AND THE GROWING SUPPORT OF THE 'NEO-MIDDLE CLASS'

> Due to development in Gujarat in the last 10 years, there has been substantial rise in this neo-middle class.
>
> BJP election manifesto before the 2012 state elections in Gujarat[1]

If polarisation is the trademark of national-populist leaders—in cultural as well as social terms—it is not an end in itself: it helps them to win elections and to maintain a majoritarian hegemony as well as the social status quo. National populism is conservative, and it attracts the support of elite groups not only because of the traditionalist cultural values it conveys, but also because of its power to diffuse attempts by emerging social categories to transform the social order. This paradox of populism is epitomised by Narendra Modi in Gujarat: while the leader claimed that he represented the people against the Establishment, he in fact worked hand in glove with the economic elite (as we've seen in chapter 5) and defended the interest of the middle class—a group designated as a social elite in India. Moreover, Modi attracted new emerging social groups, which could have mobilised against the upper castes and dominant class, by instrumentalising religion and exploiting their aspirations. A case in point here is the political trajectory of the low castes of Gujarat, which used to support the Congress and which rallied around Modi as members of a new 'neo-middle class'.

In the 2000s, the growing importance of this class at the expense of caste was clearly related to urbanisation, a process more pronounced in Gujarat than in almost any other Indian state. While the social coalition supporting Modi was vast and differentiated, it shared a relatively coherent world view, whose model was an urban middle-class ethos. Such an ethos was greatly influenced by the mindset of the diaspora and the desire to emulate Western lifestyles. Indeed, Modi's national populism epitomised a second paradox during his Gujarat years: in spite of eulogising the virtues of Hindu culture, the brand of modernity he promoted—and that the (neo-)middle class found so attractive—was imported from abroad and was influenced by Modi's trips across the world.

NARENDRA MODI, CHAMPION OF THE GUJARATI ELITES

From as early as his first term as Gujarat chief minister, the most explicit supporters of Modi came from the business community. Subsequent to the objections that some members of the CII expressed towards Modi in relation to the events of 2002, the organisation extended a kind of apology,[2] and all chambers of commerce in India rallied around him. Gradually, the 'Vibrant Gujarat' event attracted the most influential businessmen of India, who seized on the occasion to congratulate the chief minister of a state which had become more and more attractive for investors.

In 2007, Mukesh Ambani declared: 'Narendrabhai is a leader with a grand vision ... amazing clarity of purpose with determination ... strong ethos with a modern outlook, dynamism and passion'.[3] His brother Anil maintained that 'Narendrabhai is one of India's biggest leaders, a man who inspires loyalty and attracts followers wherever he goes … a political visionary'.[4] The billionaire industrialist K.M. Birla went even further: 'Gujarat is vibrant because of its political leadership and Modi is a fulltime Chief Minister of the state and genuinely the Chief Executive Officer of Gujarat.'[5] During the 2013 Vibrant Gujarat meeting, Anil Ambani, who had already projected Modi as the next prime minister of India, likened him to Mahatma Gandhi, Sardar Patel, Dhirubhai Ambani (his father) and Arjun, the hero of the Mahabharata, before calling him 'king of kings'.[6]

Businessmen had their own reasons for supporting Modi, but even though they extended him financial support, they were not in a position to have the BJP elected—only voters could do so, and the BJP's electoral successes in Gujarat can only be explained by the party's evolving support base, which expanded beyond the core group of its middle-class supporters.

The Middle Class as BJP's Core Group

In India, the notion of a middle class is counter-intuitive (and even a misnomer) since it designates the upper layer of society. This social category stands below the economic elite formed by the super-rich, but not in the 'middle'.[7] As surveys from the early 2000s have shown, the Indian middle class coincided then with the top 20 per cent of society.[8]

In Gujarat, this segment of society tended to support the BJP even before Modi's time. In the 1996 Lok Sabha election, according to the CSDS exit poll, 70 per cent of the 'middle' category of the Gujarati society and 72.4 per cent of the 'upper' category voted for the party—as against 27.3 per cent of the very poor (who supported the Congress, at 66 per cent).[9] This correlation remained the rule under Modi. In 2007 and 2012, the richer they were, the more likely (the relation was not fully linear) Gujarati voters were to support the BJP and the less likely they were to vote for the Congress (see Table 9.2). But the proportion of poor voters supporting the BJP was now as large as in the case of the Congress—a change we'll return to below.

Table 9.2: Voting pattern of different socio-economic groups in the 2007 and 2012 state elections in Gujarat (per cent)

Class	*Congress*		*BJP*		*GPP*		*Other*	
	2007	*2012*	*2007*	*2012*	*2007*	*2012*	*2007*	*2012*
Upper	31	28	60	57	n/a	8	9	7
Middle	37	34	53	54	n/a	5	11	7
Lower	40	45	39	41	n/a	2	21	13
Poor	42	44	45	43	n/a	1	14	11

Source: 'Gujarat Assembly election 2012: post-poll survey by Lokniti, Centre for the Study of Developing Societies', p. 13, http://www.lokniti.org/pdfs_dataunit/Questionairs/gujarat-postpoll-2012-survey-findings.pdf.

How can we explain the affinities between the middle class and the Hindu nationalist movement? Pravin Sheth offers a socio-psychological interpretation of this phenomenon and its political implications by emphasising the role of religiosity, as a sequel to prosperity and materialism:

> In Gujarat, the trading class has a wide social base. Unlike in other parts of India, it has spread among many castes. This class has become rich by any means, even by flouting the accepted norms of business ethics. In this context, it was nursing a sort of 'guilt sense'. In order to soothe the sense of guilt, this vast trading class found the shelter of 'kathakars' (interpreters of religious scriptures and traditions) and the temples. The material progress co-exist with the sense of guilt. It seeks the catharsis by sponsoring religious functions, religious recitals by revered saints and sadhus and patronizing the institutions and spiritual/religious movements. Thus, because of increase in religious practices, Hindutva propaganda got a lot of encouragement

> in Gujarat. Nowhere do the sects, cults or missions such as Jainism, Swaminarayan, Swadhyaya, Asharam Bapu, Gayatri Parivar, Chinmayananda Mission, Jalaram Bapu, Gita study centres, Adhyatma Vidhya Mandir, Santram Mandir, etc. have such a huge following and well-resourced establishments as in Gujarat. Some of them are inclined to prefer the moderate interpretation of broad-based Hinduism, but subtly distancing from the minority. Many among the OBCs are drawn towards Swaminarayan, Swadhyaya, and Asharam Bapu because of their liberal social preaching and inclusive approach to co-opt all the castes of the Hindu society. This suits BJP well for carrying out its project of political integration of all the Hindu castes/classes.[10]

Here Sheth describes a social milieu which gave rise to what can be defined as a class not only because of its socio-economic position, but also because of its ethos and lifestyle. Whether its sense of guilt was the real reason for its religiosity or not, this religiosity was indeed more pronounced than in most other states of India, where it gained momentum anyway.[11] Among the most popular 'modern gurus' of Gujarat, Morari Bapu and Asharam Bapu were known for their proximity to the Sangh Parivar.[12]

In 2007, Ashis Nandy offered another socio-psychological interpretation that went one step further: he did not explain the affinities between the Hindu middle class of Gujarat and the BJP in terms of religiosity only, but also their support for anti-Muslim violence in the aftermath of the 2002 riots:

> [this] class has found in militant religious nationalism a new self-respect and a new virtual identity as a martial community, the way Bengali babus, Maharashtrian Brahmins and Kashmiri Muslims at different times have sought salvation in violence. In Gujarat this class has smelt blood, for it does not have to do the killings but can plan, finance and coordinate them with impunity. The actual killers are the lowest of the low, mostly tribals and Dalits. The middle class controls the media and

> education, which have become hate factories in recent times. And they receive spirited support from most non-resident Indians who, at a safe distance from India, can afford to be more nationalist, bloodthirsty, and irresponsible.[13]

In his assessment, Nandy emphasises the attraction that Hindu nationalism, and its violent manifestations, exerted over the middle class in terms of 'self-respect'. This is substantiated by several testimonies collected by Parvis Ghassem-Fachandi after 2002. Many of his middle-class interviewees approved of violence against Muslims because of a deep inferiority complex and feeling of vulnerability, which were particularly frustrating for elite groups and which were rooted in the stereotype of the muscular, meat-eating Muslim in contrast with the effete, vegetarian upper-caste Hindu. Ghassem-Fachandi's middle-class interlocutors told him about Muslims: 'They are not like us, they do this butchering business.'[14] One of his female informants expressed her 'suspicion of excessive sexuality on the part of Muslims',[15] which is part of another commonplace stereotype.

The popularity of Modi's Hindu nationalist and muscular posture among one section of the middle class was most obvious during the 2007 election campaign. The Gujarat Chamber of Commerce and Industry organised a function in his honour at the time and he seized this opportunity to deliver an unflinching speech: 'Anti-Gujarat lobby have been propagating that I killed Sohrabuddin. If AK-57 rifles are found from the residence of a person, do I go to take their advice or should I ask the lawyers, "you tell me: what should I do?", should I not kill them?' The crowd brought together by the Gujarat Chamber of Commerce and Industry responded in a frenzy: 'Kill them! Kill them!'[16]

But Nandy, in the passage quoted above, also emphasised the way the middle class related to lower-class Hindus in the context of communal violence. That the riots helped the middle class to shape a social coalition against the 'Other', the Muslim, needs some elaboration. This kind of unity, cemented by blood, blurred social tensions that might have found an outlet in attempts by 'the lowest of the low' to revolt against elite groups. Such a sociological reading of the events of 2002 fits with Ornit Shani's analysis of the 1985 riots. Communal violence is indeed one of the instruments national populists can use to defuse tensions within their community and maintain the existing social order.

Naturally, besides its Hindu militancy or its Hindu religiosity, the Gujarati middle class is also defined by socio-economic criteria. Pravin Sheth emphasises its role in trade, which, he insists, is no longer the monopoly of the merchant castes. Traders are usually supporters of the market economy and, indeed, this group has always had strong reservations about state intervention in the economy. According to them, the private sector always performs better than the public sector. For elite groups at large, state intervention in the economy is seen negatively not only because it reduces growth (this is the argument they openly make), but also because it tends to reduce inequalities and to redistribute wealth. Here, the middle-class ethos and Hindu nationalism have affinities, for the latter insists that the traditional social structure of India (including the caste system) should not be tampered with by the state, for while society is natural, the state is artificial.[17] Modi's attempt to make the state shrink thus attracted the middle class of Gujarat. His economic policy was also popular among the elite because it was growth-oriented.

Here, economic performance fitted with the new consumption patterns of the rich Gujaratis. In the context of economic liberalisation—which had started early in Gujarat—the middle class developed more American-influenced tastes and habits.[18] This assessment is supported by social scientists' surveys which have shown that what the middle class valued most in the new economic policy was the accessibility of consumer goods.[19] Gujarat, with its shopping malls, which multiplied as early as the 1990s, did not lag behind in this regard.

The Gujarati middle class shared another key (and related) commonality with the Sangh Parivar: a more or less silent opposition to positive discrimination. This group mobilised more than any other against the policy of reservations favouring the weaker sections of society, including the OBCs and Dalits, on behalf of the principle of merit.[20] Their opposition to this public policy became pervasive across India after the implementation of the Mandal Commission Report in 1990,[21] but it had emerged as early as the 1980s in Gujarat. The BJP always remained ambivalent on this issue. On the one hand, the party could not openly reject a policy that was potentially benefiting more than half of society. On the other hand, it did not support it either for fear of alienating its traditional upper-caste base, which resented the way in which this policy was reducing its access to public sector jobs. The BJP was clearly on their side when it promoted the sense of entrepreneurship at the expense of welfare programmes perceived as forms of unfair assistance. Priya Chacko convincingly argues that the party was more and more eager 'to bolster the corporate sector and recreate the middle and neo-middle classes as "market citizens", such that they view themselves as entrepreneurs and consumers and come to see the market, rather than the state, as the major provider of public services and social transformation'.[22] These views were in accord with those of the elite groups, which criticised positive discrimination and eulogised economic liberalisation. After the implementation of the Mandal Commission Report, the middle class—mostly upper caste[23]—turned to the BJP, which came to 'represent the rebellion of the elite'.[24]

In Gujarat this shift from the Congress to the BJP—at least in the case of the Patels—had occurred ten years before, after the anti-reservation movements of the 1980s. The Sangh Parivar offered a clear antidote to the rise of the lower castes in the garb of Hindutva, an ideology which invited members of the majority community to promote their religious identity (against the

Muslim 'Other') and blur caste and class. In chapter 1 we have seen how this strategy—and its communal implications, including the polarising effect of the 1985 riots—largely explained the rise of the BJP to power in the 1990s. Under Modi, it became even more sophisticated: not only were the lower castes requested to join hands with the upper castes against Muslims to defend Hinduism, but they were also co-opted sociologically as the new 'neo-middle class'.

To understand this notion and how it crystallised, one needs first to make a detour and assess the relative malleability of caste in Gujarat.

The Relative Malleability of Caste

The data of the 2011 caste census which has leaked out to the press allows us to update the data mentioned in the introduction to this book.[25] The three columns of Table 9.3 use, respectively, the figures of the 1931 census (to which we have referred above), those of the 2011 caste census, and those drawing on the post-poll Lokniti–CSDS survey of 2012.

Table 9.3: Caste distribution in Gujarat.

Castes and communities	*1931 census*	*2011 caste census*	*Lokniti–CSDS*[¶]
Higher castes	13.1	12.05	11.4
• Brahmin	4.1	3.12	3.5
• Vanya & Jain	3.0	2.41	1.6
• Rajput & Darbar	4.9	6.52	4.5
• Other	1.1		1.8
Middle castes	12.3	14.53	14.7
• Patidar & Kanbi	12.2	14.53 (incl. 8.11 Leuva Patels and 6.42 Kadva Patels)	13.9

Castes and communities	*1931 census*	*2011 caste census*	*Lokniti–CSDS*[¶]
• Other	0.1		0.8
Lower castes & OBCs	40.3	42.9	42.8
Kshatriya		15*	13.1
Thakor		7.67	
• Koli	24.2	7.79	6.8
• Other	16.1	12.4	22.9
Scheduled Castes	7.2	7.5[§]	7.7
Scheduled Tribes	17.7	12.35[§]	16
Muslims	8.5	9.89	6.2
Other minorities	1.0	1.0	0.7
Total	100	100	100

Source: Adapted from K. Dave, 'Die is caste in Gujarat, Muslims matter', *Indian Express* (Ahmedabad edition), 2 November 2012, p. 1, http://www.indianexpress.com/news/die-is-caste-in-gujarat-muslims-matter/1025654/ (last accessed 13 Dec. 2013).

* The caste census presented in the article mentioned above does not give any figure for the Kshatriyas. The figure of 15 per cent comes from 'Gujarat polls', Exit and Opinion Polls India, 11 Dec. 2012, http://exitopinionpollsindia.blogspot.fr/2012/12/gujarat-polls-tactical-voting-and.html (last accessed 13 Dec. 2013).

[§] The 2011 population Census gives different figures, 7.1 per cent for the SCs and 14.75 per cent for the STs.

[¶] 'Gujarat Assembly election 2012: post-poll survey by Lokniti, Centre for the Study of Developing Societies', pp. 10–11, http://www.lokniti.org/pdfs_dataunit/Questionairs/gujarat-postpoll-2012-survey-findings.pdf.

The data in the three columns of Table 9.3 are fairly consistent, as neither the 2011 caste census nor the CSDS figure reveals any significant shift from the 1931 census. According to the 2011 caste census, Brahmins represented 3.12 per cent of society, Vaishyas (including Vanyas and Jains) 2.41 per cent, and Rajputs (sometimes known as Darbars) 6.52 per cent. As mentioned earlier, though they are part of the Savarnas, some of these Rajputs are less prestigious than elsewhere in North India—hence the alliance some of them formed, in the 1950s and 1960s, with some low-caste Kolis to form the well-known caste federation called the 'Kshatriyas'. This alliance was intended to contain the rise of the Patels, a dominant caste which represented about 14.5 per cent of the state's population in 2011, but which is now divided into two sub-groups, the Leuva Patels (a category concentrated in Saurashtra), who make up 8.11 per cent of society, and the Kadva Patels, who make up 6.42 per cent.[26]

The more confusing category is the OBCs. While everybody seems to agree that they represent about 40 per cent of society, the composition of this huge group is unclear. This is largely due to the elusive character of the Kshatriyas, a rather fluid category, in which the same caste group may not recognise itself as part of the OBCs in one place but will do so elsewhere. For instance, Thakors in Saurashtra are likely to appear as Rajputs, but not in Ahmedabad and Mehsana districts, where they will be Kshatriyas. Similarly, the Kolis of Saurashtra and South Gujarat do not define themselves as Kshatriyas but prefer to identify themselves simply as Kolis.[27] As a result, Kolis and Thakors who have not become part of the Kshatriyas represent 7.79 per cent and 7.67 per cent respectively of society.[28] Consequently, the 'proper' Kshatriyas are only 15 per cent of the state population according to the 2011 caste census. The elusiveness of some caste contours in Gujarat, in particular the uncertain character of the definition of Kshatriyas, stands in contrast to the more robust quality of caste identities found elsewhere in India.

While the OBCs have the advantage of numbers, the Patels—who have become powerful economically—are also numerous in many pockets.[29] In 2012, the Leuva Patels could influence the outcome of 41 Assembly seats, mostly in Saurashtra, Kutch and South Gujarat,[30] whereas the Kadva Patels commanded a similar influence in 32 seats in North Gujarat and some parts of Saurashtra.

The Superficial OBC-isation of the BJP and the Making of a 'Neo-middle Class'

As we have seen, the BJP has traditionally been associated with the upper castes and the Patels, a combination known as the Savarnas. Under Modi, the party remained closely identified with the Patels. The proportion of Patel candidates fielded by the BJP dropped, from 32.5 per cent in 1998 to 28 per cent in 2002 and even 26 per cent in 2007, but rose again in the following years to return (almost) to its 1998 level at 32.2 per cent in 2012.[31] In parallel, the BJP plebeianised itself to a certain extent. First, the proportion of upper-caste candidates nominated by the BJP for state elections constantly declined from the mid-1980s (when Modi became its organising secretary) till his last re-election—from 27 per cent in 1985 to 19 per cent in 2012. And the decline of these Savarnas among the BJP MLAs was even more pronounced, from 36.4 per cent to a mere 20 per cent.[32] The OBCs were among the main beneficiaries of this trend. The proportion of OBCs among BJP candidates jumped from a mere 18 per cent in 1985 to 24.3 per cent in 1995, 26.4 per cent in 1998 and 32.5 per cent in 2002. It remained at 32 per cent in 2007 and 30.6 per cent in 2012.[33] The party made a special effort vis-à-vis the Kolis: not only were 16 of its 35 OBC MLAs Kolis in 2007, but 8 of them were made ministers, including Parshottam Solanki.

Indeed, the sociology of the Gujarat government changed under Modi. In 2001, OBCs accounted for 33 per cent of ministers and ministers of state; in 2002, 35 per cent; and in 2007, 39 per cent, as against (respectively) 18 per cent, 26 per cent and 22 per cent of the upper castes and 29 per cent, 30.5 per cent and 28 per cent of Patels.[34] But this trend needs to be qualified. For Sharik Laliwala this democratisation process was 'superficial' because the upper castes and Patels continued to dominate the cabinet (at a time when OBCs were over-represented among ministers of state only) and were still handling key portfolios such as home, finance, energy, revenue, education, food distribution, roads, petrochemicals, industries and water supply.[35] Secondly, the proportion of OBCs in Modi's government formed in 2012 returned to what it was in the late 1990s—about 30 per cent—and the share of Patels jumped to an unprecedented level—40 per cent—when Modi realised that he needed to counter the 'Patel party' that Keshubhai had just created (see Appendix B). These contradictory trends reflect the limitations of the plebeianisation process of the BJP under Modi:

> Modi did not inaugurate, if not facilitate, any brand of representative politics as he approached the OBC question in a gradualist and piecemeal manner to defuse oppositional interest groups by recognizing—and not stimulating—upward mobility among a few numerically significant OBC jatis [sub-castes]. This political strategy vis-à-vis OBCs is remarkably at odds with the approach of Congress in the early-to-mid 1980s. At that time, Congress' KHAM experiment endeavoured to radically restructure society's power dynamics, building upon a new stream of political consciousness among OBC Kshatriyas, to dismantle centuries-old entitlements of upper castes.[36]

Indeed, the idea was not to promote social change but mostly to attract electoral support by wooing various caste groups. Hence the nomination of many OBC candidates and the variations in the social profile of Modi's governments according to the electoral cycle that Sharik Laliwala has identified. That the 'numerical strength [of OBC ministers and ministers of state] remained subject to the electoral cycle'[37] reveals the tactical dimension of their modus operandi, something that fitted well with the structural rejection of caste-based quotas by the BJP. It was also evident in the way BJP played with caste politics even more explicitly during the 2012 election campaign.

At that time, this tactic appeared obligatory for him, as he had to confront two parties associated with caste groups. On the one hand, the Congress continued to have many OBC leaders, including Shankarsinh Vaghela, Shaktisinh Gohil and Bharatsinh Solanki (the son of Madhavsinh Solanki). On the other hand, Keshubhai Patel, as we'll see below, had started his own Patel-dominated party, the Gujarat Parivartan Party (GPP). Modi tried to undermine both the Congress and the GPP by wooing caste groups which supported them.[38] He made a point, for instance, of attending Patel events: in February 2012 he inaugurated the function marking the 25th anniversary of the Umiyadham temple, a sacred place of worship for the Kadva Patels, while Keshubhai Patel presided over the closing ceremony. In 2009, Modi inaugurated the Rajat Jayanti Mahotsav celebration of the caste deity, Goddess Umiya Mata, which was relaunched in the presence of 800,000 people after 25 years.[39] In parallel, he tried to court OBCs,[40] and in particular Kshatriyas,[41] by appointing some of them ministers (like Pradipsinh Jadeja) or at the helm of corporations (like Bhupendrasinh Chudasama and Jayanti Barot).[42] More importantly, he made a successful effort to attract the descendants of former princely rulers from Saurashtra who had often been closer to the Congress. In 2011, 18 of them joined the BJP.[43]

These moves partly explain the voting patterns of the 2012 elections (see Table 9.4). While the proportion of upper-caste and Patel voters supporting the BJP remained massive, with 61 per cent of the upper-caste voters, 63 per cent of Leuva Patels and 82 per cent of Kadva Patels (see Table 9.10), the main achievement came from the huge inroads the BJP made in the traditional vote banks of the Congress, the Kshatriyas and the Kolis. A majority of voters from these two groups supported the BJP. Kolis abandoned the Congress in large numbers (–13 percentage points) and rallied around the BJP (+11 percentage points). As a result, Modi's party became almost as popular among the OBCs as among the Savarnas.[44]

Table 9.4: Caste and community voting preference in 2007 and 2012 (per cent)

Party	*Congress*		*BJP*		*GPP*	
Caste and community	*2007*	*2012*	*2007*	*2012*	*2007*	*2012*
Upper caste	26	26	69	61	n/a	5
Leuva Patel	34	15	55	63	n/a	18
Kadva Patel	8	7	85	82	n/a	4
Kshatriya	39	44	47	52	n/a	1
Koli	52	39	42	53	n/a	1
Other OBCs	38	32	54	54	n/a	4
Dalit	56	65	34	23	n/a	1
Adivasi	33	46	38	32	n/a	3
Muslim	67	72	22	20	n/a	1
Others	26	24	61	69	n/a	1

Source: 'Gujarat Assembly election 2012: post-poll survey by Lokniti, Centre for the Study of Developing Societies', p. 13, http://www.lokniti.org/pdfs_dataunit/Questionairs/gujarat-postpoll-2012-survey-findings.pdf (last accessed 13 Dec. 2013).

However, the picture of caste politics that developed in the 2000s needs to be qualified. Modi's OBC supporters did not share the same social background as those who remained with the Congress. Kolis were a case in point. While the Kolis living in villages still overwhelmingly supported the Congress, those who lived in semi-urban and urban contexts had moved towards the BJP. According to the CSDS, in rural constituencies 53.5 per cent of Kolis voted for the Congress. Only 18.5 per cent did so in semi-rural constituencies, where 65.2 per cent of them supported the BJP. This is a clear indication of the impact of urbanisation that affected many OBC caste groups—to the extent that the only constituencies in which the Congress prevailed over the BJP were rural ones. And the more urban the voters were, the weaker the Congress was—as was evident from its performance, ranging from 45.7 per cent of valid votes in rural seats to 32.2 per cent in

Table 9.5: The impact of urbanisation on the voting pattern of castes and communities

Castes and communities	*Congress*			*BJP*			*GPP*			*Others*		
Categories	*Rural**	*Semi-urban*§	*Urban*¶	*Rural*	*Semi-urban*	*Urban*	*Rural*	*Semi-urban*	*Urban*	*Rural*	*Semi-urban*	*Urban*
Upper caste	n/a#	16.1	22.5	n/a	64.5	60.5	n/a	16.1	1.6	n/a	3.2	15.5
Patel	12.4	16.1	10.7	62.8	71	72.9	24.8	6.5	6.4	0	6.5	10
Kshatriya	45	41.1	36.2	51.2	51.8	53.2	0.7	0	2.1	3.1	7.1	8.5
Koli	53.2	18.5	0	44	65.2	100	0	3.3	0	2.8	13	0
Other OBC	40.7	26.6	17.9	50.9	51.6	65.5	3.1	3.5	5.5	5.2	18.4	11
Dalit	81.3	45	59.7	18.8	36.3	16.9	0	1.3	0	0	17.5	23.4
Adivasi	47.3	41.1	20	29.6	35.6	66.7	0.8	10	0	21.4	13.3	0
Muslim	70.2	81.4	68.5	20.7	7	29.6	0.8	2.3	1.9	8.3	9.3	0
Average score	45.7	32.2	27.5	43.3	50.8	57.7	3.3	4.6	3.2	7.7	12.4	11.7

Source: CSDS data unit.[45]

* Rural constituencies have 75 per cent or more village-based voters.

§ Semi urban constituencies have between 25 per cent and 75 per cent urban voters.

¶ Urban constituencies have 75 per cent or more urban voters.

The data for the rural upper-caste voters are not available.

the semi-urban ones and only 27.5 per cent in towns and cities. The relation is equally linear on the BJP side, but in the reverse order of 43.3 per cent, 50.8 per cent and 57.7 per cent (see Table 9.5).

The way OBCs rallied around the BJP in semi-urban and urban contexts needs to be explained. These urban OBCs were former peasants who had migrated to the city or who had been involved in the rapid urbanisation that Gujarat underwent. In this process, their caste identity—which had already been secularised[46] by quota politics and caste federations—and which had traditionally been malleable, further eroded. Their aspiration to join the middle class was related to the shift from cultivating the land to working in a factory or a sweatshop in the informal sector, or even in the service sector as a tea boy or *chaiwala* (as in the film *Slum Dog Millionaire*)[47] or as a driver (like the character in Aravind Adiga's novel *The White Tiger*)[48]—if not quite a proper clerk. They may not have earned much more than before, since wages were very low in Gujarat, but at least they had a job and some hope for a brighter urban future. Expectations ran high among this aspiring group, which was also imbued with forms of intense Hindu religiosity. This was true not only in Gujarat: everywhere in India the plebeians who experience some upward social mobility, especially when they come from 'a low-caste background, adhere more strongly to the ritualistic forms of Hindu practice'.[49] Minna Saavala attributes this attitude to a new form of Sanskritisation. In Gujarat, it developed at the expense of a Kshatriya identity, which derived from the old martial tradition, distinct from the Brahminical-cum-mercantile register of central Gujarat.

While OBCs form the bulk of the 'neo-middle class', some of its members were Scheduled Castes. Dyotana Banerjee and Mona Mehta show that in Ahmedabad an emerging Dalit middle class started to leave the *chawls* (tenements) of Ahmedabad's industrial belt to find better living places in the periphery of West Ahmedabad: the 'exodus of economically well-off Dalits out of

Gomtipur' is a case in point. These 'migrants' started to move to a new Dalit colony in Chandkheda in the 1980s and even more so in the 1990s 'when Hindu–Muslim polarization and violence was on the rise', as they did not want to live next to Muslims.[50] Banerjee and Mehta point out that 'Dalit builders have constructed the many Dalit housing societies in Chandkheda', as elsewhere there developed an 'upper caste vigilantism to prevent the entry of Dalit residents'.[51] Still, the new Dalit bourgeoisie was keen to emulate the upper-caste middle class. First, they developed a deep sense of casteism: while Dalit sub-castes used to mingle in the *chawls*, in Chandkheda 'one of the anxieties of the Dalit middle class is the disruption of sub-caste boundaries through inter-marriages'.[52] Second, they enthusiastically participated in forms of Sanskritisation, including vegetarianism:

> The middle-class Dalits of Chandkheda distance themselves from their poorer counterparts by explicitly referencing their own 'upper-caste-like' food practices, through claims such as: '*hum bhi non-veg khana pasand nahi karte*' (we also prefer not to eat meat). There is not a single meat shop or non-vegetarian restaurant in the IOC region of this Dalit neighbourhood. Instead, there are makeshift non-vegetarian food carts and shops, yet they only operate in the evenings. The secretive functioning of meat carts at night hints at the Dalit desire to hide their traditional food practices and display a new Dalit middle-class identity that is more in line with upper caste norms.[53]

The zeal of the new converts that is described here needs to be understood literally: while many Patels joined the Swaminarayan movement when they migrated to the city and became more affluent, many middle-class Dalits also started to join this sect or others in order to emulate upper-caste behaviour. Elaborating on the Sanskritisation of newly affluent Dalits, Ghanshyam Shah adds that although 'some of them are sensitive to the plight of poor and subjugated Dalits, on the whole many are uprooted from a larger Dalit milieu of traditional oppression'.[54] In their case 'imitation is not merely confined to the Brahminical traditional values of purity and impurity, but also the notion of 'nation', consumerist culture and political tactics'.[55]

These variants of the Sanskritisation process were equally strong among the OBCs who experienced similar upward social mobility, albeit in much larger numbers. This process had already been one of the root causes of the making of the 'Kshatriyas' in the 1950s and 1960s, when, as Ghanshyam Shah recalls, a section of Kolis 'began to don the sacred thread, performing the Vedic rite of upanayana. Mythologies around honour and insult are created and religious rituals of the Rajputs are imitated.'[56]

Narendra Modi coined a term for this emerging social category during his 2012 election campaign when he said that they formed a new 'neo-middle class'. The BJP manifesto did not define this class, but claimed that a BJP government, if elected to power again, would take care of it: 'Due to development in Gujarat in the last 10 years, there has been substantial rise in this neo-middle class. We want to address their issues. We will form a committee to define this neo-middle class. We will try to give them benefits of government schemes.'[57] Commentators speculated on this new notion and concluded that it designated 'those who have just risen above the below (sic) poverty line (BPL) but still do not qualify in the urban middle class category'.[58] Modi also remained vague on the subject. He merely said: 'A neo-middle class has evolved in the State during the past 10 years, which just needs a little push to grow to exponential levels.'[59] Many people believed him, it seems, and were grateful. Even in 2007 a survey revealed that while only 24 per cent of poor Gujarati voters considered that their economic lot had improved (whereas 36 per cent said it had deteriorated), 72 per cent of those who had seen an improvement had voted BJP.[60] Similarly, in 2012, the BJP made progress among the social categories that the CSDS defined as 'middle' and 'lower' whereas it lost a few percentage points among both extremes of 'rich' and 'poor'. Table 9.2 shows that the BJP indeed continued to make some progress among these groups in spite of the competition from the new party created by Keshubhai Patel. Interestingly, Modi represented a better future for the youth too. The only age group which supported Modi more in 2012 than in 2007 was the18–25-year-olds.[61]

The Urbanisation Factor

Urbanisation is not only a useful proxy for measuring the transformation of the political culture of formerly rural OBC groups, but it can also shed light on how modernisation affected the behaviour of all voters in Gujarat

The state registered the highest rate of urbanisation in India between 2001 and 2011, increasing from 37 per cent to 43 per cent. As a result of this process and the corresponding re-delimitation of constituencies, in 2012, out of 182 seats, only 102 (56 per cent) were rural, 35 (19 per cent) semi-rural and 45 (25 per cent) urban. Moreover, villages were increasingly exposed to the influence of cities. As Nirendra Dev, a journalist who did fieldwork in the countryside, pointed out, in Gujarat,

> the thickening of village–kasba [town] linkages has gained momentum. Old timers in rural villages near Rajkot in 2009 recollected that visiting cities like Rajkot and Ahmedabad were 'once in blue moon' [an] experience that [was felt] too by upper castes and rich [people …] But now, several vehicles move around to and fro the cities daily full of college going students, a large number of them girls, village shoppers and a neo-brand of white collared employees. Beside these, there are large armies of rural population now moving towards cities and small towns making as watchmen, domestic helps, truck drivers and construction workers.[62]

Surveys show that in 2012 this variable contributed to the systematic electoral growth of the BJP (see Table 9.6), irrespective of the socio-demographic category defined by education, and not only in the case of Kolis. For instance, the more urbanised the Adivasi voters were, the less Congress-oriented and more BJP-oriented they were (see Table 9.5). The relation was not so straightforward in the case of Dalits and Muslims, but the rural components of these two groups were still the most supportive of the Congress.

The (partial) exception was the Patels. In their case, the urban–rural divide played a role in the 2012 Gujarat elections, as is evident from the support the GPP received from rural Patels (almost 25 per cent of whom voted for the party). But the striking figures, as far as the Patels are concerned, are to be found in the Congress and BJP columns in the table. In both cases, the degree of urbanisation hardly made any difference, which can probably be explained by the fact that the Patels have been both urban and rural for a long time and thus form some sort of 'straddling' group.[63]

Patels excepted, the rural–urban variable made a more significant difference than caste and community so far as voting patterns were concerned in Gujarat. How can we explain this impact of urbanisation? The belief that Modi would improve the standard of living of urban dwellers is one factor. But urbanisation results also in less religious mixing and more exposure to Hindu nationalist propaganda. In villages, Hindus and Muslims who have been neighbours for centuries often share some rituals and beliefs. In cities, especially riot-prone ones, these practices are less likely to occur, not only because of a more individualistic lifestyle, but also because of the ghettoisation process, which diminishes the chances of inter-religious interactions. Second, urban dwellers are easily targeted by ideological messages and images. Politics are constantly played out on television, on the internet, on mobile phones and on walls, not to mention the state of quasi-permanent mobilisation we have already discussed, which is primarily an urban phenomenon.

In view of the BJP's reliance on the support of urban voters from the middle class and neo-middle class, the government tried to make voting compulsory,[64] given that the middle class tended to vote less often than other social groups in the 2000s.[65] The Gujarat Assembly passed a bill along these lines in 2009, but the governor returned it, arguing that 'forcing voters to vote is against the principles of individual liberty'.[66] The Assembly tried to pass it again in 2011, to no avail.

To sum up, in the Gujarat of this time, the typical BJP voter was no longer a man from the Savarnas. A majority of OBCs, mostly among those who had migrated to the cities, who had received some education and become richer—and expected more—now supported the party. Modi attracted the rich, the middle class and 'neo-middle class' to vote for him by promoting a vision of modernity which found expression in the cities and which, paradoxically, emanated not from the Indian or even Hindu traditions, but from the West—and also from China.

MODI'S (SINO-)AMERICAN DREAM: MAKING CITIES 'BOURGEOIS AT LAST'

The Diasporic Connection and the Foreign Quest for Modernity

Modi got in touch with Gujarati expatriates in the US during the Emergency when, as one of the RSS's underground leaders, he was a link person between Indians at home and abroad. His professor of political science at the university, Pravin Sheth, remembers: 'When Dr Mukund Mody, a US-based NRI [non-resident Indian], who had formed a vibrant forum in America to help re-establish democratic values in India, came to Gujarat in 1976, Narendrabhai had organized a meeting with him at my residence.'[67] This American connection would have continued after the Emergency had Modi been allowed to pursue his studies in the United States. Indeed, after completing his MA, in 'the beginning of the 1980s he had obtained an admission for advanced studies in Athens University of Ohio State in America. But maybe, as he was a bachelor, RSS volunteer, not having direct family and financial links to come back after his study, he was rejected a student visa by US Consulate in Mumbai.'[68] All the same, Modi continued to pay a great deal of attention to the US and visited the country in the 1990s.[69] In fact, no BJP leader has been as familiar with the US (even its rural areas) as Modi, who travelled there repeatedly in the 1980s and 1990s.

> Modi travelled far and wide in the US using NYC as a pitstop, remembers Prakash Swamy, one of several Indian scribes who Modi kept in touch with in the Big Apple where he stayed weeks at a time. He also travelled, often by road, to and around cities such as Chicago and Boston, and flew to Texas and California. Everywhere he went, he was interested in governance and infrastructure—roads and rivers and urban regeneration; how Americans were approaching problems and what India can learn from it.[70]

After the 2002 riots, Modi was refused a visa by the US administration,[71] yet he remained connected to the Gujarati diaspora through video conferences.[72] He also tried to circumvent the visa problem by organising the Vishwa Gujarati Parivar Mahotsav festival in January 2004, an event targeting non-resident Gujaratis (NRGs) likely to invest in Gujarat.[73]

Modi's diaspora policy consisted in reinvigorating the Non-Resident Gujarati Foundation, which was part of the NRI (Non-Resident Indian) division of the state government, and whose aims, among others, were 'to channelise the savings and surplus financial resources of the NRGs into the Gujarat's developmental efforts for mutual gain'.[74] US-based NRGs then became important interlocutors for Modi. He addressed them long-distance in 2008 during the World Gujarat Conference when, according to the online magazine NRI Today, '30,000 Gujaratis converged at the Raritan Expo Center in Edison, New Jersey [one of the centres of Gujaratis in the US] to celebrate Gujarati language, culture, heritage, art, history, enterprise and people in all its grandeur'.[75] In 2010, an NGO, Friends of Gujarat, based in New Jersey, organised a similar event called Swarnim Gujarat (Golden Gujarat) to celebrate the 50th anniversary of the state and to promote business relations between Gujarat and the NRGs.[76] A senior bureaucrat travelled to the East Coast with a large delegation including representatives of Reliance Industries, the Adani Group, Suzlon and GMR.[77] Narendra Modi repeated this in May 2012—mostly to attract investors—and then again in March and May 2013 (when he simultaneously addressed crowds at 18 city gatherings via 3D projections).[78]

However, after Modi was denied access to the US, he also turned to China, a country he visited on several occasions. In 2011, during his fourth visit, he went to Beijing, Shanghai and Chengdu, where he appreciated what he had already found so fascinating in the US: 'They [the Chinese] have three important qualities—scale, speed and skill. I am very impressed by their triple "S" formula.'[79] He also declared, in a public meeting in Beijing: 'China and its people have a special place in my heart. I admire their hard work, disciplined and resilient nature and above all their sense of history.'[80] Modi invited Chinese companies to invest in Gujarat to help modernise the state along the lines of what he had seen during his visit.[81] At the end of his tour, he confidently declared that he was 'expecting top Chinese companies to invest in the state'.[82] One year later, in a video conference with non-resident Gujaratis in the US, Modi pointed out that 'Gujarat and China are being compared today [...] because of the success of the manufacturing sector'.[83]

The model of development that Modi found in the US and in China was precisely the one promoted in Gujarat by NRGs, who exerted a durable influence on the BJP and Modi, especially through their long-established North American component.[84] Among them, the Patels form a large group, if not a majority. According to one estimate, they number about 1.7 million, working primarily in American hotels and motels (which are consequently sometimes nicknamed 'potels').[85]

While Gujarati politicians had cultivated their relations with the US-based non-resident Gujaratis (NRGs) for years,[86] Modi went further and tried to woo the NRGs as well as the Gujarati middle class by importing a modern (though foreign) model of urbanisation in his state.

Driving the Poor from the City and Importing Non-Indian Urban Planning

As we have seen, the Modi government focused on towns and cities, at the expense of the rural part of the state—but what were the urban plans they had in mind? The main objective was to modernise cities in line with the preferences of the middle class. This policy implied that some of the poor had to be driven out because their slums occupied too much space in city centres, as in Ahmedabad.

In the early 2000s, street vendors in Ahmedabad were harassed by the police to such an extent that one of the most famous Indian NGOs, SEWA (Self Employed Women's Association), filed a public interest litigation (PIL) petition in the Gujarat High Court. The court then ordered the Ahmedabad Municipal Corporation (AMC) to prepare a street vending scheme for the city. However, 'The resultant Street Vending Scheme is very restrictive and prohibits vending on major roads. It also does not take into consideration the natural markets in the city. According to SEWA, if the scheme were implemented unchanged then 129 out of 174 natural markets in the city would be adversely affected.'[87]

Slum dwellers were equally victimised. In 2009, 834 slums were identified in the city, housing approximately 1.31 million people in all, which was about 23 per cent of the city's total population. The official estimates by the AMC fell to 13 per cent (0.73 million) in 2010 'due to de-notification of slums after their upgrading'.[88] Jan Breman, who has conducted fieldwork in Ahmedabad for decades, argues that harassment of slum dwellers and inhabitants of *chawls* started in the early 2000s:

> More than half of Ahmedabad's population either lives in slums spread throughout the city, or are residents of chawls concentrated in the former mill districts. Evictions took place as early as 2004, with clandestinely built shacks and their occupants being cleared because they obstructed the traffic or the execution of public works. At first these were small-scale operations in different parts of the city. And the number of people who lost their makeshift shelters was limited to a few dozen at a time, too little to attract much attention.[89]

This policy gained momentum in the mid-2000s, when the government started to modernise the city for the middle class at the expense of the poor. In 2006, the Modi government created a new Gujarat Urban Development Mission aimed at 'attaining better living standards in major cities'.[90] Three years later, Modi announced a 70 billion rupee Swarnim Jayanti Mukhya Mantri Shaheri Vikas Yojana (chief minister's Gujarat Urban Development Mission) 'for providing basic infrastructure in cities and towns'.[91] The Gujarat government reformulated the regulations for residential townships accordingly in order to enable the middle-class section of the state's cities to grow. The new regulations allowed

> real estate developers to build multi-storey buildings 70 meters high, with floor space index (FSI) of 1.5 irrespective of any zone in any urban area of Gujarat [...] The developer will have to set aside 60 per cent of land for residential purpose, while the rest can be put to use for public purpose infrastructure

> including 30-metre wide roads, streets, recreational grounds, water and electric supply, street lighting, sewerage and storm water drainage. Five per cent of the space will have to be left for school, hospital and public amenities, five per cent for parks and gardens, each plot being of at least 3,000 sq. meters. Another five per cent land will have to be set aside for weaker sections.[92]

According to these new regulations, the Gujarat government explicitly reserved 5 per cent of the new townships for the poor, at a time when slum dwellers represented 23 per cent of the total urban population in 2009.[93] This gap was indicative of its attempt at making cities 'bourgeois at last', to use the formula of Partha Chatterjee, who referred to a trend that was then widespread in India.[94]

In addition to these new plans, the Modi government tried to redesign existing cities, as could be seen from its efforts to 'rehabilitate' slum dwellers by removing them from the cities in 2010. The government then introduced a public–private partnership model that was immediately appropriated by the Ahmedabad Municipal Corporation. The idea was simple: 'builders can acquire government land occupied by slums and build houses for slum dwellers. The developer may also choose an alternative site for rehabilitating the dwellers [...] If everything goes as planned, slum pockets in Ahmedabad [...] may soon be transformed into decent residential localities.'[95]

This 'slum-free Ahmedabad dream'[96] was revealing of the fatigue of the poor felt by the urban middle class. Instead of offering them living space in the new buildings, the developers strove to relocate the poor away from the city in order to sanitise the place. As a result, Gujarat was the only state—out of the 14 that have been surveyed—where the number of slums fell between 2001 and 2011—by 1.52 per cent[97]—and where the condition of slum dwellers deteriorated[98]—a reconfirmation that they were not welcome in the city. According to the 2011 census, only 48.01 per cent of the slums of Gujarat were in a 'good' condition, as against more than 56 per cent in Maharashtra, Karnataka, Tamil Nadu, Madhya Pradesh, Rajasthan and Andhra Pradesh. For instance, more than a third (35.6 per cent) of the houses in the slums of Gujarat did not have latrines, whereas the proportion of slum houses without latrines was only 6.8 per cent in Kerala and 17.7 per cent in Tamil Nadu.[99]

Indeed, the Gujarat government did not implement the sections of the plan designed by the Union government under the name of the Jawaharlal Nehru National Urban Renewal Mission (JNNURM), which was oriented towards the poorest.[100] Darshini Mahadevia, Renu Desai and Suchita Vyas made this point very clear in 2014: 'The State government has no overarching policy to address the issue of housing for the urban poor.'[101] First of all, the money meant for housing the poor was not spent. In 2012, the Comptroller and Auditor General pointed out that only 7 per cent of the 72 housing projects approved in this framework 'for the urban poor were completed in Gujarat' between 2005 and 2012. More precisely, 'Despite the availability of funds, housing projects with an estimated cost of 1.55 billion rupees of Vadodara Municipal Corporation (VMC) and housing projects with estimated cost of 530 million rupees of Surat Municipal Corporation (SMC) were not taken up due to non-availability of land and transit accommodation.'[102]

The clearest indication that the state government was not particularly interested in improving slum dwellers' living standards comes from the rejection rate of applications for electricity connections. In 2013, the energy minister, Saurabh Patel, indicated that while 352,000 applications were received from 2008–09 to 2012–13, 334,000 had been rejected. In the course of these five years, the state had provided electricity to about 3,950 slum dwellers, mostly in Kheda (1,721) and Anand (1,486).[103]

Similarly, the provisions reserving land for the Socio-Economically Weaker Sections (SEWS), which were mandatory in town planning schemes, were not used effectively: by 2006 out of '172 plots [that] had been allocated for SEWS housing [...] 27.5 per cent plots were lying vacant and 20 per cent were still under agriculture use. SEWS housing was built on merely 6.11 per cent of the land. This shows that lands are available to improve the housing stock for the poor, but they are improperly utilized and managed.'[104]

Secondly, the Modi government betrayed a key principle of the plans designed by the central government, like the JNNURM and the Basic Services for the Urban Poor (BSUP): 'in-situ rehabilitation and upgrading along with provision of tenure security of housing is a more successful approach than rehabilitating the urban poor in new housing that generally tends to be in the urban periphery. Even then, the BSUP approach in Ahmedabad has consisted of building new housing units in the city periphery, leading to relocation and uprooting of slum dwellers from their original habitats and livelihoods.'[105] Instead of keeping the poor in the city, the Gujarat government tried hard to drive them out.

That the state government granted priority to the urban middle class is evident from the promises the BJP made at election time. The 2012 party manifesto was even more oriented towards city dwellers than the previous ones. Among the relevant items one can cite was the promise to build monorails and a BRTS (Bus Rapid Transfer System) in places other than Ahmedabad (where these projects were already under way).[106] This promise was aimed at wooing the urban middle class and not the poor, who could hardly afford this means of transport. In Ahmedabad, according to a 2012 study of the BRTS, two-thirds of the users were regularly employed in the private sector:

> Of the total users, just 13.7 per cent belong to household income of up to 5,000 rupees. BRTS is being used largely by the middle-income groups, with a monthly income between Rs 10,000 to Rs 40,000 rupees. Half the BRTS users fall within

> this group. Households with income of Rs 5,000 rupees per month are the bottom half of the urban spectrum and they do not use the BRTS to any great extent.[107]

The ultimate symbol of Modi's urban dream was the Gujarat International Finance Tec-City (the 'GIFT City'), a financial capital that is under construction 30 km outside Ahmedabad and Gandhinagar, consisting of 124 skyscrapers offering 75 million square feet of office space. This is what Modi said about it: 'The vision of Gujarat would be incomplete without capitalising on the in-house financial business acumen. To tie-up with technology, to create a hub complete with infrastructure, to meet the needs of modern Gujarat, modern India and to create a space in the global financial world … that is my dream.'[108] The two main partners of the government of Gujarat in helping make this dream come true are Fairwood India and the East China Architectural Design Institute—the latter makes a lot of sense given the Shanghai-like look of the plans.[109] The plans in the promotional brochure also reflected the American dream that so many Gujaratis cultivate, since they immediately call to mind New York, and more particularly Manhattan, with its skyscrapers and waterfront.

The waterfront developed along the banks of the Sabarmati in Ahmedabad was even more explicitly designed for the middle class and imitated those of Western cities, including London, Paris and New York.[110] When interviewed by Ipsita Chatterjee, the collector of Ahmedabad district told her: 'Ahmedabad will be like New York, Tokyo, Sydney. Have you checked the SRFDC [Sabarmati River Front Development Corporation]? It is a first in India, we are very proud, it will attract foreign enterprise, when you come to Ahmedabad again you will not recognize this place.'[111]

The riverfront was not a new idea. As Jan Breman points out:

> The initiative to lay out boulevards over a distance of 11 kilometres along the banks of the Sabarmati, with a variety of

> facilities for the diversion of the bourgeoisie during their leisure hours, was daring and imaginative. The first plans, dating back to shortly after Independence, never came to fruition because the required funds were not available and because the entire stretch of land was covered with slums. Clearing them was the only solution, but it meant that the authorities would have to deprive some 14,000 people of shelter.[112]

In 1997, the BJP chairman of Ahmedabad Municipal Corporation (AMC), Surendra Patel (who was also the treasurer of the state unit of the party), relaunched the project. He received the blessing of Chief Minister Keshubhai Patel and approached the firm of the architect and urban planner Bimal Patel, Environmental Planning Collaborative. Patel's plan was approved in 1998. It was presented as 'inclusive' because it 'brought the relocation and rehabilitation of the riverfront urban poor within the ambit of the project. It recommended that affected slum residents be resettled on the riverfront itself, stating that moving them more than 2–3 kilometres from their present sites would adversely affect their livelihoods.'[113] According to the 1998 project, 10,000 households of slum dwellers were to be affected, including 4,000 'directly'.[114] A Sabarmati River Front Development Corporation (SRFDC) was created to implement this large-scale project.[115] This 'semigovernmental body' was directed by 'high-ranking officials, politicians and private consultants'.[116] In 2000 the Congress recaptured the Ahmedabad Municipal Corporation, but it made no difference, as the party supported the project. However, the main architect of the Sabarmati Riverfront was to be Narendra Modi. As chief minister, he transferred the riverbed land to the SRFDC in 2003,[117] and inaugurated the project that year, announcing that it would 'be completed within 1,000 days'.[118]

The local slum dwellers then mobilised with the support of NGOs. Lawyers initiated proceedings at the High Court of Gujarat in 2005 on their behalf,[119] and emphasised 'the crucial interrelationship between housing and work for the slum-dwellers'.[120] The court gave a stay order and asked the authorities 'to spell out their plans for resettlement and rehabilitation (R&R)'.[121] As the stay order concerned only the eviction of slum dwellers, work continued on the Riverfront, resulting in clashes with the slum dwellers.[122] Then, 'replacement accommodations' were built in 18 locations, some of them—like Odhav or Vatva[123]—several kilometres away from the Sabarmati, in the deserted former industrial area and beyond, making it impossible for the displaced to retain their jobs.[124] Whenever the AMC or SRFDC approached the court for permission to shift families, the court obliged them.[125] On 8 November 2011 the court stated that the riverfront had to be fully vacated. Renu Desai concluded that the judiciary had presided over a process of 'evisceration of rights'.[126]

Many of the places where the slum dwellers had been moved to were unliveable.[127] Ganeshnagar, for instance, was located near the city's largest waste disposal belt as well as a sewage treatment plant. Water had to be boiled before drinking.[128] The Concerned Citizens Initiative conducted a site inspection in early 2012 and their findings were compiled in a short report called *Our Inclusive Ahmedabad.* One of the depositions read: 'We are not against development but our only request is that we should be provided with an alternative space so that we could earn our livelihood.'[129] For years, there was no school at Ganeshnagar, where men were still at work when many of the 'rehoused' arrived.[130] Out of the 1,680 rehoused families, 550 had left by 2012.[131] Most of them were Dalits, Muslims and OBCs.[132] In addition, about a third of the evicted slum dwellers who had submitted an application for rehousing saw their demand rejected.[133]

Gradually, the Riverfront took shape and started to be used by visitors as well as by the inhabitants of the neighbourhood, who could enjoy the city from the promenade. It was hailed as a major achievement of the Modi government by the World Bank.[134]

However, this policy relied on a blatant misuse of central schemes, including the BSUP, and this distortion affected not only the victims of the Sabarmati Riverfront, as Mahadevia, Desai and Vyas demonstrate:

> The AMC used the BSUP houses to resettle families displaced from the city's slums for various development projects such as the Sabarmati Riverfront project, the Kankaria Lakefront project, road-widening and flyover projects and the BRTS. In other words, the BSUP sites built by AMC are resettlement sites. About 11,000 families were displaced under the Sabarmati Riverfront project, about 2,000 under the Kankaria Lakefront project, and at least 1,000 seem to have been displaced for road-widening and BRTS projects. Thus, BSUP essentially became a tool for facilitating slum displacement and, in some cases, capturing public lands from the urban poor in prime locations.
>
> A couple of the BSUP sites are located in western Ahmedabad, many are located in the former textile mill areas of eastern Ahmedabad and many are located in the eastern industrial periphery. Since most of the sites are far from the displaced slum residents' original locations, this has led to negative impacts on their livelihood and social networks. Many are unable to continue with their earlier occupations and for those who have continued, this has resulted in greater travel time and cost.[135]

Ipsita Chatterjee has focused on the eight Economically Weaker Section colonies which have been built on the periphery of western Ahmedabad for resettling those who had been evicted because of the Sabarmati Riverfront, road widening or other projects. In these 4,500 homes, she noted 'a complete absence of Muslims' (except in two cases).[136] The resettlement process ended the heterogeneity that existed in the slums, partly because of the state's inclination, and partly because those who moved were not comfortable with the idea of living next to 'others' they did not necessarily know before. Chatterjee also shows that the ordinary people resented this kind of 'elitist urban renewal'. One of her interviewees said:

> Of course, we know that there are two Ahmedabads, one across the river to the west and one in which we, the poor live. We like the government, but they have done nothing for east Ahmedabad, and why should they care? After all, it is inhabited by low caste Hindu SCs and OBCs and Muslims. The government represents the upper caste and the rich; no wonder that east Ahmedabad is undeveloped.[137]

By importing what was perceived as a Western version of the city, Modi was not only reserving the city for the middle class, but he enabled this class and non-resident Gujaratis to be proud of something that had paradoxically, given his staunch Hindu nationalism, been imported from abroad.[138] This policy did indeed boost his popularity among the middle class. In return for what he did for them, the citizens of urban Gujarat—and non-resident Gujaratis—increasingly supported a Modi at the time, not only in national and state elections but also, more pertinently, in local elections. In 2010, during the municipal elections, the six largest cities of the state—Ahmedabad, Surat, Vadodara (Baroda), Rajkot, Bhavnagar and Jamnagar—gave the BJP a two-thirds majority, which was unprecedented in the annals of the state's civic politics. More importantly, perhaps, 'in many places voters had no idea of their candidate. But they did not seem to care. All that mattered was Modi.'[139]

SUPPORT FROM NEW KINDS OF VOTERS

Like other populists, Modi, while mobilising the masses against the Establishment, was primarily supported by elite groups (including the business community) and the middle class, whose members appreciated his Hindu nationalist ideology and its social conservatism—something that had been evident since the anti-reservation movements of the 1980s. Such a core group was key to the success of BJP in the state, but it was not enough on its own. Part of the electoral success of Modi did indeed stem from his capacity to reach out to groups that were not traditional supporters of the BJP and whose members belonged to the 'neo-middle class'. This emerging category, which was largely composed of OBCs, was attracted not only by Modi's national populism (including its religious dimension), but also by his emphasis on development, especially in the urban context.

Urban voters sealed the fate of the Congress and were responsible for Modi's rise to power. They greatly appreciated his vision of the city, which drew its inspiration—paradoxically, given the BJP's ethnic nationalism—from foreign models borrowed from the West and China. Modi's urban planning offered the most obvious evidence of his pro-middle class (and pro-NRG) inclination, for it meant that the poor had to be driven out of the city, as the Sabarmati Riverfront testifies.

Another element of continuity needs to be mentioned here, regarding the way Modi has related to the diaspora. While the NRGs based in the West formed an important part of Modi's support base when he was chief minister, he similarly cultivated ties with the NRIs (non-resident Indians) while prime minister. He made a point of systematically interacting with the diasporas when he visited the US, the UK, Canada, Australia and elsewhere. While he had endeavoured to build cities replicating the Sino-American model in Gujarat, he now promised the non-resident Indians who came to listen to him that he would create 'the India of their dreams'.[140]

More importantly, when he moved to the national scene, Modi continued to rely on the same rather elitist support base, in spite of his—still populist—political repertoire. In 2014, the richer they were, the more attracted voters were to the BJP: 38 per cent of the 'rich' cast their votes in favour of Modi, as against 24 per cent of the 'poor'.[141] But the proportion of the 'lower-middle-class' people who turned to the BJP jumped by

12 percentage points between 2009 and 2014. They were part of the same emerging 'neo-middle class' that Modi had identified in Gujarat. After 2014, this category was referred to repeatedly by BJP leaders, including Arun Jaitley, the finance minister, who tried hard to cultivate this support base.[142]

This class element reflected the over-representation of urban voters among BJP supporters. The party's appeal to voters in urban constituencies increased in 2014, as it won 42 per cent of the vote in such areas (11 percentage points more than its average score), while in semi-urban constituencies its tally reached 32 per cent and in rural constituencies it fell to 30 per cent.[143] Hence, Ashok Gulati's reference to the party's 'urban consumer bias'[144] to explain Modi's not-so-pro-farmer policy. This urban leitmotif also found expression in the Central Vista Redevelopment Project, which consisted in revamping Delhi's central administrative area, starting in 2019. Interestingly, the architect in charge of this grand transformation of India's capital city was Bimal Patel, the man who had been responsible for the Sabarmati Riverfront in Ahmedabad.

The middle class and the 'neo-middle class' supporting Modi were not defined by their urban profile only: they also coincided with caste to a large extent. As in Gujarat, BJP cultivated the upper caste in 2014 and thereafter. The party nominated such a large number of upper-caste candidates that in the Hindi belt—a vast region that represents almost half of the seats of the lower house—they represented 47.6 per cent of its MPs.[145] As a result, the percentage of Hindi belt MPs from upper castes increased to 44.5 per cent, on a par with their representation in the 1980s, before the Mandal Commission Report on reservations, whereas the share of OBCs dropped to 20 per cent. In the government Modi formed in 2014, 79.4 per cent of the ministers and ministers of state came from the upper castes.[146] As K. Adeney and W. Swenden have shown, there had not been such an over-representation since the Mandal moment. However, as in Gujarat,

BJP attracted OBC voters by nominating a larger number of candidates from this milieu. Amit Shah succeeded in achieving good results on that front by reaching out to *jatis* (sub-castes) which had not benefited from reservations as much as the Yadavs, for instance.[147] The upper caste and OBCs voters supporting the BJP increased, respectively, from 28 per cent to 48 per cent and from 22 per cent to 34 per cent between 2009 and 2014, not only because of the party's caste politics, but also because of the other mainstays of Modi's strategy that had travelled from Gujarat to the national scene, including communal polarisation.

The impact of class and urbanisation on the political culture and voting patterns of Gujarat tended to dilute caste identities—in a state where they had traditionally been more malleable than elsewhere. But ascriptive groups—including castes, at least in the case of Dalits—continued to matter and political polarisation was reinforced by growing inequalities. In fact, the situation of Dalits, Adivasis and Muslims, the losers of Modi's politics, showed that under his rule social polarisation and communal polarisation had come to structure society and politics.

10

RESISTERS, DISSENTERS AND VICTIMS

The national-populist strategy of polarisation is usually analysed as relying on the demonisation of the cultural 'Other'. In Gujarat, Narendra Modi focused on Muslims as posing a threat to the majority community so as to exploit emotions such as fear and anger. But social polarisation played a role too: although he claimed that he represented 50 million (and then, after the 2011 census, 60 million) Gujaratis, his policies did little to benefit the poor in contrast to the middle class, as chapter 6 demonstrated. This polarisation is inherent in populism, which claims that it defends the populace against elite groups, while in fact it aims to defend the interests of those who have something to lose and fear for their status.

Dalits, Adivasis and Muslims were at the receiving end of the BJP's policies in Gujarat, from a socio-economic point of view. This is one of the reasons why they did not support the BJP electorally as much as other groups did. However, they were neither sufficiently united nor numerous enough to thwart the rise of Modi's majoritarian agenda, which, relying on social and communal polarisation, in fact needed their opposition to some extent in order to solidify his support base consisting of those (upper castes and Patels) who had formed an anti-KHAM coalition already in the 1980s.

The underclass and minorities were the first casualties of the Modi government, but not the only ones. Liberals, NGOs, intellectuals and all dissenting voices—besides the IPS and IAS officers mentioned above—were also attacked because they defended a vision of society that was not that of the BJP. However, when we study those who resisted the rise of the BJP, the political opposition must come first in our analysis. The Congress tried to cope with the new hegemon but failed completely, partly because of Modi's politics, and partly because of its own limitations. And this failure largely explains why the BJP government transformed Gujarat so quickly, making it more inegalitarian and less secular.

WHAT OPPOSITION?

If a favourable environment was created for the BJP by the political culture of Gujarat, socio-economic transformations—including urbanisation and the making of the neo-middle class, the support of the upper-caste middle class and the association with crony capitalists—purely political factors, such as Modi's national populism, continued to explain the success of Moditva better than any other variable, and one of those was undoubtedly a weak opposition.

The Congress's Liabilities

The Congress suffered from many limitations in Modi's Gujarat, not least its contradictions in respect of its commitment to secularism and to social justice. There was a clear chasm between the discourse of national leaders and that of Gujarat's state leaders in these two respects. In 2007, as mentioned above, Sonia Gandhi came to canvass in Gujarat and lambasted Modi as a 'merchant of death' because of the 2002 riots. But state Congress leaders found this formula embarrassing, fearing it could alienate Hindu voters.[1] In 2012, national leaders used similar language, even though they diluted it. Sonia Gandhi, who was the first national Congress leader to campaign in Gujarat, addressed issues affecting the peasantry and did not attack Modi frontally.[2] But the Delhi MP Sandeep Dixit described him as 'a blot on the nation' and mentioned riots as well as fake encounters. The state Congress leaders did not follow suit and did not articulate an alternative programme based on secularism.

The unwillingness of the Congress to give electoral tickets to Muslims reflected its reluctance to distinguish itself from the BJP on that issue. The percentage of Muslims that the party nominated at the time of state elections dropped from a meagre 2.23 per cent in 1998 to 1 per cent in 2002 and a microscopic 0.5 per cent in 2007 and 2012, when the Congress nominated only seven Muslim candidates.[3] On both occasions, no Muslim candidate could win a seat.

The Gujarat Congress was unable to defend a secular agenda not only because the BJP had built a majoritarian vote bank and dismissed those who defended the minorities as indulging in anti-Hindu 'appeasement', but also because the party had traditionally cultivated a form of Hindu traditionalism which weakened its commitment to secularism. This ideological ambivalence found expression in some aspects of its election campaigns. In 2007, it published newspaper advertisements featuring a terrorist covering his face and denouncing the complacency of Vajpayee's government towards Islamists on four grounds: first, the liberation of Masood Azhar, the Pakistani jihadist who formed Jaish-e-Mohammed after the December 1999 Indian Airlines hijacking; second, the attack on the Akshardham temple in 2001; third, the destruction of Jammu and Kashmir temples; and fourth, the assault on Hindu pilgrims in Amarnath. The Congress was clearly trying to exploit the same latent anti-

Islamist sentiment of Gujarati Hindus as the BJP, but the latter could hardly be beaten on that issue.

The Congress's difficulty in asserting a distinctive identity vis-à-vis the BJP was related to the welcome it gave to BJP renegades, including Shankarsinh Vaghela, the former Jana Sangh organising secretary, former president of the Gujarat BJP from 1980 till 1991, and one of the accused in the Babri Masjid demolition case.[4] Vaghela became the president of the Congress in Gujarat in 2002, soon after the riots. The porous boundaries between the Congress and the BJP were especially notable during elections, when members of the BJP who had been denied tickets decided to join the former. For instance, in 2009, Vitthal Radadia won a Lok Sabha seat on a Congress ticket. In December 2012 he fought the state elections as a Congressman, but in February 2013 he joined the BJP after the Congress denied him the post of leader of the opposition.[5]

Not only was the Congress unable to articulate a secular discourse to compete with the BJP, whose ideology it tended to emulate—as it had done before the 1970s—but the party did not seek any alternative to it, either in its Gandhian antecedents or in the programmes that it had explored under Madhavsinh Solanki, including quota policies. In fact, the anti-reservation discourse—like the liberal repertoire—had become part of the doxa of Hindutva-oriented Savarnas, and the Congress was wary of taking the fight to these groups. Interestingly, the profile of its candidates for the state Assembly did not significantly differ from those of BJP candidates. Like the BJP, the Congress tended to nominate a diminishing number of upper-caste candidates, from 36 per cent in 1980 to 20 per cent in 2012—a near-linear trajectory[6]—and, like the BJP, it increasingly relied on Patels: while Patels received 15 per cent of Congress nominations in 1990, they won 24 per cent of them in 2012 (see Appendix A). And, paradoxically, the party did not invest much more than the BJP in OBCs, its traditional base: its percentage of OBC candidates dropped from 33 per cent in 1998 to 31 per cent in 2002 and jumped to 35 per cent in 2007, before returning to 32 per cent in 2012—which means that the share of its OBC candidates was never more than three percentage points above the proportion on the BJP side.

Besides, the Congress did not articulate a discourse promoting social justice. Instead of returning to the tradition created by Indulal Yagnik—whose last representative was Madhavsinh Solanki—it proposed no major social reforms aiming at greater equality, nor did it defend secularism. The party's election discourse during the 2007 election campaign is a case in point.[7] When asked, in late November, about the issues the Congress was focusing on, Arjun Modhwadia, then leader of the opposition in the Vidhan Sabha, replied: 'First, law and order: fear psychosis, kidnapping of women, children and businessmen, misuse of the police, general insecurity, fake cases and encounters, misuse of investigating agencies; second, privatisation of education; third, deprivation of health; fourth, farmers' issues, including indebtedness; fifth, unemployment, especially within the youth.'[8] It was only after I asked him about 'communal harmony' that he added to his list the need to denounce the way the BJP 'sponsor[ed] riots for political purpose'. Moreover, the Congress nominated only seven Muslim candidates and welcomed a dozen BJP dissidents who, in some cases, had indulged in anti-Muslim activities in 2002. In addition, the state Congress canvassed on the same ground as the BJP.

The Congress in Gujarat also had a leadership problem that was not unrelated to the previous points. During the 2012 state election campaign, not only did the self-proclaimed 'captain'[9] of the team, Shankarsinh Vaghela, come from the RSS, but he was locked in competition with other, equally weak state leaders like Arjun Modhwadia and Shaktisinh Gohil, who were to lose their seats this time round. None of these leaders had been considered as a contender for the post of chief minister because they all lacked the requisite authority—and because, as a corollary, it would have created tensions between them and their factions.

In addition to the leadership problem at the state level, the Congress had an organisational problem at the state *and* local levels that manifested itself in two different ways. First, in contrast to Modi's state of quasi-permanent mobilisation, the party worked intermittently, so much so that 'even well-meaning people, sympathetic to the Congress, complained that the Congress leaders approached the electorate only at the time of elections and forgot it subsequently'.[10] Second, at elections the Congress was affected by a badly managed ticket distribution. This was true at the local level in 2010 when, for the municipal elections, in contrast to the 'BJP, where candidates were finalised well in advance by Chief Minister Narendra Modi himself, Congress started the process just three days before the deadline of nominations'.[11] The problem of ticket distribution was also acute at the time of state elections, to such an extent that in 2012 it resulted in mini-riots at the party headquarters in Ahmedabad and in the defection of major Congress leaders who had been denied a ticket, like Narhari Amin, who had been deputy chief minister in 1994–95.[12] However, in 2012, the performance of the Congress was even more significantly affected by the formation of the Gujarat Parivartan Party (GPP, or the Party for Change in Gujarat).

The Gujarat Parivartan Party Makes No Difference

After a ten-year tug of war between Modi and former chief minister Keshubhai Patel, the latter, notwithstanding his age (he was 84), decided to launch a new political party before the 2012 elections. Along with other dissidents, including Suresh Mehta and Kashiram Rana, he created the Gujarat Parivartan Party (GPP). Gordhan Zadaphia's Mahagujarat Janata Party merged immediately with it. Keshubhai Patel allegedly left the BJP because of Modi's 'self-centred' style of functioning. Talking to VHP members, he made a statement consistent with the RSS sense of collegial leadership:

> When he [Modi] took over the state BJP, I told him that this race is altogether different. It's called a 'relay race', in which the baton is handed over from one participant to the other. Each one uses his strength and ultimately the team wins, not an individual. But since Modi took the baton in this relay race, he has never passed it on. He refuses to loosen his grasp over the party.[13]

Keshubhai Patel had tried to have the RSS intervene in his favour before embarking on this new venture. Modi did the same. On 21 October 2012 he argued his case in Nagpur for three hours. In Gujarat, some Sangh cadres either abstained from taking part in the BJP's campaign or supported Keshubhai.[14] For instance, the 'state RSS chief, Bhaskar Rao Damle, began openly attending all meetings of Keshubhai Patel, indicating that the state RSS did not support Modi. But Damle and two others were immediately stripped from their posts with orders from Nagpur.'[15]

Keshubhai Patel attacked the chief minister vociferously. He declared that Modi was 'like Mohammed Ghaznavi', because he had 200 Hindu temples demolished in Gandhinagar in the name of urban beautification.[16] He also compared him to General Dyer, the British officer who had been responsible for the massacre of Jallianwallah Bagh in 1919: 'General Dyer killed 1,000 people, but Modi is responsible for the deaths of more than 39,000 people who have committed suicide due to unemployment and debt.'[17] Last but not least, Patel described Modi and his clique as a 'bunch of Dawoods' (a reference to the mafia don Dawood Ibrahim) because of the 'donation' they extorted from the people.[18]

Keshubhai Patel claimed that he represented the rural sector that Modi had not treated as well as the urban ones, especially in Patel's region, Saurashtra, where water had become an acute problem and where industry was lagging behind.[19] While the Narmada dam was providing drinking water to the cities, hundreds of villages were overlooked, and many of the minor and sub-minor irrigation canals that were supposed to be completed quickly, according to Modi's electoral promises, were yet to be built. Indeed, in 2013, the Comptroller and Auditor General pointed out several cases of mismanagement in this respect.[20]

Logically enough, the GPP made inroads in Keshubhai Patel's region, Saurashtra, where the party had fielded the largest number of strong candidates. The GPP's performance affected the Congress, as was evident from the voting pattern of Keshubhai's caste, the Patels: though the BJP slightly improved its vote share among them compared with 2007, the GPP's gains among the Leuva Patels (+18 percentage points) were the Congress's loss (–19).[21] Indeed, the GPP affected the prospects of the Congress, dividing the anti-BJP votes instead of significantly damaging Modi's support base (see Appendices 9.9 and 9.10).

TARGETING DISSENTING VOICES

If political opponents, including the Congress, could not resist the BJP effectively, what about civil society organisations? Among the (potential) dissenting voices, academics, teachers, artists, NGOs and journalists were priority targets of the government and among its first casualties.

Controlling Education, Saffronising Universities

Universities came under attack immediately after the change of guard in the early 2000s. In 2004, the Gujarat State Universities Ordinance prepared the ground for major reforms. First, universities were now supposed 'to promote the study of Gujarati and its use as a medium of instruction, study, research and examination, while restricting the use of English as a library language'.[22] Secondly, the governor lost his power to appoint vice chancellors (VCs), who were now chosen by the government through its search committee. And VCs were now supposed to appoint lecturers, deans and directors of various institutes with the direct approval of the government, instead of the holders of these positions being elected by university executives and academic councils.[23]

This ordinance was resisted by academics, and the Maharaja Sayajirao University (MSU) of Baroda (or Vadodara) became the rallying point of resistance. But this university, the only university in Gujarat with English as the medium of instruction, was severely punished soon after. The government captured its Syndicate first. In a letter to Professor S.K. Thorat, then chairman of the University Grants Commission, Dr I.I. Pandya, a member of the Syndicate and the president of the Baroda University Teachers' Association, wrote on 14 October 2006:

> Of the four government nominees on the new Syndicate, one is from the RSS, one is from the BJP, and the third from the VHP. The fourth nominee is from the Gaekwad family [the dynasty which ruled the princely state of Baroda and which founded the MSU during the Raj] and is said to have made his peace with the ones now ruling the roost [...] Combined with ex-officio members on the Syndicate along with 6 others elected to it from the Senate, the stranglehold of the coterie is complete.[24]

Moreover, not long before, in 2005, the new VC, Manoj Soni, who had been appointed at the unprecedentedly young age of 40 (a pan-Indian record), was an RSS fellow traveller as well as an active member of the Swaminarayan movement.[25] He had been 'hand-picked by Modi after he wrote a paper justifying post-Godhra riots as a Hindu backlash'.[26] He implemented on the campus the cultural policing that vigilante groups were imposing in the streets. In May 2007 he ordered the Fine Arts Department to be sealed[27] because, as we have seen, for the annual examination exhibition, a master's student, Chandra Mohan, had painted a picture that a Hindu vigilante, Niraj Jain, found offensive. He called the police, who arrested Chandra Mohan immediately. He then not only shut down the whole exhibit and the department, but also suspended the dean in charge of the event, Shivaji Panikkar.[28] The pro-VC, S.M. Joshi, defended Jain in eloquent terms, telling Malvika Maheshwari that by doing so, the VC 'was simply giving vent to the society's feelings'.[29]

After Manoj Soni completed his term—he then became VC of Ambedkar University—he was replaced by Yogesh Singh, who was 'considered close to Rashtriya Swayamsevak Sangh (RSS)',[30] and who made history in July 2014 when he was the first VC of MSU to be reappointed for a second term by the state government. MSU was not the only university where pro-BJP VCs were appointed. In 2009, the convener of the Gujarat BJP IT cell (who had also been connected to the party's media cell), Shashiranjan Yadav, was appointed VC of Kutch University.[31] In Rajkot, Mahendra Padalia, a BJP district president, became VC of Saurashtra University in 2011.[32] Harish Padh, the VC of Sardar Patel University (Vallabh Vidyanagar), and Daxesh Thakar, the VC of South Gujarat University in Surat, were active BJP members or Sangh Parivar fellow travellers. These VCs sometimes expressed the allegiance they paid to Narendra Modi in a very expansive manner. The VC of Gujarat University, Parimal Trivedi, 'publicly fell on Modi's feet at a function in Ahmedabad. But he justified himself saying that what he did was a part of Indian tradition and culture.'[33] Subsequently, he was the first Indian VC (and the only one to date) to be 'arrested in connection with an atrocity case lodged by a college [Dalit] teacher'.[34]

Rewriting History Textbooks

Besides the university system, primary and secondary education were also targeted by the Modi government. As mentioned above, Gujarat under Keshubhai Patel had already implemented a policy that the RSS had long cherished, namely the rewriting of history textbooks. The Modi government went further in the same direction. Implementing the education reforms proposed in 2000 by the National Council of Educational Research and Training (NCERT) under the aegis of the human resources development minister Murli Manohar Joshi, the Gujarat government changed the state curriculum, and the State Board for School Textbooks was asked to prepare new material for certain classes and subjects.[35] In 2005, the Gujarat Board introduced a new social sciences textbook for Class IX which 'presented Nazism in a positive manner and did not mention the Holocaust'.[36] Hitler was presented as a former soldier who led the 'Patriotic youth [which] organized to take revenge of it [the Treaty of Versailles]', and Nazism was described as a 'co-ordination of nationalism and socialism'.[37] The first chapter of this textbook, titled, 'Present currents of world history', claimed that 'Hitler led the Germans towards ardent nationalism'.[38] It also said: 'The Nazi soldiers were wearing blue dress and were adorning the symbol of "SWASTIK". They considered Hitler as their "FUHRER" (Saviour).'[39] The government withdrew these editions after a visit to Gujarat by the consul general of Israel in India.[40] But a social science textbook for Class X praised Adolf Hitler in similar terms. It said:

> Hitler lent dignity and prestige to the German government within a short time by establishing a strong administrative set up. He created the vast state of Greater Germany. He adopted the policy of opposition towards the Jewish people and advocated the supremacy of the German race. He adopted a new economic policy and brought prosperity to Germany. He began efforts for the eradication of unemployment. He started constructing public buildings, providing irrigation facilities, building railways, roads and production of war materials. He made untiring efforts to make Germany self-reliant within one decade. Hitler discarded the Treaty of Versailles by calling it just 'a piece of paper' and stopped paying the war penalty. He instilled the spirit of adventure in the common people, but in doing so it led to extreme nationalism and caused the Second World War.[41]

There was no mention of the Holocaust. The same textbook contended that Mussolini 'established a strong, stable government in Italy. He made Italy prosperous and powerful.'[42] In both cases, Nazi Germany and Fascist Italy, Hitler and Mussolini were praised, not only for their strong nationalism, but also for the economic development that was attributed to their authoritarian rule.

The Gujarat government continued to rewrite school textbooks in a systematic manner during Modi's last term as chief minister, commissioning Dinanath Batra to write nine books.[43] Batra, long-time general secretary of the Sangh Parivar network of religious schools, Vidya Bharati, devoted most of his energy to combating perceived errors in history textbooks written by secularist authors. In his book published in 2001, *The Enemies of Indianisation: The Children of Marx, Macaulay and Madrasa*, he listed 41 major flaws that reflected the historical tropes of the Hindu nationalists (including their version of the Muslim invasions).[44] In 2010, he filed a civil suit to ban Wendy Doniger's *The Hindus*, which, he felt, gave Hinduism a bad image (particularly owing to her comment on Hinduism's open relationship to sexuality). Penguin India, fearing reprisals, pulped the book even before a court decision was handed down. Batra also pressured the University of Delhi to remove from its syllabus an essay by the well-known Indian anthropologist, A.K. Ramanujan, 'Three hundred Ramayanas', which contradicted the Hindu nationalist idea that there is a single version of the epic poem.[45]

In March 2014, the Gujarat education minister, Bhupendrasinh Chudasama, released nine books by Batra. In one of them, *Shining India*, one could read: 'Do you know that countries like Pakistan, Afghanistan, Nepal, Bhutan, Tibet, Bangladesh, Sri Lanka and Burma are part of undivided India? These countries are part of Akhand Bharat.' In another book, *Indianisation of Education*, the author wrote: 'Undivided India is the truth, divided India is a lie. Division of India is unnatural and it can be united again.'[46]

In June 2014, the Gujarat government issued a circular directing 42,000 primary and secondary government schools to make these books part of the curriculum's 'supplementary literature'.[47] Simultaneously, the Gujarat State Board of School Textbooks released social sciences textbooks for Classes 6, 7 and 8 reflecting 'a clear-cut political bias', according to Achyut Yagnik,[48] who added: 'the GCERT [Gujarat Council of Education Research and Training] books have only a paragraph on 350 years of Mughal rule in India, while they wax eloquent on the Solanki and Vaghela dynasties in Gujarat. The first semester textbook of class seven has a chapter on the medieval age but only one paragraph on Mughal rule. And that too speaks of how Mahmud of Ghazni plundered "India and Saurashtra".'[49]

Freedom of Expression Under Attack

Soon after Narendra Modi won the 2007 election, journalists and intellectuals came under attack while defending freedom of expression. In 2008, in reaction to the way the *Times of India* had portrayed him (see chapter 4), the Ahmedabad police commissioner O.P. Mathur filed charges of sedition and conspiracy against the newspaper's editor. Media workers immediately demonstrated to defend freedom of expression and went to court. The High Court granted anticipatory bail to the resident editor of the *Times of India* and other journalists named in the case,[50] and reacted strongly to the demand for 'guidelines for newspapers' that the additional public prosecutor, representing the government of Gujarat, had made. The judges responded: 'This court feels that the learned additional public prosecutor is not properly instructed. He should seek instructions from his employer whether they are interested in providing guidelines to newspapers.' For the court, this 'case [was] not of any regular criminal nature. It involve[d] expression of opinion in media.' Referring to the Emergency, Justice Bhagwati Prasad recalled that at the time, 'this High Court upheld the freedom of Press in the wake of charges of breach of censorship laws. The Press is the fourth estate and, in a democracy, freedom of expression has to be protected.'[51] The court provided protection to the *Times of India* against any action by the police in future cases, but the five existing cases dragged on. Journalists, therefore, fought for their rights. In 2009, they received the support of the Indian Association of Lawyers, which argued that 'the police commissioner could have filed a complaint of his defamation, but a complaint of conspiracy against the state is like strangulating the democracy's neck'.[52] The government of Gujarat, however, continued to support O.P. Mathur. Instead of letting him leave the scene quietly in 2009 when he reached retirement age, it asked for an extension, which New Delhi refused.[53]

Similarly, another case showed that the Modi government was eager to limit freedom of expression. In reaction to the op-ed that Ashis Nandy had written in January 2008 in which he denounced the militant religious nationalism of the Gujarat middle class (see chapter 9), this internationally renowned social scientist was booked under sections 153(a) and (b) 'for promoting enmity between different groups on grounds of religion, race, place of birth etc.'. Immediately, Gujarati intellectuals mobilised across the world and signed a letter asking for the charges to be dropped and defending freedom of expression. Among the signatories were Lord Bhikhu Parekh, Lord Meghnad Desai, Jawaharlal Nehru University professor Ghanshyam Shah and People's Union of Civil Liberties (PUCL) president Professor J.S. Bandukwala.[54] In an interview he gave to *Outlook*, Nandy declared that 'the Gujarat government has officially permitted the police to begin criminal proceedings against me'.[55]

THE OTHER GUJARAT: DALITS, ADIVASIS AND RELIGIOUS MINORITIES

Besides politicians, intellectuals, artists, journalists and some lawyers, opponents of Modi were to be found among social groups that did not benefit from his regime as much as the urban middle (and neo-middle) classes and the upper as well as dominant castes. This other side of Gujarat was primarily made up of Adivasis, Dalits and Muslims, who voted less and less for the BJP during Modi's chief ministership: in these three groups the BJP registered a decline in percentage points of 11, 6 and 2, respectively, between the 2007 and 2012 elections. Only a fifth to a third of the members of these groups voted for the party on average. Proportions were usually higher in urban contexts.

The Congress made steady progress among these traditional vote banks of the party. Its share of the Dalit vote increased from 56 per cent to 65 per cent between 2007 and 2012, that of the Adivasis from 33 per cent to 46 per cent, and that of the Muslims from 67 per cent to 72 per cent (see Table 9.4). Their socio-economic situation—and the policies that partly flowed from this—explained to a large extent why these three groups did not support the BJP. The communal subtext—or overtone—of the last three election campaigns was an obvious, additional factor in the case of Muslims.

Scheduled Tribes and Scheduled Castes at the Receiving End

Adivasis and Dalits, who represented 14.75 per cent and 7.1 per cent respectively of the state's population in the 2011 census, form the weakest sections of Gujarati society, especially in rural areas, where they mostly live. For this reason, they have often been the first to be evicted from their land.[56] Using the 1999–2000 and 2009–10 National Sample Survey reports, Surjit Bhalla established that Gujarat had performed no better than an average Indian state so far as Dalits and Adivasis were concerned. He made these observations on the basis of three social indicators affecting the Schedules Tribes and Scheduled Castes vis-à-vis 'non-minority' groups: (1) the number of years spent in education by the 8–24 age group: Gujarat's performance was ranked 12th for males and 16th for females; (2) consumption:

Gujarat came 12th; and (3) poverty reduction: the state ranked 11th.[57] Gujarat was one of the few states where non-Scheduled Tribe, non-Scheduled Caste and non-OBC groups represented a tiny minority of those below the poverty line. In 2004–05 only 4.2 per cent of those living in rural Gujarat and 7 per cent of urban dwellers belonged to this group, a clear indication of caste-based social polarisation—and this polarisation would have been even more pronounced if religion had been taken into account, given the socio-economic decline experienced by Muslims, another group of 'losers'.

Polarised Adivasis

Access to land is a particularly acute problem for Adivasis. Gujarat is one of the states least inclined to distribute to them Ceiling Surplus Land. As of March 2005, of the (already meagre) 782,411 acres that had been distributed to Scheduled Tribes, only 31,579 acres had been given to Gujarati Adivasis (many other states with a similar percentage of Scheduled Tribes, such as Bihar, Madhya Pradesh, Maharashtra, Tamil Nadu and West Bengal, had acted differently).[58] In 2006 the state government passed a new law, the Scheduled Tribes and Other Traditional Forest Dwellers (Recognition of Forest Rights) Act, according to which each family would be entitled to 4 ha of forest land. This law was supposed to benefit 30,000 families,[59] and could have helped the Adivasis to acquire land in some localities.[60] But the law was hardly applied, and in many districts land remained a key issue. In Tapi, where 11,947 Adivasis had applied for forest land, the state government allotted such land to only 728 of them in three years.[61]

In addition, the Comptroller and Auditor General reproached the Modi government for failing to ensure that development funds allocated to Adivasis were in proportion to their population, as per the guidelines of the Planning Commission. While Adivasis represented 14.75 per cent of the state's population, they had been repeatedly allocated a smaller fraction of the total outlay: 11.01 per cent in 2007–08, 14.06 per cent in 2008–09, 13.14 per cent in 2009–10 and 12.73 per cent in 2010–11. Things changed in 2011–12 when Adivasis received 16.48 per cent of the total outlay. Still, the actual expenditures were lower.[62] In the tribal district of Dangs (where Adivasis represented 94 per cent of the population), which in 2007 benefited (on paper) from the second highest allocation (226.4 million rupees) under the National Rural Employment Guarantee Scheme (NREGS), only 34.8 million rupees had been spent one month before the end of the fiscal year.[63] When he listed ten pro-Adivasi programmes, Bibek Debroy admitted that 'some of these are still intentions and are in the pipeline'.[64]

A clear indication of the socio-economic backwardness of Adivasis in Gujarat was the extent of their indebtedness. Among Adivasis, indebted households soared from 32.90 per cent to 60.10 per cent.[65] This high level of indebtedness was one of the contributory factors in farmer suicides in Gujarat in the late 1990s and early 2000s. While this phenomenon in the state was not as serious as that of Maharashtra, Andhra Pradesh, Karnataka and Madhya Pradesh, according to the National Crime Records Bureau (NCRB) of the Ministry of Home Affairs, Gujarat ranked fifth in India, with between 487 and 653 farmer suicides per annum from 1997 to 2006.[66]

The high level of indebtedness of Adivasis in Gujarat was naturally related to their poverty. Although the proportion of Scheduled Tribes living below the poverty line remained below the national average between 1993–94 and 2004–05, it did not follow the general trend but instead increased from 31.2 per cent to 34.7 per cent. Gujarat was not the only state where this counter-intuitive development took place since Andhra Pradesh, Madhya Pradesh, Maharashtra, Orissa, Punjab and Kerala were all in the same boat.

Notwithstanding this state of affairs, a large number of Adivasis voted for the BJP, even in 2012, as we have seen. This support partly came from the social and religious activism of the Sangh Parivar in the tribal belt of South Gujarat. As early as the 1990s, the Parivar—via the VHP, in particular—tried to reach out to Dalits and Adivasis through the vector of religion. In the tribal belt of South Gujarat, they started to build Hindu temples in large numbers. In Dangs district, '41 temples [had] been constructed between 1998 and 2005; while 28 of these [were] Hanuman temples, the remaining [were] Shiva temples'.[67] Around the same time, in 1994–95, a VHP figure, Swami Aseemanand,[68] visited Dangs as a leader of the Vanavasi Kalyan Ashram. He wanted to oppose the Christian missionaries who had established a mission in 1996–97 at Waghai. Aseemanand developed 'a close rapport by communicating with the Adivasis in their own dialect' and by sharing food with poor families: 'This had a great impact on the Dangis; so far no Hindu religious leader had visited their homes; hence they developed a lot of respect for him.'[69]

More importantly, Aseemanand used religion and other religious figures to relate even more effectively to the Adivasis. He brought to them Morari Bapu, Gujarat's most popular Ramayana reciter.[70] On 22 October 2002, the recitation (*katha*) began outside the Jesuit Centre of Subir, after it was inaugurated by Narendra Modi. Pralay Kanungo and Satyakam Joshi point out that 'Free transport, lodging, and food were provided for tribals; 45,000 people, out of whom 25,000 were from the Dangs, came to attend the *katha*, which continued for a week. About 6 million rupees were raised, out of which 4 million rupees were spent on the arrangement of *katha* itself and the rest was kept for temple construction.'[71] Indeed, temple construction was Aseemanand's priority. He dedicated a huge temple to Shabari, an Adivasi woman in the Ramayana, who suddenly became part of 'the Hindu pantheon of goddesses'.[72] In 2006, Narendra Modi and many Hindu dignitaries took part in the *kumbh* (festival) inaugurating the temple. During this function, one of them, the *shankaracharya* of Joshimath, claimed that 'All tribals are Hindus'.[73] Modi, for his part, declared that 'it was his constitutional duty to prevent conversions'.[74] The festival—during which the RSS chief also spoke—was of an unprecedented magnitude: about 500,000 pilgrims took part in it and a live telecast of the event appeared on huge screens in six different places.[75] Soon after, for the first time, the BJP won the Dangs seat reserved for Adivasis.

Dalits and Caste-based Discrimination

As with the Adivasis, the Comptroller and Auditor General reproached the Modi government for failing to ensure that development funds allocated to Scheduled Castes were in proportion to their population. Dalits, who represented 7.1 per cent of the state's population, according to the 2011 census, were allotted 1.41 per cent of the budget in 2007–08, 3.93 per cent in 2008–09, 4.51 per cent in 2009–10, 3.65 per cent in 2010–11 and 3.20 per cent in 2011–12.[76] A clear indication of the socio-economic plight of Dalits in Gujarat, as for Adivasis, is given by their indebtedness. While the overall percentage of indebted rural households increased from 35.70 per cent in 1999–2000 to 56 per cent in 2004–05, among Dalits this proportion rose from 44.80 per cent to 62.95 per cent (only in two other states out of 15 were Dalits worse off in this regard).[77]

Among Dalits, poverty went together with bonded labour: in 2006, the website of the Gujarat government mentioned that there were 249,414 bonded labour families in the state, which meant that 3.63 per cent of rural families of Gujarat were in this slave-like situation, and they were mostly Dalits.[78]

Without any significant support from the state, Dalits continued to suffer from traditional practices of discrimination, as was evident from a remarkable report, *Understanding Untouchability*, based on a survey conducted in the late 2000s in 1,589 villages.[79] The report partly attributed the plight of the

Dalits of Gujarat to the non-implementation of the Scheduled Castes and Scheduled Tribes (Prevention of Atrocities Act) of 1989, for which Dalit pressure groups had lobbied more successfully in other states.[80]

More importantly, in 2013, a 'government of Gujarat-sponsored study'[81] was published by a team of scholars from the Centre for Environmental Planning and Technology (CEPT) to counter *Understanding Untouchability*, which had been reviewed at length in local newspapers. The CEPT team echoed the official Hindu nationalist view of caste. Criticising the report's methodology, its authors argued that caste was all about 'perceptions'—and ignored discrimination. For them, there was nothing wrong if upper castes invited 'Harijans' with their utensils to a wedding party: 'They take meals in their vessels to their home and eat it there.' Similarly, there was nothing abnormal if the 'celebration of festivals by different communities [was] confined to their respective localities and especially SC [Scheduled Caste] and non-SC usually do not mingle apart from remaining spectators'. And such aloofness happened because the elderly members of the SC community '[did] not want to create any tension between them and non-SC'.

This approach dovetailed with Modi's views of Dalits, which were made public in 2007 in a book entitled *Karmayog*. Giving a spiritualist interpretation of the caste system, he singled out the Valmikis (scavengers) in a significant way:

> I do not believe that they have been doing this job [scavenging] just to sustain their livelihood. Had this been so, they would not have continued this type of work generation after generation [...] At some point of time, somebody must have got the enlightenment that it is their duty to work for the happiness of the entire society and the Gods; that they have to do this job bestowed upon them by Gods; and that this job of cleaning up should continue as an internal spiritual activity for centuries. This should have continued generation after generation. It is impossible to believe

> that their ancestors did not have the choice of adopting any other work or business.[82]

Such an interpretation is part of the Hindu nationalist discourse—while also carrying some Gandhian connotations—that presents society as potentially harmonious and permeated by the legacy of its divine origins. Each group is supposed to fulfil complementary functions without suffering from any hierarchical arrangement. Modi's views were strongly rejected by Dalits, who asked for the book to be banned. Its release was postponed, officially because to launch it a few weeks before the polls would have transgressed the electoral code of conduct.[83] Till now, it has not been made available in bookshops.

Muslims' Marginalisation and the Making of a De Facto Hindu Rashtra

The situation of Muslims in Gujarat,[84] who represented 9.7 per cent of the state population in 2011, according to the census, is unique given the communal violence from which they have repeatedly suffered. This form of violence was associated with stereotypes 'othering' Muslims in a radical manner. Even their language was often considered very different by non-Muslims, though they generally knew Gujarati. An English-speaking middle-class informer told Parvis Ghassem-Fachandi after the 2002 riots: 'They speak not our mother tongue. Our mother tongue is Gujarati, not Urdu,' or 'They will ask me '*Tame* Gujarati?' [Are you Gujarati?] as if they were not from here. This all has been going on since Partition.'[85] This form of estrangement and communal rioting went together with socio-economic and educational decline, as well as political obliteration and ghettoisation—all these processes being caused by or accompanied by government policies.

Socio-economic and Educational Decline

In the mid-2000s, the Sachar Committee Report showed that Gujarati Muslims were lagging behind other communities in terms of poverty, and that this state of affairs derived from their socio-economic status as well as their level of education. Indeed, the report revealed that they were under-represented in the formal sector, in particular the public sector. Muslims were also under-represented in most of the state government departments: they occupied 1.7 per cent of higher positions and 4.5 per cent of lower positions in the Education Department, as well as 5.6 per cent and 5.6 per cent respectively of the Home Department, 2.2 per cent and 1.5 per cent of the Health Department, and 9.4 per cent and 16.3 per cent of the Transport Department (probably because of their skills as mechanics).[86] Marginal in the government service, Gujarati Muslims resorted to working in the informal sector more than others: 54 per cent of them were self-employed, as against 39 per cent of Hindus.[87]

The situation of Muslims in the job market continued to deteriorate under Modi, and they had to look increasingly for jobs in the informal sector. The proportion of Muslims occupying salaried positions dropped from 17 per cent in 2004–05 to 14 per cent in 2009–10, whereas the share of those occupying casual employment jumped from 23.5 per cent to 32.1 per cent.[88] According to the Periodic Labour Force Survey of the National Sample Survey Office (NSSO), Muslims represented only 0.68 per cent of employees in the government and public sectors in 2017–18, as against 1.45 per cent among the Scheduled Caste Hindus and 1.02 per cent among upper-caste Hindus.[89]

Low levels of educational achievement compounded this problem. First, the community's literacy rate almost stagnated from 73.5 per cent in the 2001 census to 74.3 per cent, according to the 2007–08 NSSO 64th round,[90] whereas the average rate in the state increased from 69.1 per cent to 74.9 per cent: as a result, 'Gujarat's Muslim literacy rate relative to its overall literacy rate experienced a decline in 2007–08 compared to 2001'.[91] The dropout rate of Muslims students increased too. While 89.1 per cent of 6–10-year-old Muslim children attended school in 2007–08 according to the NSSO's 64th round (as against a national average of 92.5 per cent), only 60.4 per cent of the 11–14-year-olds attended (as against an average of 79.3 per cent).[92] Only 26 per cent of Muslims in Gujarat reached matriculation, the same proportion as for Scheduled Tribes and Scheduled Castes—as against 41 per cent for others.[93]

The 66th round of the NSSO showed no improvement. In the age group 5–14, 78.7 per cent of Muslims went to school in 2009–10—as against 78.9 per cent in 2007–08.[94] This percentage was almost as high as that of Hindus, but when young Muslims turned 15, the dropout rate was such that in the 15–19 age group they lagged behind Hindus by ten percentage points and by eight percentage points in the 20–24 age group (see Table 10.1). The situation continued to deteriorate in post-Modi's Gujarat. According to the 2017–18 NSSO Periodic Labour Force Survey, among 21–29-year-old Muslims, graduates made up only 13 per cent (as against 20 per cent among Scheduled Caste Hindus and 39 per cent among upper-caste Hindus of the same age).[95]

The occupations and educational levels of Gujarati Muslims largely accounted for their poverty, especially in towns and cities. While almost 60 per cent of the Muslims of Gujarat were town and city dwellers, 24 per cent of them lived below the poverty line according to the Sachar Committee Report—as against 17 per cent of Scheduled Tribes and Scheduled Castes, 18 per cent of OBCs, and 3 per cent of other urban dwellers.[96] The most dramatic expression of urban Gujarati Muslims' poverty was their monthly per capita expenditure, as measured by the NSSO in 2004–05 and cited by the Sachar Committee Report: at 875 rupees, this was lower than that of Scheduled Castes and Schedules Tribes (1,045), OBCs (905) and other Hindus (1,470).[97]

In 2009–10 Gujarati Muslims also remained poorer than other Muslims in most Indian states. Based on data collected in 2009–10, the Planning Commission pointed out that in urban areas the percentage of Gujarati Muslims living below the poverty line (42.4 per cent) was not only higher than the national average, but also exceeded that of West Bengal (34.9 per cent) and Rajasthan (29.5 per cent). In rural areas, the percentage of Gujarati Muslims living below the poverty line (31.4 per cent) was not far removed from that of Muslims in West Bengal (34.4 per cent).[98] In the villages of Gujarat, poverty among Muslims was largely due to the smallness of their landholdings: 70 per cent of rural Muslims owned less than 0.4 ha, as against 55.5 per cent among Hindus[99] (see Table 10.2). Using the data of the 66th round of the NSSO for 2009–10, Surjit Bhalla established that Gujarat performed badly as far as Muslims in relation to 'non-minority' groups were concerned, in terms of three social indicators: (1) for number of years spent by 8–24-year-olds in education, the performance of Gujarati Muslims was ranked 16th for males and 16th for females; (2) for consumption by Muslims, Gujarat ranked 15th; and (3) for reduction of poverty among Gujarati Muslims, the state also came in 15th place.[100]

Notwithstanding this situation, the Modi government did not design policies aimed at helping the Muslims. On the contrary: the BJP's policies and politics were in fact partly responsible for their plight.

Discriminating against Muslims

Unlike Muslims in some other states, Muslims of Gujarat were explicit victims of discrimination since funds and schemes (sometimes marked specifically for them by the central government) were not granted to them by the state government.

The Gujarat government showed its non-responsiveness towards Muslim claims when it refused to give any financial help to rebuild or repair the religious sites and buildings that had been destroyed in 2002. This issue was taken to court by Muslim organisations, but the Gujarat government objected in an affidavit before the High Court that it had not even given this kind of assistance to the Akshardham temple after the 2002 attack.[101] Financial compensation for the victims of the Gujarat riots was also a bone of contention because in 2002 the Gujarat government decided to give 200,000 rupees per Hindu victim and 100,000 rupees per Muslim victim. This decision was challenged and had to be reversed; eventually, both Hindu and Muslim victims were entitled to 100,000 rupees. Victims had to wait until 2008, when the central government announced a compensation package of 350,000 rupees for the next of kin of each of the 1,169 identified victims and 125,000 rupees for each of the 2,548 individuals injured. In addition, Rs 2.62 billion was allocated to compensate for loss of and damage to property.[102] Compensation came more from the central than from the state government, which dragged its feet in many individual cases,[103] even after Modi became prime minister.[104]

The Gujarat government under Modi also abstained from distributing scholarships that the central government had allocated for Muslims in the wake of the Sachar Committee Report. Muslim students who had achieved 50 per cent in annual exams and whose families had an annual income of less than Rs 100,000 rupees were eligible for these pre-matriculation scholarships. The amount in question was between 800 rupees and 1,000 rupees a year. Originally, 55,000 students were eligible. The central government's contribution was supposed to amount to about Rs 37.5 million and that of the state government to some 12.5 million rupees. The Modi government refused to pay on the grounds that the scheme was discriminatory towards other poor students. The matter went to the Gujarat High Court, where a division bench of three judges ruled in favour of the scheme. Later, another bench ruled against it. Finally, it went to a full bench of five judges who ruled in favour of the scheme. In response, the

Modi government appealed to the Supreme Court, which upheld the decision of the High Court in May 2013, five years after the scheme had been initiated.[105] Five months later, the Gujarat government filed an affidavit claiming that the pre-matriculation minority scholarship scheme was 'arbitrary and discriminatory' and that the Sachar Committee Report from which it derived was 'neither constitutional nor statutory' because it was intended to benefit Muslims only: 'It has not taken into consideration other religious communities, i.e. Sikhs, Christians, Buddhists and Parsis. Therefore, it cannot form the basis of the scheme [...] The Committee's target was to help the Muslims only.' It added: 'The scheme causes hostile discrimination between citizens since a far more meritorious student, who does not belong to any of the five religions [note the contradiction here], will be deprived of the benefits only on the ground that he does not belong to one of these religions.'[106] This affidavit echoed the usual hostility of the BJP to positive discrimination, which was even more strident when Muslims were likely to be the main beneficiaries.[107]

Ghettoisation by Law

Other policies discriminated against Muslims through ghettoisation in many cities of Gujarat. Ahmedabad is a case in point. In this riot-prone city, communal violence led Muslims living in Hindu-dominated neighbourhoods to regroup in their ghettos and to form new ones. This process started after the 1969 riots and gained momentum after the 1985 violence,[108] before culminating in the events of 2002. At that time, the Muslim-dominated locality of Juhapura—seven kilometres away from Old Ahmedabad—became a large ghetto of more than 300,000 people where middle-class Muslims found refuge.[109] This process was then consolidated by the state in two ways. First, the government refused to extend public amenities to the inhabitants of Juhapura, who had to develop schools, hospitals, roads and so on privately with the help of their own associations and NGOs.[110] Bus services were also minimal, forcing the inhabitants to use comparatively expensive rickshaws to commute to the city. Darshini Mahadevia, Renu Desai and Suchita Vyas 'note that in contrast to the poor level of services in Juhapura, Praveen Nagar–Gupta Nagar slum settlements just across the road are provided with good level of services and even recently with gas pipelines'.[111] Similarly, 'informal societies are mainly served by informal water providers who charge around 200 rupees per month per household for the supply'.[112] The rights naturally enjoyed by citizens of India were denied to those who lived in Juhapura, transforming them into de facto second-class citizens, partly because the place was a no man's land, a locality that did not belong to any administrative unit—until 2006, when it was finally amalgamated with the Ahmedabad Municipal Corporation.[113]

Secondly, and more importantly for us, BJP promoted ghettoisation by exploiting, and subsequently amending, the Disturbed Areas Act of 1991. This law had been passed to replace the Gujarat Prohibition of Transfer of Immovable Property and Provision for Protection of Tenants from Eviction from Premises in Disturbed Areas Act, 1986, which had been passed in the wake of the 1985 riot. At that time, communal violence had resulted in 'distress sale of properties in riot-prone localities', where families living in minority pockets had decide to flee, selling their houses or flats at give-away prices.[114] According to the 1991 law, 'any person intending to transfer immovable property situated in a disturbed area [...] [had] to make an application to the Collector for obtaining previous sanction'. The collector then had to enquire 'whether the transfer of immovable property [was] proposed to be made by free consent of the persons intending to be the transferor and the transferee and for a fair value of the immovable property'.[115] The Disturbed Areas Act prescribed six months' imprisonment and a fine of 10,000 rupees if one broke the law.[116] The new law assigned a great deal of power to the bureaucracy, who used it in a selective manner: 'Muslims have been allowed to sell their place to Hindus whereas the reverse has not been possible and the Act has become a tool to stop Muslims from mixing with others in major cities: They cannot expand in the pockets they still occupy in Ahmedabad and those who fled the city at the time of riots have not been allowed to come back.'[117] In 2009, the Gujarat Assembly amended the law to further enhance the powers granted to collectors, who could now hold an inquiry of their own accord and take temporary possession of a property that its owner intended to sell. This amendment made the acquisition of properties in mixed areas even more difficult for members of the local minority.[118]

The 1991 law was misinterpreted from another viewpoint: while section 3(1) of the Act allowed the state government to declare an area disturbed when 'public order [...] was disturbed for a substantial period by reason of riot or violence of mob', this emergency measure had continued in peacetime, more than fifteen years after the last major riot or incident of mob violence in Gujarat. Not only that, but the list of disturbed areas kept expanding. In 2013, as the map published by Sheba Tejani shows, in Ahmedabad, 'east of the river [Sabarmati] the entire walled city and the sections north and east of it [were] designated as disturbed'.[119] New areas, where no riot had ever taken place, in Surat and Vadodara, were also classified as communally disturbed; more were likely to come as, during state elections, BJP candidates even canvassed on the theme, claiming that the coming of new Hindu-dominated localities under this law would bring people security. As Sheba Tejani points out, this systematic creation of Muslim ghettos was possible because the law was 'being used to prevent the formation of mixed neighbourhoods even when there [was] no present disturbance of public order, on the pretext of pre-empting future violence'.[120] In other words, what has come to pass is that "disturbance' emanates from the mere presence of Muslims, an eventuality from which Hindus must be protected'.[121] As a result, the locations where Muslims can live became restricted, to such an extent that they had to pay 'a premium of about 67–70%' in places like West Ahmedabad.[122]

That Hindus and Muslims no longer lived next door in the way they had in the Old City only helped perpetuate stereotypes of the 'Other' and transformed both communities into strangers to each other.[123] Howard Spodek sensed this deterioration of community relations during his five-decade engagement with Gujarat, writing in his book on Ahmedabad: 'All—from the most devoted advocate of a composite society to the general secretary of the Vishwa Hindu Parishad—have agreed that this perception of the decline in personal relationships across religious lines is accurate.'[124]

In 2014, the VHP leader himself, Praveen Togadia, was seen on camera offering advice on how to prevent Muslims from buying property in areas where Hindus were in the majority. 'We should have it in us to take the law in our own hands in an area where we are a majority and scare them.'[125] This revealing quote lays bare the role of Hindu nationalist vigilante groups in their efforts to culturally police Muslims.

Vigilante Groups against 'Love Jihad' and 'Cow Slaughter'

Vigilante groups played a major role in the marginalisation of Muslims in Gujarat. They engaged routinely in anti-Muslim activities, not only during riots. The VHP and its youth movement, the Bajrang Dal, are cases in point here.

In 2015, a group of Hindu vigilantes whose chief was also the leader of the local VHP decided to bar 'entry of Muslims at Garba-raas events during the upcoming Navratri festival at Mandvi town in Gujarat's Kutch district to prevent "love jihad" incidents'.[126] A year earlier Praveen Togadia had said that Muslims should not be allowed inside the Garba events and had insisted that the identity cards of each and every participant or visitor be checked: 'We must be alert so that not a single Muslim person can enter in our Garba festival,'[127] he said, primarily so as to fight 'love jihad'.

The notion of 'love jihad'—an expression intended to shock—dates back to the 2000s. It purportedly first appeared in Gujarat in 2007,[128] and describes the alleged strategy of Muslim men who seduce Hindu women supposedly in order to marry them and persuade them to convert to Islam (and then produce Muslim offspring). The Garba appeared vulnerable to such 'attacks' on Hinduism because girls and boys of all religions mixed freely on this occasion every year. Indeed, this form of expressive popular culture allowed Hindu girls and Muslim boys to mingle.[129] The Garba, according to Rita Kothari, is

> a quintessentially Gujarati and cultural experience of the state. The nine days of Garba are many things to many people—to the young it is time for licit liaisons, to the girls flaunting backless cholis on two-wheelers it is a time for gay abandon, to the ones shy about their bodies, it is the time to let loose in the name of religious devotion. In most cases, the Garba, despite its genesis in fertility rites, has ceased to be a religious event, if it was ever one. And therefore those of us who object to its blaring music and disruptive presence in our nights, console ourselves with the fact that it is an important and inclusive festival [...] This year's Navratri is not available to Muslims. Vishwa Hindu Parishad's diktat to keep Muslims out of Garba is being followed zealously. Garba organizers are poised to check identity cards, some have had the brilliant idea of putting tilak on every forehead and thereby fortifying the symbolic walls through religion.[130]

As early as 2003, Gujarati VHP activists mobilised against Garba performances organised by some Christian churches at Christmas, with the result that many of them preferred to shut down the event rather than face harassment. Ten years later, Muslim boys had become the main targets.[131]

However, they were targeted by the Sangh Parivar more systematically when the Garba was celebrated during the festival of Navratri. In September 2014, the VHP of Gujarat distributed a leaflet asking Hindu girls to be wary of Muslim boys seeking to 'trap them into prostitution': 'Muslim teachers, doctors and lawyers seek to entrap Hindu girls.' Parents of Hindu girls were requested to contact the offices of the VHP, the Bajrang Dal and Durga Vahini (the women's wing of the VHP) when they became aware of such 'dirty tricks'.[132] The leaflet also referred to Muslim mafia dons like Dawood Ibrahim, thereby reactivating the old sentiment of vulnerability that had emerged in the 1980s. Interestingly, this campaign took place just before important by-elections.

In the Gujarat of this time, the collaboration between vigilante groups and the police to resist 'love jihad' gained momentum. This is evident from the case of Amir Raza (21) and Swati Khare (19), who fell in love in June 2006, eloped, got married in Bangalore in terms of the guidelines of the Special Marriage Act, but returned to Kosamba, their native place, in September:

> When Swati went to meet her parents, they reportedly contacted Durga Vahini and Bajrang Dal activists over phone. Kosamba-based activist, Bhavna Gajjar and her husband Nagin Gajjar arrived at the Khare residence and forced her to go with them. As per a written declaration to the Police Commissioner, Swati was taken in a car to Kosamba police station where she was forced to sign a police complaint against her husband. Sub Inspector JK Rabari reportedly aligned with the activists, telling her that she and her husband would be killed in an encounter. A case of dowry and assault was thus registered. The next day, Swati was reportedly taken to Riddhi Siddhi Maternity Hospital in Bharuch town where she was made to undergo an abortion [...] Swati was brought back to Kosamba where she was threatened by Hindu activists and asked to sign divorce papers. According to her statement to the police, when she refused to sign the

> document, she was kept in confinement at her brother's house in Vadodara.[133]

Swati managed to flee, and submitted a petition in the High Court to quash the false case registered against Amir. This collaboration between Sangh Parivar activists and men in uniform became commonplace across India after 2014.[134]

Another of the VHP's warhorses, namely cow protection, resulted in anti-Muslim mobilisation during Bakra Eid, when, according to Hindu nationalists, Muslims do not sacrifice goats but cows (because they are cheaper). Here again, the VHP, Bajrang Dal and police worked together during crackdowns on the sale of beef in the name of cow protection in Ahmedabad and Vadodara: 'these police raids were conducted following pressure by VHP activists on the local security apparatus'.[135] The VHP even 'held protests against cow slaughter'. But the VHP took an active part in this cultural policing too. A VHP office-bearer told the *Indian Express* that there were 62 teams of four to five cattle protectors in Ahmedabad: during Bakra Eid, 'we deploy the teams at entry points to the city and work in close coordination with the police'.[136]

Obliterating (Some) Muslims Politically and Socially

The BJP also discriminated against Muslims to make them invisible in Gujarat's politics. No Muslim candidates were nominated by the party for the 2007 and 2012 elections. In 2012, this decision may be explained by the fact that the party Keshubhai Patel had just created, the Gujarat Parivartan Party (GPP), had not given tickets to any Muslim candidate either—and the BJP was probably eager not to lag behind by diluting its Hindu identity. But this decision reflects a larger, long-term strategy, as a party leader pointed out when asked about the absence of Muslim candidates:

> It was too risky a gamble. This symbolic gesture may have confused the majority who see Modi as a saviour of the Hindus. More importantly, the conciliatory gesture towards the minorities could have alienated the party cadre [...] If this election is a springboard for 2014, it is important to keep Gujarat's majority sentiment in mind. There will be enough time for symbolic gestures later. The party may think of nominating a Muslim to the Rajya Sabha [upper house of the Indian parliament] when the time is right.[137]

The Muslim president of the party's minority wing in Gujarat resigned in protest, but this defection hardly made a difference. Eventually, the only mention of Muslims in the BJP's manifesto—and the first one in an election manifesto of the Gujarat BJP under Modi—referred to the modernisation of Koranic schools and to financial support for Muslims' artisanal specialities (like making kites, incense sticks, *rakhi* bands and firecrackers), two items that reinforced the stereotype of Muslims as a backward community. Nothing was said about the pre-matriculation minority scholarship scheme.[138]

However, Narendra Modi tended to distinguish 'good Muslims' from 'bad Muslims'. While the allegedly disastrous historical role of Muslims in India was one of his recurrent themes, as was evident from his repeated evocation of the '1200 years of slavery' (including the Mughal Empire) that India underwent,[139] Modi's Hindu majoritarianism did not entail systematic reservations vis-à-vis *all* Muslims. Among this minority, the one group he expressed sympathy for were the Bohras. He first established a channel of communication with the Dawoodi Bohras, who form a specific sub-group and descend from upper-caste Hindu converts. A small number of them, for instance, do not register as 'Muslims' in the census, but as Bohras.[140] The chief of the Bohra community, Sayyidna Muhammad Burhanuddin, who had taken over from his predecessor in 1965 and who was known for his very conservative style,[141] kept a low profile in relations with the BJP. He never protested against Modi or the 2002 riots and even tried 'to appease' the chief minister, according to a Bohra reformist, J.S. Bandukwala, a former professor at MSU in Baroda.[142] The Sayyidna distanced himself from the victims of the 2002 events and never even mentioned that Ehsan Jafri was a member of his community.[143] Modi paid him a courtesy visit in 2008,[144] and in 2011 Modi also opened the first trade exhibition of this community in Ahmedabad. On this occasion, he described the Bohras as the 'embodiment of peace'.[145]

Modi was much less comfortable with other Muslim groups, as was evident from a couple of episodes during his Sadbhavana Mission.[146] This programme was part of his attempts to reach out to Sunni Muslims, an effort already visible in his strategy in the 2009 local elections.[147] As mentioned above, it was aimed at promoting social harmony beyond caste, class and religious divisions. Muslims attended these functions in large numbers, but there were a few revealing incidents. The first occurred in the Convention Hall of Gujarat University (Ahmedabad) where Modi was launching the 'Mission' in September 2011. Maulvi Sayed Imam, a cleric from a small *dargah* in a nearby village, came on stage to greet him. But when 'he took out a skull cap from his pocket and offered it to Modi, the latter's expression changed in a flash' and he refused to wear it. The Imam said later: 'Modi's refusal to the cap is not my insult but an insult of Islam [...] He might have thought that wearing a skull cap will dent his image.'[148] BJP leaders congratulated themselves that Modi had not repeated the 'mistake' of L.K. Advani, who had been offered a *chadar* at the mausoleum of Jinnah in Pakistan. They explained that 'BJP doesn't believe in accepting religion in its real existence'[149]—a very revealing phrase. In Navsari, a few days later, one of Modi's Muslim supporters jumped on stage and tried to offer him a *keffiyeh*, a scarf, which he again refused.[150]

An even more powerful symbol of Modi's rejection of multiculturalism was the way he discontinued the tradition of *iftar* parties. These parties were traditionally hosted by his predecessors—Madhavsinh Solanki, Amarsinh Chaudhary and Chimanbhai Patel—to celebrate the end of the fast each day during Ramadan. Ajay Umat recalls: 'When BJP came to power in 1995, the then CM Keshubhai Patel was in two minds about hosting *Iftar* lest he would invite the ire of Sangh Parivar hardliners. But former prime minister A.B. Vajpayee [who hosted such parties himself as prime minister] asserted that Keshubhai had hosted *Iftar*. He played host twice—but avoided non-vegetarian food.'[151] In contrast, Modi never hosted *iftar* parties because he saw it 'as a form of appeasement'.[152]

Modi routinely applied to Muslims the same kind of sarcasm that he expressed towards Christian public figures. In 2003, when he explained to non-resident Indians visiting Gujarat how he was curbing power thefts, he chose the example of Juhapura, the Muslim ghetto near Ahmedabad, and said:

> there is an area in Ahmedabad called Juhapura where each lane has many power ministers. Since 20 years, no government authority, not even my predecessors, could take any stringent action here. So we had a Yusuf Lightwala, a Karim Lightwala and other Ali Lightwalas—all power ministers. It is only my government that took action against the so-called power ministers and within 10 days caught 8000 power thieves impounding truckloads of wires some 35 km long.[153]

This discourse is typical of the style of Narendra Modi, who targeted the Muslims of Juhapura as if there were no other poor slum dwellers from other communities who could only obtain electricity in this manner.

Prohibiting Conversion

That the Modi government was determined not to let people freely change their religion affected not only the religious minorities (Muslims and Christians) but also the Dalits, who were more likely than other groups to want to escape the caste system. As early as March 2003, the Modi government had the Orwellian-sounding Freedom of Religion bill passed. The new Act made conversion to another religion more difficult than before. According to the provisions of Article 5 of this new law:

> (1) Whoever converts any person from one religion to another either by performing any ceremony by himself for such conversion as a religious priest or takes part directly or indirectly in such ceremony shall take prior permission for such proposed conversion from the District Magistrate concerned by applying in such form as may be prescribed by rules. (2) The person who is converted shall send an intimation to the District Magistrate of the District concerned in which the ceremony has taken place of the fact of such conversion within such period and in such form as may be prescribed by rules. (3) Whoever fails, without sufficient cause, to comply with the provisions of sub-sections (1) and (2) shall be punished with imprisonment for a term, which may extend to one year or with fine which may extend to rupees one thousand or with both.[154]

In 2006, the state Assembly passed an amendment to the Freedom of Religion Act, grouping together Jainism, Buddhism and Hinduism, so that the adoption of any faith within this trio was not considered as conversion. The National Commission for Minorities (NCM) demanded a reversal of the decision,[155] the Catholic Church of Gujarat submitted a memorandum to the governor of the state asking him not to approve the law and started a signature campaign, and the Jamiat-e-Ulema-e-Hind of Gujarat, the organisation of Islamic scholars, asserted: 'The matter of choosing faith is a personal matter and guaranteed by the constitution. There is no need to seek anyone's permission.'[156] The right to convert to another religion is indeed guaranteed by Article 25 of the Constitution of India. The proposed amendment was withdrawn,[157] but the 2003 Act, which had not yet been implemented, was revived and in 2008 'the Gujarat Government form[ed] the rules to start implementing it'.

As a result, half of those who tried to convert to another religion between 2011 and 2016—no data is available for the previous period—were forbidden to do so: 'in five years, the state government received 1,838 applications from people of various religions to convert to another religion [...] The state government has not approved half of these applicants, only 878 persons got permission to convert.'[158] Interestingly, 1,735 applications (94.4 per cent) were filed by Hindus who wanted to renounce the religion of their birth to embrace some other creed. Among them were mostly low-caste people.

That the Gujarat government was keen to keep Dalits in the framework of the caste system was indeed evident from the new rules regarding conversions. They were confronted with new hurdles when they tried to convert to religions others than Hinduism, including Buddhism and Christianity.[159] In October 2013, 60 Dalit families of Junagadh converted to Buddhism.[160] But, according to the state, these Dalits had not obtained the permission of the district magistrate before conversion. The organisers claimed that they did, but a probe was initiated.[161] In many other cases, the new law dissuaded Dalits from leaving Hinduism.[162]

MAKING MINORITIES POLITICALLY INVISIBLE

Several of the policies of Modi's government in Gujarat that we have reviewed in this chapter were replicated when he became prime minister, adding new dimensions to the state's status as a testing ground for Hindutva. First, opposition parties were destabilised, like the Congress in Gujarat, when the BJP replicated in other states and at the Centre its strategy of attracting some of their leaders, MLAs and MPs to its fold. It resorted to intimidation practices as well as techniques of allurement. Such a 'strategy of cannibalization of its adversaries',[163] to use Gilles Verniers's words, was first used in Karnataka.[164] Here, the chief minister and Janata Dal (Secular) leader, H.D. Kumaraswamy, alleged that the BJP had offered Rs 100 million to some of his MLAs.[165] These allegations have remained unsubstantiated, but one of these turncoats, M.T.B. Nagaraj, did purchase a Rolls-Royce soon after he shifted to the BJP.[166] The second state on the BJP list was Madhya Pradesh, where the scenario was very similar. In early March 2020, former Madhya Pradesh chief minister Digvijay Singh claimed that the BJP was trying to topple the Congress state government by offering potential defectors from Rs 250 million to Rs 350 million.[167]

Second, universities were targeted across India after 2014, in the same way they had been in Gujarat under Modi. As with the IPS and IAS Gujarat cadres who followed Narendra Modi to the Centre, the new prime minister also appointed some of those who had been at the helm of institutions in Gujarat, as heads of prestigious Delhi-based universities. Yogesh Singh, who had been VC of the MSU, became VC of Delhi University, for instance,[168] and Manoj Soni became Union Public Service Commission chairman in 2022. Then again, the Modi government targeted key universities by appointing VCs who had no Gujarati connection but were close to the Hindu nationalist movement. JNU is a case in point. In this iconic university, in 2016, the Modi government appointed Mamidala Jagadesh Kumar as vice chancellor. An electrical engineering professor who had been teaching at the nearby Indian Institute of Technology until then, he had played an active role in Vijnana Bharati, an organisation under the Sangh Parivar umbrella that aims at promoting indigenous Indian science.[169] The progressive traditions of JNU came under attack after this appointment.[170]

Similarly, the rewriting of history textbooks, which had been pioneered in Gujarat, gained momentum at the centre, and

Dinanath Batra continued to play a key role in this regard. The textbooks put out by the NCERT, which can be used in schools affiliated with the Central Board of Secondary Education, were extensively rewritten. According to the *Indian Express*, 1,334 changes were made to 182 textbooks put out by the NCERT between 2005 and 2009.[171]

Beyond intellectuals, the three groups on which this chapter focused, Dalits, Adivasis and Muslims, were also at the receiving end of the post-2014 dispensation, as was evident from the government's attitude regarding positive discrimination. While India has resorted to affirmative action for emancipating the lower (and the lowest) castes for decades, the Modi government diluted this project by introducing a new quota for the Economically Weaker Sections (EWS). In fact, this quota was designed for the upper castes at large because by setting an income limit of Rs 800,000 per annum, below which households are classified under EWS, the government made this quota accessible to about 99 per cent of the upper castes—and not to the poor only. For Ashwini Deshpande and Rajesh Ramachandran, it 'completely overturn[ed] the original logic of reservations on its head':[172]

> By stipulating a quota for non-SC–ST–OBC (Other Backward Class) families earning Rs 800,000 or less, the government is effectively creating a quota exclusively for Hindu upper castes who are not in the top 1% of the income distribution. This means that despite being presented as a quota on economic criteria and not caste, the reality is that this is very much a caste based quota, targeted towards castes that do not suffer any social discrimination; on the contrary, these rank the highest on the social scale of ritual purity.[173]

However, the main targets of the Modi governments, before and after 2014, have been the Muslims—and the modus operandi used in Gujarat, in this regard too, was replicated at the Centre to a large extent. Just as the Modi government denied some scholarships to minority students, including Muslims, in Gujarat in 2022, the Union government stopped the Maulana Azad Scholarship for minority students.[174] Symbols matter too and, while A.B. Vajpayee had hosted an Eid Milan at his residence and an *iftar* party when he was prime minister,[175] Modi, who had already discontinued this tradition when he was chief minister, stopped it also at the Centre. Likewise, forms of exclusion that had emerged in Gujarat, including the economic boycott of Muslim traders or the ban on festivals like Garba, became commonplace across India after 2014. This transformation of the public sphere had, naturally, more to do with the role of vigilante groups, which were not brought to book by the state authorities when they engaged in anti-'love jihad' campaigns or other types of coercion. By transforming Muslims into de facto second-class citizens, Gujarat became the test site for the kind of Hindu Rashtra that India was destined to become under his premiership after 2014.

In Gujarat, Christians were also targeted even before Modi became chief minister. In the 1990s, while Modi was in charge of the organisation of the state BJP, as *sangathan mantri*, the VHP and the activist group Hindu Jagran Manch attacked priests who were accused of promoting conversions to Christianity.[176] In 1998 and 1999, Christians were assaulted over Christmas. Several churches were burned or damaged. The National Commission for Minorities investigated and submitted to President K.R. Narayan a report in which the state government was held responsible for its handling of the situation.[177] Christians continued to be at the receiving end when Modi became prime minister. Attacks on priests, nuns and churches multiplied after 2014, so much so that NGOs started compiling reports about hundreds of incidents,[178] and clerics began to mobilise.[179] As early as 2015, the retired police officer and author Julio Ribeiro wrote: 'As a Christian, suddenly I am a stranger in my own country.'[180] To transform Muslims and Christians into second-class citizens was the very objective of Hindu majoritarianism, an ideology whose politics first emerged in Gujarat and then became dominant in the rest of the nation.

CONCLUSION

My main objective in writing this book—which I began in the early 2000s—was to account for the politics of Narendra Modi in Gujarat in order to explain his rise to power, as well as to identify the specific characteristics of his strategy that allowed him to rule the state for a record number of years. It was intended to be, in a way, the political biography of an Indian state through the personality and actions of its most resilient ruler. As time passed, my aim evolved as it also became important to understand how Gujarat had been a Hindu nationalist test site, the crucible of a new form of Hindutva politics that was to unfold at the national level after 2014. I have explored this question in the conclusions to each chapter—which echo those of my book *Modi's India*—to demonstrate that since 2014 the prime minister of India has replicated the modus operandi he had fine-tuned as chief minister. Never before had a regional leader been able to re-scale a political repertoire rooted in a particular state and transpose it to an all-India level. In this conclusion we will focus on this process and list the techniques that Modi successfully used first in Gujarat and then in India at large.

The five parts of the book deal with the five mainstays of Modi's politics in Gujarat that were to prevail subsequently at an all-India level. Their themes overlap and there is more than one idea in each part, and in each chapter even. But these five parts remain relevant entry points for mapping Modi's politics.

Communal polarisation was the first pillar of Modi's politics in Gujarat. This approach was not new to the state, but it acquired an unprecedented scale under Modi. While this form of polarisation had traditionally been fostered by means of Hindu–Muslim riots in the past, in 2002 it resulted from mass violence. That the BJP could win state elections in this very specific context, whereas it had registered several electoral setbacks since 2000, showed that polarisation 'worked' politically, as BJP party leaders in the state had anticipated. Polarisation subsequently remained a major factor in the government's strategy, but in a different mode, as no major riot has occurred in Gujarat since 2002. Instead, polarisation was sustained by a reactivation of the politics of fear. This kind of politics had been mobilised by the BJP in the 1980s and 1990s when it targeted Latif's 'Muslim mafia': 'fake encounters', or extra-judicial killings of alleged Pakistan-supported Islamic terrorists accused of targeting the chief minister, helped to perpetuate fear of the 'Other' and the stigmatisation of Muslims. After 2014, polarisation remained Modi's trump card in national politics. There have been few episodes of mass violence (the Delhi riots in 2020 being the most significant), but alternative forms of violence, including the lynching of Muslims, have taken over. In addition, stigmatisation of the 'Other' has found expression in recurrent campaigns (against 'love jihad'; for reconversion; in the name of cow protection), not to mention the transformation of the legal framework through the Citizenship Amendment Act (according to which Muslim refugees from Bangladesh, Pakistan and Afghanistan are ineligible for Indian citizenship), or the laws making inter-religious marriages and conversions almost impossible.

The de-institutionalisation of the rule of law was the second instrument of Modi's arsenal in Gujarat. This was partly a consequence of the events of 2002, but it became a strategy for strengthening Modi's political control over the state. This process translated into the saffronisation of Gujarat institutions: policemen who took part in anti-Muslim violence were rewarded, and the government ensured that a proper judicial process would not be pursued. But the rule of law was damaged in many other ways and for other reasons under Modi. Hindu nationalist vigilante groups, including the Bajrang Dal, were given the freedom to exert forms of cultural policing by resorting to intimidation and even physical violence against those who opposed the Sangh Parivar and its world view. Moreover, instead of strengthening key institutions like the police, the judiciary and the Lokayukta, the state government left many posts vacant. Crime and corruption remained at a very high level, and these two evils continued to plague the police as well as the political parties, including the BJP. The BJP government itself took the law into its own hands by engaging in illicit forms of surveillance. After 2014, the de-institutionalisation of the rule of law has been one of Prime Minister Modi's main priorities, as is evident from the way police officers in his entourage in Gujarat followed him to Delhi and independent minded officers were dislodged from key positions in the CBI and other institutions. If the collegium-based procedure that was used for appointing the Supreme Court justices could not be reformed, lawyers sympathetic to the BJP (who had sometimes been close to Modi and Amit Shah since their Gujarat days) were promoted at the Centre, whereas those who could not be trusted by the government were not appointed even after the collegium nominated them more than once. Last but not least, surveillance techniques were adopted, as in Gujarat, even before Amit Shah became home minister of the Government of India.

A third characteristic feature of Modi's politics in Gujarat lay in his (socio-)economic policies. In a state known for its industrial dynamism, the business community could not be ignored and Modi had no intention of ignoring it. Instead, he attracted investors in a big way. His policy, in this regard, stood in stark contrast with that of his predecessors: instead of capitalising on the Gujaratis' sense of entrepreneurship, which had given birth to a dense network of SMEs, he promoted big projects by wooing large Indian companies, which were lured by all kinds of new advantages and concessions, within SEZs and outside them. Modi himself called Gujarat 'the SEZ of India'.[1] In return, some of these businessmen, including Gautam Adani, supported Modi. At the same time, the Modi government invested more in infrastructure—roads, ports and energy—than in developmental expenditure, including health and education. The political economy of Gujarat was so supply-side-oriented and capitalistic in nature that good jobs remained very few in number: the new projects were not labour-intensive and Gujarat experienced a rapid casualisation of work. Inequalities increased, especially in rural areas where cash crops—monopolised by large farmers—were promoted, whereas the small peasants lagged behind. A third defining feature of Gujarat was thus a political economy based on crony capitalism and social polarisation. These two formulas apply to India at large since 2014, suggesting that, against all odds, the political economy of a particular state could be extended on a subcontinental scale. The economic policy followed by the current Indian government is clearly supplied-side-oriented (as is evident from the fiscal measures taken as early as 2015), and crony capitalism is definitely the order of the day. Gautam Adani, who experienced a meteoric rise in Modi's Gujarat, continued to rise in Modi's India. Similarly, the gap between the rich and the poor has widened, partly because villagers bear the brunt of government policies, be they landless peasants (who do not benefit from the Rural Employment Guarantee scheme as much as they did under Manmohan Singh) or farmers (who do not sell their product at the right prices). Modi's pro-rich policies have favoured the middle class at the expense, not only of the peasantry but also of the urban poor, both in Gujarat and in India at large after 2014. The modernisation of cities—witness the manner in which Ahmedabad has been transformed—remains the order of the day, as is evident from the Central Vista project in Delhi.

The fourth distinctive feature of Modi's politics in Gujarat is probably the most obvious: his style, which resulted in a stark personalisation of power. One of the reasons for Modi's political success lies in his capacity to saturate the public sphere by using high-tech communications and maintaining a semi-permanent state of political mobilisation. The image and the message which were thus projected enabled the chief minister to portray himself as an embodiment of Gujarat against the Centre and against the Nehru–Gandhi family. These techniques also allowed him to relate directly to voters in a new form of high-tech populism. In contrast to the tradition of collegiality, inherited from the RSS, that the BJP cultivated under Vajpayee and Advani, Modi gradually captured all power within the government and his party. He emancipated himself from elements of the Sangh Parivar—including the VHP and the BKS, which he confronted—by relying on the bureaucracy (after promoting civil servants who eventually became part of the core group of Gujarat's administration) and by relating directly to the people. Indeed, Modi resorted to typically populist techniques of mobilisation by short-circuiting intermediate bodies (including his party, until he captured it) and by talking directly to voters from the platform, by means of holograms and on social media. His discourse was also populist in that he projected himself as a victim of the Establishment and the defender of the Gujarati people against a Delhi-based elite. This style was not only populist, but also *national* populist, for the people he claimed to represent were the sons of the soil—the Hindus. His enemies were not only the national rulers, but their cosmopolitan faces, including Sonia and Rahul Gandhi, at the head of what he called 'the Delhi Sultanate'. Hence the notion of 'Moditva', bracketing together his personal relationship to the people and his Hindu nationalist ideology.

The continuity between Modi's political style before and after 2014 is fascinating. It suggests that only minor adjustments were needed for shifting from state-level to national-level politics. The means of communication remained the same, allowing Modi to relate directly to 'his' people. Instead of 60 million Gujaratis, he now spoke in the name of 1.3 billion Indians; instead of adopting the dress code of the peasants of Saurashtra, as he did when he was campaigning in Kathiawar, he now changed his costume according to whichever province he visited. But the body language was the same and the general overtone too. More importantly, the targets were the same, be they Pakistan and the Islamists (or Muslims) or, on the domestic scene, the Congress and Nehru (his bête noire) as well as the latter's descendants. Such a transposition was made easier because of Gujarat's affinities with the rest of North and West India. In the South and the East, where Modi is much less popular, the dominant political culture is less conducive to the kind of Hindutva that Modi could develop in Gujarat, a province whose identity (*asmita*) is rooted in Hinduism. That Modi could centralise as well as personalise power at a pan-Indian level, as he had done at the state level, is more surprising. He successfully marginalised not only his rivals from the old guard in the BJP (including his old mentor, L.K. Advani), as he had done with Keshubhai Patel and his colleagues, but also the RSS leaders (including Mohan Bhagwat). The latter realised—in Nagpur as, before, in Ahmedabad—that they needed him more than he needed them because he had built his own parallel power structure (made up of private consultants and 'vote mobilisers') and had become remarkably popular among Hindu nationalist foot soldiers, including grassroots *swayamsevaks*.

The fifth part of the book focuses on the social and political contexts which have made the rise to power of Modi possible and the consequences of his rule for Gujarat society. This part harks back to social issues already dealt with at the beginning of the book. In chapter 1, we saw how the BJP started to grow at the expense of the Congress when the party capitalised on new developments like the saffronisation of the upper castes and Patels, who resented Madhavsinh Solanki's reservation policy in the 1980s. This core group of supporters—which coincided with Gujarat's middle class—remained staunchly behind the BJP in the 1990s, but during his terms Modi added the 'plus vote' of a new social category: the 'neo-middle class'. This group of aspiring Gujaratis was mostly made up of people who, like him, came from the lower castes, had migrated to urban centres and wanted to benefit from the state's economic growth. Modi's political strategy relied on social polarisation in the sense that not only was the rural part of the state neglected, but in the urban context the poor were marginalised, with the result that cities became 'bourgeois at last'. Meanwhile, ascriptive groups like Adivasis and Dalits did not enjoy the state support they were entitled to, partly because the state government adhered to a Hindu nationalist vision of society (and the caste system in particular). The last chapter echoes the first: in the 1980s, upper castes and Patels rallied around the Hindu nationalist movement in order to resist the social agenda initiated by state Congress leaders. Hindutva became the antidote to reservation politics: lower castes were invited to consider the Muslim as the 'Other' and to close ranks with their co-religionists, at the expense of social welfare. As in post-Congress Gujarat, the BJP in post-Mandal India has been the instrument of the politics of elite revenge. This has relied not only on anti-minority national populism but also on the making of a new social coalition including the upper and dominant castes of the middle class as well as the emerging neo-middle class drawn from OBCs (and often consisting, paradoxically, of beneficiaries of reservations). Dalits and Adivasis have been at the receiving end of new, conservative policies.

Yet, of all communities, the Muslims were the most discriminated against, as is evident from state policies which amplified, and sometimes even fostered, their socio-economic and cultural marginalisation. Victims of social exclusion and ghettoisation, Muslims—who had already been badly affected by communal violence—were turned into de facto second-class citizens. This scenario—another entry point to the social polarisation issue—has been unfolding in India at large since 2014. Muslims are directly targeted by some state measures (including the post-2014 laws mentioned above) and, even more, by vigilante groups fighting against 'love jihad' or 'land jihad'. These groups, which often work hand in glove with the police, are largely responsible for the fear, socio-economic decline and ghettoisation that Muslims are experiencing today across India. There is one difference between the situation that prevailed in Gujarat under Modi and the state of things in India today that needs to be highlighted here: while the BJP could not attract many Dalit and Adivasi voters in a sustained manner in Gujarat, it did so in the 2019 Lok Sabha elections, partly because of Modi's national-populist aura, and partly because of pro-poor schemes which have given birth to a new kind of welfarism.[2]

The five pillars of Modi's strategy in Gujarat continued to operate after he became prime minister. In fact, he literally remote-controlled the BJP and the state from New Delhi, as was evident from his frequent visits (especially before the 2017 and 2022 elections)[3] and the way the chief ministers who succeeded him were selected.

The fifth part of the book also deals with another dimension: the fight against Modi's opponents. The plebeian groups listed above were not his only victims: dissenters were also targeted in Gujarat, and still are. Intellectuals (including academics) and journalists are cases in point. The continuity, here again, is striking: the way Gujarat universities like MSU in Baroda were dealt with after the appointment of new vice chancellors by Modi prepared the ground for the way Central universities like

JNU were treated after their vice chancellors were also changed. This state of things reflects a form of authoritarianism that permeates the five parts of the book but needs to be highlighted on its own.

GUJARAT, A CRUCIBLE OF INDIA'S ELECTORAL AUTHORITARIANISM AND DEEPER STATE

There is one thing that could not be scaled up from Gujarat to the national scene, and that is the centralisation of power in the hands of a few people in New Delhi. By definition, in Gandhinagar Modi could not concentrate power beyond his state, and this is therefore a domain where he has innovated after 2014. The way he decided on demonetisation in 2016 and the COVID-19–related lockdown in 2020 without consulting the chief ministers reflected a clear concentration of power in his person.

However, the weakening of some of the key institutions of the Indian Republic echoes the way he behaved in Gujarat: the Lokpal and the Indian parliament have remained marginal players under Modi as prime minister, just as in Gujarat the office of the Lokayukta was eroded and the state Assembly declined. This body met on no more than 150 days during the life of the 12th Assembly from 2007 to 2012, that is, 30 days a year on average, and on 154 days during the life of the 11th Assembly, in stark contrast to the 1980s and 1990s, when it met on more than 200 days.[4] To top it all, as the NGO network Gujarat Social Watch mentioned in its presentation to the governor:

> In Gujarat assembly, most of the reports like the ones by the Comptroller and Auditor General of India, the State Human Rights Commission, the State Information Commission, the State Vigilance Commission, several inquiry reports, are tabled only on the last day. Thus contentious issues are not discussed properly in the assembly, and that is why contents of such reports do not reach up to the public.[5]

Moreover, the post of deputy speaker was not filled for 12 years. This state of affairs prefigured the way the Indian parliament was to be sidelined after 2014. Modi, who hardly visits the Lok Sabha and the Rajya Sabha,[6] has issued a record number of ordinances. While ordinances are usually resorted to by minority governments or coalition governments, Modi has used them more frequently than any of his predecessors in spite of enjoying an absolute majority in the Lok Sabha.[7] The Lok Sabha and the Rajya Sabha are gradually ceasing to be places for debate. First, the number of bills that have been referred to parliamentary committees—the deliberative core of parliamentary work—has shrunk dramatically, from 68 (71 per cent of the total) in the 15th Lok Sabha to 24 (25 per cent) in the 16th Lok Sabha[8]—and none in 2020.[9]

This marginalisation of the Gujarat state Assembly and the Indian parliament is in accord with a political culture where debates and even elections are seen as dividing society and therefore the nation. In Gujarat, such a view of politics and society found expression in the concept of '*samaras* [social assimilation] villages'. These villages were not invited to organise local elections and were assumed to have 'no discussions, no disputes, but unanimous decisions taken harmoniously'.[10] Ghanshyam Shah points out: 'Besides financial incentives, the government used its administrative machinery to build pressure on the villages to become samaras. Pro-BJP NGOs were "roped in to spread the samaras message and help achieve the targets"' [...] The 2009 election advertisement of the BJP was: "No discussion, vikas [development] is the mantra of BJP. Rashtravad [nationalism] is BJP's mahamantra."'[11] This motto justified some limits on debate and even the suspension of elections for appointing local leaders, 'in the name of development'.

Such an undemocratic approach did not seem to be a concern for a large proportion of Gujarat society. A 2007 CSDS survey revealed that 34 per cent of interviewees (including 37 per cent of

BJP voters) considered Modi's 'style of functioning' 'dictatorial'. But 48 per cent of those who disapproved of this dictatorial style were prepared to vote for his party (whereas among those who approved of this style, 61 per cent were prepared to do the same).[12] These figures reflect a substantial predilection for non-democratic forms of governance, which is particularly evident among the middle class,[13] a group over-represented among the supporters of Modi. The rise of an illiberal political culture in Gujarat made Modi more acceptable to the state's society as, according to Ashis Nandy, he fulfilled all the criteria of an authoritarian personality. In 2003 Nandy wrote:

> Modi, it gives me no pleasure to tell the readers, met virtually all the criteria that psychiatrists, psycho-analysts and psychologists had set up after years of empirical work on the authoritarian personality. He had the same mix of puritanical rigidity, narrowing of emotional life, massive use of the ego defence of projection, denial and fear of his own passions combined with fantasies of violence—all set within the matrix of clear paranoid and obsessive personality traits. I still remember the cool, measured tone in which he elaborated a theory of cosmic conspiracy against India that painted every Muslim as a suspected traitor and a potential terrorist.[14]

Nandy's analysis suggests that Modi was popular in Gujarat, not only because of his anti-Muslim doctrine (which attracted middle-class Gujaratis in particular, as Nandy argues elsewhere), but also because of his authoritarian personality.

This observation can be transposed to the national level. In 2017, the Pew Research Center conducted a survey in 34 countries to measure 'pro-democracy attitudes' as well as 'openness to nondemocratic forms of governance, including rule by experts, a strong leader or the military'.[15] Commenting upon the result, the Pew team pointed out that 'support for autocratic rule is higher in India than in any other nation surveyed', and India is 'one of only four nations where half or more of the public supports governing by the military'. An even larger proportion—two-thirds—believes that 'a good way to govern the country would be experts, not elected officials, making decisions according to what they think is best for the nation'. Indeed, in this survey, 55 per cent of Indian respondents backed 'a governing system in which a strong leader can make decisions without interference from parliament or the courts', while 53 per cent supported military rule. Interestingly, supporters of the Hindu nationalist party, the BJP, were over-represented in the three groups—of those who support personal rule, military governance and a technocratic regime.[16]

The demand for a strong leader was related to an acute feeling of vulnerability.[17] According to the Pew survey of India, while 'crime takes the top spot on the list, with 84% of Indians seeing it as a *very* big problem', 'terrorism' follows immediately after for 76% of the respondents (before corruption and unemployment).[18] This was well in tune with the finding that ISIS appeared as the main threat facing India to 66 per cent of the respondents, ahead of every other threat.[19] The need for a strong state further arose from the drive to stifle unresolved issues and conflicts, as was evident from the fact that a '63 per cent majority believe[d] the government should be using more military force' in Kashmir.[20] Such results suggest that the politics of fear, and the strategy of polarisation that Modi initiated in Gujarat and used at the national level, explain his political resilience and his capacity to attract supporters across society.

This fascination for the strong leader has been fostered by the national-populist techniques mentioned above, but it resulted too from the relations Modi cultivated with foreign leaders. Here again, counter-intuitively, Gujarat was a launch pad. The many observers who were amazed by the way Modi travelled widely to meet some of the most influential statesmen in the world—and acquired a prestigious image in return—could have anticipated this development if they had followed his trips abroad as chief minister. Not only did Modi as chief minister visit many countries in spite of being banned from the West after 2005, but he orchestrated a systematic campaign of publicity around these trips. When he travelled to China, his website included something that would become commonplace in the mainstream media after 2014—though no longer about China:

> The visit of Chief Minister Mr. Narendra Modi to China has been a grand success. The Government of the People's Republic of China and the ruling Community Party of China (CPC) accorded unprecedented importance and highest level of protocol to the Chief Minister going beyond the established norms. Special arrangements for reception, escort, banquets, visits, security and high level of meetings were made.
>
> The visit generated huge interest among business and industrial community as well as the Chinese political leadership. Chinese being diligent to the core, having seen all round development and spectacular growth of Gujarat, and the leadership provided by Mr. Narendra Modi, wants to build a strong and enduring relationship with Gujarat.[21]

Modi made a hundred chartered trips between 2003 and 2007, the year when he went to China, South Korea, Japan and Switzerland[22]—and the year after he went to Kenya and Uganda. But he also invited prime ministers and presidents of the world to Gujarat, on the occasion of Vibrant Gujarat in particular.[23] In other words, the transition from chief minister to prime minister was also surprisingly easy for Modi from the viewpoint of his international exposure.

While Narendra Modi epitomises the strongman type of ruler, even strongmen lose elections. And Modi, like today's other strongmen, needs to organise elections, not only to cultivate India's international reputation as 'the world's largest democracy', but also to renew his legitimacy every five years, by gaining yet another popular mandate. This is the risk all populist leaders have to take in order to prevail over unelected institutions, including the judiciary.[24] The five pillars of the Gujarat model reviewed above, which have been transposed to the national level, make Modi's electoral defeat rather unlikely, but not impossible. However, one of these pillars suggests that his defeat may not make any return to the pre-2014 situation easy, and this is the de-instutionalisation of the state, a process which goes together with the making of a 'deeper state'. The main actors here are the activists of the Sangh Parivar, including the militants of vigilante groups like the Bajrang Dal, which are policing society at the grassroots level with the blessings of the political rulers. The official police are either neutralised or accomplices. If the BJP loses power, these organisations, which have permeated society and gained momentum since 2014, may continue to prevail, claiming that their (illegal) deeds are legitimised by the sacredness of their (Hindu) cause and endorsed by the majority. A militant said, as early as 2015: 'This is Hindustan and it does not matter which party is running the government. In a democratic country like this, there are many other ways to get things done. The police know it well that we will do picketing, hold demonstration and all this will lead to rioting. So, they perforce co-operate with us.'[25]

Under the aegis of the Modi government, Hindu nationalists penetrated Gujarati society so deeply that they came to form a state deeper than the official one, while connected to it, and a control system that was well entrenched at the societal level. This modus operandi has been replicated at the national level since 2014. It would make any return to the status quo ante difficult, even if the BJP loses elections. Only a mass movement could probably counter such a majoritarian osmosis with society.[26]

APPENDICES

Appendix A: Gujarat ministries by

Caste/Religion	1962–3 Jivraj Mehta	1963–5 Balvantrai Mehta	1965 Hitendra Desai 1	1965–7 Hitendra Desai 2	1967–71 Hitendra Desai 3	1971 Hitendra Desai 4	1972–3 Ghanshyam Oz	1973–4 Chimanbhai Patel 1	1975–6 Babubhai Patel 1
Intermediate Castes (ICs)	15.38%	3.70%	7.69%	11.76%	15.38%	20.00%	12.90%	22.73%	27.27%
Patel	15.38%	3.70%	7.69%	1.76%	15.38%	20.00%	12.90%	18.18%	27.27%
Other ICs (Maratha, Jat, etc.)	0.00%	0.00%	0.00%	0.00%	0.00%	0.00%	0.00%	4.55%	0.00%
Other Backward Classes (OBCs)	7.69%	37.04%	15.38%	11.76%	3.85%	4.00%	6.45%	9.09%	21.21%
Kshatriya-Thakor (including Koli)	3.85%	14.81%	7.69%	5.88%	0.00%	0.00%	6.45%	4.55%	9.09%
Anjana Patel (Anjana Chaudhary)	0.00%	0.00%	0.00%	0.00%	0.00%	0.00%	0.00%	0.00%	9.09%
Other OBCs (Ahir, Mer, Charan-Gadhvi, etc.)	3.85%	22.22%	7.69%	5.88%	3.85%	4.00%	0.00%	4.55%	3.03%
Unidentified OBCs	0.00%	0.00%	0.00%	0.00%	0.00%	0.00%	0.00%	0.00%	0.00%
Scheduled Castes (SCs; Dalits)	3.85%	3.70%	7.69%	11.76%	3.85%	8.00%	6.45%	4.55%	9.09%
Scheduled Tribes (STs: Tribals)	3.85%	7.41%	7.69%	11.76%	3.85%	8.00%	12.90%	9.09%	3.03%
Upper Castes (UCs)	69.23%	48.15%	61.54%	52.94%	71.15%	56.00%	54.84%	50.00%	39.39%
Brahmin	38.46%	37.04%	46.15%	41.18%	34.62%	24.00%	22.58%	13.64%	15.15%
Banya/Jain	30.77%	11.11%	15.38%	11.76%	21.15%	16.00%	19.35%	18.18%	15.15%
Rajput	0.00%	0.00%	0.00%	0.00%	9.62%	12.00%	3.23%	13.64%	6.06%
Other UCs (Sindhi, Lohana, etc.)	0.00%	0.00%	0.00%	0.00%	5.77%	4.00%	9.68%	4.55%	3.03%
Others (Muslim, Parsi, Sikh, etc.)	0.00%	0.00%	0.00%	0.00%	1.92%	4.00%	6.45%	4.55%	0.00%

caste and religion (1962–1995)

1976–7 Madhavsinh Solanki 1	*1977–80 Babubhai Patel*	*1980–5 Madhavsinh Solanki 2*	*1985 Madhavsinh Solanki 3*	*1985–9 Amarsinh Chaudhary*	*1989-90 Madhavsinh Solanki 4*	*1990-4 Chimanbhai Patel 2*	*1994 Chimanbhai Patel 3*	*1994-5 Chabbildas Mehta*
24.14%	27.27	12.12%	12.50%	23.68%	9.68%	37.62%	22.22%	18.18%
24.14%	27.27%	12.12%	12.50%	23.68%	9.68%	32.67%	18.52%	15.91%
0.00%	0.00%	0.00%	0.00%	0.00%	0.00%	4.95%	3.70%	2.27%
6.90%	12.73%	27.27%	29.17%	13.16%	22.58%	18.81%	22.22%	25.00%
0.00%	1.82%	9.09%	12.50%	5.26%	12.90%	15.84%	18.52%	15.91%
0.00%	1.82%	0.00%	0.00%	0.00%	3.23%	0.00%	0.00%	2.27%
6.90%	9.09%	18.18%	16.67%	7.89%	6.45%	2.97%	3.70%	6.82%
0.00%	0.00%	0.00%	0.00%	0.00%	0.00%	0.00%	0.00%	0.00%
13.79%	7.27%	12.12%	4.17%	13.16%	6.45%	7.92%	11.11%	9.09%
6.90%	0.00%	6.06%	8.33%	13.16%	6.45%	6.93%	3.70%	9.09%
44.83%	52.73%	30.30%	41.67%	28.95%	41.94%	27.72%	37.04%	34.09%
24.14%	20.00%	18.18%	20.83%	2.63%	16.13%	8.91%	14.81%	11.36%
6.90%	25.45%	0.00%	4.17%	13.16%	12.90%	6.93%	3.70%	6.82%
13.79%	5.45%	12.12%	16.67%	13.16%	12.90%	11.88%	18.52%	15.91%
0.00%	1.82%	0.00%	0.00%	0.00%	0.00%	0.00%	0.00%	0.00%
3.45%	0.00%	12.12%	4.17%	7.89%	12.90%	0.99%	3.70%	4.55%

Appendix B: Gujarat ministries by

Caste/Religion	*1995 Keshubhai Patel 1*	*1995–6 Suresh Mehta*	*1996–7 Shankarsinh Vaghela*	*1997–8 Dilip Parikh*	*1998–2001 Keshubhai Patel 2*
Intermediate Castes	25.00%	22.92%	25.81%	20.83%	36.49%
Patel	22.73%	18.75%	25.81%	20.83%	32.43%
Other ICs (Maratha, Jat, etc.)	2.27%	4.17%	0.00%	0.00%	4.05%
Other Backward Classes	22.73%	22.92%	16.13%	29.17%	27.03%
Kshatriya-Thakor (including Koli)	4.55%	6.25%	4.84%	16.67%	12.16%
Anjana Patel (Anjana Chaudhary)	2.27%	2.08%	1.61%	4.17%	2.70%
Other OBCs (Ahir, Mer, Charan-Gadhvi)	13.64%	12.50%	9.68%	8.33%	12.16%
Unidentified OBCs	2.27%	2.08%	0.00%	0.00%	0.00%
Scheduled Castes	11.36%	10.42%	12.90%	10.42%	4.05%
Scheduled Tribes	9.09%	6.25%	16.13%	10.42%	8.11%
Upper Castes	31.82%	37.50%	29.03%	27.08%	24.32%
Brahmin	15.91%	16.67%	3.23%	2.08%	13.51%
Bania/Jain	2.27%	6.25%	12.90%	12.50%	8.11%
Rajput	13.64%	14.58%	11.29%	10.42%	1.35%
Other UCs (Sindhi. Lohana. etc.)	0.00%	0.00%	1.61%	2.08%	1.35%
Others (Muslim. Parsi. Sikh. etc.)	0.00%	0.00%	0.00%	2.08%	0.00%

Sources: Sharik Laliwala, 'In the Hindutva heartland: Bharatiya Janata Party's superficial democratization in Gujarat', *Studies in Indian Politics*, 8, no. 2 (2020); and Christophe Jaffrelot and Sharik Laliwala, 'Elite resistance in Gujarat' (forthcoming).

caste and religion (1995–2021)

2001–2 Narendra Modi 1	*2002–7 Narendra Modi 2*	*2007–12 Narendra Modi 3*	*2012-14 Narendra Modi 4*	*2014-16 (Anandiben Patel's Ministry)*	*2016-17 (Vijay Rupani's 1st Ministry)*	*2017- 2021 (Vijay Rupani's 2nd Ministry)*
28.89%	30.43%	27.78%	40.00%	38.46%	29.63%	35.48%
28.89%	30.43%	27.78%	40.00%	38.46%	29.63%	35.48%
0.00%	0.00%	0.00%	0.00%	0.00%	0.00%	0.00%
33.33%	34.78%	38.89%	30.00%	30.77%	33.33%	32.26%
17.78%	17.39%	16.67%	16.67%	15.38%	22.22%	16.13%
4.44%	2.17%	8.33%	3.33%	7.69%	3.70%	9.68%
11.11%	15.22%	13.89%	10.00%	7.69%	7.41%	6.45%
0.00%	0.00%	0.00%	0.00%	0.00%	0.00%	0.00%
6.67%	4.35%	5.56%	3.33%	2.56%	3.70%	3.23%
13.33%	4.35%	5.56%	6.67%	7.69%	7.41%	9.68%
17.78%	26.09%	22.22%	20.00%	20.51%	25.93%	19.35%
8.89%	6.52%	5.56%	10.00%	2.56%	3.70%	3.23%
4.44%	8.70%	5.56%	0.00%	2.56%	3.70%	3.23%
4.44%	10.87%	8.33%	10.00%	15.38%	14.81%	12.90%
0.00%	0.00%	2.78%	0.00%	0.00%	3.70%	0.00%
0.00%	0.00%	0.00%	0.00%	0.00%	0.00%	0.00%

APPENDICES TO CHAPTERS 4 TO 10

To chapter 4:

Table 4.1: Sanctioned strength and vacancies in the state police of Indian states in 2012

States	*Sanctioned strength of state police*	*Actual strength of state police*	*Ratio (%)*
Andhra Pradesh	132,712	89,325	67.3
Assam	62,174	55,692	89.5
Bihar	87,314	67,964	77.8
Chhattisgarh	62,836	47,628	75.8
Gujarat	103,545	57,889	55.9
Haryana	61,584	41,018	66.6
Himachal Pradesh	17,185	14,676	85.4
Jharkhand	73,270	55,403	75.6
Karnataka	90,722	79,226	87.3
Kerala	50,375	46,226	91.7
Madhya Pradesh	83,665	76,506	91.4
Maharashtra	181,803	134,696	74
Orissa	55,073	45,976	83.4
Punjab	79,446	72,063	90.7
Rajasthan	84,059	76,454	90.9
Tamil Nadu	112,363	95,745	85.2
Uttar Pradesh	368,618	173,341	47
West Bengal	77,047	55,159	71.6
All India	2,121,596	1,585,117	74.1

Source: Bureau of Police Research and Development, *Data on Police Organisation in India as on 1 January 2012*, New Delhi, 2012, p. 38.

Table 4.2: Vacancies in High Courts in 2012

Name of High Court	*Sanctioned strength*	*Working strength*	*Vacancies*	*Ratio (Vacancies/ sanctioned strength)*
Allahabad	160	75	85	53
Andhra Pradesh	49	32	17	34.7
Bombay	75	60	15	20
Calcutta	58	37	21	36.2
Chhattisgarh	18	12	6	33.3
Delhi	48	36	12	25
Gauhati	24	23	1	4.2
Gujarat	42	28	14	33.3
Himachal Pradesh	11	11	0	0
Jammu & Kashmir	14	7	7	50
Jharkhand	20	12	8	40
Karnataka	50	40	10	20
Kerala	38	34	4	10.5
Madhya Pradesh	43	34	9	20.1
Madras	60	54	6	10
Orissa	22	15	7	31.8
Patna	43	37	6	13.9
Punjab & Haryana	68	42	26	38.2
Rajasthan	40	27	13	32.5
Sikkim	3	2	1	33.3
Uttarakhand	9	8	1	1.1
Total	895	626	269	30

Source: *Court News*, vol. VII, no. 1 (Jan.–March 2012), p. 3, http://supremecourtofindia.nic.in/courtnews/2012_issue_1.pdf (last accessed 4 Dec. 2013).

Table 4.3: Crimes in Gujarat (2001–11)

Year	*Murder*	*Dacoity*	*Riots*	*Arson*
2001	1,226	327	1,930	449
2002	1,532	804	3,665	1,915
2003	1,114	338	1,824	516
2004	1,113	360	1,599	388
2005	1,033	282	1,628	320
2006	1,165	290	1,534	321
2007	1,166	245	1,668	330
2008	1,106	256	1,809	362
2009	1,020	246	1,539	240
2010	1,048	186	1,623	260
2011	1,126	221	1,615	263

Source: Milan Vaishnav, *Database on State Level Governance in India*, Washington, DC, Carnegie Endowment for International Peace, 2013.

Table 4.4: Incidence of total cognisable crimes in 2006–11 in Gujarat

Year	*2006*	*2007*	*2008*	*2009*	*2010*	*Quinquennial average 2006–10*	*2011*
Gujarat	120,972	123,195	123,808	115,183	116,439	119,919	123,371

Source: National Crime Records Bureau, *Crime in India, 2011: Statistics*, New Delhi, Ministry of Home Affairs, 2011, p. 198, http://ncrb.nic.in/CD-CII2011/Statistics2011.pdf (last accessed 4 Dec. 2013).

Table 4.5: Incidence of cognisable crimes in states in 2011

States	*Quinquennial average 2006–10*	*Population*	*Ratio QA/ Population*
Andhra Pradesh	178,030	84,655,533	0.0021
Assam	51,854	31,169,272	0.0016
Bihar	116,628	103,804,637	0.0011
Chhattisgarh	49,758	25,540,196	0.0019
Gujarat	119,919	60,383,628	0.0019
Haryana	54,560	25,353,081	0.0021
Himachal Pradesh	13,531	6,856,509	0.0019
Jammu & Kashmir	21,606	12,548,926	0.0017
Jharkhand	37,973	32,966,238	0.0011
Karnataka	128,444	61,130,704	0.0021
Kerala	118,217	33,387,677	0.0035
Madhya Pradesh	205,137	72,597,565	0.0028
Maharashtra	200,301	112,372,972	0.0017
Orissa	55,324	41,947,358	0.0013
Punjab	35,074	27,704,236	0.0012
Rajasthan	154,312	68,621,012	0.0022
Tamil Nadu	171,786	72,138,958	0.0023
Uttar Pradesh	158,664	199,581,477	0.0007
Uttarakhand	8,982	10,116,752	0.0008
West Bengal	99,445	91,347,736	0.0018
Total India*	2,061,504	1,210,193,422	0.0017

Source: National Crime Records Bureau, Crime in India, 2011: Statistics, New Delhi, Ministry of Home Affairs, 2011, p. 198, http://ncrb.nic.in/CD-CII2011/Statistics2011.pdf.

Appendices to chapter 5:

Table 5.1: Vibrant Gujarat, proposed and actual investments (Rs)

Vibrant Gujarat	*MoUs announced*	*Proposed investments*	*Actual investments*	*%*
2003	5	66,068	37,746	57.13
2005	22	106,160	37,940	35.74
2007	152	465,309	1,07,897	23.19
2009	8,860	1,239,562	1,04,490	8.43
2011	8,380	2,083,047	29,815	1.43

Source: *Socio-economic Review 2011–12*, Government of Gujarat, 2012, http://financedepartment.gujarat.gov.in/budget12_13_pdf/34_Socio_Economic_Review_English.pdf.

Table 5.2: Growth rate of different states at different periods

Period	*1982/3–1991/2*	*1992/3–2001/2*	*2002/3–2011/12*	*2006/7–2012/13*
Gujarat	3.67	7.41	10.28	9.34
Maharashtra	5.80	6.39	9.90	10.34
Andhra	5.36	5.41	8.23	9.18
Tamil Nadu	4.88	5.76	8.92	9.42
Karnataka	5.67	6.21	8.39	8.72
West Bengal	5.36	6.42	6.75	7.46

Source: Sonali Ranade and Shaelja Sharma, 'Can Gujarat's growth be attributed to Modi?', Rediff News, 25 July 2012, http://www.rediff.com/money/column/can-gujarats-growth-story-be-attributed-to-modi-column/20120725.htm.

Table 5.3: Growth of the net state domestic product at constant (2004/5) prices

State	*2005/6*	*2006/7*	*2007/8*	*2008/9*	*2009/10*	*2010/11*	*2011/ 2012*
Andhra	9.74	10.72	11.50	7.16	3.90	9.63	7.77
Assam	3.01	4.52	4.27	5.96	9.21	8.13	6.43
Bihar	–0.43	16.73	5.36	12.59	6.71	11.02	13.26
Chhattisgarh	1.63	19.02	8.08	6.56	2.78	8.79	6.71
Gujarat	14.52 n° 1	8.46 n° 13	11.82 n° 4	4.27 n° 17	14.13 n° 2	10.90 n° 4	8.34 n° 6
Haryana	9.03	11.37	7.83	7.70	12.49	9.26	8.16
Himachal Pradesh	8.59	7.87	6.22	4.88	5.43	8.70	6.56
J&K	4.63	5.84	6.18	6.26	4.85	6.53	6.11
Jharkhand	–4.48	1.68	22.28	–4.02	9.91	9.08	9.29
Karnataka	10.29	10.40	12.55	7.11	0.03	9.28	5.75
Kerala	10.24	7.90	8.92	6.15	9.04	8.35	9.85
Madhya Pradesh	5.04	9.12	4.73	12.64	9.85	6.76	12.19
Maharashtra	14.49	13.77	11.64	1.57	9.50	11.83	10.21
Orissa	4.44	12.45	8.58	7.52	0.80	5.89	2.43
Punjab	4.90	10.78	8.66	5.54	6.39	6.49	5.58
Rajasthan	6.72	11.77	4.56	8.41	5.83	15.53	6.09
Tamil Nadu	14.43	15.66	6.26	4.66	9.94	9.74	7.39
Uttar Pradesh	5.84	7.94	6.41	7.60	6.22	7.92	6.85
Uttarakhand	14.18	12.05	17.48	10.65	17.11	9.86	5.23
West Bengal	6.30	7.85	7.78	4.03	7.77	9.40	6.77
India	9.45	9.53	9.13	6.36	8.25	9.28	5.82

Source: Planning Commission, Data for use of Deputy Chairman, 3 May 2013, p. 137, http://planningcommission.nic.in/data/datatable/0205/databook_comp0205.pdf.

Table 5.4: Per capita net state domestic product at constant (2004/5) prices (Rs) and its growth rate (%)

State	*2004/5*	*2005/6*	*2006/7*	*2007/8*	*2008/9*	*2009/10*	*2010/11*	*2011/12*
Andhra Pradesh	25,321	27,486	30,114	33,239	35,272	36,303	39,434	42,119
		8.55	9.56	10.38	6.12	2.92	8.63	6.81
Assam	16,782	17,050	17,579	18,089	18,922	20,406	21,793	22,910
		1.59	3.11	2.90	4.61	7.84	6.80	5.13
Bihar	7,914	7,749	8,900	9,233	10,241	10,771	11,792	13,178
		–2.09	14.86	3.74	10.92	5.18	9.48	11.75
Chhattisgarh	18,559	18,530	21,580	22,929	23,926	24,189	25,788	26,979
		–0.16	16.46	6.25	4.35	1.10	6.61	4.62
Gujarat	32021	36,102	38,568	42,498	43,685	49,168	53,789	57,508
		n° 3	n° 4	n° 3	n° 3	n°3	n° 3	n° 3
		12.75	6.83	10.19	2.79	12.55	9.40	6.91
		n° 2	n° 14	n° 5	n° 17	n° 2	n° 4	n° 6
Haryana	37,972	40,627	44,423	47,046	49,780	55,044	59,140	62,927
		6.99	9.34	5.90	5.81	10.57	7.44	6.40
Himachal Pradesh	33,348	35,806	38,195	40,143	41,666	43,492	46,821	48,923
		7.37	6.67	5.10	3.79	4.38	7.65	4.49
Jammu & Kashmir	21,734	22,406	23,375	24,470	25,641	26,519	27,881	29,215
		3.09	4.32	4.68	4.79	3.42	5.14	4.78
Jharkhand	18,510	17,406	17,427	20,996	19,867	21,534	23,168	24,974
		–5.96	0.12	20.48	–5.38	8.39	7.59	7.80
Karnataka	26,882	29,295	31,967	35,574	37,687	37,297	40,332	42,218
		8.98	9.12	11.28	5.94	–1.03	8.14	4.68
Kerala	31,871	34,837	37,284	40,288	42,433	45,921	49,391	53,877
		9.31	7.02	8.06	5.32	8.22	7.56	9.08
Madhya Pradesh	15,442	15,927	17,073	17,572	19,462	21,029	22,091	24,395
		3.14	7.19	.93	10.76	8.05	5.05	10.43
Maharashtra	36,077	40,671	45,582	50,138	50,138	54,166	59,735	64,951
		12.74	12.07	9.99	0.09	7.94	10.28	8.73
Orissa	17,650	18,194	20,194	21,640	22,963	22,846	23,875	24,134
		3.08	10.99	7.16	6.11	–0.51	4.50	1.08

State	*2004/5*	*2005/6*	*2006/7*	*2007/8*	*2008/9*	*2009/10*	*2010/11*	*2011/12*
Punjab	33,103	34,096	37,087	39,567	41,003	42,831	44,783	46,422
		3.00	8.77	6.69	3.63	4.46	4.56	3.66
Rajasthan	18,565	19,445	21,342	21,922	23,356	24,304	27,625	28,851
		4.74	9.76	2.72	6.54	4.06	13.66	4.44
Tamil Nadu	30,062	34,126	39,166	41,314	42,936	46,886	51,117	54,550
		13.52	14.77	5.48	3.93	9.20	9.02	6.72
Uttar Pradesh	12,950	13,445	14,241	14,875	15,713	16,390	17,378	18,249
		3.82	5.93	4.45	5.63	4.31	6.02	5.02
Uttarakhand	24,726	27,781	30,644	35,444	36,621	44,557	48,240	50,045
		12.36	10.30	15.67	8.96	15.37	8.27	3.74
West Bengal	22,649	23,808	25,400	27,094	27,914	29,799	32,299	34,166
		5.12	6.69	6.67	3.03	6.75	8.39	5.78
India	24,143	26,015	28,067	30,332	31,754	33,901	36,342	38,037
		7.75	7.89	8.07	4.69	6.76	7.20	4.66

Source: Reserve Bank of India, http://dbie.rbi.org.in/DBIE/dbie.rbi?site=statistics.

Appendices to chapter 6:

Table 6.1: Average wages of casual workers and unemployment rates in urban and rural areas in some Indian states in 2011

States	*Average daily wages of casual labourers aged 15–59 (Rs)*		*Unemployment rate (per 1,000)*	
	Urban (other than public works)	*Rural (engaged in public works other than MGNREG)*	*Urban*	*Rural*
Kerala	309.90	147.49	123	169
Himachal Pradesh	167.23	127.40	36	22
J&K	210.47	154.44	84	61
Haryana	204.46	128.27	44	46
Rajasthan	173.67	116.84	52	35
Punjab	187.95	_	43	52
Andhra	178.34	108.80	64	52
Tamil Nadu	208.34	94.73	68	111
Uttarakhand	170.41	148.76	71	51
Chhattisgarh	106.16	109	89	48
Maharashtra	154.62	142.92	37	42
Uttar Pradesh	143.20	132.01	61	51
Karnataka	174.05	135.51	41	34
Bihar	157.33	133.23	74	48
Assam	155.38	171.43	60	54
Gujarat	144.52	130	16	29
India	170.10	121.46	55	57

Source: Based on *Key Indicators of Employment and Unemployment in India*, National Sample Survey, 2011, pp. 66, 102 and 103, http://www.indiaenvironmentportal.org.in/files/file/key%20indicators%20of%20employment%20and%20unemployment%20India%202011-12.pdf.

Table 6.2: Literacy rate and gender gap in literacy in Gujarat (1961–2011)

Years	*1961*	*1971*	*1981*	*1991*	*2001*	*2011*
Total	39.33	45.22	53.30	61.29	69.14	79.31
Males	53	58.16	66.36	73.13	79.66	87.23
Females	24.73	31.32	39.42	48.64	57.80	70.73
Gender gap	28.28	26.84	26.94	24.49	21.87	16.50

Source: Manish Bharadwaj, Director of Census Operation, Census of India, 2011: Provisional population totals, Paper 2, vol. 1 of 2011, Gandhinagar, 2011, p. 41.

*Table 6.3: Expenditure on education as proportion of aggregate expenditure**

Year	*2000/ 1*	*2001/ 2*	*2002/ 3*	*2003/ 4*	*2004/ 5*	*2005/ 6*	*2006/ 7*	*2007/ 8*	*2008/ 9*	*2009/ 10*	*2010/ 11*	*2011/- 12*	*2012/ 13*	*Average*
Andhra	13.3	12.5	11.7	11.6	9.8	11.1	10.8	9.0	9.0	10.0	12.5	14.0	13.6	11.45
Assam	25.5	21.9	22.4	22.3	17.0	20.8	20.4	20.1	18.8	16.4	22.0	18.7	21.1	20.56
Bihar	23.7	20.7	18.4	18.9	15.8	19.6	19.7	17.6	18.5	18.1	16.3	16.6	19.5	17.22
Chhattisgarh	13.1	12.4	11.0	10.8	12.3	13.4	12.9	13.5	14.4	15.6	18.6	19.0	17.8	14.21
Goa	11.9	10.5	12.0	12.1	13.9	12.3	13.7	12.3	13.3	14.1	15.4	16.6	15.4	13.34
Gujarat	13.6	12.7	13.5	11.2	11.5	12.6	12.7	13.4	11.7	13.8	15.9	16.1	13.4	13.22
Haryana	14.6	13.8	13.7	10.2	11.6	13.4	11.9	12.9	15.0	16.3	17.3	16.6	18.3	14.27
HP	17.0	16.2	14.5	12.4	13.5	14.1	14.1	15.4	16.2	16.3	17.9	18.8	17.5	14.69
J&K	11.1	11.6	10.9	11.1	9.7	9.3	10.0	9.2	10.0	11.3	12.6	13.4	13.0	11.01
Jharkhand	-	16.2	19	14.2	14.9	15.8	15.2	15.1	18.6	15.4	15.8	17.0	17.0	16.18
Karnataka	17.7	16.0	14.8	12.9	12.7	14.0	13.1	14.4	16.1	14.0	15.6	15.5	14.8	14.73
Kerala	20.0	19.0	17.6	15.7	16.2	16.6	17.1	15.9	16.7	16.8	17.0	17.6	17.0	17.16
MP	16.3	12.5	12.2	9.9	8.8	10.2	12.4	11.1	12.8	13.0	14.2	13.3	14.8	12.42
Maharashtra	22.3	22.1	18.9	15.5	14.0	15.7	16.4	17.2	17.0	19.1	20.8	19.9	19.8	18.36

Year	2000/1	2001/2	2002/3	2003/4	2004/5	2005/6	2006/7	2007/8	2008/9	2009/10	2010/11	2011/-12	2012/13	Average
Orissa	15.9	14.6	14.3	12.2	12.6	14.7	12.8	14.3	16.9	18.2	18.3	16.9	15.7	15.18
Punjab	13.2	11.7	12.1	10.2	10.1	11.3	8.9	10.3	11.3	12.2	11.7	15.6	14.2	11.75
Rajasthan	18.8	18.2	15.5	14.1	13.8	17.2	15.6	14.6	17.9	19.0	19.1	18.0	18.5	16.94
Tamil Nadu	18.0	17.3	13.8	12.6	11.2	13.6	12.2	12.7	13.1	15.2	15.2	14.5	15.0	14.18
UP	16.8	16.0	14.6	9.1	12.5	15.2	14.7	14.1	13.2	13.8	16.1	17.4	17.6	14.73
Uttarakhand	21.5	21.1	20.0	17.6	18.4	17.2	18.1	17.6	18.2	22.6	23.5	18.2	20.8	19.6
West Bengal	17.1	16.2	15.9	11.8	14.9	13.7	15.2	15.2	13.1	17.7	19.7	19.4	17.8	15.97
India¶	17.4	16.2	15.1	12.6	12.7	14.2	14.0	13.8	14.3	15.3	16.6	16.6	16.5	15.02

Includes expenditure on sports, art and culture under revenue expenditure and capital outlay.

¶ Including seven other states and Union territories.

Source: Budget Documents of the State Governments, State Finance Accounts.

Table 6.4: Poverty reduction in nine Indian states between 2004/5 and 2009/10

State	*2004/5*	*2009/10*	*% reduction in BPL population*
Orissa	57.2	37	20.2
Maharashtra	38.2	24.5	13.7
Tamil Nadu	29.4	17.1	12.3
Madhya Pradesh	48.6	36.7	11.9
Karnataka	33.3	23.6	9.7
Rajasthan	34.4	24.8	9.6
Gujarat	31.6	23	8.6
Andhra Pradesh	29.6	21.1	8.5
West Bengal	34.2	26.7	7.5
India	37.2	29.8	7.4

Source: Planning Commission of India, 'State specific poverty lines, number and percentage of population below poverty line by states, 2004/5 & 2009/10', http://planningcommission.nic.in/data/datatable/0904/tab_45.pdf.

Table 6.5: Percentage of children aged 0–6 of normal weight in 2011

States	%
Andhra	50.04
Assam	64.47
Chhattisgarh	46.97
Gujarat	43.13
Haryana	56.09
Himachal	62.72
J&K	68.88
Jharkhand	56.43
Karnataka	48
Kerala	62.82
Madhya Pradesh	56.14
Maharashtra	62.11
Orissa	47.33
Punjab	65.15
Rajasthan	52.69
Tamil Nadu	63.53
Uttar Pradesh	47.34
India	54.16

Source: A. Kapur Mehta, A. Sheperd, S. Bhide, A. Shah and A. Kumar, *India Chronic Poverty Report*, New Delhi, Indian Institute of Public Administration, 2011, p. 84, http://www.chronicpoverty.org/uploads/publication_files/India%20Chronic%20Poverty%20Report.pdf.

Table 6.6: Infant mortality rate (by state)

States and Union territories	*2001*	*2011*	*Difference*
A & N Islands	18	23	5
Andhra Pradesh	66	43	-23
Arunachal Pradesh	39	32	-7
Assam	74	55	-19
Bihar	62	44	-18
Chandigarh	24	20	-4
Chhattisgarh	77	48	-29
D&N Haveli	58	35	-23
Daman & Diu	40	22	-18
Delhi	29	28	-1
Goa	19	11	-8
Gujarat	60 n° 25	41 n° 22	-19 n° 14
Haryana	66	44	-22
Himachal Pradesh	54	38	-16
Jammu and Kashmir	48	41	-7
Jharkhand	62	39	-23
Karnataka	58	35	-23
Kerala	11	12	1
Lakshadweep	33	24	-9
Madhya Pradesh	86	59	-27

States and Union territories	*2001*	*2011*	*Difference*
Maharashtra	45	25	-20
Manipur	20	11	-9
Meghalaya	56	52	-4
Mizoram	19	34	15
Nagaland	13	21	8
Orissa	91	57	–34
Pondicherry	22	19	–3
Punjab	52	30	–22
Rajasthan	80	52	–28
Sikkim	42	26	–16
Tamil Nadu	49	22	–27
Tripura	39	29	–10
Uttar Pradesh	83	57	–26
Uttarakhand	48	36	–12
West Bengal	51	32	–19
India	66	44	–22

Source: *SRS Bulletin*, 46, no. 1 (Dec. 2011) and *SRS Bulletin*, 47, no. 2 (Oct. 2012), http://censusindia.gov.in/vital_statistics/SRS_Bulletins/SRS_Bulletin-Oct._2012.pdf.

Table 6.7: Monthly per capita expenditures in urban and rural India, by state (1993–4–2011–12)

Year	*1993–4*			*2007–8*			*2011–12*			*Diff. 1993–4–2011–12*
Urban/Rural	*Rural*	*Urban*	*% difference*	*Rural*	*Urban*	*% difference*	*Rural*	*Urban*	*% difference*	
Haryana	385	474	23.1	1034,	1,628	57.4	2,176	3,817	75.4	52.3
Karnataka	269	423	57.2	819	1,668	103.6	1,561	3,026	93.5	36.3
Uttar Pradesh	274	389	41.9	680	1,121	64.8	1,156	2,051	77.4	35.5
West Bengal	279	474	69.9	702	1,452	106.8	1,291	2,591	100.7	30.8
Rajasthan	322	425	31.9	801	1,265	57.9	1,598	2,442	52.9	21
Gujarat	303 n° 4	454 n° 7	49.8 n° 7	875 n° 4	1,471 n° 8	68.1 n° 5	1,536 n° 9	2,581 n° 9	68 n° 7	18.2 n°9
Madhya Pradesh	252	408	61.9	634	1,190	87.7	1,152	2,058	78.6	16.7
Andhra Pradesh	289	409	41.5	816	1,550	89.9	1,754	2,685	53.1	11.6
Orissa	220	403	83.1	559	1,438	157.2	1,003	1,941	93.6	10.5
Tamil Nadu	294	438	49	834	1,410	69	1,693	2,622	54.9	5.9
Maharashtra	273	530	94	868	1,709	96.9	1,619	3,189	97	3
Assam	258	459	77.9	799	1,452	81.7	1,219	2,189	79.6	1.7

Year	*1993–4*			*2007–8*			*2011–12*			*Diff. 1993–4–2011–12*
Urban/Rural	*Rural*	*Urban*	*% difference*	*Rural*	*Urban*	*% difference*	*Rural*	*Urban*	*% difference*	
Punjab	433	511	18	1,273	1633	28.3	2,345	2,794	19.2	1.2
Kerala	390	494	26.6	1,383	1948	40.8	2,669	3,408	27.7	1.1
Bihar	218	353	61.9	598	1,080	80.6	1,127	1,507	33.7	–28.2
Jharkhand	n/a	n/a	n/a	592	1,395	135.6	1,006	2,018	100.7	n/a
Chhattisgarh	n/a	n/a	n/a	582	1,503	158.3	1,027	1,868	81.9	n/a
India	281	458	62.9	772	1,472	90.7	1,430	2,630	83.9	21

Sources: 'Key results on household consumer expenditure 1993–94, NSS 15th round', National Sample Survey, Organisation Department of Statistics, Govt. of India, March 1996; 'Household consumer expenditure in India, 2007-08', National Sample Survey Organisation, Ministry of Statistics and Programme Implementation, Govt. of India, March 2010; and National Sample Survey, 'Key indicators of household consumer expenditure in India', NSS 68th Round, July 2011–June 2012, New Delhi, Govt. of India, 2013, p. 9, http://www.indiaenvironmentportal.org.in/files/file/key%20indicators%20of%20household%20consumer%20expenditure%202011-12.pdf.

Table 6.8: Percentage of population below th

Year	*1993/4*§				*1999/2000*¶			
Urban/Rural	*Rural*	*Urban*	*Diff*°	*Total*	*Rural*	*Urban*	*Diff.*°	*Total*
Andhra Pradesh	15.92	38.33	–22.41	22.19	11.05	26.63	–15.58	15.7
Assam	45.01	7.73	37.28	40.86	40.04	7.47	32.57	36.0
Bihar	58.21	34.50	23.71	54.96	44.30	32.91	11.39	42.6
Gujarat	22.18 n° 3	27.89 n°6	–5.71 n°5	24.21 n°3	13.17 n°7	7.52 n°4	5.65 n°10	14.0 n°6
Haryana	28.02	16.38	11.64	25.05	8.37	9.99	–1.62	8.7
Himachal Pradesh	30.34	9.18	21.16	28.44	7.94	4.63	3.31	7.6
J & K	30.34	9.18	21.16	25.17	3.97	1.98	1.99	3.4
Karnataka	29.88	40.14	-10.26	33.16	17.38	25.25	–7.87	20.0
Kerala	25.76	24.55	1.21	25.43	9.38	20.27	-10.89	12.7
Madhya Pradesh	40.64	48.38	–7.74	42.52	37.06	38.44	–1.38	37.4
Maharashtra	37.93	35.15	2.78	36.86	23.72	26.81	–3.09	25.0
Orissa	49.72	41.64	8.08	48.56	48.01	42.83	5.18	47.1
Punjab	11.95	11.35	0.6	11.77	6.35	5.75	0.6	6.1
Rajasthan	26.46	30.49	–4.03	27.41	13.74	19.85	–6.11	15.2
Tamil Nadu	32.48	39.77	–7.29	35.03	20.55	22.11	–1.56	21.1
Uttar Pradesh	42.28	35.39	6.89	40.85	31.22	30.89	0.33	31.1
West Bengal	40.80	22.41	18.39	35.66	31.85	14.86	16.99	27.0
India*	37.27	32.36	4.91	35.97	27.09	23.62	3.47	26.1

° 'Diff.' refers to the difference between % of rural and % of urban people living below the poverty line.

The figures for India include other states and Union territories which have not been included in the table.

§ Source: Planning Commission, 'Press note on poverty estimates', New Delhi, Govt. of India, 20 11, http://planningcommission.nic.in/reports/genrep/Press_pov_27Jan11.pdf.

¶ Source: Planning Commission, *National Human Development Report 2001*, New Delhi, Govt. of India, 2002, p. 165.

† Source: Planning Commission, 'Review of the expert group to review the methodology for estimation of poverty', New Delhi, Govt. of India, 2009, p. 17, http://planningcommission.nic.in/reports/genrep/rep_pov.pdf.

‡ Planning Commission, 'Press note on poverty estimates, 2009–10', New Delhi, Govt. of India, 2012, p. 6, http://planningcommission.nic.in/news/press_pov1903.pdf.

** Planning Commission, 'Press note on poverty estimates, 2011–12', New Delhi, Govt. of India, 2013, p. 6, http://planningcommission.nic.in/news/pre_pov2307.pdf.

poverty line by states (1993/4 to 2011/12)

2004/5†				*2009/10*‡				*2011/12***			
Rural	*Urban*	*Diff.*°	*Total*	*Rural*	*Urban*	*Diff.*°	*Total*	*Rural*	*Urban*	*Diff.*°	*Total*
32.3	23.4	8.9	29.6	22.8	17.7	5.1	21.1	10.96	5.81	5.15	9.20
36.4	21.8	14.6	34.4	39.9	26.1	13.8	37.9	33.89	20.49	13.4	31.98
55.7	43.7	12	54.4	55.3	39.4	15.9	53.5	34.06	31.23	2.83	33.74
39.1 n°11	20.1 n°6	19 n°13	31.6 n°8	26.7 n°10	17.9 n°5	8.8 n°11	23.0 n°8	21.54 n°9	10.14 n°8	11.4 n°13	16.63 n°9
24.8	22.4	2.4	24.1	18.6	23.0	–4.4	20.1	11.64	10.28	1.36	11.16
25	4.6	20.4	22.9	9.1	12.6	–3.5	9.5	8.48	4.33	4.15	8.08
14.1	10.4	3.7	13.1	8.1	12.8	–4.7	9.4	11.54	7.20	4.34	10.35
37.5	25.9	11.6	33.3	26.1	19.6	6.5	23.6	24.53	15.25	9.28	20.91
20.2	18.4	1.8	19.6	12.0	12.1	-0.1	12.0	9.14	4.97	4.17	7.05
53.6	35.1	18.5	48.6	42.0	22.9	19.1	36.7	35.74	21.00	14.74	31.65
47.9	25.6	22.3	38.2	29.5	18.3	11.2	24.5	24.22	9.12	15.1	17.35
60.8	37.6	23.2	57.2	39.2	25.9	13.3	37.0	35.69	17.29	18.4	32.59
22.1	18.7	3.4	20.9	14.6	18.1	–3.5	15.9	7.66	9.24	–1.58	8.26
35.8	29.7	6.1	34.4	26.4	19.9	6.5	24.8	16.05	10.69	5.36	14.71
37.5	19.7	17.8	29.4	21.2	12.8	8.4	17.1	15.83	6.54	0.29	11.28
42.7	34.1	8.6	40.9	19.8	31.7	–11.9	37.7	30.40	26.06	4.34	29.43
38.2	24.4	13.8	34.2	28.8	22.0	6.8	26.7	22.52	14.66	7.86	19.98
42.0	25.5	16.5	37.20	33.8	20.9	12.9	29.8	25.70	13.70	12	21.92

Appendices to chapter 9:

Table 9.1: Trends in vote shares and seats won of BJP, Congress and others during the Gujarat state elections (1980–2012)

Parties	*1980*	*1985*	*1990*	*1995*	*1998*	*2002*	*2007*	*2012*
BJP	14 % 9	15 % 11	26.7% 67	42.5% 121	44.8 % 117	49.8 % 127	49 % 117	48 % 115
Congress	51 % 141	55.6 % 149	30.7% 33	32.9 % 45	34.8 % 53	39.3 % 51	38 % 59	39 % 60
Others	35 % 32	29.4 % 22	42.6% 82	24.6 % 16	20.4 % 12	10.9 % 4	13 % 6	13% 7

Source: Srijit Mishra, 'Gujarat elections 2002. Vote share across regions', *Economic and Political Weekly*, 3 May 2003, p. 1804; and Election Commission of India statistical report of 2012 Gujarat Assembly election, http://eci.nic.in/eci_main/StatisticalReports/SE_2012/Reports_Index%20Card_ECIApplication_GujaratState_CEO.pdf.

Table 9.6: Percentage of urban population in Gujarat and in India (1961–2011)

Year	*1961*	*1971*	*1981*	*1991*	*2001*	*2011*
Gujarat	25.77	28.08	31.10	34.49	37.36	42.58
India	17.97	19.91	23.08	25.49	27.81	31.16

Source: Manish Bharadwaj, Director of Census Operation, *Census of India, 2011*, Provisional population totals, Paper 2, vol. 1 of 2011, Gandhinagar, 2011, p. 14.

Appendices to chapter 10:

Table 10.1: Current attendance rates of Hindus and Muslims of Gujarat in education institutions for different age groups (%)

Age groups	*5–14*	*15–19*	*20–24*
Hindus	81.4	42	9.3
Muslims	78.7	32.5	1.32

Source: National Sample Survey Office, *Employment and Unemployment Situation among the Religious Groups in India: NSS 66th round, July 2009–June 2010*, New Delhi, Govt. of India, 2010, pp. 70–1, http://mospi.nic.in/mospi_new/upload/nss_report_552.pdf.

Table 10.2: Distribution of households of Hindus and Muslims by size of landholdings in Gujarat

Size of households (ha)	*0*	*0.001–0.004*	*0.005–0.40*	*0.41–1.00*	*1.01–2.00*	*2.01–4.00*	*4.01 and above*	*Total*
Muslims	8.9	20.4	41.1	1.15	8.6	2.6	6.9	100
Hindus	5.1	16	34.4	20.8	7.5	10	6.2	100

Source: National Sample Survey Office, *Employment and Unemployment Situation among the Religious Groups in India: NSS 66th round, July 2009–June 2010*, New Delhi, Govt. of India, 2010, pp. 70–1, http://mospi.nic.in/mospi_new/upload/nss_report_552.pdf.

NOTES

INTRODUCTION

1. See the section entitled 'Gujarat, a laboratory for Hindu nationalism', in Christophe Jaffrelot, 'The BJP at the Centre: a central and centrist party?', in T.B. Hansen and Christophe Jaffrelot (eds), *The BJP and the Compulsions of Politics in India*, Delhi, Oxford University Press, 2001, pp. 356–63.
2. H. Spodek, 'In the Hindutva laboratory: pogroms and politics in Gujarat', *Modern Asian Studies*, 44, no. 2 (March 2010).
3. Cited in T.T. Kumar, 'Where entrepreneurship is almost a religion', *Hindu BusinessLine*, 25 May 2013, p. 6.
4. Achyut Yagnik and Suchitra Sheth, *The Shaping of Modern Gujarat*, New Delhi, Penguin, 2005, p. 21.
5. Harald Tambs-Lyche, *Power, Profit, Poetry: Traditional Society in Kathiawar, Western India*, New Delhi, Manohar, 1997.
6. See Pravin Sheth and Ramesh Menon, *Caste and Communal Time-Bomb*, Ahmedabad, Golwala Publications, 1986, p. 119.
7. Harald Tambs-Lyche, 'Reflections on caste in Gujarat', in Edward Simpson and Aparna Kapadia (eds), *The Idea of Gujarat: History, Ethnography and Text*, Hyderabad, Orient Blackswan, 2010, p. 101.
8. Of the 562 states recognised by the 1935 Government of India Act, 323 were in what is today Gujarat. See Nagindas Sanghavi, 'From Navnirman to the anti-Mandal riots: the political trajectory of Gujarat (1974–1985)', in Nalin Mehta and Mona G. Mehta (eds), *Gujarat beyond Gandhi: Identity, Society and Conflict*, London, Routledge, 2012, p. 15.

9. A.M. Shah and I.P. Desai, *Division and Hierarchy: An Overview of Caste in Gujarat*, Delhi, Hindustan, 1988.
10. David F. Pocock, *Kanbi and Patidar: A Study of the Patidar Community of Gujarat*, London, Oxford University Press, 1972.
11. Tambs-Lyche, 'Reflections on caste in Gujarat', p. 105.
12. Ibid., p. 109.
13. R.B. Williams, *A New Face of Hinduism: The Swaminarayan Religion*, Cambridge, Cambridge University Press, 1984.
14. Hanna H. Kim, 'The Swaminarayan movement and religious subjectivity', in Edward Simpson and Aparna Kapadia (eds), *The Idea of Gujarat: History, Ethnography and Text*, Hyderabad, Orient Blackswan, 2010, p. 209.
15. Edward Simpson, 'The parable of the Jakhs', in Edward Simpson and Aparna Kapadia (eds), *The Idea of Gujarat: History, Ethnography and Text*, Hyderabad, Orient Blackswan, 2010, p. 18.
16. J.J. Roy Burman, *Gujarat Unknown: Hindu–Muslim Syncretism and Humanistic Forays*, New Delhi, Mittal Publications, 2005.
17. Yagnik and Sheth, *The Shaping of Modern Gujarat*, p. 40.
18. Ibid., p. 47.
19. Samira Sheikh, *Forging a Region: Sultans, Traders, and Pilgrims in Gujarat, 1200–1500*, Delhi, Oxford University Press, 2010.
20. Yagnik and Sheth, *The Shaping of Modern Gujarat*, pp. 50–1.
21. The Maul-e-Salaam Garasiyas, a religious sect at the interface of Islam and Hinduism, is a fascinating symbol of this cultural synthesis. 'Maul-e-Salaam Garasiyas of Gujarat creates a happy synthesis of their own', *India Today*, 31 Dec. 1990, https://www.indiatoday.in/magazine/religion/story/19901231-maul-e-salaam-garasiyas-of-gujarat-creates-a-happy-synthesis-of-their-own-813455-1990-12-30.
22. On the emergence of the Gujarati regional identity, see Sudhir Chandra, 'Regional consciousness in 19th century India: a preliminary note', *Economic and Political Weekly* [henceforth *EPW*], 17, no. 32 (7 Aug. 1982), pp. 1278–85.
23. Yashachandra Sitansu, 'Towards Hind Svaraj: an interpretation of the rise of prose in nineteenth-century Gujarati literature', *Social Scientist*, 23, nos. 10–12 (Oct.–Dec. 1995); Riho Isaka, 'Gujarati intellectuals and history writing in the colonial period', *EPW*, 37, no. 48 (30 Nov.–6 Dec. 2002), pp. 4867–72; and Riho Isaka, 'Language

and dominance: the debates over the Gujarati language in the late nineteenth century', *South Asia: Journal of South Asia Studies*, 25, no. 1 (April 2002), pp. 1–19.

24. Interestingly, while these authors codified the Gujarati *asmita* by referring to the Hindu high tradition of the upper castes, in Saurashtra the most popular poet remained Jhaverchand Meghani, who showed great respect for popular forms of Hinduism, including the shakta cults. I am grateful to Harald Tambs-Lyche for this observation.
25. Cited in Yagnik and Sheth, *The Shaping of Modern Gujarat*, p. 201.
26. Mehta and Mehta, *Gujarat beyond Gandhi*, p. 4.
27. Ghanshyam Shah, 'Colonial modernity and construction of community', in Jan Breman and Ghanshyam Shah, *Gujarat, Cradle and Harbinger of Identity Politics: India's Injurious Frame of Communalism*, New Delhi, Tulika Books, 2022, p. 13.
28. Yagnik and Sheth, *The Shaping of Modern Gujarat*, p. 202.
29. As Ganesh Devy points out, 'You do not become a bad man in Gujarat if you hate Muslims; you are normal. Decent people hate Muslims.' Cited in 'Hating Muslims is a natural thing in Gujarat', *Tehelka*, 20 May 2006. See http://archive.tehelka.com/story_main18.asp?filename=Ne052006view_point_CS.asp (last accessed 5 Dec. 2013).
30. As Nagindas Sanghavi points out, 'Four major attempts to establish and nurture regional outfits have failed to flower for any length of time. MahaGujarat Janata Parishad was formed by Indulal Yagnik in 1955 [*sic*] to demand a linguistic state of Gujarat and it showed its strength in the 1957 elections. But it withered away after 1960. The Kisan Mazdoor Lok Party (KIMLOP) was organized by Chimanbhai Patel after he was thrown out of the Congress (R) in 1974 and it captured 12 seats in the Assembly elections of 1975. It was the supporting prop for the Janata Morcha ministry of Babubhai Patel (1975–1976) but it died of its own ambitions in 1976. Ratubhai Adani's Rashtriya Congress (1982) was a stillborn baby and never took wings. Chimanbhai Patel's Janta Dal (G) was no party at all as it was floated with no other purpose except to get the support of the Congress. The Rashtriya Janata Party of Shankarsinh Vaghela (1997) split the Gujarat BJP and toppled its government. It formed its ministry in 1997 and ruled Gujarat for a year. But it was given

a mortal blow by the voters in 1998 and disappeared in 1999.' Sanghavi, 'From Navnirnam to the anti-Mandal riots', p. 15.

31. Parvis Ghassem-Fachandi, *Pogrom in Gujarat: Hindu Nationalism and Anti-Muslim Violence in India*, Princeton, NJ, Princeton University Press, 2012, p. 132.
32. K.S. Shekhar, 'When a Gujarat chief minister was shot dead by Pakistani fighter pilot', *India Today*, 10 Nov. 2017, https://www.indiatoday.in/india/story/gujarat-chief-minister-balwantrai-mehta-pakistani-fighter-pilot-1083749-2017-11-10.
33. This section draws from Christophe Jaffrelot, 'The invention of an ethnic nationalism', in Christophe Jaffrelot (ed.), *Hindu Nationalism: A Reader*, Princeton, NJ, Princeton University Press, 2007, pp. 3–26.
34. On the Arya Samaj, the best source remains K. Jones, *Arya Dharm: Hindu Consciousness in 19th-century Punjab,* Berkeley, University of California Press, 1976.
35. Richard Gordon, 'The Hindu Mahasabha and the Indian National Congress, 1915 to 1926', *Modern Asian Studies*, 9, no. 2 (1975).
36. On the Hindu nationalist (use of the) fear of the Muslims, see Dibyesh Anand, *Hindu Nationalism in India and the Politics of Fear*, New York, Palgrave, 2011.
37. For a detailed analysis of this process, see Christophe Jaffrelot, *Hindu Nationalism and Indian Politics*, London, Hurst, 1996.
38. Vinayak Damodar Savarkar, *Hindutva: Who is a Hindu?*, New Delhi, Bharatiya Sahitya Sadan, 1989 [1923].
39. While in England in 1906–10, Savarkar stayed at India House, a guest house founded by Shyamji Krishna Varma, a Gujarati Brahmin who had been a close disciple of Dayananda. See Dhananjay Keer, *Veer Savarkar*, Bombay, Popular Prakashan, 1988, p. 29.
40. On the Hindu nationalist 'tolerance' of the Muslims, see Peter van der Veer, *Religious Nationalism: Hindus and Muslims in India*, Berkeley, University of California Press, 1994. See also Jaffrelot, *Hindu Nationalism and Indian Politics*, ch. 1.
41. B.V. Deshpande and S.R. Ramaswamy, *Dr Hedgewar, the Epoch-maker*, Bangalore, Sahitya Sindhu, 1981.
42. J.A. Curran, *Militant Hinduism in Indian Politics: A Study of the RSS*, New York, Institute of Pacific Relations, 1951.

43. Walter Andersen and Shridhar D. Damle, *The Brotherhood in Saffron: The Rashtriya Swayamsevak Sangh and Hindu Revivalism*, New Delhi, Vistaar Publications, 1987; and Pralay Kanungo, *RSS's Tryst with Politics: From Hedgewar to Sudarshan*, Delhi, Manohar, 2000.
44. Recently, Dhirendra K. Jha has shown that, in fact, Godse had never left RSS. See Dhirendra K. Jha, *Gandhi's Assassin: The Making of Nathuram Godse and His Idea of India*, New Delhi, Penguin India, 2022.
45. Bruce Graham, *Hindu Nationalism and Indian Politics: The Origins and Development of the Bharatiya Jana Sangh*, Cambridge, Cambridge University Press, 1990; and Craig Baxter, *The Jana Sangh: A Biography of an Indian Political Party*, New Delhi, Oxford University Press, 1971.
46. Chetan Bhatt, *Hindu Nationalism: Origins, Ideologies and Modern Myths*, Oxford, Berg, 2001, ch. 7; Christophe Jaffrelot, 'The Vishva Hindu Parishad: a nationalist but mimetic attempt at federating the Hindu sects', in Vasudha Dalmia, Angelika Malinar and Martin Christof (eds), *Charisma and Canon: Essays on the Religious History of the Indian Subcontinent*, Delhi, Oxford University Press, 2001.
47. For more details, see Christophe Jaffrelot (ed.), *The Sangh Parivar: A Reader*, Delhi, Oxford University Press, 2005.
48. Krishna Jha and Dhirendra K. Jha, *Ayodhya: The Dark Night; The Secret History of Rama's Appearance in Babri Masjid*, New Delhi, HarperCollins, 2012.
49. On this 'saffron wave', see Thomas Blom Hansen, *The Saffron Wave: Democracy and Hindu Nationalism in Modern India*, Princeton, NJ, Princeton University Press, 1999.
50. Hansen and Jaffrelot, *The BJP and the Compulsions of Politics in India*.
51. Kingshuk Nag, *The NaMo Story: A Political Life*, New Delhi, Roli Books, 2013, p. 64.
52. Ministers and chief ministers need to be members of one of their state assemblies, but they can be appointed before and be elected within six months.
53. The word 'pogrom' was used by specialists of communal violence in India immediately after this mass massacre took place. See Paul Brass, 'The Gujarat pogrom of 2002' and Ashutosh Varshney, 'Understanding Gujarat violence', *Items* (New York, SSRC), 4, no. 1

(2002–3), pp. 1–2. In contrast to a riot, a pogrom is characterised by the involvement of the state (including the police) and the fact that the main casualties, in a minority, are victims of a radically asymmetric form of violence.

1. GUJARAT BEFORE MODI

1. On the importance of this item in the party's agenda, see Christophe Jaffrelot, *The Hindu Nationalist Movement and Indian Politics*, London, Hurst, 1996, pp. 169ff.
2. See the section entitled 'Mahatma Gandhi as a union leader', in Jan Breman, *The Making and Unmaking of an Industrial Working Class: Sliding down the Labour Hierarchy in Ahmedabad, India*, New Delhi, Oxford University Press, 2004, pp. 40–7.
3. Ibid., p. 217.
4. Eleanor Zelliot 'Congress and the Untouchables, 1917–1950', in Richard Sisson and Stanley Wolpert (eds), *Congress and Indian Nationalism:The Pre-independence Phase*, New Delhi, Oxford University Press, 1988, p. 186.
5. Mahatma K. Gandhi, 'The sin of untouchability', *Young India*, 19 Jan. 1921, in *The CollectedWorks of Mahatma Gandhi*, vol. XIX, Ahmedabad, Navajivan Trust, 1966, pp. 242–3.
6. Mahatma Gandhi, 'The caste system', *Young India*, 8 Dec. 1920, in *The CollectedWorks of Mahatma Gandhi*, vol. IX, Ahmedabad, Navajivan Trust, 1966, pp. 83–5.
7. Ajay Skaria, 'Homeless in Gujarat and India: on the curious love of Indulal Yagnik', in William R. Pinch (ed.), *Speaking of Peasants: Essays on Indian History and Politics in Honour of Walter Hauser*, Delhi, Manohar, 2008, p. 377.
8. Howard Spodek, *Ahmedabad: Shock City of Twentieth-century India*, Hyderabad, Orient Blackswan, 2012, p. 42.
9. Indulal Yagnik, *The Autobiography of Indulal Yagnik*, vol. 1, translated by D.N. Pathak, H. Spodek and J.R. Wood, Delhi, Manohar, 2011, p. 391.
10. Skaria, 'Homeless in Gujarat and India', pp. 358–9.
11. Ibid. On this episode, see Spodek, *Ahmedabad*, pp. 81–2.

12. Cited in Indulal Yagnik, *The Autobiography of Indulal Yagnik*, vol. 2, translated by D.N. Pathak, H. Spodek and J.R. Wood, Delhi, Manohar, 2011, p. 30.
13. Indulal Yagnik, *Gandhi as I Know Him*, Delhi, Danish Mahal, 1943, pp. 209–11.
14. For a more detailed analysis of Indulal Yagnik's political role and the other progressive faces of the Gujarat Congress, see Christophe Jaffrelot, 'The Congress in Gujarat (1917–1969): conservative face of a progressive party', in Christophe Jaffrelot (ed.), 'Political conservatism in India', *Studies in Indian Politics*, 5, no. 2 (Special Issue, Nov. 2017), pp. 248–61.
15. See the chapter entitled 'Vallabhbhai Patel builds the Congress political machine', in Howard Spodek, *Ahmedabad: Shock City of Twentieth-century India*, Hyderabad, Orient Blackswan, 2012, pp. 70–93.
16. Ibid., p. 83.
17. Beatriz Martinez-Saavedra, 'Shaping the "community": Hindu nationalist imagination in Gujarat, 1880–1950', unpublished PhD, University of Warwick, 2013, p. 131.
18. After the First World War, Indian Muslims mobilised in the Khilafat Movement in support of the deposed Ottoman Sultan, the Caliph.
19. Rafiq Zakaria, *Sardar Patel and Indian Muslims: An Analysis of His Relations with Muslims before and after India's Partition*, Bombay, Bharatiya Vidya Bhawan, 1996, p. 5.
20. Cited in Martinez-Saavedra, 'Shaping the "community"', p. 195.
21. Zakaria, *Sardar Patel and Indian Muslims*, p. 18.
22. Ghanshyam Shah, 'Freedom movement: Hindu and Hindutva nationalism', in Jan Breman and Ghanshyam Shah, *Gujarat, Cradle and Harbinger of Identity Politics: India's Injurious Frame of Communalism*, New Delhi, Tulika Books, 2022, p. 33.
23. He adds in the same letter: 'We have also, during the last six or eight months, been giving arms liberally to non-Muslim applicants.' Martinez-Saavedra, 'Shaping the "community"', p. 205.
24. *Hindustan Times*, 15 Nov. 1947, p. 6.
25. Vapal Pangunni Menon, *The Story of the Integration of the Indian States,* Bombay, Orient Longmans, 1969, p. 141.

26. Quoted in Peter van der Veer, 'Ayodhya and Somnath: eternal shrines, contested histories', *Social Research*, 59, no. 1 (Spring 1992), p. 91.
27. Mahatma Gandhi asked that the reconstruction of the Somnath temple be carried out with public subscriptions and not from government funds.
28. Letter to Gangadhar Rao, 21 Dec. 1947, in P.N. Chopra (ed.), *The Collected Works of Sardar Vallabhbhai Patel*, vol. XII, Delhi, Konark, 1998, p. 265.
29. *Hindustan Standard*, 8 Jan. 1948, pp. 1 and 8. N.V. Gadgil, one of Patel's colleagues in government, confirmed that in the late 1940s Patel regarded the RSS members as patriots. D.V. Tahmankar, *Sardar Patel*, London, George Allen and Unwin, 1970, p. 248.
30. Letter to S.P. Mookerjee, 18 July 1948, in P.N. Chopra (ed.), *The Collected Works of Sardar Vallabhbhai Patel*, vol. XIII, Delhi, Konark, 1999, p. 170.
31. 'Sardar Patel warns RSS', *Hindustan Times*, 20 Dec. 1948, cited in P.N. Chopra (ed.), *The Collected Works of Sardar Vallabhbhai Patel*, vol. XII, Delhi, Konark, 1998, p. 349.
32. Letter to V. Shastri, 16 July 1949, cited in P.N. Chopra (ed.), *The Collected Works of Sardar Vallabhbhai Patel*, vol. XII, Delhi, Konark, 1998, p. 187.
33. On this episode, see *Hitavada*, 11 Oct. 1949, p. 1, 12 Oct. 1949, p. 1, 1 Nov. 1949, p. 1, 6 Nov. 1949, p. 3, 17 Nov. 1949, p. 1, and 18 Nov. 1949, p. 1.
34. 'Sardar Patel justifies India's policy towards states and silences critics who described it as weak', *Hindustan Times*, 18 Jan. 1948, in P.N. Chopra (ed.), *The Collected Works of Sardar Vallabhbhai Patel*, vol. XIII, Delhi, Konark, p. 54.
35. Christophe Jaffrelot, 'Composite culture is not multiculturalism: a study of the Indian Constituent Assembly debates', in Ashutosh Varshney (ed.), *India and the Politics of Developing Countries: Essays in Memory of Myron Weiner*, New Delhi, Sage, 2004, pp. 126–49.
36. Bruce Graham, *Hindu Nationalism and Indian Politics: The Origins and Development of the Bharatiya Jana Sangh*, Cambridge, Cambridge University Press, 1990, p. 6.

37. Manu Bhagavan, 'The Hindutva underground: Hindu nationalism and the Indian National Congress in late colonial and early post-colonial India', *EPW*, 43, no. 37 (13 Sept. 2008), p. 41.
38. Jaffrelot, *The Hindu Nationalist Movement and Indian Politics*, pp. 98ff.
39. Rita and Abhijit Kothari, 'Past continuous: K.M. Munshi, Gujarat and the Patan trilogy', *EPW*, 56, no. 18 (1 May 2021). See the translation of the Patan trilogy by Rita and Abhijit Kothari, *The Glory of Patan*, New Delhi, Penguin Viking, 2017; *Lord and Master of Gujarat*, New Delhi, Penguin Viking, 2019; and *King of Kings*, New Delhi, Penguin Viking, 2019.
40. Skaria, 'Homeless in Gujarat and India', p. 352.
41. Meghnad Desai, 'Not a nice Gujarati to know', *Seminar*, no. 470 (Oct. 1998), p. 14.
42. The Salt March was a mass protest which, in 1931, took Gandhi and his supporters from his ashram to the sea where the Mahatma picked up some grains of salt, which led to his arrest since salt was a monopoly of the colonial state.
43. Cited in Martinez-Saavedra, 'Shaping the "community"', p. 241.
44. The guru of the RSS is the saffron flag.
45. Martinez-Saavedra, 'Shaping the "community"', p. 233.
46. Shah, 'Freedom movement', p. 33.
47. Bhagavan, 'The Hindutva underground', p. 41.
48. V.B. Kulkarni, *K.M. Munshi*, New Delhi, Govt. of India, 1983, pp. 89, 94 and 100.
49. Bhagavan, 'The Hindutva underground', p. 43.
50. For more details, see Jaffrelot, 'Composite culture is not multiculturalism', pp. 126–49.
51. Munshi apparently relied on Hindu nationalist activists to complete this mission. See Bhagavan, 'The Hindutva underground', p. 46.
52. Romila Thapar, *Somnatha: The Many Voices of a History*, London, Verso, 2005, p. 185.
53. K.M. Munshi, *Somnatha: The Shrine Eternal*, 4th edn, Bombay, 1976, p. 39.
54. Sarvepalli Gopal, *Jawaharlal Nehru: A Biography*, vol. 2, London, Jonathan Cape, 1979, p. 155.
55. Cited in Bhagavan, 'The Hindutva underground', p. 44.
56. Published by Bharatiya Vidya Bhavan.

57. K.M. Munshi, 'Preface', in C. Rajagopalachari, *Ramayana*, Bombay, Bharatiya Vidya Bhavan, 1957, p. 6.
58. K.M. Munshi, *Our Greatest Need and Other Addresses*, Bombay, Bharatiya Vidya Bhavan, 1953, p. 57.
59. Ibid., p. 43.
60. Ibid.
61. See, for instance, J.J. Roy Burman, *Gujarat Unknown: Hindu–Muslim Syncretism and Humanistic Forays*, New Delhi, Mittal Publications, 2005, pp. 33–88.
62. Howard L. Erdman, *The Swatantra Party and Indian Conservatism*, Cambridge, Cambridge University Press, 1967, p. 133.
63. K.M. Munshi, 'Wanted: an active Hindu religion', *Organiser*, Diwali Special issue, 1963.
64. N.B. Lele, 'Shri Shiv Shankar Apte', in *Shraddhanjali Smarika*, New Delhi, Vishva Hindu Parishad, n.d., pp. 26–8 (Hindi).
65. Some sources (e.g. https://www.indiainfoline.com/prime-ministers-of-india/gulzari-lal-nanda) mention that he was elected from Bombay in 1952, mistakenly. See Trilochan Singh (ed.), *Indian Parliament (1952–57)*, New Delhi, Arunam and Sheel, n.d., p. 198.
66. 'Note from secretary, Bharat Sadhu Samaj', *Report on the Hindu Endowment Commission, 1960–1962*, New Delhi, Ministry of Law, n.d., p. 510.
67. This traditional form of Indian medicine was not then officially recognised. See Paul Brass, 'The politics of Ayurvedic education: a case study of revivalism and modernization in India', in Susanne Hoeber Rudolph and Llyod Rudolph (eds), *Education and Politics in India: Studies in Organisation, Society and Policy*, New Delhi, Oxford University Press, 1972, pp. 361–2. In 1962, Nanda appointed as president of the Ayurvedic Congress a man who would later be elected an MP in 1967 with the support of the Jana Sangh, Pandit Shiv Sharma.
68. *Organiser*, 10 July 1964, p. 16.
69. Ibid., p. 1.
70. *Organiser,* 27 Nov. 1964.
71. *Organiser*, 21 June 1965, p. 1.
72. Pupul Jayakar, *Indira Gandhi: A Biography*, New Delhi, Viking, 1988, p. 184.

73. *Organiser*, 9 Jan. 1983, p. 13.
74. The circumstances of this episode are not entirely clear, but he apparently 'resigned as deputy collector of Godhra in May 1930 after being found guilty of going soft on Hindus during the riots of 1927–28 there'. Ajay Umat and Harit Mehta, 'Can Modi follow in Morarji's footsteps?', *The Times of India*, 10 Jan. 2013, http://articles.timesofindia.indiatimes.com/2013-06-10/india/39872327_1_keshubhai-patel-narendra-modi-l-k-advani (last accessed 5 Dec. 2013). Subsequently, Morarji Desai vetoed the wedding of his daughter with a Muslim classmate of hers at the medical college where she studied. She died by suicide. Indru Advani, *Sur les pas d'Indru Advani dans l'Asie en mutation*, Paris, Riveneuve, 2009, p. 103.
75. *Indian Express*, 15 May 1979. A similar law was passed in Arunachal Pradesh, a Union territory, with the blessing of the then home minister of Gujarat, H.M. Patel. Cabinet secretary under Sardar Patel in 1946–50, H.M. Patel had joined the Swatantra Party in 1959 and in 1977 was elected MP for Sabarkantha in Gujarat.
76. *National Herald*, 31 June 1977; A.R.G. Tiwari, 'A true history of India is yet to be written', *Organiser*, 23 July 1978, pp. 8–9.
77. Susanne Hoeber Rudolph and Lloyd Rudolph, 'Cultural policy, the textbooks controversy and Indian identity', in A. Jeyaratnam Wilson and Dennis Dalton (eds), *The States of South Asia*, London, Hurst, 1982, p. 139.
78. Ghanshyam Shah, 'Communal riots in Gujarat: report of a preliminary investigation', in Jan Breman and Ghanshyam Shah, *Gujarat, Cradle and Harbinger of Identity Politics: India's Injurious Frame of Communalism*, New Delhi, Tulika Books, 2022, p. 63. Shah (p. 43) also cites a Congress social worker who had told him: 'For the first time, Hindus are able to teach a lesson to Muslims.'
79. In addition to his campaigns on behalf of the labouring poor, Yagnik's popularity was mostly derived from his campaign in favour of creating a separate state of Gujarat. Neither Munshi nor Nanda nor Desai was in favour of partitioning the old Bombay province. That was another thing they shared in common with the RSS, which opposed redrawing the Indian administrative map according to linguistic criteria because of its 'dangerous potential for secession'—the fear that regionalisms would divide the nation. *Organiser*, 26 Jan. 1956, p. 5.

80. See http://www.visionjafri.org/webpages/pg_ahsanjafri.html (last accessed May 2010).
81. Breman, *The Making and Unmaking of an Industrial Working Class*, pp. 141ff.
82. The analysis that follows is based on the extremely perceptive analysis of Ghanshyam Shah, 'Polarised communities', *Seminar*, no. 470, Oct. 1998, p. 31.
83. A comprehensive study based on about 10,000 interviews in the 1980s revealed that illiteracy among Rajputs (15 per cent) was almost twice what it was among Vanyas and Brahmins. Ghanshyam Shah, 'Caste, class and reservation', *EPW*, 20, no. 3 (19 Jan. 1985).
84. Shah, 'Polarised communities', p. 31.
85. Rajni Kothari and Rushikesh Maru, 'Federating of political interests: the Kshatriyas of Gujarat', in Rajni Kothari (ed.), *Caste in Indian Politics*, New Delhi, Orient Longmans, 1986 [1970], p. 72.
86. Ghanshyam Shah, *Caste Association and Political Process in Gujarat: A Study of Gujarat Kshatriya Sabha*, Bombay, Popular Prakashan, 1975, p. 33.
87. 'I wondered why I had to work exclusively for the Rajputs. Why not work for all the members of the Kshatriya class. The Kshatriyas are a class, not a caste.' Cited in Myron Weiner, *Party Building in a New Nation: The Indian National Congress*, Chicago, University of Chicago Press, 1967, p. 97. Solanki obviously plays on the relative ambiguity of the varna system since, by contrast with *jati* (which is usually translated as 'caste'), varnas are generally presented as being more flexible and based on the criteria of socio-economic functions.
88. Lancy Lobo, 'Koli Kshatriyas of North Gujarat: a shift from Sanskritised mobility to politicised mobility', *Eastern Anthropologist*, 42, no. 2 (April–June 1989), pp. 176–7.
89. Kothari and Maru, 'Federating of political interests', p. 73.
90. Lobo, 'Koli Kshatriyas of North Gujarat', p. 188.
91. In addition, Congress leadership feared 'communalisation' of the party, and therefore declared that dual membership of a caste association and Congress was incompatible.
92. Shah, *Caste Association*, p. 127.
93. See Christophe Jaffrelot and Sharik Laliwala, 'Elite resistance in Gujarat' (forthcoming). See also John Wood, 'Congress restored?

The KHAM strategy and Congress recruitment in Gujarat', in John Wood (ed.), *State Politics in Contemporary India: Crisis or Continuity?*, Boulder, CO, Westview Press, 1985, p. 212.

94. Ghanshyam Shah, 'Caste sentiments, class formation and dominance in Gujarat', in Francine Frankel and M.S.A. Rao (eds), *Dominance and State Power in Modern India*, vol. 2, New Delhi, Oxford University Press, 1990, pp. 59–114.
95. Christophe Jaffrelot and Sharik Laliwala, 'Elite resistance in Gujarat', in Christophe Jaffrelot and Gilles Verniers (eds), *Resilient Elitism: The Changing Profile of India's Regional Assemblies* (forthcoming). See also Kiran Desai and Ghanshyam Shah, 'When Patels resist the Kshatriyas', in Christophe Jaffrelot and Sanjay Kumar (eds), *Rise of the Plebeians? The Changing Face of Indian Legislative Assemblies*, New Delhi, Routledge, 2009, p. 198.
96. Jaffrelot and Laliwala, 'Elite resistance in Gujarat'.
97. The state of Saurashtra, which had merged with Gujarat when it was created, had appointed a Backward Classes Commission in 1953, but in Kutch no list of OBCs existed.
98. Yagnik not only gave him a scholarship for covering his college fees, but he let him work in his newspaper for two years. Interview with Madhavsinh Solanki in January 2019, Gandhinagar.
99. One-third of the government was made of Kshatriyas. Ghanshyam Shah, 'Gujarat politics in the post-Emergency period', *Indian Journal of Political Science*, 55, no. 3 (July–Sept. 1994), p. 237.
100. *Report of the Socially and Educationally Backward Class Commission*, Government of Gujarat, 1976, pp. 126–7.
101. 'Darji: A poor man's Congressman', *The Times of India*, 31 Aug. 2004, http://timesofindia.indiatimes.com/articleshow/834014.cms?utm_source=contentofinterest&utm_medium=text&utm_campaign=cppst.
102. Solanki also said: 'I was also from a poor family just like Darji. He saw the exploitation of the poor people by the rich when he was working in Surat district. So wherever Jinabhai Darji went, he took up the cause of the poor people. Therefore, naturally we were on the same side.' Interview with Madhavsinh Solanki, Jan. 2019, Gandhinagar.
103. Kingshuk Nag, 'It's disadvantage Cong in South Gujarat', *The Times of India*, 27 Nov. 2002, http://articles.timesofindia.indiatimes.

com/2002-11-27/ahmedabad/27318523_1_hemant-chapatwala-naishadh-desai-tushar-chaudhary (last accessed 5 Dec. 2013).

104. Nagindas Sanghavi, 'From Navnirman to the anti-Mandal riots: the political trajectory of Gujarat (1974–1985)', in Nalin Mehta and Mona G. Mehta (eds), *Gujarat beyond Gandhi: Identity, Society and Conflict*, London, Routledge, 2012, p. 22.

105. Desai and Shah, 'When Patels resist the Kshatriyas', pp. 196 and 198.

106. Jaffrelot and Laliwala, 'Elite resistance in Gujarat'.

107. I.P. Desai, 'Anti-reservation agitation and structure of Gujarat society', in *Caste, Caste Conflict and Reservations*, New Delhi, Ajanta, 1985, pp. 124–36.

108. Ibid., p. 135; and Pradip Kumar Bose, 'Social mobility and caste violence: a study of Gujarat riots', in Desai, *Caste, Caste Conflict and Reservations*, p. 144. These attacks against Dalits could hardly have been motivated by the inroads they were making in the medical college: in 1979–80, SC and ST students accounted for only 507 out of 4,500 (instead of the 945 they should have had, according to the quotas, which were obviously not filled). Similarly, out of 742 teaching positions, 22 were held by SCs and 2 by STs, barely representing 3 per cent of their total entitlement. Desai, 'Anti-reservation agitation and structure of Gujarat society', p. 127. Similarly, in 1984, only 34 per cent of seats reserved for OBCs were effectively occupied (of a total of 10 per cent). See Upendra Baxi, 'Reflections on the reservations crisis in Gujarat', in V. Das (ed.), *Mirrors of Violence: Communities, Riots and Survivors in South Asia*, New Delhi, Oxford University Press, 1990, p. 217.

109. Christophe Jaffrelot, *India's Silent Revolution: The Rise of the Lower Castes in North India*, London: Hurst, 2003.

110. Desai, 'Anti-reservation agitation and structure of Gujarat society', pp. 135–6.

111. Pravin Sheth and Ramesh Menon, *Caste and Communal Time-Bomb*, Ahmedabad, Golwala Publications, 1986, p. 47.

112. On 'quota politics', see Jaffrelot, *India's Silent Revolution*, Part 3: 'Quota politics and Kisan politics'.

113. It is hard to know whether Solanki was serious about these reservations or whether he was only using them for electoral

purposes since no government resolution was passed to implement them. Sheth and Menon, *Caste and Communal Time-Bomb*, p. 18. See also Baxi, 'Reflections on the reservations crisis in Gujarat', pp. 215–39.

114. Jaffrelot and Laliwala, 'Elite resistance in Gujarat'.
115. Sheth and Menon, *Caste and Communal Time-Bomb*, p. 92.
116 'Vadodara: the context and a profile', p. 25, http://www.onlinevolunteers.org/gujarat/reports/pucl/vv_chapter3.pdf (last accessed 30 Oct. 2013).
117. Ornit Shani, *Communalism, Caste and Hindu Nationalism*, Cambridge, Cambridge University Press, 2007, p. 82.
118. Sheth and Menon, *Caste and Communal Time-Bomb*, p. 24.
119. Ibid., p. 27.
120. Ashok Bhatt, a BJP MLA from Ahmedabad, secured court injunctions forbidding policemen from entering some localities. But on 22 April 1985 one policeman was killed in a middle-class area of Khadia, in Bhatt's constituency. In retaliation policemen attacked and burnt the *Gujarat Samachar* office, since this paper—whose coverage of events was allegedly biased in favour of anti-reservationists—was accused of portraying the police action subjectively. It was time for the army to intervene.
121. Sheth and Menon, *Caste and Communal Time-Bomb*, p. 44.
122. Ibid., p. 22.
123. Interview with M.S. Solanki, Jan. 2019, Gandhinagar.
124. Sunita Parikh, *The Politics of Preference: Democratic Institutions and Affirmative Action in the United States and India*, Ann Arbor, MI, University of Michigan Press, 1997, p. 183.
125. Sheth and Menon, *Caste and Communal Time-Bomb*, p. 45.
126. Ibid., p. 86.
127. Shani, *Communalism, Caste and Hindu Nationalism*, p. 132.
128. Ibid., p. 123.
129. Ibid., p. 113.
130. Ibid., p. 118.
131. On the use of processions by Hindu nationalist organisation for uniting their community against the Muslims and instigating riots, see Christophe Jaffrelot, 'The politics of processions and Hindu–Muslim riots', in Atul Kohli and Amrita Basu (eds), *Community*

Conflicts and the State in India, New Delhi, Oxford University Press, 1998, pp. 58–92.

132. Sheth and Menon, *Caste and Communal Time-Bomb*, p. 59.
133. Christophe Jaffrelot and Charlotte Thomas, 'Facing ghettoisation in "riot-city": Old Ahmedabad and Juhapura between victimisation and self-help', in Laurent Gayer and Christophe Jaffrelot (eds), *Muslims in India's Cities: Trajectories of Marginalisation*, London, Hurst, 2012, pp. 43–79.
134. Shani, *Communalism, Caste and Hindu Nationalism*, p. 117.
135. Dave Commission report cited in ibid., p. 88.
136. Sheth and Menon, *Caste and Communal Time-Bomb*, pp. 151–2.
137. Swaminarayan Bliss, *BAPS Youth Activities 60th Anniversary Celebration*, March–April 2013, p. 52, www.baps.org/CreateDownloads/download.aspx (last accessed 5 Dec. 2013).
138. Chaudhary appointed a new commission, presided over by R.C. Mankad, in June 1987. But in 1990, when the Mandal Report controversy arose, the Mankad Commission had not yet submitted its report, which remained a dead letter thereafter.
139. Jaffrelot and Laliwala, 'Elite resistance in Gujarat'.
140. Ibid.
141. Walter Andersen and Shridhar D. Damle, *The Brotherhood in Saffron: The Rashtriya Swayamsevak Sangh and Hindu Revivalism*, New Delhi, Vistaar Publications, 1987, p. 38.
142. M.V. Kamath and K. Randeri, *Narendra Modi: The Architect of a Modern State*, New Delhi, Rupa, 2009, p. 21.
143. While the Maharajah of Baroda was not known for his Hindu nationalist sympathies, in 1932 he 'allowed the playing of music before mosques without providing any further explanation', whereas Hindu processions playing music outside mosques proved to be a major cause of communal riots. See Martinez-Saavedra, 'Shaping the "community"', p. 109.
144. Ibid., p. 22.
145. Arafaat A. Valiani, *Militant Publics in India: Physical Culture and Violence in the Making of a Modern Polity*, New York, Palgrave Macmillan, 2011, p. 150.
146. Achyut Yagnik and Suchitra Sheth, *The Shaping of Modern Gujarat*, New Delhi, Penguin, 2005, p. 214.

147. Ibid.
148. Martinez-Saavedra, 'Shaping the "community"', p. 115; see also pp. 130 and 133.
149. Ghanshyam Shah, 'The spread of the Hindutva gospel and electoral mobilization in the pre-Modi phase', in Jan Breman and Ghanshyam Shah, *Gujarat, Cradle and Harbinger of Identity Politics: India's Injurious Frame of Communalism*, New Delhi, Tulika Books, 2022, p. 226.
150. The notion of *samskara* plays a key role in the RSS culture. For the organisation this key concept of the Hindu civilisation designates all the good influences which can be exerted in the formation of the individual's character, especially on children—one of its meanings according to Indologists well versed in the Hindu traditions. See Lakshmi Kapani, *La notion de samskara*, vol. 1, Paris, De Boccard, 1992, p. 43; and A.K. Ramanuja's afterword to U.R. Ananthamurthy, *Samskara: A Rite for a Dead Man*, Delhi, Oxford University Press, 1992 [1976], pp. 139–47.
151. Shah, 'The spread of the Hindutva gospel', p. 228.
152. Ibid.
153. Ghanshayam Shah, 'Caste, Hindutva and hideousness', in Jan Breman and Ghanshyam Shah, *Gujarat, Cradle and Harbinger of Identity Politics: India's Injurious Frame of Communalism*, New Delhi, Tulika Books, 2022, p. 147.
154. Ibid.
155. Andersen and Damle, *Brotherhood in Saffron*, pp. 128 and 152 (n. 65).
156. Ibid., p. 171.
157. Pravin N. Sheth, 'Elections in Gujarat: the emerging pattern', in S.P. Varma and Iqbal Narain (eds), *Fourth General Election in India*, Bombay, Orient Longmans, 1968, p. 181.
158. Graham, *Hindu Nationalism and Indian Politics*, p. 158.
159. P.N. Sheth, 'Elections in Gujarat', p. 181.
160. Ghanshyam Shah, *Protest Movements in Two Indian States: A Study of the Gujarat and Bihar Movements*, New Delhi, Ajanta, 1977.
161. For more detail, see Christophe Jaffrelot and Pratinav Anil, *India's First Dictatorship: The Emergency, 1975–77*, London, Hurst; New York, Oxford University Press; New Delhi, HarperCollins, 2020.
162. David Butler, Ashok Lahiri and Prannoy Roy (eds), *India Decides. Elections 1952 – 1989*, New Delhi, Living Media India, 1989, p. 127.

163. Howard Spodek calls it a 'communal pogrom'. See Spodek, *Ahmedabad*, p. 180.
164. See Shah, 'Communal riots in Gujarat: report of a preliminary investigation', pp. 187–200; and Howard Spodek, 'From Gandhi to Modi: Ahmedabad, 1915–2007', in Edward Simpson and Aparna Kapadia (eds), *The Idea of Gujarat: History, Ethnography and Text*, Hyderabad, Orient Blackswan, 2010, p. 139.
165. Justice P. Jaganmohan Reddy, *Inquiry into the Communal Disturbances at Ahmedabad and Other Places in Gujarat on and after 18th September 1969*, Ahmedabad, Government of Gujarat, 1970, pp. 179–82.
166. Ashutosh Varshney, *Ethnic Conflict and Civic Life: Hindus and Muslims in India*, New Haven, CT, Yale University Press, 2002, ch. 10; and Violette Graff and Juliette Galonnier, 'Hindu–Muslim communal riots in India I (1947–1986)', https://www.sciencespo.fr/mass-violence-war-massacre-resistance/fr/document/hindu-muslim-communal-riots-india-i-1947-1986.html.
167. Such as 'Every Muslim is a traitor, send him to Pakistan'. Reddy, *Inquiry into the Communal Disturbances at Ahmedabad*, p. 58.
168. Ibid., pp. 151–66.
169. Megha Kumar, 'Communal riots, sexual violence and Hindu nationalism in post-independence Gujarat, 1969–2002', DPhil, University of Oxford, 2009, p. 98. This thesis has been published as Megha Kumar, *Communalism and Sexual Violence in India: The Politics of Gender, Ethnicity and Conflict*, London and New York, I.B. Tauris, 2016.
170. Ghanshyam Shah, 'The BJP's riddle in Gujarat: caste, factionalism and Hindutva', in T.B. Hansen and Christophe Jaffrelot (eds), *The BJP and the Compulsions of Politics in India*, Delhi, Oxford University Press, 2001, p. 245.
171. In between, the average number of people who died every year because of communal violence in Gujarat rose from 48.4 in 1961–70 to 63.4 in 1990. *Muslim India*, no. 81 (Sept. 1989), and no. 3 (July 1991); and Gopal Krishna, 'Communal violence in India', *EPW*, 12 Jan. 1985, p. 74.
172. Christophe Jaffrelot, 'The Hindu nationalist reinterpretation of pilgrimage in India: the limits of yatra politics', *Nations and Nationalism*, 15, no. 1 (2008), pp. 1–19.

173. Jan Breman, 'Anti-Muslim pogrom in Surat', in Jan Breman and Ghanshyam Shah, *Gujarat, Cradle and Harbinger of Identity Politics: India's Injurious Frame of Communalism*, New Delhi, Tulika Books, 2022, pp. 76–90.
174. Varshney, *Ethnic Conflict and Civic Life*, p. 97.
175. Ornit Shani, 'Bootlegging, politics and corruption: state violence and the routine practices of public power in Gujarat (1985–2002)', *South Asian History and Culture*, 1, no. 4 (2010), pp. 496–7.
176. Shah, 'Communal riots in Gujarat', p. 49.
177. Shani, 'Bootlegging, politics and corruption', p. 499.
178. Ibid.
179. Howard Spodek, 'Crises and response: Ahmedabad 2000', *EPW*, 36, no. 19 (12–18 May 2001), p. 1629.
180. Prashant Dayal, *Latif: Daarubandhi nu Arthtkarana ane Komvaad nu Rajkaran* [Latif: The Economy of Prohibition and the Politics of Communalism] Ahmedabad, Sarthak Prakashan, 2017. I am grateful to Sharik Laliwala for his translation of the sentences cited above.
181. Ibid., pp. 38–9.
182. Ornit Shani, 'The rise of Hindu nationalism in India: the case study of Ahmedabad in the 1980s', *Modern Asian Studies*, 39, no. 4 (Oct. 2005), p. 884.
183. Dayal, *Latif*, p. 26.
184. Ibid., pp. 70–1.
185. TNN, 'Latif was state BJP's first whipping boy', *The Times of India*, 12 June 2008, https://timesofindia.indiatimes.com/city/ahmedabad/latif-was-state-bjps-first-whipping-boy/articleshow/3121443.cms.
186. Cited in ibid.
187. R.B. Sreekumar, *Gujarat: Behind the Curtain*, New Delhi, Manas Publications, 2016, p. 23.
188. TNN, 'Latif was state BJP's first whipping boy'.
189. 'Throwback: when India's fifth richest man was kidnapped for ransom', ETNowNews, 14 June 2020, https://www.timesnownews.com/business-economy/companies/article/throwback-when-indias-fifth-richest-man-survived-a-kidnapping-and-terrorist-attack/606122.

190. Express News Service, 'Two accused of abducting Gautam Adani 20 years ago acquitted', *The Indian Express*, 1 Dec. 2018, https://indianexpress.com/article/cities/ahmedabad/two-accused-of-abducting-gautam-adani-20-years-ago-acquitted-5473592/.
191. Cited in Shah, 'Caste, Hindutva and hideousness', p. 145.
192. Ghanshyam Shah, 'The Dalit and Hindutva: underprivileged and communal carnage', in Jan Breman and Ghanshyam Shah, *Gujarat, Cradle and Harbinger of Identity Politics: India's Injurious Frame of Communalism*, New Delhi, Tulika Books, 2022, p. 200.
193. Ibid., p. 201.
194. Ibid.
195. Ibid., p. 203.
196. Christophe Jaffrelot and Smita Gupta, 'The Bajrang Dal: the new Hindu nationalist brigade', in Mushirul Hasan (ed.), *Living with Secularism: The Destiny of India's Muslims*, Delhi, Manohar, 2007, pp. 197–222.
197. See the section entitled 'Gujarat, a laboratory for Hindu nationalism', in Hansen and Jaffrelot, *The BJP and the Compulsions of Politics in India*, pp. 356–63.
198. Jaffrelot and Laliwala, 'Elite resistance in Gujarat'.
199. Ibid.
200. Shah, 'The BJP's riddle in Gujarat', p. 261.
201. Jaffrelot and Laliwala, 'Elite resistance in Gujarat'; see also Desai and Shah, 'When Patels resist the Kshatriyas', p. 199.
202. Sharik Laliwala, 'In the Hindutva heartland: Bharatiya Janata Party's superficial democratization in Gujarat', *Studies in Indian Politics*, 8, no. 2 (2020), p. 252.
203. Priyavadan Patel, 'Sectarian mobilization: factionalism and voting in Gujarat', *EPW*, 34, no. 34/35 (21 Aug.–3 Sept. 1999), p. 2426.
204. According to Ghanshyam Shah, 'Supporters of Keshubhai Patel, mainly Patidars, saw the entire revolt as an anti-Patidar conspiracy. Leuva-Patidars of Saurashtra and central Gujarat closed their ranks to fight back at the Kshatriya and OBC lobbies, thus recasting the traditional rivalry between Patidars and Rajput-cum-Kolis.' Shah, 'The BJP's riddle in Gujarat', p. 262.
205. Patel, 'Sectarian mobilisation', pp. 2423–33.
206. Christophe Jaffrelot, 'The BJP at the Centre: a central and centrist party?', in Thomas Blom Hansen and Christophe Jaffrelot (eds), *The*

BJP and the Compulsions of Politics in India, Delhi, Oxford University Press, 2001, pp. 315–69.

207. Its youth wing, the Bajrang Dal, also burnt copies of the New Testament that had been distributed in a school in Rajkot.
208. Cited in Kamal Mitra Chenoy (ed.), *Violence in Gujarat: Test Case for a Larger Fundamentalist Agenda*, New Delhi and Bangalore, National Alliance of Women, 1999, p. 43.
209. Ibid., p. 7.
210. Cited in *The Statesman*, 3 Feb. 1999, p. 8.
211. Chenoy, *Violence in Gujarat*, p. 6.
212. Ghanshyam Shah, 'Hate propaganda in Gujarat press and Bardoli riots', *EPW*, 33, no. 33–34, 15 Aug. 1998, p. 2218.
213. Cited in Chenoy, *Violence in Gujarat*, pp. 53–4.
214. See *Frontline*, 24 Sept. 1999, p. 87.
215. Ibid.
216. *The Hindu*, 17 March 2000, p. 8.
217. R. Das, 'In Gujarat's textbooks, minorities are foreigners', *Hindustan Times*, 25 July 1999.
218. Desai, 'Not a nice Gujarati to know', p. 16.

2. HINDUTVA VERSUS 'ISLAMIST THREATS'

1. Cited in Nilanjan Mukhopadhyay, *Narendra Modi: The Man, the Times*, Chennai, Westland, 2013, p. 106.
2. This defeat took place in spite of the fact that the government postponed the village panchayat elections three times. See Dionne Bunsha, 'A new oarsman', *Frontline*, 26 Oct. 2001, p. 32; Achyut Yagnik and Suchitra Sheth, *The Shaping of Modern Gujarat*, New Delhi, Penguin, 2005, p. 270.
3. See Edward Simpson, *The Political Biography of an Earthquake: Aftermath and Amnesia in Gujarat, India*, London, Hurst, 2014.
4. Kingshuk Nag, *The NaMo Story: A Political Life*, New Delhi, Roli Books, 2013, pp. 79–80.
5. Bunsha, 'A new oarsman', p. 32.
6. Manas Dasgupta, 'Pracharak in power', *The Hindu*, 14 Oct. 2001, http://www.thehindujobs.com/thehindu/2001/10/14/stories/05141342.htm (last accessed 9 Dec. 2013).

7. See his interview in *Gram Garjana*, 1 Jan. 2006, cited in Pravin Sheth, *Images of Transformation: Gujarat and Narendra Modi*, Ahmedabad, Team Spirit, 2007, p. 203.
8. Mukhopadhyay, *Narendra Modi*, p. 52.
9. M.V. Kamath and Kalindi Randeri, *Narendra Modi: The Architect of a Modern State*, New Delhi, Rupa, 2009, p. 17.
10. Cited in Mukhopadhyay, *Narendra Modi*, p. 102.
11. See ch. 1 of Christophe Jaffrelot, *The Hindu Nationalist Movement and Indian Politics*, London, Hurst, 1996.
12. Nag, *The NaMo Story*, p. 36.
13. Kamath and Randeri, *Narendra Modi*, p. 22.
14. He published his biography in 2001 under the title *Jyoti Punj*.
15. Mukhopadhyay, *Narendra Modi*, p. 122. There is a controversy about Modi's degrees, including his MA in 'Entire Political Science'. According to some political opponents, these degrees have been 'forged'. See 'PM's degree forged, says AAP, after BJP shows Modi's BA and MA degree', *The Times of India*, 9 May 2016, https://timesofindia.indiatimes.com/india/pms-degree-forged-says-aap-after-bjp-shows-modis-ba-and-ma-degree/articleshow/52186709.cms; and Sayandeb Chowdhury, 'PM Modi's educational degree should neither be a national shame nor a state secret', *The Wire*, 12 April 2023, https://thewire.in/government/narendra-modi-degree-entire-political-science.
16. Sheth, *Images of Transformation*, p. 57.
17. Kamath and Randeri, *Narendra Modi*, p. 37.
18. Mukhopadhyay, *Narendra Modi*, p. 125.
19. He tells Nilanjan Mukhopadhyay: 'I had to tour the entire country and meet everyone and take interviews on the basis of their experiences during the Emergency [...] There were some former chief ministers and there were those who were in power even at that time.' See Mukhopadhyay, *Narendra Modi*, p. 126.
20. Kamath and Randeri, *Narendra Modi*, p. 38.
21. Nag, *The NaMo Story*, p. 53.
22. Cited in ibid., p. 71.
23. Cited in ibid., pp. 71–2.
24. Mukhopadhyay, *Narendra Modi*, p. 180.
25. Cited in Nag, *The NaMo Story*, p. 60.

26. Mukhopadhyay, *Narendra Modi*, p. 147.
27. Sheth, *Images of Transformation*, p. 53.
28. Christophe Jaffrelot and Charlotte Thomas, 'Facing ghettoisation in "riot-city": Old Ahmedabad and Juhapura between victimisation and self-help', in Laurent Gayer and Christophe Jaffrelot (eds), *Muslims in India's Cities: Trajectories of Marginalisation*, London, Hurst, 2012, pp. 43–79.
29. Yagnik and Sheth, *The Shaping of Modern Gujarat*, p. 266.
30. Ajay Umat and Harit Mehta, '3-day fast rocks 30-year bond', *The Times of India* (Ahmedabad edn), 25 Sept. 2011, http://articles.timesofindia.indiatimes.com/2011-09-25/ahmedabad/30200558_1_narendra-modi-keshubhai-patel-anti-modi-forces (last accessed 8 Nov. 2013).
31. Mukhopadhyay, *Narendra Modi*, p. 202.
32. Ibid.; and Nag, *The NaMo Story*, p. 61.
33. Ibid., p. 62.
34. Ibid., p. 64.
35. On the career of Thakre, see Christophe Jaffrelot, *Hindu Nationalism and Indian Politics*, London, Hurst, 1996.
36. Nag, *The NaMo Story*, pp. 77–8.
37. Kamath and Randeri, *Narendra Modi*, p. 69.
38. Sheth, *Images of Transformation*, p. 57.
39. Vinod Mehta, *Lucknow Boy: A Memoir*, New Delhi, Penguin, 2011, p. 209.
40. Kamath and Randeri, *Narendra Modi*, p. 82.
41. When Modi took over in Gandhinagar, a senior correspondent noted: 'it seems unlikely that Modi will be able to reverse the sharp decline in public support in the State for the BJP in time for the Assembly elections to be held in early 2003.' Bunsha, 'A new oarsman', p. 31.
42. Cited in Kamath and Randeri, *Narendra Modi*, p. 83.
43. This section summarises the argument I make in one of the chapters of a forthcoming book that analyses the way Hindu nationalists relate to violence—and implement it. It draws from Christophe Jaffrelot, 'The 2002 pogrom in Gujarat: the post-9/11 face of Hindu nationalist anti-Muslim violence', in John Hinnels and Richard King (eds), *Religion and Violence in South Asia*, London and New York, Routledge, 2006, pp. 173–92. The word 'pogrom', as already mentioned above, describes more aptly than any other what happened in Gujarat in

2002 because of the magnitude of violence, because of the fact that most of the victims belonged to the minority community which had been attacked by members of the majority community, and because the state did not protect the victims. In fact, the attitude of the police largely explains why the victims came almost entirely from the Muslim minority—in contrast to what happens, usually, in a riot. As mentioned above, this form of violence calls to mind the 'communal pogrom' (Howard Spodek, *Ahmedabad: Shock City of Twentieth-century India*, Hyderabad, Orient Blackswan, 2012, p. 180) of 1969 and the anti-Sikh pogrom that occurred in Delhi after the assassination of Indira Gandhi in 1984.

44. On what happened in Godhra and on the pogrom that followed, the best source remains the report that the Concerned Citizens Tribunal published in 2002. This Tribunal comprised eight senior citizens of India. Its chairman was the former chief justice of the Supreme Court, V.R. Krishna Iyer. Its other members were Justice P.B. Sawant (a retired judge from the Supreme Court); Justice Hosbet Suresh (a retired judge of the Mumbai High Court); a lawyer, K.G. Kannabiran (president of the People's Union for Civil Liberties); Aruna Roy, the founder of the famous NGO Mazdoor Kisan Shakti Sangathan; Dr K.S. Subramanian, a retired Indian Police Service officer, and former director general of police of Tripura; Prof. Ghanshyam Shah, then teaching at Jawaharlal Nehru University; and Prof. Tanika Sarkar, also from JNU. This Tribunal prepared its report on the basis of '2,094 oral and written testimonies, both individual and collective, from victim-survivors and also independent human rights groups, women's groups, NGOs and academics'. See Concerned Citizens Tribunal, Gujarat 2002, *Crime against Humanity*, vol. II: *An Inquiry into the Carnage in Gujarat: Findings and Recommendations*, Mumbai, Citizens for Justice and Peace, 2002, p. 9. See http://www.sabrang.com/tribunal/tribunal2.pdf (last accessed 8 Nov. 2013). See also the meticulous work by Manoj Mitta, *The Fiction of Fact-finding: Modi and Godhra*, Noida, HarperCollins, 2014. The main argument of the book about the Godhra incident is summarised in Manoj Mitta, '"Preplanned inhuman collective violent act of terrorism": what Modi got away with in the Godhra case', *Scroll.in*, 27 Feb. 2017, https://scroll.

in/article/830319/preplanned-inhuman-collective-violent-act-of-terrorism-what-modi-got-away-with-in-the-godhra-case.

45. Concerned Citizens Tribunal, *Crime against Humanity*, vol. II: *An Inquiry into the Carnage in Gujarat*, p. 12.

46. For a complete study of these events, see Siddarth Varadarajan (ed.), *Gujarat: The Making of a Tragedy*, New Delhi, Penguin, 2002. Another remarkable source book of more than 1,000 pages drawn from many official (and unofficial) reports is John Dayal (ed.), *Gujarat 2002: Untold and Re-told Stories of the Hindutva Lab*, vol. 1, New Delhi, Media House, 2003. Martha Nussbaum has devoted the first chapter of her book on India to what she calls 'Genocide in Gujarat'. See Martha Nussbaum, *The Clash Within: Democracy, Religious Violence and India's Future*, Cambridge, MA, Harvard University Press, 2007. Harsh Mander's articles on the Gujarat pogrom have been published in the form of an evocative book, *Cry, My Beloved Country: Reflections on the Gujarat Carnage 2002 and Its Aftermath*, Noida, Rainbow Publishers, 2004. See also, Harsh Mander, *Fear and Forgiveness: The Aftermath of Massacre*, Delhi, Penguin, 2009. More recent invaluable testimonies are Rana Ayyub, *Gujarat Files: Anatomy of a Cover Up*, n.p., 2016; Harsh Mander, *Between Memory and Forgetting: Massacre and the Modi Years in Gujarat*, New Delhi, Yoda, 2019; and Ashish Khetan, *Undercover: My Journey into the Darkness of Hindutva*, Chennai, Westland, 2021. See also Moyukh Chatterjee, *Composing Violence: The Limits of Exposure and the Making of Minorities*, Durham and London, Duke University Press, 2023.

47. Parvis Ghassem-Fachandi, *Pogrom in Gujarat: Hindu Nationalism and Anti-Muslim Violence in India*, Princeton, NJ, Princeton University Press, 2012, p. 59. One month later, Narendra Modi reiterated this interpretation in a long interview with *The Times of India* in which he said that 'the attack on the Sabarmati Express' was 'a deep-rooted conspiracy and a pre-planned, cold-blooded attack'. Interview with Narendra Modi by S. Balakrishnan, 'Peace has returned to Gujarat, claims Modi', *The Times of India*, 29 March 2002, http://timesofindia.indiatimes.com/city/ahmedabad/Peace-has-returned-to-Gujarat-claims-Modi/articleshow/5307572.cms (last accessed 8 Nov. 2013). The idea that the Godhra attack was 'premeditated' was also expressed in the report that the Gujarat state government submitted

to the National Human Rights Commission after this body had sent it a notice on 1 March 2002 asking for 'the protection of human rights of the people in the state of Gujarat irrespective of their religion'. See 'Suo motu case no. 1150/6/2001-2002', 1 March 2002, http://nhrc.nic.in (last accessed 8 Nov. 2013). See also *Communalism Combat*, 8, nos. 77–78 (March–April 2002), p. 12. The Hindu nationalists' interpretation focusing on the ISI remained their standard explanation. In 2004 I found a very revealing publication in the bookstore of the RSS's headquarters in Delhi. It reads: 'On the 27 Feb. 2002, innocent, unarmed kar sevaks including women and children were burnt alive in the S-6 compartment of Sabarmati Express. From information available so far, the whole episode was planned. Had the train reached there as per its scheduled time, it was planned to burn the whole train near village Chanchelav. A mob of 2000 strong men with petrol bombs, enough quantity of kerosene, cannot be mustered all at once. As per the investigating agencies, it is felt that the threads of all this operation appear to be pointing towards ISI involvement here [...] The masterminds behind this plan are those people of terroristic mentality who had the courage to carry out an attack on the Parliament House. Their intention was not only to burn the kar sevaks but in a wider effect, they wanted to spread unrest in the country and to destabilize it through insurrections within the country. The army be required to be shifted from the Indo-Pak borders and to tarnish the international image of Bharat as also to increase the inimical rift between the Hindus and Muslims. All this was a wisely planned action.' *Godhra Terrorism Unmasked*, Ahmedabad, Vishwa Samvad Kendra, 2002, p. 1.

48. Haren Pandya, the former home minister of state in Keshubhai Patel's government who had become minister of state for revenue after Modi took over, told Kingshuk Nag that after the Godhra tragedy he had 'advised against a move to bring the bodies to Ahmedabad, but was shouted down by cabinet colleagues who said that a "reaction" in Ahmedabad would benefit the BJP in the next elections'. Nag, *The NaMo Story*, p. 97.
49. See the article 'Godhrano banav ekaj kommi ek tarafi himsanu trasvadi krutya: Modi', *Sandesh*, 28 Feb. 2002, p. 1, cited in Ghassem-Fachandi, *Pogrom in Gujarat*, p. 59.

50. Ibid.
51. National Human Rights Commission, 'Suo motu case no. 1150/6/2001-2002', 1 April 2002, http://nhrc.nic.in (last accessed 8 Nov. 2013).
52. Parvis Ghassem-Fachandi, walking across Ahmedabad on 28 February, points out 'the frustration and humiliation that many policemen must have felt, as they had been given unambiguous orders not to intervene in the violent action unfolding in front of their eyes'. See Ghassem-Fachandi, *Pogrom in Gujarat*, p. 41.
53. Ibid., p. 37. One must keep in mind here that of the state's 65 IPS (Indian Police Service, a national elite corps) officers in 2002, only one was a Muslim. All the others had been transferred to training duties, railroad surveillance, etc. *Communalism Combat*, 8, nos. 77–78 (March–April 2002), p. 119.
54. Concerned Citizens Tribunal, *Crime against Humanity*, vol. I, p. 26, http://www.sabrang.com/tribunal/volI/inciahmed.html (last accessed 8 Nov. 2013).
55. In one of his Rajkot speeches, Jafri 'had urged people not to vote for him because he was an RSS man, and to vote for the Congress instead'. Ibid., p. 32.
56. Concerned Citizens Tribunal, *Crime against Humanity*, vol. I, pp. 26–7.
57. Jaffrelot, 'The 2002 pogrom in Gujarat', pp. 173–92.
58. Concerned Citizens Tribunal, *Crime against Humanity*, vol. II, p. 85.
59. 'Report on the visit of NHRC team headed by chairperson, NHRC to Ahmedabad, Vadodara and Godhra from 19–22 March 2002', Annexure 1, appended to National Human Rights Commission, 'Suo motu case no. 1150/6/2001-2002', 1 April 2002, http://nhrc.nic.in/guj_annex_1.htm (last accessed 8 Nov. 2013).
60. Cited in *Communalism Combat*, 8, nos. 77–78 (March–April 2002), p. 136, http://www.sabrang.com/cc/archive/comapril2002.pdf (last accessed 8 Nov. 2013).
61. Cited in ibid., p. 137.
62. Ibid.
63. Sadeja Momin, 'Gagging the press', *The Statesman*, 18 April 2002, p. 4.
64. Press Council of India, 'Communal violence in Gujarat: role of the media, adjudications rendered on 30.06.2003 in 24 cases', Hindu Vivek Kendra, http://www.hvk.org/specialreports/pci/index.

html. Paradoxically (or not), this report is available on a website promoting the Hindutva ideology.

65. In a fifty-word report published by the Baroda edition of *Gujarat Samachar*, the expression 'pre-planned like Godhra' is repeated five times. See PUCL, 'The role of newspapers during the Gujarat carnage', PUCL, Vadodara, 2002, p. 6, http://www.pucl.org/Topics/Religion-communalism/2002/gujarat-media.htm (last accessed 8 Nov. 2013).
66. Ibid., p. 4
67. Ibid., p. 6.
68. Ibid.
69. Dionne Bunsha, 'Peddling hate', *Frontline*, 19, no. 15 (20 July–2 Aug. 2002).
70. Cited in PUCL, 'The role of newspapers during the Gujarat carnage', p. 25.
71. 'We can increase our understanding of these networks if we see their operations during riots in the light of the functions that the same networks perform when there are no riots.' See Ward Berenschot, *Riot Politics: Hindu–Muslim Violence and the Indian State*, London, Hurst, 2011, p. 167.
72. 'As the local Congress networks and affiliated organizations like the TLA gradually collapsed, people became more dependent on the patronage structures that developed around the BJP, the RSS and the VHP.' Ibid., p. 69.
73. Ibid., p. 191.
74. The report of the Concerned Citizens Tribunal points out that on 28 February, a '20–25,000 strong mob surrounded the Chamanpura area in the heart of Ahmedabad city'. Concerned Citizens Tribunal, *Crime against Humanity*, vol. I, p. 26.
75. The Concerned Citizens Tribunal gathered from several testimonies that trishuls had been freely distributed, whereas swords cost Rs. 310 (Concerned Citizens Tribunal, *Crime against Humanity*, vol. II, p. 56). Vinod Mall, then SP of Surendranagar, saw the VHP and the Bajrang Dal distributing trishuls before the riots. Interview with Vinod Mall in Ahmedabad, 5 April 2007.
76. 'LPG blasts baffle riot investigators', *The Times of India*, 17 July 2002, http://timesofindia.indiatimes.com/articleshow/16199590.

cms?utm_source=contentofinterest&utm_medium=text&utm_campaign=cppst.

77. The Gujarat VHP president, K.K. Shastri, explained to Sheela Bhatt, a Rediff News reporter, that the list of Muslim targets had been established shortly beforehand. 'It had to be done, VHP leader says of riots', Rediff, 12 March 2002, http://www.rediff.com/news/2002/mar/12train.htm (last accessed 8 Nov. 2013). Hence the fact that, sometimes, only one shop or one house among many others had been attacked and burned. See Ghassem-Fachandi, *Pogrom in Gujarat*, pp. 125 and 129.
78. A retired High Court judge and an active High Court judge had to leave their houses under attack.
79. Megha Kumar, *Communalism and Sexual Violence in India: The Politics of Gender, Ethnicity and Conflict*, London and New York, I.B. Tauris, 2016.
80. International Initiative for Justice, *Threatened Existence: A Feminist Analysis of the Genocide in Gujarat*, December 2003, https://www.onlinevolunteers.org/gujarat/reports/iijg/2003/.
81. *Muslim India*, no. 235 (July 2002), p. 305. The Concerned Citizens Tribunal mentions the destruction of 270 mosques and *dargahs*. See Concerned Citizens Tribunal, *Crime against Humanity*, vol. II, p. 48. The inquiry team of the National Human Rights Commission has produced more alarming figures: 'Over 100 mosques and dargahs were desecrated and damaged in Ahmedabad and about 500 in other parts of Gujarat. Two members of the team saw the site of Dargah of Sufi poet Wali Gujarati, revered by both the communities, near the underground bridge of Shahibag, which has been razed to the ground. Allegedly, the Govt., instead of protecting the site for reconstruction of the Dargah, has got the old historic Dargah ground flattened and now one sees an asphalt road with vehicle moving over it.' 'Report on the visit of NHRC team headed by chairperson, NHRC to Ahmedabad, Vadodara and Godhra from 19–22 March 2002', http://nhrc.nic.in/guj_annex_1.htm.
82. Hindu–Muslim riots for a long time remained basically an urban phenomenon in Gujarat and elsewhere: from 1950 to 1995, 80 per cent of the victims of all the rioting in Gujarat were in Ahmedabad and Vadodara. See Ashutosh Varshney, *Ethnic Conflict and Civic Life:*

Hindus and Muslims in India, New Haven, CT, Yale University Press, 2002, p. 7.

83. According to official figures, out of 755 casualties, 454 took place in urban areas and 301 in rural areas. Raheel Dhattiwala and Michael Biggs, 'The political logic of ethnic violence: the anti-Muslim pogrom in Gujarat, 2002', *Policy and Society*, 40, no. 4 (2012), pp. 505–6.

84. Dipankar Gupta, 'The limits of tolerance: prospects of secularism in India after Gujarat', Prem Bathia Memorial Lecture, 11 Aug. 2002. See also Dipankar Gupta, *Justice before Reconciliation: Negotiating a 'New Normal' in Post-riot Mumbai and Ahmedabad*, London and New York, Routledge, 2011.

85 Bela Bhatia, 'A step back in Sabarkantha', *Seminar*, no. 513, http://www.india-seminar.com/2002/513/513%20bela%20bhatia.htm (last accessed 8 Nov. 2013).

86. 'Report on the visit of NHRC team headed by chairperson, NHRC to Ahmedabad, Vadodara and Godhra from 19–22 March 2002', http://nhrc.nic.in/guj_annex_1.htm (last accessed 8 Nov. 2013).

87. Ganesh Devy, 'Tribal voice and violence', *Seminar*, no. 513, http://www.india-seminar.com/2002/513/513%20bela%20bhatia.htm (last accessed 8 Nov. 2013).

88. Lancy Lobo, 'Adivasis, Hindutva and post-Godhra riots in Gujarat', *EPW*, 37, no. 48 (30 Nov. 2002), p. 4848. See also Stany Pinto, 'Communalisation of Tribals in South Gujarat', *EPW*, 30, no. 39 (30 Sept. 1995), pp. 2416–19; and A.M. Shah, 'The tribes—so-called—of Gujarat', *EPW*, 38, no. 02 (11 Jan. 2003), pp. 95–7.

89. Christophe Jaffrelot, 'Communal riots in Gujarat: the state at risk?', *Heidelberg Papers in South Asian and Comparative Politics*, no. 13, May 2003, https://d-nb.info/1203741847/34.

90. These figures were supplied in 2002 by the additional director general of police R.B. Sreekumar to the chief election commissioner J.M. Lyngdoh, who deduced from them that 154 of the 182 Assembly constituencies in the state had been affected. Ashish Khetan, 'The truth about the Godhra SIT report', *Tehelka*, 12 Feb. 2011, p. 40.

91. Concerned Citizens Tribunal, *Crime against Humanity*, vol. II, p. 17.

92. This is also the figure Yagnik and Sheth give in *The Shaping of Modern Gujarat*, p. 282.

93. Mass graves were found years after the events, but grounds where others are believed to lie have still not been inspected, in all likelihood, so as not to raise the human death toll. Many bodies were also thrown into wells. Such was the case in Naroda Patiya.
94. This sentence that was allegedly heard from the police by Gujarati Muslims has become the title of a report of Human Rights Watch, India, '"We have no order to save you": state participation and complicity in communal violence in Gujarat', 14, no. 3 (April 2003), http://www.hrw.org/reports/2002/india/India0402-03.htm (last accessed 8 Nov. 2013). See also Human Rights Watch, New York, 'Compounding injustice: the government's failure to redress massacres in Gujarat', 15, no. 3 (July 2003), http://www.hrw.org/reports/2003/india0703/India0703full.pdf (last accessed 8 Nov. 2013).
95. For a complete account of Khetan's sting operation, see Khetan, *Undercover: My Journey into the Darkness of Hindutva*.
96. 'CBI authentication of Tehelka tapes pursuant to the NHRC order dated March, 5, 2008', http://www.cjponline.org/gujaratTrials/statecomp/pdf (accessed 25 Nov. 2011).
97. For more information on the role of the Bajrang Dal and Babu Bajrangi in Gujarat, see 'The militias of Hindutva: communal violence, terrorism and cultural policing', in Laurent Gayer and Christophe Jaffrelot (eds), *Armed Militias of South Asia: Fundamentalist, Maoists and Separatists*, London, Hurst; New York, Columbia University Press; New Delhi, Foundation Books, 2009, pp. 199–236.
98. In fact, Zadaphia was the home minister of state as the home minister was Narendra Modi himself.
99 'Gujarat 2002: the truth in the words of the men who did it', *Tehelka* (Special issue), 3 Nov. 2007, pp. 12–14. In addition to Zadaphia, Bajrangi told Khetan that he called Jaideep Patel (a senior VHP leader) '11 or 12 times' while attacking Muslims.
100. In Naroda, as in so many other places, Dalits were encouraged to attack their Muslim neighbours. A BJP leader from Baroda, Deepak Shah, testifies that this is the usual pattern: they 'are the warring communities ... the Kharvas, the Baakris ... They always come forward at such times ... They are meat-eating people ... They have the tools and they usually lead from the front ... So they were channelized ... There were Kahars ... A lot of Rabaris were

there this time ... Bhadris, Parmars and Marathi-speaking people, who have a lot of passion.' 'Gujarat 2002: the truth in the words of the men who did it', p. 26. In the words of Jan Breman, 'Dalits have lost their "beyond the pale"' classification and are supposed to pay for their acceptance within the Hindutva fold by joining the hunt against the excluded minority made to live at the margins of society as a new category of untouchables.' Jan Breman, *The Making and Unmaking of an Industrial Working Class: Sliding down the Labour Hierarchy in Ahmedabad, India*, New Delhi, Oxford University Press, 2004, p. 289. The VHP president in Gujarat, K.K. Shastri, stated that the most active thugs in the violence were Waghri Dalits whose 'payoff' came in the form of looting Muslim shops (Rediff News, 12 March 2002). But Dalits were not in the least *systematically* involved. Undeniably, they were part of the clientelistic networks built by the BJP. However, Dhattiwala and Biggs found that there was no correlation between the proximity of Scheduled Castes to Muslim neighbourhoods and the number of casualties, and that out of 74 Hindus convicted of killing Muslims, 53 were Patidars. Dhattiwala and Biggs, 'The political logic of ethnic violence', p. 501.

101. 'Gujarat 2002: the truth in the words of the men who did it', p. 22.
102. Ibid., p. 35.
103. And consistent with the slogans shouted on the streets in Gujarat: '*Yeh andar ki baat hai / Police hamarey saath hai* (This is inside information, the police are with us). *Jaan se maar dengey / Bajrang Dal zindabad / Narendra Modi zindabad* (We will kill. Long live the Bajrang Dal. Long live Narendra Modi).' Cited in Human Rights Watch, '"We have no order to save you"', http://www.hrw.org/reports/2002/india/India0402-03.htm (last accessed 8 Nov. 2013).
104. 'Gujarat 2002: the truth in the words of the men who did it', p. 41.
105. Ibid., p. 43.
106. Ibid., p. 44.
107. 'Report on the visit of NHRC team headed by chairperson, NHRC to Ahmedabad, Vadodara and Godhra from 19–22 March 2002', Annexure 1.
108. Ashok Bhatt was in the control room of Ahmedabad and I.K. Jadeja in the Gandhinagar one. Interview with a former Gujarat cadre IPS officer under the cover of anonymity in Ahmedabad on 5 April 2007.

109. Concerned Citizens Tribunal, *Crime against Humanity*, vol. II, p. 18; see also pp. 82–3.
110. The source in question, as it turned out, was none other than Haren Pandya (see below), who gave the same information to *Outlook* under the cover of anonymity again on two occasions. 'A midnight meeting on Feb. 27 and a murdered minister', *Outlook*, 5 Feb. 2022, https://www.outlookindia.com/magazine/story/a-midnight-meeting-on-feb-27-and-a-murdered-minister/235982.
111. 'In the Supreme Court of India. Special leave petition no. 1088 of 2008, Smt Zakia Ahsan Jafri and Citizens for Justice and Peace ... Petitioners versus State of Gujarat and others respondents. Affidavit of Sanjiv Rajendra Bhatt, IPS, April 14, 2011, Ahmedabad', NDTV, http://drop.ndtv.com/common/pdf/Sanjiv_Bhatt.pdf?from=NDTV (last accessed 8 Nov. 2013).
112. Lt Gen. Zameer Uddin Shah, *The Sarkari Mussalman: The Life and Travails of a Soldier Educationist*, New Delhi, Konark Publishers, 2019, p. 117.
113. Human Rights Watch, '"We have no order to save you"'.
114. The nine affidavits that R.B. Sreekumar has submitted to the Nanavati Commission are among the most useful sources for understanding Modi's Gujarat. See 'Affidavit before Justice K.G. Shah and Justice G.T. Nanavati Commission enquiring into communal disturbances after the incident of train burning at Godhra on 27-02-2002', 15 July 2002, https://cjp.org.in/wp-content/uploads/2018/11/RB-Sreekumar-Affidavit-1-15-JUL-2002.pdf; and 'A representation in the public interests for initiation of departmental action against those responsible for culpable negligence in maintenance of public order and investigation of genocidal crimes', 9 Dec. 2012, https://counterviewfiles.files.wordpress.com/2021/09/letter-to-governor-2012.pdf. See also, 'Gujarat genocide: the state, law and subversion; R.B. Sreekumar', 27 February 2012, https://kafila.online/2012/02/27/gujarat-genocide-the-state-law-and-subversion-r-b-sreekumar/.
115. Soon before, R.B. Sreekumar had submitted to the chief minister a very detailed note called 'Current communal scenario in Ahmedabad City'.
116. Shah, *The Sarkari Mussalman*, p. 125.

117. See Shanta Kumar, *Autobiography: Living My Convictions*, New Delhi, Prabhat Prakashan, 2022, p. 345.
118. 'PM assures economic revival package for state', *Economic Times* (Ahmedabad edn), 5 April 2002, p. 1. Vajpayee had also told, in Hindi, 'there is one message for the CM and that is, he should follow the raj dharma ... By raj dharma I mean there should be no difference between caste and caste, between religion and religion'. P. Saghal, 'Minor modification', *Outlook*, 15 April 2002, https://www.outlookindia.com/magazine/story/minormodification/215185.
119. L.K. Advani, *My Country, My Life*, Delhi, Rupa, 2008, p. 843.
120. Ibid.
121. Sri Krishna, 'BJP rejects demand for Modi's removal', Rediff News, 12 April 2002, https://www.rediff.com/news/2002/apr/12bjp2.htm.
122. Ibid.
123. Kamath and Randeri, *Narendra Modi*, pp. 141–3.
124. *India Today*, 19 April 2002.
125. Vinod K. Jose, 'The emperor uncrowned', *The Caravan*, 1 March 2012, http://caravanmagazine.in/reportage/emperor-uncrowned?page=0,9 (last accessed 8 Nov. 2013).
126. Kumar, *Autobiography*, p. 345.
127. Rajiv Shah, 'I'm ready to kiss the gallows: Modi', *The Times of India* (Ahmedabad edn), 13 June 2004, https://timesofindia.indiatimes.com/city/ahmedabad/im-ready-to-kiss-the-gallows-modi/articleshow/736310.cms?from=mdr.
128. Ibid.
129. Kamath and Randeri, *Narendra Modi*, p. 138.
130. Steven I. Wilkinson, 'Froids calculs et foules déchaînées: les émeutes intercommunautaires en Inde', *Critique Internationale*, no. 6 (Winter 2000), p. 132.
131. Steven Wilkinson, *Votes and Violence: Electoral Competition and Ethnic Riots in India*, Cambridge, Cambridge University Press, 2004, p. 139.
132. Kamal Mitra Chenoy, S.P. Shukla, K.S. Subramanian and Achin Vanaik, *Gujarat Carnage 2002: A Report to the Nation*, April 2002, p. 19.
133. Some of the most senior party members were probably aware that this phenomenon was not politically counterproductive. Indeed, the

Concerned Citizens Tribunal has established a correlation between the intensity of communal violence and the geographical strongholds of the members of the state government: 'Electoral constituencies of ministers in the state cabinet were more prone to violence; in some cases, ministers themselves were leading the mobs.' Concerned Citizens Tribunal, *Crime against Humanity*, vol. II, pp. 76–7.

134. For more details, see Ghanshyam Shah, 'Contestation and negotiations: Hindutva sentiments and temporal interests in Gujarat elections', *EPW*, 37, no. 48 (30 Nov. 2002), pp. 4838–43.
135. Saghal, 'Minor modification'.
136. 'PM opposes snap poll in Gujarat', *The Times of India*, 5 April 2002, p. 7.
137. It seems that this decision was precipitated by the appointment of former BJP leader, Shankarsinh Vaghela, as state Congress chief. According to Rathin Das, 'Modi had to speed up the process of holding fresh elections, to make sure that the GPCC chief did not get much time to rebuild and reorganize the fragmented state Congress he inherited.' Rathin Das, 'Modi resigns, seeks fresh vote', *Hindustan Times*, 20 July 2002, p. 1.
138. 'Modi flies flag of Gujarat pride in open letter', *The Telegraph*, 20 July 2002, p. 8.
139. In three months, the government registered the return home of 73,500 refugees (52,500 in Ahmedabad) to pretend that law and order had been restored and that elections could be held.
140. On the role of the NGOs, see Christophe Jaffrelot, 'Communal riots in Gujarat: the state at risk?', *Heidelberg Papers in South Asian and Comparative Politics*, no. 13 (May 2003), p. 20.
141. Indian Constitution, Part XVIII Emergency Procedures, article 356 dealing with 'Provisions in case of failure of constitutional machinery in state'.
142. 'SC upholds EC order on Gujarat', *The Times of India*, 28 Oct. 2002, http://timesofindia.indiatimes.com/articleshow/26544721.cms?utm_source=contentofinterest&utm_medium=text&utm_campaign=cppst.
143. Deepal Trivedi, 'Is Lyngdoh from Italy, asks Modi', *The Asian Age*, 22 Aug. 2002, pp. 1–2. In fact, in 2012 there were still more than 16,000 refugees in relief camps, according to an NGO's report.

See Janvikas, *Gujarat's Internally Displaced: Ten Years Later*, Ahmedabad, 2012, p. 10.

144. 'Sena refuses to bestow Hindu Hriday Samrat title to Modi', *The Indian Express*, 13 July 2013, http://www.indianexpress.com/news/sena-refuses-to-bestow-hindu-hriday-samrat-title-on-modi/1141340/ (last accessed 8 Nov. 2013).
145. Sheela Bhatt, 'Gujarat IB officers transferred for putting Modi's controversial speech on record', Rediff News, 18 Sept. 2002, http://www.rediff.com/news/2002/sep/18guj2.htm (last accessed 8 Nov. 2013).
146. Ibid. The additional director general R.B. Sreekumar was transferred to the police reforms department. The deputy inspector general of police E. Radhakrishna, in charge of political and communal affairs, was transferred to Junagadh as principal of the Police Training College, while the deputy commissioner of police Sanjeev Bhatt, in charge of internal security, was transferred as principal of the State Reserve Police Training College.
147. 'Modi blasts Pak terrorism, urges people to stand united', *The Asian Age*, 29 May 2002, p. 9.
148. 'Modi accuses Pakistan of spreading "semi-terrorism"', *The Asian Age*, 25 May 2002, p. 3.
149. 'Pakistan responsible for Gujarat unrest: Modi', *The Times of India* (Ahmedabad edn), 9 June 2002, p. 4.
150. Sanjay Basak, 'Modi to reform Gujarat madrasas', *The Asian Age* (Ahmedabad edn), 14 June 2002, p. 2.
151. R.B. Sreekumar, *Gujarat: Behind the Curtain*, New Delhi, Manas Publications, 2016, p. 59.
152. Manas Dasguta, 'Death sentence for Akshardham temple attack convicts upheld', *The Hindu*, 2 June 2010, http://www.thehindu.com/news/national/death-sentence-for-akshardham-temple-attack-convicts-upheld/article443455.ece (last accessed 8 Nov. 2013).
153. Sanjeev Bhatt considered that 'Akshardham was an engineered attack'. Interview with Sanjeev Bhatt in Ahmedabad on 24 Feb. 2012. Bhatt, whose testimony about the 2002 pogrom had implicated the chief minister and other ministers, as mentioned above, was sentenced to life in 2019 in a 1990 case of custodial death.

154. 'Dham attack case: three years after SC rejects probe, new arrest', *The Indian Express*, 5 Nov. 2017, http://indianexpress.com/article/india/akshardham-attack-case-three-years-after-sc-rejects-probe-new-arrest-4922689/ (last accessed 19 March 2018).
155. Cited in Darshan Desai, 'That missing healing touch', *Outlook*, 14 Oct. 2002, https://www.outlookindia.com/magazine/story/that-missing-healing-touch/217544 (last accessed 26 Sept. 2020).
156. Sanjay Kumar, 'Gujarat Assembly elections 2002: analysing the verdict', *EPW*, 38, no.4 (25 Jan. 2003), p. 272.
157. Ibid.
158. Aseem Prakash, 'Re-imagination of the state and Gujarat's electoral verdict', *EPW*, 38, no. 16 (19 April 2003), pp. 1604–5.
159. Dhattiwala and Biggs, 'The political logic of ethnic violence', pp. 501–2.
160. Cited in Berenschodt, *Riot Politics*, p. 158.
161. Kumar, 'Gujarat Assembly elections 2002', p. 275.
162. *India Today*, 16 Dec. 2002, p. 27.
163. *India Today*, 26 Aug. 2002, p. 33.
164. For more details, see Jaffrelot, *Hindu Nationalism and Indian Politics*, ch. 1.
165. Howard Spodek, 'In the Hindutva laboratory: pogroms and politics in Gujarat', *Modern Asian Studies*, 44, no. 2 (March 2010), p. 378.
166. Ghassem-Fachandi, *Pogrom in Gujarat*, p. 124.
167. Jaffrelot, *The Hindu Nationalist Movement*, ch. 1.
168. For a more detailed analysis focusing on the British Raj years, see ibid.
169. The strategy of emulation of the Muslim, the 'threatening' Other, is also evident from culinary practices. More than one century ago, the young M.K. Gandhi secretly ate meat to be as strong as his Muslim friend. Similarly, Parvis Ghassem-Fachandi pointed out: 'I have seen many men from middle-class Hindu and Jain communities consume meat at night, out of the view of their wives, in the predominantly Muslim-owned meat stands and restaurants of the old city [...] Meat seemed to enable the Hindu consumer to cross a certain boundary and confront the image of the ever-powerful masculine Muslim either as a co-conspirator in festive consumption or as a rival.' Ghassem-Fachandi, *Pogrom in Gujarat*, p. 180.

170. Nag, *The NaMo Story*, p. 97. The reporter of *India Today* had been struck by the same thing after the 1985 riots: 'In spite of such horrible violence, there is no feeling of shame or sadness in anyone. The communal elements among the Hindus consisting of many traders and professionals believe that this was going to happen. One businessman said: 'Muslims will never dare to raise their heads in Surat now. They will have to learn to live in an inferior position as befits a minority.' Cited in Yagnik and Sheth, *The Shaping of Modern Gujarat*, p. 264.
171. Ashis Nandy, 'Obituary of a culture', *Seminar*, no. 513, http://www.india-seminar.com/2002/513/513%20ashis%20nandy.htm (last accessed 9 Dec. 2013).
172. The report resulting from the inquiry conducted by the British government, which was made public in the BBC documentary *India: the Modi question* (https://www.dailymotion.com/video/x8iziwy), stated: 'The aim of the perpetrators of the violence, the VHP and other Hindu extremist groups, was to purge Muslims from Hindu and mixed localities in order to ghettoize them. Their systematic campaign of violence has all the hallmarks of ethnic cleansing. The attack of the train at Godhra on 27 February provided the pretext. If it had not occurred, another one would have been found.' Hartosh Singh Bal, 'BBC row: UK report states VHP planned Gujarat violence in advance, Godhra a "pretext"', *The Caravan*, 23 January 2023, https://caravanmagazine.in/politics/uk-government-modi-gujarat-2002-riots-report-bbc-documentary.
173. For a sophisticated analysis of the words Modi used, see Ghassem-Fachandi, *Pogrom in Gujarat*, p. 62.
174. https://www.youtube.com/watch?v=c2KBmB0FKzc.
175. Srinath Jagannathan, Rajnish Rai and Christophe Jaffrelot, 'Fear and violence as organizational strategies: the possibility of a Derridean lens to analyze extra-judicial police violence', *Journal of Business Ethics*, 175 (2022), pp. 465–84, https://doi.org/10.1007/s10551-020-04655-6.
176. He thus paid obeisance at a Vaishno Devi shrine prior to a rally in Jammu and Kashmir. 'Modi kicks-off "Bharat Vijay" campaign from Jammu', *Jagran Post*, 26 March 2014, http://post.jagran.com/modikicksoff-bharat-vijay-campaign-from-jammu-1395818051 (last accessed 22 Sept. 2020).

177. Abantika Ghosh, 'Saffron in the atmosphere, Narendra Modi praises Ramdev', *The Indian Express*, 24 March 2014, https://indianexpress.com/article/political-pulse/saffron-in-the-atmosphere-modi-makes-it-up-to-ramdev/. For more details on these figures of the Sangh Parivar, see my articles 'Ramdev, Swami without sampradaya', *The Caravan*, 1 July 2011, http://www.caravanmagazine.in/perspectives/ramdev-swami-without-sampradaya (last accessed 4 Feb. 2015); 'The other saffron', *The Indian Express*, 6 Oct. 2014, http://indianexpress.com/article/opinion/columns/the-other-saffron/ (last accessed 4 Feb. 2015); and the remarkable biography by Priyanka Pathak-Narain, *Godman to Tycoon: The Untold Story of Baba Ramdev*, New Delhi, Juggernaut, 2017.
178. Prashant Pandey, 'Narendra Modi in Varanasi: I'm here on the call of Ganga Mata', *The Indian Express*, 25 April 2014, https://indianexpress.com/article/india/politics/modi-in-varanasi-im-here-on-the-call-of-ganga-mata/ (last accessed 26 Sept. 2020).
179. Cited in Lalmani Verma, 'Hindutva is backdrop for Modi in UP', *The Indian Express*, 21 Dec. 2013, https://indianexpress.com/article/cities/lucknow/hindutva-is-backdrop-for-narendra-modi-in-up/ (last accessed 22 Sept. 2020).
180. 'Modi returns fire, calls Arvind Kejriwal Pakistan agent "AK-49"', *Hindustan Times*, 26 March 2014, https://www.hindustantimes.com/india/modi-returns-fire-calls-arvind-kejriwal-pakistan-agent-ak-49/storyoTrX1M43uYZFWRR7oeDdoI.html (last accessed 22 Sept. 2020).
181. Hilal Ahmed, 'Muzaffarnagar 2013: meanings of violence', *EPW*, 48, no. 40 (5 Oct. 2013), pp. 10–12; and 'No respite for Muzaffarnagar', *The Hindu*, 25 Dec. 2013, https://www.thehindu.com/opinion/editorial/no-respite-for-muzaffarnagar/article5497971.ece (last accessed 22 Sept. 2020).
182. Ravish Tiwari, 'UP BJP wants tickets for four riot-accused MLAs', *The Indian Express*, 10 March 2014, https://indianexpress.com/article/cities/lucknow/uttar-pradesh-bjp-wants-tickets-for-four-riot-accused-mlas/ (last accessed 22 Sept. 2020).
183. Two of them got elected, one of whom was given a ministerial portfolio in the Modi government.

184. Sharat Pradhan, 'At Ayodhya Bhoomi Pujan, Modi became all-in-one: proper rituals not followed, allege pundits', *The Wire*, 7 Aug. 2020, https://thewire.in/politics/ayodhya-bhoomi-pujan-narendra-modi-priests-pundits (last accessed 8 Sept. 2020).
185. For more details, see Christophe Jaffrelot, *Modi's India: Hindu Nationalism and the Rise of Ethnic Democracy*, Princeton, NJ, Princeton University Press; Chennai, Westland, 2021, pp. 439 and 113–15.

3. THE CAPTURE OF INSTITUTIONS

1. 'Modi lauds his cops on I-Day', *The Indian Express* (Ahmedabad edn), 15 Aug. 2010, p. 5.
2. Ghanshyam Shah, 'Communal riots in Gujarat: report of a preliminary investigation', in Jan Breman and Ghanshyam Shah, *Gujarat, Cradle and Harbinger of Identity Politics: India's Injurious Frame of Communalism*, New Delhi, Tulika Books, 2022, p. 61.
3. In the present volume, the amounts given in rupees have been converted into US dollars using a conversion rate of 80 rupees per US$.
4. 'Cheers: "Malt March" in Gandhi's Gujarat', *The Times of India*, 27 Jan. 2007, http://articles.timesofindia.indiatimes.com/2007-01-27/india/ 27877061_1_prohibition-salt-march-malt-march (last accessed 4 Dec. 2013).
5. Ornit Shani, 'Bootlegging, politics and corruption: state violence and the routine practices of public power in Gujarat (1985–2002)', in Nalin Mehta and Mona G. Mehta (eds), *Gujarat beyond Gandhi: Identity, Society and Conflict*, London, Routledge, 2012, p. 31.
6. Ibid.
7. Julius Ribeiro, *Bullet for Bullet: My Life as a Police Officer*, New Delhi, Penguin, 1998, p. 256.
8. Ibid., p. 258.
9. Lt Gen. Zameer Uddin Shah, *The Sarkari Mussalman: The Life and Travails of a Soldier Educationist*, New Delhi, Konark Publishers, 2019, p. 122.
10. Modi continued to stick to this line of defence in the years that followed. In 2004, Shekhar Gupta interviewed him on NDTV for

Walk the Talk and asked him whether he had any 'regret' about the way he had handled the post-Godhra situation. He responded: 'I am waiting for the inquiry commission so that we can get a third party's objective view and then work on the shortcomings.' He added, 'As far as the results are concerned, I managed to protect 98% of Gujarat where not a single untoward incident occurred.' When asked why senior police officers had not been suspended, he responded: 'Rather than me handing out a punishment, it is better if the legal system takes action.' The transcript of this interview has been reproduced in *The Indian Express* on 17 Sept. 2013 as 'The riots took place when I was in power, so I know I can't detach myself from them'. When asked similar questions after this interview, Modi usually made similar responses. However, he sometimes refused to respond. He even left the stage in 2007 when Karan Thapar became too insistent to his taste on a CNN-IBN programme. 'Narendra Modi's run away from studio during interview by Karan Thapar', http://www.youtube.com/watch?v=QHS_eSoOBzg. In July 2013, in an interview with Reuters, he said: 'I would feel guilty if I did something wrong' and 'Up till now, we feel that we used our full strength to set out to do the right thing'. 'Interview with BJP leader Narendra Modi', by Ross Colvin and Sruthi Gottipati, Reuters, 12 July 2013, http://blogs.reuters.com/india/2013/07/12/interview-with-bjp-leader-narendra-modi/?print=1&r= (last accessed 8 Nov. 2013).

11. The main ranks in the Indian Police Service (IPS), from local to state levels of responsibility, are superintendent of police (an IPS officer in charge of a district), inspector general of police (an IPS officer in charge of a range, a territorial unit made of several districts), additional director general of police (a category from which come the commissioners of police in charge of a city as well as officers assisting the director general of police at the state level) and the director general of police, in charge of the state police. Note that the SPs and the commissioners generally report directly to the Chief Minister's Office.
12. 'Report on the visit of NHRC team headed by chairperson, NHRC to Ahmedabad, Vadodara and Godhra from 19–22 March 2002', Annexure 1, appended to National Human Rights Commission, 'Suo motu case no. 1150/6/2001-2002', 1 April 2002, http://nhrc.nic.

in/guj_annex_1.htm (last accessed 8 Nov. 2013). For the original quote, from *The Telegraph*, 2 March 2002, http://www.outlookindia.com/printarticle.aspx?218024 (last accessed 8 Nov. 2013).
13. R.B. Sreekumar, *Gujarat: Behind the Curtain*, New Delhi, Manas Publications, 2016, p. 140.
14. Ibid.
15. During the pogrom, Babu Bajrangi allegedly communicated through his mobile phone with the inspector of police Mysorewala. 'Gujarat 2002: the truth in the words of the men who did it', *Tehelka* (Special issue), 3 Nov. 2007, p. 41.
16. Sreekumar, *Gujarat: Behind the Curtain*, p. 140.
17. Ibid.
18. Ibid., pp. 138–43.
19. Ibid., p. 143.
20. Ibid., p. 145.
21. Ibid.
22. Ibid., pp. 143–6.
23. Steven I. Wilkinson, 'Communal and caste politics and conflicts in India', in Paul R. Brass (ed.), *Routledge Handbook of South Asian Politics: India, Pakistan, Bangladesh, Sri Lanka and Nepal*, London and New York, Routledge, 2009.
24. See the definition given by Jagannathan and Rai: 'A police encounter is a term used in India as a shorthand for dubious police actions resulting in the killing of person(s) whom police allege to be criminal(s), but where police narratives of exchange of firing and self-defence appear to be prima facie unbelievable.' Srinath Jagannathan, Rajnish Rai and Christophe Jaffrelot, 'Fear and violence as organizational strategies: the possibility of a Derridean lens to analyze extra-judicial police violence', *Journal of Business Ethics*, 175 (2022), pp. 465–84, https://doi.org/10.1007/s10551-020-04655-6.
25. 'SC orders probe into 21 "fake" encounters in Guj', *The Times of India* (Ahmedabad edn), 26 Jan. 2012, p. 1. For an overview of these fake encounters, see Amnesty International, India, 'A pattern of unlawful killings by the Gujarat police: urgent need for effective investigations', 24 May 2007, http://www.amnesty.org/en/library/asset/ASA20/011/2007/en/1c189822-d393-11dd-a329-2f46302a8cc6/asa200112007en.pdf (last accessed 4 Dec. 2013).

26. Cited in 'Justice Bedi to probe case of 2003-06 Gujarat fake encounters deaths', *The Hindu*, 3 March 2012.
27. 'Gujarat govt in the line of SC fire again', *The Times of India* (Ahmedabad edn), 25 Feb. 2012. In 2010 Justice Vyas was the first choice of Narendra Modi for the post of Gujarat Lokayukta, but the governor had rejected him, as we shall see later.
28. 'Gujarat encounter killings: SC for sharing of Justice's Bedi Report', *The Hindu*, 26 July 2013, http://www.thehindu.com/news/national/gujarat-encounter-killings-sc-for-sharing-of-justice-bedis-report/article4956594.ece (last accessed 4 Dec. 2013).
29. 'In 10 cases, encounter cops get STF clean chit', *The Indian Express*, (Ahmedabad edn), 10 July 2014, https://indianexpress.com/article/cities/ahmedabad/in-10-cases-encounter-cops-get-stf-clean-chit/.
30. 'What is Justice Bedi Report on Gujarat fake encounters, why SC order could spell trouble for several policemen', *The Indian Express*, 9 Jan. 2019, https://indianexpress.com/article/explained/explained-justice-bedi-report-on-gujarat-fake-encounters-5530501/.
31. Note that some cases, including the killing of four Kashmiri students in an encounter in Ganga Row House in the Vatva area of Ahmedabad in 2006, were not part of Justice Bedi's list. Prashant Dayal, 'One STF, two bosses!', *The Times of India* (Ahmedabad edn), 29 April 2012, p. 1.
32. 'Writ Petition (Criminal) no. 31 of 2007 B.G. Verghese vs Union of India and others with Writ Petition (Criminal) no. 83 of 2007 Javed Akhtar and others vs State of Gujarat & others. Final Report by Justice H.S. Bedi (former Judge, Supreme Court of India), Chairman, Monitoring Authority, Ahmedabad (Gujarat)', known as 'the Justice Bedi Report', p. 193.
33. Ibid., p. 208.
34. Ibid., 219.
35. The Maharashtra Control of Organised Crime Act (1999) is a special law designed by this state, primarily for fighting terrorism. Under this law, confessions before senior police officers are admissible not only against the accused but also against other accused (which is not the case under normal law) and there is no provision for granting anticipatory bail for six months.

36. Sub-inspector of police Daya Nayak became one of the encounter 'specialists' in the Maharashtra police in Mumbai. In the early 2000s, he was known for having killed more than 80 criminals. 'I've done 83 encounters', Rediff News, 23 Oct. 2003, http://www.rediff.com/news/2003/oct/27inter.htm (last accessed 4 Dec. 2013). However, he was suspended in 2006 because he had amassed wealth disproportionate to his income. He was reinstated in the Maharashtra police in 2012. '"Encounter specialist" Daya Nayak reinstated in police department', *The Times of India*, 16 June 2012, http://articles.timesofindia.indiatimes.com/2012-06-16/mumbai/32268943_1_daya-nayak-encounter-specialist-disproportionate-assets-case (last accessed 4 Dec. 2013).
37. An aide of Dawood Ibrahim, Tariq Parveen, was arrested in Dubai and deported to India in July 2004.
38. Cited in Mukul Sinha, 'Countless encounters: death in uniform', *Elaan* (blog), no. 3 (Oct. 2009), p. 1, http://elaanmonthly.blogspot.fr/2009_10_01_archive.html (last accessed 4 Dec. 2013).
39. Rana Ayyub, 'Ishrat Jahan encounter: CBI probe nails IB officer's role', *Tehelka*, 29 June 2013, http://www.tehelka.com/amit-shah-rajendra-kumar-ordered-ishrat-jahan-encounter/ (last accessed 4 Dec. 2013).
40. Sukanya Shantha, 'Sadiq Jamal encounter: CBI names four Mumbai cops', *The Indian Express*, 28 Nov. 2013.
41. FIR of Ahmedabad City Department Crime Branch, PS I CR no. 8/2004 (15 June 2004), Appendix A1 of Jagannathan, Rai and Jaffrelot, 'Fear and violence as organizational strategies'.
42. In November 2013 the CBI sent letters rogatory to Pakistan to gather information on Rana and Johar. 'Ishrat case: CBI sends judicial request to Pakistan', *The Indian Express*, 15 Nov. 2013, http://www.indianexpress.com/story-print/1195357/ (last accessed 4 Dec. 2013).
43. 'Tamang's magisterial enquiry report', Appendix A2 of Jagannathan, Rai and Jaffrelot, 'Fear and violence as organizational strategies'.
44. Manas Dasgupta, 'Ishrat Jahan killing also a fake encounter: probe report', *The Hindu*, 8 Sept. 2009, http://www.hindu.com/2009/09/08/stories/2009090856670100.htm (last accessed 4 Dec. 2013); 'DySP Tarun Barot brought AK-56 to Ishrat encounter

site', *The Indian Express*, 10 July 2013, http://www.indianexpress.com/news/dysp-tarun-barot-brought-ak56-to-ishrat-encounter-site/1139938/ (last accessed 4 Dec. 2013); and R.K. Mishra, 'Ishrat killed in staged encounter: CBI', *Outlook*, 3 July 2013, http://www.outlookindia.com/printarticle.aspx?286652 (last accessed 4 Dec. 2013).

45. 'Amin, Amit Shah spoke 32 times in week before Sohrab killing', *The Times of India*, 27 July 2007, http://articles.timesofindia.indiatimes.com/2010-07-27/india/28281769_1_fake-encounter-case-sohrabuddin-sheikh-g-c-raige (last accessed 4 Dec. 2013).

46. Satish Verma was not only transferred to the post of principal of the Police Training College of Junagadh, but the High Court, revisiting a 15-year-old case, ordered a probe into his involvement in an encounter killing and two custodial deaths in Porbandar district, where he was posted in 1996–97. See Ujjwala Nayudu, 'Satish Verma: the next cop in the firing line?', *The Indian Express* (Ahmedabad edn), 20 April 2012, p. 3.

47. Ilyas Abbas, '14 facts about Ishrat Jahan encounter case', *Niti Central*, 18 June 2013, http://www.niticentral.com/?p=91693 (last accessed 4 Dec. 2013).

48. 'FIR filed by the SIT', Appendix A3 of Jagannathan, Rai and Jaffrelot, 'Fear and violence as organizational strategies'.

49. 'CBI takes charge of Ishrat encounter case', *The Indian Express* (Ahmedabad edn), 7 Jan. 2012, p. 4.

50. 'Summary of the first charge sheet filed by the CBI in Ishrat Jahan encounter case', Appendix A4 of Jagannathan, Rai and Jaffrelot, 'Fear and violence as organizational strategies'.

51. The CBI director, Ranjit Sinha, declared in June 2013: 'We have evidence against Kumar and the agency's proceedings are as per the law.' Rahul Tripathi, 'Ishrat Jahan case: CBI says it has evidence against IB officer', *The Indian Express*, 14 June 2013, http://www.indianexpress.com/news/ishrat-case-cbi-says-it-has-evidence-against-ib-officer/1128936/ (last accessed 4 Dec. 2013). See also Ayyub, 'Ishrat Jahan encounter'.

52. In his biography of Narendra Modi, Nilanjan Mukhopadhyay gives interesting details in this respect. Mukhopadhyay, *Narendra Modi: The Man, the Times*, Chennai, Westland, 2013, p. 302.

53. On the politics of fear, see Haleh Afshar, 'The politics of fear: what does it mean to those who are otherized and feared?', *Ethnic and Racial Studies*, 36 (2013), pp. 9–27; D.L. Altheide, 'Notes towards a politics of fear', *Journal for Crime, Conflict and the Media*, 1 (2003), pp. 37–54; D.L. Altheide, 'Terrorism and the politics of fear', *Cultural Studies Critical Methodologies*, 6 (2006), pp. 415–39; A. Gore, 'The politics of fear', *Social Research*, 71 (2004), pp. 779–98.
54. Cited in Jagannathan, Rai and Jaffrelot, 'Fear and violence as organizational strategies', p. 474.
55. Cited in R. Ayyub, 'Dead man talking', *Tehelka*, 3 December 2011, http://old.tehelka.com/dead-man-talking/ (last accessed 18 May 2020). The report that Justice Bedi submitted in 2018 gives some additional information: 'As per the police version the deceased had come in contact with Muslim Jehadi organizations and on the basis of a passport illegally obtained from Bhopal had got one month's visa to visit Pakistan, had gone, stayed there and had [*sic*] in that country for three years during which period he had obtained training in weapons from the Jaish-e-Mohammed at places such as Karachi, Lahore, Rawalpindi etc. and had thereafter re-entered India through Nepal with the assistance of the ISI and established hide outs in Mumbai, Rajkot and Bhopal etc. It is further the police version that after the attack on the Akshardham Mandir, the deceased had been directed by Rizvan of the Jaish-e-Mohammed who was a resident of Pakistan to go to Ahmedabad and kill the then Chief Minister Mr. Narendrabhai Modi.' The Justice Bedi Report, p. 193.
56. 'Conspiracy to kill Modi: court acquits three', *The Indian Express* (Ahmedabad edn), 25 July 2009, p. 3.
57. 'Police failed to provide evidence in "kill Modi" plot', *The Times of India* (Ahmedabad edn), 24 July 2009, p. 3.
58. 'Fidayeen may be closing in on Modi: intelligence', *DNA* (Ahmedabad edn), 3 Dec. 2008, p. 1.
59. 'Dawood planned to kill Narendra Modi for '02 riots' and 'Dawood had sent 3 men to kill Modi', *DNA*, 3 June 2009, p. 1.
60. 'After 26/11, LeT target was Modi', *The Indian Express* (Ahmedabad edn), 6 Dec. 2010, p. 1.
61. S. Bhattacharya, 'Indian mujahideen: "Modi is one to 10 in the list of targets"', *Outlook*, 29 Oct. 2013, https://www.outlookindia.

com/website/story/modi-is-one-to-10-in-the-list-of-targets/288375 (last accessed 2 Nov. 2013).

62. Cited in Jagannathan, Rai and Jaffrelot, 'Fear and violence as organizational strategies', p. 475.
63. 'Kill-Modi plot falls flat', *The Times of India* (Ahmedabad edn), 24 July 2009, p. 1.
64 Prashant Dayal, 'Modi was on Viquar's hit list', *The Times of India* (Ahmedabad edn), 9 Aug. 2010, p. 4.
65. Jagannathan, Rai and Jaffrelot, 'Fear and violence as organizational strategies', p. 478.
66. 'Tamang's magisterial enquiry report', Appendix A2 of Jagannathan, Rai and Jaffrelot, 'Fear and violence as organizational strategies'.
67. 'Statement of Mr R.B. Sreekumar former DGP Gujarat on 12.09.2013.' See also Jagannathan, Rai and Jaffrelot, 'Fear and violence as organizational strategies', p. 469; and Jahnavi Sen, 'The second killing of Ishrat Jahan', *The Wire*, 2 March 2016, https://thewire.in/politics/the-secon d-killing-of-ishrat-jahan (last accessed 12 Feb. 2018).
68. The Justice Bedi Report, p. 212. In his report, Tirth Raj also indicted 'persons from the Chief Minister's office' (ibid., p. 214). The information compiled in the report of Tirth Raj was also part of what he told Ashish Khetan in the course of a sting operation. See Ashish Khetan, *Undercover: My Journey into the Darkness of Hindutva*, Chennai, Westland, 2021.
69. The Justice Bedi Report, p. 215.
70. Kauser Bi was cremated in Illol (Sabarkantha district), the native village of D.G. Vanzara. 'Kauser Bi killed, body burnt; Gujarat govt to SC', Rediff India Abroad, 30 April 2007, http://www.rediff.com/news/2007/apr/30fake.htm (last accessed 4 Dec. 2013); and Z. Qureshi and V. Zaia, 'Arham farmhouse owner held by CBI', *Ahmedabad Mirror*, 28 July 2010, http://www.ahmedabadmirror.com/article/3/2010072820100728034823923f3076389/Arham-farmhouse-owner-held-by-CBI.html (last accessed 4 Dec. 2013).
71. 'DG Vanzara: all you need to know about Gujarat's former "supercop"', *Firstpost*, 3 Sept. 2013, http://www.firstpost.com/politics/dg-vanzara-all-you-need-to-know-about-gujarats-former-supercop-1082183.html (last accessed 4 Dec. 2013).

72. Syed Khalique Ahmed, 'We hope to get justice', *The Indian Express*, 13 Jan. 2010.
73. 'The journalist who cracked Gujarat fake encounter case', Rediff India Abroad, 25 April 2007, http://www.rediff.com/news/2007/apr/25spec.htm (last accessed 4 Dec. 2013).
74. Atul Dev, 'His master's voice', *The Caravan*, 1 October 2020, https://caravanmagazine.in/law/tushar-mehta-holds-court.
75. 'Who is Geetha Johri?', *NDTV*, 30 July 2010, http://www.ndtv.com/article/india/who-is-geeta-johri-41009 (last accessed 4 Dec. 2013).
76. Ajay Umat emphasises that 'This decision to transfer Vanzara could not have been taken by Amit Shah as per the rules of the business and it was only the Chief Minister who could have finally passed the order.' Ajay Umat, 'CBI encounters "Modi hand" in triple-murder', *Sunday Times of India* (Ahmedabad edn), 19 May 2013, p. 1.
77. Cited in Neena Vyas, 'Geetha Johri report speaks of "collusion of state government"', *The Hindu*, 5 May 2007, http://www.hindu.com/2007/05/05/stories/2007050510410100.htm (last accessed 4 Dec. 2013).
78. According to the CBI, 'Following instructions from Shah, Johri directed investigating officer V.L. Solanki to make changes in the enquiry papers and to prepare a report.' 'Tulsiram Prajapati encounter case: the plot, as "cracked" by CBI', *The Indian Express* (Ahmedabad edn), 21 Sept. 2012, p. 5.
79. 'SC slams Gujarat police probe', *The Indian Express*, 13 Jan. 2010.
80. 'Amit and coterie ran extortion racket', *Hindustan Times*, 24 July 2010, http://www.hindustantimes.com/India-news/Ahmedabad/Amit-amp-coterie-ran-extortion-racket/Article1-576856.aspx (last accessed 4 Dec. 2013).
81. *Tehelka* emphasised the impact of Chudasama's arrest: 'Chudasama was one of the most well-connected police officers in Gujarat's home Ministry, under which the police department falls. Right after his arrest, Modi flew down to Delhi to meet BJP party president and confidant Nitin Gadkari and L.K. Advani at his residence. Subsequently, Modi travelled to Nagpur to discuss the developments with RSS head Mohan Bhagwat. The effect showed in the form of L.K. Advani along with BJP party MPs sitting on a dharna outside

parliament to protest against the mishandling of CBI by the UPA government. Subsequently, Gadkari also issued a three-and-a-half-page statement on this, of which two pages were devoted to defending the Modi government's record.' Rana Ayyub, 'All's not well with your home, minister', *Tehelka*, 7, no. 22 (5 June 2010), http://archive.tehelka.com/story_main45.asp?filename=Ne050610alls_not.asp (last accessed 4 Dec. 2013).

82. See also Rana Ayyub, 'Gujarat home minister Amit Shah called cops arrested for killing Tulsi Prajapati', *Tehelka*, 7, no. 26 (3 July 2010), http://archive.tehelka.com/story_main45.asp?filename=Ne030710gujrat.asp (last accessed 4 Dec. 2013).
83. 'Sohrabuddin: where Gujarat police erred', *The Indian Express* (Ahmedabad edn), 14 Jan. 2010, https://indianexpress.com/article/news-archive/web/sohrabuddin-where-gujarat-police-erred/.
84. Ayyub, 'Gujarat home minister Amit Shah called cops arrested for killing Tulsi Prajapati'.
85. Vinod K. Jose, 'The emperor uncrowned', *The Caravan*, 1 March 2012, http://caravanmagazine.in/reportage/emperor-uncrowned?page=0,9 (last accessed 4 Dec. 2013).
86. Dilip Patel, 'Modi keeps entire home, distributes other portfolios', *Ahmedabad Mirror*, 28 July 2010, p. 4.
87. Sheela Bhatt, 'What Amit Shah's fall really means', Rediff News, 28 July 2010, http://news.rediff.com/special/2010/jul/24/what-amit-shahs-fall-really-means.htm.
88. On the relationship between Amit Shah and Narendra Modi, see Rana Ayyub, 'Breakthrough exposé: so why is Narendra Modi protecting Amit Shah?', *Tehelka*, 7, no. 28 (17 July 2010), http://www.tehelka.com/breakthrough-expose-so-why-is-narendra-modi-protecting-amit-shah/ (last accessed 4 Dec. 2013).
89. Rebecca Samervel, 'Shah appears before Mumbai court', *The Times of India* (Ahmedabad edn), 10 Nov. 2012, p. 3.
90. Cited in 'Out in the open', *Ahmedabad Mirror*, 29 March 2013, p. 9.
91. Cited in Thufail Pt and Sunha Dutta, 'Gujarat's shame', *Tehelka*, 7, no. 29 (24 July 2010), http://www.tehelka.com/breakthrough-expose-so-why-is-narendra-modi-protecting-amit-shah/ (last accessed 4 Dec. 2013).

92. Ibid.
93. Josy Joseph, *The Silent Coup: A History of India's Deep State*, Chennai, Westland, 2021, p. 232.
94. Ujjwala Nayudu, 'D.G. Vanzara arrested by CBI team probing the Ishrat Jahan encounter case', *The Indian Express*, 3 June 2013, http://m.indianexpress.com/news/d-g-vanzara-arrested-by-cbi-team-probing-the-ishrat-jahan-encounter-case/1124497/ (last accessed 4 Dec. 2013).
95. 'The resignation letter of D.G. Vanzara, Gujarat IPS officer', *Biharprabha News*, 3 Sept. 2013, http://news.biharprabha.com/2013/09/senior-gujarat-police-d-g-vanzara-resigns-from-ips-blaming-amit-shah/ (last accessed 4 Dec. 2013).
96. Joseph, *The Silent Coup*, p. 232.
97. This section draws from an article which it also updates: Christophe Jaffrelot, 'Gujarat 2002: what justice for the victims? The Supreme Court, the SIT, the police and the state judiciary', *EPW*, 47, no. 8 (25 Feb. 2012), pp. 77–89.
98. See Teesta Setalvald, 'For healing you need justice', *The Times of India*, 4 Dec. 2002, p. 3. Harsh Mander, a former cadre in the elite Indian Administrative Service, who campaigns for a major Nyayagraha (grip of justice) movement on the model of Gandhi's satyagraha, has written an interesting article on the subject, 'Living in times of fear and hate: failures of reconciliation in Gujarat', *EPW*, 42, no. 10 (10 March 2007), and *Beyond Memory and Forgetting: Massacre and the Modi Years in Gujarat, Delhi*, Yoda Press, 2019.
99. Rowena Robinson, *Tremors of Violence: Muslim Survivors of Ethnic Strife in Western India*, New Delhi, Sage, 2005, p. 45.
100. '"KG Shah is our man: Nanavati is only after money", Advocate General Arvind Pandya claims the accused have nothing to fear from the Nanavati–Shah Commission', *Tehelka*, 8 June 2007, http://www.Tehelka.com/story_main35.asp?filename=Ne031107KG.asp (last accessed 4 Dec. 2013).
101. 'No police lapse in Gujarat riots: Justice Nanavati', Rediff News, 18 May 2003, http://www.rediff.com/news/2003/may/18guj.htm (last accessed 4 Dec. 2013).
102. 'Godhra Inquiry Commission in March 2002', *News Track*, 14 May 2007; 'Nanavati-Mehta Commission gets 18th extension', *The*

Times of India, 30 March 2012, http://www.newstrackindia.com/newsdetails/158 (last accessed 4 Dec. 2013).

103. D.P. Bhattacharya, 'Gujarat riots: How IPS officer Rahul Sharma exposed "rioters"', *India Today*, 12 Aug. 2011 (https://www.indiatoday.in/india/west/story/gujarat-riots-modi-government-rahul-sharma-139188-2011-08-11).
104. In June 2013, the commission closure date was extended for the 20th time until the month of December 2013. 'Nanavati panel gets its 20th extension', *The Indian Express*, 3 July 2013, http://www.indianexpress.com/news/nanavati-panel-gets-its-20th-extension/1136987/ (last accessed 4 Dec. 2013).
105. The transcript of this interview was reproduced in *The Indian Express* on 17 Sept. 2013: 'The riots took place when I was in power, so I know I can't detach myself from them.'
106. See 'Excerpts from the Justice U.C. Banerjee Committee report', *DNA*, 19 Nov. 2019, http://www.dnaindia.com/india/report_excerpts-from-the-justice-u-c-banerjee-committee-report_1016092 (last accessed 4 Dec. 2013).
107. See 'Gujarat High Court stays action on UC Banerjee report', *DNA*, 19 Nov. 2019, http://www.dnaindia.com/india/report_gujarat-high-court-stays-action-on-uc-banerjee-report_1016665 (last accessed 4 Dec. 2013).
108. 'Banerjee panel on Godhra riots illegal: Gujarat HC', *EconomicTimes*, 14 Oct. 2006, https://economictimes.indiatimes.com/news/politics-and-nation/banerjee-panel-on-godhra-riots-illegal-gujarat-hc/articleshow/2170889.cms?utm_source=contentofinterest&utm_medium=text&utm_campaign=cppst.
109. See Manoj Mitta, *The Fiction of Fact-finding: Modi and Godhra*, Noida, HarperCollins, 2014.
110. 'Godhra report says train carnage a conspiracy', CNN-IBN, 25 Sept. 2008, https://web.archive.org/web/20140503015616/http://ibnlive.in.com/news/godhra-report-says-train-carnage-a-conspiracy/74309-3.html (last accessed 10 Nov. 2022).
111. 'Nanavati panel report on 2002 riots tabled in Guj Assembly', *Business Standard*, 11 Dec. 2019, https://www.business-standard.com/article/pti-stories/nanavati-panel-report-on-2002-riots-tabled-in-guj-assembly-119121100355_1.html.

112. '2002 Godhra riots: key points of Justice Nanavati–Mehta Commission report that gave clean chit to Narendra Modi govt', *Firstpost*, 12 Dec. 2019, https://www.firstpost.com/india/2002-godhra-riots-key-points-of-justice-nanavati-mehta-commission-report-that-gave-clean-chit-to-narendra-modi-govt-7772521.html.
113. 'Dilip Trivedi: "some cases were so weak: by God's grace we managed"', *Tehelka*, 3 Nov. 2007, p. 58.
114. Basant Rawat, 'Gujarat riot prosecutors', *The Telegraph*, 12 Oct. 2003.
115. https://www.sabrang.com/news/cjp18oct03.htm.
116. Bharat Bhatt, 'I never took money from the accused', *Tehelka*, 3 Nov. 2007, p. 61, http://archive.tehelka.com/story_main35.asp?filename= Ne031107I_NEVER.asp.
117. Ibid., pp. 60–1.
118. Cited in Janyala Sreenivas, 'Justice? When P in VHP stands for prosecution', *The Indian Express*, 19 Sept. 2003, p. 3.
119. Cited in ibid.
120. Ibid.
121. Amit Mukherjee and Robin David, 'Riots and aftermath: "prosecuting" justice', *The Times of India*, 10 July 2003, https://timesofindia.indiatimes.com/india/riots-and-aftermath-prosecuting-justice/articleshow/68364.cms.
122. 'Statement by Teesta Setalvad, Secretary *Citizens for Justice and Peace* before the Special Investigation Team (SIT) appointed by the Hon'ble Supreme Court through its Order dated 26.3.2008', https://cjp.org.in/wp-content/uploads/2017/05/080509%20SETALVAD%20STATEMENT%20TO%20SIT%20PART%20III.pdf; and 'Appointing Lawyers with Tainted Credentials as Law Officers began in Gujarat: 2002', *Sabrang*, 20 July 2018, https://sabrangindia.in/appointing-lawyers-tainted-credentials-law-officers-began-gujarat-2002/.
123. Arvind Pandya, 'Were Modi not a minister, he would have burst bombs', *Tehelka*, 3 Nov. 2007, p. 53.
124. Ibid., p. 62.
125. 'It's all in the Parivar for some prosecutors', *The Times of India* (Ahmedabad edn), 10 July 2003.
126. Ashish Khetan, 'The truth about the Godhra SIT report', *Tehelka*, 12 Feb. 2011, p. 38.

127. 'Ghodasar case does not go the best way', *The Times of India*, 24 Nov. 2004, https://timesofindia.indiatimes.com/city/ahmedabad/ghodasar-case-does-not-go-the-best-way/articleshow/301724.cms; and Vikram Rautela, 'Ghodasar riot case: police clueless as six convicts jump parole', *The Indian Express*, 8 Jan. 2009, https://indianexpress.com/article/cities/ahmedabad/ghodasar-riot-case-police-clueless-as-six-convicts-jump-parole/.
128. Raghuvir Pandya's anti-Muslim bias led the SIT to point out in its report to the Supreme Court in 2010 that 'the Supreme Court of India has passed serious strictures on the role played by Pandya in this trial which deserves to be brought to the notice of the Bar Association for suitable action as deemed fit.' Cited in Khetan, 'The truth about the Godhra SIT report', p. 37.
129. Amnesty International press release on 26 February 2004 titled 'Gujarat: denial of justice for victims' (Index AI: ASA 20/03/2004), https://www.amnesty.org/fr/documents/asa20/003/2004/fr/.
130. 'Best Bakery case: dateline', Centre for Justice and Peace, https://cjp.org.in/wp-content/uploads/2017/05/bestfactfile.htm; and 'Teesta at SC door with probe plea', *The Telegraph*, 6 Nov. 2004 https://www.telegraphindia.com/india/teesta-at-sc-door with-probe-plea/cid/699836.
131. Quoted in the Amnesty International report 'India: justice, the victim' (Index AI: ASA 20/002/2005), https://www.amnesty.org/fr/wp-content/uploads/sites/8/2021/08/asa200022005fr.pdf.
132. Quoted in Robinson, *Tremors of Violence*, p. 26.
133. The judgment against Zahira, paradoxically, incriminated Shrivastava, but also the state of Gujarat's functionaries. 'Supreme Court on Zahira contempt of court punishment, 8.3.2006', https://cjp.org.in/wp-content/uploads/2017/05/SC8March06Judgment.pdf.
134. See 'Genocide in rural Gujarat: the experience of Dahod district', Mumbai, Forum Against Oppression of Women and Aawaaz-E-Niswaan, n.d., http://www.onlinevolunteers.org/gujarat/reports/rural/rural-gujarat.pdf (last accessed 4 Dec. 2013).
135. Kavita Srivastava, 'The twenty-two-year-old struggle of Bilkis Bano: a journey of hope, courage and camaraderie', *PUCL*, 1 Feb. 2024, https://pucl.org/manage-writings/the-twenty-two-year-

old-struggle-of-bilkis-bano-a-journey-of-hope-courage-and-camaraderie/.

136. S. Anand, 'Bilkis Bano's brave fight', *Tehelka*, 5, no. 4 (2 Feb. 2008).
137. 'Gujarat riot cases to be reopened', BBC News, 8 Feb. 2006, http://news.bbc.co.uk/2/hi/south_asia/4693412.stm; and 'Gujarat riot probe panel moves against 41 cops', *The The Indian Express,* 9 February 2006.
138. Shiv Visvanathan made a most suggestive comment in this regard: 'When the Supreme Court established the Special Investigation Team, the victim and survivor, almost dormant with despair, felt that finally something different was happening.' S. Visvanathan, 'The unmaking of an investigation', *Seminar*, no. 605 (Jan. 2010), p. 3.
139. To concentrate on a few cases only was not an easy decision to make for the NGOs which, since 2002, had been helping the victims to get some justice. Interviews with Gagan Sethi, in Ahmedabad, 6 April 2007. Over two decades, I've met more than once not only Gagan Sethi, but also Father Cedric Prakash, Shabnam Hashmi, Malika Sarabhai and, once, in Ahmedabad, Teesta Setalvad. The question of the quest for justice gradually faded away in our conversations.
140. The SIT could do nothing more than hear witnesses' testimony—it was not authorised to order searches, for instance.
141. Visvanathan, 'The unmaking of an investigation', p. 3.
142. 'SIT to verify antecedents of advocates', *The Indian Express*, 9 May 2009, https://indianexpress.com/article/cities/ahmedabad/sit-to-verify-antecedents-of-advocates/.
143. 'The Gulberg case judge used to browbeat witnesses', Rediff News, 25 March 2010, http://news.rediff.com/interview/2010/mar/25/gulbarg-society-case-prosecutor-speaks-out.htm (last accessed 25 Nov. 2011). Eventually, ten months later, after witnesses and the NGOs supporting them approached the High Court, the court transferred Joshi to the Himmatnagar sessions court and appointed a new judge, B.J. Dhandha.
144. I am grateful to Ashish Khetan for sharing this piece of information with me.
145. In the late 2000s, in Gujarat, '239 Muslims and one Sikh were booked under POTA on charges of waging war against the country,

conspiring to kill BJP leaders, and participating in the ISI's plans of destabilisation'. Anand, 'Bilkis Bano's brave fight'. See also Leena Misra, 'Only minorities figure in Gujarat's POTA list', *The Times of India*, 15 Sept. 2003, p. 5. While the UPA government had repealed the POTA in 2004, very few of the POTA accused were freed on bail in Gujarat.

146. 'They've left Patiya, they don't have the guts to stay here, defying us ... The rest have gone to Karnataka.' 'Gujarat 2002: the truth in the words of the men who did it', p. 13.
147. Mallika Sarabhai, 'Nadeem Saiyed: yet another truth seeker', *Daily News Analysis*, 9 Nov. 2011, https://www.dnaindia.com/analysis/column-nadeem-saiyed-yet-another-truth-seeker-silenced-1608334.
148. 'Death threat: Ode witnesses yet to get protection', *The Indian Express*, 13 Nov. 2011, p. 3.
149. See Dev, 'His master's voice'.
150. He even leaked official reports on the investigation to the RSS. P. Joshi and G. Singh, 'Cop says post-Godhra riots report leaked to RSS man to help accused plan defence', *India Today*, 5 Aug. 2011, https://www.indiatoday.in/india/west/story/gujarat-godhra-riots-report-leaked-to-rss-138809-2011-08-05.
151. See Dev, 'His master's voice'.
152. Ibid.
153. Ibid. In 2013, when the Gujarat High Court heard the case of the extra-judicial killing of Ishrat Jahan—in which Amit Shah was one of the accused—Mehta appeared as the state's counsel to argue against the CBI.
154. 'SIT arrests DySP for Gulberg killing role', *DNA* (Ahmedabad edn), 9 Feb. 209, p. 1.
155. Mustafa Khan, 'Maya Kodnani: conceiving and aborting career in misdeeds', *Countercurrents*, 28 March 2009, https://countercurrents.org/khan280309.htm. See also 'First Modi minister arrested for 2002 riots', *The Indian Express*, 28 March 2009, http://archive.indianexpress.com/news/first-modi-minister-arrested-for-2002-riots/440098/.
156. Besides Modi, the SIT also questioned Praveen Togadia in 2010. Immediately afterwards, he filed a complaint against Zakia Jafri and

her son for 'attempting to create communal hatred and endangering the peace of Gujarat'. *The Hindu*, 16 May 2010, p. 3.

157. FIR against Modi and others lodged by Mrs Jafri, 8 June 2006, https://cjp.org.in/wp-content/uploads/2017/05/060608%20Zakia%20FIR.pdf.
158. The Supreme Court was to exclude Geetha Johri and Shivanand Jha from the SIT on 6 April 2010, a decision Raghavan contested in a memo to the court ten days later.
159. He also claimed that he had no idea his party had joined the *bandh* of 28 February that was behind the violence: 'In the night only I came to know that bandh call had been given by the VHP. However, on 28.02.2002, I came to know from newspaper reports that the bandh had been supported by BJP.' See the transcription of the exchange in *Tehelka*, 12 Feb. 2011, pp. 42–7.
160. Quoted by Ashish Khetan, 'Here's the smoking gun: so how come the SIT is looking the other way?', *Tehelka*, 12 Feb. 2011, p. 29.
161. Cited in ibid., p. 31.
162. Interview with one of the lawyers, M.M. Tirmizi, in Ahmedabad on 26 Feb. 2010.
163. POTA was repealed by the Manmohan Singh government after the BJP was defeated in the 2004 elections, but the effect of this decision was not automatically retroactive.
164. Cited in D.P. Bhattacharya, 'Godhra train fire: lawyers slam Nanavati report', *India Today*, 25 Feb. 2011, https://www.indiatoday.in/india/west/story/godhra-train-fire-lawyers-slam-nanavatis-report-129277-2011-02-24. See also, 'Nanavati panel, Gujarat HC divided on Godhra killings', CNN-IBN, http://ibnlive.in.com/videos/85390/nanavati–panel–gujarat–hc–divided–on–godhra–killings.html (accessed 28 Dec. 2011).
165. Cited in Ashish Khetan, 'Twice burnt, still simmering', *Tehelka*, 3 Nov. 2007, p. 94. This article offers an exhaustive account of the Godhra investigation.
166. 'Gujarat HC notice to SIT on admitting Godhra sting op as evidence', Rediff News, http://www.rediff.com/news/report/gujarat-hc-notice-tosit-on-admitting-godhra-sting-op-as-evidence/20111229.htm (last accessed 4 Dec. 2013)

167. Ashish Khetan, 'The Godhra verdict, burn after reading', *Tehelka*, 5 March 2011, pp. 33–43.
168. Vidya Subrahmaniam, 'Godhra "witness" escapes to tell his story', *The Hindu*, 25 Feb. 2005, p. 3.
169. The author emphasises that 'Other than Jabir's confession there is no material to show that there was a prior plan'. Nitya Ramakrishnan, 'Godhra: the verdict analysed', *EPW*, 46, no. 15 (9 April 2011), p. 42.
170. On the role of Teesta Setalvad after the Gujarat pogrom, see Teesta Setalvad, *Foot Soldier of the Constitution*, New Delhi, LeftWord, 2017.
171. 'No conspiracy, rioters intended to kill: Sardarpura verdict', *The Indian Express*, 10 Nov. 2011, https://indianexpress.com/article/news-archive/latest-news/no-conspiracy-rioters-intended-to-kill-sardarpura-verdict/.
172. This feeling was especially strong among Muslims whose trust in the judiciary has been rekindled. *Radiance*, for instance, wrote: 'It is for the first time in the history of communal riots in India that 31 persons have been convicted for mob violence and mass murder. Otherwise, invariably, in almost all communal massacres the criminals were let off. The monitoring by the Supreme Court, the generally better atmosphere in the country and the feeling that the wheels of justice must move full circle raises the hope that, inshAllah, in other cases also justice would be done.' See 'Sardarpura verdict first step to justice', *Radiance Weekly*, 26 Nov. 2011, http://www.radianceweekly.com/282/7911/ruining-innocent-liveguilt-of-investigating-agencies/2011-11-20/editorial (last accessed 4 Dec. 2013).
173. Parimal Dabhi, 'Sardarpura verdict: why the conspiracy theory fell', *The Indian Express*, 26 Nov. 2011, p. 3.
174. '2002 Gujarat riots: 18 get life term for Ode village massacre', *The Indian Express*, 12 April 2012, http://www.indianexpress.com/news/2002-gujarat-riots-18-get-life-term-for-ode-village-massacre/935868/ (last accessed 4 Dec. 2013).
175. 'Nine get life term in second Ode case', *Hindustan Times*, 4 May 2012, http://www.hindustantimes.com/india-news/nine-get-life-term-in-second-ode-case/article1-850456.aspx.
176. 'Verdict blasts Ahmedabad cops for poor investigation', *The Times of India*, 4 Sept. 2012, http://articles.timesofindia.indiatimes.

com/2012-09-04/ahmedabad/33581467_1_court-verdict-naroda-patia-case-elephantine-task (last accessed 4 Dec. 2013).

177. Ajay Umat, 'Patia judge hinted at Narendra Modi govt's bid to shield Kodnani', *The Times of India*, 2 Sept. 2012, http://articles.timesofindia.indiatimes.com/2012-09-02/india/33548078_1_kodnani-naroda-patia-judge-jyotsna-yagnik (last accessed 4 Dec. 2013).
178. 'In the Supreme Court of India. Special leave petition no. 1088 of 2008, Smt Zakia Ahsan Jafri and Citizens for Justice and Peace … Petitioners versus State of Gujarat and other respondents. Affidavit of Sanjiv Rajendra Bhatt, IPS, April 14, 2011, Ahmedabad.' This document is accessible on the website of NDTV, http://drop.ndtv.com/common/pdf/Sanjiv_Bhatt.pdf?from=NDTV (last accessed 4 Dec. 2013).
179. Ibid. Bhatt also said: 'I submit that on 25th March 2011, when I again tried to bring up the issue of a larger conspiracy or official orchestration behind the Gujarat Riots 2002, as also the ongoing attempts at cover-up, I faced unconcealed hostility from the members of SIT. This was even more obvious when I gave names of witnesses who could corroborate the fact of my having attended the said meeting with the Chief Minister on 27.2.2002.'
180. See 'Ex-BBC journo supports Sanjeev Bhatt's claim', *TwoCircles*, 28 May 2011, http://twocircles.net/2011may28/exbbc_journo_supports_sanjeev_bhatt%E2%80%99s_claim.html (accessed on 30 May 2011 (last accessed 4 Dec. 2013).
181. Ankur Jain, 'Sanjiv Bhatt says SC has opened new doors for him', *The Times of India*, 18 Nov. 2011, https://timesofindia.indiatimes.com/india/sanjiv-bhatt-says-sc-has-opened-new-doors-for-him/articleshow/10780301.cms.
182. Rahul Kripalani, 'Meaning of Supreme Court order on Jafri petition', *EPW*, 46, no. 39 (24 Sept. 2011), p. 11.
183. 'Full text: amicus curiae's report on Gujarat riots', IBN Live, 7 May 2012, http://ibnlive.in.com/news/full-text-amicus-curiaes-report-on-gujarat-riots/255578-53.html. See also 'Gujarat riots: amicus curiae says Modi can be prosecuted', *The Indian Express*, 7 May 2012, http://www.indianexpress.com/news/gujarat-riots-amicus-curiae-says-modi-can-be-prosecuted/946400/0 (last accessed 4 Dec. 2013).

184. Manas Dasgupta, 'SIT rejects amicus curiae's observations against Modi', *The Hindu*, 10 May 2012, http://www.thehindu.com/news/national/sit-rejects-amicus-curiaes-observations-against-modi/article3401728.ece (last accessed 4 Dec. 2013).
185. 'Supreme Court permits Jafri to file fresh petition against Narendra Modi clean chit', *The Times of India*, 8 Feb. 2013, http://articles.timesofindia.indiatimes.com/2013-02-08/india/36992351_1_protest-petition-congress-leader-ehsan-jafri-jakia-jafri (last accessed 4 Dec. 2013).
186. 'Zakia makes final submission challenging SIT's clean chit to Modi', *The Hindu*, 19 Sept. 2013, http://www.thehindu.com/news/national/other-states/zakia-makes-final-submission-challenging-sits-clean-chit-to-modi/article5142910.ece.
187. 'Modi lauds his cops on I-Day', *The Indian Express* (Ahmedabad edn), 15 Aug. 2010, p. 5.
188. Uttam Sengupta, 'Little Gujarat in CBI headquarters', *Outlook*, 27 July 2015, https://magazine.outlookindia.com/story/little-gujarat-in-cbi-headquarters/294874 (last accessed 22 Aug. 2020).
189. The judge even said, 'The investigating officers concerned ought to be held accountable for their ineptitude resulting in injustice, huge harassment of many persons concerned and enormous waste of public resources and public time of the courts.' Cited in Jose, 'The emperor uncrowned'. See also 'The Haren Pandya judgment: dissection of a botched investigation', *EPW*, 46, no. 38 (17 Sept. 2011). Also in 2015, Arun Kumar Sharma, another IPS officer of the Gujarat cadre, was transferred to the CBI as joint director. According to 'highly placed officials' of the CBI, Narendra Modi wanted to give him the key charge of the Policy Division (known as JPC), making him the number two of the CBI. Sharma, however, had a controversial past. He was one of the Gujarat police officers who had been accused of derailing the investigations into the killing of Ishrat Jahan in 2004. The post of 'special commissioner' of the Ahmedabad Detection of Crime Branch had been created for him. The then CBI director, Anil Sinha, refused to appoint him JPC. Dhirendra K. Jha, 'Modi wants CBI to hand over sensitive division to officer with controversial past', *Scroll.in*, 6 July 2015, https://scroll.in/article/739017/modi-wants-cbi-to-hand-over-sensitive-

division-to-officer-with-controversial-past (last accessed 22 July 2020).

190. Paranjoy Guha Thakurta, 'All eyes on SC hearing challenging Rakesh Asthana's appointment as CBI special director', *The Wire*, 11 Nov. 2017, https://thewire.in/law/eyes-sc-hearing-challenging-rakesh-asthanas-appointment-cbi-special-director (last accessed 10 Aug. 2020).

191. Imran Ahmed Siddiqui, 'Godhra probe officer gets CBI charge', *The Telegraph*, 3 Dec. 2016, https://www.telegraphindia.com/india/godhra-probe-officer-gets-cbi-charge/cid/1514419.

192. Vijaita Singh, '"Asthana elevated despite dissent note"', *The Hindu*, 27 Oct. 2017, https://www.thehindu.com/news/national/asthana-elevated-despite-dissent-note/article19927505.ece (last accessed 10 Aug. 2020).

193. See the FIR filed by the CBI against Asthana, the number two of the organisation: 'Full text of FIR against CBI special director Rakesh Asthana for bribery', *The Wire*, 22 Oct. 2020, https://thewire.in/government/full-text-of-fir-against-cbi-special-director-rakesh-asthana-for-bribery (last accessed 10 Aug. 2020).

194. 'Modi ousts CBI chief Alok Verma as Asthana case reaches breakpoint', *The Wire*, 24 Oct. 2018, https://thewire.in/government/centre-intervenes-in-cbis-civil-war-director-alok-verma-sent-on-leave (last accessed 10 Aug. 2020). The CBI director was allegedly eased out—on the recommendation of a secret CVC interim report—because he had met Prashant Bhushan, Arun Shourie and Yashwant Sinha, the three public figures who had filed a complaint at that time, urging the CBI to investigate the Rafale fighter aircraft deal on the grounds of suspected corruption. Neeta Sharma, 'CBI chief meeting Arun Shourie, Prashant Bhushan on Rafale upsets Centre', NDTV, 10 Oct. 2020, https://www.ndtv.com/india-news/narendra-modi-government-upset-with-cbi-director-alok-verma-for-meeting-arun-shourie-and-prashant-bh-1929413 (last accessed 10 Aug. 2020).

195. 'Tried to uphold CBI integrity, attempts were being made to destroy it: Alok Verma on being removed as chief', *India Today*, 11 Jan. 2019, https://www.indiatoday.in/india/story/tried-to-uphold-cbi-integrity-attempts-were-being-made-to-destroy-it-alok-verma-

on-being-removed-as-chief-1428424-2019-01-11 (last accessed 10 Aug. 2020).

196. 'SV Raju appointed additional solicitor general of SC', *The Indian Express*, 30 June 2020, https://indianexpress.com/article/india/sv-raju-appointed-additional-solicitor-general-of-sc-6482332/.
197. See Christophe Jaffrelot, *Modi's India: Hindu Nationalism and the Rise of Ethnic Democracy*, Princeton, NJ, Princeton University Press; Chennai, Westland, 2021, and in particular the section titled 'The Supreme Court, from resistance to surrender', pp. 276–97.
198. Utkarsh Anand, 'Rejected for judgeship, Gopal Subramanium hits out at NDA govt, Supreme Court', *The Indian Express*, 26 June 2014, http://archive.indianexpress.com/news/rejected-for-judgeship-gopal-subramanium-hits-out-at-nda-govt-supreme-court/1264310/0 (last accessed 14 Aug. 2020).
199. Kian Ganz, 'Gopal Subramanium's heartbreakingly honest 9-page withdrawal letter: bows out to avoid clouding others' appointments. "Judiciary compromised" because gov't feared he wouldn't "toe their line"', *Legally India*, 25 June 2014, https://www.legallyindia.com/the-bench-and-the-bar/gopal-subramanium-withdraws-writes-judiciary-compromised-because-gov-t-feared-he-wouldn-t-toe-their-line-20140625-4821 (last accessed 14 Aug. 2020).
200. Ibid.
201. Geeta Pandey, 'Bilkis Bano: India PM Modi's government okayed rapists' release', BBC, 18 Oct. 2022, https://www.bbc.com/news/world-asia-india-62574247.
202. Sohini Ghosh, 'Naroda Gam massacre case: court acquits former BJP minister Maya Kodnani, 66 other accused', *The Indian Express*, 20 April 2023, https://indianexpress.com/article/cities/ahmedabad/naroda-gam-massacre-case-2002-gujarat-riots-8566964/.

4. CREATING A DEEPER STATE

1. Ribeiro was the director general of police in Gujarat in the mid-1980s after completing his term as Mumbai police chief. Julio Ribeiro, *Bullet for Bullet: My Life as a Police Officer*, New Delhi, Penguin, 1998.
2. Himanshu Kaushik, 'Police dept most corrupt', *The Times of India* (Ahmedabad edn), 7 March 2007, p. 3.

3. 'SC upholds lifer in former RS member Abdul Rauf murder case', *One India*, 21 Nov. 2008, https://www.oneindia.com/2008/11/21/sc-uphelds-lifer-in-former-rs-member-abdul-rauf-murder-case-1227278341.html?story=2.
4. Prashant Dayal, 'How can A'bad be safe in his hands?', *The Times of India* (Ahmedabad edn), 28 May 2008, p. 1.
5. Prashant Dayal, 'Crooked path to the crown', *The Times of India* (Ahmedabad edn), 30 May 2008, p. 1.
6. 'Fight terror, show him the door', *The Times of India* (Ahmedabad edn), 31 May 2008, p. 1.
7. Centre for Media Studies and Transparency International India, *India Corruption Study, 2008*, New Delhi, Transparency International India, 2008, p. 254, http://www.transparencyindia.org/resource/survey_study/India%20Corruptino%20Study%202008.pdf (last accessed 4 Dec. 2013).
8. Kaushik, 'Police dept most corrupt', p. 3.
9. Roxy Gagdekar, 'Beware! Criminals in Khaki', *DNA* (Ahmedabad edn), 22 March 2010, p. 3.
10. Parth Shastri, 'Now, a rogues gallery of Ahmedabad cops', *The Times of India* (Ahmedabad edn), 10 April 2010, p. 1. The judiciary was almost equally tainted, partly because of the state government's practices. In 2008, 27 judges, sitting and retired, were allotted residential plots in illegal circumstances, according to the Gujarat High Court, which raised this issue in 2015.
11. In 2010, the average monthly salary for a police constable was Rs. 8,000, compared to Rs. 12,000 in Haryana (and about the same amount in Bihar and Uttar Pradesh). Parth Shastri, 'Gujarat police one of the least paid in the country', *The Times of India* (Ahmedabad edn), 5 Feb. 2010, p. 2.
12. Himanshu Kaushik, 'One cop to protect 1,000 in Gujarat', *The Times of India* (Ahmedabad edn), 4 Feb. 2010, p. 4; '27 judges, sitting and retired, get High Court notice for plots they got from Gujarat govt', *The Indian Express*, 11 Aug. 2015, pp. 1 and 2.
13. Ujjwala Nayudu, 'Modi govt to recruit 5,000 policemen ahead of '14 LS poll, create SI squad', *The Indian Express*, 25 May 2013, http://www.indianexpress.com/news/modi-govt-to-recruit-

5000-policemen-ahead-of-14-ls-poll-create-si-squad/1120483/ (last accessed 4 Dec. 2013).

14. 'First night court', *The Times of India*, 6 Nov. 2006, http://articles.timesofindia.indiatimes.com/2006-11-06/ahmedabad/27793515_1_gujarat-high-court-evening-courts-rules-court-proceedings (last accessed 18 Nov. 2013).
15. Uday Mahurkar, 'After-hours gavel gazing', *India Today*, 27 March 2007, http://indiatoday.intoday.in/story/evening-courts-for-pending-cases/1/156163.html (last accessed 18 Nov. 2013).
16. Ibid.
17. Tables have been included in the Appendix, at the end of the book.
18. See Bibek Debroy, *Gujarat: Governance for Growth and Development*, New Delhi, Academic Foundation, 2012, p. 122.
19. C. Choudhury, 'Courts in slow motion', *Ahmedabad Mirror*, 15 March 2014, p. 2.
20. Bibek Debroy and Laveesh Bhandari, *Economic Freedom for States*, New Delhi, International Management Institute, n.d., p. 23.
21. 'Narendra Modi's open letter to Anna Hazare', 11 April 2011, Narendra Modi website, http://www.narendramodi.in/narendra-modi's-open-letter-to-anna-hazare (last accessed 4 Dec. 2013).
22. 'The Gujarat Lokayukta Act, 1986', http://www.lawsofindia.org/pdf/gujarat/1986/1986GUJARAT31.pdf (last accessed 4 Dec. 2013).
23. It seems Vora was preferred by Modi because, as a member of a division bench of the Gujarat High Court, he had upheld the verdict of the Vadodara fast-track court, acquitting all the accused involved in the Best Bakery massacre case from the 2002 communal riots. 'Why did Modi prefer Justice (retd) J.R. Vora for Lokayukta post?', *TwoCircles*, 5 Sept. 2011, http://twocircles.net/2011sep05/why_did_modi_prefer_justice_retd_j_r_vora_lokayukta_post.html (last accessed 4 Dec. 2013).
24. S. Muralidhar, 'The curious case of Gujarat Lokayukta', Centre Right India, 7 April 2013, https://swarajyamag.com/analysis/the-curious-case-of-gujarat-lokayukta.
25. 'Why did Modi prefer Justice (retd) J.R. Vora for Lokayukta post?'
26. Manas Dasgupta, 'Court comes down on Modi's "false sense of invincibility"', *The Hindu*, 20 Jan. 2012, http://www.thehindu.

com/news/national/court-comes-down-on-modis-false-sense-of-invincibility/article2815109.ece (last accessed 4 Dec. 2013).

27. Cited in 'Lokayukta row: Modi govt challenges Guj HC order in SC', Rediff News, 19 Jan. 2012, http://www.rediff.com/news/report/lokayukta-row-modi-govt-challenges-guj-hc-order-in-sc/20120119.htm (last accessed 4 Dec. 2013).
28. 'Modi govt has done nothing wrong, says panel set up by it', *The Times of India*, 4 Oct. 2012, http://articles.timesofindia.indiatimes.com/2012-10-04/ahmedabad/34259599_1_gujarat-government-bjp-leader-gujarat-congress (last accessed 4 Dec. 2013).
29. 'Proposed bill puts all Lokayukta strings in hands of chief minister', *The Times of India* (Ahmedabad edn), 26 March 2013, p. 3.
30. Darshan Desai, 'Lokayukta: Gujarat bill ending role of governor, CJ passed', *The Hindu*, 2 April 2013, http://www.thehindu.com/news/national/other-states/lokayukta-gujarat-bill-ending-role-of-governor-cj-passed/article4573056.ece (last accessed 4 Dec. 2013).
31. Kapil Dave, 'Justice R.A. Mehta refuses to take the charge as Gujarat Lokayukta', *The Times of India*, 7 Aug. 2013, http://articles.timesofindia.indiatimes.com/2013-08-07/india/41166364_1_gujarat-lokayukta-a-mehta-justice-mehta (last accessed 4 Dec. 2013).
32. 'Gujarat Congress demands full power for Lokayukta', *DNA*, 29 Nov. 2013, http://www.dnaindia.com/ahmedabad/report-gujarat-congress-demands-full-power-for-lokayukta-1926692 (last accessed 4 Dec. 2013).
33. See 'DP Buch to take oath as Lokayukta today', *The Indian Express*, 11 Dec. 2013, http://m.indianexpress.com/news/d-p-buch-to-take-oath-as-lokayukta-today/1206169/ (last accessed 13 Dec. 2013).
34. 'Lokayukta toothless to probe Modi corruption', *The Statesman*, 29 Nov. 2013, http://www.thestatesman.net/news/27388-lokayukta-toothless-to-probe-modi-corruption.html (last accessed 4 Dec. 2013).
35. Sanjay Kumar and Sanjeer Alam, 'Has corruption increased in Gujarat?', *The Indian Express*, 6 Dec. 2007, http://www.indianexpress.com/news/has-corruption-increased-in-gujarat-/247160/ (last accessed 4 Dec. 2013).

36. Centre for Media Studies and Transparency International India, *India Corruption Study, 2008*, p. 250.
37. Ibid., p. 51.
38. Ibid., p. 254.
39. Ibid., p. 252.
40. 'Anti-Corruption Bureau springs five traps across Gujarat', *The Times of India*, 25 Oct. 2013, http://articles.timesofindia.indiatimes.com/2013-10-25/ahmedabad/43393807_1_acb-officials-kalpesh-solanki-deposits-rs (last accessed 4 Dec. 2013).
41. We are referring here to the total annual number of cognisable crimes as compiled by the National Crime Records Bureau.
42. Ministry of Home Affairs, *Crime in India* annual reports, http://www.systemicpeace.org/inscr/inscr.htm (last accessed 4 Dec. 2013).
43. 'Missing kids' parents vent ire at Modi', *DNA* (Ahmedabad edn), 24 June 2012, p. 3.
44. On rapes, see Kumar Anand, 'Gujarat in 2006: state of one rape per day', *The Indian Express*, 9 March 2009, p. 1; '1 rape every week in Ahmedabad', *DNA* (Ahmedabad edn), 3 March 2012, p. 8.
45. Zahid Qureshi, 'Gayab!', *Ahmedabad Mirror*, 10 Jan. 2008, p. 4.
46. This development is particularly obvious among diamond merchants and other traders. 'Fear drives Gujarat's traders to self-protection', *DNA* (Ahmedabad edn), 29 March 2007, p. 1.
47. In 2007, in two months, the total value of thefts reached almost 20 million rupees, for instance. 'Thieves turned crorepatis [millionaires]', *The Times of India*, 9 March 2007, p. 3.
48. Darshini Mahadevia, Renu Desai and Suchita Vyas, 'City Profile: Ahmedabad', Ahmedabad, CEPT University, CUE Working Paper 26, September 2014, p. 2, https://www.academia.edu/24733900/City_Profile_Ahmedabad.
49. Ibid., p. 48.
50. Syed Khalique Ahmed, 'Human Rights Commission reports violations by state police', *The Indian Express* (Ahmedabad edn), 31 March 2010, p. 5.
51. 'Criminal cops: Gujarat killings show up police–underworld nexus', *The Times of India* (Ahmedabad edn), 2 May 2007, p. 10.
52. Deepal Trivedi, Ojas Mehta and Shramana Ganguly, 'Assembly of 34 criminals', *The Asian Age* (Ahmedabad edn), 19 Sept. 2004, p. 1.

53. '27% of new MLAs face criminal charges', *DNA* (Ahmedabad edn), 26 Dec. 2007, p. 2.
54. ADR, *Asset Comparison of Newly Elected MLAs Who Also Contested in Gujarat 2007 Assembly Elections*, 24 Dec. 2012, https://adrindia.org/content/gujarat-assembly-election-2012-asset-comparison-re-elected-mlas-english.
55. ADR, *Analysis of Criminal, Financial and Other Details of MLAs of the Gujarat Assembly Elections 2012*, 24 Dec. 2012, p. 4, https://adrindia.org/content/gujarat-assembly-elections-2012-mla-background-report-english. The 2012 report reads: 'The top three [*sic*] candidates from major parties who have declared serious criminal cases of murder, kidnapping and theft against them are: (1) Chhotubhai Amarsinh Vasava of JD (U) from Jhagadia (ST) constituency who has declared 9 charges related to dacoity, 7 charges related to theft and 3 charges related to murder. (2) Amit Anil Chandra Shah (of BJP from Naranpura constituency) has declared 2 charges related to murder and 2 charges related to kidnapping. (3) Shankarbhai Lagdhirbhai Chaudhary (of BJP from Vav constituency) has declared 3 charges related to murder and 3 charges related to attempt to murder. (4) Jethabhai G. Ahir (of BJP from Shehra constituency) has declared 1 charge related to rape and 1 charge related to kidnapping. (5) Jashubhai Dhanabhai Barad (of INC from Talala constituency) has declared 1 charge related to attempt to murder. ADR, *Analysis of Criminal, Financial and Other Details of MLAs of the Gujarat Assembly Elections 2012*, p. 1. The previous report gave similar results: of the 47 MLAs with criminal cases—there were 36 in 2002—who had been elected in 2007 (out of 182), 25 were from BJP and 20 from Congress. Vikram Rautela, 'Long runs the list of tainted candidates', *The Indian Express*, 25 Dec. 2007, p. 3.
56. Milan Vaishnav, *The Merits of Money and 'Muscle': Essays on Criminality, Elections and Democracy in India*, New York, Columbia University, 2012.
57. On the coding of the affidavit data, see ibid., pp. 263ff.
58. We have explained this distinction elsewhere: 'To separate "serious" crimes, we discard minor charges, such as those that might be related to elections, campaigning, opinion, lifestyle, speech or assembly—or those plausibly related to a politician's vocation.

We are left with charges of a serious nature (a subset of "serious" charges can be called "heinous", which is even narrower in scope). For instance, assault to deter a public servant from discharging his duty is a "serious" charge, while murder and attempted murder qualify for the "heinous" category.' Christophe Jaffrelot and Milan Vaishnav, 'Party in the dock', *The Indian Express*, 9 May 2013, http://www.indianexpress.com/news/party-in-the-dock/1113228/ (last accessed 4 Dec. 2013).

59. I am most grateful to Milan Vaishnav for allowing me to access his database. For biographical details, see 'Law makers or law breakers?', *DNA* (Ahmedabad edn), 26 Nov. 2012, p. 1.
60. 'Gujarat minister, kin get three years in jail for illegal mining', *The Indian Express*, 16 June 2013, https://indianexpress.com/article/cities/ahmedabad/gujarat-minister-kin-get-three-years-in-jail-for-illegal-mining/.
61. Meera Ahmed, 'The curious case of Parshottam Solanki', *Truth of Gujarat*, 8 Aug. 2013, http://www.truthofgujarat.com/the-curious-case-of-parshottam-solanki/ (last accessed 4 Dec. 2013).
62. 'Congress welcomes Gujarat HC decision on Solanki trial', *Global Gujarat News*, 20 Sept. 2012, http://english.globalgujaratnews.com/article/congress-welcomes-gujarat-hc-decision-on-solanki-trial/ (last accessed 4 Dec. 2013).
63. 'Katara's human cargo', *The Times of India*, 20 April 2007, p. 1.
64. 'Tainted ex-Dahod MP in BJP National Council', *The Indian Express*, 4 April 2013, https://indianexpress.com/article/cities/ahmedabad/tainted-exdahod-mp-in-bjp-national-council/.
65. Rautela, 'Long runs the list of tainted candidates', p. 3.
66. Bibek Debroy and Laveesh Bhandari, 'Corruption in India', *The World Financial Review*, 3 March 2012, http://www.worldfinancialreview.com/?p=1575 (last accessed 4 Dec. 2013).
67. This section draws from Christophe Jaffrelot and Basim-U-Nissa, 'The struggle of RTI activists in Gujarat', *EPW*, 53, no. 33 (18 Aug. 2018), pp. 62–7.
68. 'An indicative list of RTI users attacked so far (maintained for the NCPRI)', National Campaign for People's Right to Information, 4 Sept. 2017, https://docs.google.com/spreadsheets/

d/1FTKRkFmsXN1lYHEVUx7-O7OeaRZLNakf2Fn9MII1C1A/edit#gid=0.

69. Kunal Majumder, 'The dead will not seek power', *Tehelka*, 8, no. 11 (26 Feb. 2011), http://www.tehelka.com/2011/02/the-dead-will-not-seek-power/?singlepage=1.
70. Interestingly, an RTI activist also filed a similar petition in Ahmedabad, but the commission in charge said that private companies are not supposed to share information according to the RTI Act. This limitation of the RTI Act is well explained by Prashant Sharma, *Democracy and Transparency in the Indian State: The Making of the Right to Information Act*, London, Routledge, 2015.
71. He was active in many other ways. For a detailed account of his achievements see https://en.wikipedia.org/wiki/Amit_Jethwa.
72. For NGOs of RTI activists the case of Jethwa is different, however, because they suspect he was using RTIs for extorting money. Indeed, he settled down in Ahmedabad and started to file RTIs for one of the two companies against the other—and his lifestyle changed in the process.
73. Satish Jha, 'Amit Jethva murder case: blow to ex-BJP MP Dinu Solanki as Gujarat HC orders fresh trial', *The Indian Express*, 29 June 2017, http://indianexpress.com/article/india/rti-activist-amit-jethva-murder-case-blow-to-ex-bjp-mp-dinu-solanki-as-gujarat-hc-orders-fresh-trial-4727347/.
74. Cited in Pankti Jog, 'Cost of filing RTI with police in Gujarat: activist-journalist Shailesh Patel "murdered" by bootleggers', *Counterview*, 20 June 2015, http://www.counterview.net/2015/06/cost-of-filing-rti-with-police-in.html. See also a short TV report, https://www.youtube.com/watch?v=YYDulaF6pYU.
75. 'Meet Manisha', Namati, https://namati.org/stories/meet-manisha/.
76. Josy Joseph, *The Silent Coup: A History of India's Deep State*, Chennai, Westland, 2021, pp. 230–44.
77. Once again, the Centre asked the Modi government to amend the text of the GujCOC, and once again Modi refused. 'No, no, no says Modi to Centre's 3 GujCOC changes', *DNA* (Ahmedabad edn), 21 June 2009, p. 1.

78. 'Few tears for GujCOC', *DNA* (Ahmedabad edn), 20 June 2009, p. 3; and Rajiv Shah, 'Phone tapping to come back in GujCOC', *The Times of India* (Ahmedabad edn), 3 July 2009, p. 3.
79. See also 'Modi has a snooping habit, I was told to tap Vaghela: Sreekumar', *The Indian Express*, 20 Nov. 2013, https://indianexpress.com/article/news-archive/web/modi-has-a-snooping-habit-i-was-told-to-tap-vaghela-sreekumar/.
80. 'Cong alleges phone tapping by state govt', *Ahmedabad Mirror*, 29 April 2009, p. 9.
81. Dilip Patel, 'Modi's budget: 200 million rupees to spy on friends, foes', *Ahmedabad Mirror*, 4 March 2008, p. 2.
82. 'Gujarat phone tapping spikes to 90,000 cases, intrigues central intelligence agencies', *The Indian Express*, 25 June 2013, http://www.indianexpress.com/news/gujarat-phone-tapping-spikes-to-90000-cases-intrigues-central-intelligence-agencies/1133637/ (last accessed 4 Dec. 2013).
83. 'For "saheb", Amit Shah used cops to snoop on woman: news portals', *The Indian Express*, 15 Nov. 2013, https://indianexpress.com/article/cities/ahmedabad/for-saheb-amit-shah-used-cops-to-snoop-on-woman-news-portals/.
84. Ashish Khetan and Raja Chowdhury, 'The stalkers: Amit Shah's illegal surveillance exposed', Cobrapost, 15 Nov. 2013, https://cobrapost.com/blog/stalkers-amit-shahs-illegal-surveillance-exposed/904.
85. Pradeep Sharma was the younger brother of an IPS officer who was also at loggerheads with the Modi government.
86. Cited in Khetan and Chowdhury, 'The stalkers'.
87. 'No one's family', *Outlook*, 2 Dec. 2013, https://www.outlookindia.com/magazine/story/no-ones-family/288625.
88. Series of transcripts are available on the website of Cobrapost and another one was accessible, at least till 2014, on the website of *Outlook*.
89. 'Don't worry, sir. She won't escape', *Outlook*, 2 Dec. 2013, https://www.outlookindia.com/magazine/story/dont-worry-sir-she-wont-escape/288623 (last accessed 13 Jan. 2014).
90. 'No one's family'.
91. In 2010, his brother, Kuldip Sharma—who had denounced alleged collusion between Amit Shah and Ketan Parekh, the prime accused

in the Madhavpura Mercantile Cooperative Bank scam, and who then guided the probe in the Sohrabuddin case—was charged for an extra-judicial killing that occurred in 1984 when he was SP of Kutch district: in both cases (as in so many others) old stories were resurrected in order to put officers behind bars. 'Top cop Kuldip Sharma booked for 1984 encounter killing', *The Times of India* (Ahmedabad edn), 11 Aug. 2010, p. 10.

92. A. Raman and R.K. Misra, 'These streets have eyes', *Outlook*, 2 Dec. 2013, https://www.outlookindia.com/national/these-streets-have-eyes-news-288624.
93. Khetan and Chowdhury, 'The stalkers'.
94. Gilles Favarel-Garrigues and Laurent Gayer, *Proud to Punish: The Global Landscape of Rough Justice*, Stanford, Stanford University Press (forthcoming).
95. Gilles Favarel-Garrigues and Laurent Gayer, 'Violer la loi pour maintenir l'ordre: le vigilantisme en débat', *Politix*, 29, no. 115 (2016), p. 9.
96. One of the first 'vigilance committees' was established in 1856 by WASPs in San Francisco to watch and discipline the Irish, who were supposedly criminally inclined.
97. Smita Gupta and Christophe Jaffrelot, 'The Bajrang Dal: the new Hindu nationalist brigade', in Mushirul Hasan (ed.), *Living with Secularism: The Destiny of India's Muslims*, New Delhi, Manohar, 2007, pp. 197–222; and Christophe Jaffrelot, 'The militias of Hindutva: communal violence, terrorism and cultural policing', in Laurent Gayer and Christophe Jaffrelot (eds), *Armed Militias of South Asia: Fundamentalist, Maoists and Separatists*, London, Hurst; New York, Columbia University Press; New Delhi, Foundation Books, 2009, pp. 199–236.
98. Malvika Maheshwari, *Art Attacks: Violence and Offence-taking in India*, Delhi, Oxford University Press, 2019, pp. 223–4.
99. Praveen Swami, 'Predatory pursuit of power', *Frontline*, 23 May 1998, https://frontline.thehindu.com/politics/article30161515.ece.
100. Many years after the events, policemen are still stationed in neighbourhoods where clashes occurred and they patrol those refugee camps that remain in operation.

101. Interview with N.K. Singh, Ahmedabad, 4 April 2007.
102. 'Parzania: case against Bajrang Dal leader', *The Times of India*, 7 Feb. 2007, http://timesofindia.indiatimes.com/articleshow/1574339.cms?utm_source=contentofinterest&utm_medium=text&utm_campaign=cppst; and *The Indian Express* (Ahmedabad edn), 22 March 2007, p. 3.
103. Acharya mentioned 'in his complaint that Bajrangi seems to be running a parallel government in the state'. 'Case against Bajrang Dal leader over screening of 'Parzania", *Zeenews*, 7 Feb. 2007, https://zeenews.india.com/home/case-against-bajrang-dal-leader-over-screening-of-parzania352686.html.
104. Bajrangi paid particular attention to the girls of his caste, the Patels. See D.P. Bhattacharya, 'Bajrangi goes gung-ho with "rescue operations"', *The Indian Express* (Ahmedabad edn), 14 April 2007, p. 3.
105. Syed Khalique Ahmed, 'From Naroda-Patiya to Parzania: he's the one calling the shot', *The Indian Express* (Ahmedabad edn), 18 Feb. 2007, p. 3.
106. A telling story was reported in the press in 2006, that of Swati Khare (19) and Amir Raza (21) who hailed from Kosamba. They eloped and got married in Bangalore but returned to visit Swati's parents soon after. They then called the Bajrang Dal: 'Swati was taken in a car to Kosamba police station where she was forced to sign a police complaint against her husband. Sub-Inspector J.K. Rabari reportedly aligned with the [Bajrang Dal] activists, telling her [that she] and her husband would be killed in an encounter. A case of dowry and assault was thus registered with Kosamba police. The next day Swati was reportedly taken to Riddhi Siddhi Maternity Hospital in Bharuch town where she was made to undergo an abortion.' Soumik Dey, 'Muslim boy weds Hindu girl, Dal ensures they won't live happily ever after', *The Indian Express* (Ahmedabad edn), 10 Oct. 2010, p. 1. Swati managed to flee and submit a writ petition in the Gujarat High Court.
107. *The Indian Express* (Ahmedabad edn), 21 Feb. 2007; and *The Times of India* (Ahmedabad edn), 22 Feb. 2007, p. 3.
108. See 'Civil society organisation demands Bajrangi's arrest', *The Indian Express*, 26 April 2007, p. 3.

109. Ranjit Hoskote, 'The mob as censor', *The Hindu*, 11 Feb. 2004, p. 3.
110. Maheshwari, *Art Attacks*, pp. 1–2 and 284.
111. One of his canvases represented a goddess giving birth to a man, and another showed penises forming a Christian cross, which the local church also criticised.
112. Madanjeet Singh, 'Cultures and vultures: wake-up call from Vadodara', *The Hindu*, 18 May 2007, https://www.southasiafoundation.org/SAF-News/Article-1213-Cultures-and-Vultures-wake-up-call-from-Vadodara.htm. For a complete overview, see Anupama Katakam, 'Attack on art', *Frontline*, 1 June 2007, pp. 26–32.
113. Interview with a former Gujarat cadre IPS officer under cover of anonymity in Ahmedabad on 5 April 2007.
114. Lt Gen. Zameer Uddin Shah, *The Sarkari Mussalman: The Life and Travails of a Soldier Educationist*, New Delhi, Konark Publishers, 2019, p. 123.
115. Moyukh Chatterjee, 'The ordinary life of Hindu supremacy: in conversation with a Bajrang Dal activist', *EPW–Engage*, 53, no. 4 (27 Jan. 2018), https://www.epw.in/engage/article/ordinary-life-hindu-supremacy (last accessed 26 Sept. 2020).
116. Pavan Dahat, Gopal Sathe and Aman Sethi, 'Bhima Koregaon lawyers were targeted in WhatsApp spyware scandal', HuffPost, 31 Oct. 2019, https://www.huffingtonpost.in/entry/whatsapp-hacking-bhima-koregaon-lawyers-targeted_in_5dba8e9ae4b066da552c5028; and Sukanya Shantha, 'Indian activists, lawyers were "targeted" using Israeli spyware Pegasus', *The Wire*, 31 Oct. 2019, https://thewire.in/tech/pegasus-spyware-bhima-koregaon-activists-warning-whatsapp (last accessed 18 Sept. 2020). WhatsApp—the application used by the attackers to break into phones—has sued NSO Group. R. Satter and E. Culliford, 'WhatsApp sues Israel's NSO for allegedly helping spies hack phones around the world', Reuters, 29 Oct. 2019, https://www.reuters.com/article/us-facebook-cyber-whatsapp-nsogroup-idUSKBN1X82BE (last accessed 18 Sept. 2020).
117. Anuj Srivas and Kabir Agarwal, 'Snoop list has 40 Indian journalists, forensic tests confirm presence of Pegasus spyware on some', *The Wire*, 18 July 2021, https://thewire.in/media/pegasus-project-spyware-indian-journalists; 'Pegasus: Rahul Gandhi, Prashant Kishor among those allegedly targeted', *Business Standard*, 19 July 2021,

https://www.business-standard.com/article/current-affairs/pegasus-rahul-gandhi-prashant-kishore-among-those-allegedly-targeted-121071901045_1.html; Aashish Aryan and Pranav Mukul, 'Phones of 2 ministers, 3 opp leaders among many targeted for surveillance: report', *The Indian Express*, 19 July 2021, https://indianexpress.com/article/india/project-pegasus-phones-of-2-ministers-3-opp-leaders-among-many-targeted-for-surveillance-report-7411027/.

118. Martand Kaushik and Anjaneya Sivan, 'Bhima Koregaon case: prison-rights activist Rona Wilson's hard disk contained malware that allowed remote access', *The Caravan*, 12 March 2020, https://caravanmagazine.in/politics/bhima-koregaon-case-rona-wilson-hard-disk-malware-remote-access (last accessed 14 Sept. 2020).
119. Vijaita Singh, '1,100 rioters identified using facial recognition technology: Amit Shah', *The Hindu*, 12 March 2020, https://www.thehindu.com/news/cities/Delhi/1100-rioters-identified-using-facial-recognition-technology-amit-shah/article31044548.ece (last accessed 18 Sept. 2020).
120. Ibid.
121. Gautam Bhatia, 'India's growing surveillance state', *Foreign Affairs*, 19 Feb. 2020, https://www.foreignaffairs.com/articles/india/2020-02-19/indias-growing-surveillance-state (last accessed 18 Sept. 2020).
122. In October 2020, Vivek Raghavan, the chief product manager and biometric architect of the Unique Identification Authority of India, declared that the UIAI was 'developing face authentication system which will be available to all the Aadhaar holders'. The UIAI had 'allowed face recognition as an additional means of Aadhaar authentication' in 2018. 'Aadhaar authentication via face recognition from July: how it will work', NDTV, 15 Jan. 2018, https://www.ndtv.com/business/aadhaar-authentication-via-face-recognition-from-july-how-it-will-work-1800194 (last accessed 6 Oct. 2020).
123. I elaborated upon this question of the making (or 'formation') of a parallel state, resulting in a de facto Hindu Rashtra, in ch. 7 of Christophe Jaffrelot, *Modi's India: Hindu Nationalism and the Rise of Ethnic Democracy*, Princeton, NJ, Princeton University Press; Chennai, Westland, 2021, pp. 211–47.

124. 'In our judiciary, anybody can be bought, says Gujarat CJ', *The Times of India*, 6 March 2010, http://articles.timesofindia.indiatimes.com/2010-03-06/india/28137253_1_court-judges-judicial-officers-judiciary (last accessed 4 Dec. 2013).
125. On this phenomenon, see an interesting article by Kapil Dave, 'In the last seven years, the state has paid over Rs. 120 million to the advocate general (AG) and the additional advocate general (AAG) for appearing in important cases, including lucrative ones like the Lokayukta's appointment and the petition filed by Zakia Jafri [...] In 2011, present AAG Tushar Mehta received Rs. 53.5 million and AG Kamal Trivedi Rs. 17 million from the government.' See Kapil Dave, '2 top Guj lawyers made Rs. 7 cr. fighting for Modi in 2011', *The Times of India* (Mumbai edn), 21 Nov. 2012, p. 9.
126. Cited in Manas Dasgupta, 'Hazare: Gujarat is a "land of scams", more liquor than milk in the state', *The Hindu*, 27 May 2011, http://www.thehindu.com/news/national/hazare-gujarat-is-a-land-of-scams-more-liquor-than-milk-flows-in-the-state/article2052073.ece (last accessed 11 Dec. 2013). Hazare made a similar statement from Bihar in 2013: 'Narendra Modi for PM? Gujarat is not corruption-free, says Anna Hazare', NDTV, 31 Jan. 2013, http://www.ndtv.com/article/india/narendra-modi-for-pm-gujarat-is-not-corruption-free-says-anna-hazare-324740 (last accessed 11 Dec. 2013).
127. This goes well with the fact that, while Gujarat has the second largest number of Indian criminals on the list of Interpol (after Delhi—68 as against 73), a majority of them are involved in 'white-collar crime', including the creation of bogus companies. See Paul John, 'Gujarat's hall of shame', *The Times of India* (Ahmedabad edn), 3 Feb. 2012, p. 2.
128. Cited in Aseema Sinha, *Regional Roots of Developmental Politics in India: A Divided Leviathan*, New Delhi, Oxford University Press, 2005, p. 228.
129. Jennifer Bussell, *Corruption and Reform in India*, Cambridge, Cambridge University Press, 2013, pp. 43, 107 and 188.
130. Ibid., p. 184.

PART THREE: DEVELOPMENT OR GROWTH?

1. Sinha, *The Regional Roots of Developmental Politics in India.*

2. John Wood, 'On the periphery but in the thick of it: some recent political crises viewed from Gujarat', in Philip Oldenburg (ed.), *India Briefing: Staying the Course*, Armonk, NY, M.E. Sharpe, 1995, p. 158.
3. In 1991, Gujarat was clearly in a position to benefit fully from the new liberalisation policy. It then displayed a much more dynamic economy than most other states of the Indian Union. Indeed, in the 1990s, it was ahead of other dynamic states like Maharashtra, Andhra Pradesh and Tamil Nadu by a margin of one to two percentage points in terms of annual growth rate.
4. Aseema Sinha, 'Reforming public services in a high growth state', in Vikram K. Chand (ed.), *Public Service Delivery in India: Understanding the Reform Process*, New Delhi, Oxford University Press, 2010, p. 134.
5. It was used, for instance, 'to institute a generous voluntary retirement scheme (VRS) for around 14,000 employees, especially those of the Gujarat State Textile Corporation'. Ibid., p. 138. This corporation was closed down, as were four others.
6. Ibid., p. 142.

5. A NEW BRAND OF CRONY CAPITALISM

1. 'Advantage Gujarat, once again', *The Pioneer* (Ahmedabad edn), 17 Feb. 2002.
2. Dionne Bunsha, 'A new oarsman', *Frontline*, 26 Oct. 2001, p. 32.
3. 'Modi unveils 10-point plan to reinvigorate economy', *The Economic Times* (Ahmedabad edn), 22 Dec. 2001, p. 3.
4. In an interview, Prof. Bakul Dholakia (IIM Ahmedabad) estimated the loss at 1 billion rupees. 'Economic impact of riots will differ for different factors', *The Times of India* (Ahmedabad edn), 22 March 2002, p. 2.
5. 'PM assures economic revival package for state', *The Economic Times* (Ahmedabad edn), 5 April 2002, p. 1.
6. Ibid.
7. Nandini Oza, 'Gujarat stands to lose 300 billion rupees annually', *The Asian Age* (Ahmedabad edn), 26 April 2002, p. 6. According to another estimate, the 'industry in Gujarat had lost 20 billion rupees in the riots.' Cited in Vinod K. Jose, 'The emperor uncrowned', *The*

Caravan, 1 March 2012, http://caravanmagazine.in/reportage/emperor-uncrowned?page=0,9 (last accessed 18 Nov. 2013).

8. Kingshuk Nag, *The NaMo Story: A Political Life*, New Delhi, Roli Books, 2013, p. 108. In November Azim Premji declared similarly at an IIM-A seminar: 'Investors are wary of coming to Gujarat due to the lingering communal tensions in the state apart from its proximity to Pakistan.' 'Communal Gujarat scares investors: Premji', *The Asian Age* (Ahmedabad edn), 21 Nov. 2003, p. 9.
9. Himanshu Kaushik, 'Now, BJP harps on development mantra', *The Indian Express*, 20 Jan. 2003, p. 3.
10. 'Narendra Modi unveils "BIG 2020" document for 19 infrastructure sectors in Gujarat', *DNA*, 1 July 2010, https://www.dnaindia.com/india/report-narendra-modi-unveils-big-2020-document-for-19-infrastructure-sectors-in-gujarat-1403731.
11. Bibek Debroy, *Gujarat: Governance for Growth and Development*, New Delhi, Academic Foundation, 2012, p. 51.
12. Atul Sood, 'Rousing growth amid raging disparities', in Atul Sood (ed.), *Poverty amidst Prosperity: Essays on the Trajectory of Development in Gujarat*, Delhi, Aakar Books, 2012, p. 14.
13. N. Madhavan, 'Gujarat's power sector turnaround story', *Business Today*, 31 Jan. 2012, http://businesstoday.intoday.in/storyprint/21750 (last accessed 18 Nov. 2013).
14. P. Vashisht and G. Arya, 'Public–private partnership: insights from infrastructure development', in Sood, *Poverty amidst Prosperity*, p. 78.
15. Ibid.
16. Directorate of Economics and Statistics, *Socio-economic Review, 2012–2013*, Gujarat State, Gandhinagar, Government of Gujarat, Feb. 2013, p. 32. Bibek Debroy offers two figures. For him, the share of the private sector in total installed capacity is between 25 per cent and 40 per cent. See Debroy, *Gujarat*, p. 48.
17. Ibid., p. 80.
18. Directorate of Economics and Statistics, *Socio-economic Review, 2012–2013*, p. xiii.
19. S. Khanna, 'Guj sold 14.5 billion rupees power to other states in 3 years', *DNA* (Ahmedabad edn), 3 March 2011, p. 1.

20. Rajiv Shah, 'State govt mulls raising power tariff for farmers', *The Times of India* (Ahmedabad edn), 26 July 2011, p. 7.
21. Vashisht and Arya, 'Public–private partnership', p. 82.
22. Ibid., pp. 81–2.
23. M.V. Kamath and Kalindi Randeri, *Narendra Modi: The Architect of a Modern State*, New Delhi, Rupa, 2009, p. 256.
24. Nandan Nilekani, co-founder of Infosys, made this point in his book *Imagining India*: 'Despite all his baggage and his unappealing Hindutva triumphalism, Modi may have been the first politician to demonstrate to his voters how markets could work better than any corrupt subsidy system in accessing electricity, water and roads.' Nandan Nilekani, *Imagining India: Ideas for the New Century*, New Delhi, Penguin Books, 2008, p. 310.
25. Chaitanya Kalbag, 'Gujarat chief minister Narendra Modi on the state's development', *Business Today*, 6 Jan. 2011, http://businesstoday.intoday.in/storyprint/11910 (last accessed 18 Nov. 2013). Nirendra Dev points out in the same vein: 'Like his critics and admirers admit, Modi functions like a modern-day CEO laying emphasis on the outcome and often allegedly putting the rules and normal norms into backburner.' Nirendra Dev, *Modi to Moditva*, New Delhi, Manas Publications, 2012, p. 169.
26. Vashisht and Arya, 'Public–private partnership', p. 67.
27. Ibid.
28. 'Gujarat's roads to success', *TrafficInfraTech Magazine*, 3 June 2013, https://www.trafficinfratech.com/gujarat's-roads-to-success/.
29. Arnab Bandyopadhyay and Natalya Stankevich, *Institutional Development and Good Governance in the Highway Sector: Learning from Gujarat*, Washington, World Bank, 2010, https://openknowledge.worldbank.org/handle/10986/27815.
30. Ibid., p. 8.
31. Ibid., p. 21.
32. 'Gujarat's state highways: the roads leading to the state's progress!', 27 Dec. 2012, Narendra Modi website, https://www.narendramodi.in/gujarat's-state-highways-the-roads-leading-to-the-state's-progress-4888.
33. Bandyopadhyay and Stankevich, *Institutional Development and Good Governance in the Highway Sector*, p. 19.

34. Ibid., p. 45.
35. Vashisht and Arya, 'Public–private partnership', p. 69.
36. Ibid., p. 73.
37. Ibid., p. 65.
38. Ibid., p. 64.
39. Sood, 'Rousing growth amid raging disparities', p. 13.
40. This section and the two following ones draw from Christophe Jaffrelot, 'Business-friendly Gujarat under Narendra Modi: the implications of a new political economy', in Christophe Jaffrelot, Atul Kohli and Kanta Murali (eds), *Business and Politics in India*, New York, Oxford University Press; Delhi, Oxford University Press, 2019, pp. 211–33.
41. Besides industrialists, the business community comprised many small-scale enterprises reflecting the strength of the urban economy, a development fostered by the shift of the Patidars from villages to towns. See Véronique Dupont, *Decentralized Industrialisation and Urban Dynamics*, New Delhi, Sage, 1995; and P.G. Pathak, 'Industrial structure in Gujarat: a study in spatial dimension', in D.T. Lakdawala (ed.), *Gujarat Economy: Problems and Prospects*, Ahmedabad, Sardar Patel Institute of Economic and Social Research, 1982, pp. 441–75. See also Shobha Bondre, *How Gujaratis Do Business*, New Delhi, Random House, 2013. The Gujarat development pattern even relied on what Mario Rutten called 'rural industrialists'. Mario Rutten, *Farms and Factories: Social Profile of Large Farmers and Rural Industrialists in West India*, Delhi, Oxford University Press, 1995.
42. Archana Dholakia and Ravindra Dholakia, 'Policy reform in economic sectors', in Arvind Panagarya and M. Govinda Rao (eds), *The Making of Miracles in Indian States: Andhra Pradesh, Bihar and Gujarat*, New Delhi, Oxford University Press, 2015, p. 251.
43. For instance, in 2010-11, the government of Gujarat spent only 39.88 per cent of the grants given by the Centre for backward regions. Rajiv Shah, 'Govt spending in backward areas nosedives, says report', *The Times of India*, 14 Dec. 2011, http://timesofindia.indiatimes.com/articleshow/11103575.cms?utm_source=contentofinterest&utm_medium=text&utm_campaign=cppst.
44. Dholakia and Dholakia, 'Policy reform in economic sectors', p. 252.

45. Government of Gujarat, 'Gujarat Act no. 2 of 2009', January 2009, p. 20, http://www.gidb.org/pdf/sirord.pdf.
46. Government of Gujarat, *Industrial Policy, 2009*, January 2009, p. 3, http://www.ic.gujarat.gov.in/pdf/industrial-policy-2009-at-a-glance.pdf.
47. Indira Hirway, Neha Shah and Rajeev Sharma, 'Political economy of subsidies and incentives to industries in Gujarat', in Indira Hirway, Amita Shah and Ghanshyam Shah (eds), *Growth or Development: Which Way Is Gujarat Going?*, New Delhi, Oxford University Press, 2014, p. 147.
48. Government of Gujarat, *Industrial Policy, 2009*, p. 13.
49. Hirway, Shah and Sharma, 'Political economy of subsidies and incentives to industries in Gujarat', pp. 161–3.
50. Ibid., p. 149.
51. Ibid., p. 156.
52. See Debroy, *Gujarat*, p. 165.
53. Atul Kohli, *Poverty amid Plenty in the New India*, Cambridge, Cambridge University Press, 2012, p. 192.
54. Sanjay Gupta, the CEO of the Adani Group, uses the same words in an interview of 2003: 'The industry friendly, hassle free, single door clearance policy of the government has ensured that the investment flow continues in the state.' See 'Industrial policy to usher investment in Gujarat', *The Pioneer*, 8 Nov. 2003, p. 11.
55. As Nikita Sud herself says in *Liberalization, Hindu Nationalism and the State: A Biography of Gujarat*, New Delhi, Oxford University Press, 2012, p. 63. The manner in which Gujarat's government related to the corporate sector was illustrated by the way it retained control over the merging and acquisition of enterprises. For instance, when British Gas put up one of its subsidiaries, Gujarat Gas, for sale, not only were Adani Gas and Torrent Power, 'two private companies interested in the purchase […] advised to keep away', but in the end the state company GSPC 'took over Gujarat Gas at a cost of 26.94 billion, a heavy discount from the market price of 40 billion rupees.' Kingshuk Nag, *The NaMo Story: A Political Life*, New Delhi, Roli Books, 2013, p. 16.
56. Sud, *Liberalization, Hindu Nationalism and the State*, p. 85.
57. Ibid., p. 87.

58. Ibid.
59. Narendra Modi used this formula in one of the Vibrant Gujarat meetings. See George Hype, 'In Gujarat, sow a rupee & reap a dollar: Modi', Rediff News, 8 Jan. 2008, http://www.rediff.com/news/2006/jan/08pbd1.htm (last accessed 18 Nov. 2013).
60. 'Investors back out, vibrant plans go awry', *The Times of India* (Ahmedabad edn), 4 March 2008, p. 1.
61. Nag, *The NaMo Story*, p. 113.
62. Ibid.
63. Ibid., p. 116.
64. Ibid., p. 121.
65. Debroy, *Gujarat*, p. 71.
66. In addition to SEZs, the Modi government created a Special Economic Region in 2009 on the Delhi–Mumbai corridor in order to facilitate investments in this area too.
67. Debroy, *Gujarat*, p. 71.
68. Bibek Debroy and Laveesh Bhandari, *Economic Freedom for States*, New Delhi, International Management Institute, n.d., p. 11.
69. 'The Rajiv Gandhi Foundation finds Gujarat no. 1 state', *The Economic Times*, 21 May 2005, http://articles.economictimes.indiatimes.com/2005-05-21/news/27510532_1_economic-freedom-gsdp-total-cases (last accessed 18 Nov. 2013).
70. Dholakia and Dholakia, 'Policy reform in economic sectors', p. 255.
71. Manshi Asher, 'Gujarat and Punjab: the entrepreneur's paradise and the land of the farmer', in Rob Jenkins, Loraine Kennedy and Partha Mukhopadhyay (eds), *Power, Policy, and Protest: The Politics of India's Special Economic Zones*, Oxford: Oxford University Press, 2014, p. 140.
72. '15 minutes and Gujarat had won over Tatas', *DNA* (Ahmedabad edn), 3 Nov. 2012, p. 6
73. Pravin Mishra, 'Whose Gujarat is vibrant', *Ahmedabad Mirror*, 28 March 2011, p. 3.
74. Nag, *The NaMo Story*, p. 119.
75. *'Development' versus People: Gujarat Model of Land Acquisition and People's Voices*, Ahmedabad, Behavioural Science Centre, 2012, p. 65. A Gujarati version of the text of the agreement is available as Appendix 7 of this document (pp. 100–1). When it leaked, Modi

ordered an inquiry. 'Did Modi offer 320 billion rupees in sops to Tata Motors?', *The Hindu*, 12 Nov. 2008, p. 15. In December 2011, while he was about to retire, Ratan Tata came to Gandhinagar in order to introduce his successor, Cyrus P. Mistry, to him. 'Ratan Tata takes Mistry to Modi', *The Indian Express* (Ahmedabad edn), 30 Dec. 2011.

76. Mishra, 'Whose Gujarat is vibrant'.
77. M. Mehta, 'Corporate cronyism in "vibrant Gujarat"', *Hardnews*, July 2012, http://hardnewsmedia.com/2012/07/5445?page-show (last accessed in Nov. 2103).
78. 'Forest land allotted to corporates in Gujarat', *DNA*, 7 March 2012, http://www.dnaindia.com/india/1659613/report-forest-land-allotted-to-corporates-in-gujarat; and *'Development' versus People*, p. 47.
79. *Report No. 2 of 2013, Government of Gujrat: Report of the Comptroller and Auditor General of India on Revenue Receipts*, http://saiindia.gov.in/english/home/Our_Products/Audit_Report/Government_Wise/state_audit/recent_reports/Gujarat/2012/Report_2/Overview.pdf (last accessed 18 Nov. 2013).
80. 'CAG indicts Modi govt. for "undue" favours to firm', *The Hindu*, 15 April 2013, p. 10.
81. 'CAG finds state's public land policy poor, suggests immediate reforms', *The Times of India*, 4 April 2013, p. 3.
82. 'State lost, big business gained from govt's land policy: CAG', *DNA* (Ahmedabad edn), 3 April 2013, p. 1.
83. 'The unanswered CAG queries across departments, if quantified, pertain to suspected irregularities to the tune of 90 billion rupees.' Kapil Dave, 'Over 5,000 CAG queries awaiting Modi govt reply!', *The Times of India* (Ahmedabad edn), 27 Nov. 2012, p. 1.
84. *Critical Concerns: Deciphering Gujarat's Development*, Mumbai and Bangalore, Centre for Education and Documentation, 2013, p. 2, http://www.doccentre.net/cc/gujarat-final7.pdf (last accessed 10 Dec. 2013).
85. The rise of the Adani Group accelerated in 2013 and 2014 when Modi became a strong contender for the post of prime minister: the market capitalisation of its companies increased by 250 per cent between September 2013—when Narendra Modi was declared the BJP's official candidate for prime-ministership—and September

2014. Between September 2013 and May 2014, the wealth of Gautam Adani had already increased by 501.31 billion rupees because of the market capitalisation of his companies (it increased by 18 billion rupees every day during the week that followed Modi's electoral success). Mukesh Ambani's wealth increased by 'only' 305.03 billion rupees during the same period. 'Fortunes of Indian promoters rise significantly: Gautam Adani witnesses the maximum surge', *The Economic Times*, 17 May 2014, http://economictimes.indiatimes.com/markets/stocks/fortunes-of-indian-promoters-rise-significantly-gautam-adani-witnesses-the-maximum-surge/articleshow/35226427.cms. Graphs published by *Business Today* help to visualise this surge, which was mostly due to two major components of the Adani Group: Adani Enterprises, and Adani Ports and Economic Zone. Tony Joseph, 'Adani's $10-billion gamble', *Business Today*, 18 January 2015, p. 48.

86. On 22 May 2014, the day he was sworn in as prime minister, he flew to New Delhi from Ahmedabad in the private aircraft of Adani, the Indian flag embossed on the aircraft to his right, and on his left an embossed logo of the Adani Group.
87. Paranjoy Guha Thakurta, 'The incredible rise and rise of Gautam Adani: part one', *The Citizen*, 26 April 2015, http://www.thecitizen.in/NewsDetail.aspx?Id=3375&The/Incredible/Rise/and/Rise/of/Gautam/Adani:/Part/One.
88. 'Gautam Adani biography', Business Maps of India, http://business.mapsofindia.com/business-leaders/gautam-adani.html.
89. M. Rajshekhar, 'The other big', *The Economic Times* (Mumbai edn), 5 Sept. 2013, p. 3.
90. Ibid.
91. 'Industry attacks Modi's Gujarat', *The Asian Age* (Ahmedabad edn), 24 April 2002, p. 14.
92. 'Gujarat Inc. guns for CII', *The Times of India* (Ahmedabad edn), 20 Feb. 2003, p. 3.
93. If Modi was relatively isolated in 2002–03, Gautam Adani was not part of the business establishment either, as is evident from his marginal position in terms of interlocking directorates. Jules Naudet, Adrien Allorant and Mathieu Ferry, 'Heirs, corporate aristocrats and

"meritocrats": the three worlds of top CEOs and chairmen in India', *Socio-economic Review*, 16, no. 2 (2018), pp. 307–39.

94. Thakurta, 'The incredible rise and rise of Gautam Adani'.
95. *'Development' versus People*, p. 16.
96. P.T. George, *Special Economic Zones and People's Struggles in Gujarat*, New Delhi, Intercultural Resources, 2011, http://base.d-p-h.info/fr/fiches/dph/fiche-dph-8854.html (last accessed 18 Nov. 2013). See also 'Gujarat state government gifts Adani Group land in Kutch for peanuts', *Ahmedabad Mirror*, 29 Feb. 2012, p. 3.
97. Megha Bahree, 'Doing big business in Modi's Gujarat', *Forbes*, 24 March 2014, http://www.forbes.com/sites/meghabahree/2014/03/12/doing-big-business-in-modis-gujarat/.
98. Anumeha Yadav, 'Vibrant Gujarat? Your coast is not clear Mr. Adani', *Tehelka*, 8, no. 8 (26 Feb. 2011), http://archive.tehelka.com/story_main48.asp?filename=Ne260211DEVELOPMENT_CONFLICTS.asp (last accessed 18 Nov. 2013).
99. CAG, *Audit Report (Revenue Receipts) for the Year Ended 31 March 2012: Report no. 2 of 2013*, p. 96, http://saiindia.gov.in/english/home/Our_Products/Audit_Report/Government_Wise/state_audit/recent_reports/Gujarat/2012/Report_2/Chap_3.pdf (last accessed 18 Nov. 2013).
100. CAG, 'Chapter III, Transaction Audit Observations', p. 91, http://saiindia.gov.in/english/home/Our_Products/Audit_Report/Government_Wise/state_audit/recent_reports/Gujarat/2012/Report_1/Chap_3.pdf (last accessed 18 Nov. 2013).
101. 'Kejriwal targets Modi, alleges favouritism in giving away gas wells, land allotments', *The Indian Express*, 5 Dec. 2012, p. 5.
102. 2,000 MW from Adani Power Ltd, 1,000 MW from Essar Power Gujarat Ltd, 1,805 MW from Coastal Power Gujarat Ltd, and 200 MW from Aryan Coal Beneficiation Private Ltd.
103. CAG, *Report of the Comptroller and Auditor General of India on Public Sector Undertakings for the Year Ended 31 March 2013* (Report no. 3 of the year 2014), p. 23.
104. *Report of the Committee for Inspection of M/s Adani Port & SEZ Ltd., Mundra, Gujarat*, New Delhi, Ministry of Environment and Forests, April 2013, pp. 19ff.
105. Bahree, 'Doing big business in Modi's Gujarat'.

106. Arindam Mukherjee, 'Mundra: the port of no call', *Outlook*, 29 July 2016, http://www.outlookindia.com/magazine/story/mundra-the-port-of-no-call/297572.
107. Cited in ibid.
108. CAG, *Audit Report no. 1 (State Finances), for the Year Ended 31 March 2012*, p. 28, http://saiindia.gov.in/english/home/Our_Products/Audit_Report/Government_Wise/state_audit/recent_reports/Gujarat/2012/SF/Chap_1.pdf (last accessed 18 Nov. 2013).
109. In 2009, the debt of Gujarat was 'only' 1.04 trillion rupees as against 1.88 trillion rupees for UP, 1.77 trillion rupees for Maharashtra, 1.47 trillion rupees for West Bengal, and 1.27 trillion rupees for Andhra. Rajiv Shah, 'State debt set to cross 1 trillion rupees', *The Times of India* (Ahmedabad edn), 2 Jan. 2009, p. 8.
110. Ajay Umat, 'Modi mortgage model', *The Times of India* (Ahmedabad edn), 6 April 2013, p. 1; and 'Gujarat's per capita debt set to rise by 46%', *India Tribune*, http://www.indiatribune.com/index.php?option=com_content&view=article&id=8498:gujarats-per-capita-debt-set-to-rise-by-46-&catid=125:general-news&Itemid=400 (last accessed 10 Dec. 2013).
111. 'Gujarat's revenue-debt ratio second highest in nation', *DNA*, 3 July 2011, http://www.dnaindia.com/india/report-gujarats-revenue-debt-ratio-second-highest-in-nation-1561796 (last accessed 18 Nov. 2013).
112. Sumit Khanna, 'Guj to use Rs. 19K cr loan to pay off old debts', *DNA* (Ahmedabad edn), 16 March 2013, p. 1.
113. Asher, 'Gujarat and Punjab', p. 140.
114. Sud, *Liberalization, Hindu Nationalism and the State*, p. 65.
115. CAG, 'Chapter II: Value Added Taxes/Sales Taxes', 2013, p. 14, http://saiindia.gov.in/english/home/Our_Products/Audit_Report/Government_Wise/state_audit/recent_reports/Gujarat/2012/Report_2/Chap_2.pdf (last accessed 18 Nov. 2013). VAT was particularly high on some items: on natural gas, for instance, it represented 15 per cent of the price.
116. CAG, 'Chapter III: Executive summary', 2013, p. 65, http://saiindia.gov.in/english/home/Our_Products/Audit_Report/Government_Wise/state_audit/recent_reports/Gujarat/2012/Report_2/Chap_3.pdf (last accessed 18 Nov. 2013).

117. See Debroy, *Gujarat*, p. 40.
118. Kapil Dave, 'Firms owe 120 billion rupees in taxes to state govt', *The Indian Express* (Ahmedabad edn), 11 Feb. 2011, p. 3.
119. Sumit Khanna, 'Has Essar's proximity to Modi become too taxing?', *DNA* (Ahmedabad edn), 18 July 2012, p. 1.
120. Satish Jha, 'A'bad owes 48 billion rupees to the income tax department', *DNA*, 19 March 2010, p. 1.
121. CAG, Audit Report no. 1 (State Finances), for the Year Ended 31 March 2012, p. 4.
122. Atri Mukherjee, 'Regional inequality in Foreign Direct Investment flows to India: the problem and the prospects', Reserve Bank of India Occasional Papers, 32, no. 2 (2011) and 'Statement on RBI's regional offices year-wise (with state covered) received FDI inflows from January 2000 to September 2012', http://dipp.nic.in/English/Publications/SIA_Newsletter/2012/dec2012/index.htm (last accessed 10 Dec. 2013).
123. Aseema Sinha, 'Ideas and institutions in policy change', in Rob Jenkins (ed.), *Regional Reflections: Comparing Politics in India's States*, New Delhi, Oxford University Press, 2004, p. 75.
124. Nag, *The NaMo Story*, 2013, p. 11.
125. Maitreesh Ghatak and Sanchari Roy, 'Did Gujarat's growth rate accelerate under Modi?', *EPW*, 49, no. 15 (12 April 2014), https://www.epw.in/journal/2014/15/commentary/did-gujarats-growth-rate-accelerate-under-modi.html.
126. See the Planning Commission's statistics, http://planningcommission.nic.in/data/datatable/data_2110/table_57.pdf (last accessed 10 Dec. 2013).
127. Dev, *Modi to Moditva*, p. 157.
128. See the Planning Commission's statistics, http://planningcommission.nic.in/data/datatable/data_2110/table_59.pdf.
129. It reached 121,92 m in 2008, but Modi wanted to take it even higher, to 138,68 m, against the wish of NGOs defending peasants who would have had to be displaced. 'Height of Narmada dam should not be raised', *The Hindu*, 18 May 2008, p. 10.
130. 'Mum on riots, he sticks to N-word', *The Indian Express* (Ahmedabad edn), 29 Aug. 2002, p. 3.

131. 'Narmada, the lifeline of Gujarat', http://www.sardarsarovardam.org/Client/Index.aspx (last accessed 18 Nov. 2013).
132. Directorate of Economics and Statistics, *Socio-economic Review, 2012–2013: Gujarat State*, p. 14.
133. Ibid., p. 60.
134. 'Gujarat records highest decadal agricultural growth rate of 10.97%', *The Times of India*, 16 July 2011, http://articles.economictimes.indiatimes.com/2011-07-16/news/29781759_1_farm-sector-primary-sector-decadal.
135. Bhalchandra Mungekar, 'Figuring out Gujarat', *The Indian Express*, 29 July 2013, http://www.indianexpress.com/news/figuring-out-gujarat/1147944/ (last accessed 18 Nov. 2013).
136. See Planning Commission's statistics, http://planningcommission.nic.in/data/datatable/data_2110/table_55.pdf.
137. Ashok Gulati, Tushaar Shah and Ganga Shreedhar, *Agriculture Performance in Gujarat since 2000*, New Delhi, International Food Policy Research Institute, 2009, p. 2, http://ebrary.ifpri.org/cdm/singleitem/collection/p15738coll2/id/126224/rec/2 (last accessed 18 Nov. 2013). The IFPRI suggests that Narmada water was not a major factor in agricultural growth, at least in the initial years of the Modi government, when most of the canals had not been built, compared with the myriad of check dams.
138. Pravin Sheth, *Images of Transformation: Gujarat and Narendra Modi*, Ahmedabad, Team Spirit, 2007, p. 233.
139. Pravin Sheth and Pradeep Mallick, *Happening State: Gujarat; A Live Case of Can-Doism*, Mumbai and Ahmedabad, R.R. Sheth and Co., 2012, pp. 122–3.
140 Aseem Gaurav, 'Top ten Gujarati billionaires', India TV, 10 Dec. 2012, http://www.indiatvnews.com/business/india/top-Gujarati-billionaires-3732.html (last accessed 18 Nov. 2013).
141. Interestingly, Mukesh Ambani is the chairman of the Ahmedabad-based Pandit Deendayal Petroleum University, whereas Deendayal Upadhyaya did not favour big companies but rather agriculture and cottage industries. See 'Modi has put Gujarat on world map, says Mukesh Ambani', *The Times of India* (Ahmedabad edn), 28 Sept. 2011, p. 2.

142. 'Gautam Adani becomes world's second richest person, surpasses Jeff Bezos', *Outlook*, 17 Sept. 2022, https://www.outlookindia.com/business/gautam-adani-world-richest-person-news-gautam-adani-becomes-world-s-second-richest-person-surpasses-jeff-bezos-news-223974.
143. Mahesh Langa, 'Gautam Adani, PM Modi's constant companion on overseas trips', *Hindustan Times*, 16 April 2015, http://www.hindustantimes.com/india/gautam-adani-pm-modi-s-constant-companion-on-overseas-trips/story-CMDqyMTSNxoewGpQVqEeDK.html.
144. See Christophe Jaffrelot, *Modi's India: Hindu Nationalism and the Rise of Ethnic Democracy*, Princeton, NJ, Princeton University Press; Chennai, Westland, 2021, p. 147.
145. 'Jaitley gave 2 trillion rupees bonanza to corporates: Chidambaram', *Business Standard*, 1 March 2015, http://scroll.in/article/710729/jaitley-gave-rs-2-lakh-crore-bonanza-to-corporations-says-chidambaram (last accessed 27 Sept. 2020).
146. Tadit Kundu, 'How Modi government's budgets have differed from UPA's', *Mint*, 25 Dec. 2019, https://www.livemint.com/Politics/Tq0rrXZsEOA64o9I1Q5pgP/How-Modi-governments-budgets-have-differed-from-UPA.html (last accessed 24 Sept. 2020).
147. Ayaskant Das, 'Incremental dilution of India's environment regulatory regime for benefit of corporates?', *Newsclick*, 26 April 2022, https://www.newsclick.in/incremental-dilution-india-environment-regulatory-regime-benefit-corporates.

6. SOCIAL POLARISATION

1. Narendra Modi, 'How did Gujarat emerge as a model of development?', 7 Oct. 2011, Narendra Modi website, https://www.narendramodi.in/how-did-gujarat-emerge-as-a-model-for-development-4142.
2. See Arvind Panagariya, 'Why the Gujarat miracle matters', *The Times of India* (Ahmedabad edn), 29 June 2013, p. 12. Interestingly, Panagariya attributes the growth rate of Gujarat to Narendra Modi almost exclusively: 'The Gujarat experience matters precisely because Modi, who nurtures national ambition, leads it and he

matters precisely because he is the man behind the Gujarat miracle. Without Modi at its helm, Gujarat would not be the centre of attention; and without the accomplishments of Gujarat, Modi would not command the attention he does.'

3. 'How did Gujarat emerge as a model for development?', 7 Oct. 2011, Narendra Modi website, http://www.narendramodi.in/how-did-gujarat-emerge-as-a-model-for-development/ (last accessed 18 Nov. 2013).
4. Jagdish Bhagwati and Arvind Panagariya, 'We are impressed by Modi's economic policies', *The Economic Times*. For more details, see their book *India's Tryst with Destiny*, New York, HarperCollins, 2012.
5. Jean Drèze and Amartya Sen, *An Uncertain Glory: India and Its Contradictions*, Princeton, NJ, Princeton University Press, 2013.
6. See Bibek Debroy, *Gujarat: Governance for Growth and Development*, New Delhi, Academic Foundation, 2012, p. 23.
7. Christophe Jaffrelot, 'What Gujarat model? Growth without development and with socio-political polarization', *South Asia: Journal of South Asian Studies*, 38, no. 4 (2015), pp. 820–38.
8. Atul Sood, 'Rousing growth amid raging disparities', in Atul Sood (ed.), *Poverty amidst Prosperity: Essays on the Trajectory of Development in Gujarat*, Delhi, Aakar Books, 2012, p. 49.
9. Sunil R. Parekh, 'Some facets of industrialisation in Gujarat (1999–2009)', in Indira Hirway, Amita Shah and Ghanshyam Shah (eds), *Growth or Development: Which Way Is Gujarat Going?*, New Delhi, Oxford University Press, 2014, p. 198.
10. The Reliance refinery of Jamnagar, the largest in the world, has only 2,500 employees, for instance.
11. Sangeeta Ghosh, 'Selective development in Gujarat: a study of the manufacturing sector', in Atul Sood (ed.), *Poverty amidst Prosperity: Essays on the Trajectory of Development in Gujarat*, Delhi, Aakar Books, 2012, p. 134.
12. Govindraj Ethiraj, 'Quietly, Maharashtra and Tamil Nadu outrace Gujarat', IndiaSpend, 16 Jan. 2015, http://www.indiaspend.com/cover-story/quietly-maharashtra-tamil-nadu-outrace-gujarat-25529.
13. ISED Small Enterprise Observatory, *Gujarat Micro, Small and Medium Enterprises Report 2013*, Cochin, Institute of Small Enterprises and Development, 2013, p. 39.

14. Ghosh, 'Selective development in Gujarat', p. 167.
15. ISED Small Enterprise Observatory, *Gujarat Micro, Small and Medium Enterprises Report 2013*, p. 99.
16. Ibid., p. 80.
17. The eight cooperative banks in question were: Madhavpura Mercantile Cooperative Bank, Charotar Cooperative Bank, Visnagar Cooperative Bank, Laxmi Cooperative Bank, Diamond Jubilee Cooperative Bank, Suryapur Cooperative Bank, General Cooperative Bank and Baroda People's Cooperative Bank. See 'Another co-operative bank in Gujarat in liquidity crisis', *The Economic Times,* 4 Sept. 2002, http://articles.economictimes.indiatimes.com/2002-09-04/news/27357001_1_liquidity-crisis-suryapur-co-operative-bank-diamond-jubilee-cooperative-bank.
18. Piyush Mishra, 'Only UP has more sick MSMEs than Gujarat', *The Times of India* (Ahmedabad edn), 4 Dec. 2015, p. 2.
19. Pragya Singh, 'How much growth can absorb all?', *Outlook*, 14 Sept. 2015, http://www.outlookindia.com/printarticle.aspx?295246.
20. One could read in the document presenting the 2009 industrial policy of Gujarat: 'Though the state has been witnessing very high levels of industrial activity, employment generation activities have not kept pace with the same.' Government of Gujarat, *Industrial Policy, 2009*, January 2009, p. 10, http://www.ic.gujarat.gov.in/pdf/industrial-policy-2009-at-a-glance.pdf. But the remedy proposed—'mega projects'—was a reflection of the 'more of the same' syndrome.
21. The state government officially recognised that there were '612,000 educated-unemployed persons' in the state. Avinash Nair, 'Over 1,395,000 new jobs in Gujarat since July 2011', *The Indian Express*, 11 April 2017, http://indianexpress.com/article/cities/ahmedabad/over-13-95-lakh-new-jobs-in-gujarat-since-july-2011-4608227/. Among them, the engineers were well represented according to the All India Council for Technical Education. 'More than 80% engineers are without jobs', *Ahmedabad Mirror*, 28 March 2017, http://ahmedabadmirror.indiatimes.com/ahmedabad/cover-story/more-than-80-engineers-are-without-jobs/articleshow/57880536.cms?prtpage=1.

22. For more detail and an analysis of the impact of the job problem on the Patel movement, see Christophe Jaffrelot, 'Quota for Patels? The neo-middle class syndrome and the (partial) return of caste politics in Gujarat', *Studies in Indian Politics*, 4, no. 2 (2016), pp. 1–15.
23. Ghosh, 'Selective development in Gujarat', p. 140.
24. Darshini Mahadevia, 'Dynamics of urbanization in Gujarat', in Indira Hirway, Amita Shah and Ghanshyam Shah (eds), *Growth or Development: Which Way Is Gujarat Going?*, New Delhi, Oxford University Press, 2014, p. 347.
25. 'Workers strike at Tata Motors, Sanand, Gujarat, in India', Libcom, 14 March 2016, https://libcom.org/news/workers-tata-motors-sanand-gujarat-14032016; and Arefa Johari, 'Casteism, brides and a failed Gujarat model: what the Patel demand for reservations is really about', *Scroll.in*, 14 Sept. 2015, http://scroll.in/article/753595/casteism-brides-and-a-failed-gujarat-model-what-the-patel-demand-for-reservations-is-really-about.
26. Deepal Trivedi, 'How vibrant is our Gujarat', *Ahmedabad Mirror*, 9 Oct. 2012.
27. 'Govt to revise daily wagers' pay scale after 11 years', *The Sunday Express* (Ahmedabad edn), 30 Aug. 2009, p. 5.
28. Ghosh, 'Selective development in Gujarat', p. 141.
29. 'Gujarat tops in labour unrest: survey', *The Indian Express*, 25 Feb. 2011, http://archive.indianexpress.com/news/gujarat-tops-in-labour-unrest-survey/754803/.
30. 'Workers' strike: Guj tops the list in India', *DNA*, 11 Aug. 2015, p. 7.
31. 'Strike at Tata Nano Sanand plant ends', *Firstpost*, 23 March 2016, http://www.firstpost.com/business/strike-at-tata-nano-sanand-plant-ends-2692166.html.
32. Directorate of Economics and Statistics, *Socio-economic Review, 2012–2013*, Gujarat State, Gandhinagar, Government of Gujarat, Feb. 2013, p. x. This point had been made very clearly in 2012, during a conference which took place on this question in Ahmedabad. See Trivedi, 'How vibrant is our Gujarat?'
33. See Debroy, *Gujarat*, pp. 82–4.
34. Ghanshyam Shah, 'Politics of governance: a study of Gujarat', *Studies in Indian Politics*, 1, no. 1 (2013), p. 73.

35 Pratham, *Annual Status of Education Report (Rural) 2011*, p. 33, http://images2.asercentre.org/aserreports/ASER_2011/north_east_report_final_for_mail.pdf (last accessed 18 Nov. 2013). According to another Pratham survey, 55 per cent of rural pupils in standard V cannot read a standard II-level text and 65 per cent cannot do simple subtraction. See http://www.pratham.org/M-40-5-Gujarat.aspx (last accessed 18 Nov. 2013).

36. Sangeeta Ghosh, 'An analysis of state education in Gujarat', in Atul Sood (ed.), *Poverty amidst Prosperity: Essays on the Trajectory of Development in Gujarat*, Delhi, Aakar Books, 2012, p. 194.

37 Reserve Bank of India, *State Finances: A Study of Budgets*, p. 173, http://www.rbi.org.in/scripts/PublicationsView.aspx?id=14834 (last accessed 31 July 2023).

38. Ibid.

39. *DISE 2011–12: Elementary Education*, New Delhi, National University of Educational Planning and Administration, 2013, p. 2, http://www.dise.in/Downloads/Publications/Publications%202011-12/Flash%202011-12.pdf (last accessed 18 Nov. 2013).

40. In rural Gujarat, the proportion of children from 6 to 14 years old going to private schools is limited (11.8 per cent). *Annual Status of Education Report (Rural) 2012*, p. 55, http://img.asercentre.org/docs/Publications/ASER%20Reports/ASER_2012/fullaser2012report.pdf (last accessed 10 Dec. 2013).

41. Bhalchandra Mungekar, 'Gujarat: myth and reality', *The Times of India*, 12 June 2012, http://timesofindia.indiatimes.com/articleshow/14032015.cms?utm_source=contentofinterest&utm_medium=text&utm_campaign=cppst. Mungekar also emphasised that on 'three important social indicators, viz life expectancy at birth (LEB), mean years of schooling (MYS) and school life expectancy (SLE), Gujarat is far behind some other states. In Gujarat, the LEB during 2002–6 was 64.1 years and it ranked ninth among major Indian states. In the areas of MYS and SLE, during 2004–5, it ranked seventh and ninth, respectively. Kerala ranked first in all three indicators. Even Maharashtra, Himachal Pradesh, Punjab, Haryana, Tamil Nadu and Karnataka performed much better than Gujarat.'

42. Ghanshyam Shah points out that in 2007 Ahmedabad had 'the lowest labour costs among the major cities in India, with labour costs

less than 50% of those of Delhi and 40% below those of Pune.' Ghanshyam Shah, 'Politics of governance: a study of Gujarat', *Studies in Indian Politics*, 1, no. 1 (2013), p. 70.

43. Rajiv Shah, 'Bihar pays better than Gujarat', *The Times of India*, 8 Aug. 2010, http://timesofindia.indiatimes.com/articleshow/6272874.cms?utm_source=contentofinterest&utm_medium=text&utm_campaign=cppst.
44. Purnima Menon, Anil B. Deolikar and Anjor Bhaskar, *India State Hunger Index: A Comparison of Hunger across States*, Washington, DC, International Food Policy Institute, 2009, p. 15, http://www.ifpri.org/sites/default/files/publications/ishi08.pdf (last accessed 18 Nov. 2013).
45. Rajiv Shah, 'Gujarat seeks 4.5 billion rupees aid to fight malnourishment', *The Times of India*, 6 Sept. 2012, https://reliefweb.int/report/india/gujarat-seeks-rs-450-crore-aid-fight-malnourishment.
46. Ibid.
47. According to the International Food Policy Research Institute's 2008 Global Hunger Index, Gujarat is ranked 69th, at the same level as Haiti.
48. Avinash Nair, 'Every third child in Gujarat is underweight', *The Indian Express*, 24 Oct. 2013, http://www.indianexpress.com/news/-every-third-child-in-gujarat-is-underweight-/1178189/ (last accessed 18 Nov. 2013).
49. 'Monthly average quantity of consumption of different cereals per person', NSSO, Household Consumer Expenditures in India, 66th round, July 2009–June 2010, Report no. 538.
50. Sandeep Sharma, 'Rich state with poor health: disappointing status of public health in Gujarat', in Atul Sood (ed.), *Poverty amidst Prosperity: Essays on the Trajectory of Development in Gujarat*, Delhi, Aakar Books, 2012, p. 201.
51 Reserve Bank of India, *State Finances: A Study of Budgets*.
52. Sharma, 'Rich state with poor health', pp. 209 and 282.
53. D. Mavalankar and J. Satia, 'Medical scenario in Gujarat', www.icci.com/events/20425/ISP/vibrant_gujarat_PwC.pdf (last accessed in Nov. 2013). Cited in Shah, 'Politics of governance', p. 71.
54. Mahendra Singh, 'State no hot potato for Ahluwalia', *The Times of India* (Ahmedabad edn), 19 June 2013, p. 5.

55. Manish Bharadwaj, Director of Census Operation, *Census of India, Provisional Population Totals*, Paper 2, vol. 1 of 2011, Gandhinagar, 2011, p. 17.
56. Govt. of India, *Economic Survey 2011-12*, New Delhi, 2012, p. 313, http://indiabudget.nic.in/es2011-12/echap-13.pdf (last accessed 18 Nov. 2013).
57. Bhavesh Shah, '12,000 of India's "super rich" are in Gujarat', *DNA* (Ahmedabad edn), 13 March 2013, p. 1.
58. Naturally, the definition of the BPL was not the same in both contexts. In the rural part of Gujarat it was fixed at Rs. 202.11 while in the urban part it was fixed at Rs. 297.22.
59. Sharma, 'Rich state with poor health', p. 203; see also p. 275.
60. Rajiv Shah, 'Gujarat health sector: a lurking rural–urban gap', *The Times of India*, 19 Nov. 2014, https://timesofindia.indiatimes.com/blogs/true-lies/gujarat-health-sector-a-lurking-rural-urban-gap/.
61. See M. Dinesh Kumar, A. Narayanamoorthy, O.P. Singh, M.V.K. Sivamohan, Manoj Sharma and Nitin Bassi, 'Gujarat Agriculture's Growth Story: Exploding Some Myths', Hyderabad, Institute for Resource Analysis and Policy, 2010, Occasional Paper no. 2-0410, p. 13, https://www.researchgate.net/publication/312160581_Gujarat%27s_Agricultural_Growth_Story_Exploding_Some_Myths.
62. Rajiv Shah, 'Gujarat: dilemma of low income from agriculture', *The Times of India*, 25 Dec. 2014, https://timesofindia.indiatimes.com/blogs/true-lies/gujarat-dilemma-of-low-income-from-agriculture/.
63. Rajiv Shah, 'Gujarat's rural indebtedness', *The Times of India*, 27 Dec. 2014, https://timesofindia.indiatimes.com/blogs/true-lies/gujarats-rural-indebtedness/.
64. 'Rs 91 cr more for urban poor', *DNA* (Ahmedabad edn), 30 May 2011, p. 4.
65. Jennifer Bussell, *Corruption and Reform in India*, Cambridge, Cambridge University Press, 2013, pp. 140–1.
66. Ajoy Ashirwad Mahaprashasta, 'The great land grab', *Frontline*, 1 May 2013, www.frontline.in/cover-story/the-great-land-grab/article4666181.ece?css=print (last accessed 18 Nov. 2013). Indeed, the SEZ Act allows the owners of large SEZs (above 1,000

ha) to use 75 per cent of their land for non-industrial purposes (for the smaller ones, up to 50 per cent of an SEZ can be devoted to non-processing areas, including education and residential complexes). SEZ owners have been quick to indulge in real-estate speculation and to lease at market price land that they'd bought at a throwaway price. 'SEZs and land acquisition: factsheet for an unconstitutional economic policy', Citizens' Research Collective, http://www.sacw.net/Nation/sezland_eng.pdf (last accessed 18 Nov. 2013). In 2011 IAS officer Pradeep Sharma, accused of having granted land at a low price to a company, Welspun, near Anjar, demanded 'that chief minister Narendra Modi be made co-accused in the case as the decision for granting land was that of the chief minister's and he had only acted as per his instructions'. D.V. Maheshwari, 'Modi gave the order on land', *DNA* (Ahmedabad edn), 16 Feb. 2011, p. 4.

67 'Modi thinks I'm another Medha Patkar', *Outlook*, 2 Sept. 2013, http://www.outlookindia.com/article.aspx?287500 (last accessed 18 Nov. 2013).

68. For an overview, see Debarshi Dasgupta, 'The plough in the works', *Outlook*, 2 Sept. 2013, http://www.outlookindia.com/article.aspx?287499 (last accessed 18 Nov. 2013).

69. Nikita Sud, *Liberalization, Hindu Nationalism and the State: A Biography of Gujarat*, New Delhi, Oxford University Press, 2012, p. 89.

70. *'Development' versus People: Gujarat Model of Land Acquisition and People's Voices*, Ahmedabad, Behavioural Science Centre, 2012, p. 54.

71. See Debroy, *Gujarat*, pp. 129 and 137.

72. S. Sen and C. Mallik, 'Understanding Gujarat's agricultural growth and liberalizing environment: signs of a redefined margin?', in Atul Sood (ed.), *Poverty amidst Prosperity: Essays on the Trajectory of Development in Gujarat*, Delhi, Aakar Books, 2012, p. 102.

73. Ibid., p. 107.

74. Ibid., p. 235.

75. BT cotton, whose seeds were expensive, has become dominant in Gujarat. Ibid., p. 119.

76. Ibid., p. 123.

77. Mohan Guruswamy, 'Myth of the Gujarat model miracle', The Observer Research Foundation, 13 Feb. 2013, http://orfonline.

org/cms/sites/orfonline/modules/analysis/AnalysisDetail.html?cmaid=48115&mmacmaid=48116 (last accessed 18 Nov. 2013).

78. In March 2010, for instance, 6.42 billion rupees had not been spent 20 days before the end of the fiscal year. 'Govt helping rich at the cost of poor', *DNA* (Ahmedabad edn), 10 March 2010, p. 4.
79. Rajiv Shah, '42% of plan money remains unutilized', *The Times of India*, 20 Feb. 2010.
80. See the first chapter of Christophe Jaffrelot, *The Hindu Nationalist Movement and Indian Politics, 1925 to the 1990s*, New York, Columbia University Press; London, Hurst; New Delhi, Penguin India, 1996.
81. Bibek Debroy and Laveesh Bhandari, *Economic Freedom for States*, New Delhi, International Management Institute, n.d., p. 21.
82. 'World Bank chief gives thumbs up to Gujarat model', *The Times of India*, 24 July 2014, http://timesofindia.indiatimes.com/articleshow/38949869.cms?utm_source=contentofinterest&utm_medium=text&utm_campaign=cppst.
83. Kapil Dave, 'We failed to reach out to the poor: state govt', *DNA* (Ahmedabad edn), 14 Dec. 2009, p. 3.
84. John Echeverry-Gent, Aseema Sinha and Andrew Wyatt, 'Economic distress amidst political success: India's economic policy under Modi, 2014–2019', *India Review*, 20, no. 4 (2021), pp. 402–35, https://www.tandfonline.com/doi/abs/10.1080/14736489.2021.1958582.
85. Srirang Jha and Amiya Kumar Mohapatra, 'Jobless growth in India: the way forward', SSRN, 28 Oct. 2019, https://papers.ssrn.com/sol3/papers.cfm?abstract_id=3476599.
86. On this question of the non-performing assets of public banks and their political dimension, see Christophe Jaffrelot, *Modi's India: Hindu Nationalism and the Rise of Ethnic Democracy*, Princeton, NJ, Princeton University Press; Chennai, Westland, 2021, pp. 146–7.
87. It was one of the most ambitious programmes to help the rural poor that India (and therefore the world) had ever known. The method was a novel one that aimed to minimise dependence on government aid, as the state committed to providing 100 days of actual *work* paid at minimum wage for any rural family suffering from chronic underemployment. See Rob Jenkins and James Manor, *Politics and the*

Right to Work: India's National Rural Employment Guarantee Act, London, Hurst, 2017.

88. An analysis by Jean Drèze shows that the growth rate for agricultural wages for men increased to 2.7 per cent per year and for women to 3.7 per cent per year during 2005/6–2010/11 as compared with 0.1 per cent per year for men and negative for women in the pre-MGNREGA (2000/1–2005/6). See Mann Neelakshi and Jairam Ramesh, 'Rising farm wages will lift all boats', *The Hindu*, 14 May 2013, http://www.thehindu.com/opinion/op-ed/rising-farm-wages-will-lift-all-boats/article4712302.ece (last accessed 27 Sept. 2020); and Harish Damodaran Surabhi, 'Rural wage growth lowest in 10 years, signals farm distress, falling inflation', *The Indian Express*, 7 Jan. 2015, http://indianexpress.com/article/india/india-others/rural-wage-growth-lowest-in-10-years-signals-farm-distress-falling-inflation (last accessed 27 Sept. 2020).

89. Pushparaj Deshpande, 'NDA destroying MGNREGA: has Modi forgotten "sabka saath, sabka vikas"?', *The Indian Express*, 3 Feb. 2016, https://indianexpress.com/article/blogs/mgnrega-surprising-to-see-nda-so-determined-to-destroy-it/ (last accessed 27 Sept. 2020).

90. 'MNREGA, a "monument to failure of Congress govts": Modi', *The Hindu*, 27 Feb. 2015, https://www.thehindu.com/news/national/mnrega-monument-to-failure-of-congress-govts-modi/article10701735.ece (last accessed 27 Sept. 2020).

91. Shalini Nair, 'Fund crunch: 88% of NREGA budget over, 6 months left', *The Indian Express*, 19 Oct. 2017; see also Ashok Gulati, 'Adrift and directionless: can MGNREGA move from being a "living monument of UPA's failure" to a development scheme?', *The Times of India*, 24 Feb. 2017, https://timesofindia.indiatimes.com/blogs/toi-edit-page/adrift-and-...m-being-a-living-monument-of-upas-failure-to-a-development-scheme/ (last accessed 27 Sept. 2020).

92. Himanshu Kaushik, 'A Union budget for the village', *The Indian Express*, 27 Feb. 2016, https://indianexpress.com/article/opinion/columns/a-union-budget-for-the-village-rural-economy/ (last accessed 27 Sept. 2020).

93. Himanshu Kaushik, 'India's farm crisis: decades old and with deep roots', *India Forum*, 29 April 2019, https://www.theindiaforum.in/

article/farm-crisis-runs-deep-higher-msps-and-cash-handouts-are-not-enough (last accessed 27 Sept. 2020).

94. Abhishek Waghmare, 'Farm distress: markets, not MSP, the key', *Business Standard*, 5 Feb. 2018, https://www.business-standard.com/budget/article/farm-distress-markets-not-msp-is-the-budget-focus-118020300800_1.html (last accessed 27 Sept. 2020).
95. On the case of wheat—one among many others—see M. Bhardwaj and R. Jadhav, 'India scraps wheat import duty, purchases may hit decade high', Reuters, 8 Dec. 2016, https://in.reuters.com/article/india-wheat-import-duty-idINKBN13X0GG (last accessed 27 Sept. 2020).
96. Roshan Kishore, 'Worse price slump in 18 years shows scale of farm crisis', *Hindustan Times*, 15 Jan. 2019, https://www.hindustantimes.com/india-news/worst-price-slump-in-18-years-shows-scale-of-farm-crisis/story-P2niBeuqAcaxgms3HmFCTK.html (last accessed 27 Sept. 2020).
97. Ashok Gulati, 'Dismayed farmers, defunct policies', *The Indian Express*, 31 Aug. 2015, https://indianexpress.com/article/opinion/columns/dismayed-farmers-defunct-policies/ (last accessed 27 Sept. 2020).

7. PERSONAL POWER VERSUS HINDUTVA'S COLLEGIALITY

1. *India Today*, 6 Jan. 2003, p. 12.
2. See Christophe Jaffrelot and Pratinav Anil, *India's First Dictatorship: The Emergency, 1975–77*, London, Hurst; New York, Oxford University Press; New Delhi, HarperCollins, 2020.
3. 'Create distinct work culture: Modi to officials', *The Indian Express* (Ahmedabad edn), 21 June 2002.
4. 'Modi's review has babus on their toes', *The Times of India*, 26 Oct. 2003, https://timesofindia.indiatimes.com/india/modis-review-has-babus-on-their-toes/articleshow/251665.cms.
5. Chaitanya Kalbag, 'Gujarat chief minister Narendra Modi on the state's development', *Business Today*, 6 Jan. 2011, http://businesstoday.intoday.in/storyprint/11910 (last accessed 18 Nov. 2013).
6. Rajiv Shah, 'Why are so many babus leaving CMO?', *The Times of India*, 16 July 2006, http://timesofindia.indiatimes.com/

articleshow/1761909.cms?utm_source=contentofinterest&utm_medium=text&utm_campaign=cppst.

7. Rajiv Shah, 'Babus in exit mode', *The Times of India*, 1 Nov. 2006, http://timesofindia.indiatimes.com/articleshow/263904.cms?utm_source=contentofinterest&utm_medium=text&utm_campaign=cppst.
8. 'Exodus of IAS officers on, one more puts in papers', *The Indian Express* (Ahmedabad edn), 30 Sept. 2008, p. 1.
9. Elaborating on this practice which makes the bureaucrats responsible for the state's decisions, Modhwadia added: 'Modi just signs "Narendra" after receiving the file. Earlier, chief ministers would take bold decisions, overruling the officials' viewpoints. He only uses yellow post-it notes to give instructions. This is the only reason why so many officials have left the IAS in Gujarat and many more are likely to leave.' 'Modi's style forcing babus into exit mode', *The Times of India* (Ahmedabad edn), 3 Nov. 2006, p. 2.
10. Bashir Pathan, 'Tale of missing heads: 6 key departments running without chief functionaries', The *Sunday Express Newsline* (Ahmedabad edn), 16 Nov. 2008.
11. Kapil Dave, 'Over a dozen IAS babus face probe', *DNA* (Ahmedabad edn), 24 Jan. 2010, p. 2.
12. Cited in Nilanjan Mukhopadhyay, *Narendra Modi: The Man, the Times*, Chennai, Westland, 2013, p. 359.
13. 'Major's Modi commander comment angers army', *DNA* (Mumbai edn), 15 March 2011, p. 15.
14. Pathan, 'Tale of missing heads', p. 3.
15. '2,600 posts vacant in state finance department', *DNA* (Ahmedabad edn), 3 Oct. 2011, p. 5.
16. 'Who is G.C. Murmu, Modi aide and now J&K's first Lt Governor?', *The Week*, 25 October 2020, https://www.theweek.in/news/india/2019/10/25/who-is-gc-murmu-modi-aide-and-now-jks-first-lt-governor.html.
17. Arshu John, 'The professional fortunes of cops, bureaucrats and SIT members associated with the 2002 Godhra investigation', *The Caravan*, 22 Sept. 2017, https://caravanmagazine.in/vantage/postings-cops-bureaucrats-sit-members-godhra-2002-investigation.

18. 'PK Mishra is back in Gujarat', *The Times of India*, 8 Sept. 2008, https://timesofindia.indiatimes.com/city/ahmedabad/p-k-mishra-is-back-in-gujarat/articleshow/3456784.cms.
19. In 2015, Sanjay Gupta was sent to judicial custody because of accusations of corruption. 'Fall of Sanjay Gupta: from IAS to conman', *The Economic Times*, 20 May 2015, http://articles.economictimes.indiatimes.com/2015-05-20/news/62413387_1_gujarat-state-petroleum-corporation-sanjay-gupta-neesa-group.
20. 'Gautam Adani: meet the man who built 470 billion rupees infrastructure empire', *The Economic Times*, 5 Sept. 2013, https://economictimes.indiatimes.com/industry/indl-goods/svs/construction/gautam-adani-meet-the-man-who-built-rs-47000-crore-infrastructure-empire/articleshow/22304960.cms.
21. Rajiv Shah, 'Vipul Mittra quits IAS; it's three in a row', *The Times of India*, 4 Nov. 2006, https://rajivnews.wordpress.com/2006/11/04/vipul-mittra-quits-ias-its-three-in-a-row/.
22. M. Rajshekhar, 'The other big', *The Economic Times* (Mumbai edition), 5 Sept. 2013.
23. Ghanshyam Shah, 'Modi's power play and mega-marketing in the 2009 Lok Sabha elections', in Jan Breman and Ghanshyam Shah, *Gujarat, Cradle and Harbinger of Identity Politics: India's Injurious Frame of Communalism*, New Delhi, Tulika Books, 2022, p. 264. Narendra Modi did not get a mobile phone when he was chief minister but used the phones of others, according to a senior Ahmedabad-based journalist.
24. Bharat Desai, 'The Parivar's "punishment" Modi baiters are waiting for', *The Times of India* (Ahmedabad edn), 24 June 2013, https://timesofindia.indiatimes.com/india/the-parivars-punishment-narendra-modi-baiters-are-waiting-for/articleshow/20736884.cms.
25. A few years later 'on the eve of the BJP national executive meeting in Dec. 2005, sleazy CDs appeared in Mumbai which gave the impression of Joshi being in a compromising position with a woman'. See ibid. Joshi was relieved of his responsibilities before the meeting but the Madhya Pradesh government, which investigated the case because the CDs had been posted from Bhopal, established that these CDs had been doctored. 'It is on record that crime branch

officials from Gujarat had distributed the CDs at the venue of the national executive.' Ibid.

26. 'CM makes punching bag out of Haren', *The Asian Age*, 29 July 2002, pp. 9–11.
27. 'Modi vs Pandya: who'll blink first', *The Times of India* (Ahmedabad edn), 22 Nov. 2002, p. 1.
28. Vinod K. Jose, 'The emperor uncrowned', *The Caravan*, 1 March 2012, http://caravanmagazine.in/reportage/emperor-uncrowned?page=0,9 (last accessed 21 Nov. 2013).
29. 'The Haren Pandya judgment: dissection of a botched investigation', *EPW*, 46, no. 38 (17 Sept. 2011), pp. 10–12.
30. Roxy Gagdekar, 'Was it Tulsiram Prajapati who killed Haren Pandya', *DNA* (Ahmedabad edn), 30 Aug. 2011, http://www.dnaindia.com/india/1581624/report-was-it-tulsiram-prajapati-who-killed-haren-pandya (last accessed 21 Nov. 2013).
31. 'In the High Court of Gujarat at Ahmedabad (District Jamnagar), Special Criminal Application no. 2101 of 2011, Sanjiv Rajendra Bhatt, IPS vs State of Gujarat and Others', http://www.cjponline.org/SBArrest/SCrA%202101%20of%202011%20additional%20affidavit%20110927.pdf (last accessed 12 Dec. 2013).
32. Ibid.
33. 'D.G. Vanzara sings about Haren Pandya's murder, says it was political conspiracy: CBI', *The Times of India*, 21 Sept. 2013, http://articles.timesofindia.indiatimes.com/2013-09-21/india/42271814_1_sadiq-jamal-encounter-case-tulsiram-prajapati (last accessed 21 Nov. 2013). A few weeks before Vanzara's statement the CBI 'found three men are common to cases pertaining to the assassination of BJP leader Haren Pandya and the encounters of Ishrat Jahan and Sadiq Jamal'. Satish Jha, 'CBI finds common link in Pandya murder, Ishrat, Sadiq encounters', *The Indian Express*, 15 Aug. 2013, http://www.indianexpress.com/news/cbi-finds-common-link-in-pandya-murder-ishrat-sadiq-encounters/1155731/ (last accessed 12 Dec. 2013). On the murder of Pandya, see Shastri Ramachandaran, 'Haren Pandya's murder: questions without answers', *EPW*, 46, no. 52 (24 Dec. 2011), pp. 10–12.
34. Jose, 'The emperor uncrowned'.

35. In 2002, as chairman of the BJP Election Campaign Committee, he simply showed quietly that he was 'unhappy about Modi taking all the credit for development works initiated by him'. Himanshu Kaushik, 'At BJP meet, Keshubhai "warns" Modi', *The Indian Express* (Ahmedabad edn), 9 Oct. 2002, p. 3.
36. N.K. Singh, 'In Gujarat, BJP is quite Modi-fied', *The Indian Express*, 21 Oct. 2006, p. 3.
37. Mahesh Langa, 'Modi has last word: Rupala's BJP president', *The Indian Express* (Ahmedabad edn), 27 Oct. 2006, p. 3.
38. Ibid.
39. Ibid.
40. According to Rajiv Shah in June 2004, while A.B. Vajpayee was considering that the BJP's defeat in the Lok Sabha elections was partly due to the 2002 violence in Gujarat, 'as many as 80–85 MLAs in the BJP Legislature Party of 128 may want Modi out'. Rajiv Shah, 'I'm ready to kiss the gallows: Modi', *The Times of India* (Ahmedabad edn), 13 June 2004, https://timesofindia.indiatimes.com/city/ahmedabad/im-ready-to-kiss-the-gallows-modi/articleshow/736310.cms?from=mdr.
41. Rajendrasinh Rana, a rebel who was Gujarat BJP president in 2001, had already been eased out and replaced by Vajubhai Vala. But as early as 2004, it was clear that Purshottam Rupala was 'the CM's choice for the post of state BJP president'. 'Modi overtures soften BKS stand on ouster', *The Times of India* (Ahmedabad edn), 22 June 2004, http://articles.timesofindia.indiatimes.com/2004-06-22/ahmedabad/27155290_1_bharatiya-kisan-sangh-bks-chief-minister-narendra-modi (last accessed 21 Nov. 2013).
42. In 2002 he had lost his seat as MLA, but this setback did not dissuade Modi from supporting him. 'Modi pits Rupala against Keshubhai for BJP chief's post', *The Times of India* (Ahmedabad edn), 12 Oct. 2006, p. 4.
43. 'Wait continues for state BJP chief', *The Indian Express* (Ahmedabad edn), 15 Oct. 2006, p. 3.
44. Pravin Sheth, *Images of Transformation: Gujarat and Narendra Modi*, Ahmedabad, Team Spirit, 2007, p. 227.
45. 'Keshubhai fires an I-Day salvo at Modi', *The Times of India* (Ahmedabad edn), 17 Aug. 2007, p. 4.

46. Ibid.
47. 'Modi is a dictator: Govindacharya', *The Times of India* (Ahmedabad edn), 29 Aug. 2011, p. 5.
48. Mahesh Langa, 'BJP plays it safe, repeats sitting MLAs to avoid defection', *Hindustan Times*, 22 Nov. 2012, http://www.hindustantimes.com/specials/coverage/gujarat-assembly-elections-2012/chunk-ht-ui-gujaratassemblyelections2012-topstories/bjp-plays-it-safe-repeats-sitting-mlas-to-avoid-defection/sp-article10-962977.aspx (last accessed 21 Nov. 2013).
49. Nilanjan Mukhopadhyay, *Narendra Modi: The Man, the Times*, Chennai, Westland, 2013, p. 305.
50. Parimal Dabhi, 'In Maya Kodnani U-turn, Narendra Modi white flag to right wing', *The Indian Express*, 17 May 2013, http://m.indianexpress.com/news/in-maya-kodnani-uturn-narendra-modi-white-flag-to-right-wing/1116803/ (last accessed 21 Nov. 2013).
51. 'VHP wants Modi to spare Bajrangi', *The Indian Express*, 17 Sept. 2013, http://m.indianexpress.com/news/vhp-wants-modi-to-spare-bajrangi/1170234/ (last accessed 21 Nov. 2013).
52. Avinash Nair, 'Modi's criticisms were love bytes: VHP's Singhal', *The Economic Times* (Ahmedabad edn), 25 April 2009, p. 2.
53. 'VHP slams policies of Gujarat govt', *The Times of India* (Ahmedabad edn), 7 Nov. 2011, p. 3.
54. N.B. Ahuja, 'Modi visits Sangh HQ', *The Asian Age*, 27 Nov. 2008, p. 4.
55. 'CM bows before RSS, drops law to regulate trusts', *The Times of India* (Ahmedabad edn), 9 Feb. 2012, p. 1.
56. 'Govt bows to pressure, will scrap Trust Act', *The Indian Express* (Ahmedabad edn), 9 Feb. 2012, p. 3.
57. 'Don't pay electricity bills, BKS tells farmers', *The Times of India* (Ahmedabad edn), 4 July 2003, http://articles.timesofindia.indiatimes.com/2003-07-04/ahmedabad/27197597_1_maganbhai-patel-bharatiya-kisan-sangh-price-rise (last accessed 21 Nov. 2013).
58. Cited in ibid.
59. 'Farmers plough into Modi's parade', *The Times of India* (Ahmedabad edn), 25 Sept. 2003, http://articles.timesofindia.indiatimes.

com/2003-09-25/ahmedabad/27193446_1_maganbhai-patel-bks-bharatiya-kisan-sangh (last accessed 21 Nov. 2013).

60. 'Modi ousts Sangh Parivar outfit', *The Times of India* (Ahmedabad edn), 1 Jan. 2004, http://articles.timesofindia.indiatimes.com/2004-01-01/india/28332665_1_bharatiya-kisan-sangh-bks-leaders-jiyanbhai-patel (last accessed 21 Nov. 2013).
61. 'Central leaders coming to sort out BKS dispute', *The Times of India* (Ahmedabad edn), 24 Jan. 2004, http://articles.timesofindia.indiatimes.com/2004-01-24/ahmedabad/28325679_1_bjp-leaders-laljibhai-patel-bharatiya-kisan-sangh (last accessed 21 Nov. 2013).
62. 'Govt invites BKS for negotiations, mum on tariff', *The Times of India* (Ahmedabad edn), 28 Jan. 2004, http://articles.timesofindia.indiatimes.com/2004-01-28/ahmedabad/28335298_1_power-tariff-tariff-hike-bharatiya-kisan-sangh (last accessed 21 Nov. 2013).
63. 'BKS sends letter to government for talks', *The Times of India* (Ahmedabad edn), 1 Feb. 2004, http://articles.timesofindia.indiatimes.com/2004-02-01/ahmedabad/28333337_1_dams-narmada-water-bks (last accessed 21 Nov. 2013).
64. 'Sangh farmers' body says Modi must go', *The Times of India* (Ahmedabad edn), 18 May 2004, http://articles.timesofindia.indiatimes.com/2004-05-18/india/28339993_1_cm-narendra-modi-sangh-parivar-maganbhai-patel (last accessed 21 Nov. 2013).
65. Rajiv Shah, 'BKS sends letter to government for talks', *The Times of India*, 1 Feb. 2004, http://timesofindia.indiatimes.com/articleshow/468069.cms?utm_source=contentofinterest&utm_medium=text&utm_campaign=cppst.
66. 'Power cuts will affect crops: BKS', *The Times of India* (Ahmedabad edn), 15 June 2007, http://articles.timesofindia.indiatimes.com/2007-06-15/ahmedabad/27972099_1_farmer-suicides-bks-president-prafull-senjalia-bharatiya-kisan-sangh (last accessed 12 Dec. 2013). For more articles on the BKS, see http://articles.timesofindia.indiatimes.com/keyword/bharatiya-kisan-sangh.
67. 'Modi is a propagandist: Bhartiya Kisan Sangh', CNN-IBN, 26 Nov. 2007, http://ibnlive.in.com/news/modi-is-a-propagandist-bhartiya-kisan-sangh/53045-37.html (last accessed 21 Nov. 2013).
68. 'Lack of co-ordination in Guj govt depts affecting crops: BKS', *Business Standard*, 13 Dec. 2011, http://www.business-standard.com/article/

economy-policy/lack-of-coordination-in-guj-govt-depts-affecting-crops-bks-111121300010_1.html (last accessed 21 Nov. 2013).

69. The basic demand of the BKS was to get the eight hours of electricity that farmers were receiving not during the night or, sometimes, in the afternoon, but only in the morning. Ibid.

70. 'State govt ignoring farmer suicides', *The Times of India* (Ahmedabad edn), 8 March 2007, http://articles.timesofindia.indiatimes.com/2007-05-08/ahmedabad/27876439_1_farmer-suicides-bks-general-secretary-maganbhai-patel (last accessed 21 Nov. 2013).

71. Ibid.

72. 'Watch where the water flows in Gujarat', *The Indian Express*, 1 April 2013, http://www.indianexpress.com/story-print/1095812/ (last accessed 21 Nov. 2013).

73. 'Gujarat farmers to intensify their stir if SIR is not scrapped', *Tehelka*, 13 Aug. 2013, http://www.tehelka.com/gujarat-farmers-to-intensify-their-stir-if-sir-is-not-scrapped/ (last accessed 21 Nov. 2013); and 'Gujarat farmers protest against land acquisition for Maruti plant', *Hindu BusinessLine*, 18 June 2013, http://www.thehindubusinessline.com/news/states/gujarat-farmers-protest-against-land-acquisition-for-maruti-plant/article4827095.ece (last accessed 21 Nov. 2013).

74. Cited in Mukhopadhyay, *Narendra Modi*, p. 303.

75. Ibid., p. 307. Manmohan Vaidya is the son of a very senior RSS leader, M.G. Vaidya, who has been publicly critical of Narendra Modi. See Sanjay Singh, 'Vaidya vs Vaidya: how the BJP is caught in a bind', *Firstpost*, 12 Nov. 2012, http://www.firstpost.com/politics/vaidya-vs-vaidya-how-the-bjp-is-caught-in-a-bind-522986.html?utm_source=ref_article (last accessed 21 Nov. 2013).

76. Mukhopadhyay, *Narendra Modi*, p. 334.

77. Cited in ibid., p. 335.

78. Cited in ibid., p. 352.

79. Rajiv Shah, 'Sangh pressure causes delay in BJP chief selection', *The Times of India*, 7 Feb. 2004, https://timesofindia.indiatimes.com/city/ahmedabad/sangh-pressure-causes-delay-in-bjp-chief-selection/articleshow/482450.cms.

80. Rajiv Shah, 'Modi's rift with Sangh Parivar widening', *The Times of India*, 29 Aug. 2006, https://timesofindia.indiatimes.com/india/

modis-rift-with-sangh-parivar-widening/articleshow/1933901.cms. See also Rajiv Shah, 'Modi's rift with pro-rebel Parivar widens in Gujarat', *The Times of India*, 4 Sept. 2005, p. 3.

81. Rajiv Shah, 'Is rift widening between RSS, Modi?', *The Times of India*, 26 Aug. 2006, https://timesofindia.indiatimes.com/city/ahmedabad/is-rift-widening-between-rss-modi/articleshow/1929374.cms.
82. Rajiv Shah, 'RSS mediates to keep Keshubhai in BJP', *The Times of India*, 7 Oct. 2007, p. 3.
83. Mukhopadhyay, *Narendra Modi*, p. 53.
84. 'BJP ignores RSS for polls', *The Times of India* (Ahmedabad edn), 6 Nov. 2007, p. 3.
85. 'RSS will back Keshubhai's oust-Modi campaign: Maniar', *The Times of India*, 6 Aug. 2012, http://articles.timesofindia.indiatimes.com/2012-08-06/rajkot/33064500_1_pravin-maniar-rss-top-brass-rss-man (last accessed 12 Dec. 2013).
86. Interview with Pravin Maniar by Tina Parekh, 'RSS to keep away from poll work', *DNA* (Ahmedabad edn), 25 Nov. 2007, p. 3.
87. *The Indian Express* (Ahmedabad edn), 11 Dec. 2007, p. 3.
88. Ibid.
89. Ibid.
90. Ajay Umat, 'Pracharak blooms, Parivar wilts', *The Times of India* (Ahmedabad edn), 3 Oct. 2012, p. 1.
91. Ibid.
92. Ibid.
93. Singh, 'Vaidya vs Vaidya'.
94. Mohua Chatterjee, 'Modi gets the better of Gadkari, Sanjay Joshi quits BJP National Executive', *The Times of India*, 24 May 2012, http://articles.timesofindia.indiatimes.com/2012-05-24/india/31839911_1_gadkari-joshi-sanjay-joshi-national-executive (last accessed 12 Dec. 2013).
95. The way it had done in 1984 when senior RSS leaders including Nanaji Deshmukh had found it more appropriate to support Rajiv Gandhi's Congress than A.B. Vajpayee's BJP. See Christophe Jaffrelot, *Hindu Nationalism and Indian Politics*, London, Hurst, 1996, p. 329.
96. Shah, 'Modi's power play and mega-marketing', p. 274.
97. This interest in local politics may appear ironical given his initial stand on Panchayat elections. In 2001, when 10,000 villages were going

to the polls he 'declared that all villages choosing their members unanimously would be suitably rewarded by giving additional funds development. More than 45 percent villages chose to go in for unanimous elections and each of those villages was rewarded with 200,000 rupees in addition to the allotted development fund.' Interview with Narendra Modi by Ajay Singh, 'Modi on Mahatma, economy and strengths of India', *Governance Now*, 17 Sept. 2013, http://www.governancenow.com/news/regular-story/modi-mahatma-economy-and-strengths-india (last accessed 21 Nov. 2013). This interview first appeared in the 1–15 Feb. 2011 issue of *Governance Now* magazine.

98. Profiling Modi in the preface of an interview in 2007, *Organiser* interestingly hailed him for this reason: 'A true people's person, he has personally campaigned for all polls—from panchayat elections to those of municipal corporations never losing touch with the common man.' 'Special interview', *Organiser*, 2 Dec. 2007, p. 2.
99. Nikunj Soni, 'Modi harps on 5-pt plan', *DNA* (Ahmedabad edn), 21 Oct. 2010, p. 1.
100. Such as Nadiad, Kapadvanj, Anand, Bharuch, Dabhoi and Porbandar where the Congress was almost decimated. See Rathin Das, 'Vanquished Cong ponders reasons for Gujarat defeat', *The Pioneer*, 26 Oct. 2010, p. 6.
101. Similarly, in 2011, after the BJP won 67 seats out of 105 (Congress got 39) in civic elections, Narendra Modi tweeted: 'Thankful to voters for reposing faith in BJP in the civic by-polls across Gujarat.' 'Civic election poll results: BJP leads with 67 seats', *Ahmedabad Mirror*, 8 Dec. 2011, p. 10.
102. D.P. Bhattacharya, 'From turning weak co-ops to economic gains, Shah knows it all', *The Economic Times*, 10 July 2021, https://economictimes.indiatimes.com/news/politics-and-nation/from-turning-weak-co-ops-to-economic-gains-shah-knows-it-all/articleshow/84278292.cms?from=mdr.
103. Ibid.
104. Atul Dev, 'His master's voice', *The Caravan*, 1 October 2020, https://caravanmagazine.in/law/tushar-mehta-holds-court.
105. Kingshuk Nag, *The NaMo Story: A Political Life*, New Delhi, Roli Books, 2013, p. 59.

106. Ibid.; and Nikita Sud, *Liberalization, Hindu Nationalism and the State: A Biography of Gujarat*, New Delhi, Oxford University Press, 2012, p. 53.
107. Ibid.
108. Ibid.
109. Bhattacharya, 'From turning weak co-ops to economic gains, Shah knows it all'.
110. Ibid.
111. Ibid.
112. Anirban Ganguly and Shiwanand Dwivedi, *Amit Shah and the March of BJP*, New Delhi, Bloomsbury, 2019, p. 47.
113. Stanley A. Kochanek, 'Mrs Gandhi's pyramid: the new Congress', in H.C. Hart (ed.), *Indira's Gandhi India: A Political System Reappraised*, Boulder, CO, Westview, 1976.
114. There are very few articles on APCO and the way the company operates as a lobbyist. One of the best pieces of investigative journalism is Ken Silverstein, 'Their men in Washington: undercover with D.C.'s lobbyists for hire', *Harper's Magazine*, July 2007, https://harpers.org/archive/2007/07/their-men-in-washington/.
115. G. Vishnu, 'What lies on the other side of US' praise of Modi', *Tehelka*, 19 Sept. 2011. This article, like many *Tehelka* articles, cannot be retrieved. Aradhna Wal offers some explanations for the disappearance of *Tehelka* archives: 'Into the void', *The Caravan*, 1 Dec. 2018, https://caravanmagazine.in/media/curious-case-of-tehelkas-missing-archives.
116. *The Times of India*, 17 Nov. 2007, p. 3. See also Shelley Kasli, 'Mechanics of Narendra Modi's PR agency: APCO worldwide; orchestrating our future', *Beyond Headlines*, 26 June 2013, https://beyondheadlines.in/2013/06/mechanics-of-narendra-modis-pr-agency-apco-worldwide-orchestrating-future/.
117. Aou Esthose Suresh, 'The Modi machine: makeover gurus', *The Indian Express*, 20 Oct. 2013, http://www.indianexpress.com/story-print/1184809/ (last accessed 21 Nov. 2013).
118. Including (ex-)ministers like Anandiben Patel, Vaju Vala and Amit Shah, BJP veterans like Purshottam Rupala, R.C. Faldu, Surendra Patel and Parindu Bhagat (in charge of financial and legal matters) and RSS cadres (including V. Satish, the joint general secretary of the

BJP). See Shishir Gupta, 'Team Narendra Modi: the strategists who run his campaign', *Hindustan Times*, 17 Nov. 2013, http://www.hindustantimes.com/StoryPage/Print/968485.aspx (last accessed 21 Nov. 2013).

119. Sunil Khilnani, 'Finely slicing the electorate: with clever use of technology, Narendra Modi plans to customise messages to voters', *The Times of India*, 24 May 2013, http://articles.timesofindia.indiatimes.com/2013-05-24/edit-page/39476042_1_personal-data-campaigns-rajesh-jain (last accessed 12 Dec. 2013).
120. Dhanya Ann Thoppil, 'Meet Modi's social media men', *India Real Time* (blog), 5 July 2013, http://blogs.wsj.com/indiarealtime/2013/07/05/meet-modis-social-media-men/ (last accessed 21 Nov. 2013).
121. Pratik Sinha, 'Who runs Narendra Modi's website?', *Truth of Gujarat*, 15 Oct. 2013, http://www.truthofgujarat.com/runs-narendra-modis-website/ (last accessed 21 Nov. 2013); and 'Narendra Modi campaign runs website that justifies Gujarat riots', *Dainik Bhaskar*, 8 Oct. 2013, http://daily.bhaskar.com/article/GUJ-AHD-revealed-narendra-modi-campaign-runs-website-that-justifies-gujarat-riots-4396624-NOR.html (last accessed 21 Nov. 2013).
122. Harit Mehta, 'New Team Modi', *The Times of India* (Ahmedabad edn), 23 Sept. 2012, p. 1.
123. See Amogh Sharma, 'The backstage of democracy: exploring the professionalisation of politics in India', DPhil thesis, Oxford University, 2020, p. 244ff.
124. 'Modi's key media advisor Avashia quits', *The Indian Express*, 2 Feb. 2012, http://www.indianexpress.com/story-print/906940/ (last accessed 21 Nov. 2013).
125. B. Raman, 'Mr. Modi's problem', *Outlook*, 3 Sept. 2012, http://www.outlookindia.com/article.aspx?282128 (last accessed 12 Dec. 2013). Elsewhere, B. Raman wrote:

> Since the beginning of last year, I have been drawing attention to the Nazi Storm Trooper-like methods adopted by many followers of NaMo to impose their will on their party and then the nation. Anyone aware of the methods used by the Nazi Storm Troopers to force the German people to accept

Hitler as their leader would be struck by the similarity of the rhetoric and PSYWAR methods used by these pro-NaMo elements whom I have been referring to as the NaMo Brigade. They do not call themselves the NaMo Brigade, but they make no secret of the fact that they support NaMo as the next prime minister of India. Their worrisome methods, reminiscent of the methods used by the Storm Troopers, consist largely of abuse, vituperation, disinformation, character assassination and psychological pressure. Whereas the Nazi Storm Troopers did not have the benefit of the computer and the Internet, the NaMo Brigade, which has established a dominance over the means of propaganda through the Net in the absence of any opposition to their methods from secular and liberal elements, has been using the social media networks in their PSYWAR.

Nobody can object to their campaign in favour of NaMo as the prime minister despite his perceived misdeeds of the past. But one has reasons to be concerned over the ways adopted by these elements in an attempt to enforce their will on the nation. If they succeed due to lack of adequate public knowledge of the sinister implications of their strategy and the inadequate attempts to counter their methods, the nation may have to pay a heavy price. India needs a strong, efficient and effective ruler, but not a Hitler.

See B. Raman, 'A wake up call', *Outlook*, 4 June 2012, http://www.outlookindia.com/article.aspx?281135 (last accessed 13 Dec. 2013).

126. 'CM wasted taxpayers' money on global agriculture meet: Vaghela', *The Indian Express*, 11 Sept. 2013, http://m.indianexpress.com/news/cm-wasted-taxpayers-money-on-global-agriculture-meet-vaghela/1167502/ (last accessed 21 Nov. 2013).
127. Mukhopadhyay, *Narendra Modi*, p. 54.
128. In 2013, Narendra Modi gave an interview in which he said: 'I am nationalist. I am patriotic. Nothing is wrong. I am born Hindu. Nothing is wrong. So I'm a Hindu nationalist.' See Deepshika Ghosh, 'Narendra Modi's "Hindu nationalist" posters should be banned, says Samajwadi Party', NDTV, 24 July 2013, http://www.ndtv.com/

article/india/narendra-modi-s-hindu-nationalist-posters-should-be-banned-says-samajwadi-party-396494 (last accessed 12 Dec. 2013). In 1994 I had a long discussion with L.K. Advani, who wanted to know whether the French title of my book meant 'nationalist Hindus' or 'Hindu nationalists'. He had a clear preference for the first translation.

129. See the section entitled 'Secularism' in Jaffrelot, *Hindu Nationalism*, pp. 313–41.
130. 'RSS bats for Modi', *The Indian Express* (Ahmedabad edn), 25 June 2012, p. 5.
131. Christophe Jaffrelot, 'The militias of Hindutva: communal violence, terrorism and cultural policing', in Laurent Gayer and Christophe Jaffrelot (eds), *Armed Militias of South Asia: Fundamentalist, Maoists and Separatists*, London, Hurst; New York, Columbia University Press; New Delhi, Foundation Books, 2009, pp. 199–236.
132. In 2007, Acharya Dharmendra, a VHP leader, took part in the BJP election campaign in Gujarat and said something that became the title of an article: 'I back Modi because he has never been apologetic', *The Indian Express*, 11 Dec. 2007, p. 3.
133. 'Abhinav Bharat, the Malegaon blast and Hindu nationalism: resisting and emulating Islamist terrorism', *EPW*, 45, no. 36 (4–10 Sept. 2010), pp. 51–8.
134. Christophe Jaffrelot and Malvika Maheshwari, 'Paradigmatic shifts by the RSS? Lessons from Aseemanand's confession', *EPW*, 46, no. 6 (5–11 Feb. 2011), pp. 42–6.
135. D.K. Jha, 'Bhagwat eclipsed', *The Caravan*, 31 Oct. 2022, https://caravanmagazine.in/politics/bhagwat-modi-supreme.
136. Ibid.
137. Diksha Munjal, 'Who is Girish Chandra Murmu, CAG and trusted aide of PM Modi since Gujarat days?', *The Hindu*, 8 June 2023, https://www.thehindu.com/news/national/who-is-girish-chandra-murmu-cag-and-trusted-aide-of-pm-modi-since-gujarat-days/article66913528.ece.
138. R.K. Misra, 'How Modi's Margdarshak Mandal became parking place for discarded, elderly egos', *Counterview*, 17 April 2019, https://www.counterview.net/2019/04/how-modis-margdarshak-mandal-became.html.

139. Jha, 'Bhagwat eclipsed'.
140. Ibid.
141. See Sharma, 'The backstage of democracy', pp. 244ff.
142. Uday Mahurkar and Kunal Pradhan, 'Meet the men behind Modi's audacious election campaign', *India Today*, 24 Feb. 2014, p. 39, http://indiatoday.intoday.in/story/narendra-modi-bjpprime-ministerial-candidate-campaign-social-media/1/343517.html (last accessed 4 Feb. 2015).
143. Pradeep K. Chhibber and Susan L. Ostermann, 'The BJP's fragile mandate: Modi and vote mobilizers in the 2014 general elections', *Studies in Indian Politics*, 2, no. 2 (2014), pp. 1–15.
144. Ibid., p. 3.
145. Chhibber and Ostermann, 'The BJP's fragile mandate', p. 10.

8. RELATING TO THE PEOPLE THE NATIONAL-POPULIST WAY

1. Cited in Rajiv Shah, 'Modi only mascot for BJP: Rupala', *The Times of India*, 5 Nov. 2007, p. 3.
2. Cas Mudde and Cristóbal Rovira Kaltwasser, *Populism: A Very Short Introduction*, New York, Oxford University Press, 2017, p. 6.
3. Gino Germani, *Authoritarianism, Fascism and National Populism*, New Brunswick, NJ, Transactions Books, 1978.
4. On Modi's high-tech populism as chief minister, see Christophe Jaffrelot, 'Gujarat elections: the sub-text of Modi's "hattrick"; high tech populism and the "neo-middle class"', *Studies in Indian Politics*, 1, no. 1, 2013, https://journals.sagepub.com/doi/full/10.1177/2321023013482789?journalCode=inpa#fn4- 2321023013482789.
5. In 2012, he had 1.1 million followers on Twitter, for instance. A. Raman, 'Drawing his map in mega pixels', *Outlook*, 31 Dec. 2012, https://www.outlookindia.com/magazine/story/drawing-his-map-in-mega-pixels/283392.
6. Kapil Dave, 'Unsure of 3-D effect will work, Modi to hit the road', *The Times of India* (Ahmedabad edn), 25 Nov. 2012, p. 1.
7. Christophe Jaffrelot, 'Narendra Modi and the power of television in Gujarat', *Television and New Media*, 16 (May 2015), pp. 346–53.
8. Avinash Nair, 'And they were 26: Modi scripts his "victory sequel" in 3D now', *The Indian Express* (Ahmedabad edn), 3 Dec. 2012, p. 1.

9. When taking my children to Ahmedabad Zoo in 2009, I was welcomed by a huge photograph of a smiling Modi.
10. This inclination is evident from the—very sophisticated—website of Narendra Modi, which he has commissioned from a private company and which comprised 373 photographs of him in 2007. Rajdeep Sardesai once asked Narendra Modi 'Why do you have only your pictures on all the Gujarat government websites? Why do your photographs appear so frequently?' Cited in Aakar Patel, 'Meet Narendra Modi's no. 1 fan: himself', *DNA*, 3 March 2013, http://www.dnaindia.com/analysis/1806729/column-meet-narendra-modi-s-no-1-fan-himself (last accessed 21 Nov. 2013).
11. Cited in Nilanjan Mukhopadhyay, *Narendra Modi: The Man, the Times*, Chennai, Westland, 2013, p. 359.
12. He may say otherwise, though. He declared, 'I never spent a single minute for my image' in response to Karan Thapar in 2007. Cited in ibid., p. 14.
13. Zee TV, 'Mahatma Gandhi was India's biggest brand ambassador: Narendra Modi', 30 Sept. 2013, http://zeenews.india.com/news/maharashtra/mahatama-gandhi-was-india-s-biggest-brand-ambassador-narendra-modi_880259.html (last accessed 12 Dec. 2013).
14. Manas Dasgupta, 'Amitabh Bachchan volunteers to be Gujarat's brand ambassador', *The Hindu*, 7 Jan. 2010, http://www.hindu.com/2010/01/07/stories/2010010760511400.htm (last accessed 12 Dec. 2013).
15. Nilanjan Mukhopadhyay writes that the young 'Narendra was conscious of what he wore. "He liked to dress properly and took care of his clothes—did not allow them to get frayed and ruffled like other children. He spent a lot of time in grooming", the uncle [of Narendra Modi] reminiscences.' See Mukhopadhyay, *Narendra Modi*, p. 31.
16. Cited in ibid., p. 281.
17. This inclination is also evident from several other pieces of 'information' provided by Nilanjan Mukhopadhyay: 'As far as his looks are concerned, besides the stated fondness for stylish clothes—there is no "compromise" on this front—Modi is also particular about perfect and timely trimming of his facial hair and locks.' Ibid., p. 286.

18. In 2013, 4,500 schoolbags and 138,000 notebooks with the pictures of Narendra Modi and A.B. Vajpayee or with those of Modi and Swami Vivekananda were distributed to pupils in Gujarat with the logo of the government programme known as Sarva Shiksha Abhiyan at the back. Kumar Anand, 'Evolution of Narendra Modi's self-branding: CM rubs shoulders with Atal on schoolbags', *The Indian Express*, 21 June 2013, http://www.indianexpress.com/news/evolution-of-narendra-modis-selfbranding-cm-rubs-shoulders-with-atal-on-schoolbags/1131976/ (last accessed 12 Dec. 2013).
19. See Partha Chatterjee, *I Am the People: Reflections on Popular Sovereignty Today*, New York, Columbia University Press, 2019.
20. Radha Sharma, 'Who's behind the Modi-mask?', *The Times of India*, 27 Dec. 2007, http://timesofindia.indiatimes.com/articleshow/2653760.cms?utm_source=contentofinterest&utm_medium=text&utm_campaign=cppst.
21. See ibid.
22. Pierre Ostiguy, 'Populism: a socio-cultural approach', in Cristóbal Rovira Kaltwasser, Paul A. Taggart, Paulina Ochoa Espejo and Pierre Ostiguy (eds), *The Oxford Handbook of Populism*, Oxford, Oxford University Press, 2017, p. 74.
23. For a more detailed analysis of the mimetic dimension of Modi's populist style in India, see Jean-Thomas Martelli and Christophe Jaffrelot, 'Do populist leaders mimic the language of ordinary citizens? Evidence from India', *Political Psychology*, January 2023, https://onlinelibrary.wiley.com/doi/epdf/10.1111/pops.12881.
24. *The Times of India* (Ahmedabad edn), 11 Dec. 2007, p. 3.
25. Subsequently, in 2010, the 50th anniversary of the creation of the state of Gujarat was celebrated in a grand manner during the Swarnim Gujarat (Golden Gujarat) functions, besides many other celebrations.
26. Ghanshyam Shah, 'Modi's power play and mega-marketing in the 2009 Lok Sabha elections', in Jan Breman and Ghanshyam Shah, *Gujarat, Cradle and Harbinger of Identity Politics: India's Injurious Frame of Communalism*, New Delhi, Tulika Books, 2022, p. 268.
27 Mahesh Langa, 'Gujarat vibrancy costs Rs 25 cr', *Tehelka*, 1 Oct. 2005, http://archive.tehelka.com/story_main14.asp?filename=Ne100105Gujarats_vibrancy.asp (last accessed 21 Nov. 2013).

28. See the way he announced it on TV: http://www.youtube.com/watch?v=z5MT91Gckf0 (last accessed 21 Nov. 2013).
29 Narendra Modi, 'Sadbhavana Mission: a touching people's movement', 16 Feb. 2012, Narendra Modi website, http://www.narendramodi.in/sadbhavana-mission-a-touching-people's-movement (last accessed 21 Nov. 2013).
30. Mukhopadhyay, *Narendra Modi*, p. 282.
31. Nalin Mehta, 'Ashis Nandy vs the state of Gujarat: authoritarian developmentalism, democracy and the politics of Narendra Modi', in Nalin Mehta and Mona G. Mehta (eds), *Gujarat beyond Gandhi: Identity, Society and Conflict*, London, Routledge, 2012, p. 122.
32. Ibid.
33. Prashant Dayal, 'Shutter-bug's delight and fit for the ramp', *The Times of India* (Ahmedabad edn), 27 Nov. 2007, p. 3.
34. Mukhopadhyay, *Narendra Modi*, p. 283.
35. Cited in 'Modi attacks Cong on 2G, Coalgate', *The Times of India* (Ahmedabad edn), 12 Sept. 2012, p. 5.
36. The transcript of this interview was reproduced in *The Indian Express* in 2013. 'The riots took place when I was in power, so I know I can't detach myself from them', *The Indian Express*, 17 Sept. 2013, http://m.indianexpress.com/news/the-riots-took-place-when-i-was-in-power-so-i-know-i-cant-detach-myself-from-them/1170181/ (last accessed 21 Nov. 2013).
37. Ostiguy, 'Populism', p. 74.
38. See Pravin Sheth, *Images of Transformation: Gujarat and Narendra Modi*, Ahmedabad, Team Spirit, 2007, p. 249.
39. Ostiguy, 'Populism', p. 74.
40. Cited in E. San Juan, Jr., 'Orientations of Max Weber's concept of charisma', *Centennial Review*, 11, no. 2 (Spring 1967), pp. 270–85, https://www.jstor.org/stable/23738015.
41. See Narendra Modi website, http://www.narendramodi.in/the-cm/ (last accessed 21 Nov. 2013).
42. Morwadia had said about Modi: 'He is like a monkey who is challenging the king [Manmohan Singh—'singh' means lion] of jungle to a duel from the top of a tree.' 'Narendra Modi called monkey by Gujarat Congress chief', *The Indian Express*, 8 Nov. 2012,

http://archive.indianexpress.com/news/narendra-modi-called-monkey-by-gujarat-congress-chief/1028853/.

43. 'I'm Hanuman, says 3D Modi', *The Times of India* (Ahmedabad edn), 19 Nov. 2012, p. 1.
44. *The Times of India*, 23 Nov. 2007, p. 1.
45. Radha Sharma, 'Young Modi wanted crocodile as a pet', *The Times of India* (Ahmedabad edn), 24 Nov. 2007, p. 1.
46. Radha Sharma, 'I can digest all kinds of poison', *The Times of India* (Ahmedabad edn), 25 Nov. 2007, p. 1.
47. *The Times of India* (Ahmedabad edn), 26 Nov. 2007, p. 1.
48. Harish Khare, 'Modi, the man and the message', *The Hindu*, 4 April 2013, http://www.thehindu.com/opinion/lead/modi-the-man-and-the-message/article4577674.ece (last accessed 12 Dec. 2013).
49. S. Prasannarajan, 'Narendra Modi, master divider', *India Today*, 6 Jan. 2003, p. 6.
50. Ostiguy, 'Populism', p. 74.
51. Vibrant Gujarat lecture series, 17 June 2013, Sabarmati Auditorium, Swarnim Sankul-1, Gandhinagar, Shri Modi's speech during interactive session on 'Achieving India's full economic potential' with Mr Jim O'Neill, Narendra Modi website, https://www.narendramodi.in/shri-modi-attends-interactive-session-on-%E2%80%98achieving-india%E2%80%99s-full-economic-potential%E2%80%99-with-mr-jim-o%E2%80%99niell-renowned-economist-who-headed-goldman-sachs-5339 (last accessed 12 Dec. 2013).
52. Interview with Narendra Modi by Ajay Singh, 'Modi on Mahatma, economy and strengths of India', *Governance Now*, 17 Sept. 2013, http://www.governancenow.com/news/regular-story/modi-mahatma-economy-and-strengths-india (last accessed 21 Nov. 2013). This interview first appeared in the 1–15 Feb. 2011 issue of *Governance Now* magazine.
53. In 2007, the media were struck by the volte-face. See Uday Mahurkar, 'Back to Hindutva', *India Today*, 3 Dec. 2007, pp. 35–7.
54. On the notion of subnationalism in the Indian context, see Prerna Singh, 'Subnationalism and social development: a comparative analysis of Indian states', *World Politics*, June 2015, p. 2, doi:10.1017/S0043887115000131. See also Prerna Singh, *How Solidarity Works for*

Welfare: Subnationalism and Social Development in India, Cambridge, Cambridge University Press, 2016.

55. Mona G. Mehta, 'A river of no dissent: Narmada movement and coercive Gujarati nativism', in Nalin Mehta and Mona G. Mehta (eds), *Gujarat beyond Gandhi: Identity, Society and Conflict*, London, Routledge, 2012, p. 45.
56. Ibid., p. 49.
57. Ibid., p. 51.
58. Cited in ibid., p. 52.
59. Ibid., p. 53.
60. Ajay Singh, 'Modi on Mahatma, economy and strengths of India'.
61. Cited in 'Modi mocks PM as "Maun Mohan Singh"', *The Indian Express* (Ahmedabad edn), 30 Oct. 2012.
62. 'Modi addresses farmers, blames Centre for delay in Narmada', *The Indian Express*, 6 May 2013, p. 4. The 16-metre-tall gates that Narendra Modi wanted to install would increase the reservoir's capacity from 1.27 million acre feet (mcft) to 4.75 mcft by taking the height of the dam from 121.92 m to 138.62 m.
63. Cited in 'Modi attacks Cong on 2G, Coalgate', p. 5.
64. 'UPA released more funds to Gujarat than NDA govt', *The Indian Express* (Ahmedabad edn), 6 Oct. 2010, p. 5.
65. The agriculture minister, Dileep Sanghani, 'requested the Union minister to provide the money of crop insurance to the farmers immediately'. 'Gujarat govt declares crop failure, writes to Centre', *The Indian Express* (Ahmedabad edn), 13 Sept. 2012, p. 1.
66. Christophe Jaffrelot, 'Populism against democracy or people against democracy?', in Alain Dieckhoff, Christophe Jaffrelot and Elise Massicard (eds), *Contemporary Populists in Power*, New York, Palgrave, 2022, pp. 35–54.
67. 'Modi mocks PM as 'Maun Mohan Singh', p. 1.
68. Note that what the Hindu nationalists insist on calling a 'structure'—because they looked at it as a temple (were not the statues of Ram and Sita which were inside worshipped by Hindus?)—was here described as a mosque.
69. Cited in 'Modi slams Malik for Babri comments', *Ahmedabad Mirror*, 16 Dec. 2012, p. 4.

70. Cited in ibid. See also Rathin Das, 'Gujarat CM raps UPA on Sir Creek', *Sunday Pioneer* (New Delhi edn), 16 Dec. 2012, p. 6.
71. 'Shri Narendra Modi in New Delhi at BJP national headquarter on Gujarat victory', 27 Dec. 2012, Narendra Modi website, http://www.narendramodi.in/shri-narendra-modi-in-new-delhi-at-bjp-national-headquarter-on-gujarat-victory/ (last accessed 21 Nov. 2013).
72. Abheek Barman, 'Modi's Himalayan miracle', *The Times of India* (Ahmedabad edn), 26 June 2013. The author shows that in 2013 Narendra Modi's claim that he had had 15,000 Gujarati pilgrims rescued from the landslides which had taken place in the Himalayas revealed 'his hype machine at work'. He also narrates a well-known story about Modi: 'In 2005 he announced that state-owned company GSPC had made India's biggest gas discovery: 20 trillion cubic feet (tcf) valued at more than US$50 billion, off Andhra Pradesh. This was 40 per cent more than what Reliance had found in the same area. Modi then egged on GSPC to grab projects in Egypt, Yemen and Australia. Many suspected that Modi's gas claim was hot air, but in the absence of evidence few could say so. But in 2012, the Centre's directorate general of hydrocarbon (DGH), which analyses and certifies all energy finds, said that it could vouch only a tenth of Modi's claim: there was only 2 tcf of gas.'
73. Summit Khanna, 'Sadbhavana sops exceed annual plan', *DNA* (Ahmedabad edn), 17 Feb. 2012, p. 1; and Hirlal Dave, Kamaal Saiyed, Gopal Kateshiya and Kapil Dave, '170 billion rupees and counting ...: figure the magic in Modi maths', *The Indian Express* (Ahmedabad edn), 18 Jan. 2012, p. 5.
74. Cited in 'Modi mocks PM as "Maun Mohan Singh"', p. 3.
75. 'Modi slams Cong for ad goof-up', *The Indian Express* (Ahmedabad edn), 30 Nov. 2012, p. 3.
76. 'Modi says it loud and clear: it's Congress vs CM', *The Indian Express* (Ahmedabad edn), 2 Dec. 2012, p. 3.
77. Cited in Mukhopadhyay, *Narendra Modi*, p. 293.
78. 'Modi slams Malik for Babri comments', p. 4.
79. 'Modi takes a dig at dynasty politics, UPA policies', *The Indian Express* (Ahmedabad edn), 3 Sept. 2012, p. 3.

80. 'Mixed response to CM attack on Nehru family', *Ahmedabad Mirror*, 27 Oct. 2012, p. 6.
81. Ravish Tiwari, 'Narendra Modi as a "backward leader", Nitish Kumar as an upper-caste "hero"', *The Indian Express*, 16 April 2013, http://www.indianexpress.com/news/narendra-modi-as-a-backward-leader-nitish-kumar-as-an-upper-caste-hero/1102578/ (last accessed 12 Dec. 2013); and 'Narendra Modi: from tea vendor to PM candidate', *The Times of India*, 13 Sept. 2013, http://articles.timesofindia.indiatimes.com/2013-09-13/india/42040411_1_narendra-modi-nilanjan-mukhopadhyay-railway-station (last accessed 12 Dec. 2013).
82. Manas Dasgupta, 'Insult to India', *The Hindu*, 19 March 2005, p. 3.
83. A. Baruah, 'U.S. denied entry to Modi: Centre protests', *The Hindu*, 19 March 2005, p. 3.
84. 'Modi immobilized', *The Economist*, 26 March 2005, https://www.economist.com/asia/2005/03/23/modi-immobilised.
85. Cited in Shah, 'Modi power play and mega marketing', p. 276.
86. A.M. Shah, Pravin J. Patel and Lancy Lobo, 'A heady mix: Gujarati and Hindu pride', *EPW*, 43, no. 08 (23 Feb. 2008), p. 21.
87. 'Patan to be focus of Modi-fied I-Day fete', *The Times of India*, 18 July 2003, http://articles.timesofindia.indiatimes.com/2003-07-18/ahmedabad/27213865_1_patan-jana-gana-mana-national-anthem (last accessed 12 Dec. 2013).
88. Shah, Patel and Lobo, 'A heady mix', p. 21.
89. 'Gujarat: Sardar Patel statue to be twice the size of Statue of Liberty', CNN-IBN, 30 Oct. 2010, http://m.ibnlive.com/news/gujarat-sardar-patel-statue-to-be-twice-the-size-of-statue-of-liberty/431317-3-238.html.
90. Mukhopadhyay, *Narendra Modi*, p. 343.
91. Subhamoy Das, 'Uttarayan and the kite festival of Gujarat', http://hinduism.about.com/cs/festivals/a/aa011103a.htm (last accessed 21 Nov. 2013).
92. Shah, 'Modi's power play and mega-marketing', p. 268.
93. Ibid.
94. Parvis Ghassem-Fachandi, *Pogrom in Gujarat: Hindu Nationalism and Anti-Muslim Violence in India*, Princeton, NJ, Princeton University Press, 2012, p. 153.

95. '"Techno-savvy" Modi to welcome Narmada-Sabarmati Sangam', *Asian Age*, 28 Aug. 2002, p. 9.
96. D.V. Maheshwari, 'CM opens Swaminarayan Temple', *DNA* (Ahmedabad edn), 19 May 2010, p. 4.
97. As mentioned above, BAPS is the acronym of the official name of the Swaminarayan movement. It stands for Bochasanwasi Akshar Purushottam Sanstha.
98. *Swaminarayan Bliss*, March–April 2013, p. 20.
99. 'Godmen swamp poll-bound Gujarat', *The Indian Express* (Ahmedabad edn), 8 Nov. 2012.
100. Achyut Yagnik and Suchitra Sheth, *The Shaping of Modern Gujarat*, New Delhi, Penguin, 2005, p. 290.
101. For a more detailed analysis of Modi's version of subnationalism, see Christophe Jaffrelot, 'Narendra Modi between Hindutva and subnationalism: the Gujarati *asmita* of a Hindu Hriday Samrat', *India Review*, 15, no. 2 (2016), pp. 196–217.
102. Shah, Patel and Lobo, 'A heady mix', p. 21.
103. Mukhopadhyay, *Narendra Modi*, p. 330.
104. Here Sonia Gandhi alludes to the arrest of Muslims—after the Godhra events especially—on behalf of POTA.
105. *The Indian Express* (Ahmedabad edn), 4 Nov. 2007, p. 3.
106. *The Indian Express* (Ahmedabad edn), 9 Dec. 2007, p. 3.
107. Ibid.
108. C.L. Manoj, 'BJP must come clean on "Hindu terror": Digvijay', *The Economic Times*, 25 Oct. 2008, https://economictimes.indiatimes.com/news/politics-and-nation/bjp-must-come-clean-on-hindu-terror-digvijay/articleshow/3638913.cms?from=mdr.
109. On the Ram Sethu issue, see Christophe Jaffrelot, 'Hindu nationalism and the (not so easy) art of being outraged: the Ram Setu controversy', *Samaj*, no. 2 (2008), http://samaj.revues.org/1372 (last accessed 22 Nov. 2013).
110. *The Times of India*, 19 Nov. 2007, p. 3.
111. Mahurkar, 'Back to Hindutva', p. 35. Modi also declared: 'I have given you a curfew-free Gujarat' and 'I won't allow the Congress to reach Gandhinagar through the Sohrabuddin route'. Ibid.
112. Note here that Modi speaks as if Gujarat were not in India.
113. *The Times of India* (Ahmedabad edn), 6 Dec. 2007, p. 3.

114. See Arundhati Roy, *The Hanging of Afzal Guru and the Strange Case of the Attack on the Indian Parliament*, New Delhi, Penguin Books, 2013.
115. Here Modi alludes to the debate about whether the encounter had taken place in Gujarat or in Rajasthan.
116. *The Times of India* (Ahmedabad edn), 6 Dec. 2007, p. 3.
117. K.T.S. Tulsi, the lawyer representing Modi in the Supreme Court, let it immediately be known that he withdrew from the case: 'On the one hand, the Gujarat government has filed a number of affidavits in the Supreme Court saying that it's a cold-blooded murder and it has filed a chargesheet against its own police officers and is prosecuting them for murder. And now the Chief Minister says that the murder is justified. In this situation, the stand of the government and the Chief Minister is completely contradictory. I cannot defend such a case. I cannot accept that any police officer has the right to murder anyone. It's a mockery of law.' Ibid.
118. By imposing the President's Rule, the Union government dismisses a state government and dissolves the state Assembly.
119. *The Times of India* (Ahmedabad edn), 6 Dec. 2007, p. 3.
120. *The Indian Express*, 9 Dec. 2007, p. 3.
121. See, for instance, *DNA* (Ahmedabad edn), 10 Dec. 2007, p. 3.
122. Mahurkar, 'Back to Hindutva', p. 37.
123. See, for instance, *DNA* (Ahmedabad edn), 10 Dec. 2007.
124. 'Modi pats himself', *The Indian Express* (Ahmedabad edn), 9 Oct. 2012, p. 4.
125. 'Modi slams UPA over beef subsidies', *Ahmedabad Mirror*, 29 Oct. 2012, p. 6.
126. This is a very old technique in the 'Cow Belt', namely the Hindi heartland: Madan Mohan Malaviya used it against Motilal Nehru in 1926.
127. Hirlal Dave, 'Sidhu attack turned into self-goal', *The Indian Express* (Ahmedabad edn), 3 Dec. 2012, p. 5.
128. 'Ramdev lands in state, backs CM for PM post', *The Indian Express* (Ahmedabad edn), 30 Oct. 2012, p. 4. See Christophe Jaffrelot, 'Ramdev: Swami without Sampradaya', *The Caravan*, 1 July 2011, http://caravanmagazine.in/perspectives/ramdev-swami-without-sampradaya (last accessed 22 Nov. 2013).

129. Satish Jha, 'Modi calls Patel "Ahmedmian", says his denial sounds fishy', *The Indian Express* (Ahmedabad edn), 3 Dec. 2012, p. 5.
130. On Modi's use of propaganda, see Ghanshyam Shah, 'Goebbels's propaganda and governance: the 2009 Lok Sabha elections in Gujarat', in Paul Wallace and Ramashray Roy (eds), *India's 2009 Elections: Coalition Politics, Party Competition and Congress Continuity*, New Delhi, Sage, 2011, pp. 167–91.
131. In the course of an interview in 2006 he declared: 'I am an *apolitical* CM.' Sheth, *Images of Transformation*, p. 203.
132. Swapan Dasgupta, 'Modi, inept pragmatist', *The Indian Express*, 24 Nov. 2007, http://www.indianexpress.com/news/modi-inept-pragmatist/242902/ (last accessed 28 Nov. 2013).
133. In 2014, his campaign's watchword was 'development', at a time when an economic slump—and the correlative drop in job offers—was causing anxiety in public opinion. Moreover, a Carnegie Endowment survey showed that growth was the main campaign issue for voters, who clearly saw jobs behind this stated objective. Milan Vaishnav, Devesh Kapur and Neelanjan Sircar, 'Growth is no. 1 poll issue for voters, survey shows', Carnegie Endowment, 16 March 2014, http://carnegieendowment.org/2014/03/16/growth-is-no.-1-poll-issue-for-voters-survey-shows/h4gh (last accessed 26 Sept. 2020).
134. Amogh Sharma, 'The backstage of democracy: exploring the professionalisation of politics in India', DPhil thesis, Oxford University, 2020, p. 103.
135. Narendra Modi website, 15 May 2014, cited in ibid., p. 103.
136. 'Modi's "chai pe charcha"? What's that all about?', Rediff News, 12 Feb. 2014, http://www.rediff.com/news/report/slide-show-1-modis-chai-pe-charcha-whats- that-all-about/20140212.htm#3 (last accessed 4 Feb. 2015).
137. The Muslims who attended the Jaipur meeting of Modi in September 2013 were requested to wear sherwanis and skull caps if they were males and burqas if they were females. According to observers of Rajasthan's politics, 'the dress code idea has been put forward to "polish" the BJP's pro-Muslim image in the state.' 'BJP's Jaipur rally to display Modi's "burqa of secularism",' *Business Standard*, 10 Sept. 2013, https://www.business-standard.com/

article/politics/bjp-s-jaipur-rally-to-display-modi-s-burqa-of-secularism-113091000201_1.html (last accessed 4 Feb. 2015).

138. On 14 February 2019, barely a few weeks before the beginning of the official campaign, a deadly attack in Pulwama (Jammu and Kashmir) led by a jihadi group based in Pakistan claimed the lives of 41 Indian Centre Reserve Police Force personnel. By way of response, Modi ordered air strikes to be conducted on Pakistani territory. A Jaish-e-Mohammed training camp was allegedly destroyed in Balakot. In the operation, the Indian Air Force lost a plane and a pilot, Wing Commander Abhinandan Varthaman (who would eventually be returned to India and came back as a hero), and mistakenly shot down one of its own helicopters, killing six airmen. 'IAF missile brought down Mi-17 helicopter in Budgam, says probe', *Deccan Chronicle*, 24 Aug. 2019, https://www.deccanchronicle.com/nation/current-affairs/240819/iaf-missile-brought-down-mi-17-helicopter-in-budgam-says-probe.html (last accessed 30 Sept. 2020).

139. See Christophe Jaffrelot, *Modi's India: Hindu Nationalism and the Rise of Ethnic Democracy*, Princeton, NJ, Princeton University Press; Chennai, Westland, 2021, pp. 311ff.

140. 'Hang me if I have committed a crime', *Ahmedabad Mirror*, 17 April 2014, p. 1, https://ahmedabadmirror.indiatimes.com/ahmedabad/cover-story/hang-me-if-i-have-committed-crime/articleshow/35643182.cms (last accessed 26 Sept. 2020).

141. Narendra Modi also dismissed the role the Central Bureau of Investigation (CBI) was playing in investigations regarding former members of his government in Gujarat, including Amit Shah, by saying that it was an instrument in the hands of the ruling Congress. He even renamed it the Congress Bureau of Investigation. 'CBI will fight upcoming polls, not Congress, says Narendra Modi', *The Indian Express*, 26 Sept. 2013, p. 12. By the end of the election campaign he was to make similar remarks about the Election Commission. See https://indianexpress.com/article/india/politics/cbi-will-fight-upcoming-polls-not-congress-says-narendra-modi/ (last accessed 26 Sept. 2020).

142. 'Throw out Congress, save the nation: Modi', *The Hindu*, 3 May 2013, www.thehindu.com/todays-paper/tp-national/tp-karnataka/

throw-out-congress-save-the-nation-modi/article4679005.ece (last accessed 26 Sept. 2020).

143. 'Narendra Modi: the Times Now interview', Mid-Day, 8 May 2014, http://www.mid-day.com/articles/full-text-of-narendra-modis-interview-the-bjp-leader-opens-up/15282184 (last accessed 26 Sept. 2020).

9. THE BACKING OF THE ELITE AND THE GROWING SUPPORT OF THE 'NEO-MIDDLE CLASS'

1. 'Poll-bound Modi banks on "neo-middle class"', *The Times of India* (Ahmedabad edn), 4 Dec. 2012.
2. Tarun Das, then director general of the CII, went to Gandhinagar one month after the meeting of the organisation during which Narendra Modi had been criticised in Delhi (see ch. 3) and told him that the CII leaders 'were very sorry for all that had happened'. 'CII says sorry to Narendra Modi', *The Times of India*, 7 March 2003, http://articles.timesofindia.indiatimes.com/2003-03-07/ahmedabad/27277328_1_cii-s-gujarat-tarun-das-gujarat-industry (last accessed 28 Nov. 2013).
3. *The Indian Express* (Ahmedabad edn), 27 Nov. 2007, p. 3.
4. Ibid.
5. Ibid.
6. Rathin Das, 'Anil Ambani says Modi king of kings, India Inc adds praise', *The Pioneer*, 12 Jan. 2013, p. 1. The day before, Mukesh Ambani had hailed Narendra Modi as 'a leader with a grand vision'. 'India Inc hails Narendra Modi's "vision"', *The Indian Express*, 11 Jan. 2013, p. 3. For more details, see 'Vibrant Gujarat', *The Economic Times* (Ahmedabad edn), 12 Jan. 2013, p. 10.
7. Leela Fernandes and Patrick Heller, 'Hegemonic aspirations: new middle class and India's democracy in comparative perspective', *Critical Asian Studies*, 38, no. 4 (2006), p. 500, http://www.patrickheller.com/uploads/1/5/3/7/15377686/hegemonic_aspirations.pdf (last accessed 13 Dec. 2013).
8. This figure draws from surveys of the Centre for the Study of Developing Societies. See E. Sridharan, 'The growth and sectoral composition of India's middle class: its impact on the politics of

economic liberalization', *India Review*, 3, no. 4 (Aug. 2004); and D.L. Sheth, 'Secularisation of caste and making of new middle class', *EPW*, 34, no. 34/35 (21 Aug.–3 Sep. 1999), http://jan.ucc.nau.edu/~sj6/epwshethmclass1.htm (last accessed 28 Nov. 2013).

9. Priyavadan Patel, 'Sectarian mobilisation, factionalism and voting in Gujarat', *EPW*, 34, no. 34/35 (21 Aug.–3 Sept. 1999), p. 2449.
10. Pravin Sheth, *Images of Transformation: Gujarat and Narendra Modi*, Ahmedabad, Team Spirit, 2007, p. 20.
11. Lise McKean, *Divine Enterprise: Gurus and the Hindu Nationalist Movement*, Chicago, Chicago University Press, 1996.
12. Uday Mehta, *Religion and Gurus in Traditional and Modern India*, Delhi, Kalpaz, 2018, pp. 155–222.
13. Ashis Nandy, 'Blame the middle class', *The Times of India* (Ahmedabad edn), 8 Jan. 2008, p. 14.
14. Parvis Ghassem-Fachandi, *Pogrom in Gujarat: Hindu Nationalism and Anti-Muslim Violence in India*, Princeton, NJ, Princeton University Press, 2012, p. 130. Another informant said: 'They do not see what is right, what is wrong. They see blood. If they can kill animals without a thought, how can they have problems killing humans?' Cited in ibid., p. 127. Another one said that 'Every young Muslim boy of five years of age is taught by his father to slaughter a chicken halal-style [...] To slaughter an animal halal—according to Islamic injunction—is considered particularly cruel in Gujarat, as the knife has to cut the throat while the heart still pumps out the blood (considered impure by Muslims).' Cited in ibid., p. 135.
15. Ibid., p. 132.
16. *The Times of India* (Ahmedabad edn), 18 Nov. 2007, p. 3.
17. See Christophe Jaffrelot, *Hindu Nationalism and Indian Politics*, London, Hurst, 1996, ch. 1.
18. Pavan K. Varma, *The Great Indian Middle Class*, New Delhi, Penguin, 1998, p. 174. Interestingly, the critical overtone of Varma's assessment is also found among the Hindu nationalists. In 2005, *Organiser* published a similar indictment of the middle class: 'The [problem with the] middle class is that it wants many things—money, comforts, entertainment, prestige and, above all, a clean environment and good government—all at once on a platter. But anything in return? Probably none. It negates the ever true "demand

and duty" relationship which holds the mankind together.' S.N. Saxena, 'A role for middle class', *Organiser*, 24 April 2005, p. 15.

19. See Leila Fernandes, '"Nationalising the global": media images, economic reform and the middle class in India', *Media, Culture and Society*, 22, no. 5 (Nov. 2000), pp. 611–28.
20. This emphasis on merit is partly due to the fact that, as André Béteille emphasised, the Indian middle class 'is defined not only by occupation, but also by education'. See André Béteille, 'The social character of the Indian middle class', in Imtiaz Ahmad and Helmut Reifeld (eds), *Middle Class Values in India and Western Europe*, New Delhi, Social Science Press, 2002, p. 77.
21. Christophe Jaffrelot, *India's Silent Revolution: The Rise of the Lower Castes in North India*, London, Hurst, 2003, chs. 7, 8 and 9.
22. Priya Chacko, 'Marketizing Hindutva: the state, society, and markets in Hindu nationalism', *Modern Asian Studies*, 53, no. 2 (2019), p. 380.
23. See Satish Deshpande, *Contemporary India: A Sociological View*, New Delhi, Penguin India, 2004.
24. Yogendra Yadav, Sanjay Kumar and Oliver Heath, 'The BJP's new social bloc', *Frontline*, 16, no. 23 (Nov. 1999), pp. 6–19, http://www.frontline.in/static/html/fl1623/16230310.htm (last accessed 28 Nov. 2013).
25. Kapil Dave, 'Die is caste in Gujarat, Muslims matter', *The Indian Express* (Ahmedabad edn), 2 Nov. 2012, p. 1, http://www.indianexpress.com/news/die-is-caste-in-gujarat-muslims-matter/1025654/ (last accessed 28 Nov. 2013).
26. Achyut Yagnik interviewed by Sheila Bhatt, 'Understanding Gujarat: why the Patels won't be decisive', Rediff News, 13 Aug. 2012.
27. I am grateful to Ghanshyam Shah for these explanations—and for many others, emerging from our conversations over the last 20 years.
28. The Kolis sometimes call themselves 'Koli Patels'. They have started an All Gujarat Koli Patel Samaj, which, in 2012, asked for more tickets to the BJP as well as the Congress. See Himansshu Bhatt, 'Koli Patels armtwist parties for more tickets', *The Indian Express* (Ahmedabad edn), 21 Nov. 2012, p. 2.
29. According to press reports, they represent 21 per cent to 46 per cent of the voters in 12 constituencies. See Ajay Umat, 'As Bapa

rages, Modi hunts for Leuva love', *The Times of India* (Ahmedabad edn), 30 Oct. 2012, p. 1.

30. 'Gujarat polls', Exit and Opinion Polls India, 11 Dec. 2012, http://exitopinionpollsindia.blogspot.fr/2012/12/gujarat-polls-tactical-voting-and.html (last accessed 28 Nov. 2013).
31. Christophe Jaffrelot and Sharik Laliwala, 'Elite resistance in Gujarat' (forthcoming).
32. Ibid.
33. Ibid.
34. Ibid.
35. Sharik Laliwala, 'In the Hindutva heartland: Bharatiya Janata Party's superficial democratization in Gujarat', *Studies in Indian Politics*, 8, no. 2 (2020), p. 254.
36. Ibid., p. 261.
37. Ibid., p. 248.
38. On the resilience of caste politics in Gujarat, see Jumana Shah, 'Casteist politics takes sheen off progressive Gujarat', *DNA* (Ahmedabad edn), 24 April 2012, p. 1.
39. 'Grand Kadva fest begins today in Jamnagar', *The Indian Express* (Ahmedabad edn), 9 Feb. 2012, p. 4. See 'Umiya Mata draws 800,000 devotees', *DNA* (Ahmedabad edn), 29 Nov. 2009, p. 1.
40. H. Dave and G. Kateshiya, 'Kshatriyas, a larger vote bank waiting for parties to invest', *The Indian Express*, 26 Nov. 2012, p. 4.
41. 'OBCs demand their pound of flesh, call for Modi's ouster', *Ahmedabad Mirror*, 13 June 2012, p. 8.
42. Dilip Patel, 'Modi eyes Cong vote banks', *Ahmedabad Mirror*, 25 May 2011, p. 12.
43. 'Gujarat ex-royals project Modi as PM-in-waiting', *The Indian Express* (Ahmedabad edn), 20 June 2011, p. 3.
44. Christophe Jaffrelot, 'Gujarat elections: the sub-text of Modi's "hattrick"; high tech populism and the "neo-middle class"', *Studies in Indian Politics*, 1, no. 1 (June 2013), pp. 79–96.
45. I am grateful to Sanjay Kumar for providing me with these data in the context of the work we did on the impact of urbanisation on electoral politics in India. See Christophe Jaffrelot and Sanjay Kumar, 'The impact of urbanization on the electoral results of the 2014 Indian elections: with special reference to the BJP vote', in

'Understanding India's 2014 elections', *Studies in Indian Politics*, 3, no. 1 (June 2015), pp. 39–49.
46. D.L. Sheth, 'Secularisation of caste and making of new middle class', *EPW*, 21–28 Aug. 1999, http://jan.ucc.nau.edu/~sj6/epwshethmclass1.htm.
47. Adapted from the 2005 novel by Vikas Swarup, the film *Slumdog Millionaire* was released in 2008.
48. Arvind Adiga, *The White Tiger*, New Delhi, HarperCollins, 2008.
49. Minna Saavala, *Middle-Class Moralities: Everyday Struggle over Belonging and Prestige in India*, Hyderabad, Orient BlackSwan, 2010, p. 156.
50. D. Banerjee and M.G. Mehta, 'Caste and capital in the remaking of Ahmedabad', *Contemporary South Asia*, 2017, p. 6, http://dx.doi.org/10.1080/09584935.2017.1329278.
51. Ibid., p. 8.
52. Ibid., p. 10.
53. Ibid., p. 11.
54. Ghanshyam Shah, 'The Dalit and Hindutva: underprivileged and communal carnage', in Jan Breman and Ghanshyam Shah, *Gujarat, Cradle and Harbinger of Identity Politics: India's Injurious Frame of Communalism*, New Delhi, Tulika Books, 2022, p. 191.
55. Ibid., 192.
56. Ghanshyam Shah, 'Caste, Hindutva and hideousness', in Jan Breman and Ghanshyam Shah, *Gujarat, Cradle and Harbinger of Identity Politics: India's Injurious Frame of Communalism*, New Delhi, Tulika Books, 2022, p. 147.
57. 'Poll-bound Modi banks on "neo-middle class"', *The Times of India* (Ahmedabad edn), 4 Dec. 2012.
58. Maulik Pathak and Sahil Makkar, 'Narendra Modi seeks support of "neo middle-class" voters', *Mint* (Bangalore edn), 4 Dec. 2012, p. 3.
59. Darshan Desai, 'In manifesto, Modi targets urbanites, youth', *The Hindu* (Bangalore edn), 4 Dec. 2012, p. 12.
60. Praveen Rai and Dhananjaj Joshi, 'The Indian Express–CNN-IBN–Divya Bhaskar–CSDS pre-poll survey: a poor show in Gujarat', *The Indian Express* (Ahmedabad edn), 7 Dec. 2007, p. 4.
61. 'Gujarat Assembly election 2012: post-poll survey by Lokniti, Centre for the Study of Developing Societies', p. 13, http://www.

lokniti.org/pdfs_dataunit/Questionairs/gujarat-postpoll-2012-survey-findings.pdf (last accessed 28 Nov. 2013).

62. Nirendra Dev, *Modi to Moditva*, New Delhi, Manas Publications, 2012, p. 104.
63. As early as the first half of the twentieth century, Patels have migrated to the cities for developing their businesses and joining colleges. Sardar Patel, a lawyer, was elected mayor of Ahmedabad, having, as a child, worked in the fields with his father, an indication of the one-century-old transition of the Patels to urban life. After Independence, these agrarian capitalists who were so good at commercial agriculture invested in industrial ventures such as diamond cutting in Surat. They were clearly the main beneficiaries of the state policy supporting small-scale enterprises—and resisting the Licence Raj. See Christophe Jaffrelot, 'Quota for Patels? The neo-middle class syndrome and the (partial) return of caste politics in Gujarat', *Studies in Indian Politics*, 4, no. 2 (2016), pp. 1–15.
64. 'Controversial local bodies' bill passed in Assembly', *DNA* (Ahmedabad edn), 20 Dec. 2009, http://www.dnaindia.com/india/report-controversial-local-bodies-bill-passed-in-gujarat-assembly-1325517 (last accessed 28 Nov. 2013).
65. Christophe Jaffrelot, '"Why should we vote?" The Indian middle class and the functioning of the world's largest democracy', in Christophe Jaffrelot and Peter van der Veer (eds), *Patterns of Middle Class Consumption in India and China*, New Delhi, Sage, 2008, pp. 35–54.
66. 'Compulsory voting bill passed again by Gujarat Assembly', *Zee News*, 1 March 2011, http://zeenews.india.com/news/gujarat/compulsory-voting-bill-passed-again-by-gujarat-assembly_690404.html (last accessed 28 Nov. 2013).
67. Sheth, *Images of Transformation*, p. 54. Mukund Mody died in New York in 2013 after decades of association with the Sangh Parivar in the US. See http://www.haindavakeralam.com/HKPage.aspx?PageID=17426 (last accessed 8 Nov. 2013). Indeed, Mukund Mody had established the Overseas Friends of BJP in the US in 1991. See http://www.newsindia-times.com/NewsIndiaTimes/20130607/5223698173563886880.htm (last accessed 8 Nov. 2013).

68. Sheth, *Images of Transformation*, pp. 57–8.
69. 'Summer of '93: check out young Narendra Modi hanging out in US', *Firstpost*, 28 Sept. 2014, https://www.firstpost.com/world/summer-of-93-check-out-young-narendra-modi-hanging-out-in-us-1730697.html.
70. Chidanand Rajghatta, 'Narendra Modi returns to his stomping ground as prime minister after a 14-year exile', *The Times of India*, 25 Sept. 2014, http://timesofindia.indiatimes.com/world/us/Narendra-Modi-returns-to-his-stomping-ground-as-Prime-Minister-after-a-14-year-exile/articleshow/43441558.cms.
71. On the US refusal of issuing a visa to Narendra Modi, see Kingshuk Nag, *The NaMo Story: A Political Life*, New Delhi, Roli Books, 2013, p. 114.
72. In fact, he was refused a visa in 2005 when he tried to attend the Annual Convention and Trade Show of the Asian American Hotel Owners Association in Florida and eventually addressed them by video. A section of Narendra Modi's website is devoted to this activity. See 'Shri Narendra Modi addressing the Global Indian diaspora through video conferencing', Narendra Modi website, http://www.narendramodi.in/category/speeches/page/7/.
73. Ajaya Kumar Sahoo, 'Issues of identity in the Indian diaspora: a transnational perspective', in Eliezer Ben-Rafael and Yitzhak Sternberg (eds), *Transnationalism: Diasporas and the Advent of a New (Dis)order*, Leiden, Brill, 2009, p. 535. See also 'Govt pulls out all stops to ensure NRG participation', *The Times of India*, 14 Jan. 2004, http://articles.timesofindia.indiatimes.com/2004-01-14/ahmedabad/28330588_1_Gujaratis-nrgs-kites-vishwa-Gujarati-parivar-mahotsav (last accessed 28 Nov. 2013).
74. 'Objectives', NRI Gujarat, http://www.nri.gujarat.gov.in/objective-nrg-found.htm (last accessed 13 Dec. 2013).
75. 'World Gujarati Conference in New Jersey', http://www.nritoday.net/community-news/554-world-Gujarati-conference-in-new-jersey (last accessed 28 Nov. 2013).
76. Christophe Jaffrelot, 'From holy sites to web sites: Hindu nationalism, from sacred territory to diasporic ethnicity', in Patrick Michel, Adam Possamai and Bryan Turner (eds), *Religions, Nations,*

and Transnationalism in Multiple Modernities, Basingstoke, Palgrave, 2017, pp. 153–74.

77. Lakshmi Ajay, '3D Modi plans US blitz, to address "Global Gujaratis"', *The Indian Express*, 3 July 2013, http://www.indianexpress.com/news/3d-modi-plans-us-blitz-to-address-global-Gujaratis/1136996/0 (last accessed 28 Nov. 2013).
78. Ibid. See also Sudhir Vyas, 'Friends of Gujarat to organize 3-day Gujarati meet in NJ: friends of Gujarat announce a 3-day conference to unite and showcase the Gujarati community', http://www.desiclub.com/community/culture/culture_article.cfm?id=1183 (last accessed 28 Nov. 2013).
79. Cited in 'China charms Modi with its "scale, speed and skill"', *The Indian Express* (Ahmedabad edn), 13 Nov. 2011, p. 5.
80. Cited in ibid.
81. Ananth Krishnan, 'Modi courts Chinese investment, showcasing "Gujarat model"', *The Hindu*, 10 Nov. 2011, p. 15.
82. Cited in 'China charms Modi'.
83. 'Narendra Modi praises China before US non-resident Gujaratis', *The Times of India*, 21 May 2012, https://timesofindia.indiatimes.com/city/ahmedabad/narendra-modi-praises-china-before-us-non-resident-gujaratis/articleshow/13323200.cms.
84. See Sharmina Mawani and Anjoom A. Mukadam (eds), *Gujaratis in the West: Evolving Identities in Contemporary Society*, Newcastle, Cambridge Scholars Press, 2007.
85. Govind Bhatka, *Patels: A Gujarati Community History in the United States*, Los Angeles, UCLA Asian American Studies Press, 2003. See also Pawan Dhingra, *Life behind the Lobby: Indian American Motel Owners and the American Dream*, Los Angeles, Stanford University Press, 2012.
86. Modi's biographers M.V. Kamath and Kalindi Randeri mention that in the 1990s his predecessor, Keshubhai Patel, used to go to the US 'to mobilise funds from NRIs for the development of Gujarat'. See M.V. Kamath and Kalindi Randeri, *Narendra Modi: The Architect of a Modern State*, New Delhi, Rupa, 2009, p. 64.
87. Darshini Mahadevia, Renu Desai and Suchita Vyas, 'City Profile: Ahmedabad', Ahmedabad, CEPT University, CUE Working Paper 26, September 2014, p. 32, https://www.academia.edu/24733900/

City_Profile_Ahmedabad. They also write: 'Number of times the authorities also lathicharge the vendors and abuse them verbally. To avoid or resolve conflicts with the authorities the most common practice by vendors is to pay bribes and protection money (known as hafta). During festivals like Uttarayan, Diwali and Holi, the frequency and amount of bribes to be paid also increase.' Ibid., p. 33.

88. Ibid., p. 16.
89. Jan Breman, 'Clearing the city of the undeserving underclass', in Jan Breman and Ghanshyam Shah, *Gujarat, Cradle and Harbinger of Identity Politics: India's Injurious Frame of Communalism*, New Delhi, Tulika Books, 2022, p. 288.
90. 'Govt has a new mission: urban development', *The Indian Express* (Ahmedabad edn), 30 Jan. 2006, p. 3.
91. 'Rs 7K cr for Mukhya Mantri's urban plan', *The Times of India* (Ahmedabad edn), 1 July 2009, p. 1.
92. 'Finally, govt announces township policy', *The Times of India* (Ahmedabad edn), 4 Dec. 2009, p. 1.
93. Rajiv Shah, 'Urban poor worse off than rural population: Govt', *The Times of India* (Ahmedabad edn), 3 Oct. 2009, p. 10.
94. Partha Chatterjee, 'Are Indian cities becoming bourgeois at last?', in Indira Chandrasekhar and Peter C. Seel (eds), *Body City: Siting Contemporary Culture in India*, Berlin, Haus der Kulturen der Welt; New Delhi, Tulika Books, 2003.
95. Niyati Rana and Kuldeep Tiwari, 'Slum-free A'bad dream now reality', *DNA* (Ahmedabad edn), 6 March 2010, p. 1.
96. Ibid.
97. Paras K. Jha, 'For Gujarat slum no longer glum story', *DNA*, 14 July 2013, http://www.dnaindia.com/ahmedabad/report-for-gujarat-slum-no-longer-glum-story-1861032 (last accessed 22 Nov. 2013). The percentage of the urban population of Gujarat living in slums has been disputed. It seems that it is kept artificially low because of the non-notification of slum areas, which are, therefore, not recognised officially. In Ahmedabad, for instance, the real proportion should not be considered as the official 12 per cent, but twice that figure. See Rajiv Shah, 'Gujarat slums are worse off than most states say latest census data: comments', *Counterview*, 18 May 2013, http://counterview.org/2013/05/18/gujarat-

slums-are-worse-off-than-most-states-say-latest-census-data/ (last accessed 22 Nov. 2013).

98. To such an extent that, for instance, the percentage of underweight children was higher among the urban poor than among the rural poor and the infant mortality rate was also higher. See Shah, 'Urban poor worse off than rural population', p. 10.

99. Shah, 'Gujarat slums are worse off than most states'. These aggregated data are largely corroborated by an interesting survey: Benjamin Stanwix, *Urban Slums in Gujarat and Rajasthan: A Study of Basic Infrastructure in Seven Cities*, Ahmedabad, Mahila Housing SEWA Trust, 2009. See also the report by the National Sample Survey Office, *Some Characteristics of Urban Slums*, New Delhi, Ministry of Statistics and Programme Implementation, Govt. of India, 2010.

100. On the other hand, in 2010, 'The Centre announced that only Gujarat completed 23 of the 26 schemes under the Jawaharlal Nehru National Urban Renewal Mission'. Pravin Sheth and Pradeep Mallick, *Happening State: Gujarat; A Live Case of Can-Doism*, Mumbai and Ahmedabad, R.R. Sheth and Co., 2012, p. 92.

101. Mahadevia, Desai and Vyas, 'City Profile: Ahmedabad', p. 24.

102. Avinash Nair, 'Only 7% JNNURM housing projects finished in Gujarat', *The Indian Express*, 5 Oct. 2013, http://www.indianexpress.com/news/-only-7--jnnurm-housing-projects-finished-in-gujarat-/1178696/ (last accessed 22 Nov. 2013).

103. 'Gujarat provides power to 3,950 slum-dwellers in 5 yrs', *The Indian Express*, 4 Oct. 2013, http://www.indianexpress.com/news/-gujarat-provides-power-to-3950-slumdwellers-in-5-yrs-/1178181/ (last accessed 22 Nov. 2013).

104. Mahadevia, Desai and Vyas, 'City Profile: Ahmedabad', pp. 24–5.

105. Ibid., p. 24.

106. In July 2012 already Modi introduced a medical scheme in favour of the (lower) middle class (those who earned less than 200,000 rupees): according to this concession scheme, three hospitals of Ahmedabad would now bear 50 per cent of the medicine and hospital expenses of patients and/or of five members of their immediate family suffering from life-threatening diseases. These benefits were bound to go primarily to the (lower) middle class simply because the poor had not enough money to pay for the other 50 per cent. Vipul

Rajput, 'Guj govt woos middle class, to fund 50% treatment cost of life-threatening diseases', *Ahmedabad Mirror*, 5 July 2012, p. 6.

107. Mahadevia, Desai and Vyas, 'City Profile: Ahmedabad', p. 36.
108. This document is not available any longer, but the website of Gift features a video in which Narendra Modi uses similar words and a home page where one can read: 'Witness the fruition of a vision to create an epicentre for Indian and global financial and IT businesses. It is a pre-eminent, futuristic city built on the foundation of sustainability. GIFT City presents an unprecedented ecosystem for crucial economic activities with globally benchmarked regulations, taxation, policies and more, supported by Govt. of India and Gujarat.' See https://www.giftgujarat.in (last accessed 31 July 2023).
109. See ibid. The Statue of Unity, representing Sardar Patel, the world's tallest statue at 182 m, was also partly made by the Chinese. 'Statue of Unity to be "made in China", Gujarat govt says it's contractor's call', *The Indian Express*, 20 Oct. 2015, https://indianexpress.com/article/india/india-news-india/statue-of-unity-to-be-made-in-china-gujarat-govt-says-its-contractors-call/.
110. I am grateful to Bimal Patel, the main architect of this project, for showing his vision to me on several occasions between 2015 and 2019.
111. Ipsita Chatterjee, 'Social conflict and the neoliberal city: a case of Hindu–Muslim violence in India', *Transactions of the Institute of British Geographers*, NS, 34, no. 2 (April 2009), p. 153.
112. Breman, 'Clearing the city of the undeserving underclass', p. 289.
113. Renu Desai, 'Municipal Politics, Court Sympathy and Housing Rights: A Post-mortem of Displacement and Resettlement under the Sabarmati Riverfront Project, Ahmedabad', Ahmedabad, Centre for Urban Equity, CEPT University, CUE Working Paper 23, May 2014, pp. 5–6, https://www.academia.edu/26248720/Municipal_Politics_Court_Sympathy_and_Housing_Rights_A_Post_Mortem_of_Displacement_and_Resettlement_under_the_Sabarmati_Riverfront_Project_Ahmedabad.
114. Ibid., p. 6.
115. Ibid., p. 5.
116. Breman, 'Clearing the city of the undeserving underclass', p. 289.
117. Desai, *Municipal Politics, Court Sympathy and Housing Rights*, p. 6.

118. Breman, 'Clearing the city of the undeserving underclass', p. 292.
119. A public interest litigation petition was filed by Girish Patel. Desai, *Municipal Politics, Court Sympathy and Housing Rights*, pp. 7 and 14.
120. Breman, 'Clearing the city of the undeserving underclass', p. 291.
121. Desai, *Municipal Politics, Court Sympathy and Housing Rights*, pp. 7 and 15.
122. Ibid., p. 16.
123. On the resettlement operations in Vadva, see Shrey Kapoor, 'From riots to dispossession', PhD dissertation (forthcoming); and Shrey Kapoor, 'Resisting a hegemonic spatiotemporal order: Hindu nationalist violence and subterranean agency in Ahmedabad', in Mara Albrecht and Alke Jenss (eds), *The Spatiality and Temporality of Urban Violence: Histories, Rhythms and Ruptures*, Manchester, Manchester University Press, 2023.
124. 'Most of the families, before resettlement, were earning their livelihood in the informal sector, often within walking/cycling distances of their home. Majority of women worked as domestic maids, street vendors or were engaged in home-based work such as kite-making and stitching garments, while majority of men were engaged in daily-wage labour, low-wage regular work (for instance, in small shops and workshops) and street vending. The resettlement had profound impacts on their livelihood due to the distance of the resettlement sites. The average distance of the resettlement sites from the central city area is seven kilometers. Some of the sites like Vatwa and Odhav (which comprise of almost one-third of the BSUP houses built by AMC) are more than 12 kilometers from the central city area. After resettlement, travel distances, travel time, and travel costs have increased tremendously, the latter cutting into their savings. For some, the increased travel costs left so little to save that it simply did not make sense to continue work.' Mahadevia, Desai and Vyas, 'City Profile: Ahmedabad', p. 40.
125. Desai, *Municipal Politics, Court Sympathy and Housing Rights*, p. 8.
126. Ibid., p. 24.
127. Mahadevia, Desai and Vyas, 'City Profile: Ahmedabad', p. 40.
128. Breman, 'Clearing the city of the undeserving underclass', p. 298.
129. Cited in ibid., p. 285.
130. Ibid., p. 307.

131. Ibid.
132. Ibid., p. 309.
133. Ibid., p. 304.
134. Rana Amirtahmasebi, Mariana Orloff, Sameh Wahba and Andrew Altman, *Regenerating Urban Land: A Practitioner's Guide to Leveraging Private Investment*, Washington, DC, World Bank, 2016, pp. 253–83.
135. Mahadevia, Desai and Vyas, 'City Profile: Ahmedabad', p. 26.
136. Chatterjee, 'Social conflict and the neoliberal city', p. 155.
137. Cited in ibid., p. 152.
138. This paradox is not new. I have shown that the ideology of Hindu nationalism itself has been imported from Western Europe. See Jaffrelot, *Hindu Nationalism and Indian Politics*, ch. 1.
139. '6/6 for Modi in urban Gujarat', *The Times of India* (Ahmedabad edn), 13 Oct. 2010, p. 1.
140. 'I will work towards achieving India of your dreams: PM Modi to Indian diaspora in US', *The Times of India*, 26 June 2017, https://timesofindia.indiatimes.com/i-will-work-towards-achieving-india-of-your-dreams-pm-modi-to-indian-diaspora-in-us/videoshow/59315037.cms?mobile=no; and 'Will make India of your dreams: PM Narendra Modi tells Indian diaspora in United States', *Free Press*, 30 May 2019, https://www.freepressjournal.in/cmcm/will-make-india-of-your-dreams-pm-narendra-modi-tells-indian-diaspora-in-united-states.
141. Christophe Jaffrelot, 'The class element in the 2014 Indian election and the BJP's success with special reference to the Hindi belt', in 'Understanding India's 2014 elections', *Studies in Indian Politics*, 3, no. 1 (June 2015), pp. 19–38.
142. '"Neo middle class" is the new "aam aadmi"', *The Indian Express*, 11 July 2014, https://indianexpress.com/article/india/india-others/neo-middle-class-is-the-new-aam-aadmi-2/; and Udit Misra, 'How Jaitley went from neo-middle class to farmers, jobs to welfare', *The Indian Express*, 1 March 2016, https://indianexpress.com/article/explained/how-jaitley-went-from-neo-middle-class-to-farmers-jobs-to-welfare/.
143. Jaffrelot and Kumar, 'The impact of urbanization on the electoral results of the 2014 Indian elections', pp. 9–49.

144. Ashok Gulati, 'Dismayed farmers, defunct policies', *The Indian Express*, 31 Aug. 2015, https://indianexpress.com/article/opinion/columns/dismayed-farmers-defunct-policies/ (last accessed 27 Sept. 2020).
145. Christophe Jaffrelot and Gilles Verniers, 'The representation gap', *The Indian Express*, 24 July 2015, https://indianexpress.com/article/opinion/columns/the-representation-gap-2/ (last accessed 27 Sept. 2020).
146. Katharine Adeney and Wilfried Swenden, 'Power sharing in the world's largest democracy: informal consociationalism in India (and its decline?)', *Swiss Political Science Review*, 25, no. 4 (2019), p. 458.
147. On the caste politics of Modi and Shah, see Christophe Jaffrelot, *Modi's India: Hindu Nationalism and the Rise of Ethnic Democracy*, Princeton, NJ, Princeton University Press; Chennai, Westland, 2021, pp. 329ff.

10. RESISTERS, DISSENTERS AND VICTIMS

1. Christophe Jaffrelot, 'The meaning of Modi's victory', *EPW*, 43, no. 15 (12 April 2008), https://www.epw.in/journal/2008/15/commentary/gujarat-meaning-modis-victory.html.
2. Hiral Dave, 'Sonia targets Modi's record, avoids taking him on directly', *The Indian Express*, 4 Oct. 2012, p. 1.
3. Christophe Jaffrelot and Sharik Laliwala, 'Elite resistance in Gujarat', in Christophe Jaffrelot and Gilles Verniers (eds), *Resilient Elitism: The Changing Profile of India's Regional Assemblies* (forthcoming).
4. Kingshuk Nag, *The NaMo Story: A Political Life*, New Delhi, Roli Books, 2013, pp. 62–3.
5. 'Narendra Modi welcomes gun-toting ex-Congressman Vitthal Radadia into BJP', *The Indian Express*, 8 March 2013, http://www.indianexpress.com/news/narendra-modi-welcomes-guntotting-excongressman-vitthal-radadia-into-bjp/1085234/ (last accessed 4 Dec. 2013).
6. Jaffrelot and Laliwala, 'Elite resistance in Gujarat' (forthcoming).
7. Jaffrelot, 'The meaning of Modi's victory'.
8. Interview with Arjun Modhwadia, 25 November 2007, in Gandhinagar.

9. 'I'm captain of Congress, says Vaghela', *DNA* (Ahmedabad edn), 6 Dec. 2012, p. 3.
10. A.M. Shah, Pravin J. Patel and Lancy Lobo, 'A heady mix: Gujarati and Hindu pride', *EPW*, 43, no. 08 (23 Feb. 2008), p. 38.
11. '6/6 for Modi in urban Gujarat', *The Times of India* (Ahmedabad edn), 13 Oct. 2010, p. 1.
12. Darshan Desai, 'Narhari Amin joins BJP', *The Hindu*, 6 Dec. 2012, https://www.thehindu.com/news/national/Narhari-Amin-joins-BJP/article15616974.ece.
13. 'Keshubhai seeks RSS, VHP support', *Ahmedabad Mirror*, 24 Oct. 2012, p. 8.
14. The octogenarian general secretary of the Gujarat branch of the RSS, Pravin Maniar, took part in the Saurashtra convention of the GPP in November 2012 at Rajkot and was all praise for Keshubhai. But on this occasion a VHP leader, on condition of anonymity, told journalists: 'Not all of us are ready to openly work against Modi. But a section is quietly conducting a campaign.' *The Indian Express* (Ahmedabad edn), 20 Nov. 2012, p. 3.
15. 'Gujarat polls', Exit and Opinion Polls India, 11 Dec. 2012, http://exitopinionpollsindia.blogspot.fr/2012/12/gujarat-polls-tactical-voting-and.html (last accessed 28 Nov. 2013); and 'RSS axes its Narendra Modi-baiter veteran, 2 others', *The Indian Express*, 3 July 2012, https://indianexpress.com/article/cities/gujarat/rss-axes-its-narendra-modibaiter-veteran-2-others/.
16. 'Keshubhai seeks RSS, VHP support', p. 8.
17. 'Modi worse than General Dyer', *The Times of India* (Ahmedabad edn), 19 Nov. 2012, p. 1.
18. 'Dawood amassed 5.5 billion rupees as donations: Bapa', *DNA* (Ahmedabad edn), 6 Dec. 2012, p. 3.
19. 'Saurashtra has got only injustice in 10 years', *The Times of India* (Ahmedabad edn), 6 Nov. 2012.
20. It showed that 'Non-commencement of construction of canals simultaneously with the head works of Macchu-III Water Resources Project led to non-achievement of the targeted irrigation benefits even after investment of 256.2 million rupees', and that 'Commencement of construction of spreading channel without ensuring the acquisition of required land led to unproductive

expenditure of 22.3 million rupees and irregular parking of Twelfth Finance Commission funds of 40 million rupees.' CAG, *Audit Report (Economic Sector) for the Year Ended 31 March 2012: Report no. 3 of 2013*, pp. 8 and 9, http://saiindia.gov.in/english/home/Our_Products/Audit_Report/Government_Wise/state_audit/recent_reports/Gujarat/2012/Report_2/Chap_5.pdf (last accessed 28 Nov. 2013).

21. 'Gujarat Assembly election 2012: post-poll survey by Lokniti, Centre for the Study of Developing Societies', p. 13, http://www.lokniti.org/pdfs_dataunit/Questionairs/gujarat-postpoll-2012-survey-findings.pdf (last accessed 13 Dec. 2013).
22. 'Ordinance to hit MSU hardest', *The Times of India*, 25 Sept. 2004, https://timesofindia.indiatimes.com/city/ahmedabad/ordinance-to-hit-msu-hardest/articleshow/863073.cms.
23. Ibid.
24. I am grateful to Professor Thorat for sharing this correspondence with me.
25. A.P. Singh, 'Meet "Karmayogi" Dr Manoj Soni, the new UPSC chairman', Indian Masterminds, 9 April 2022, https://indianmasterminds.com/news/upsc-news/know-the-new-upsc-chief-dr-manoj-soni-who-was-countrys-youngest-university-vice-chancellor-once-selling-incense-sticks-12th-failed/.
26. Abdul Hafiz Lakhani, 'Gujarat universities have saffron VCs', *The Milli Gazette*, 14 Nov. 2021, https://www.milligazette.com/news/4-national/2672-gujarat-universities-have-saffron-vcs/; 'MSU V-C Manoj Soni: dark horse who turned into steed overnight', *The Times of India*, 16 April 2005, http://articles.timesofindia.indiatimes.com/2005-04-16/ahmedabad/27846031_1_ms-university-appointment-vadodara (last accessed 4 Dec. 2013).
27. 'MSU V-C seals fine arts dept', *The Times of India*, 12 May 2007, http://archive.indianexpress.com/news/msu-vc-seals-fine-arts-dept/30702/.
28. The VC also wanted to terminate his contract, something he could counter before the court. Interview with Shivaji Panikkar, in Vadodara on 3 March 2010. See also Anupama Katakam, 'Attack on art', *Frontline*, 1 June 2007, pp. 26–32; and Anil Dharker, 'Beauty and the beast', *The Times of India* (Ahmedabad edn), 17 May 2007, p. 12.

29. Cited in Malvika Maheshwari, *Art Attacks: Violence and Offence-taking in India*, Delhi, Oxford University Press, 2019, p. 289.
30. 'DTU's Yogesh Singh appointed 23rd vice chancellor of Delhi University', *Hindustan Times*, 22 Sept. 2021, https://www.hindustantimes.com/cities/delhi-news/dtus-yogesh-singh-appointed-23rd-vice-chancellor-of-delhi-university-101632331058482.html.
31. P.K. Jha, 'Government appoints BJP man to top post of Kutch varsity', *DNA*, 19 Nov. 2013, https://www.dnaindia.com/academy/report-government-appoints-bjp-man-to-top-post-of-kutch-varsity-1310055.
32. Lakhani, 'Gujarat universities have saffron VCs'.
33. Syed Khalique Ahmed, 'Many rows later, Parimal Trivedi exits as GU V-C', *The Indian Express*, 27 June 2012, https://indianexpress.com/article/cities/gujarat/many-rows-later-parimal-trivedi-exits-as-gu-vc/.
34. Ibid.; and 'Gujarat University vice-chancellor Parimal Trivedi in caste row', *India Today*, 22 Feb. 2012, https://www.indiatoday.in/mail-today/story/gujarat-university-vice-chancellor-parimal-trivedi-in-caste-row-93855-2012-02-22.
35. Sylvie Guichard, *The Construction of History and Nationalism in India: Textbooks, Controversies and Politics*, Abingdon, Routledge, 2010, pp. 84–5.
36. Ibid.
37. Cited in ibid.
38. Jumana Shah, 'Gujarat textbooks hail Hitler', *DNA* (Mumbai edn), 16 June 2006, p. 13.
39. Cited in Guichard, *The Construction of History and Nationalism in India*, p. 85.
40. Ibid.
41. 'In Modi's Gujarat, Hitler is a textbook hero', *The Times of India*. 30 Sept. 2004, http://m.timesofindia.com/articleshow/msid-868469,curpg-2.cms (last accessed 13 Dec. 2013); and Akshaya Mukul, 'Modi ignores on books glorifying Hitler', *The Times of India*, 22 Oct. 2005, http://articles.timesofindia.indiatimes.com/2005-10-22/india/27842647_1_class-x-book-nationalism-and-socialism-hitler (last accessed 13 Dec. 2013).

42. Monobina Gupta, 'In Gujarat, Adolf catches 'em in schools', *The Telegraph*, 29 April 2002, p. 6.
43. Ritu Sharma, 'Man who got Wendy Doniger pulped is made "must reading" in Gujarat schools', *The Indian Express*, 25 July 2014, https://indianexpress.com/article/india/india-others/man-who-got-wendy-doniger-pulped-is-made-must-reading-in-gujarat-schools/.
44. Aarefa Johari, 'The textbook vigilante: meet the man who got Doniger's book on Hinduism withdrawn', *Scroll.in*, 12 Feb. 2014, https://scroll.in/article/656157/the-textbook-vigilante-meet-the-man-who-got-donigers-book-on-hinduism-banned (last accessed 12 Feb. 2018).
45. Vijetha S.N., 'Historians protest as Delhi University purges Ramayana essay from syllabus', *The Hindu*, 15 Oct. 2011, https://www.thehindu.com/news/national/Historians-protest-as-Delhi-University-purges-Ramayana-essay-from-syllabus/article13372074.ece (last accessed 27 Sept. 2020).
46. Sharma, 'Man who got Wendy Doniger pulped'.
47. Ibid.
48. Darshan Desai, 'A textbook case of howlers in Gujarat', *The Hindu*, 26 Feb. 2014, https://www.thehindu.com/news/national/other-states/a-textbook-case-of-howlers-in-gujarat/article5726783.ece.
49. Ibid.
50. 'HC grants anticipatory bail to TOI staffers in sedition case', *The Times of India* (Ahmedabad edn), 6 June 2008, p. 1.
51. 'Uphold freedom of press, HC tells govt', *The Times of India* (Ahmedabad edn), 19 June 2008, p. 1.
52. 'A show of solidarity', *The Times of India*, 3 June 2009, https://timesofindia.indiatimes.com/city/ahmedabad/a-show-of-solidarity/articleshow/3094918.cms.
53. 'IPS officers PC Pandey, OP Mathur retire', *The Indian Express* (Ahmedabad edn), 1 April 2009, https://indianexpress.com/article/cities/ahmedabad/ips-officers-p-c-pande-o-p-mathur-retire/.
54. 'Litterateurs demand dropping of charges against Ashis Nandy', *The Times of India* (Ahmedabad edn), 25 June 2008, p. 2.
55. 'Democracy is now psephocracy', interview with Ashis Nandy by Sheela Reddy, *Outlook*, 30 June 2008, https://magazine.outlookindia.com/story/amp/democracy-is-now-psephocracy/237806.

56. This is not a new situation: in a 2009 publication covering the period 1947–2004, Lobo and Kumar showed that of the 4 million people who have been 'displaced' in Gujarat, 45 per cent were Adivasis and 11 per cent Dalits. See Nancy Lobo and Shashikant Kumar, *Land Acquisition, Displacement and Resettlement in Gujarat, 1947–2004*, New Delhi, Sage, 2009, p. 9.
57. Surjit Bhalla, 'The Modi metric', *The Indian Express*, 13 Dec. 2012, http://archive.indianexpress.com/news/the-modi-metric/1044536/0.
58. *'Development' versus People: Gujarat Model of Land Acquisition and People's Voices*, Ahmedabad, Behavioural Science Centre, 2012, pp. 44–5, 51.
59. Tina Parekh, 'Tribal Rights Bill to benefit 30,000 families', *DNA* (Ahmedabad edn), 27 Dec. 2006, p. 12.
60. Out of the 4,661,000 of farmers holding 10,269,000 hectares of agricultural land, the STs are 487,000 (10.45 per cent) owning 969,000 ha (9.4 per cent) while the SCs are 161,000 (3.45 per cent) owning 310,000 ha (3.01 per cent). CAG, *Audit Report (Economic Sector) for the Year Ended 31 March 2012: Report no. 3 of 2013*, p. 22.
61. 'Land for Tribals: Cong stages walkout', *DNA* (Ahmedabad edn), 10 March 2011, p. 4.
62. CAG, *Audit Report (Economic Sector) for the Year Ended 31 March 2012: Report no. 3 of 2013*, p. 23.
63. Mahesh Langa, 'Dangs gets second highest fund but utilises the least', *The Indian Express*, 4 March 2007, p. 2.
64. See Bibek Debroy, *Gujarat: Governance for Growth and Development*, New Delhi, Academic Foundation, 2012, p. 114.
65. Govt. of India, *Rural Labour Enquiry Report on Indebtedness among Rural Labour Households, 2004–05*, Shimla and Chandigarh, Ministry of Labour and Employment, 2010, p. 59, http://labourbureaunew.gov.in/UserContent/RLE_Indebtedness_RLH_2004_05.pdf (last accessed 30 Nov. 2022).
66. G. Gruère, P. Mehta-Bhatt and D. Sengupta, 'BT cotton and farmer suicides in India', IFPRI Discussion Paper 00808, p. 4, http://www.ifpri.org/sites/default/files/publications/ifpridp00808.pdf (last accessed 18 Nov. 2013).
67. Pralay Kanungo and Satyakam Joshi, 'Carving out a white marble deity from a rugged black stone? Hindutva rehabilitates Ramayan's

Shabari in a temple', *International Journal of Hindu Studies*, 13, no. 3 (2009), p. 284.

68. See Christophe Jaffrelot and Malvika Maheshwari, 'Paradigm shifts by the RSS? Lessons from Aseemanand's confession', *EPW*, 46, no. 6 (5 Feb. 2011), p. 42.
69. Kanungo and Joshi, 'Carving out a white marble deity', p. 285.
70. On Morari Bapu, see ch. 6 of Uday Mehta, *Religion and Gurus in Traditional and Modern India*, Delhi, Kalpaz, 2018, pp. 155–86.
71. Kanungo and Joshi, 'Carving out a white marble deity', p. 287.
72. Ibid., p. 279. But in this temple, 'Shabari has no existence independent of Ram. She was an ordinary Bhil Adivasi woman before she met Ram and became extraordinary only because Ram blessed her. Hence, the Shabari temple could not be conceived without Ram. Ram appears majestic and Shabari marginal, though both share the space in the sanctum sanctorum.' Ibid., p. 289.
73. Ibid., p. 291.
74. Ibid., p. 292.
75. Ibid., p. 294.
76. CAG, Audit Report (Economic Sector) for the Year Ended 31 March 2012: Report no. 3 of 2013, p. 23.
77. Govt. of India, *Rural Labour Enquiry Report on Indebtedness among Rural Labour Households, 2004–05*, p. 59.
78. Rajiv Shah, 'Gujarat still has bonded labourers', *The Times of India*, 27 Sept. 2006, p. 3.
79. *Understanding Untouchability: A Comprehensive Study of Practices and Conditions in 1589 Villages*, Navsarjan and Robert F. Kennedy Center for Justice and Human Rights, n.d., np., http://navsarjan.org/Documents/Untouchability_Report_FINAL_Complete.pdf (last accessed 18 Nov. 2013). On the atrocities against Dalits in Gujarat, see also Jenny Paleaz, *A Legally Immune Form of Discrimination: Report on Socio-economic Boycotts of Dalits in Gujarat*, Ahmedabad, Navsarjan Trust, 2009, http://navsarjan.org/Documents/Social%20Boycott%20Report%20-%20Jenny%20Paleaz.doc/view (last accessed 18 Nov. 2013).
80. This non-implementation is well documented in *Justice Undelivered: Public Hearing on the Lack of Enforcement of the Scheduled Castes and the Scheduled Tribes (Prevention of Atrocities) Act, 1989 in Gujarat, 31*

March 2008, Town Hall, Ahmedabad, Gujarat, Navsarjan, Center for Dalit Human Rights, http://navsarjan.org/Documents/Public%20Hearing%20Report.pdf (last accessed 18 Nov. 2013).

81. Rajiv Shah, 'Gujarat government-sponsored study by CEPT University scholars justifies caste discrimination as an issue of "perceptions"', *Counterview*, 3 July 2013, https://counterview.org/2013/07/03/gujarat-government-sponsored-study-by-cept-university-scholars-justifies-caste-discrimination-as-an-issue-of-perceptions/.

82. Cited in Rajiv Shah, '"Karmayogi" swears by caste order "scavenging a spiritual experience for Valmikis"', *The Times of India* (Ahmedabad edn), 24 Nov. 2007, http://epaper.timesofindia.com/Repository/ml.asp?Ref=VE9JQS8yMDA3LzExLzI0I0FyMDA3MDA=& (last accessed 18 Nov. 2013).

83. Ibid.; and Rajiv Shah, 'Modi's spiritual potion to woo karmayogis', *The Times of India*, 1 Dec. 2012, http://blogs.timesofindia.indiatimes.com/true-lies/entry/modi-s-spiritual-potion-to-woo-karmayogis (last accessed 18 Nov. 2013). See also Ashok Bagriya, 'Modi's book Karmayog offends Dalits', IBN Live, 26 Nov. 2007, http://ibnlive.in.com/news/modis-book-karmayog-offends-dalits/53024-3.html.

84. For more details, see Christophe Jaffrelot, 'The Muslims of Gujarat during Narendra Modi's chief ministership', in Riaz Hassan (ed.), *Indian Muslims: Struggling for Equality and Citizenship*, Melbourne, Melbourne University Publishing, 2016, pp. 235–58.

85. Parvis Ghassem-Fachandi, *Pogrom in Gujarat: Hindu Nationalism and Anti-Muslim Violence in India*, Princeton, NJ, Princeton University Press, 2012, p. 130.

86. *Social, Economic and Educational Status of the Muslim Community of India: A Report*, New Delhi, Govt. of India, 2006 [hereafter, Sachar Committee Report], pp. 370–1 and, for aggregate figures, p. 170, https://www.minorityaffairs.gov.in/WriteReadData/RTF1984/7830578798.pdf.

87 Summary of Sachar Committee, http://www.prsindia.org/administrator/uploads/general/1242304423~~Summary%20of%20Sachar%20Committee%20Report.pdf (last accessed 18 Nov. 2013).

88. R. Rani and A. Kalaiyarasan, 'Galloping growth stagnant employment: mapping regional and social differences', in Atul Sood (ed.), *Poverty amidst Prosperity: Essays on the Trajectory of Development in Gujarat*, Delhi, Aakar Books, 2012, pp. 177 and 268.
89. For more details, see Christophe Jaffrelot and A. Kalaiyarasan, 'Indian Muslims: varieties of discrimination and what affirmative action can do', in Ashwini Deshpande (ed.), *Handbook on Economics of Discrimination and Affirmative Action*, Springer, Singapore, 2023, pp. 1–22.
90. Rani and Kalaiyarasan, 'Galloping growth stagnant employment', p. 270.
91. Sangeeta Ghosh, 'An analysis of state education in Gujarat', in Atul Sood (ed.), *Poverty amidst Prosperity: Essays on the Trajectory of Development in Gujarat*, Delhi, Aakar Books, 2012, p. 185.
92. Rani and Kalaiyarasan, 'Galloping growth stagnant employment', p. 271.
93. Abusaleh Shariff, 'An empirical note on relative development of Gujarat and socio-religious differentials', New Delhi, NCAER, 2011, p. 8, http://www.cjponline.org/GujaratReview070311.pdf (last accessed 18 Nov. 2013).
94. See the Sachar Committee Report, p. 292.
95. For a comparison with other states, see Christophe Jaffrelot and A. Kalaiyarasan, 'On socio-economic indicators, Muslim youth fare worse than SCs and OBCs', *The Indian Express*, 1 Nov. 2019, https://indianexpress.com/article/opinion/columns/muslim-community-youth-india-marginalisation-6096881/.
96. Sachar Committee Report, p. 159.
97. Ibid., p. 364.
98. Information Bureau, *Improvement in Conditions of Muslims*, New Delhi, Govt. of India, 7 Dec. 2012, http://pib.nic.in/newsite/erelease.aspx?relid=90229 (last accessed 18 Nov. 2013).
99. In 2013, on the basis of the NSS survey conducted in 2011-12, Surjit Bhalla pointed out that the 'sharpest decline in poverty between 2009–10 and 2011–12 is observed for Muslims'. 'The poverty ratio for Muslims, which had not shown much change between 1999–2000 and 2009–10, now collapses to only a 11.4 per cent level from the high 37.6 per cent level observed two years

earlier.' Surjit Bhalla, 'Lessons from the Gujarat model', *The Indian Express*, 26 Oct. 2013, http://www.indianexpress.com/news/lessons-from-the-gujarat-model/1187332/0 (last accessed 18 Nov. 2013). However, Bhalla points out that 'the large decline in poverty shown between 2009–10 and 2011–12 is statistically suspect and deserved further investigation.' Surjit Bhalla, 'Gujarat's Muslims: in a politically correct trap?', *The Indian Express*, 2 Nov. 2013, http://www.indianexpress.com/news/gujarat-s-muslims-in-a-politically-correct-trap-/1190232/0 (last accessed 18 Nov. 2013).

100. Bhalla, 'The Modi metric'.
101. 'Can't give aid to religious places damaged in riots', *DNA* (Ahmedabad edn), 25 Jan. 2011, p. 3.
102. 'Rs 3.3bn compensation offered, but Gujarat riots victims sceptical', *TwoCircles*, 23 May 2008, http://twocircles.net/2008may22/rs3_3_bn_compensation_offered_gujarat_riots_victims_sceptical.html (last accessed 18 Nov. 2013).
103. 'Consider greater relief measures to Gujarat riot victims on lines of court order for victims of Muzzafarnagar riots', *Counterview*, 8 July 2015, https://counterview.org/2015/07/08/consider-greater-relief-measures-to-gujarat-riot-victims-on-lines-of-court-order-for-victims-of-muzzafarnagar-riots/.
104. For instance, in September 2019 the Supreme Court 'asked the Gujarat government as to why it has not given the compensation, job and accommodation to Bilkis [Bano] despite the apex court's April 23 order'. *The Indian Express*, 30 Sept. 2019, https://indianexpress.com/article/india/2002-riots-sc-asks-gujarat-to-give-compensation-job-accommodation-to-bilkis-bano-6040714/.
105. 'SC won't stay Centre's minority scholarship scheme in Gujarat', *The Hindu*, 7 May 2013, http://www.thehindu.com/news/national/other-states/sc-wont-stay-centres-minority-scholarship-scheme-in-gujarat/article4690136.ece (last accessed 18 Nov. 2013).
106. Utkarsh Anand, 'Gujarat to Supreme Court: Sachar panel illegal, only to help Muslims', *The Indian Express*, 28 Nov. 2013, http://www.indianexpress.com/news/gujarat-to-supreme-court-sachar-panel-illegal-only-to-help-muslims/1200518/ (last accessed 10 Dec. 2013).
107. In 2012, the government of Gujarat made another move affecting some linguistic and religious minorities: the column for Sindhi-,

Tamil-, Marathi- and Urdu-medium graduates was left out in the form for the Teacher Eligibility Test. As a result, those graduates who wanted to teach in these languages could not apply for the upper primary teacher posts. 'No mention of Urdu, 3 other languages in Guj application form', *The Indian Express* (Ahmedabad edn), 4 June 2012, p. 5.

108. On the ghettoisation process in twentieth century Ahmedabad, see Tommaso Bobbio, *Urbanization, Citizenship and Conflict in India: Ahmedabad, 1900–2000*, London and New York, Routledge, 2015.

109. On Juhapura and the ghettoisation process in post-2002 Ahmedabad, see Jan Breman, 'Ghettoization in Ahmedabad', in Jan Breman and Ghanshyam Shah, *Gujarat, Cradle and Harbinger of Identity Politics: India's Injurious Frame of Communalism*, New Delhi, Tulika Books, 2022, pp. 112–14; Christophe Jaffrelot and Charlotte Thomas, 'Facing ghettoisation in "riot-city": Old Ahmedabad and Juhapura between victimisation and self-help', in Laurent Gayer and Christophe Jaffrelot (eds), *Muslims in India's Cities: Trajectories of Marginalisation*, London, Hurst, 2012, pp. 43–79; and Raphael Susewind, 'Muslims in Indian cities: degrees of segregation and the elusive ghetto', *Environment and Planning*, 49, no. 6 (2017), pp. 1286–307.

110. See Jaffrelot and Thomas, 'Facing ghettoisation in "riot-city"', pp. 43–79; and Sharik Laliwala, Christophe Jaffrelot, Priyal Thakkar and Abida Desai, 'Paradoxes of ghettoization: Juhapura 'in' Ahmedabad', in *Indian Exclusion Report, 2019–2020*, New Delhi, Three Essays Collective with Centre for Equity Studies, 2020, pp. 103–36, https://spire.sciencespo.fr/hdl:/2441/1ni56132699n1r9hm18of0urkr/resources/2021-jaffrelot-paradoxes-of-ghettoization-india-exclusion-report-2019-20.pdf.

111. Darshini Mahadevia, Renu Desai and Suchita Vyas, 'City Profile: Ahmedabad', Ahmedabad, CEPT University, CUE Working Paper 26, September 2014, p. 43.

112. Ibid., p. 44.

113. Laliwala, Jaffrelot, Thakkar and Desai, 'Paradoxes of ghettoization', p. 112.

114. Sheba Tejani, 'Saffron geographies of exclusion: the Disturbed Areas Act of Gujarat', *Urban Studies*, 60, no. 4 (2022), pp. 1–23.

115. 'Gujarat Act No. 12 of 1991. The Gujarat Prohibition of Transfer of Immovable Property and Provision for Protection of Tenants from Eviction from Premises in Disturbed Areas Act, 1991', https://www.indiacode.nic.in/bitstream/123456789/4609/1/disturbedareasact.pdf.
116. Sharik Laliwala, 'Gujarat's enduring Muslim ghettoes: laws like Disturbed Areas Act (1991) and amendments severely segregate the minority', *Daily O*, 15 July 2019, https://www.dailyo.in/politics/gujarat-disturbed-areas-act-1991-muslim-ghettoisation-juhapura/story/1/31485.html.
117. Christophe Jaffrelot and Sharik Laliwala, 'The segregated city', *The Indian Express*, 26 May 2018, https://indianexpress.com/article/opinion/columns/muslims-in-india-hindus-jains-gujarat-love-jihad-5191304/.
118. Sheba Tejani, 'Saffron geographies of exclusion: the Disturbed Areas Act of Gujarat', *Urban Studies*, 60, no. 4 (2022), pp. 1–23.
119. Tejani, 'Saffron geographies of exclusion'.
120. Ibid.
121. Ibid.
122. Ibid.
123. Fahad Zuberi, 'Apartheid by law: sustaining conflict, producing divided cities; the case of Disturbed Areas Act, 1991', in A. Srivathsan, Seema Khanwalkar and Kaiwan Mehta (eds), *CEPT Essay Prize 2019*, CEPT University Press, 2020, pp. 9–21.
124. Howard Spodek, 'In the Hindutva laboratory: pogroms and politics in Gujarat', *Modern Asian Studies*, 44, no. 2 (March 2010), p. 380.
125. Rohit Bhan, 'Remarks on Muslims by Praveen Togadia, VHP, trigger new controversy', NDTV, 21 April 2014, https://www.ndtv.com/elections-news/remarks-on-muslims-by-pravin-togadia-vhp-trigger-new-controversy-558217.
126. 'Won't allow Muslims at Garba to prevent love jihad: right-wing group in Gujarat', *Firstpost*, 5 Oct. 2015, https://www.firstpost.com/india/wont-allow-muslims-at-garba-to-prevent-love-jihad-right-wing-group-in-gujarat-2455198.html.
127. Ibid.
128. Lalmani Verma and T.A. Johnson, 'Who loves love jihad', *The Indian Express*, 7 Sept. 2014, http://indianexpress.com/article/india/india-others/who-loves-love-jihad/ (last accessed 29 Jan. 2022).

129. Jessica Marie Falcone, 'Dance steps, nationalist movement: how Hindu extremists claimed Garba-raas', *Anthropology Now*, 8, no. 3 (Dec. 2016), p. 51, https://www.academia.edu/38845011/Dance_Steps_Nationalist_Movement_How_Hindu_Extremists_Claimed_Garba_raas.
130. Rita Kothari, 'Koni koni chhe Gujarat', *Kafila*, 26 Sept. 2014, https://kafila.online/2014/09/26/koni-koni-chhe-gujarat-rita-kothari/.
131. Harit Mehta and Himanshu Bhayani, 'Santa trades carols for Garba', *The Times of India*, 25 Dec. 2003, https://timesofindia.indiatimes.com/india/santa-trades-carols-for-garba-in-gujarat/articleshow/380929.cms.
132. 'VHP's anti-love jihad campaign in Gujarat: aggressive leaflet distributed ahead of ten by-polls', *Counterview*, 9 Sept. 2014, https://www.counterview.net/2014/09/vhps-anti-love-jihad-campaign-in.html.
133. Soumik Dey, 'Muslim boy weds Hindu girl, Dal ensures they don't live happily ever after', *The Indian Express*, 10 Oct. 2006, pp. 1 and 2.
134. See Christophe Jaffrelot, *Modi's India: Hindu Nationalism and the Rise of Ethnic Democracy*, Princeton, NJ, Princeton University Press; Chennai, Westland, 2021, in particular ch. 7: 'A de facto Hindu Rashtra: Indian-style vigilantism', pp. 211–36.
135. 'Common thread in Gujarat clashes: VHP "aiding" police', *The Indian Express*, 8 Oct. 2014, https://indianexpress.com/article/india/gujarat/common-thread-in-gujarat-clashes-vhp-aiding-police/.
136. Ibid.
137. Harinder Baweja, 'Modi selects his side, rejects Muslim candidates', *Hindustan Times*, 10 Dec. 2012, http://www.hindustantimes.com/StoryPage/Print/970716.aspx (last accessed 22 Nov. 2013).
138. https://fr.scribd.com/document/115453938/Gujarat-BJP-Manifesto-for-Assembly-Election-2012-in-Gujarati-language.
139. See his speech at Fergusson College, for instance. 'Hon. Chief Minister's speech at Fergusson College, Pune', 14 July 2013, Narendra Modi website, http://www.narendramodi.in/shri-narendra-modi-speech-at-fergusson-college-pune/ (last accessed 21 Nov. 2013).
140. Primary census data accessed at the Gujarat Census Office (Gandhinagar) in 2011.

141. He opposed, for instance, the attempts at reforming the community that intellectuals like Asghar Ali Engineer had undertaken. Engineer, the son of a Bohra *amil* (priest), initiated a socio-religious reform movement within the Bohra community in 1972 in Udaipur. He was elected general secretary of the Central Board of the Dawoodi Bohra Community in 1977. See http://dawoodi-bohras.com/about_us/people/engineer/ (last accessed 22 Nov. 2013).
142. Interview with J.S. Bandukwala, 2 March 2010 at Baroda. Prof. Bandukwala, who taught physics at the MSU (Baroda) for decades, had given up any hopes of reforming the Bohra community from the inside after the 1972 events in Udaipur. He was also targeted by Hindu nationalist militants in 2002 by the auditor of the MSU, who was one of his neighbours, as well as by Dalits who looted his house.
143. Jafri was a Bohra and the reactions of his community to his death are very revealing of its inner divisions. While there was no comment on the conservative leaders' side, a website of the Dawoodi Bohras launched a forum called 'Progressive Dawoodi Bohras'. The discussion on Jafri was initiated by 'Awarebohra', who posted a very interesting piece of writing called 'A valiant Bohra family's battle against Modi', where one could read: 'If you happen to talk to the Muslims (not Bohras) [*sic*], who survived the fateful day, they address Ahsan Jafri as 'shaheed' Ahsan Jafri, whereas you talk to any other Dawoodi Bohra who happened to be present there on that day (there are quite a few who survived, in fact Ahsan Jafri was the only Dawoodi Bohra to have laid down his life that day, remaining all 54 or so who died in Gulberg Society were Muslims), they don't even seem to acknowledge the great act this gentlemen [*sic*] succeeded in putting off. See http://dawoodi-bohras.com/forum/viewtopic.php?f=1&t=5025 (last accessed 22 Nov. 2013). Reacting to this message, several Bohras attacked the 'Adbes' and their leader the 'Syedna'. Not only do Bohras not always consider themselves as Muslims (as evident from Awarebhora's formulas), but they are also obviously divided.
144. For a picture of the scene, see http://www.flickr.com/photos/76720863@N08/7064011289/ (last accessed 22 Nov. 2013).
145. 'Bohras by his side, Modi talks peace', *The Sunday Express* (Ahmedabad edn), 20 Feb. 2011, p. 4.

146. Many of the press photographs taken in this context show Narendra Modi on stage with Bohras. See, for instance, 'Now, Muslims "in" Modi's Gujaratis', *DNA* (Ahmedabad edn), 18 Sept. 2011, p. 1.
147. In 2009, the BJP nominated Muslim candidates in two by-elections and for the municipal elections in Junagadh—and lost. 'BJP bait fails to lure Junagadh Muslims', *DNA*, 22 July 2009, http://www.dnaindia.com/india/report-bjp-bait-fails-to-lure-junagadh-muslims-1276263 (last accessed 22 Nov. 2013). But one year later, 117 Muslim candidates won local polls on the BJP ticket. Rajiv Shah, '117 Muslims won local polls on party ticket in Gujarat: BJP', *The Times of India* (Ahmedabad edn), 28 Oct. 2010.
148. 'Wary of Jinnah fiasco, Modi refuses skull cap', *Hindustan Times* (New Delhi), 20 Sept. 2011, p. 11.
149. 'The Sadbhavana? Modi's no to skullcap is insult to Islam: imam', *DNA* (Ahmedabad edn), 20 Sept. 2011, p. 5.
150. Yagnesh Mehta, 'After skullcap, Narendra Modi refuses keffiyeh: a traditional Arab head-dress', *The Times of India*, 21 Oct. 2011, http://articles.timesofindia.indiatimes.com/2011-10-21/ahmedabad/30305691_1_sadbhavana-mission-damage-control-mode-fadia (last accessed 22 Nov. 2013).
151. Ajay Umat, 'Official iftars in Gujarat an all-veg affair', *The Times of India*, 15 Aug. 2012, http://articles.timesofindia.indiatimes.com/2012-08-15/ahmedabad/33216269_1_iftar-jain-monk-vegetarian-outlet (last accessed 22 Nov. 2013).
152. Nilanjan Mukhopadhyay, *Narendra Modi: The Man, the Times*, Chennai, Westland, 2013, p. 315.
153. Prashant Rupera, 'Modi takes a dig at Juhapura's "power ministers"', *The Times of India* (Ahmedabad edn), 27 Dec. 2003, p. 5.
154. 'The Gujarat Freedom of Religion Act, 2003 Act 22 of 2003', https://prsindia.org/files/bills_acts/acts_states/gujarat/2003/Act%20No.%2022%20of%202003%20Gujarat.pdf.
155. 'Minorities protest against Gujarat's conversion law', *The Economic Times*, 21 Sept. 2006, https://economictimes.indiatimes.com/news/politics-and-nation/minorities-protest-against-gujarats-conversion-law/articleshow/2011955.cms?utm_source=contentofinterest&utm_medium=text&utm_campaign=cppst) (last accessed 24 Jan. 2022).

156. Ayesha Khan, 'Religion bill stirs up an unholy mess', *Ahmedabad Newsline*, 4 Oct. 2006, https://web.archive.org/web/20080502163701/http://cities.expressindia.com/fullstory.php?newsid=203711# (last accessed 24 Jan. 2022).
157. 'Gujarat withdraws Freedom of Religion Amendment Bill', *The Indian Express*, 11 March 2008, http://archive.indianexpress.com/news/gujarat-withdraws-freedom-of-religion-amendment-bill/282818/2 (last accessed 24 Jan. 2022).
158. 'In Gujarat, 94.4% of those seeking to convert are Hindu', *The Times of India*, 16 March 2016, https://timesofindia.indiatimes.com/city/ahmedabad/In-Gujarat-94-4-of-those-seeking-to-convert-are-Hindu/articleshow/51419977.cms (last accessed 24 Jan. 2022).
159. The Modi government was in principle against the granting of reservations to Muslim Dalits and Christian Dalits. The Gujarat Assembly voted a resolution on this issue in 2009. See 'State to urge Centre against reservation for Dalit Muslims, Christians', *The Indian Express* (Ahmedabad edn), 15 Dec. 2009, p. 3.
160. One of the new converts justified his decision by explaining that he resented the fact that the Dalit children had 'to sit separately while eating their lunch'. Gopal Kateshiya, 'Became Buddhist for haircut, shave … mental untouchability persists', *The Indian Express*, 21 Oct. 2013, http://www.indianexpress.com/story-print/1185035/ (last accessed 18 Nov. 2013).
161. Syed Khalique Ahmed, 'Dalit conversions: Gujarat govt orders probe', *The Indian Express*, 16 Oct. 2013, http://www.indianexpress.com/story-print/1183094/ (last accessed 18 Nov. 2013).
162. The government also tried to dissuade Hindu Dalits from converting to Christianity by asking the Church to disclose the list of the baptised, as some of them continued to claim that they were still Hindus in order to retain access to reservations. The Church refused to show the registers. Interview with Father Cedric Prakash, in Ahmedabad, on 27 February 2012.
163. 'Karnataka and Goa Congress defections: political opportunism or did ideology never matter?', *The Print*, 11 July 2019, https://theprint.in/talk-point/karnataka-goa-congress-defections-political-opportunism-or-did-ideology-never-matter/261701/ (last accessed 3 Oct. 2020).

164. In fact, the BJP engineered similar defections in Goa in 2017, but in contrast to what happened in Karnataka, it was already in office in the state as part of the ruling coalition. In Goa, in February 2017, the BJP played the defection card to prevent the Congress, which had the largest number of MLAs, from forming the government. But in July 2019, in order to consolidate its strength in parliament and to discard its coalition partner, the Goa Forward Party, which was cobbled together in haste after the 2017 state election, the BJP 'acquired' ten other MLAs from the Congress.
165. 'BJP offered Rs 10 crore to JDS MLA, says Karnataka CM Kumaraswamy', *The Indian Express*, 10 June 2019. After losing the 2018 Karnataka election, BJP had already tried to reach out to Congress and JD(S) MLAs, offering them inducements to leave their party. 'Congress releases more tapes: Yeddyurappa, son allegedly caught luring Cong MLAs', News Minute, 19 May 2018, https://www.thenewsminute.com/article/congress-releases-more-tapes-yeddyurappa-son-allegedly-caught-luring-cong-mlas-81573 (last accessed 3 Oct. 2020).
166. 'Disqualified Karnataka MLA buys India's most expensive car worth Rs 11 crore', News 18, 20 Aug. 2019, https://www.news18.com/news/auto/disqualified-karnataka-mla-buys-india-most-expensive-car-worth-rs-11-crore-2272641.html (last accessed 3 Oct. 2020).
167. Milind Ghatwai, 'Bid to topple MP govt? Congress says its MLAs confined in Gurugram hotel, BJP denies', *The Indian Express*, 4 March 2020, https://indianexpress.com/article/india/madhya-pradesh-kamal-nath-congress-bjp-6297845/ (last accessed 24 Aug. 2020).
168. 'DTU's Yogesh Singh appointed 23rd vice chancellor of Delhi University', *Hindustan Times*, 22 Sept. 2021, https://www.hindustantimes.com/cities/delhi-news/dtus-yogesh-singh-appointed-23rd-vice-chancellor-of-delhi-university-101632331058482.html.
169. Ashok Swain, 'JNU VC Jagadesh Kumar does not seem fit for his job', *Daily O*, 26 July 2017, https://www.dailyo.in/voices/jnu-vc-rss-tanks-patriotism-hypernationalism/story/1/18597.html (last accessed 27 Sept. 2020).
170. For more detail, see Jaffrelot, *Modi's India*, pp. 176–83.

171. Science textbooks underwent 573 modifications and social science textbooks 316. Ritika Chopra, 'From Swachh Bharat, noteban to Ganga and Digital India: govt schemes enter NCERT textbooks', *The Indian Express*, 1 June 2018, https://indianexpress.com/article/education/from-modis-swachh-bharat-noteban-to-ganga-and-digital-india-govt-schemes-enter-ncert-textbooks-5199426/ (last accessed 27 Sept. 2020).
172. Ashwini Deshpande and Rajesh Ramachandran, 'The 10% quota: is caste still an indicator of backwardness?', *EPW*, 54, no. 13 (30 March 2019), p. 27.
173. Ibid., p. 30.
174. Esha Roy, 'Maulana Azad Fellowship for minority students not available anymore: Irani', *The Indian Express*, 10 Dec. 2022, https://indianexpress.com/article/india/maulana-azad-fellowship-for-minority-students-not-available-anymore-irani-8316212/.
175. 'Vajpayee to host Eid Milan Sunday', *The Times of India*, 7 Dec. 2002, http://articles.timesofindia.indiatimes.com/2002-12-07/india/27305758_1_host-communal-violence-minister-atal-bihari-vajpayee (last accessed 22 Nov. 2013).
176. Interview with Father Cedric Prakash in February 2001 in Ahmedabad.
177. K.M. Chenoy, *Violence in Gujarat: Test Case for a Larger Fundamentalist Agenda; Report of the Citizens Commission on Persecution of Christians in Gujarat*, New Delhi and Bangalore, National Alliance of Women, 1999, https://cjp.org.in/wp-content/uploads/2020/07/Violence-in-Gujarat-Final_pdf.
178. *Official India: On the Side of the Militants; An Analysis of the Persecution of Christians in India with the Tacit Approval of Police and Government Officials (July–December 2017)*, Church in Chains, http://www.churchinchains.ie/wp/wpcontent/uploads/2018/01/India-Persecution-Report-Jul-Dec-2017-WEB.pdf; https://layreadersbookreviews.wordpress.com/2018/03/25/official-india-on-the-side-of-the-militants-an-analysis-of-the-persecution-of-christians-in-india-with-the-tacit-approval-of-police-and-government-officials/ (last accessed 4 April 2018).
179. The Archbishop of Goa, Filipe Neri Ferrão, stated in April 2018 before an assembly organised by the Catholic Bishops' Conference

of India that 'the idea of India with its strongest pillars of diversity and pluralism is being threatened by several emerging trends', starting with 'the emergence of both majoritarian hegemony and the growth of terror and extremism engendered by the growth of exclusivist religious fundamentalism'. Gary Azavedo, 'Rising communal violence in India most dangerous of all social distrusts: Archbishop Ferrão', *The Times of India*, 5 April 2018, https://timesofindia.indiatimes.com/india/rising-communal-violence-in-india-most-dangerous-of-all-social-distrusts-archbishop-ferrao/articleshow/63633384.cms (last accessed 27 Sept. 2020).

180. Julio Ribeiro, 'As a Christian, suddenly I am a stranger in my own country, writes Julio Ribeiro', *The Indian Express*, 17 March 2017, http://indianexpress.com/article/opinion/columns/i-feel-i-am-on-a-hit-list/ (last accessed 4 April 2018).

CONCLUSION

1. 'Gujarat now India's SEZ: Narendra Modi', *The Times of India*, 6 Sept. 2007, http://articles.timesofindia.indiatimes.com/2007-09-06/india/27992794_1_chief-minister-narendra-modi-india-s-sez-chinese-sezs.
2. Christophe Jaffrelot, *Modi's India: Hindu Nationalism and the Rise of Ethnic Democracy*, Princeton, NJ, Princeton University Press; Chennai, Westland, 2021, pp. 112–48.
3. See Christophe Jaffrelot and Mahesh Langa, 'Gujarat 2022 elections: explaining BJP's hegemony', *Studies in Indian Politics*, 11, no. 1, 2023, pp. 118–33.
4. 'No. 1 CM has the lowest average Assembly sittings', *Dainik Bhaskar*, 19 July 2012, http://daily.bhaskar.com/article/GUJ-AHD-no-3543600.html (last accessed 28 Nov. 2013).
5. 'Gujarat Social Watch asks governor to ensure state Assembly becomes "meaningful" for democracy', *Counterview*, 29 Aug. 2013, http://www.counterview.net/2013/08/gujarat-social-watch-asks-governor-to.html (last accessed 28 Nov. 2013).
6. Christophe Jaffrelot and Vihang Jumle, 'Bypassing parliament', *The Indian Express*, 15 Oct. 2020, https://indianexpress.com/article/opinion/columns/narendra-modi-government-parliament-lok-

sabha-rajya-sabha-6725428/ (last accessed 16 Oct. 2020); and P.B. Mehta, 'Betrayal of procedure in parliament is not just about technicalities: deference to process builds trust', *The Indian Express*, 22 Sept. 2020, https://indianexpress.com/article/opinion/columns/parliament-monsoon-session-farm-bills-modi-govt-railroading-the-bill-6605281/ (last accessed 7 Oct. 2020).

7. During his first term, the number of ordinances jumped from six per year under Manmohan Singh to eleven per year under Modi. See *List of Ordinances Promulgated, Text of the Central Ordinances: Legislative References*, Legislative Department, Ministry of Law and Justice, Government of India, http://legislative.gov.in/documents/legislative-references (last accessed 7 Oct. 2020).
8. Valerian Rodrigues, 'Parliamentary scrutiny on the back burner', *The Hindu*, 26 Sept. 2020, https://www.thehindu.com/opinion/lead/parliamentary-scrutiny-on-the-back-burner/article32699224.ece (last accessed 7 Oct. 2020).
9. 'Bills referred to committees' for 15th, 16th, 17th Lok Sabha under all committees, Lok Sabha, Parliament of India, http://loksabhaph.nic.in/Committee/Bill_Search.aspx (last accessed 3 Oct. 2020).
10. Ghanshyam Shah, 'Modi's power play and mega-marketing in the 2009 Lok Sabha elections', in Jan Breman and Ghanshyam Shah (eds), *Gujarat, Cradle and Harbinger of Identity Politics: India's Injurious Frame of Communalism*, New Delhi, Tulika Books, 2022, p. 270.
11. Ibid.
12. 'Dictating the trend', *The Indian Express*, 27 Nov. 2007, http://www.indianexpress.com/news/dictating-the-trend/243904/ (last accessed 28 Nov. 2013).
13. Patrick Heller and Leila Fernandes, 'Hegemonic aspirations: new middle class politics and India's democracy in comparative perspective', *Critical Asian Studies*, 38, no. 4 (2006), pp. 495–522.
14. Ashis Nandy, 'Obituary of a culture', *Seminar*, no. 513 (2002), http://www.india-seminar.com/2002/513/513%20ashis%20nandy.htm.
15. Richard Wike, Katie Simmons, Bruce Stokes and Janell Fetterolf, 'Globally, broad support for representative and direct democracy', in Pew Research Center, *Global Attitudes and Trends*, 16 Oct. 2017,

https://www.pewresearch.org/global/2017/10/16/globally-broad-support-for-representative-and-direct-democracy/.

16. Bruce Stokes, Dorothy Manevich and Hanyu Chwe, 'The state of Indian democracy', in Pew Research Center, *Global Attitudes and Trends*, 15 Nov. 2017, http://www.pewglobal.org/2017/11/15/the-state-of-indian-democracy/ (last accessed 26 June 2018). To compare India with other countries, see http://www.pewglobal.org/2017/10/16/globally-broad-support-for-representative-and-direct-democracy/.
17. I have elaborated on this point in Christophe Jaffrelot, 'Populism against democracy or people against democracy?', in Alain Dieckhoff and Elise Massicard (eds), *Contemporary Populists in Power*, New York, Palgrave, 2022, pp. 35–54.
18. Bruce Stokes, Dorothy Manevich and Hanyu Chwe, 'Indians satisfied with country's direction but worry about crime, terrorism', in Pew Research Center, *Global Attitudes and Trends*, 15 Nov. 2017, https://www.pewresearch.org/global/2017/11/15/indians-satisfied-with-countrys-direction-but-worry-about-crime-terrorism/.
19. Bruce Stokes, Dorothy Manevich and Hanyu Chwe, 'India and the world', in Pew Research Center, *Global Attitudes and Trends*, 15 Nov. 2017, http://www.pewglobal.org/2017/11/15/india-and-the-world/ (last accessed 26 June 2018).
20. Stokes, Manevich and Chwe, 'India and the world'.
21. 'Gujarat chief minister Mr. Narendra Modi's historic visit to the People's Republic of China', 13 Nov. 2011, Narendra Modi website, https://www.narendramodi.in/gujarat-chief-minister-mr-narendra-modi's-historic-visit-to-the-people's-republic-of-china-4188.
22. 'Congress has a question: who paid for Narendra Modi's chartered flights as Gujarat chief minister?', *The Indian Express*, 19 Oct. 2017, https://indianexpress.com/article/india/who-paid-for-modis-chartered-flights-as-gujarat-cm-asks-congress/.
23. J.K. Pathak, 'Three eras of visits by foreign leaders to Gujarat', DeshGujarat, 19 April 2022, https://www.deshgujarat.com/2022/04/19/three-eras-of-visits-of-foreign-leaders-to-gujarat/.
24. On the electoral compulsions of populism, see Jaffrelot, 'Populism against democracy or people against democracy?', pp. 35–54.

25. 'Operation Juliet: busting the bogey of 'love jihad'', *Cobrapost*, 4 Oct. 2015, http://cobrapost.com/blog/operation-juliet-busting-the-bogey-of-love-jihad-2/900 (last accessed 9 April 2018).
26. See Christophe Jaffrelot, 'Bajrang Dal and making of the deeper state: in the name of faith and state', *The Indian Express*, 5 June 2023, https://indianexpress.com/article/opinion/columns/karnataka-election-result-poll-campaign-congress-bjp-8645595/.

INDEX

Note: Page numbers followed by '*n*' refer to notes, '*t*' refer to tables.